Lecture Notes in Computer Science 537

Edited by G. Goos and J. Hartmanis

Advisory Board: W. Brauer   D. G

Lecture Notes in Computer Science   537

Edited by G. Goos and J. Hartmanis

Advisory Board: W. Brauer D. Gries J. Stoer

A. J. Menezes   S. A. Vanstone (Eds.)

Advances in Cryptology – CRYPTO '90

Proceedings

Springer-Verlag

Berlin Heidelberg New York
London Paris Tokyo
Hong Kong Barcelona
Budapest

Series Editors

Gerhard Goos
Universität Karlsruhe
Postfach 69 80
Vincenz-Priessnitz-Straße 1
W-7500 Karlsruhe, FRG

Juris Hartmanis
Department of Computer Science
Cornell University
Upson Hall
Ithaca, NY 14853, USA

Volume Editors

Alfred J. Menezes
Scott A. Vanstone
Department of Combinatorics and Optimization
University of Waterloo, Waterloo, Ontario, Canada N2L 3G1

CR Subject Classification (1991): E.3

ISBN 3-540-54508-5 Springer-Verlag Berlin Heidelberg New York
ISBN 0-387-54508-5 Springer-Verlag New York Berlin Heidelberg

This work is subject to copyright. All rights are reserved, whether the whole or part of
the material is concerned, specifically the rights of translation, reprinting, re-use of
illustrations, recitation, broadcasting, reproduction on microfilms or in any other way,
and storage in data banks. Duplication of this publication or parts thereof is permitted
only under the provisions of the German Copyright Law of September 9, 1965, in its
current version, and permission for use must always be obtained from Springer-Verlag.
Violations are liable for prosecution under the German Copyright Law.

© Springer-Verlag Berlin Heidelberg 1991
Printed in Germany

Printing and binding: Druckhaus Beltz, Hemsbach/Bergstr.
45/3140-543210 - Printed on acid-free paper

CRYPTO '90

A Conference on the Theory and Application of Cryptography

held at the University of California, Santa Barbara,
August 11-15, 1990
through the cooperation of the Computer Science Department

Sponsored by:

International Association for Cryptologic Research

in cooperation with

*The IEEE Computer Society Technical Committee
On Security and Privacy*

General Chair
Sherry McMahan, Cylink

Program Chair
Scott Vanstone, University of Waterloo

Program Committee

Gordon Agnew	University of Waterloo
Thomas Berson	Anagram Laboratories
Johannes Buchmann	Universität des Saarlandes
Yvo Desmedt	University of Wisconsin
Amos Fiat	Tel-Aviv University
Kenji Koyama	NTT Basic Research Lab
Ronald Rivest	Massachusetts Institute of Technology
Rainer Rueppel	Crypto AG
Marijke De Soete	Philips Research Labs
Doug Stinson	University of Nebraska
Hugh Williams	University of Manitoba

Foreword

Crypto '90 marked the tenth anniversary of the Crypto conferences held at the University of California at Santa Barbara. The conference was held from August 11 to August 15, 1990 and was sponsored by the International Association for Cryptologic Research, in cooperation with the IEEE Computer Society Technical Committee on Security and Privacy and the Department of Computer Science of the University of California at Santa Barbara.

Crypto '90 attracted 227 participants from twenty countries around the world. Roughly 35% of attendees were from academia, 45% from industry and 20% from government. The program was intended to provide a balance between the purely theoretical and the purely practical aspects of cryptography to meet the needs and diversified interests of these various groups.

The overall organization of the conference was superbly handled by the general chairperson Sherry McMahan. All of the outstanding features of Crypto, which we have come to expect over the years, were again present and, in addition to all of this, she did a magnificent job in the preparation of the book of abstracts. This is a crucial part of the program and we owe her a great deal of thanks.

Each year the number and quality of submissions to Crypto has been increasing. This is of course very good for the conference but it does make the task of the program committee more difficult. This year we had 104 papers and abstracts submitted from 18 countries. In anticipation of this larger number, the committee was expanded to twelve members representing seven countries. Having a bigger committee and a wider global representation poses certain problems with communication, but we believe these problems are minute in comparison to the benefits obtained from having each paper scrutinized by more people and by involving a much larger cross-section of the cryptographic community in this process. Each paper was assigned to three committee members who were then responsible for its refereeing. Of the 104 submissions, one was withdrawn, 43 were accepted for presentation and, of these 43, two were merged into one presentation. All papers and abstracts accepted for presentation which contained sufficient detail for the committee to make a reasonably accurate evaluation of the final form of the paper have not been been re-refereed. Rump session contributions and papers accepted for presentation based on abstracts with very little detail have been refereed.

As in other years, Whitfield Diffie kindly agreed to coordinate the Rump Session. We would like to take this opportunity to thank Whit for running this very important aspect of Crypto over the years and for graciously accepting to do it again. In an effort to contain the number of short talks given in this session, a much harder line was adopted this year. Of the 22 abstracts submitted only 12 were accepted for presentation. Of these 12, only 6 were submitted for the proceedings and all of these have gone through a thorough refereeing process.

For this conference there were three invited speakers and each was given fifty minutes to lecture. It was our goal to have topics of current interest, given by noted authorities in the area and presented in a manner which would make the lectures accessible to a large audience of diversified backgrounds. With this in mind we approached Whitfield Diffie (Bell Northern Research), Adi Shamir (Weizmann Institute) and Gus Simmons (Sandia National Laboratories) and all accepted. We thank them for their outstanding presentations and the enthusiasm which they conveyed for the subject.

We would also like to thank Dr. Tatsuaki Okamoto (NTT Tokyo) for the very valuable assistance he provided to us. Dr. Okamoto was on sabbatical leave from NTT and was spending this time (August 1989 – August 1990) at the University of Waterloo. He kindly volunteered his services and made many very important and significant contributions to our efforts with the program.

Finally, we thank the members of the program committee itself for the very fine job they did. Theirs is a task which takes a great deal of time and effort and which receives a disproportionate amount of gratitude. Without a complete commitment by all members, the task would be impossible. We thank each of them for a very thorough and conscientious effort and also for their very deep dedication in making Crypto '90 successful. Many thanks to Gordon Agnew, Thomas Berson, Johannes Buchmann, Yvo Desmedt, Amos Fiat, Kenji Koyama, Ronald Rivest, Rainer Rueppel, Marijke De Soete, Doug Stinson, and Hugh Williams.

Alfred J. Menezes and Scott A. Vanstone
University of Waterloo
December 1990

Table of Contents

Session 4: Signatures and Authentication
Chair: D. Stinson

Session 5: Secret Sharing
Chair: M. De Soete

Session 6: Key Distribution
Chair: T. Berson

Session 7: Hash Functions
Chair: R. Rueppel

Session 8: Zero-Knowledge
Chair: A. Fiat

Session 9: Randomness
Chair: R. Rivest

Session 10: Applications
Chair: G. Agnew

Session 11: Design and Analysis I
Chair: K. Koyama

Session 12: Design and Analysis II
Chair: J. Buchmann

Rump Session: Impromptu Talks
Chair: W. Diffie

Cryptanalysis

Chair: S. Vanstone, University of Waterloo

Differential Cryptanalysis
of
DES-like Cryptosystems

(Extended Abstract)

Eli Biham   *Adi Shamir*

The Weizmann Institute of Science
Department of Applied Mathematics

Abstract

The Data Encryption Standard (DES) is the best known and most widely used cryptosystem for civilian applications. It was developed at IBM and adopted by the National Buraeu of Standards in the mid 70's, and has successfully withstood all the attacks published so far in the open literature. In this paper we develop a new type of cryptanalytic attack which can break DES with up to eight rounds in a few minutes on a PC and can break DES with up to 15 rounds faster than an exhaustive search. The new attack can be applied to a variety of DES-like substitution/permutation cryptosystems, and demonstrates the crucial role of the (unpublished) design rules.

1   Introduction

Iterated cryptosystems are a family of cryptographically strong functions based on iterating a weaker function n times. Each iteration is called a *round* and the cryptosystem is called an *n round cryptosystem*. The *round function* is a function of the output of the previous round and of a *subkey* which is a key dependent value calculated via a *key scheduling* algorithm. The round function is usually based on S boxes, bit permutations, arithmetic operations and the exclusive-or (denoted by $\oplus$ and XOR) operations. The *S boxes* are nonlinear translation tables mapping a small number of input bits to a small number of output bits. They are usually the only part of the cryptosystem that is not linear and thus the security of the cryptosystem crucially depends on their choice. The bit permutation is used to rearrange the output bits of the S boxes in order to make the input bits of each S box in the following round depend on the output of as many S boxes as possible. The XOR operation is often used to mix the subkey with the data. In most applications the encryption algorithm is assumed to be known and the secrecy of the data depends only on the secrecy of the randomly chosen key.

An early proposal for an iterated cryptosystems was Lucifer[7], which was designed at IBM to resolve the growing need for data security in its products. The round function of Lucifer has a combination of non linear S boxes and a bit permutation. The input bits are divided into groups of four consecutive bits. Each group is translated by a reversible S box giving a four bit result. The output bits of all the S boxes are permuted in order to mix them when they become the input to the following round. In Lucifer only two fixed S boxes (S_0 and S_1) were chosen. Each S box can be used at any S box location and the choice is key dependent. Decryption is accomplished by running the data backwards using the inverse of each S box.

The Data Encryption Standard (DES) [14] is an improved version of Lucifer. It was developed at IBM and adopted by the U.S. National Bureau of Standards (NBS) as the standard cryptosystem for sensitive but unclassified data (such as financial transactions and email messages). DES has become a well known and widely used cryptosystem. The key size of DES is 56 bits and the block size is 64 bits. This block is divided into two halves of 32 bits each. The main part of the round function is the *F function*, which works on the right half of the data using a subkey of 48 bits and eight (six bit to four bit) S boxes. The 32 output bits of the F function are XORed with the left half of the data and the two halves are exchanged. The complete specification of the DES algorithm appears in [14]. In this paper the existence of the initial permutation and its inverse are ignored, since they have no cryptanalytic significance.

An extensive cryptanalytic literature on DES was published since its adoption in 1977. Yet, no short-cuts which can reduce the complexity of cryptanalysis to less than half of exhaustive search were ever reported in the open literature.

The 50% reduction[9] (under a chosen plaintext attack) is based on a symmetry under complementation. Cryptanalysis can exploit this symmetry if two plaintext/ciphertext pairs (P_1, T_1) and (P_2, T_2) are available with $P_1 = \bar{P}_2$.

Diffie and Hellman[6] suggested an exhaustive search of the entire key space in one day on a parallel machine. They estimate the cost of this machine to be $20-million and the cost per solution to be $5000.

Hellman[8] presented a time memory tradeoff method for a chosen plaintext attack. A special case of this method takes about 2^{38} time and 2^{38} memory, with a 2^{56} preprocessing time. Hellman suggests a special purpose machine which produces 100 solutions per day with an average wait of one day. He estimates that the machine costs about $4-million and the cost per solution is about $1–100. The preprocessing is estimated to take 2.3 years on the same machine.

The *Method of Formal Coding* in which the formal expression of each bit in the ciphertext is found as a XOR sum of products of the bits of the plaintext and the key was suggested in [9]. Schaumuller-Bichl[15,16] studied this method and concluded that it requires an enormous amount of computer memory which makes the whole approach impractical.

In 1987 Chaum and Evertse[2] showed that a meet in the middle attack can reduce the key search for DES with a small number of rounds by the following factors:

Number of Rounds	Reduction Factor
4	2^{19}
5	2^9
6	2^2
7	–

They also showed that a slightly modified version of DES with seven rounds can be solved with a reduction factor of 2. However, they proved that a meet in the middle attack of this kind is not applicable to DES with eight or more rounds.

In the same year, Donald W. Davies[3] described a known plaintext cryptanalytic attack on DES. Given sufficient data, it could yield 16 linear relationships among key bits, thus reducing the size of a subsequent key search to 2^{40}. It exploited the correlation between the outputs of adjacent S boxes, due to their inputs being derived from, among other things, a pair of identical bits produced by the bit expansion operation. This correlation could reveal a linear relationship among the four bits of key used to modify these S box input bits. The two 32-bit halves of the DES result (ignoring IP) receive these outputs independently, so each pair of adjacent S boxes could be exploited twice, yielding 16 bits of key information.

The analysis does not require the plaintext P or ciphertext T but uses the quantity $P \oplus T$ and requires a huge number of random inputs. The S box pairs vary in the extent of correlation they produce so that, for example, the pair S7/S8 needs about 10^{17} samples but pair S2/S3 needs about 10^{21}. With about 10^{23} samples, all but the pair S3/S4 should give results (i.e., a total of 14 bits of key information). To exploit all pairs the cryptanalyst needs about 10^{26} samples. The S boxes do not appear to have been designed to minimize the correlation but they are somewhat better than a random choice in this respect. The large number of samples required makes this analysis much harder than exhaustive search for the full DES, but for an eight round version of DES the sample size of 10^{12} or 10^{13} (about 2^{40}) is on the verge of practicality. Therefore, Davies' analysis had penetrated more rounds than previously reported attacks.

During the last decade several cryptosystems which are variants of DES were suggested. Schaumuller-Bichl suggested three such cryptosystems [15, 17]. Two of them (called C80 and C82) are based on the DES structure with the replacement of the F function by nonreversible functions. The third one, called The Generalized DES Scheme (GDES), is an attempt to speed up DES. GDES has 16 rounds with the original DES F function but with a larger block size which is divided into more than two parts. She claims that GDES increases the encryption speed of DES without decreasing its security.

Another variant is the Fast Data Encryption Algorithm (Feal). Feal was designed to be efficiently implementable on an eight bit microprocessor. Feal has two versions. The first[19], called Feal-4, has four rounds. Feal-4 was broken by Den-Boer[4] using a chosen plaintext attack with 100–10000 encryptions. The creators of Feal reacted by creating a new version, called Feal-8, with eight rounds and additional XORs of the plaintext and the ciphertext with subkeys[18,13]. Both versions were described as cryptographically better than DES in several aspects.

In this paper we describe a new kind of attack that can be applied to many DES-like iterated cryptosystems. This is a chosen plaintext attack which uses only the resultant ciphertexts. The basic tool of the attack is the *ciphertext pair* which is a pair of ciphertexts whose plaintexts have particular differences. The two plaintexts can be chosen at random, as long as they satisfy the difference condition, and the cryptanalyst does not have to know their values. The attack is statistical in nature and can fail in rare instances.

2   Introduction to differential cryptanalysis

Differential cryptanalysis is a method which analyses the effect of particular differences in plaintext pairs on the differences of the resultant ciphertext pairs. These differences can be used to assign probabilities to the possible keys and to locate the most probable key. This method usually works on many pairs of plaintexts with the same particular difference using only the resultant ciphertext pairs. For DES-like cryptosystems the difference is chosen as a fixed XORed value of the two plaintexts. In this introduction we show how these differences can be analyzed and exploited.

Let us recall how the DES F function behaves in these terms. The F function takes a 32 bit input and a 48 bit key. The input is expanded (by the E expansion) to 48 bits and XORed with the key. The result is fed into the S boxes and the resultant bits are permuted.

Although DES seems to be very non linear in its input bits, when particular combinations of input bits are modified simultaneously, particular intermidiate bits are modified in a usable way with a relatively high probability after several rounds. We describe this property by means of the particular XOR value of the two plaintexts, the particular XOR value of the intermidiate round and the corresponding probability. Two such encryptions are called a pair.

The XOR of pairs is invariant in the XORing of the key and is linear in the E expansion, the P permutation and the XOR operation between the left half of the data and the output of the F function. Therefore, it is very easy to push the knowledge of such a XOR in the input over these operations.

DES contains also S boxes which are non linear tables. Knowledge of the input XOR of a pair cannot guarantee knowledge of its output XOR. However, every input XOR of an S box suggests a probabilistic distribution of the possible output XORs. In this distribution several output XORs have a relatively high probability. Table 1 describes the distribution of the output XORs for several input XORs in S1. The table counts the number of possible pairs that lead to each of the entries. Each input XOR has 64 possible pairs which are divided among the 16 entries in a row. The average entry is thus four, representing a probability of $\frac{4}{64} = \frac{1}{16}$. We see that a zero input XOR has only one possible output XOR, which is zero. Many entries are impossible or have a small probability. However, there are several entries with probability $\frac{1}{4}$ (i.e., 16 out of 64) or close to it.

Input XOR	Output XOR															
	0_x	1_x	2_x	3_x	4_x	5_x	6_x	7_x	8_x	9_x	A_x	B_x	C_x	D_x	E_x	F_x
0_x	64	0	0	0	0	0	0	0	0	0	0	0	0	0	0	0
1_x	0	0	0	6	0	2	4	4	0	10	12	4	10	6	2	4
2_x	0	0	0	8	0	4	4	4	0	6	8	6	12	6	4	2
3_x	14	4	2	2	10	6	4	2	6	4	4	0	2	2	2	0
4_x	0	0	0	6	0	10	10	6	0	4	6	4	2	8	6	2
5_x	4	8	6	2	2	4	4	2	0	4	4	0	12	2	4	6
6_x	0	4	2	4	8	2	6	2	8	4	4	2	4	2	0	12
7_x	2	4	10	4	0	4	8	4	2	4	8	2	2	2	4	4
8_x	0	0	0	12	0	8	8	4	0	6	2	8	8	2	2	4
9_x	10	2	4	0	2	4	6	0	2	2	8	0	10	0	2	12
A_x	0	8	6	2	2	8	6	0	6	4	6	0	4	0	2	10
B_x	2	4	0	10	2	2	4	0	2	6	2	6	6	4	2	12
C_x	0	0	0	8	0	6	6	0	0	6	6	4	6	6	14	2
D_x	6	6	4	8	4	8	2	6	0	6	4	6	0	2	0	2
E_x	0	4	8	8	6	6	4	0	6	6	4	0	0	4	0	8
F_x	2	0	2	4	4	6	4	2	4	8	2	2	2	6	8	8
								$\vdots$								
30_x	0	4	6	0	12	6	2	2	8	2	4	4	6	2	2	4
31_x	4	8	2	10	2	2	2	2	6	0	0	2	2	4	10	8
32_x	4	4	6	4	4	2	2	4	6	4	0	4	8	2	2	8
33_x	4	4	6	2	10	8	4	2	4	0	2	2	4	6	2	4
34_x	0	8	16	6	2	0	0	12	6	0	0	0	0	8	0	6
35_x	2	2	4	0	8	0	0	0	14	4	6	8	0	2	14	0
36_x	2	6	2	2	8	0	2	2	4	2	6	8	6	4	10	0
37_x	2	2	12	4	2	4	4	10	4	4	2	6	0	2	2	4
38_x	0	6	2	2	2	0	2	2	4	6	4	4	4	6	10	10
39_x	6	2	2	4	12	6	4	8	4	0	2	4	2	4	4	0
$3A_x$	6	4	6	4	6	8	0	6	2	2	2	6	2	2	6	4
$3B_x$	2	6	4	0	0	2	4	6	4	6	8	6	4	4	6	2
$3C_x$	0	10	4	0	12	0	4	2	6	0	4	12	4	4	2	0
$3D_x$	0	8	6	2	2	6	0	8	4	4	0	4	0	12	4	4
$3E_x$	4	8	2	2	2	4	4	14	4	2	0	2	0	8	4	4
$3F_x$	4	8	4	2	4	0	2	4	4	2	4	8	8	6	2	2

Table 1: Partial pairs XOR distribution table of S1(values subsripted with x are in hexadecimal)

We can use this property as a tool to identify key bits. If we can find the output XOR of the F function of the last round, we can filter the set of possible subkeys entering this F function when the pair of ciphertexts is known. Using both ciphertexts it is easy to calculate the input XOR of the F function of the last round and its output XOR. Then the input XOR and output XOR of each S box in the last round are known. In case k input pairs can lead to that entry in the table, exactly k values of the corresponding six subkey bits are possible. Most subkey values are suggested by only few pairs. However, the real value of the subkey bits is suggested by all the pairs and thus can be identified.

The following introductory example breaks a three round DES. The attack uses pairs of ciphertexts whose corresponding plaintext XORs consist of a zero right half and an arbitrary left half. The main part of the algorithm counts the number of pairs which suggest each possible value of the six key bits entering each S box. For each ciphertext pair we do the following: The input XOR of the F function in the first round is zero and thus its output XOR must be zero. The left half of the ciphertext is calculated as the XOR value of the left half of the plaintext, the output of the first round and the output of the third round ($l = L \oplus A \oplus C$, where L is the left half of the plaintext and l is the left half of the ciphertext. See figure 1). Since the plaintext XOR is fixed and the ciphertext XOR is known and the output XOR of the first round is zero, the output XOR of the F function in the third round can be calculated as the XOR of the left half of the plaintext XOR and the left half of the ciphertext XOR. The inputs of the F function in the third round are easily extractable from the ciphertext pair.

The following analysis can be done for each S box in the third round. In this example we only show how to find the six key bits entering S1 in the third round. The input XOR and output XOR of S1 can be easily derived from the input XOR and output XOR of the F function. Let k be the number of possible input pairs to S1 with those input XOR and output XOR. The value of the input bits (denoted by S_E) which are XORed with the six key bits (denoted by S_K) to make the actual value of the input of the S box (denoted by S_I) is extractable from the ciphertext. Therefore, there are exactly k key values suggested by the pair via $S_K = S_E \oplus S_I$. For

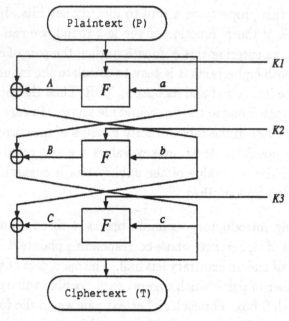

Figure 1: DES with three rounds

S box input		Possible Keys	
06,	32	07,	33
10,	24	11,	25
16,	22	17,	23
1C,	28	1D,	29

Table 2: Possible keys for $34 \to D$ by S1 with input 1, 35 (in hexadecimal)

example, if the ciphertext bits entering S1 in the third round of the two encryptions are $S_E = 1$, $S_E^* = 35$ and the output XOR is D then the value of S_K must appear in table 2. Each line in the table describes two pairs with the same two inputs but with two possible orders. Each pair leads to one key, so each line leads to two keys (which are $S_E \oplus S_I$ and $S_E^* \oplus S_I$). Given many pairs we can count the number of pairs suggesting each possible value of the key bits entering S1. The value which is suggested by all the pairs must be the real value of the key bits.

We now describe the basic tool which allows us to push the knowledge of the plaintext XOR to a knowledge of an intermidiate XOR after as many rounds as possible, which is called an n round characteristic. Every n round characteristic has a particular plaintext XOR Ω_P, a particular XOR of the data in the nth round Ω_T and a probability p^Ω in which the XOR of the data in the nth round is Ω_T when random pairs whose plaintext XOR is Ω_P are used. Any pair whose plaintext XOR is Ω_P and whose XOR of the data in the nth round (using a particular key) is Ω_T is called a right pair. Any other pair is called a wrong pair. Therefore, the right pairs form a fraction p^Ω of all the possible pairs. In the following examples of characteristics we denote the input and output XORs of the F function in the first round by a' and A' respectively, the input and output XORs of the F function in the second round by b' and B' respectively, etc.

The following one round characteristic has probability 1 (for any L'). This is the only one round characteristic with probability greater than $\frac{1}{4}$.

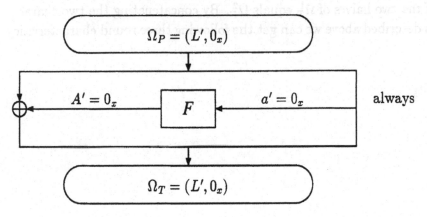

This characteristic has special importance since it plays a role in all the characteristics used to break DES-like cryptosystems.

The following one round characteristic has probability $\frac{14}{64}$ (for any L').

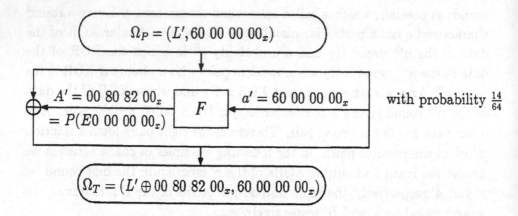

The concatenation of two characteristics lets us build a longer characteristic with probability which is close to the product of their probabilities. A concatenation of characteristics Ω^1 and Ω^2 can be done if the swapped value of the two halves of Ω_T^1 equals Ω_P^2. By concatenating the two characteristics described above we can get the following three round characteristic with probability $\left(\frac{14}{64}\right)^2 \approx 0.05$:

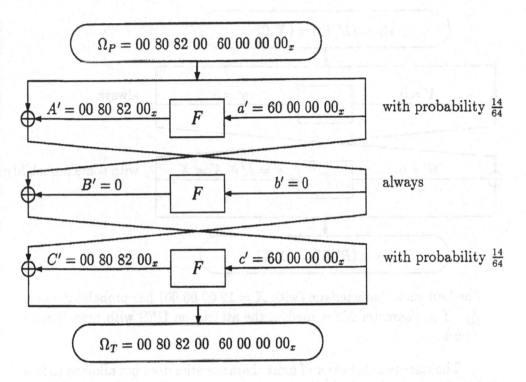

Several characteristics can be concatenated to themselves. These characteristics are called iterative characteristics. We can concatenate an iterative characteristic to itself any number of times. The advantage of iterative characteristics is that we can build an n round characteristic for any large n with a fixed reduction rate of the probability for each additional round, while in non iterative characteristics the reduction rate of the probability usually increases due to the avalanche effect.

There are several kinds of iterative characteristics but the simplest ones are the most useful. These characteristics are based on a non zero input XOR to the F function that may cause a zero output XOR (i.e., two different inputs yield the same output). This is possible in the F function of DES if at least three neighboring S boxes differ in the pair (see also at [5,1]). The structure of these characteristics is as follows. The input XOR of the F function is marked by X, s.t. there are as many pairs as possible whose input XOR is X and the output XOR is zero.

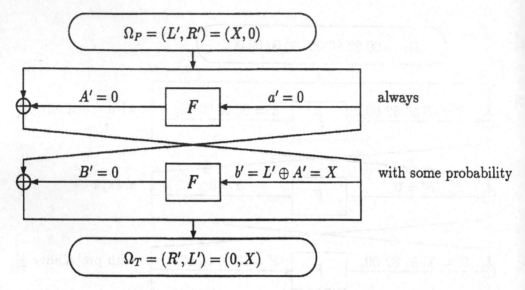

The best such characteristic (with $X = 19\ 60\ 00\ 00$) has probability about $\frac{1}{234}$. This characteristic is used in the attacks on DES with nine or more rounds.

The statistical behavior of most characteristics does not allow us to look for the intersection of all the keys suggested by the various pairs as we did before, since the intersection is usually empty: the wrong pairs do not necessarily list the right key as a possible value. However, we know that the right key value should result from all the right pairs, which occur with the characteristic's probability. All the other possible key values are fairly randomly distributed: the expected XOR value (which is usually not the real value in the pair) with the known ciphertext pair can cause any key value to be possible, and even the wrong key values suggested by the right pairs are quite random. Consequently, the right key appears with the characteristic's probability (from right pairs) plus other random occurrences (from wrong pairs). To find the key we just have to count the number of occurrences of each of the suggested keys. When the number of pairs is large enough, the right key is likely to be the one that occurs most often.

3 Breaking DES with six rounds

The cryptanalysis of DES with six rounds is more complex than the crypt-analysis of the three round version. We use two statistical characteristics with probability $\frac{1}{16}$, and choose the key value that is counted most often. Each one of the two characteristics lets us find the 30 key bits of K6 which are used at the input of five S boxes in the sixth round, but three of the S boxes are common so the total number of key bits found by the two characteristics is 42. The other 14 key bits can be found later by means of exhaustive search or by a more careful counting on the key bits entering the eighth S box in the sixth round.

The first characteristic Ω^1 is:

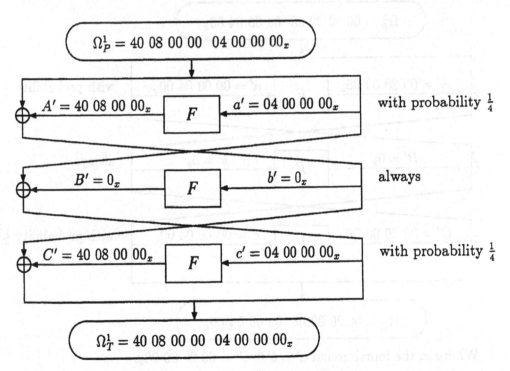

$$\Omega^1_P = 40\ 08\ 00\ 00\ \ 04\ 00\ 00\ 00_x$$

$A' = 40\ 08\ 00\ 00_x$ — F — $a' = 04\ 00\ 00\ 00_x$ — with probability $\frac{1}{4}$

$B' = 0_x$ — F — $b' = 0_x$ — always

$C' = 40\ 08\ 00\ 00_x$ — F — $c' = 04\ 00\ 00\ 00_x$ — with probability $\frac{1}{4}$

$$\Omega^1_T = 40\ 08\ 00\ 00\ \ 04\ 00\ 00\ 00_x$$

Where in the fourth round $d' = b' \oplus C' = 40\ 08\ 00\ 00_x$.

Five S boxes in the fourth round (S2, S5, ..., S8) have zero input XORs ($S'_{Ed} = 0$) and thus their output XORs are zero ($S'_{Od} = 0$). The corresponding output XORs in the sixth round can be found by $F' = c' \oplus D' \oplus l'$. Since the right key value is not suggested by all the pairs (due to the probabilistic nature of the characteristic). We should simultaneously count on subkey bits entering several S boxes. The best approach is to count on all the 30 countable subkey bits together, which maximizes the probability that the right key value is the one counted most often. A straightforward implementation of this method requires 2^{30} counters, which is impractical on most computers. However, the improved counting procedure described in the full paper achieves exactly the same result with much smaller memory (the program size is about 100K bytes on a personal computer).

The same efficient algorithm is used to find the 30 key bits of S1, S2, S4, S5 and S6 using the second characteristic Ω^2 which is:

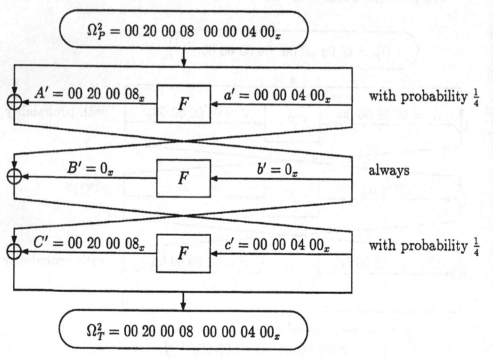

$$\Omega_P^2 = 00\ 20\ 00\ 08\ \ 00\ 00\ 04\ 00_x$$

$A' = 00\ 20\ 00\ 08_x$ F $a' = 00\ 00\ 04\ 00_x$ with probability $\frac{1}{4}$

$B' = 0_x$ F $b' = 0_x$ always

$C' = 00\ 20\ 00\ 08_x$ F $c' = 00\ 00\ 04\ 00_x$ with probability $\frac{1}{4}$

$$\Omega_T^2 = 00\ 20\ 00\ 08\ \ 00\ 00\ 04\ 00_x$$

Where in the fourth round $d' = b' \oplus C' = 00\ 20\ 00\ 08_x$.

Again, five S boxes in the fourth round (S1, S2, S4, S5 and S6) have zero input XORs. The computed key values of the common S boxes S2, S5 and S6 should be the same in both calculations (otherwise we should analyze more pairs or consider additional candidate keys with almost maximal counts). If this test is successful, we have probably found 42 bits of K6.

DES has 56 key bits and 14 of them are still missing. We can find them by searching all the 2^{14} possibilities for the expected plaintext XOR value of the decrypted ciphertexts.

4 Results

We now describe the results we get by this kind of attacks. Due to space limitations, we are not describing the attacks in detail in this extended abstract. Note that the complexities we quote are the number of encryptions needed to create all the necessary pairs while the attacking algorithm itself uses fewer and simpler operations.

DES with six rounds was broken in less than 0.3 seconds on a personal computer using 240 ciphertexts. DES with eight rounds was broken in less than two minutes on a computer by analysing 15000 ciphertexts chosen from a pool of 50000 candidate ciphertexts. DES with up to 15 rounds is breakable faster than exhaustive search. DES with 15 rounds can be broken in about 2^{52} steps but DES with 16 rounds still requires 2^{58} steps (which is slightly higher than the complexity of an exhaustive search). A summary of the cryptanalytic results on DES with intermidiate number of rounds appears in table 3.

Some researchers have proposed to strengthen DES by making all the subkeys Ki independent (or at least to derive them in a more complicated way from a longer actual key K). Our attack can be carried out even in this case. DES with eight rounds with independent subkeys (i.e., with $8 \cdot 48 = 384$ independent bits which are not compatible with the key scheduling algorithm) was broken in less than two minutes using the same ciphertexts as in the case of dependent subkeys. DES with independent subkeys (i.e., with $16 \cdot 48 = 768$ independent bits) is breakable within 2^{61} steps. As a result, any modification of the key scheduling algorithm cannot make DES much stronger. The attacks on DES with 9–16 rounds are not

Rounds	Complexity
4	2^4
6	2^8
8	2^{16}
9	2^{26}
10	2^{35}
11	2^{36}
12	2^{43}
13	2^{44}
14	2^{51}
15	2^{52}
16	2^{58}

Table 3: Summary of the cryptanalysis of DES

influenced by the P permutation and the replacement of the P permutation by any other permutation or function can't make them less successful. On the other hand, the replacement of the order of the eight DES S boxes (without changing their values) can make DES much weaker: DES with 16 rounds with a particular replaced order is breakable in about 2^{46} steps. The replacement of the XOR operation by the more complex addition operation makes this cryptosystem much weaker. DES with random S boxes is shown to be very easy to break. Even a minimal change of one entry in one of the DES S boxes can make DES easier to break. GDES is shown to be trivially breakable with six encryptions in less than 0.2 seconds, while GDES with independent subkeys is breakable with 16 encryptions in less than 3 seconds.

This attack is applicable also to a wide variety of DES-like cryptosystems. Lucifer with eight rounds can be broken using less than 60 ciphertexts (30 pairs). The Feal-8 cryptosystem can be broken with less than 2000 ciphertexts (1000 pairs) and the Feal-4 cryptosystem can be broken with just eight ciphertexts and one of their plaintexts. As a reaction to our attack on Feal-8, its creators introduced Feal-N[11], with any even number of rounds N. They suggest the use of Feal-N with 16 and 32 rounds.

Nevertheless, Feal-N can be broken for any $N \leq 31$ rounds faster than an exhaustive search.

Differential cryptanalytic techniques are applicable to hash functions, in addition to cryptosystems. For example, the following messages hash to the same value in Merkle's Snefru[10] function with two pass:

- 00000000 00000000 00000000 00000000 00000000 00000000 0000000(
  00000000 00000000 00000000 00000000 00000000

- 00000000 f1301600 13dfc53e 4cc3b093 37461661 ccd8b94d 24d9d35:
  71471fde 00000000 00000000 00000000 00000000

- 00000000 1d197f00 2abd3f6f cf33f3d1 8674966a 816e5d51 acd9a90!
  53c1d180 00000000 00000000 00000000 00000000

- 00000000 e98c8300 1e777a47 b5271f34 a04974bb 44cc8b62 be4b0ef(
  18131756 00000000 00000000 00000000 00000000

and the following two messages hash to the same value in a variant of Miyaguchi's N-Hash[12] function with six rounds:

- CAECE595 127ABF3C 1ADE09C8 1F9AD8C2

- 4A8C6595 921A3F3C 1ADE09C8 1F9AD8C2.

References

[1] E. F. Brickell, J. H. Moore, M. R. Purtill, *Structure in the S-Boxes of the DES*, Advances in cryptology, proceedings of CRYPTO 86, pp. 3–7, 1986.

[2] David Chaum, Jan-Hendrik Evertse, *Cryptanalysis of DES with a reduced number of rounds, Sequences of linear factors in block ciphers*, technical report, 1987.

[3] D. W. Davies, private communications.

[4] Bert Den Boer, *Cryptanalysis of F.E.A.L.*, Advances in cryptology, proceedings of EUROCRYPT 88, 1988.

[5] Yvo Desmedt, Jean-Jacque Quisquater, Marc Davio, *Dependence of output on input in DES: small avalanche characteristics*, Advances in cryptology, proceedings of CRYPTO 84, pp. 359–376, 1984.

[6] W. Diffie and M. E. Hellman, *Exhaustive cryptanalysis of the NBS Data Encryption Standard*, Computer, Vol. 10, No. 6, pp. 74–84, June 1977.

[7] H. Feistel, *Cryptography and data security*, Scientific american, Vol 228, No. 5, pp. 15–23, May 1973.

[8] M. E. Hellman, *A Cryptanalytic Time-Memory Tradeoff*, IEEE Trans. Inform. Theory, Vol. 26, No. 4, pp. 401–406, July 1980.

[9] M. E. Hellman, R. Merkle, R. Schroppel, L. Washington, W. Diffie, S. Pohlig and P. Schweitzer, *Results of an Initial Attempt to Cryptanalyze the NBS Data Encryption Standard*, Stanford university, September 1976.

[10] Ralph C. Merkle, technical report, March 1990.

[11] Shoji Miyaguchi, *Feal-N specifications*.

[12] S. Miyaguchi, K. Ohta, M. Iwata, *128-bit hash function (N-Hash)*, proceedings of SECURICOM90, March 1990.

[13] Shoji Miyaguchi, Akira Shiraishi, Akihiro Shimizu, *Fast data encryption algorithm Feal-8*, Review of electrical communications laboratories, Vol. 36 No. 4, 1988.

[14] National Bureau of Standards, *Data Encryption Standard*, U.S. Department of Commerce, FIPS pub. 46, January 1977.

[15] Ingrid Schaumuller-Bichl, *Zur Analyse des Data Encryption Standard und Synthese Verwandter Chiffriersysteme*, thesis, May 1981.

[16] Ingrid Schaumuller-Bichl, *Cryptanalysis of the Data Encryption Standard by the Method of Formal Coding*, Cryptologia, proceedings of CRYPTO 82, pp. 235–255, 1982.

[17] Ingrid Schaumuller-Bichl, *On the Design and Analysis of New Cipher Systems Related to the DES*, technical report, 1983.

[18] Akihiro Shimizu, Shoji Miyaguchi, *Fast Data Encryption Algorithm Feal*, Advances in cryptology, proceedings of EUROCRYPT 87, pp. 267, 1987.

[19] Akihiro Shimizu, Shoji Miyaguchi, *Fast Data Encryption Algorithm Feal*, Abstracts of EUROCRYPT 87, Amsterdam, April 1987.

A STATISTICAL ATTACK OF THE FEAL-8 CRYPTOSYSTEM

Henri Gilbert and Guy Chassé

Centre National d'Etudes des Télécommunications (CNET)

PAA-TIM

38-40, rue du Général Leclerc

92131 Issy les Moulineaux

FRANCE

ABSTRACT.

This paper presents a chosen plaintext cryptanalysis of the FEAL-8 cryptosystem. The attack requires the ciphertext corresponding to approximately 10000 pairs of 64 bit plaintext blocks. The difference (bitwise xor) between the two blocks of each pair is equal to an appropriately selected constant. We first state that some differential statistics for intermediate values of the data randomizer are non uniform and independent of the encryption key. We then show that these statistics can be used to compute gradually the expanded key of the data randomizer.

In 1989 some announcements were made that the so-called FEAL-8, 8 round version of the FEAL cryptosystem, was vulnerable to a chosen plaintext attack [1]. So far, however, only the cryptanalysis of the 4 round version FEAL-4 by Bert Den Boer [2] was published. In this paper we present a chosen plaintext attack of FEAL-8 based on some differential statistics of its data randomization scheme.

1 Description of the FEAL-8 randomizer and first remarks.

We are using the following notations.

- If A represents a 32 bit word $(a_0, a_1, ..., a_{31})$, A_0 is the byte $(a_0 a_1 ... a_7)$, A_1 is the byte $(a_8 a_9 ... a_{15})$,... etc. We also write $A = (A_0, A_1, A_2, A_3)$.

- If A and A' are two binary strings (e.g. bits or bytes or 32 bit words, etc...), $A \oplus A'$ is the bitwise "exclusive or" ("xor" or addition modulo 2) between A and A'.

- If B is the byte $(b_7, b_6, b_5, b_4, b_3, b_2, b_1, b_0)$, the right side bit b_0 is also referred to as $B[0]$, the bit b_1 as $B[1]$,... etc. The byte $(b_5 b_4 b_3 b_2 b_1 b_0 b_7 b_6)$ is denoted by $ROT_2(B)$.

- If B and B' are two bytes, they will be sometimes considered as two integers in the usual way (the right side bit is equal to the integer modulo 2) and the byte $B + B'$ will be the sum modulo 256 of these 2 integers. We also define the ternary operator SBOX : $SBOX(B, B', \epsilon) = ROT_2(B + B' + \epsilon)$ where ϵ is equal to 0 or 1.

The FEAL-8 algorithm, which is specified in the reference [3], can be divided in two components : the key schedule and the data randomizer. We do not need here to consider the details of the key schedule : let us only tell that the key schedule transforms the 64 bit secret key K in an expanded key of 32 bytes $K_0, K_1, ..., K_{31}$.

The data randomizer operates on a 64 bit plaintext block I divided into a left 32 bit word I^0 and a right one I^1. It produces the 64 bit ciphertext block O divided into a left 32 bit word O^0 and a right one O^1. The data randomization can be split in the three following steps.

The initial step.

We start with a 64 bit word (I^0, I^1) as input. The we compute a new 64 bit word (X^0, X^1) defined by :

$$X^0 = I^0 \oplus (K_{16}, K_{17}, K_{18}, K_{19})$$
$$X^1 = I^1 \oplus I^0 \oplus (K_{16} \oplus K_{20}, K_{17} \oplus K_{21}, K_{18} \oplus K_{22}, K_{19} \oplus K_{23})$$

The main step.

The 64 bit word (X^0, X^1) is taken as the input to an 8 round Feistel scheme. The rounds are numbered from 0 to 7. At round i, a new 32 bit word X^{i+2} is produced, given by the relation :

$$X^{i+2} = f_i(X^{i+1}) \oplus X^i.$$

The function f_i is defined by :

$$\{0,1\}^{32} \longrightarrow \{0,1\}^{32}$$

$$X = (X_0, X_1, X_2, X_3) \longmapsto Y = (Y_0, Y_1, Y_2, Y_3)$$

where the bytes of Y are computed in the following order :

$$Y_1 = SBOX(X_0 \oplus X_1 \oplus K_{2i}, X_2 \oplus X_3 \oplus K_{2i+1}, 1),$$
$$Y_0 = SBOX(X_0, Y_1, 0),$$
$$Y_2 = SBOX(Y_1, X_2 \oplus X_3 \oplus K_{2i+1}, 0),$$
$$Y_3 = SBOX(Y_2, X_3, 1).$$

It is easier to understand such a transformation with a diagram.

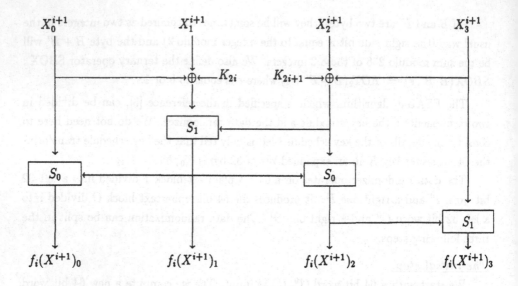

Figure 1 : diagram of the f function.

The function f_i is one to one and only depending on the two expanded key bytes K_{2i} and K_{2i+1}. In the (traditional) 64 bit representation of the Feistel scheme, the round i output is the 64 bit word (X^{i+1}, X^{i+2}).

The final step.

The 64 bit word (X^8, X^9) is taken as input to this final step. The intermediate 64 bit word $(X^9, X^8 \oplus X^9)$ is xored with the 64 bit word $(K_{24}, K_{25}, ...K_{31})$, giving the 64 bit output (O^0, O^1).

It is worth making two elementary remarks on the FEAL randomizer. We state them in an intentionnaly informal manner.

• If we consider bytes as elements of the GF(2) vector space $GF(2)^8$, the only nonlinear elementary operation of the whole randomization is the modulo 256 addition + (the ROT_2 function and the xor operation $\oplus$ are linear).

• The diffusion introduced by an f_i function is quite poor for some of the input bits. The f_i functions are built with the $SBOX$ operator. Notice that if two bytes B and B' are taken as input to an $SBOX$, the ouput is equal, up to the ROT_2 rotation, to a byte B'' which takes one of the values $B + B'$ and $B + B' + 1$. Each bit of B or B' only influences the bits of equal or higher weight in B''. The diffusion between bits of different weight is entirely based on the carry propagation phenomenon and the diffusion effect decreases fastly as the distance between the bit positions is increasing. In fact, the modulo 256 sum $B + B'$ of two bytes B and B' has in most cases many bits equal to the corresponding ones of $B \oplus B'$: roughly speaking the two operations $+$ and $\oplus$ do not strongly differ.

These properties will be very useful in the Sections 3 and 4 where we show that an attacker can take advantage from them by a suitable choice of the plaintext.

2 Outline of our attack method.

The FEAL-8 data randomizer belongs to the quite large family of the layered blockciphers. We are calling "statistical meet in the middle attack" the following chosen plaintext attack method, which is appropriate for some layered blockciphers with a limited number of rounds.

The attacker first chooses the plaintext blocks, later referred to as plaintext samples. This selection is the crucial issue of the attack. The plaintext samples must be chosen in such a way that the distribution of some "last round input bits" (i.e. bits which appear in the enciphering scheme as input bits of the last round) is not uniform and independent of the actual secret key K. The number n of plaintext blocks must be taken sufficiently large to prevent the concealment of this phenomenon. The n selected plaintext samples are encrypted with the secret key K, providing n ciphertext samples.

Observing these n ciphertext samples, the attacker tries to guess the last round input bits, using the upward calculation scheme given by the deciphering algorithm. For that purpose he makes an exhaustive trial of all the expanded key bits involved in the upward calculation scheme. Denote by "last round key bits" these unknown expanded key bits. For each assumption on the last round key bits, the attacker makes n upward calculations of the last round input bits (one calculation for each ciphertext sample) and finally obtains a distribution of their values. One may reasonably expect that only the right last round key bits lead to the expected non uniform distribution, and that any wrong hypothesis leads to a much more uniform, or at least different distribution. If this happens to be true, once having computed the distribution associated to each assumption, the attacker is able to guess the last round key bits.

Once the last round key bits have been correctly guessed, the problem of obtaining the remaining expanded key bits is more or less similar to finding a chosen plaintext attack against the same blockcipher with a reduced number of rounds. Of course there exist many variants of this attack method.

In the two following sections, we apply the statistical meet in the middle attack method to the FEAL-8 algorithm. We first show how to choose the plaintext samples in order to obtain a non uniform statistical distribution of some intermediate bits. We then show how to use these properties to guess the expanded key.

3 Choice of the plaintext samples.

Our strategy for the choice of the plaintext samples is based on the previous remark concerning the diffusion in the FEAL randomizer. In the + operation between two bytes, the diffusion of the highest weight bit of each input byte is limited to the highest weight bit of the output byte since there is no carry propagation at the left of this bit. In other words, if two samples are such that at any stage of the calculation the input bytes to an $SBOX$ operator of the f function differ only by their highest weight bit, the output bytes will only differ by their second lowest weight bit.

In order to take advantage from this weakness, it seems appropriate to select the plaintext samples in pairs. We use the notations I^0, I^1, X^0,..., X^9, O^0, O^1 introduced in Section 1 for the first component of a sample pair and the notations I'^0, I'^1, X'^0,...,X'^9, O'^0, O'^1 for the second one. If A represents any variable related to the first element of a sample pair and A' the similar variable for the second element, the notation ΔA will be used instead of $A \oplus A'$.

It is easy to generate random sample pairs (I, I') with the constraints :

$$\Delta I^0 = (2, 0, 0, 2),$$
$$\Delta I^1 = (130, 128, 128, 130).$$

There are 2^{63} such pairs because the order is irrelevant . So we only need to randomly generate the first 64 bit word $I = (I^0, I^1)$, then we deduce $I' = (I'^0, I'^1)$ using the constraints.

The following observations are the basis of our results.

• Looking at the corresponding values of X^0 and X^1 we notice immediately from the initial step of the algorithm that for every value of the secret key :

$$\Delta X^0 = (2, 0, 0, 2),$$
$$\Delta X^1 = (128, 128, 128, 128).$$

(what means, for instance, that only the highest weight bit of the bytes X_i^1 and $X_i'^1$ differ for the integers i, $0 \le i \le 3$).

• The 32 bit word :

$$\Delta X^2 = f^0(X^1) \oplus X^0 \oplus f^0(X'^1) \oplus X'^0$$

is equal for every key to the quadruple of bytes $(0, 0, 0, 0)$.

Similarly we obtain :

$$\Delta X^3 = (128, 128, 128, 128)$$

and then :

$$\Delta X^4 = (2, 0, 0, 2).$$

• Some bits of $\Delta X^5, \Delta X^6$ and ΔX^7 are not uniformly distributed in a way which does not strongly depend on the actual key.

The last statement can be deduced from computations similar to those made for $\Delta X^2, \Delta X^3$ and ΔX^4. Nevertheless, experiments are necessary to describe with precision the statistics for the bits of $\Delta X^5, \Delta X^6$ and ΔX^7. These statistics, which are the framework of our cryptanalysis are gathered in the annex, at the end of the paper. The four arrays contain the observed frequency of 0 for each bit of the 32 bit words ΔX^0, ΔX^1, ΔX^2, ΔX^3, ΔX^4, ΔX^5, ΔX^6 and ΔX^7 for random input pairs (I^0, I^1) and (I'^0, I'^1) with the above described constraints. It appears for instance that, even after the seventh round, two bits are not uniformly distributed : $\Delta X_1^7[7]$ and $\Delta X_1^7[6]$. Their 0 frequency is printed in boldface.

The occurence rates in the annex have been obtained by computing the empirical 0 frequency of the corresponding bits with $n = 20000$ sample pairs for a given fixed key K. Let Ω be the set of the 2^{63} inputs respecting the constraints. Considering the set Ω equipped with the uniform probability, we can consider the n trials :

$$\Omega \longrightarrow \{0, 1\}$$

$$\omega \longmapsto \Delta X_j^i[k]$$

mapping one sample pair ω to the corresponding bit $\Delta X_j^i[k]$ (the integer i, j, k being fixed to a chosen value) as n independant random variables of same law. So applying the approximation suggested by the Central Limit Theorem we can get an order of magnitude of the error on the experimentally obtained 0 frequency using n samples. Using the Central Limit Theorem to the finite value $n = 20000$ leads to the conclusion that, for the key used in an experiment, the absolute value of the error on each estimated occurence rate is less than 0.01 with a probability larger than 0.99. In order to check that those occurence rates do not strongly depend on the secret key used, we have simply made experiments with different keys : the order of magnitude of the discrepancies between the obtained results is less than 0.01.

Through the same method, we have estimated the occurence rate of the value 0 for the bit $b = \Delta X_0^7[7] \oplus \Delta X_1^7[5]$. The rate of 0.54, was found for several different keys.

We have shown that if an attacker chooses n samples pairs according to the described constraints, he is able to predict some irregularities in the statistics of some intermediate outputs even after seven rounds of the Feistel scheme.

A similar phenomenon can be obtained with other choices of the constraints, for instance :

- $\Delta I^0 = (2, 0, 0, 0)$ and $\Delta I^1 = (130, 128, 0, 0)$,
- $\Delta I^0 = (0, 0, 0, 2)$ and $\Delta I^1 = (0, 0, 128, 130)$.

These two alternative choices for the constraints are not used in the attack described in the next section.

4 Estimation of the expanded key.

We now show how to guess stepwise the secret expanded key from, say, 10000 plaintext sample pairs selected as explained in Section 3 and from the corresponding ciphertext.

The key estimation process can be subdivided in several elementary steps. At each step, one of the statistical properties stated in Section 3 is used for guessing some new bits or new linear bit combinations of the unknown expanded key by an exhaustive search on these new bits.

The splitting of the estimation process in steps is somewhat arbitrary. The division presented here seemed convenient to us for showing the feasablility of the attack, although it is far from being optimal from a performance point of view.

The first step, which provides the 10 first linear bit combinations of the expanded key, is explained in some detail in Section 4.1. In Section 4.2 we summarize the subsequent steps more briefly; it is mainly intended for readers interested in details. Since all the steps are very similar to the first one, section 4.2 is not essential for the understanding of our attack. Section 4.3 gives the outcome of our attack.

4.1 Description of the first step.

Step 1 uses the non uniform distribution of bit $\Delta X_1^7[7]$. This bit is related to the ciphertext samples (O^0, O^1) and (O'^0, O'^1) by the following relations :

$$X_1^7 = SBOX(X_0^8 \oplus X_1^8 \oplus K_{14}, X_2^8 \oplus X_3^8 \oplus K_{15}, 1) \oplus X_1^9,$$
$$X_0^8 = O_0^0 \oplus O_0^1 \oplus K_{24} \oplus K_{28},$$
$$X_1^8 = O_1^0 \oplus O_1^1 \oplus K_{25} \oplus K_{29},$$
$$X_2^8 = O_2^0 \oplus O_2^1 \oplus K_{26} \oplus K_{30},$$
$$X_3^8 = O_3^0 \oplus O_3^1 \oplus K_{27} \oplus K_{31},$$
$$X_1^9 = O_1^0 \oplus K_{25}.$$

Let us replace in the first relation the bytes $X_0^8, X_1^8, X_2^8, X_3^8$ and X_1^9 using the subsequent relations. Let us do the same for the second component of a sample pair and let us "xor" the two obtained relations. We can see that the unknown byte ΔX_1^7 can be expressed in terms of the observed ciphertext bytes and of the two unknown bytes $B_1 = K_{14} \oplus K_{24} \oplus K_{28} \oplus K_{25} \oplus K_{29}$ and $B_2 = K_{15} \oplus K_{26} \oplus K_{30} \oplus K_{27} \oplus K_{31}$. More precisely, considering the details of the binary operations (addition and $SBOX$ operation) we see that bit $\Delta X_1^7[7]$ depends only on the 5 lowest weight bits of B_1 and B_2 , i.e. on 10 unknown bits.

For each of the 2^{10} possible assumptions about these 10 bits, the attacker performs 10000 estimations of bit $\Delta X_1^7[7]$ (one for each ciphertext sample pair). For the correct assumption, his estimations will be distributed according to the rates indicated in Section 3 (i.e. the value 0 will occur with probability almost equal to .54), otherwise, for a wrong assumption, his estimations will be more uniformly distributed. So the attacker is able to recognise the right value of the 5 lowest weight bits of B_1 and the 5 lowest weight bits of B_2 in less than 2^{24} upward computations of bit $\Delta X_1^7[7]$.

4.2 Description of the further steps.

Step 2 uses the non uniform distribution of bit $b = \Delta X_0^7[7] \oplus \Delta X_1^7[5]$ for which the value 0 occurs with a probability .54 (see Section 3). In order to relate bit b to the ciphertext, we need the six relations used in the step 1 and the two following additional ones :

$$X_0^7 = SBOX(SBOX(X_0^8 \oplus X_1^8 \oplus K_{14}, X_2^8 \oplus X_3^8 \oplus K_{15}, 1), X_0^8, 0) \oplus X_0^9,$$
$$X_0^9 = O_0^0 \oplus K_{24}.$$

It follows from these eight relations that bit b is a function of the ciphertext and of the three bytes : $B_1 = K_{14} \oplus K_{24} \oplus K_{28} \oplus K_{25} \oplus K_{29}$, $B_2 = K_{15} \oplus K_{26} \oplus K_{30} \oplus K_{27} \oplus K_{31}$ and $B_3 = K_{24} \oplus K_{28}$.

More precisely, one can check that b actually depends on the 5 lowest weight bits of byte B_3, on the 7 lowest weight bits of B_1 and B_2 and on the bit $(B_1[7] \oplus B_2[7])$. Since the 5 lowest weight bits of B_1 and B_2 have been already guessed at step 1, b only depends on 10 new unknown bits. An exhaustive search on these 10 bits provides the right solution.

Step 3 uses the non uniform distribution of bit $\Delta X_1^6[2]$ (for which the value 0 occurs with a probability .62). One can check that this bit only depends on :
- the 6 lowest weight bits of byte B_3,
- the 6 lowest weight bits of byte $B_4 = K_{27} \oplus K_{31}$,
- and on all the bits of B_1 and B_2.

There are 8 new unknown bits : 6 for B_4, and one for B_3 and B_1. An exhaustive search provides the right solution .

Step 4 uses the non uniform distribution of bit $\Delta X_1^6[5]$ (which takes the value 0 with a probability .17). This bit can be expressed in terms of the ciphertext, of the already determined key bits, and of the following 8 new unknown key bits :
- bit $B_3[6]$,
- bit $B_4[6]$,
- the bits 0 and 2 of bytes $B_5 = K_{12} \oplus K_{24} \oplus K_{25}$ and $B_6 = K_{13} \oplus K_{26} \oplus K_{27}$,

- and the two bits $(B_3[7] \oplus B_5[1])$ and $(B_4[7] \oplus B_6[1])$.
An exhaustive search provides the right value for those 8 bits.

Let us summarize the outcome of the four first steps. We have now determined all the bits of bytes B_1, B_2, B_3 and B_4 (except the highest weight bit of B_3 and B_4, which will be determined later on). This implies (as may be checked in using the relations between the 4 byte words X^7, X^8 and X^9) that X^7 is now known up to four unknown constant bytes, so we have gained one round with respect to the initial situation, where only X^8 and X^9 were known up to four unknown constant bytes. So, roughly speaking, the problem of guessing the remaining expanded key bits is now easier than breaking the FEAL-7 cryptosystem.

Steps 5, 6 and 7 use the non uniform distribution of bits $\Delta X_1^6[1], \Delta X_1^5[2]$ and $\Delta X_1^5[5]$ (which take the value 0 with probability .55, 1 and .75 respectively). They enable us to determine :

- the whole bytes $B_7 = K_{12} \oplus K_{25}$ and $B_8 = K_{13} \oplus K_{26}$,
- the not yet known bits of the partially known bytes B_5 and B_6, except the 4 bits $B_5[1], B_6[1], B_5[7]$ and $B_6[7]$ which will be determined later,
- the two bits $(B_5[7] \oplus B_9[1])$ and $(B_6[7] \oplus B_{10}[1])$, which are combinations of the bytes B_5, B_6 and of the unknown bytes $B_9 = K_{10} \oplus K_{14}$ and $B_{10} = K_{11} \oplus K_{15}$,
- the bits number 0 and 2 of the bytes B_9 and B_{10}.

Consequently, the 4 byte word X^6 is now known for each sample up to four unknown constant bytes and we have now gained two rounds with respect to the situation at the beginning of step 1.

Step 8 uses the unbalanced distribution of the 3 lowest weight bits of ΔX_0^5 and of the 4 lowest weight bits of ΔX_1^5 (the probability that all of these 7 bits take the value 0 is about .83) for recovering all the still unknown bits of bytes $B_9 = K_{10} \oplus K_{14}$ and $B_{10} = K_{11} \oplus K_{15}$. Only 100 sample pairs do now suffice for making the correct guess.

The following steps enable us to guess successively :

- the unknown bytes $B_{11} = K_8 \oplus K_{12}$ and $B_{12} = K_9 \oplus K_{13}$ and the two still unknown bits $B_3[7]$ and $B_4[7]$, using the statistics of the 4 bytes word ΔX^4, which is constant and equal to $(2,0,0,2)$; less than 100 sample pairs are sufficient ;
- the unknown bytes $B_{13} = K_6 \oplus K_{10}$ and $B_{14} = K_7 \oplus K_{11}$, due to the statistics on the 4 bytes word ΔX^3, which is constant and equal to $(128,128,128,128)$; less than 100 sample pairs are sufficient.

At this point of the attack, the use of the ciphertext alone does no longer suffice. This is because the statistics on the 4 byte words $\Delta X^2, \Delta X^1$ and ΔX^0 are trivial consequences of the statistics on the 4 byte words ΔX^3 and ΔX^4. So the statistics on $\Delta X^2, \Delta X^1$ and ΔX^0 do not allow to guess any new unknown expanded key bit. There are two ways to solve this slight difficulty :

- the first approach is to use, say, 100 additional sample pairs, selected according to other constraints, e.g. according to the relations $\Delta I^0 = (128, 128, 128, 128)$ and $\Delta I^1 = (130, 128, 128, 130)$. The statistics on $\Delta X^2, \Delta X^1$ and ΔX^0 are no longer trivial consequences of those on ΔX^3 and ΔX^4; they enable us to guess new unknown expanded key bits based on the new ciphertext. Also the plaintext for at least one of the ciphertext samples is required at the end of the attack;

- the second approach is now to take the plaintext and the ciphertext of the initial samples into account (instead of the ciphertext samples alone); the property that, for each sample bit $X_1^1[2]$ differs from the plaintext bit $(I_1^1[2] \oplus I_1^0[2])$ by one constant bit can be first used for recovering new expanded key bits, etc...

We summarize here the last steps of the attack with the first method. The following bytes are successively guessed :

- the unknown bytes $B_{15} = K_4 \oplus K_8$ and $B_{16} = K_5 \oplus K_9$ (using the statistics on ΔX^2);

- the unknown bytes $B_{17} = K_2 \oplus K_6$ and $B_{18} = K_3 \oplus K_7$ (using the statistics on ΔX^1);

- the unknown bytes $B_{19} = K_0 \oplus K_4$ and $B_{20} = K_1 \oplus K_5$ (using the statistics on ΔX^0).

The eight unknown bytes $B_{21} = K_{16} \oplus K_{20}, B_{22} = K_0 \oplus K_{17} \oplus K_{21}, B_{23} = K_1 \oplus K_{18} \oplus K_{22}, B_{24} = K_{19} \oplus K_{23}, B_{25} = K_{16}, B_{26} = K_2 \oplus K_{17}, B_{27} = K_3 \oplus K_{18}$ and $B_{28} = K_{19}$ are now available with almost no calculation, using one single plaintext sample and the corresponding ciphertext.

4.3 Outcome of the attack.

The two previous sections have described a complete attack. Not surprisingly, this estimation process has provided the 28 combinations $B_1, B_2, ...B_{28}$ instead of the 32 bytes $K_0, K_1, ...K_{31}$: this is because the encryption and decryption functions associated with any 32-uple of expanded key bytes $K_0, K_1, ...K_{31}$ is entirely determined by the bytes $B_1, B_2, ...B_{28}$.

According to our simulations on the thirteen steps of the above attack, it does not require more than two hours computing time on a SUN4 workstation.

As already stated, we have not tried to optimize the performance of the attack. It seems feasible to us to split the computation of the expanded key in much more steps, each of them requiring an exhaustive search on substantially fewer bits. Indeed, instead of performing at each step an exhaustive search on all the new unknown involved expanded key bits, it is feasible to first perform an exhaustive search on the bits which have the major impact due to their position in the addition processes and, after that, to determine the remaining ones by another exhaustive search. This would save much computing time.

5 Conclusions.

In this paper we have presented a statistical attack method which we propose to call "statistical meet in the middle". We have shown how to apply this method to a complete attack on the FEAL-8 enciphering algorithm. Our attack is based on the analysis of about 10000 sample pairs, and requires a rather limited computational expense.

Remaining open questions include :

- how to extend our attack to FEAL-N, when $N > 8$;
- whether our methods are applicable to a known plaintext attack on FEAL-8.

6 Acknowledgements.

We are grateful to our colleagues Mireille Campana and David Arditti, from CNET. The content of this paper is directly related to some previous studies on blockciphers carried out in collaboration with them.

REFERENCES

[1] A. Shamir *Lecture at Securicom 89.*

[2] Bert Den Boer *Cryptanalysis of F.E.A.L.*, Proceedings of Eurocrypt'88, pp 293-299.

[3] S. Miyaguchi, S. Shiraishi, S. Shimizu *Fast Data Encipherment Algorithm FEAL-8* Review of the Electrical Communication Laboratories, Vol. 36, N°4 (1988).

ANNEX

$j =$	7	6	5	4	3	2	1	0
$\Delta X_0^0[j]$	1	1	1	1	1	1	1	1
$\Delta X_0^1[j]$	0	1	1	1	1	1	0	1
$\Delta X_0^2[j]$	1	1	1	1	1	1	1	1
$\Delta X_0^3[j]$	0	1	1	1	1	1	1	1
$\Delta X_0^4[j]$	1	1	1	1	1	1	1	1
$\Delta X_0^5[j]$	.277	.506	.745	.497	.016	.969	.930	.860
$\Delta X_0^6[j]$	.406	.496	.351	.571	.555	.494	.476	.502
$\Delta X_0^7[j]$	.492	.498	.497	.508	.497	.499	.500	.500
$\Delta X_0^8[j]$	.505	.502	.496	.501	.496	.497	.507	.509
$\Delta X_0^9[j]$	.494	.501	.499	.499	.500	.504	.500	.495

$j =$	7	6	5	4	3	2	1	0
$\Delta X_1^0[j]$	1	1	1	1	1	1	1	1
$\Delta X_1^1[j]$	0	1	1	1	1	1	1	1
$\Delta X_1^2[j]$	1	1	1	1	1	1	1	1
$\Delta X_1^3[j]$	0	1	1	1	1	1	1	1
$\Delta X_1^4[j]$	1	1	1	1	1	1	1	1
$\Delta X_1^5[j]$	.063	.871	.750	.504	1	1	.984	.969
$\Delta X_1^6[j]$	.474	.499	.176	.718	.690	.624	.556	.498
$\Delta X_1^7[j]$	.536	.514	.497	.497	.507	.496	.494	.501
$\Delta X_1^8[j]$	.502	.501	.500	.504	.500	.497	.497	.498
$\Delta X_1^9[j]$	.495	.505	.501	.503	.497	.502	.501	.499

$j =$	7	6	5	4	3	2	1	0
$\Delta X_2^0[j]$	1	1	1	1	1	1	1	1
$\Delta X_2^1[j]$	1	1	1	1	1	1	1	1
$\Delta X_2^2[j]$	1	1	1	1	1	1	1	1
$\Delta X_2^3[j]$	0	1	1	1	1	1	1	1
$\Delta X_2^4[j]$	1	1	1	1	1	1	1	1
$\Delta X_2^5[j]$	.310	.506	.742	.491	.015	.969	.920	.844
$\Delta X_2^6[j]$	.577	.502	.650	.591	.553	.501	.493	.503
$\Delta X_2^7[j]$	.497	.493	.497	.502	.502	.504	.502	.497
$\Delta X_2^8[j]$	.500	.492	.504	.498	.507	.503	.503	.498
$\Delta X_2^9[j]$	.499	.496	.503	.498	.503	.501	.499	.502

$j =$	7	6	5	4	3	2	1	0
$\Delta X_3^0[j]$	1	1	1	1	1	1	1	1
$\Delta X_3^1[j]$	0	1	1	1	1	1	0	1
$\Delta X_3^2[j]$	1	1	1	1	1	1	1	1
$\Delta X_3^3[j]$	0	1	1	1	1	1	0	1
$\Delta X_3^4[j]$	1	1	1	1	1	1	1	1
$\Delta X_3^5[j]$	.248	.496	.265	.485	.080	.844	.689	.503
$\Delta X_3^6[j]$	.456	.499	.469	.500	.487	.502	.522	.495
$\Delta X_3^7[j]$	.499	.496	.496	.500	.496	.492	.502	.506
$\Delta X_3^8[j]$	.495	.499	.505	.500	.500	.497	.502	.501
$\Delta X_3^9[j]$	.502	.502	.502	.499	.508	.503	.504	.502

Frequency of 0 on the bits $\Delta X_j^i[k]$ observed for 20000 sample pairs with constraints described in section 3

An Improved Linear Syndrome Algorithm in Cryptanalysis With Applications *

Kencheng Zeng[1], C.H. Yang[2], and T.R.N. Rao[2]

[1]Graduate School of USTC
Academia Sinica
P.O. Box 3908
Beijing
People's Republic of China

[2]The Center for Advanced Computer Studies
University of Southwestern Louisiana
P.O. Box 44330
Lafayette, LA 70504-4330

Abstract. *A new algorithm is developed for making attacks to certain comparatively simple LFSR based ciphersystems. Special attention is paid towards minimizing the solution distance and guaranteeing the success probability of the attacks. The algorithm is then applied to crack the random bit generators of Geffe (1973) and Beth-Piper (1984).*

I. Introduction

The linear syndrome (LS) method was discussed in [1] for the purpose of solving cryptanalytic problems reducible to the following mathematical setting: What is given is a certain segment of a binary sequence of the form $B = A + X$, where A is a linear recursive sequence with known feedback polynomial $f(x)$ and the sequence X is unknown but sparse in the sense that $Prob\left[x(t) = 1\right] = s_0 < \dfrac{1}{2}$, s_0 being called the *initial error rate* of the sequence A in the sequence B. What is required to

---
* This research is supported by Board of Regents of Louisiana Grant #86-USL(2)-127-03

do is to recover from the captured segment of B the sequence A and hence the sequence X.

The method suggests to fix an integer $r \geqslant 3$, find out a set of r-nomial multiples

$$g(x) = 1 + x^{i_1} + \cdots + x^{i_{r-1}} \tag{1}$$

of the feedback polynomial $f(x)$, compute an odd number, say $2m + 1$, of *syndromes*

$$\sigma_{i,k}\left[g(x)\right] \triangleq \sum_{p=0}^{r-1} b(i + i_p - i_k), \tag{2}$$

and revise the signals $b(i)$ to new signals $b'(i)$ according to the rule of majority decision, namely, put $b'(i) = \overline{b(i)}$ if at least $m + 1$ syndromes are 1, otherwise $b'(i) = b(i)$.

It has been shown that the error rate s_1 of the sequence A in the sequence $B' = \{b'(i)\}$ is

$$s_1 = f_m(s_0) = p - (1 - 2p) \sum_{k=0}^{m-1} C_{2k+1}^k (pq)^{k+1}, \tag{3}$$

where

$$p \triangleq p(s_0) = \frac{1 - (1 - 2s_0)^{r-1}}{2}, \qquad q \triangleq 1 - p. \tag{4}$$

Further for any s_0, there exists an integer m_c, called the *critical number*, such that

$$\lim_{k \to \infty} f_m^{(k)}(s_0) = \begin{cases} 0, & \text{if } m \geqslant m_c, \\ 1/2, & \text{if } m < m_c, \end{cases} \tag{5}$$

where $f_m^{(k)}$ denotes the k-fold self-composite of the function f_m.

Of course, the applicability of the convergence theorem (5), which suggests making iterated revision using a **fixed** number of $2m + 1$ syndromes, is based on the tacitly made assumption that during each iteration the error pattern is well-modelled as being independent so that the relation (3) between the old and new error rates s_i and s_{i+1} remains valid. However, the main disadvantage of the method is that it provides no way towards minimizing the *solution distance* and guaranteeing the *success probability*. The solution distance here refers to the length of the captured segment needed in solving the problem. The success probability is the probability of identifying the correct solution after a certain finite number of revisions.

In this paper, we give a new algorithm for solving the same problem, which will make up the above defects. We assume that $r = 3$ and the feedback polynomial $f(x)$ itself is a primitive trinomial. If $f(x)$ is not a trinomial, we can replace it by its trinomial multiple of the least possible degree, which can always be found by computing discrete logarithms [2].

We point out that some of these concepts can be found in [7] with some numerical experiments reported. However, their paper gave no consideration to such important issues of cryptanalysis as convergence of the method, solution distance, success probability, and possible applications. Beside the applications, the present paper is interesting in that the algorithm proposed here contains in itself a proof of its convergence much simpler than that given in [1].

II. The Improved LS Algorithm

(1) Supercritical and cleansing numbers

We start the new algorithm with the following.

Lemma. The function $w(s) \triangleq f_1(s) - s$ has in $\left[0, \dfrac{1}{2}\right]$ a single root

$\alpha \approx 0.1294$. We have $w(s) < 0$ in $\left[0, \alpha\right)$, $w(s) > 0$ in $\left(\alpha, \dfrac{1}{2}\right]$, and

$\lim\limits_{k \to \infty} f_1^{(k)}(s) = 0$ if $0 \leqslant s < \alpha$.

Proof. Let $u = 1 - 2s$. We have

$$w(s) = p^2(3 - 2p) - s = \frac{(1-u^2)^2}{4}\left[3-(1-u^2)\right] - \frac{1-u}{2}$$

$$= \frac{u(u-1)(u^4 + u^3 + u^2 + u - 2)}{4} = \frac{u(u-1)h(u)}{4}.$$

But $h(u)$ increases strictly with u and $h(0) = -2$, $h(1) = 2$, so we see $h(u)$ has only

one zero β in the open u-interval $(0, 1)$, which can be found by Newton's method of

successive approximation to be $\beta \approx 0.7412$. From here we get the conclusion about

the zero α and the sign of $w(s)$. Further, if $s \in \left[0, \alpha\right)$ and we define $s_0 \triangleq s$,

$s_k \triangleq f_1(s_{k-1})$, then the sequence s_k, $k \geqslant 0$, decreases strictly to a certain limit

$s^* \in \left[0, \alpha\right)$, and $w(s^*) = 0$. So we must have $s^* = 0$. This proves the lemma.

The main idea in the improved LS algorithm is to make the revisions with a

reducing number of syndromes, with the length of the segment under processing

being reduced correspondingly. The central role is played by the concept of *supercri-*

tical and *cleansing* numbers.

Definition. By the supercritical number m_{sc} corresponding to the initial error

rate s_0, we mean the least integer m such that the inequalities

$$s_k \triangleq f_{m-k+1}(s_{k-1}) < s_{k-1} \tag{6}$$

hold true for all $1 \leqslant k \leqslant m$. By the t-th cleansing number l_t corresponding to s_0

we mean the least integer l such that

$$f_1^{(l)}(s_{m_{sc}}) < 10^{-t}.\tag{7}$$

Theorem 1. For any $s_0 \in \left(0, \dfrac{1}{2}\right]$ and any $t \geqslant 0$, the supercritical number m_{sc}

and the cleansing number l_t exist.

Proof. As pointed out in [1],

$$\lim_{m \to \infty} f_m(s_0) = p - (1 - 2p) \sum_{k=0}^{\infty} C_{2k+1}^k (pq)^{k+1} = 0.$$

Therefore, for m sufficiently large we have

$$s_1 = f_m(s_0) < \min(\alpha, s_0).$$

But we know from (3)

$$f_i(s) \leqslant f_1(s), \qquad \forall i \geqslant 1,$$

So we have

$$s_2 = f_{m-1}(s_1) < f_1(s_1) < s_1 < \alpha,$$
$$s_3 = f_{m-2}(s_2) < f_1(s_2) < s_2 < \alpha,$$

etc. This means the set of positive integers m, for which the condition (6) holds, is not empty, and the existence of the m_{sc} corresponding to s_0 follows from the well-ordering principle of the set of all non-negative integers. The existence of l_t is an easy consequence of the lemma given above, for we see from $f_1(s_{m_{sc}-1}) < s_{m_{sc}-1}$ that

$$s_{m_{sc}-1} < \alpha.$$

Theorem 1 provides a natural justification to the following algorithm for finding m_{sc}:

Step 1: $1 \to m_{sc}, 1 \to k, s_0 \to s$.

Step 2: If $k = 0$, stop. Otherwise compute $s' = f_k(s)$.

Step 3: If $s' < s$ then $k - 1 \to k, s' \to s$, and return to Step 2.

Step 4: $m_{sc} + 1 \to m_{sc}, \; m_{sc} \to k, s_0 \to s$, go to Step 2.

s_0	m_c	m_{sc}	l_4	$c(s_0, 4)$
0.03125	1	1	2	7
0.0625	1	1	3	9
0.09375	1	1	5	13
0.125	1	1	10	23
0.15625	2	2	8	23
0.1875	2	3	4	19
0.21875	3	4	2	23
0.25	3	5	1	37
0.28125	4	6	0	51
0.3125	6	7	1	85
0.34375	8	10	0	339
0.375	13	14	0	2387
0.40625	22	24	0	218451

The above is a table of critical, supercritical, and cleansing numbers, together with the numbers $c(s_0, t)$ to be defined later in Theorem 2, computed for values of s_0 at step length equal to $\dfrac{1}{32}$. It may be of some interest to note that $m_{sc} - m_c \leqslant 2$.

(2) The improved LS algorithm

Now we can state the new LS algorithm.

Theorem 2. There exists an algorithm which, when given as input the number t and a captured B-segment of length

$$N(s_0, t) = \left[1 + 2l_t + 2\sum_{m=1}^{m_{sc}} L(m)\right] n = c(s_0, t)\, n, \tag{8}$$

where $n = \deg f(x)$ and $L(m) \triangleq 2^{\lfloor \frac{4m-1}{6} \rfloor}$, will give as output the state vector of the attacked LFSR at a certain moment i with success probability

$$P_{success} > (1 - 10^{-t})^n. \tag{9}$$

The computational complexity of the algorithm in terms of bit operations is

$$Q(s_0, t) = \left[6l_t^2 + 2m_{sc}(m_{sc} + 2)(2l_t + 1) + 4\sum_{j=1}^{m_{sc}} (2j+1)D(j-1)\right] n \tag{10}$$

$$= q(s_0, t)\, n,$$

where

$$D(j) \triangleq L(1) + L(2) + \cdots L(j), \qquad D(0) = 0. \tag{11}$$

Proof. The required algorithm is divided into two phases: the *reducing* phase, at which the initial error rate s_0 is reduced to $s_{m_{sc}} < \alpha$; and the *cleansing* phase, at which the remanent error rate $s_{m_{sc}}$ is rendered below 10^{-t}.

At the reducing phase we need $p = \lceil \dfrac{2m_{sc} + 1}{3} \rceil$ trinomial multiples of $f(x)$ to form the syndromes, which we choose to be

$$g_0(x) = f(x), \quad g_{i+1}(x) = g_i^2(x), \quad 0 \leqslant i \leqslant p - 2.$$

Observe that each trinomial $g(x) = 1 + x^{i_1} + x^{i_2}$ provides three syndrome formulas

$$\sigma_{i,k}(g) = \sum_{p=0}^{2} b(i + i_p - i_k), \quad k = 0, 1, 2$$

for checking the same ciphertext signal $b(i)$. We arrange the $3p$ syndrome formulas in the following two different ways:

(i) $\sigma_{i,0}(\mathcal{G}_0), \sigma_{i,1}(\mathcal{G}_0), \sigma_{i,2}(\mathcal{G}_0), \sigma_{i,0}(\mathcal{G}_1), \sigma_{i,1}(\mathcal{G}_1), \sigma_{i,2}(\mathcal{G}_1), \cdots, \sigma_{i,0}(\mathcal{G}_{p-1}), \sigma_{i,1}(\mathcal{G}_{p-1}), \sigma_{i,2}(\mathcal{G}_{p-1})$

(ii) $\sigma_{i,2}(\mathcal{G}_0), \sigma_{i,1}(\mathcal{G}_0), \sigma_{i,0}(\mathcal{G}_0), \sigma_{i,2}(\mathcal{G}_1), \sigma_{i,1}(\mathcal{G}_1), \sigma_{i,0}(\mathcal{G}_1), \cdots, \sigma_{i,2}(\mathcal{G}_{p-1}), \sigma_{i,1}(\mathcal{G}_{p-1}), \sigma_{i,0}(\mathcal{G}_{p-1})$

Reducing Phase

Step 1: $c(s_0, t) n \to N, m_{sc} \to m, nL(m) \to L$.

Step 2: For $L \leqslant i \leqslant N - L - 1$, compute the syndromes needed by the first $2m + 1$ formulas of (i) or (ii) according to $i \leqslant \dfrac{N}{2}$ or $i > \dfrac{N}{2}$,

do $\overline{b(i)} \to b(i)$, if at least $m + 1$ syndromes are 1.

Step 3: $m - 1 \to m$. If $m = 0$, go to Step 5.

Step 4: $nL(m) + L \to L$, return to Step 2.

Cleansing Phase

Step 5: $l_t \to m, L + n \to L$.

Step 6: $m - 1 \to m$. If $m < 0$, stop.

Step 7: For $L \leqslant i \leqslant N - L - 1$, compute $\sigma_{i,0}(f), \sigma_{i,1}(f), \sigma_{i,2}(f)$,

do $\overline{b(i)} \to b(i)$, if at least two syndromes are 1. Return to Step 6.

Observe that at the $(m_{sc} - m + 1)$-th round of the reducing phase, the signals $b(i)$ with

$$L \leqslant i \leqslant N - L - 1 \tag{12}$$

are revised according to majority decision with $2m + 1$ syndromes computed from the wider range of signals $b(j)$ with

$$L - nL(m) \leqslant j \leqslant N - L + nL(m) - 1. \tag{13}$$

So we can conclude by reverse induction on m that after the $(m_{sc} - m + 1)$-th round

of work

$$Prob\left[b(i) \neq a(i)\right] - s_m,$$

for all i satisfying (12), provided at the start of the round we have in the signals

$b(j)$, with j satisfying (13), all the necessary data for computing the $2m + 1$ syn-

dromes needed. Evidently, it suffices to check the point for the case

$$i - \lfloor \frac{N}{2} \rfloor, \quad 2m + 1 \equiv 1 \mod 3.$$

Using the easily checkable fact that $\sum_{k-1}^{m} L(k) \geqslant 2^{\lceil \frac{2m+1}{3} \rceil}$, it is easy to show that in

this case the largest j, for which the signal $b(j)$ is used in computing the syndromes

is

$$j_{max} - \lceil \frac{N}{2} \rceil + n 2^{\frac{2m+1}{3}} \leqslant N - L + nL(m) - 1.$$

This means the proviso is fulfilled at each round and the initial error rate s_0 definitely

will be rendered below α after the reducing phase. That it will be further reduced to

below 10^{-t} can be proved in a similar way. Thus we see that, after $m_{sc} + l_t$ rounds

of iterated revision, the algorithm will output the n-bit vector

$$\left[b(\frac{N-n}{2}), \ b(\frac{N-n}{2} + 1), \ \cdots, \ b(\frac{N-n}{2} + n - 1)\right],$$

which coincides with the $\frac{N-n}{2}$-th state vector of the attacked LFSR with proba-

The formula (10) for the computational complexity can be derived by straight-forward manipulations, and is omitted here. □

III. Cracking the Generators of Geffe and Beth-Piper

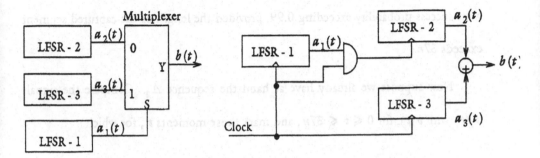

Figure 1. Generator **G**   Figure 2. Generator **BP**

The Geffe [3] generator **G** and the Beth-Piper [4] generator **BP** (as described by Figures 1 and 2, respectively), are designed on the basis of quite different cryptographical ideas; but they can be cracked by one and the same method, at the expense of nearly the same amount of computation. It is assumed that all the feedback polynomials are primitive.

Theorem 3. If in the **G**-generator the feedback polynomials $f_i(x)$, $1 \leqslant i \leqslant 3$, of the LFSRs are *all known to the cryptanalyst* and $f_2(x)$ is a *trinomial* of degree n, then the system can be broken on a captured segment of length $N = 37\,n$, at the computational expense of $Q = 896\,n$ bit operations, disregarding the work not directly related to the LS algorithm.

Proof. The output signal of the **G**-generator at the moment t is

$$b(t) = a_1(t)a_3(t) + \overline{a_1(t)}a_2(t)$$

$$= a_2(t) + a_1(t)\Big[a_2(t) + a_3(t)\Big].$$

It follows from the balanced property of m-sequences that

$$s_0 = Prob\left[b(t) \neq a_2(t)\right] = \frac{1}{4}.$$

So we see LFSR-2 is the Achilles heel in the system. If, for example, $n \leqslant 100$ and we choose $t = 4$, then the sequence $A_2 = \{a_2(t)\}$ can be recovered by our algorithm with success probability exceeding 0.99, provided the length of the captured segment exceeds $37n$.

Now suppose we already have at hand the sequence A_2. Compare the signals $a_2(t)$ with $b(t)$, for $0 \leqslant t \leqslant 37n$, and mark those moments t_i, for which

$$a_2(t_i) + b(t_i) = 1.$$

It is easy to see that at these moments

$$a_1(t_i) = 1, \quad a_3(t_i) = b(t_i).$$

Divide each power x^{t_i} by $f_1(x)$ and $f_3(x)$ respectively to obtain the remainders

$$x^{t_i} = r_{i,0} + r_{i,1}x + \cdots + r_{i,n_1-1}x^{n_1-1} \quad mod \ f_1(x)$$

and

$$x^{t_i} = s_{i,0} + s_{i,1}x + \cdots + s_{i,n_3-1}x^{n_3-1} \quad mod \ f_3(x).$$

Then we shall have two linear systems, each containing the same number of approximately $9n$ equations

$$r_{i,0}a_1(0) + r_{i,1}a_1(1) + \cdots + r_{i,n_1-1}a_1(n_1-1) = 1,$$

and

$$s_{i,0}a_3(0) + s_{i,1}a_3(1) + \cdots + s_{i,n_3-1}a_3(n_3-1) = b(t_i).$$

If $n_1, n_2 \ll 9n$, then these systems will determine with probability nearly 1 (see [5]), the initial states of LFSR-1 and LFSR-3.

Theorem 4. If in the **BP**-generator, $f_1(x)$ and $f_3(x)$ are *known* trinomials of degrees not greater than n, while $f_2(x)$ is *arbitrary and unknown*, then the system can be broken on a captured segment of length $N = 37\,n$, at the computational expense of $Q = 1792\,n$ bit operations, disregarding the work not directly related to the LS algorithm.

Proof. Denote the output signal of the clock-controlled LFSR-2 at the moment t by $a_2{}'(t)$, then we have

$$Prob\Big[a_2{}'(t) = a_2{}'(t+1)\Big] = Prob\Big[a_1(t) = 0\Big] + Prob\Big[a_1(t) = 1\Big]\,Prob\Big[a_2(t) = a_2(t+1)\Big]$$

$$= \frac{1}{2} + \frac{1}{2} \times \frac{1}{2} = \frac{3}{4}.$$

Thus if we write

$$a_2^*(t) = a_2{}'(t) + a_2{}'(t+1), \qquad b^*(t) = b(t) + b(t+1) \qquad a_3^*(t) = a_3(t) + a_3(t+1),$$

then we will encounter with the cracking problem $B^* = A_3^* + A_2^*$, where A_3^* is an m-sequence with the known trinomial feedback $f_3(x)$ and

$$s_0 = Prob\Big[a_2^*(t) = 1\Big] = \frac{1}{4}.$$

After cracking it with the improved LS algorithm, we will get at the sequence A_3^*. The signals $a_3(t)$ can be determined recursively by

$$a_3(0) = \epsilon, \qquad a_3(t) = a_3^*(t-1) + a_3(t-1)$$

where $\epsilon = 0$ or 1. The actual value of ϵ can be decided by the linear relations the signals of A_3 should satisfy, for here $f_3(x)$ is a trinomial.

Now suppose we have done this and have $A_2{}'$ at hand. Define

$$a_1^*(t) \triangleq \begin{cases} 0, & \text{if } a_2'(t) = a_2'(t+1), \\ 1, & \text{if } a_2'(t) \neq a_2'(t+1). \end{cases}$$

Since, as can be easily seen,

$$Prob\left[a_1(t) = 1 \mid a_2'(t) = a_2'(t+1)\right] = \frac{1}{3},$$

we have

$$s_0 = Prob\left[a_1^*(t) \neq a_1(t)\right]$$

$$= Prob\left[a_2'(t) = a_2'(t+1)\right] Prob\left[a_1(t) = 1 \mid a_2'(t) = a_2'(t+1)\right] = \frac{1}{4}.$$

Once again, we meet with the problem

$$A_1^* = A_1 + X, \quad s_0 = \frac{1}{4},$$

with the trinomial $f_1(x)$ assumed known. So we can recover the sequence A_1.

Finally, the sequence A_2 can be recovered by removing the repeating signals which appear when $a_1(t) = 1$. The unknown feedback polynomial $f_2(x)$ can then be found by the well-known Massey [6] synthesis algorithm, provided $deg \, f_2(x) \leqslant 18n$.

References

1. Kencheng Zeng and Minqiang Huang, *On the Linear Syndrome Method in Cryptanalysis*, CRYPTO 88, 1988.

2. Don Coppersmith, *Fast Evaluation of Logarithms in Fields of Characteristic Two*, IEEE Trans. Information Theory, IT-30, July 1984, pp. 587-594.

3. Philip R. Geffe, *How to Protect Data with Ciphers That Are Really Hard to Break*, Electronics, Jan. 4, 1973, pp. 99-101.

4. T. Beth and F.C. Piper, *The Stop-and-Go-Generator*, EUROCRYPT 84, 1984, pp. 88-92.

5. K.C. Zeng, C.H. Yang, and T.R.N. Rao, *On the Linear Consistency Test in Cryptanalysis*, to appear.

6. J. L. Massey, *Shift-Register Synthesis and BCH Decoding*, IEEE Trans. Information Theory, IT-15, Jan. 1969, pp. 122-127.

7. W. Meier and O. Staffelback, *Fast Correlation Attacks on Certain Stream Ciphers*, Journal of Cryptology, Vol. 1, pp. 159-176, 1989.

Session 2
Protocols
Chair: Y. Desmedt, University of Wisconsin

Quantum Bit Commitment
and Coin Tossing Protocols

Gilles Brassard *

Département d'informatique et de R.O.
Université de Montréal
C.P. 6128, succ. "A"
Montréal, Québec CANADA H3C 3J7

Claude Crépeau [†]

Laboratoire de Recherche en Informatique
Université de Paris – Sud
Bâtiment 490
91405 Orsay FRANCE

1 Introduction

In the late 1960's a physicist, Stephen Wiesner, had the idea that the uncertainty principle could be used for cryptography (though he published his result much later [Wie83]). One of his ideas was that it would be possible to use a stream of polarized photons to transmit two messages in a way that would make only one of them readable at the receiver's choosing. This notion, which he called "multiplexing", is remarkably similar to the "one-out-of-two oblivious transfer" to be reinvented many years later [EGL83], and it even predates Rabin's notion of oblivious transfer [Rab81] by more than a decade. In the late 1970's, Wiesner's invention was brought back to life by the work of Charles H. Bennett and Gilles Brassard, which resulted in a CRYPTO '82 paper [BBBW82]. Subsequently, Bennett and Brassard used quantum cryptographic principles to implement basic cryptographic protocols, such as secret key exchange and coin tossing by telephone [BB84]. There has been recently much excitement in the field of quantum cryptography because a working prototype of the quantum key exchange channel has been successfully built at the IBM T. J. Watson Research Laboratory, Yorktown Heights [BBBSS90].

In recent times, the importance of cryptographic primitives has been brought to light by the work of many researchers whose goal is to characterize precisely the primitives sufficient for the implementation of various cryptographic protocols. One of these primitives is a Bit Commitment Scheme. The importance and usefulness of such a primitive is enlightened by the work of [GMW86, BCC88] to mention just a few.

---

*Supported in part by Canada NSERC grant A4107.

[†]Supported in part by NSERC Postgraduate and Postdoctorate Scholarships. This research was performed in part while the author was a graduate student at M.I.T. and while visiting the IBM Almaden Research Center.

While such primitives are usually built under computational complexity assumptions, it is sometimes possible to build them based on assumptions of a different nature, as pointed out by [Wie83, BBBW82, BB84, CK88]. The current paper presents the state-of-the-art in the technology of building a bit commitment scheme on a quantum mechanical assumption. The applications are numerous, including secure two-party computation.

2 Physics background

For a complete coverage of the physics of quantum cryptography, please consult [BB84] or chapter 6 of [Bra88]. The linear polarization of photons is a quantum state. In general, the value of this variable cannot be determined exactly. According to quantum mechanics, although the value of the polarization can be any angle in the (real) interval $[0°, 180°)$, only specific boolean (two states) predicates can be measured about this variable. Moreover, only one such measurement can be performed on any given photon because the measurement itself necessarily destroys the information. For instance, let Θ be the polarization of a photon. Assuming that it is known *a priori* that Θ is either $0°$ or $90°$, the predicate "Is $\Theta = 0°$?" can be measured accurately for these two quantum states (at least in principle). On the other hand, even if Θ is known to be either $0°$ or $45°$, then no measuring apparatus can distinguish between these two states with certainty, although some probabilistic information can be obtained. If we have no constraint on the set of possible values for Θ, then the result of *any* apparatus designed to decide whether $\Theta = 0°$ will be a probabilistic answer dependent on the value of Θ, but no certainty can be achieved. It is not a matter of technology, it is not that no one has a good enough apparatus to figure out Θ; quantum theory tells us that it is **impossible** to determine this value with certainty.

It is however possible (in principle) to build a device that always says "yes" if $\Theta = 0°$ and always says "no" when $\Theta = 90°$. In general, with such a device, Prob(device says "yes"$|\Theta$) $= \cos^2(\Theta)$. This can be obtained by combining a Wollaston prism with two photomultipliers (photon detectors). See figure 1. Consider a Wollaston prism set for distinguishing polarization angles ϕ from $\phi + 90°$. A photon polarized at angle Θ will come out of this Wollaston prism on the left side with probability $\cos^2(\Theta - \phi)$ (and will then be repolarized at angle ϕ) and on the right side with complementary probability $\sin^2(\Theta - \phi)$ (and will then be repolarized at angle $\phi + 90°$). According to quantum mechanics, this device is the best that can be built with respect to measuring the polarization Θ of a single photon.

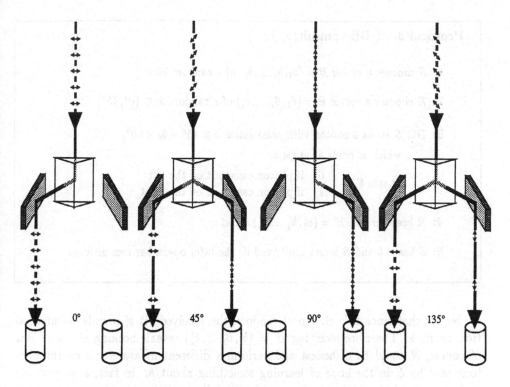

Figure 1: Photons passing through a Wollaston prism set at angle $0°$.

3 Review of earlier quantum protocols

3.1 A bit commitment scheme

Consider two parties: a *sender* S and a *receiver* R. Assume that S has a bit b in mind, to which she[1] would like to be committed toward R. That is, S wishes to provide R with a piece of evidence that she has a bit in mind and that she cannot change it. Meanwhile, R should not be able to tell from that evidence what b is. At a later time, however, it must be possible for S to *open* the commitment, that is to show R which bit she had committed to, and convince him that this is indeed the genuine bit that she had in mind when she committed.

The first quantum bit commitment scheme ever proposed is due to Bennett and Brassard [BB84] (actually, the protocol they describe is only claimed to implement coin tossing, but it is obvious how to modify it in order to implement bit commitment; here, we proceed the other way around). Let us briefly review this protocol and its main weaknesses before describing our new scheme in Section 4. Let s be a security parameter. In order to commit to bit b toward R, S initiates the following protocol.

---

[1] For the sake of convenience, we shall refer to S as a "she" and to R as a "he".

Protocol 3.1 (BB-commit(b))

1: S chooses a vector $B = (b_1, b_2, ..., b_s)$ of s random bits

2: R chooses a vector $\Theta = (\theta_1, \theta_2, ..., \theta_s)$ of s random $\theta_i \in \{0°, 45°\}$

3: $\overset{s}{\underset{i=1}{DO}}$ S sends a photon with polarization $b \times 45° + b_i \times 90°$,
which R reads at angle θ_i;

R sets $b'_i \leftarrow \begin{cases} 0 & \text{if photon came out on the left} \\ 1 & \text{if photon came out on the right} \end{cases}$

4: R keeps Θ and $B' = (b'_1, b'_2, ..., b'_s)$ secret

5: S keeps b and B secret until (and if) she later opens her commitment

---

Notice that since b_i is chosen at random, the received bit b'_i reveals no information about b. Therefore receiving $B' = (b'_1, b'_2, ..., b'_s)$ reveals nothing about b. But of course, R could be dishonest and perform a different measurement on the photons sent by S in the hope of learning something about b. In fact, a very strong statement can be proved: quantum mechanics tells us that *no* measuring apparatus can distinguish a commitment to 0 from a commitment to 1, unless it is possible to communicate information faster than the speed of light. It is impossible to obtain even a probabilistic bias about which bit was committed to. Therefore, the privacy of S's bit b is unconditionally protected. But why is S committed?

To open her commitment, S initiates the following protocol with R.

Protocol 3.2 (BB-open($(B, b), (B', \Theta)$))

1: S reveals b and B to R

2: $\overset{s}{\underset{i=1}{DO}}$ R checks that $b'_i = b_i$ whenever $\theta_i = b \times 45°$

3: **if** this condition is satisfied for all i **then** R outputs "accept"
$\qquad\qquad\qquad\qquad\qquad\qquad\qquad\qquad$ **else** R outputs "reject"

First note that if S is honest then the condition is always satisfied, provided that no transmission errors have occurred due to imperfections of the apparatus (the possibility of transmission errors in practice is addressed in section 3.3). Now suppose that a cheating S tries to "commit" in a way that will enable her to open B as 0 or 1 at her later choice. In order to achieve this, she may prefer to send her photons at angles that are not among $\{0°, 45°, 90°, 135°\}$. A *strategy* for a cheating S consists of a vector $\Phi = (\phi_1, \phi_2, ..., \phi_s)$ of values in the real interval $[0°, 180°)$ together with two binary vectors $B^0 = (b_1^0, b_2^0, ..., b_s^0)$ and $B^1 = (b_1^1, b_2^1, ..., b_s^1)$. In order to use this strategy, S sends her i^{th} photon with polarization angle ϕ_i during protocol BB-commit. If she wishes to open the commitment as $b \in \{0, 1\}$, she runs BB-open with (B^b, b) as her share of the input. The strategy is *successful* if

$$\forall i \left[(\theta_i = 0°) \Rightarrow (b_i^0 = b_i') \text{ and } (\theta_i = 45°) \Rightarrow (b_i^1 = b_i') \right]. \tag{1}$$

An *optimal* strategy is one that has the highest probability of being successful.

We leave it for the reader to verify that for all choices of B^0 and B^1, there is exactly one choice of Φ that will maximize S's probability of success. In that optimal choice, it is always the case that all ϕ_i's belong to $\{22\frac{1}{2}°, 67\frac{1}{2}°, 112\frac{1}{2}°, 157\frac{1}{2}°\}$. For example, if $b_i^0 = 1$ and $b_i^1 = 0$, then it is best to set $\phi_i = 67\frac{1}{2}°$ because b_i' is likely to be 1 if R's reading angle θ_i was $0°$ whereas b_i' is likely to be 0 if θ_i was $45°$. With this strategy, S's probability of failure is $\sin^2(22\frac{1}{2}°) \approx 15\%$ for each i. Therefore, whichever strategy is used, the probability that equation 1 holds is at most $(\cos^2(22\frac{1}{2}°))^s$, which can be made arbitrarily small. (If R follows his protocol blindly, S's simplest optimal strategy is to set $\phi_i = 22\frac{1}{2}°$ and $b_i^0 = b_i^1 = 0$ for all i. However, a human R might become suspicious. Therefore, it is safer to choose B^0 and B^1 randomly and to set Φ accordingly.)

3.2   Coin tossing

Bennett and Brassard used this technique in order to implement a protocol for coin tossing by (quantum!) "telephone" [Blu81] as follows.

Protocol 3.3 (BB-cointoss)

   1: S chooses a random bit b_0 and uses BB-commit(b_0) with R

   2: R chooses a random bit b_1 and sends it to S

   3: S runs BB-open(b_0) with R

   4: R wins the coin toss if and only if $b_1 = b_0$

This protocol can be broken exactly if the bit commitment scheme can be broken. Of course, S could refuse to cooperate at step 3 if she decides that she does not wish the result of the coin toss to become known to R.

3.3 The problems with this scheme

The bit commitment scheme of section 3.1 and the resulting coin tossing protocol have major defects both in principle and in practice.

As mentioned in [BB84], these schemes can be defeated in theory using the consequences of the Einstein – Podolsky – Rosen so-called "EPR paradox" [EPR35]. The interested reader can consult [BB84] for a more detailed explanation. Let us only say here that this kind of attack is rather implausible in practice because the apparatus necessary to perform it is far beyond the current available technology, and because even a small failure in the cheater's technology will result in the loss of her [2] possibility of cheating. Nevertheless, from a theoretical point of view, it is important to design a protocol that is not subject to the EPR threat. This is precisely the main purpose of the current paper, as we shall proceed to explain in the next section.

In addition to the theoretical weakness described above, the schemes of [BB84] suffer from two problems in practice. One of these problems is easy to deal with but the other is not. The first practical problem is that it is not reasonable to expect in protocol BB-open that $b_i' = b_i$ every single time that $\theta_i = b \times 45°$. Indeed, transmission errors will necessarily occur in practice. Such errors can be due to misalignment of S's and R's apparatuses, to dark currents in R's photomultipliers and to photons repolarizing for one reason or another while in transit. Also, photomultipliers do not have perfect efficiency, and therefore R will receive nothing at all most of the time (in which case he knows that he did not receive the photon, unless he is fooled by his own photomultipliers' dark current — a reasonably rare event). Fortunately, the actual apparatus built in Yorktown Heights to demonstrate the feasibility of the quantum key exchange protocol [BBBSS90] shows that it is entirely reasonable to expect an error rate below 5 % when a photon is received (or thought to be received). On the other hand, recall that S's optimal cheating strategy would give her the value of each relevant b_i' with probability roughly 85 % (even if no transmission errors occur). Therefore, the protocol remains safe against S's cheating attempts even if R accepts provided that $b_i' = b_i$ at least 90 % of the times when the photon is detected and $\theta_i = b \times 45°$. The only price to pay for this increased robustness is that the security parameter s must be chosen larger in order to attain the same small probability of undetected cheating.

The other practical problem with the schemes of [BB84] is much more serious. Recall that the protocol calls for S to send single polarized photons to R. Although this is possible in principle, it is very difficult to achieve in practice. It is much easier to send very dim pulses of polarized photons, as with the experimental quantum key exchange apparatus. Unfortunately, such dim pulses will sometimes contain more than one photon, and all the photons in any single pulse will be polarized at the same angle. These multiphoton pulses are of no consequences for key exchange, but they spell doom on the bit commitment scheme described above. Indeed, whenever

---

[2] Only S can take advantage of the EPR loophole. As previously stated, R has no possibility of cheating whatsoever.

$\mathcal{R}$ reads a pulse at angle θ_i and detects photons coming out *both* on the right and the left, it is very likely to mean that the pulse contained more than one photon and that they were all polarized either at angle $45° - \theta_i$ or $135° - \theta_i$. In either case, the value of b becomes known to $\mathcal{R}$. There is no known way to get around this difficulty in practice with the bit commitment scheme of Bennett and Brassard. In sharp contrast, the new scheme that we now describe remains secure even if a small number of multiphoton pulses occur.

4 A new bit commitment scheme

4.1 How to commit

In order to commit to a bit b, S builds an $s \times s$ boolean matrix:

$$B = \begin{pmatrix} b_{1,1} & \cdots & b_{1,s} \\ \vdots & \ddots & \vdots \\ b_{s,1} & \cdots & b_{s,s} \end{pmatrix},$$

which is random subject to the following property:

$$\forall 1 \leq i \leq s \quad \left[\bigoplus_{j=1}^{s} b_{i,j} = b \right]. \tag{2}$$

She sends it to $\mathcal{R}$ using the following protocol.

Protocol 4.1 (BC-commit(b))

1: S builds a random $s \times s$ boolean matrix B as indicated above

2: $\overset{s}{\underset{i=1}{\mathrm{DO}}}\,\overset{s}{\underset{j=1}{\mathrm{DO}}}$ S chooses a random $\phi_{i,j} \in \{0°, 45°\}$ and

$\mathcal{R}$ chooses a random $\theta_{i,j} \in \{0°, 45°\}$

3: $\overset{s}{\underset{i=1}{\mathrm{DO}}}\,\overset{s}{\underset{j=1}{\mathrm{DO}}}$ S sends a photon with polarization $\phi_{i,j} + b_{i,j} \times 90°$,

which $\mathcal{R}$ reads at angle $\theta_{i,j}$

$\mathcal{R}$ sets $b'_{i,j} \leftarrow \begin{cases} 0 & \text{if photon came out on the left} \\ 1 & \text{if photon came out on the right} \end{cases}$

4: $\mathcal{R}$ keeps B' and Θ (see below) secret

5: S keeps b, B and Φ (see below) secret until (and if) she later opens her commitment

---

where

$$B' = \begin{pmatrix} b'_{1,1} & \cdots & b'_{1,s} \\ \vdots & \ddots & \vdots \\ b'_{s,1} & \cdots & b'_{s,s} \end{pmatrix}, \Theta = \begin{pmatrix} \theta_{1,1} & \cdots & \theta_{1,s} \\ \vdots & \ddots & \vdots \\ \theta_{s,1} & \cdots & \theta_{s,s} \end{pmatrix}, \text{ and } \Phi = \begin{pmatrix} \phi_{1,1} & \cdots & \phi_{1,s} \\ \vdots & \ddots & \vdots \\ \phi_{s,1} & \cdots & \phi_{s,s} \end{pmatrix}.$$

If both participants are honest, B' is such that

$$\forall 1 \le i \le s, 1 \le j \le s \; [\text{Prob}(b'_{i,j} = b_{i,j}) = \tfrac{3}{4}].$$

However, if $\mathcal{R}$ uses angle $\theta_{i,j} = 22\frac{1}{2}^\circ$, he will end up getting more information about B. It is an easy exercise to prove that this is the optimal strategy for a cheating $\mathcal{R}$. With such measurements, $\forall 1 \le i \le s, 1 \le j \le s \; [\text{Prob}(b'_{i,j} = b_{i,j}) = \cos^2(22\frac{1}{2}^\circ)]$. Nevertheless, even then the matrix B' reveals very little about b. We measure this fact by computing $\text{Prob}(b = 0|B')$ and $\text{Prob}(b = 1|B')$ for every possible B'. We are satisfied if there exists a positive constant $\alpha < 1$ such that

$$|\text{Prob}(b = 0|B') - \text{Prob}(b = 1|B')| \le \alpha^s$$

for every B'. Since $\text{Prob}(b = 0|B') + \text{Prob}(b = 1|B') = 1$, the following condition is sufficient for this result.

Theorem 4.1 *There exists a positive constant $\alpha < 1$ such that*

$$\tfrac{1}{2} - \alpha^s \le \text{Prob}(b = 0|B') \le \tfrac{1}{2} + \alpha^s.$$

Proof.

Provided in the journal version of the paper. □

4.2 How to open

The above theorem shows that an honest S does not reveal much about her secret bit b by sending the matrix B through the quantum channel, hence $\mathcal{R}$ may at best learn an exponentially small bias about bit b. But for this to be a commitment, it should be possible for S to convince $\mathcal{R}$ of what bit she has committed to. She should not be able to open the "commitment" to show a bit of her choice.

To open her commitment, the honest S initiates the following protocol with $\mathcal{R}$.

Protocol 4.2 (BC-open$((B, \Phi, b), (B', \Theta))$)

    1: S reveals b, B and Φ to R

    2: $\underset{i=1}{\overset{s}{\text{DO}}} R$ checks that $\bigoplus_{j=1}^{s} b_{i,j} = b$

    3: $\underset{i=1}{\overset{s}{\text{DO}}}\underset{j=1}{\overset{s}{\text{DO}}} R$ checks that $b'_{i,j} = b_{i,j}$ whenever $\theta_{i,j} = \phi_{i,j}$

    4: **if** this condition is satisfied for all i and j, **then** R outputs "accept"

                                           else R outputs "reject"

In order to prove that S cannot cheat, one must once again take account of all the possible ways in which S could deviate from her prescribed behaviour, not only in BC-open but also in BC-commit. In particular, she could bypass the choice of matrices B and Φ at steps 1 and 2 in BC-commit, and send photons with arbitrary polarization angles at step 3. In general, a *strategy* for a cheating S consists of a matrix $\tilde{\Phi}$ of arbitrary angles, together with two pairs of matrices B^0, Φ^0 and B^1, Φ^1 such that B^0 and B^1 are boolean, whereas Φ^0 and Φ^1 contain only $0°$ and $45°$. In order to use this strategy, S sends her photons with polarization angles according to $\tilde{\Phi}$ during protocol BB-commit. If she wishes to open the commitment as $b \in \{0, 1\}$, she runs BB-open with (B^b, Φ^b, b) as her share of the input. A strategy is *successful* if

$$\forall i \left[\bigoplus_{j=1}^{s} b_{i,j}^0 = 0 \text{ and } \bigoplus_{j=1}^{s} b_{i,j}^1 = 1 \right], \text{ and} \tag{3}$$

$$\forall i, j \left[(\phi_{i,j}^0 = \theta_{i,j}) \Rightarrow (b_{i,j}^0 = b'_{i,j}) \text{ and } (\phi_{i,j}^1 = \theta_{i,j}) \Rightarrow (b_{i,j}^1 = b'_{i,j}) \right]. \tag{4}$$

Theorem 4.2 *There exists a constant $\alpha < 1$ such that the probability of success of any strategy is at most α^s.*

Proof.

First notice that there are no probabilities associated with whether a strategy satisfies equation 3. Thus, we may as well assume that this equation holds, which implies that B^0 and B^1 differ at least once in each row. Therefore, there are at least s bits that are different between these two matrices. Let i and j be such that $b_{i,j}^0 \neq b_{i,j}^1$. First consider the case in which $\phi_{i,j}^0 = \phi_{i,j}^1 = \phi$. With probability $\frac{1}{2}$, the reading angle $\theta_{i,j}$ is equal to ϕ. If this occurs, equation 4 is necessarily violated. Also with probability $\frac{1}{2}$, $\theta_{i,j} \neq \phi$, in which case equation 4 is (vacuously) satisfied for such values of i and j. Therefore, the choice of $\tilde{\phi}_{i,j}$ is irrelevant when $b_{i,j}^0 \neq b_{i,j}^1$ and $\phi_{i,j}^0 = \phi_{i,j}^1$, and the probability that this will cause the strategy to be rejected is always $\frac{1}{2}$.

Now consider the case in which $\phi_{i,j}^0 \neq \phi_{i,j}^1$. In order to maximize her chances of satisfying equation 4, $\mathcal{S}$'s optimal strategy is to send the corresponding photon at an angle $\tilde{\phi}_{i,j}$ that will simultaneously maximize her chances that it will be read as $b_{i,j}^0$ if measured at angle $\phi_{i,j}^0$, whereas it will be read as $b_{i,j}^1$ if measured at angle $\phi_{i,j}^1$. That angle is easily seen to be $67\frac{1}{2}^\circ$ if $b_{i,j}^0 = 0$ and $\phi_{i,j}^0 = 45^\circ$ or if $b_{i,j}^0 = 1$ and $\phi_{i,j}^0 = 0^\circ$. The angle $157\frac{1}{2}^\circ$ is optimal for the other two cases. In all cases, equation 4 is violated with probability $\sin^2(22\frac{1}{2}^\circ) \approx 15\%$.

This shows clearly that it is always preferable to set $\phi_{i,j}^0 \neq \phi_{i,j}^1$ whenever $b_{i,j}^0 \neq b_{i,j}^1$, but that even then the probability of success is at most $\cos^2(22\frac{1}{2}^\circ) \approx 85\%$ for each such pair (i,j). Since there must be at least s such pairs in order to satisfy equation 3, we conclude that no strategy can succeed with probability greater than $(\cos^2(22\frac{1}{2}^\circ))^s$, which can be made arbitrarily small. $\square$

4.3 The problems with this new scheme

Recall that the original bit commitment scheme of Bennett and Brassard [BB84] suffered from problems in principle as well as in practice. Unfortunately, this is also the case with our new scheme. However, the new protocol is somewhat of a dual to he old one because the problems that were serious with the old scheme are of no consequence with the new scheme, and *vice versa*. Also, the only party that had a possibility of cheating in an ideal implementation of the old scheme was $\mathcal{S}$, whereas now it is $\mathcal{R}$. We shall see in section 5 how to capitalize on this role reversal.

One thing that is not ruled out by quantum mechanics is the possibility of evaluating predicates on several photons at once. Such possibility is known in the world of quantum mechanics as *coherent measurements*. For instance, there are functions f such that, given two photons of polarization ϕ_1 and ϕ_2, there might exist a way to find out more about $f(\phi_1, \phi_2)$ than what can be obtained by applying f (or perhaps another function) to what can be measured about ϕ_1 and ϕ_2 separately. Such a possibility would make the commitment scheme described above totally insecure if the $\oplus$ of the values carried by many photons could be measured at once, even if only a reasonably good estimate on the answer could be obtained. Indeed, the value of b could then be recovered easily using equation 2: $b = \bigoplus_{j=1}^{s} b_{i,j}$ and taking majority on the rows.

Fortunately, not only is no technology available to do coherent measurements, but its availability is not predicted for any foreseeable future. In fact, physicists do not even know how to get photons to interact in ways that could lead to such measurements. Therefore, although such a possibility exists in principle for $\mathcal{R}$ to cheat, there should be very little concern that the protocol be broken this way in practice. On the other hand, it is easy to see that the EPR threat that allowed $\mathcal{S}$ to cheat the protocol of Bennett and Brassard does not apply to the new scheme even in principle. (And conversely, coherent measurements could not help break the old scheme even in principle.)

From a practical point of view, however, notice that even a few transmission errors will lead $\mathcal{R}$ to believe that $\mathcal{S}$ is cheating and thus to reject her commitments even when she is honest. Because occasional transmission errors are technologically unavoidable, it is important to be able to deal with them if this scheme is ever to be used in practice. We do not know of any simple solution to solve this difficulty because it would be easy for $\mathcal{S}$ to cheat if $\mathcal{R}$ were willing to tolerate that $b'_{i,j} \neq b_{i,j}$ even occasionally when $\theta_{i,j} = \phi_{i,j}$. Nevertheless, this problem will be addressed in another paper whose purpose is to deal with transmission errors in quantum protocols. That paper, which is currently in preparation with Charles H. Bennett [BBC90], solves not only the question of practical quantum bit commitment, but also that of practical quantum oblivious transfer.

On the other hand, recall that the bit commitment scheme of Bennett and Brassard was seriously impaired in practice by the difficulty of producing single polarized photons. A more careful analysis in the proof of theorem 4.1 shows that this is not a worry with the new protocol presented here. Our protocol works just as well if multiphoton pulses happen, provided that their occurrence is not too frequent (at the cost of using a slightly larger security parameter s).

5 Have we gained anything?

As it turns out, having two different schemes is better than one even if each of them can be broken in principle. Indeed, one can build a coin tossing protocol that can be broken only if one can implement *both* the EPR attack and coherent measurements. Consider the following protocol.

Protocol 5.1 (BC-cointoss)

   1: $\mathcal{S}$ chooses a random bit b_0 and uses BB-commit(b_0) with $\mathcal{R}$

   2: $\mathcal{R}$ chooses a random bit b_1 and uses BC-commit(b_1) with $\mathcal{S}$
      (the roles of $\mathcal{R}$ and $\mathcal{S}$ are temporarily interchanged)

   3: $\mathcal{S}$ runs BB-open(b_0) with $\mathcal{R}$

   4: $\mathcal{R}$ runs BC-open(b_1) with $\mathcal{S}$

   5: $\mathcal{R}$ wins the coin toss if and only if $b_1 = b_0$

In principle, this protocol can be broken only if $\mathcal{S}$ can implement the EPR attack as well as the coherent measurement attack. $\mathcal{R}$ has no way of cheating whatsoever, unless he can design an apparatus that can transmit information faster than the speed of light. The proof of this claim will be provided in the journal version of the paper.

6 Conclusion and open problems

In the light of ongoing progress in experimental physics [AG86], it is reasonable to fear that the EPR attack on the bit commitment scheme (or coin tossing protocol) of [BB84] could be implemented. The bit commitment scheme that we have presented in this paper does not yield to this attack. Unfortunately, we can still describe an attack on this new scheme, which is possible in principle although not in practice, based on coherent measurements. Can one build a bit commitment scheme unbreakable in an absolute way, based solely on the equations of quantum mechanics? We cannot answer this question at this time even if practical considerations are not taken into account.

Still we have been able to build a coin tossing protocol that is secure unless both attacks can be implemented. This seems to indicate that maybe Bit Commitment is more than Coin Tossing since, at this time, we are unable to offer a bit commitment scheme with this same level of security.

7 Acknowledgements

We are very grateful to Charles H. Bennett and Joe Kilian for suggestions and comments on this work. Claude would especially like to thank Silvio Micali for the colossal work he contributed while writing and polishing this text, parts of which first appeared in Claude's Ph.D. thesis.

References

[AG86]   Aspect, A. and P. Grangier, "Experiments on Einstein – Podolsky – Rosen – type correlations with pairs of visible photons", in *Quantum concepts in space and time* (R. Penrose and C.J. Isham, eds.), Oxford University Press, 1986.

[BBBSS90]   Bennett, C.H., F. Bessette, G. Brassard, L. Salvail, and J. Smolin, "Experimental quantum cryptography", *Advances in Cryptology: Proceedings of Eurocrypt '90*, Aarhus, Denmark, Springer–Verlag, to appear. Submitted to *Journal of Cryptology*.

[BB84]   Bennett, C.H. and G. Brassard, "Quantum cryptography: public key distribution and coin tossing", *Proceedings of IEEE International Conference on Computers, Systems, and Signal Processing*, Bangalore, India, pp. 175–179, 1984.

[BBBW82]   Bennett, C.H., G. Brassard, S. Breidbart, and S. Wiesner, "Quantum cryptography, or unforgeable subway tokens", *Advances in Cryptology: Proceedings of Crypto 82*, Plenum Press, pp. 267–275, 1983.

[BBC90]   Bennett, C.H., G. Brassard, and C. Crépeau, "Practical Quantum Oblivious Transfer", *in preparation*, 1990.

[Bra88]   Brassard, G., *Modern Cryptology*, Lecture Notes in Computer Science, Vol. 325, Springer–Verlag, 1988.

[BCC88]   Brassard, G., D. Chaum, and C. Crépeau, "Minimum disclosure proofs of knowledge", *Journal of Computer and System Sciences*, Vol. 37, no. 2, pp. 156–189, 1988.

[Blu81]   Blum, M., "Three applications of the oblivious transfer: Part I: Coin flipping by telephone; Part II: How to exchange secrets; Part III: How to send certified electronic mail", Technical Report, Department of EECS, University of California, Berkeley, CA, 1981.

[CK88]   Crépeau, C. and J. Kilian, "Achieving oblivious transfer using weakened security assumptions", *Proceedings of the 29th IEEE Symposium on Foundations of Computer Science*, pp. 42–52, 1988.

[EPR35]   Einstein, A., P. Podolsky, and N. Rosen, "Can quantum-mechanical description of physical reality be considered complete?", *Physical Review*, Vol. 47, pp. 777–780, 1935. Reprinted in *Quantum theory and measurement* (J. A. Wheeler and W. Z. Zurek, eds.), Princeton University Press, 1983.

[EGL83]   Even, S., O. Goldreich, and A. Lempel, "A randomized protocol for signing contracts", *Advances in Cryptology: Proceedings of Crypto 82*, Plenum Press, pp. 205–210, 1983.

[GMW86]   Goldreich, O., S. Micali, and A. Wigderson, "Proofs that yield nothing but their validity and a methodology of cryptographic protocol design", *Proceedings of the 27th IEEE Symposium on Foundations of Computer Science*, pp. 174–187, 1986.

[Rab81]   Rabin, M. O., "How to exchange secrets by oblivious transfer", Technical Memo TR-81, Aiken Computation Laboratory, Harvard University, 1981.

[Wie83]   Wiesner, S., "Conjugate coding", *Sigact News*, Vol. 15, no. 1, pp. 78–88, 1983. manuscript written *circa* 1969, unpublished until it appeared in *Sigact News*.

Security with Low Communication Overhead

D. Beaver[*]   J. Feigenbaum[†]   J. Kilian[‡]   P. Rogaway[§]

(Extended Abstract)

Abstract

We consider the communication complexity of secure multiparty computations by networks of processors each with unlimited computing power. Say that an n-party protocol for a function of m bits is efficient if it uses a constant number of rounds of communication and a total number of message bits that is polynomial in $\max(m, n)$. We show that any function has an efficient protocol that achieves $(n \log n)/m$ resilience. Ours is the first secure multiparty protocol in which the communication complexity is independent of the computational complexity of the function being computed.

We also consider the communication complexity of zero-knowledge proofs of properties of committed bits. We show that every function f of m bits has an efficient *notarized envelope scheme*; that is, there is a protocol in which a computationally unlimited prover commits a sequence of bits x to a computationally unlimited verifier and then proves in perfect zero-knowledge (without decommitting x) that $f(x) = 1$, using a constant number of rounds and $poly(m)$ message bits. Ours is the first notarized envelope scheme in which the communication complexity is independent of the computational complexity of f.

Finally, we establish a new upper bound on the number of oracles needed in *instance-hiding schemes* for arbitrary functions. These schemes allow a computationally limited querier to capitalize on the superior power of one or more computationally unlimited oracles in order to obtain $f(x)$ without revealing its private input x to any one of the oracles. We show that every function of m bits has an $(m/\log m)$-oracle instance-hiding scheme.

The central technique used in all of these results is *locally random reducibility*, which was used for the first time in [7] and is formally defined for the first time here. In addition to the applications that we present, locally random reducibility has been applied to interactive proof systems, program checking, and program testing.

---

[*]AT&T Bell Laboratories, Room 2C324, 600 Mountain Avenue, Murray Hill, NJ 07974 USA, beaver@research.att.com. Work done at Harvard University, supported in part by NSF grant CCR-870-4513.

[†]AT&T Bell Laboratories, Room 2C473, 600 Mountain Avenue, Murray Hill, NJ 07974 USA, jf@research.att.com.

[‡]Harvard University and MIT Laboratory for Computer Science, 545 Technology Square, Cambridge, MA 02139 USA, joek@theory.lcs.mit.edu. Supported by an NSF Postdoctoral Fellowship.

[§]MIT Laboratory for Computer Science, 545 Technology Square, Cambridge, MA 02139 USA, rogaway@theory.lcs.mit.edu.

1 Introduction

A *resilient, multiparty protocol* allows a network of processors to compute a function of the processors' private inputs in such a way that each processor learns the result, no processor learns anything about another's private input (except what is implied by the result and its own private input), and the protocol works even if some proper subset of the processors behave in an arbitrary faulty manner. For example, a t-resilient protocol for majority-voting allows all voters to learn who won, while preventing any coalition of t or fewer anarchists from learning the vote of an honest participant or disrupting the election.

In this paper, we make no assumptions about the computing power of the individual processors in our network. Because no such assumptions are made, all proofs of the security properties of protocols must be argued on information-theoretic grounds. No complexity-theoretic hypotheses, such as the existence of one-way functions, are relevant.

Let n be the number of processors and m be the total number of input bits to the function being computed. We focus on three criteria for evaluating a protocol:

- The *resilience* $t(m,n)$ is the maximum number of faulty processors that can be tolerated.

- The *round complexity* $\rho(m,n)$ is the maximum number of communication rounds in an execution of the protocol.

- The *bit complexity* $b(m,n)$ is the maximum total number of message bits sent by *all* of the processors during an execution.

Theorem: For any positive constant c, every function of m bits has an n-party protocol that achieves $(cn\log n)/m$ resilience, *constant* round complexity, and bit complexity that is *polynomial* in $\max(m,n)$.

That is, even functions whose circuit complexity is exponential have resilient multiparty protocols whose communication complexity is polynomial.

Our actual result gives a more general tradeoff and is stated precisely in Section 5.3 below.

In a resilient multiparty protocol, the processors are equally powerful, and they must cooperate in a computation because none of them alone has all of the necessary data. An alternative view of distributed computations with private data is considered in [1, 7]. There one processor, who has all of the data, must cooperate with other processors because it lacks the power to carry out the computation. More specifically, a *μ-oracle instance-hiding scheme* for a function f is a protocol in which a polynomial-time bounded *querier* consults μ computationally-unlimited *oracles* in such a way that the querier learns the value $f(x)$, but none of the oracles learns the input x. Beaver and Feigenbaum [7] show that, for every positive constant c, every function of m bits has an $(m - c\log m)$-oracle instance-hiding scheme. In this paper, we improve this general upper bound.

Theorem: For every positive constant c, every function of m bits has an $(m/c \log m)$-oracle instance-hiding scheme.

Zero-knowledge proof systems, as originally formulated in [25], are two-party protocols in which the parties have a common input x, and one party (the prover) convinces the other (the verifier) that, say, $f(x) = 1$, without revealing a proof. *Notarized envelope schemes* allow the prover to publish a *commitment* to its private input x and then prove in zero-knowledge to the verifier that $f(x) = 1$ *without decommitting x*. Many of the cost criteria that apply to resilient multiparty protocols also apply to notarized envelope schemes. In this paper, we are most interested in the communcation costs of a scheme – that is, its round complexity and its bit complexity.

We examine notarized envelope schemes in the *ideal envelope model*; that is, both prover and verifier have unlimited computational power, no cryptographic assumptions are made, and bit commitment is assumed as a primitive. Any primitive that implements bit commitment in this model is called an *envelope scheme*. A natural question to ask is whether notarized envelope schemes exist in this model; that is, can notarized envelopes be built out of ordinary envelopes? This question was answered in the affirmative by numerous authors (e.g., [10, 32]); a written account of one scheme appears in [11].

All previously published notarized envelope schemes have the following feature in common: They have bit complexity proportional to the circuit complexity of f. Here, we achieve a more communication-efficient construction of general notarized envelope schemes.

Theorem: In the ideal envelope model, every function has a notarized envelope scheme that has *constant* round complexity and bit complexity *polynomial in the number of input bits*.

The results given here first appeared in our Technical Memorandum [8]. In this abstract, some details of proof are omitted, because of space limitations; many of these details can be found in [6], and all will appear in our final paper.

The rest of this abstract is organized as follows. Section 2 contains a brief account of previous work on secure, distributed computation, with emphasis on the results that do not involve complexity-theoretic hypotheses. Notation and terminology is given in Section 3, and several necessary building blocks are recalled from the literature. Section 4 gives a precise definition of locally random reducibility and recalls the reduction given in [7]. We present our main results in Section 5; the multiparty protocol result is given last, because it relies upon the other two.

2   Previous Work on Secure Distributed Computation

Secure distributed computation was introduced by Yao [35]. His proofs of the security properties of protocols are based on complexity-theoretic hypotheses such as the existence of one-way functions. Further work along these lines can be found in [9, 18, 23, 24, 36].

Previous results on secure distributed computation without complexity-theoretic hypotheses can be summarized as follows.

- The approach was first taken by Ben-Or, Goldwasser, Wigderson [13] and Chaum, Crépeau, Damgård [17]. Their n-party protocols for secure evaluation of a function f of m bits are based on distributed simulation of a circuit C_f for f. Their protocols achieve $(n-1)/3$-resilience, round complexity proportional to the depth of C_f, and bit complexity proportional to the size of C_f.

- T. Rabin, Ben-Or [31] and Beaver [4] give protocols that achieve $(n-1)/2$-resilience but have the same round complexity and the same bit complexity as those in [13, 17].

- The protocol of Bar-Ilan, Beaver [3] achieves $(n-1)/2$-resilience, *constant* round complexity, and bit complexity proportional to the size of C_f, if the depth of C_f is $O(\log m)$.

- Chaum [16] gives an interesting protocol that can be proven $(n-1)/2$-resilient without complexity-theoretic hypotheses and $(n-1)$-resilient with complexity-theoretic hypotheses.

Throughout this paper, we use the term "secure protocol" to mean a protocol that is "resilient" against arbitrarily (i.e., potentially malicious) faulty players. There is also a literature on a weaker notion of security – "privacy" against "honest but curious" players; refer to [5, 19, 27] for details.

3 Preliminaries

We use f to denote a function with domain $\{0,1\}^m$. The range of f is contained in $K_{m,n}$ – a finite field that is large enough but still of size polynomial in $\max(m,n)$. The meaning of "large enough" will vary but will be clear from context. The field $K_{m,n}$ will always be constructible in time polynomial in $\max(m,n)$. The constants $\alpha_1, \alpha_2, \ldots$ are distinct elements of $K_{m,n} \setminus \{0\}$.

Consider g, the "arithmetization" of f over $K_{m,n}$. For $A = (a_1, \ldots, a_m) \in \{0,1\}^m$, let

$$\delta_A(X_1, \ldots, X_m) = \prod_{j=1}^m (X_j - \overline{a_j})(-1)^{\overline{a_j}} \in K_{m,n}[X_1, \ldots, X_m].$$

Then, for any $x = (x_1, \ldots, x_m) \in \{0,1\}^m$, $\delta_A(x)$ is 1 if $A = x$ and it is 0 otherwise. Next, let

$$g(X_1, \ldots, X_m) = \sum_{A \in \{0,1\}^m} f(A)\delta_A(X_1, \ldots, X_m) \in K_{m,n}[X_1, \ldots, X_m].$$

The multivariate polynomial g has the property that it agrees with f on all inputs in $\{0,1\}^m$.

For example, if f is the boolean function

$$f(x_1, x_2, x_3) = x_1 \oplus x_2 \oplus x_3,$$

where $\oplus$ denotes exclusive-or, the arithmetization is

$$g(X_1, X_2, X_3) = X_1(1-X_2)(1-X_3)+(1-X_1)X_2(1-X_3)+(1-X_1)(1-X_2)X_3+X_1X_2X_3.$$

Our model of computation is a synchronous network of computationally unlimited processors, $P_1, \ldots, P_n$, completely connected by private channels and a broadcast channel, acted upon by a dynamic adversary. In one round of the protocol, each processor can receive a message from each other processor, perform an unlimited amount of local computation, and send a message to each other processor. Each processor P_i has a private input z_i and a private random source. The correct outcome of the protocol is, roughly, that each P_i receives the functional value while no P_i receives any information about z_j, $j \neq i$, except what is implied by the functional value and z_i. Furthermore, the malicious players' inputs do not depend on the honest players' inputs. The protocol is *t-resilient* if the correct outcome occurs even if as many as t of the processors exhibit arbitrarily faulty behavior.

The vector $(z_1, \ldots, z_n)$ of inputs contains a total of m bits, which we denote by $x_1, \ldots, x_m$. Thus the desired functional value is $f(x_1, \ldots, x_m)$.

An *envelope scheme* is a protocol in which two *computationally-unlimited* processors achieve *information-theoretically secure bit commitment*. That is, *committer P_1* can compute and send to the *receiver P_2* a sequence of *commitments*, say $c_1, \ldots, c_m$, to a sequence of bits $b_1, \ldots, b_m$. The sequence $c_1, \ldots, c_m$ conveys no information (in the Shannon sense) to the receiver about the sequence $b_1, \ldots, b_m$ (except its length). At any time after the commitment takes place, P_2 may challenge P_1 to *decommit* any c_i. The envelope scheme must have the properties that P_1 can always prove that c_i is a commitment to b_i and that P_1 can never prove that c_i is a commitment to $1 - b_i$. Notice that, by definition, the security of an envelope scheme is two-sided: P_2 cannot find out any information about b_i unless P_1 decommits, and P_1 cannot "change its mind" about what it has committed.

In Section 5.2 below, we present a result in the *ideal envelope model*, as opposed to the cryptographic model. That is, we assume that committer and receiver both have unlimited computational power and that an envelope scheme is given as a primitive.

A *notarized envelope scheme* is a protocol in which a *prover* commits to a sequence of bits $x_1, \ldots, x_m$, and then gives a *zero-knowledge proof* to a *verifier* that $f(x_1, \ldots, x_m) = 1$, *without revealing any information about* $x_1, \ldots, x_m$. Since the verifier has unlimited computational power in the ideal envelope model, a natural question to ask is why it cannot simply compute $f(x_1, \ldots, x_m)$ without the help of the prover. The answer, of course, is that the verifier does not have $x_1, \ldots, x_m$; rather it has the prover's commitments to $x_1, \ldots, x_m$.

The round complexity of a notarized envelope scheme or n-party protocol for a function f of m bits is the (worst-case) total number of rounds in an execution, as a function of n and m. Similarly, the bit complexity is the sum, over all i, of the sum of the lengths of all messages sent by P_i in a (worst-case) execution. We use the following results in our constructions in Section 5.

Theorem 3.1 ([10, 11, 32]) *If f is computable by a (possibly nondeterministic) boolean or arithmetic circuit of polynomial size, then it has a notarized envelope scheme with constant round complexity and bit complexity polynomial in the length of the input.*

Theorem 3.2 ([3]) *If f is computable by a boolean or arithmetic circuit of depth $\log m$ and size $poly(m)$, then f has an $((n-1)/2)$-resilient, n-party protocol with constant round complexity and bit complexity $poly(\max(m, n))$.*

In Section 5, we refer to the constant-round, polynomial-bit notarized envelope schemes of [10, 11, 32] for functions with poly-size circuits as the *standard notarized envelope schemes*.

A $\mu(m)$-*oracle instance-hiding scheme for f* is a $\rho(m)$-round synchronous protocol executed by a polynomial-time Turing Machine P_0 (the *querier*) and $\mu(m)$ computationally-unlimited oracle Turing Machines $P_1, \ldots, P_\mu$ (the *oracles*). Querier P_0 has a private input $x \in \{0, 1\}^m$ as well as a private source of randomness. For each oracle P_i, there is a private channel connecting P_0 to P_i. There are no communication channels at all between pairs of distinct oracles. This model is analogous in one sense to the multiprover model of interactive proofs systems (see [2, 12, 22]): The oracles (like the provers) can "meet to agree on a strategy" before the execution of the instance-hiding scheme begins, but they cannot collude during the execution of the scheme, and no oracle sees the communication between the querier and the other oracles. During one round of the scheme, P_0 can receive a message from each oracle, perform a randomized polynomial-time local computation, and send a message to each oracle. Also in one round, each oracle can receive a message from P_0, perform an unlimited amount of local computation, and send a message to P_0. In round $\rho(m)$, P_0 uses the transcript of the execution to compute $f(x)$. For $1 \leq i \leq \mu(m)$, the sequence of messages sent by P_0 to P_i is independent of x, given m.[1] Intuitively, P_0 uses the oracles to compute $f(x)$ without telling any one of them what x is.

4 Locally Random Reductions

Intuitively, a *locally random reduction* from a function f to a function g is a randomized polynomial-time mapping that takes an *arbitrary* instance x of f to a set $\{y_1, \ldots, y_\mu\}$ of *random* instances of g in such a way that $f(x)$ is easily computable from $g(y_1), \ldots, g(y_\mu)$. A function f is *random self-reducible* if there is a locally random reduction from f to itself. We now define this concept more formally.

---

[1]There is actually no need to restrict attention to instance-hiding schemes that "leak at most n." Refer to [7, Section 2] for a detailed description of the general model.

Definition 4.1 *A function f is* $(t(m), \mu(m))$**-locally random reducible** *to a function g if there are polynomial-time computable functions ϕ, σ_1, ..., $\sigma_{\mu(m)}$ and a polynomially-bounded function $w(m)$ with the following properties.*

- *For all m, all $x \in \{0,1\}^m$, and at least $3/4$ of all $r \in \{0,1\}^{w(m)}$,*

$$f(x) = \phi(x, r, g(\sigma_1(x, r)), \ldots, g(\sigma_{\mu(m)}(x, r))).$$

- *If r is chosen uniformly from $\{0,1\}^{w(m)}$, then, for any pair x_1, x_2 of distinct elements of $\{0,1\}^m$ and all $\{i_1, \ldots, i_{t(m)}\} \subset \{1, \ldots, \mu(m)\}$, the random variables $\langle \sigma_{i_1}(x_1, r), \ldots, \sigma_{i_{t(m)}}(x_1, r) \rangle$ and $\langle \sigma_{i_1}(x_2, r), \ldots, \sigma_{i_{t(m)}}(x_2, r) \rangle$ are identically distributed.*

More succinctly, we say that f is (t, μ)-lrr to g.

Informally, if T is a subset of the target instances $\{y_1 = \sigma_1(x, r), \ldots, y_{\mu(m)} = \sigma_{\mu(m)}(x, r)\}$, and $|T| \leq t(m)$, then T leaks no information about the original instance x, except its length m.

As in the definition of BPP, the fraction $3/4$ can be replaced by $1/2 + 1/poly(m)$. In the results we present below, the equation $f(x) = \phi(x, r, g(\sigma_1(x, r)), \ldots, g(\sigma_{\mu(m)}(x, r)))$ can be made to hold for all r, by appropriate choice of the field $K_{m,n}$.

Note that a $(1, \mu)$-lrr from f to g can be thought of as a one-round, μ-oracle instance-hiding scheme for f. The querier P_0 chooses r, computes the target instances $y_i = \sigma_i(x, r)$, for $1 \leq i \leq \mu$, and sends each y_i to a separate g-oracle P_i. P_i then sends back $g(y_i)$, for $1 \leq i \leq \mu$, and P_0 computes $f(x)$ using ϕ, x, r, and the values $\{g(y_i)\}$.

The following special case of Definition 4.1 is important: f is $(1, \mu)$-lrr to g, and each of the random instances $\sigma_i(x, r)$ is distributed uniformly over all g-instances of the appropriate length (although, as usual, pairs of instances $\sigma_i(x, r)$ and $\sigma_j(x, r)$ are dependent). In this case, the average-case complexity of g gives an upper bound (up to polynomial factors) on the worst-case complexity of f. This property of locally random reductions is used to prove that the permanent function is as hard on average as it is in the worst case (cf. [28]) and to show that, for every (finite) function f, there is a polynomial g such that g is as hard on average as f is in the worst case (cf. [7]).

More precisely, it is shown in [7] that every function f of m inputs bits is $(1, m+1)$-lrr to a polynomial g. We repeat this construction here and improve upon it in Section 5.1 below.

Let $x = (x_1, \ldots, x_m)$ be an element of $\{0,1\}^m$. Choose m coefficients c_1, ..., c_m independently and uniformly from $K_{m,n}$. The univariate polynomial

$$G(Z) = g(c_1 Z + x_1, \ldots, c_m Z + x_m)$$

is of degree m and has the property that

$$G(0) = g(x_1, \ldots, x_m) = f(x_1, \ldots, x_m).$$

For $1 \leq i \leq m + 1$, the function σ_i of the locally random reduction maps x to $y_i = (c_1 \alpha_i + x_1, \ldots, c_m \alpha_i + x_m)$. The function ϕ recovers $f(x)$ by interpolating the pairs $(\alpha_1, g(y_1)), \ldots, (\alpha_{m+1}, g(y_{m+1}))$; these $m+1$ points determine a unique degree-m polynomial in $K_{m,n}[Z]$ – namely $G(Z)$, which has constant term $f(x)$. Finally, each y_i is distributed uniformly over $K_{m,n}^m$ and hence leaks no information about x.

All of the results we present in Section 5 use locally random reductions in an essential way. This notion of reducibility has also been applied to interactive proof systems (cf. [2, 29, 34]), and to program checking, testing, and self correcting (cf. [14, 15, 28]). An extensive treatment of the complexity-theoretic aspects of random self-reducibility can be found in [20, 21].

5 Results

5.1 Instance-Hiding Schemes

Theorem 5.1 *For every function f and every polynomial $t(m)$, there is a polynomial h such that f is $(t(m), 1 + t(m)m/\log m)$-lrr to h.*

Proof (sketch): Clearly, it suffices to prove the following two lemmas.

Lemma 5.1 *Every function f is polynomial-time, many-one reducible to a multivariate polynomial h over $K_{m,n}$ of degree $m/\log m$.*

Lemma 5.2 *For every polynomial $t(m)$, every multivariate polynomial h over $K_{m,n}$ is $(t, 1 + dt)$-locally random self-reducible, where d is the degree of h.*

Let f be a function that maps $\{0,1\}^m$ to $K_{m,n}$. Assume without loss of generality that $\log m$ divides m; if it does not, then x can be "padded" with dummy input bits. Divide the input bits $x_1, \ldots, x_m$ into consecutive "blocks" of length $\log m$. For example, if $m = 4$, then the first block is $\{x_1, x_2\}$ and the second is $\{x_3, x_4\}$.

Proof of Lemma 5.1: The crux of this construction is a change of variables that allows us to use a degree-$(m/\log m)$ polynomial h in $m^2/\log m$ variables in place of the degree-m polynomial g in m variables that was used in Section 4.

Let $\{x_j\}_{j=(k-1)\log m+1}^{k\log m}$, for each $1 \le k \le m/\log m$, be a block of input bits, and let $\{X_j\}_{j=(k-1)\log m+1}^{k\log m}$ be the corresponding block of indeterminates over $K_{m,n}$ that are used to define the arithmetization g of f. For each subset S of the indices $\{(k-1)\log m + 1, \ldots, k\log m\}$, let the variable W_S represent the monomial $\Pi_{j\in S}X_j$. There are $m/\log m$ blocks, and hence a total of $m^2/\log m$ variables $W_1, \ldots, W_{m^2/\log m}$.

Each monomial in g can be represented as a monomial in $m/\log m$ of the W's. Let $h(W_1, \ldots, W_{m^2/\log m})$ be the degree-$(m/\log m)$ polynomial that results from summing these representations of all of the monomials in g. ∎

Proof of Lemma 5.2: Let $h(W_1, \ldots, W_s)$ be a degree-d polynomial over $K_{m,n}$, and let $w = (w_1, \ldots, w_s)$ be an element of $K_{m,n}^s$. We show how to reduce w to a collection of $1 + dt$ elements of $K_{m,n}^s$ with an appropriate distribution. For each $1 \le l \le s$, choose t elements $c_{l,1}, \ldots, c_{l,t}$ of $K_{m,n}$ independently and uniformly at random, and let $q_l(Z) = c_{l,t}Z^t + \cdots + c_{l,1}Z + w_l$. Then the univariate polynomial

$$H(Z) = h(q_1(Z), \ldots, q_s(Z))$$

is of degree at most $t(m) \cdot d$ and has the property that

$$H(0) = h(w_1, \ldots, w_s).$$

For $1 \le i \le 1 + td$, the function $\sigma_i(x, r)$ maps x to $y_i = (q_1(\alpha_i), \ldots, q_s(\alpha_i))$. The function ϕ recovers $h(w)$ by interpolating the polynomial $H(Z)$ from the pairs $(\alpha_i, h(y_i))$.

The second requirement of Definition 4.1 is satisfied for the same reason that Shamir's secret-sharing scheme works (cf. [33]): For every l, t or fewer values of the random degree-t polynomial q_l reveal no information about its constant term w_l. ∎

The relationship between the multivariate polynomial g and the univariate polynomial G in Section 4 is a special case of the relationship between the polynomials h and H that we use here; in that special case, $t = 1$. ∎

Remark 5.1 *This can be improved to a $(t(m), 1 + t(m)m/c\log m)$-lrr, for any positive constant c, by increasing the block size to $c\log m$ (and the number of w_l's per block to m^c).*

Remark 5.2 *More generally, one can use block size k, which is not necessarily $O(\log m)$. This will result in a $(t(m), 1 + t(m) \cdot \lceil m/k \rceil)$-lrr from f to a polynomial h of degree $\lceil m/k \rceil$ in $2^k \cdot \lceil m/k \rceil$ variables, but the reduction will take time $2^k \cdot poly(m)$.*

By taking $t(m) = 1$, we get the desired result on instance-hiding schemes.

Corollary 5.1 *For every positive constant c, every function has an $(m/c\log m)$-oracle instance-hiding scheme.*

5.2 Notarized Envelope Schemes

In this section, we show how to build a notarized envelope scheme with low communication complexity, starting with an ordinary envelope scheme. The notation f and g is as in Section 3.

Let P and V denote the prover and verifier of the notarized envelope scheme. In most of the literature on interactive proof systems, V denotes a probabilistic, polynomial-time verifier. Therefore, we stress that, in a notarized envelope scheme, *no limitation is placed of the computational power of V.*

Intuitively, player P in our notarized envelope scheme plays the roles of the querier and all of the oracles in the instance-hiding scheme of [7]. Player V then challenges the prover to demonstrate that it played both roles faithfully. In the following protocol, the quantifiers "for $1 \le i \le m + 1$" and "for $1 \le j \le m$" are implicit in each step in which the subscript i or j occurs.

Notarized Envelope Scheme to show that $f(x_1, \ldots, x_m) = 1$

Step 1. P commits to x_j.

Step 2. P selects random c_j uniformly at random from $K_{m,n}$ and lets $q_j(Z) = c_j Z + x_j$. Then P computes $(y_{1,i}, \ldots, y_{m,i}) = (q_1(\alpha_i), \ldots, q_m(\alpha_i))$ and $v_i = g(y_{1,i}, \ldots, y_{m,i})$.

Step 3. P commits to q_j, $(y_{1,i}, \ldots, y_{m,i})$, and v_i.

Step 4. P uses a standard notarized envelope scheme to prove to V that $q_j(0) = x_j$, that $q_j(\alpha_i) = y_{j,i}$, and that $\{(\alpha_i, v_i)\}$ interpolate a degree-m polynomial with constant term 1. V rejects (and terminates the protocol) if any of these proofs fail.

Step 5. V chooses k uniformly from $\{1, \ldots, m+1\}$ and sends it to P.

Step 6. P decommits $(y_{1,k}, \ldots, y_{m,k})$, and v_k.

Step 7. V accepts if and only if $g(y_{1,k}, \ldots, y_{m,k}) = v_k$.

Theorem 5.2 *The protocol just given is a notarized envelope scheme and has the following properties.*

(A) *If $f(x_1, \ldots, x_m) = 1$ and P is honest, then V always accepts.*

(B) *If $f(x_1, \ldots, x_m) \neq 1$ and P cheats, then V rejects with probability at least $1/(m+1)$.*

(C) *Repetitions can be performed in parallel. Thus the rejection probability in (B) can be amplified while retaining constant round complexity and polynomial bit complexity.*

Proof (sketch): The fact that this protocol satisfies the requirements of a notarized envelope scheme follows from the fact that $q_j(\alpha_i)$ is uniformly distributed over $K_{m,n}$, the properties of the standard notarized envelope schemes, the definition of envelopes, and the fact that V has the power to compute g. We first argue that this protocol satisfies the necessary security requirements. That is, we claim that no information about $x_1, \ldots, x_m$ (but for the value of m) is revealed to V. By the properties of the standard notarized envelope schemes, the bits revealed during any of these zero-knowledge proofs are independent of the values of $x_1, \ldots, x_m$. It also follows from a straightforward analysis that these revealed bits are independent of the values of $y_{1,k}, \ldots, y_{m,k}$ for $1 \leq k \leq m+1$. By the properties of our locally random reduction, we have that $y_{1,k}, \ldots, y_{m,k}$ is uniformly distributed over K_m^m, and is thus independent of $x_1, \ldots, x_m$. Finally, we note that v_k is completely determined by $y_{1,k}, \ldots, y_{m,k}$, and thus contributes no additional information about $x_1, \ldots, x_m$.

Part (A) follows from the properties of the older notarized envelope schemes, and the fact that the prover never makes an untrue assertion.

To prove (B), observe that, if P cheats, then either one of the assertions that he makes in Step 4 is wrong (and thus V will reject with high probability), or at least one of the v_i's is not equal to $g(y_{1,i}, \ldots, y_{m,i})$ (and thus V will reject with probability at least $1/(m+1)$ in Step 7).

Part (C) follows from the parallelizability of the earlier notarized envelope schemes. Note that we are working in the ideal envelope model, in which zero-knowledge proofs can be run in parallel without losing their zero-knowledge properties. ∎

5.3 Resilient Multiparty Protocols

Theorem 5.3 *For any positive constant c, every function f has a $((cn\log n)/m)$-resilient, n-party protocol with constant round complexity and bit complexity polynomial in $\max(m,n)$.*

Proof (sketch): We make use of a $((cn\log n)/m, n)$-lrr from f to a polynomial h of degree $m/c'\log n$, where $c' > c$. Such a reduction is obtained by taking block size $c'\log n$ in Remark 5.2. Let $s = n^{c'}m/c'\log n$ be the number of variables w_l in h. Recall that player P_i's input is z_i, which is some subset of the bits $x_1, \ldots, x_m$.

We first exhibit a protocol that satisfies the weaker requirement of *t-privacy*, where $t = ((cn\log n)/m)$. That is, as many as t players may collude to discover others' inputs, but all players compute and send all required values correctly. We then show how to enhance the basic protocol to achieve *t*-resilience. When we "run a subprotocol" to compute intermediate values, we use the resilient n-party protocol of Bar-Ilan and Beaver [3].

We say that a player *t-secretly shares* b when the player selects $q(Z) = c_t Z^t + \cdots + c_1 Z + b$ by choosing each c_i independently and uniformly at random, and sends $q(\alpha_i)$ to P_i, for $1 \le i \le n$. The quantifiers "for $1 \le i, j \le n$" and "for $1 \le l \le s$" are implicit in each step in which the subscripts i, j, and l occur.

An n-party protocol to compute $f(x_1, \ldots, x_m)$

Step 1. P_i t-secretly shares each bit of z_i.

Step 2. Run a subprotocol to compute w_l and t-secretly share it. Let $(y_{1,i}, \ldots, y_{s,i})$ denote the shares sent to P_i.

Step 3. P_i computes $v_i = h(y_{1,i}, \ldots, y_{s,i})$ and t-secretly shares it.

Step 4. Run a subprotocol to interpolate the polynomial $H(Z)$ from $\{(\alpha_i, v_i)\}$ and reveal to everyone the constant term, which is $f(x_1, \ldots, x_m)$.

Observe first that this basic protocol is correct, is t-private, has constant round complexity, and has polynomial bit complexity. Essentially, this follows from the properties of Shamir's secret-sharing scheme and from Theorem 3.2, because the subprotocols of Steps 2 and 4 use poly-size, log-depth circuits: change of variables, selection of random polynomials, polynomial evaluation and polynomial interpolation.

To achieve $((cn\log n)/m)$ *resilience*, we add another subprotocol between Steps 3 and 4. In this subprotocol, each player P_i proves in zero-knowledge that he has computed v_i correctly. These proofs are accomplished using the notarized envelope scheme of Section 5.2 and a (constant-round, polynomial-bits) majority-voting scheme. "Envelopes" need *not* be assumed as a primitive (as they are in the ideal envelope model of Section 5.2), because they can be implemented using verifiable secret-sharing (cf. T. Rabin [30]). In the resilient version of the protocol, verifiable secret sharing is used in all steps in which ordinary secret sharing is used in the private version. ∎

Remark 5.3 *The bound $t = (cn \log n)/m$ is needed because h has degree $d = m/c' \log n$, and we need $dt < n$ in order to interpolate the result. That is, even if the processors are "honest but curious," our protocol is only $((cn \log n)/m)$-private, because it must compute the locally random reduction. Everything except the locally random reduction could be made $(n-1)/2$ resilient. In general, any t-private, n-party protocol for f with constant round complexity and bit complexity polynomial in $\max(m,n)$ can be compiled into a t-resilient, n-party protocol for f with constant round complexity and bit complexity polynomial in $\max(m,n)$.*

Correctness proofs for multiparty protocols are both complicated and elusive. To our knowledge, no proof of correctness for any general multiparty protocol has been widely examined and found to be completely rigorous. Indeed, there is no universally accepted standard for what secure multiparty computation should actually entail. Furthermore, there are no rigorously proven composition results for these protocols. Any rigorous use of these basic protocol constructions must contend with these difficulties.

It is likely that the techniques necessary to prove the results of [3, 13, 17, 31] cleanly and rigorously will also suffice to analyze our protocol. In the meantime, our strategy is to compartmentalize these earlier results so that we can truly treat them as black boxes. Toward this end, we will first consider a *trusted servant* abstraction for multiparty protocols. In addition to the n players, of potentially infinite power, we include an auxiliary player (the servant) with the following properties.

1. The servant is guaranteed to behave honestly.

2. The servant can communicate privately with any of the other players.

3. The servant can perform polynomial time computations on its private data.

4. The servant can terminate without revealing any of its private information.

Our proof can then be divided up as follows. First, and easiest, we restate our protocol so that it uses a trusted servant and prove its correctness in that model. Then we reduce the correctness of the trusted servant protocol to the correctness of results that have already appeared in the literature. At this point, a rigorous proof of the earlier multiparty results will yield a rigorous proof of our result as well.

6 Open Problems

The obvious question is whether the bounds achieved here can be improved. Specifically:

1. Is there a better general upper bound than $m/\log m$ oracles for instance-hiding?

2. Can more than $n \log n/m$ resilience be achieved, while retaining constant round complexity and polynomial bit complexity?

3. If the answer to Question 2 is no for general f, what can be said about functions with polynomial-sized circuits?

4. Because it uses the arithmetization of f, our multiparty protocol incurs a high local computation cost, even if f has small circuit complexity. Can this be avoided?

7 Acknowledgements

The authors are grateful to Yvo Desmedt for interesting discussions of these results and to the organizers of the October, 1989 *Monte Verita Seminar on Future Directions in Cryptography*, where some of this work was done.

References

[1] M. Abadi, J. Feigenbaum, and J. Kilian. On Hiding Information from an Oracle, *J. Comput. System Sci.* 39 (1989), 21–50.

[2] L. Babai, L. Fortnow, and C. Lund. Non-Deterministic Exponential Time has Two-Prover Interactive Proofs, *Proc. of FOCS 1990*, IEEE.

[3] J. Bar-Ilan and D. Beaver. Non-Cryptographic Fault-Tolerant Computing in a Constant Number of Rounds, *Proc. of PODC 1989*, ACM, 201–209.

[4] D. Beaver. Secure Multiparty Protocols Tolerating Half Faulty Processors, to appear in *J. Cryptology*. Preliminary version in *Proc. of CRYPTO 1989*, Springer Verlag LNCS 435, 560–572.

[5] D. Beaver. Perfect Privacy for Two-Party Protocols, *Proc. of DIMACS Workshop on Distributed Computing and Cryptography* (Princeton, NJ; October, 1989), AMS, 1990.

[6] D. Beaver. Security, Fault-Tolerance, and Communication Complexity for Distributed Systems, PhD Thesis, Harvard University, 1990.

[7] D. Beaver and J. Feigenbaum. Hiding Instances in Multioracle Queries, *Proc. of STACS 1990*, Springer Verlag LNCS 415, 37–48.

[8] D. Beaver, J. Feigenbaum, J. Kilian, and P. Rogaway. Cryptographic Applications of Locally Random Reductions, AT&T Bell Laboratories Technical Memorandum, November 15, 1989.

[9] D. Beaver, S. Micali, and P. Rogaway. The Round Complexity of Secure Protocols, *Proc. of STOC 1990*, ACM, 503–513.

[10] C. Bennett, G. Brassard, and C. Crépeau. Private communication.

[11] M. Ben-Or, O. Goldreich, S. Goldwasser, J. Hastad, J. Kilian, S. Micali, and P. Rogaway. Everything Provable is Provable in Zero-Knowledge, *Proc. of CRYPTO 1988*, Springer Verlag LNCS 403, 37–56.

[12] M. Ben-Or, S. Goldwasser, J. Kilian, and A. Wigderson. Multi-Prover Interactive Proofs: How to Remove Intractability, *Proc. of STOC 1988*, ACM, 113–131.

[13] M. Ben-Or, S. Goldwasser, and A. Wigderson. Completeness Theorems for Non-Cryptographic Fault-Tolerant Distributed Computation, *Proc. of STOC 1988*, ACM, 1–10.

[14] M. Blum, M. Luby, and R. Rubinfeld. Stronger Checkers and General Techniques for Numerical Problems, *Proc. of STOC 1990*, ACM, 73–83.

[15] M. Blum, M. Luby, and R. Rubinfeld. Program Result Checking Against Adaptive Programs and in Cryptographic Settings, *Proc. of DIMACS Workshop on Distributed Computing and Cryptography* (Princeton, NJ; October, 1989), AMS, 1990.

[16] D. Chaum. The Spymasters Double-Agent Problem: Multiparty Computations Secure Unconditionally from Minorities and Cryptographically from Majorities, *Proc. of CRYPTO 1989*, Springer Verlag LNCS 435, 591–604.

[17] D. Chaum, C. Crépeau, and I. Damgård. Multiparty Unconditionally Secure Protocols, *Proc. of STOC 1988*, ACM, 11–19.

[18] D. Chaum, I. Damgård, and J. van de Graaf. Multiparty Computations Ensuring Secrecy of Each Party's Input and Correctness of the Output, *Proc. of CRYPTO 1987*, Springer Verlag LNCS 293, 87–119.

[19] B. Chor, E. Kushilevitz. A Zero-One Law for Boolean Privacy, *Proc. of STOC 1989*, ACM, 62–72.

[20] J. Feigenbaum and L. Fortnow. On the Random-Self-Reducibility of Complete Sets, University of Chicago Technical Report 90-22, Computer Science Department, August 20, 1990.

[21] J. Feigenbaum, S. Kannan, and N. Nisan. Lower Bounds on Random-Self-Reducibility, *Proc. of Structures 1990*, IEEE, 100–109.

[22] L. Fortnow, J. Rompel, and M. Sipser. On the Power of Multi-Prover Interactive Protocols, *Proc. of Structures 1988*, IEEE, 156–161.

[23] Z. Galil, S. Haber, and M. Yung. Cryptographic Computation: Secure Fault-Tolerant Protocols and the Public-Key Model, *Proc. of CRYPTO 1987*, Springer Verlag LNCS 293, 135–155.

[24] O. Goldreich, S. Micali, and A. Wigderson. How to Play ANY Mental Game, *Proc. of STOC 1987*, ACM, 218–229.

[25] S. Goldwasser, S. Micali, and C. Rackoff. The Knowledge Complexity of Interactive Proof Systems, *SIAM J. Comput.* 18 (1989), 186–208.

[26] J. Kilian. Founding Cryptography on Oblivious Transfer, *Proc. of STOC 1988*, ACM, 20–31.

[27] E. Kushilevitz. Privacy and Communication Complexity, *Proc. of FOCS 1989*, IEEE, 416–421.

[28] R. Lipton. New Directions in Testing, *Proc. of DIMACS Workshop on Distributed Computing and Cryptography* (Princeton, NJ; October, 1989), AMS, 1990.

[29] C. Lund, L. Fortnow, H. Karloff, and N. Nisan. Algrebraic Methods for Interactive Proof Systems, *Proc. of FOCS 1990*, IEEE.

[30] T. Rabin. Robust Sharing of Secrets When the Dealer is Honest or Cheating, M.Sc. Thesis, Hebrew University, 1988.

[31] T. Rabin and M. Ben-Or. Verifiable Secret Sharing and Multiparty Protocols with Honest Majority, *Proc. of STOC 1989*, ACM, 73–85.

[32] S. Rudich. Private communication.

[33] A. Shamir. How to Share a Secret, *Commun. Assoc. Comput. Machinery* 22 (1979), 612–613.

[34] A. Shamir. IP = PSPACE, *Proc. of FOCS 1990*, IEEE.

[35] A. C. Yao. Protocols for Secure Computations, *Proc. of FOCS 1982*, IEEE, 160–164.

[36] A. C. Yao. How to Generate and Exchange Secrets, *Proc. of FOCS 1986*, IEEE, 162–167.

Fair Computation of General Functions in Presence of Immoral Majority

Shafi Goldwasser*
MIT

Leonid Levin[†]
Boston University[‡], MIT

Abstract

This paper describes a method for n players, a majority of which may be faulty, to compute *correctly*, *privately*, and *fairly* any computable function $f(x_1, \ldots, x_n)$ where x_i is the input of the i-th player. The method uses as a building block an oblivious transfer primitive.

Previous methods achieved these properties, only for boolean functions, which, in particular, precluded composition of such protocols.

We also propose a simpler definition of security for multi-player protocols which still implies previous definitions of privacy and correctness.

1 Introduction

The problem of performing a distributed computation in a fault-tolerant and private manner has been addressed by many researchers in the past few years.

In a sequence of papers [Goldreich Micali Wigderson 87, Ben-Or Goldwasser Wigderson 88, Chaum Crepeau Damgaard 88, Ben-Or Rabin 89] it has been shown that when both private channels between pairs of players and broadcast channels are available, any distributed computation (e.g. function or game) can be performed privately and correctly, in spite of worst case behavior of the faulty players, if they are in minority.

When in majority, faulty players can be shown to be able to prevent the completion of certain computations by quitting early. Moreover, they may quit while being "ahead", i.e. having learned more about the output than non-faulty players.

A special computation problem where quitting early is especially harmful was addressed by [Luby Micali Rackoff 83]: the simultaneous exchange between two players of random secret bits. Each player must be protected against the case the other player

*Supported by ARO grant DAAL 03-86-K-0171 and NSF PYI grant 8657527-CCR with IBM matching funds

[†]Supported by an NSF grant , and the MIT laboratory of computer science.

[‡]Computer Science dept., 111 Cummington St., Boston, MA 02215; e-mail: Lnd@cs.bu.edu

quits early. The fairness notion they proposed (and achieved under the assumption the quadratic residue problem is hard) is that the probability that player A knows the secret bit of player B is within an ϵ of the probability that B knows the secret bit of A (the protocol is polynomial time in ϵ^{-1}).

[Yao 86] proposed (and showed how to achieve under the assumption that integer factorization problem is hard) the following notion of fairness for arbitrary two party boolean protocols. Suppose two players A and B want to compute a boolean function f privately and correctly. Informally, a protocol is fair if given any strategy of a faulty A, the non-faulty B has a strategy such that the probability that B will learn f, given that A will learn f is at any time during the protocol is as high as it is in the beginning of the protocol. The solution is based on the existence of trapdoor functions. These results were extended in ([Galil Haber Yung 89, Brickell Chaum Damgaard VanDeGraaf 87]) to the multi-player case.

The drawback of the above fairness definition is its severe limitation on the power of the faulty players. Since the strategy of the non-faulty players depends on the strategy of the faulty players, the faulty players program strategy must be chosen first and can not change depending on the program of the non-faulty players.

[Beaver Goldwasser 89] proposes a different notion of fairness, free from this limitation. A protocol to compute function f is said to be fair: if there exists a strategy for player B such that for any strategy of faulty subset of players A the ratio of the odds of B and A to compute the outcome of f is (about) the same at any time during the protocol as it is in the beginning of the protocol. It is shown how to achieve such fairness for multi-player protocols for boolean functions (as well as different boolean functions for different participants). The solution in[1] is based on trapdoor functions, and in [2] on the existence of an oblivious transfer primitive.

New Results. In this paper we show how to define and achieve fairness of any (not only boolean) function from strings to strings. This allows iteration and composition of protocols preserving fairness. In fact, we can achieve fairness for *any interactive probabilistic computation*, (i.e. games – to be defined in the journal version of this paper). The solution is based on the existence of an oblivious transfer primitive between every pair of players and a broadcast channel. The failure probability of the the protocol we propose is exponential while previously known was a polynomial.

We also propose a simpler definition of security for multi-player protocols which still implies previous definitions of privacy and correctness. [Kilian Micali Rogaway 90] have proposed independently another set of definitions of security. The relationship between the set of definitions has not been fully analyzed yet.

2 Conventions

Definition 1   • A *interactive* Turing machine is one equipped with a work-tape, input tape, random tape, output tape and several read-only and write-only communication tapes. The random tape contains an infinite sequence of random bits. *Flipping a coin* means reading the next new bit from the random tape.

- A *multi-player protocol* $\vec{P} = (P_1, P_2, \ldots, P_n)$ is a tuple of n interactive Turing machines where P_i starts up with x_i on its input tape and ends up with some output y_i on its output tape. We call $\vec{x} = (x_1, \ldots, x_n)$ the input vector to $\vec{P}$.

Inputs. We assume that the number n of players and identity i of each player P_i are included in its input. Initially coin-flips and inputs are independent. They may become correlated if their joint distribution became conditional on the information (say their sum) released by the player. Such coin-flips we call *relevant*. Players may want to keep them secret, to protect the privacy of their inputs. Other *irrelevant* coins flips may be released after the end of the protocol. The third type are *unused* coin-flips. They are kept, so that modifications of the protocol may use them and run with no extra random sources. The protocol must separate the three types before any communication starts and the unused flips must have at least constant density on the tape. We will treat the relevant coin-flips as part of the *complete* input, unless we talk of the *proper* input.

Outputs. Also, each player's output in non-faulty protocols consists of its input, relevant coin-flips, and only one more string $P(\vec{x})$, *common* to all players. This assumption does not limit generality, since we can always add one last step to any protocol $\vec{P}$ in which every player i uses a secret random string p_i and tells all other players the value of exclusive or: $y_i \oplus p_i$. Then, the common output is the concatenation of all $y_i \oplus p_i$. The new protocol is, clearly, equivalent to the old one and retains all its properties, like correctness, privacy, etc.

Notation 1 Let $\vec{x} = (x_1, \ldots, x_n)$ be the input vector to protocol $\vec{P} = (P_1, \ldots, P_n)$. Then, $\vec{P}(\vec{x})$ will denote the random variable which maps the (uniformly distributed) contents of random tapes α_i of the P_i's into the output vector $\vec{y} = (y_1, \ldots, y_n)$ where y_i is the output of machine P_i.

Let $F \subseteq \{1, \ldots, n\}$ be the set of (colluding) faulty players. An upper bound $t \geq |F|$ on their number is included in the inputs of all players. The inputs and outputs of faulty and non-faulty players we denote $\vec{x}_F, \vec{x}_{!F}, \vec{P}_F(\vec{x}), \vec{P}_{!F}(\vec{x})$, respectively.

Let us choose an arbitrary monotone unbounded *security* threshold $S(k) < k$ and call functions $k^{-S(k)/O(1)}$ *negligible*. If a family Y of random variables runs in expected polynomial time $E_\alpha T_{Y_k(\alpha)} = k^{O(1)}$, we call it *samplable*.

Definition 2 A *test* is a probabilistic algorithm $t(\omega, y)$ which maps the tested string y into the result $\{\pm 1, 0\}$, using its internal coin-flips ω. Tests must run in expected polynomial time $E_\omega T_{t(\omega,y)} = |y|^{O(1)}$. A test t *accepts* a family $Y_k(\alpha) \in \{0,1\}^k$ if its expected value $t_Y(k) = E_{\omega,\alpha} t(\omega, Y_k(\alpha))$ is negligible. We call *indistinguishable*:

- two families of random variables, if every test accepts both or none of them.[1]

- protocols $\vec{P}, \vec{P}'$, if $\vec{P}(\vec{x})$, $\vec{P}'(\vec{x})$ are indistinguishable when $\vec{x}$ is generated by any samplable family of random variables.

2.1 Faulty Versions of Protocols

Versions of a protocol capture deviations from it by the faulty players.

Definition 3 A *version* of protocol P is any protocol P', with $P_{!F} = P'_{!F}$.

Note, that no restriction is put on P'_F. They may deviate from the P_F at any time and freely exchange messages among members of F. This raises two questions.

Question 1: How does a player become faulty and enter F?

Answer: We assume an adversary who points to a player and makes it faulty.

Question 2: How does such an adversary decide who to point to?

Answer: We consider two models for such adversary.

In the first model, the adversary, called the *static adversary*, chooses the set of faulty player before the beginning of the computation.

In the second model the adversary is called the *dynamic adversary*. In this model the adversary observes the broadcast messages and private inputs/communication of any (none at the start) players which already became faulty. Based on this information, the adversary may, at any time and repeatedly, choose new players to become faulty. Once a player is faulty it remains faulty and their number is limited by t.

2.2 Legal and Moral Faults

Some faults affect the input-output behavior of a protocol but, for trivial reasons, can never be prevented by the non-faulty players.

For example, players in F may choose to misrepresent their inputs x_F as x'_F and run P_F accordingly; also they may choose to replace their output y_F with entirely different strings y'_F. We refer to such faulty behavior as *immoral* but *legal*.

Definition 4 A *legal version* of a multi-player protocol $\vec{P} = (P_1, \dots, P_n)$ is a protocol $\vec{P}' = (P'_1, \dots, P'_n)$ where P'_i is identical to P_i except for

- Before any communication with non-faulty machines, the faulty players may pull together their inputs and random tapes and transform them arbitrarily.

---

[1]For non-samplable Y, Y' one should require negligibility of $t_Y - t_{Y'}$.

- Upon termination of $\vec{P}$, all $i \in F$ may pull together their inputs, outputs, and random tapes. Then the outputs of faulty players may be replaced by a function of this pool.

Note: The dynamic adversary in the legal version is active only during the input and output stages. In these stages he corrupts players choosing them on the basis of inputs (and at the end of outputs as well) of those players he previously corrupted.

When in majority, faulty players have other non-preventable ways to affect the protocol's input-output behavior. Namely, if players quit early, they can prevent the good players from completing the computation.

Definition 5 A *legal-minority* version of a multi-player protocol $\vec{P}$ is a legal version $\vec{P'}$ of a protocol identical to $\vec{P}$ except that

- At the start of the protocols the players broadcast whether their inputs are empty. If anyone's input is empty, the protocol is aborted and players output *error*.

- At any time $n - t$ players may broadcast "I am faulty". Then the protocol is aborted and non-faulty players append to their output the identity of the players who declared themselves faulty.

2.3   Robust and Fair Protocols

Definition 6 A protocol $\vec{P} = (P_1, \ldots, P_n)$ is *robust* (respectively *semi-robust*), if for every version $\vec{P'}$ of $\vec{P}$, there exists a legal (respectively legal-minority) version $\vec{P''}$, of $\vec{P}$, indistinguishable from $\vec{P'}$.

While robustness is a "complete" quality, semi-robustness requires additional feature: quit-fairness. It insures that interrupting the protocol does not give an unfair advantage in knowledge to the perpetrating majority.

In addition to players $1, \ldots, n$, we will speak of player 0 to mean the coalition of faulty players whose joint input is $x_0 = x_F$. (from here on i ranges from 0 to n).

For generality, we assume that not all output information has equal value. Some may be useless, as the players may somehow get it for free upon termination of the protocol $\vec{P}$. Suppose this free information for player i is $V_i(\vec{x})$. The function $\vec{V}$ may not even been known to i during the protocol, but could be known to the faulty players. (The reader may ignore this extra generality, assuming $\vec{V} = 0$.)

Let $\bar{\mu}_y(i)$ be the probability (over $\vec{x}, \vec{\alpha}$) of output $y = P(\vec{x})$ given $V_i(\vec{x})$ and x_i, and $\delta(i, \vec{x}, \vec{\alpha}) = \frac{1}{\bar{\mu}_{P(x)}} E_{y \neq P(\vec{x})}(\bar{\mu}_y) = \frac{1}{\bar{\mu}_{P(x)}} \sum_{y \neq P(\vec{x})} \frac{\bar{\mu}_y^2}{1 - \bar{\mu}_{P(x)}}$ be the ratio of the average (over y) probability of a wrong answer to the probability of a correct answer (from the point of view of player i).

Let $h_{\vec{x},i,t,\vec{\alpha}}$ be the history seen by player i upto step t on input $\vec{x}$, and coin tosses $\vec{\alpha}$.

Let $\mu_t(i, \vec{x}, \vec{\alpha})$ denote the probability of the correct output $P(\vec{x})$ (taken over $\vec{x}, \vec{\alpha}$) given $V_i(\vec{x})$ and $h_{\vec{x},i,t,\vec{\alpha}}$ (from the point of view of player i).

Let $r_t(i, \vec{x}, \vec{\alpha}) = \frac{(1-\mu)}{\mu}$ be the ratio of the odds of wrong and correct values for $P(\vec{x})$ (from the point of view of player i)

Let $R_t(i, \vec{x})$ be the expectation (over $\vec{\alpha}$) of r_t and $D_t(i, \vec{x})$ be its standard deviation.

Definition 7 A protocol is *quit-fair* if

- for all $i, t, \vec{x}, \vec{\alpha}$ either $\log \frac{r_{t+1}(i,\vec{x},\vec{\alpha})}{r_t(i,\vec{x},\vec{\alpha})} < \frac{1}{|\vec{x}|}^2$ or $h_{\vec{x},i,t,\vec{\alpha}} \in H_{\vec{x},i,t}$ where $H_{\vec{x},i,t}$ is a set of histories of exponentially small probability over α.

- $\frac{R_{t+1}(i,\vec{x})}{R_t(i,\vec{x})}$ does not depend on i.

- $D_t(i, \vec{x})$ is $O(\sqrt{\delta(i, \vec{x}, \vec{\alpha}) R_t(i, \vec{x})})$.

A protocol is *robust for minority* if it is semi-robust and quit-fair.

2.4 Stable Functions and Commitment Protocols

Definition 8 A function f is *stable* if $f(\vec{x'})$ is either nil or $f(\vec{x})$, for all $\vec{x}$ in its domain and $\vec{x'}$, s.t. $x'_{!F} = x_{!F}$.

Note 1 *Faulty players can not affect the value of stable functions by misrepresenting their inputs.*

By running a *commitment* protocol on inputs $\vec{x}$ we will transform any function f into a stable function f' (on possible outcomes $\vec{y}$ of the commitment protocol), such that $f'(\vec{y}) = f(\vec{x'})$ for some $\vec{x'}$, $x'_{!F} = x_{!F}$.

3 The Merits of the Definitions

Traditionally, several properties are required of a protocol such as privacy, correctness, independent choice of the inputs by faulty players, when a minority is faulty. And, additionally, quit-fairness, when majority is faulty.

All versions of robust protocol satisfy all these properties:

Proposition 1 *Any version of a robust protocol $\vec{P}$ satisfies the following properties:*

---

[2]This can be made arbitrarily small by padding the input $\vec{x}$.

- *Correctness:* In a legal version, by definition, the non-faulty players output $P_{!F}(\vec{x'})$, and $x'_{!F} = x_{!F}$. Now, since there exists a legal version which is indistinguishable from an illegal one and in that the good guys outputs are correct, we are practically guaranteed correctness for illegal version of $\vec{P}$.

- *Privacy:* Several definitions of privacy exist. We recall one of them and demonstrate it for a robust protocol. Let $VIEW_F$ be the random variable which takes on as value the entire history of communication and coin tosses as seen by the players in F. Call a protocol *private* if there is a polynomial time algorithm M, s.t. $(M(x_F, \alpha_F, y_F), \vec{x}, \vec{y})$ is indistinguishable from $(VIEW_F, \vec{x}, \vec{y})$.

  Now, any version $\vec{P'}$ of protocol $\vec{P}$, can be modified by making its faulty players to output the $VIEW_F$. There exists a legal version $\vec{P''}$ of $\vec{P}$, with an output distribution indistinguishable from $\vec{P'}$. In a legal version, the faulty players compute their output based only on their inputs/outputs for $\vec{P}$. It follows that $VIEW_F$ can be generated given only the inputs x_F and outputs y_F for $\vec{P}$ of a faulty coalition.

- *independent commitment to inputs:* By definition, in a legal version of the protocol the faulty players decide on which value x'_i to use independently of the values of non-faulty players. Since for every illegal version of the protocol, there exists a legal version with the same output distribution, the values that faulty players choose in the illegal version would have been chosen by faulty players in a legal version independently of non-faulty inputs.

Proposition 2 *Any version of a robust for minority protocol $\vec{P}$ satisfies privacy, correctness, independent commitment to inputs, and quit-fairness.*

Proof: Privacy and independent commitment to values are shown as above. The definition of correctness for a faulty majority is an extension of correctness in the faulty minority case. Namely, we allow non-faulty players to output the special "error" output when faulty players quit in the middle of the protocol. For this extended definition, the same argument used for correctness in above theorem will work. Fairness is guaranteed as part of the definition of robust for minority protocols.

Now previous theorems in the literature can be cast in this terminology:

Theorem 1 ([Ben-Or Goldwasser Wigderson 88, Ben-Or Rabin 89])
If $|F| < n/2$, any protocol can be modified into a robust one with same outputs.

Especially interesting is the case of $\vec{P}$ computing stable functions, since in all versions of robust protocols for a stable function, non-faulty outputs are the same.

4 Main Result: Robust for Minority Protocols

Theorem 2 (Main) *If an oblivious transfer primitive exists and a broadcast channel exists, any protocol can be modified into one robust for minority, with same outputs.*

Note 2 *No restriction is made on the number of faults in the theorem. The oblivious transfer condition has previously been shown necessary for a general protocol transformation preserving privacy for a majority of faults.*

In addition to players $1, \ldots, n$, we will speak of player 0 to mean the coalition of faulty players whose joint input is $x_0 = x_F$. (from here on i ranges from 0 to n).

The x_i's for player i are chosen at random with some (not necessarily easy computable) distribution. Recall that we assume the original protocol to compute one common output $P(\vec{x})$ (in addition to x_i and relevant coin flips). This is so since at the end of the original protocol each player can choose a random string p_i, and send all other players $y_i \oplus p_i$. The common output will the concatenation of all $p_i \oplus y_i$. Clearly, the same privacy properties hold. Thus, from here on we speak of a protocol to compute a single output.

The protocol consists of four stages: preprocessing, commitment, computation, and revelation.

Preprocessing

If the number of potential faults is in minority the preprocessing stage is skipped. If the number of potential faults is in majority, then first the entire network engages in a preprocessing phase, independent of the inputs. The outcome of the preprocessing phase is either *error* or the protocol proceeds to stages of commitment, computation and revelation. An *error* implies that the protocol is aborted. A majority of faulty players can always force an early abort, but their decision to cause an early abort is independent of the non-faulty players inputs.

Commitment

The commitment stage reduces the problem to computing a stable function $P(\vec{x})$. It also creates a sequence of (committed to but hidden) coin-flips α (each the sum mod2 of coin-flips of all users).

Computation

The computation stage reveals the sum (taken over $Z_2^{|P(\vec{x})|}$) of $P(\vec{x})$ with random password w (chosen based on α). Fairness is not an issue at this stage, because any player can (were the protocol interrupted) make this sum totally random by erasing her coin-flips.

Revelation

At the revelation stage w is revealed. Privacy is not an issue at this stage, since w has no information about the inputs (beyond what the function value reveals).

Let $\varepsilon = 1/|\vec{x}|$. The revelation protocol consists of $T < 2|w|$ *macrosteps* in which the protocol reveals next unused portion of α and interprets it as a vector $v_T \in Z_2^{|w|}$. It then reveals a sequence of ε^{-3} independent bits (one per *micro step*) $b_t(\alpha)$ chosen such that $b_t = (v_T \cdot w)$ (the inner product of v_T and w) with probability $1/2 + \varepsilon$. At the end of the macro-step the actual value of $(v_T \cdot w)$ is revealed.[3]

Clearly the logarithm of $r_t(i, \vec{x}, \vec{\alpha})$ (see Definition 7) cannot change by more than $O(\varepsilon)$ per micro-step. After going through ε^{-3} micro steps with an exponentially small probability the majority of the coin flips differs from $v_T \cdot w$. Thus, at the last step of the macro step when $v_T \cdot w$ is revealed, $r_{t+1} - r_t$ is changed negligibly uness this exponentially rare failure of majority has happened. This takes care of the first requirement of quit-fairness.

Assume for generality sake that at termination of the protocol player i may even be given an extra information $V_i(\vec{x})$. (The function $\vec{V}$ to be later handed out may not necessarily be known to the non-faulty players during the protocol but could be known to the faulty players).

One can easily show that R_t decreases with almost the same speed for all $\vec{x}, i, \vec{V}$. Indeed, let the computation stage output $y = P(\vec{x}) \oplus w$. At the outset of a macro-step T, let $S_T(y, \alpha)$ be the set of w' with $(v_{T'} \cdot w') = (v_{T'} \cdot w)$ for all $T' < T$. Let $p(Y)$ be the probability at the outset (over $\vec{x}$ with given x_i and $V_i(\vec{x})$) of $y \oplus P(\vec{x}) \in Y$. Then at the end of macrostep T, $r_t = \frac{1 - \mu_t}{\mu_t} = \frac{(p(S_T) - p(w))}{p(w)}$.

Each w' has a 2^{-T} chance to satisfy all T of the above randomly chosen $v_T \cdot w$ boolean linear equations and so fall in S_T. Moreover, each u falls in or out of S_T pairwise independently of any $u' \notin \{u, u \oplus w\}$. Thus, the expectation at the end of a macro step of $p(S_T) - p(w)$ (over α) is $(1 - p(w))/2^T$, and therefore the expected value of $\frac{1 - \mu_t}{\mu_t}$ is $\frac{(1 - p(w))}{p(w) \cdot 2^T}$. No change in the expected value occurs at a micro step. Thus R_t is independent of i and the second requirement of quit-fairness is satisfied.

The standard deviation of $p(S_T) - p(w)$ is smaller than the square root of the mean of $p(\{a\})$ by a factor of $2^{-T/2}/O(1)$, and therefore $D_T \leq O(\sqrt{\delta R_T})$. (Recall that δ (in the definition of quit-fairness) is the ratio of the average probability of wrong answer to correct answer.)[4]

---

[3]The purpose of not revealing $(v_T \cdot w)$ immediately is to assure that by quitting early the faulty players can only receive one coin flip more than non-faulty ones toward the value of $(v_T \cdot w)$. After $2|w|$ macrosteps, w itself can be revealed.

Sometimes the faulty coalition can be restricted to a polynomial number of possible combinations (known to all parties). Also the parties may be confident at the start that their inputs are random and completely secret. Then a more sophisticated procedure could be used to discriminate against possible coalitions, which "know too much". We ignore this issue for now.

[4]The fairness requirement does not prevent erratic behavior at the end of the protocol, thus in special cases when it is detectable that the players doubts are concentrated on a logarithmic number of outputs we can do better by tossing a cube of all possible answers slightly biases toward the correct one.

5 How to Use the Oblivious Transfer Primitive

5.1 The Oblivious Transfer Assumption

We assume that every two players can perform an oblivious transfer.

An *oblivious transfer* [Rabin, Blum, Fischer Micali Rackoff, Even Goldreich Lempel 82] between two players A and B denoted by $\frac{1}{2} - OT^{AB}(b_0, b_1, c)$ is a process by which player A who has bits b_0, b_1 transfers bit b_c to player B, where c is chosen by B. The transfer is done obliviously: player A can not distinguish between the case player B received b_0 and the case B received b_1; player B can not distinguish between $b_{\bar{c}} = 0$ and $b_{\bar{c}} = 1$.[5] An oblivious transfer of one bit, means that the other bit is 0 and the (random) order of bits is revealed after the transfer is performed.

An oblivious transfer can be implemented if trapdoor functions exist and A and B are computationally bounded [Even Goldreich Lempel 82]; or can be derived from the existence of noisy channel and other physical means even in the presence of infinitely powerful A and B [Crepeau Kilian 88].

We show how to use an $\frac{1}{2} - OT^{AB}(b_0, b_1, c)$ protocol between every pair of players A and B to implement the preprocessing, commitment, and computation stages specified in section 4. Thus, we start with a legal protocol and transform it to one which is robust.

Many of the ideas in the transformation which lead to semi-robustness property (not quit-fairness) are similar to ones used in previous results of [Goldreich Micali Wigderson 87, Galil Haber Yung 87, Ben Or Goldwasser Wigderson 88, Kilian 88, Beaver Goldwasser 89].

In [Beaver Goldwasser 89a] a version of a protocol achieving semi-robustness for boolena functions based on the existence of trapdoor functions, is described. Here, we describe a protocol based on the existence of oblivious transfer, in which the error probability is improved from the previously known 1/polynomial [Beaver Goldwasser 89b] to 1/exponential.

We let t be the number of potential adversaries, k denote the security parameter.

5.2 Preprocessing Stage

5.2.1 Global Commitment and Decommitment

Each player globally commits to a library of 0's and 1's. A global commit has properties similar to a commit between two players. In fact, many of the the ideas are similar to the two party bit-commitment of [Kilian 88].

In particular, preprocess-global-commit(A,v,J) is a protocol for player A to globally commit to a bit v such that if the preprocessing stage is completed successfuly, then there exists a unique value $\hat{v}$ associated with J such that

---

[5]This form of oblivious transfer was shown equivalent to the original one proposed by Rabin.

- $\hat{v} = v$ if A is non-faulty.

- At any time player A can decommit $\hat{v}$ (or $\hat{v}_1 \oplus \hat{v}_2$ where $\hat{v}_1$, $\hat{v}_2$ are two previously commited bits) to a subset S of players such that either all non-faulty players in S will receive the correct value, or all non-faulty players will broadcast that A is faulty, or an exponentially rare event will happen. In the case of decommiting $\hat{v}_1 \oplus \hat{v}_2$, the privacy of $\hat{v}_1$ remains intact for the entire network.

- If non-faulty A committed a v randomly chosen in $\{0,1\}$ then the probability that the faulty players guess the value of v before it is decommitted to one of them is negligible.

This is achieved as follows.

Notation: We let $rep(v)$ be a set of k boolean vectors $\{\overline{v}_i\}, 1 \leq i \leq k$ such that for each $\overline{v}_i = (v_{i1}, ..., v_{ik})$ the $\oplus_j v_{ij} = v$. We say that $rep(v) = (\vec{v}_1, ..., \vec{v}_k)$ is *invalid* if for some s, t the $\oplus_j v_{sj} \neq \oplus_j v_{tj}$. To choose a $rep(v)$ at random means to pick the $v_{ij} \in \{0,1\}$ as above at random. To broadcast or obliviously transfer $rep(v)$ means to broadcast or run oblivious transfer each of the v_{ij}'s. We let the function $all(\{b_i\}) = b_1$ if for all $i, j, b_i = b_j$, otherwise it assumes an *error* value.

Preprocess Global Commit(A,v,J):

Step 1. For $1 \leq i \leq k^a$: A chooses $v_i^L, v_i^R \in \{0,1\}$ at random and sets $v_i = v_i^L \oplus v_i^R$. A chooses a $rep(v_i^L) = (\overline{v}_1^{iL}, ..., \overline{v}_k^{iL})$ and $rep(v_i^r) = (\overline{v}_1^{iR}, ..., \overline{v}_k^{iR})$ at random; For every player B, A oblivious transfers to B $rep(v_i^L)$ and $rep(v_i^R)$.[6]

Step 2. The network chooses at random[7] a set I containing half of the i's. For all $i \notin I$, A broadcasts $rep(v_i^L)$ and $rep(v_i^R)$. If for some i, d player B gets an invalid $rep(v_i^d)$ or inconsistent with information B received then B broadcasts a complaint and the protocol is aborted.[8] Otherwise, A broadcasts a set $\{c_i = v_i^R \oplus v_i^L \oplus v | i \in I\}$.

Step 3.[9] Repeat for every player B k times: B broadcasts indexes i, j chosen at random in I; A broadcasts $b = v_i^L \oplus v_j^L$; B chooses $d \in \{L, R\}$ at random; A broadcasts $rep(v_i^d)$ and $rep(v_j^d)$; if $b \neq v_i^d \oplus c_i \oplus v_j^d \oplus c_j$, then B broadcasts a complaint and the protocol is aborted, otherwise $I = I - \{i, j\}$.

Step 4. Each player stores $I, \{c_i, i \in I\}$ and the information he received during the global commit of player A to $v_i^L, v_i^R, i \in I$ in $BIT - COMMIT(A, J)^{10}$ and the Jth bit is declared committed. (The value of this bit is $all(v_i^R \oplus c_i \oplus v_i^l), i \in I)$.)

---

[6] each bits v_i is represented by a pair v_i^R, v_i^L such that $v_i = v_i^R \oplus v_i^L$.

[7] It suffices that players alternate in choosing elements in I

[8] if the protocol is aborted during an execution of preprocess-global-commit, then all non-faulty players output error.

[9] In this step A proves to each player B in turn that for all remaining $i, j \in I$ $v_i \oplus c_i = v_j \oplus c_j$.

[10] Clearly each player may have received different bits during the oblivious transfer and thus has different information.

At the outset of the preprocessing stage, every player runs the protocol preprocess-global-commit for a sufficient number of values $v = 0$ and $v = 1$ as will be necessary for A to commit bits during the life time of the protocol.

During the protocol player A globally commits to bit v by broadcasting index J, such that the bit committed during the preprocessing global commit stored in $BIT - COMMIT(A, J)$ is m. Once an index J is broadcast it is never reused.

To decommit to a subset S of the players, a committed bit stored in $BIT - COMMIT(A, J)$, A runs the following protocol.

Global Decommit(A,S,J):

Let v be the bit committed in $BIT - COMMIT(A, J)$ and S the subset to which it should be decommitted.

Step 1: A sends in private to each player in S, for all $i \in I$, $rep(v_i^R)$ and $rep(v_i^L)$. Players in S set $v = c_i \oplus v_i^R \oplus v_i^L$ for the smallest $i \in I$.

Step 2: If any player $B \in S$ gets for some i, d an invalid $rep(v_i^d)$ or inconsistent with information B received during the oblivious transfer stage, then B broadcasts a request that player A should broadcast $rep(v_i^R), rep(v_i^L)$ for all $i \in I$.

Step 3: If any player C detects that the information A broadcasts in step 2 is "inconsistent" or invalid, then C broadcasts that A is faulty, otherwise the value of v is taken to be the bit $c_i \oplus v_i^L \oplus v_i^R$ where v_i^L, v_i^R are defined by the information which A has broadcast at step 2.[11]

5.2.2 Decommitting Sums of Globally Committed Bits

During the protocol player A will need to prove that various bits globally committed are the same. Let v and u be two previously globally committed bits stored in $BIT - COMMIT(A, v, J_v)$ and $BIT - COMMIT(A, u, J_u)$.
Recall: Bit v has associated with it $I_v, \{c_{vi} | i \in I_v\}, rep(v_i^L), rep(v_i^R)$ for all $i \in I_v$, and bit u has associated with it $I_u, \{c_{ui} | i \in I_u\}, rep(u_i^L), rep(u_i^R)$ for all $i \in I_u$.

Protocol Prove-Equality(A,u, v)

Repeat for every player B k times: B broadcasts indexes $i \in I_v$ and $j \in I_u$ chosen at random; A broadcasts $b = v_i^L \oplus u_j^L$; B chooses $d \in \{L, R\}$ at random; A broadcasts $rep(v_i^d)$ and $rep(u_i^d)$ (if any C finds these invalid, then C broadcasts that A is faulty); if $b \neq v_i^d \oplus c_{vi} \oplus u_j^d \oplus c_{uj}$, then every player broadcasts that A is faulty, otherwise every player updates I_v to be $I_v - \{i\}$ and I_u to be $I_u - \{j\}$.

In fact, general properties of data globally committed can be proven in **zero-knowledge** using the protocols of [Kilian 89, Ben-Or et al [4]]. We chose the parameter a in the preprocess-global-commit protocol so to allow repeated zero-knowledge proofs about globally committed bits.

---

[11]By the properties of our global commit protocol all non-faulty players will either declare A faulty or agree that a bit of the same value has been decommitted.

5.2.3 Private Communication Lines

During the protocol players A and B will need to privately communicate and yet be able to prove to other players that the messages they send privately were computed correctly with respect to their committed inputs and previously received messages.

If encryption functions were available this would present no problem, however we only have the ability to perform oblivious transfers between every two players.

Thus, in the preprocessing stage every pair of players prepare and globally commit to a supply of 0's and 1's known to A and B alone which both can globally decommit. These bits will be used later for private communication.

This is done by running the following protocol.

Protocol Preprocess-Private-Communication(A,B,J)

A randomly chooses $b \in \{0, 1\}$ and runs an identical protocol to $Preprocess - Global - Commit(A, b, J)$ with the exception that the information stored normally in $BIT - COMMIT(A, J)$ is stored in $PRIVATE - COMMIT(A, B, J)$. Next A decommits b to player B by running $Global - Decommit(A, \{B\}, J)$; (Note now that both A and B can decommit the bit store in $PRIVATE - COMM(A, B, J)$.)

During the protocol A sends private message $m = m_1, ..., m_k$ to player B by broadcasting indexes J_i such that for every $i = 1, ..., k$ the value of the bit committed in $PRIVATE - COMM(A, B, J_i)$ is m_i. (Once an index J is broadcast it is never reused.)

5.2.4 Global Oblivious Transfers

During the protocol every pair of players (A,B) will need to engage in an oblivious transfer in such a way that A and B can prove to to the rest of the network that indeed they have fed the correct inputs to the oblivious transfer process, and have received claimed outputs.

This is achieved by having every pair of players (A, B) prepare a supply of oblivious transfers in which the inputs and the outputs have been globally committed.

Let $i \in \{0, 1\}^3$. Say that an oblivious transfer is of type $i = i_0 i_1 i_2$ if $b_0 = i_0$, $b_1 = i_1$ and $c = i_2$. To prepare at least L oblivious transfers of each type $i \in \{0, 1\}^3$, every pair of players (A, B) execute the following protocol $O(L + k)$ times.

Protocol Preprocess-Oblivious-Transfer(A,B, J)

Step 1. For $j = 1, ..., k^a$: Player B globally commits to c^j randomly chosen in $\{0, 1\}$; Player A globally commits to b_0^j, b_1^j, r^j randomly chosen in $\{0, 1\}$. Players A and B run an $OT^{AB}(b_0^j \oplus r^j, b_1^j \oplus r^j, c^j)$; Player B globally commits to $\hat{r}^j$ which he received as a result of the oblivious transfer. (Clearly, if A and B are non-faulty, $\hat{r}^j$ should equal $b_{c^j}^j \oplus r^j$).

Step 2. The network chooses at random [12] a set I of half of the j's. For all $j \notin I$, A globally decommits b_0^j, b_1^j, r^j to the entire network; B globally decommits c^j and $\hat{r}^j$ to the network. If any player complains during these global commits or $r^j \oplus b_{c^j}^j \neq \hat{r}^j$, the protocol is aborted. Otherwise, player B globally commits to randomly chosen $c \in \{0, 1\}$, broadcasts set $I_1 \subset I$ such that $I_1 = \{j | c^j = c\}$, and proves that $c^j = c$ iff $j \in I_1$ (using the Prove-Equality procedure defined above.) Player A globally commits to randomly chosen $b_0, b_1, r \in \{0, 1\}$, broadcasts set $I_2 \subset I_1$ such that $I_2 = \{j | b_0^j = b_0, b_1^j = b_1, r^j = r\}$, and proves that $b_0^j = b_0$, $b_1^j = b_1$, $r^j = r$ iff $j \in I_2$ (using the Prove-Equality procedure). If for some $i, j \in I_2$ $\hat{r}^j \neq \hat{r}^i$ A broadcasts a complaint and the protocol is aborted, otherwise A globally commits to $\hat{r}$ such that $\hat{r} = \hat{r}^j$, for all $j \in I_2$ and proves this fact (using the Prove-Equality procedure). Each player stores I_2 and the information obtained during the global commits of $b_0^j, b_1^j, c^j, r^j, \hat{r}^j$, for $j \in I_2$ in its copy of $OT - COMMIT(A, B, J)$.

During the computation stage when A and B need to engage in an oblivious transfer with parameters B_0, B_1 known to A and parameter C known to B they run the following protocol.

Protocol Global-Oblivious-Transfer(A, B, B_0, B_1, C)

B selects a J such that the set $\{b_0^j, b_1^j, c^j, r^j, \hat{r}^j, j \in I_2\}$ stored in $OT - COMMIT(A, B, J)$ is such that $c^j = C$ for all $j \in I_2$ (a fact B proves to the network), and broadcasts J to the network. If $B_0 = b_0^j$ and $B_1 = b_1^j$ for all $j \in I_2$ (a fact A proves to the network), A decommits $r^j, j \in I_2$ to B, else J is cast out and the step is repeated. B sets $B_C = all(\{r^s \oplus \hat{r}^s, s \in I_2\})$.

5.3 Input Commitment and Computation Stages

At this stage every player A needs to globally commit to its input x_A and a sequence of coin flips α_A.

Let $x_A \alpha_A = y_A^1...y_A^m$ (in binary). Player A broadcasts[13] indexes $J_1, ..., J_k$ such that the bit committed in $GLOBAL - COMMIT(A, J_i)$ is y_A^i.

Set $\alpha = \sum_{\text{player } A} \alpha_A \bmod 2$.

5.3.1 Computation

Let C_P be the arithmetic circuit over field of elements F computing the legal protocol P (assuming that P has already been modified to output single output to all players). Let $\gamma_B \in F$ be a unique element associated with player B.

In order to allow the network to compute with inputs x_A (and α_a), player A secret shares x_A (and α_a) as follows. A selects a random polynomial p_{x_A} of degree t such

---

[12]It suffices that players alternate in choosing elements in I

[13]once an index is broadcast it will never be reused.

that $p_{x_A}(0) = x_A$. For every player B, A globally commits to $p_{x_A}(\gamma_B)$ and privately communicates $p_{x_A}(\gamma_B)$ to B.

Note now that because of the properties of PRIVATE-COMM every player B now knows $p_{x_A}(\gamma_B)$, and every other player has received a global commitment to the value of $p_{x_A}(\gamma_B)$ which can be decommitted either by A and or B.

A now proves in zero-knowledge to the network that the values privately sent $\{p_{x_A}(\gamma_B)\}_B$ interpolate to a unique t degree polynomial whose free term is x_A.

The arithmetic circuit C_P has two types of gates: addition $(+)$, and multiplication $(\times)$ over the finite field F (scalar multiplication is a trivial extension of $+$ gate).

The circuit is evaluated in a gate by gate fashion. The invariant during the computation stage is that each player holds a share of all inputs to the next gate to be computed, which is globally committed.

Suppose the inputs to a $+$ gate are u and v. Every player A holds $P_u(\gamma_A)$ and $P_v(\gamma_A)$ (where P_u and P_v are random polynomials of degree t with free term u and v respectively). To compute a share of the output $u+v$, player A computes $P_{u+v}(\gamma_A) = P_u(\gamma_A) + P_v(\gamma_A)$. A globally commits to $P_{u+v}(\gamma_A)$.

Suppose the inputs to a $\times$ gate are u and v. Computing $P_{u\times v}(\gamma_A)$ (where $P_{u\times v}$ is a random polynomial of degree t whose free term is $u\times v$.) can be reduced to the problem of every pair of players (A,B) computing semi-robustly a two-player function on the shares they hold $P_u(\gamma_A)$ and $P_v(\gamma_B)$, (see [Galil Haber Yung 87, Van Dem Graaph etal. 87, Beaver Goldwasser 88]). To compute a two-player function semi-robustly has been reduced to two-player oblivious transfer in [Kilian 88]. Instead of the two-player oblivious tarnsfert called for in [Kilian 88]'s construction, the $Commit - Oblivious - Transfer(A, B, ...)$ protocol which was set up in the preprocessing stage is used.

Every message of the player sent while computing the $\times$ gate must be accompanied by a zero-knowledge proof that it has been computed and sent correctly with respect to the inputs globally committed and the messages previously received from other players both in private and by broadcast. This is possible as all private messages sent during the commitment and computation stage have been globally committed (as all these messages were sent using the private communication lines set up in preprocess-private-communication.)

5.4 Acknowledgements

We are grateful to Mihir Bellare, Joe Kilian, and Silvio Micali for very useful discussion.

References

[1] D. Beaver, S. Goldwasser. *Multi Party Fault Tolerant Computation with Faulty Majority*, proceedings of Crypto89, Santa Barbara, CA, August 1989.

[2] D. Beaver, S. Goldwasser. *Multi Party Fault Tolerant Computation with Faulty Majority Based on Oblivious Transfer*, proceedings of FOCS89, Duke, NC, October 1989, pp. 468-473.

[3] M. Ben-Or, S. Goldwasser, A. Wigderson. *Completeness Theorems for Non-Cryptographic Fault-Tolerant Distributed Computation.* Proc. of 20th STOC 1988, pp. 1-10.

[4] Ben-Or, Michael, Oded Goldreich, Shafi Goldwasser, Johan Hastad, Joe Kilian, Silvio Micali, Phillip Rogaway, "IP is in Zero-Knowledge," Proceedings, *Advances in Cryptology,* Crypto 1988.

[5] Rabin, T. and M. Ben-Or. "Verifiable Secret Sharing and Multiparty Protocols with Honest Majority." Proc. of 21st STOC, ACM, 1989.

[6] Blakely,T.. Security Proofs for Information Protection Systems. Proceedings of the *1980 Symposium on Security and Privacy,* IEEE Computer Society Press, NY, pp. 79-88, 1981.

[7] Brassard, Gilles, Claude Crépeau, and David Chaum, "Minimum Disclosure Proofs of Knowledge," manuscript.

[8] Brassard, Gilles, Claude Crépeau, and Jean-Marc Robert. "Information Theoritic Reductions Among Disclosure Problems," *Proceedings of the* 27th *FOCS,* IEEE, 1986, 168–173.

[9] E. Brickell, D. Chaum, I. Damgaard, J. van de Graaf. Gradual and Verifiable Release of A Secret. *CRYPTO* 1987.

[10] D. Chaum, C. Crepeau, I. Damgaard. Multiparty Unconditionally Secure Protocols. Proc. of 20th STOC 1988, pp. 11-19.

[11] Chaum, David, Ivan Damgard, and Jeroen van de Graaf. "Multiparty Computations Ensuring Secrecy of Each Party's Input and Correctness of the Output," *Proceedings of CRYPTO '85,* Springer-Verlag, 1986, 477–488.

[12] R. Cleve. Limits on the Security of Coin Flips When Half the Processors are Faulty. *STOC* 1986.

[13] Cohen, Fischer. A Robust and Verifiable Cryptographically Secure Election. *FOCS* 1985.

[14] C. Crepeau and J. Kilian. Achieving Oblivious Transfer Using Weakened Security Assumptions. *FOCS* 1988.

[15] Crépeau Claude, "On the Equivalence of Two Types of Oblivious Transfer", Crypto87.

[16] B.Chor, S. Goldwasser, S. Micali, B. Awerbuch. Verifiable Secret Sharing and Achieving Simultaneity in the Presence of Faults. *FOCS* 1985.

[17] B. Chor, M. Rabin. Achieving Independence in Logarithmic Number of Rounds. *PODC* 1986.

[18] Even S., Goldreich O., and A. Lempel, *A Randomized Protocol for Signing Contracts*, CACM, vol. 28, no. 6, 1985, pp. 637-647.

[19] Fischer M., Micali S., and Rackoff C. *Oblivious Transfer Based in Quadratic Residuosity*, Unpublished.

[20] Z.Galil, S.Haber, M.Yung. Cryptographic Computation: Secure Fault-Tolerant Protocols and the Public Key Model. Proc. *CRYPTO* 1987.

[21] O. Goldreich, S. Micali, A. Wigderson. How to Play Any Mental Game, or A Completeness Theorem for Protocols with Honest Majority. Proc. of 19th *STOC* 1987, pp. 218-229.

[22] Goldreich, O., Vainish, R. "How to Solve any Protocol Problem: An Efficiency Improvement", Crypto 87.

[23] Goldwasser, Micali, Rackoff. The Knowledge Complexity of Interactive Proof Systems. *SIAM J. of Comp* 1989.

[24] S.Haber. *Multi-Party Cryptographic Computation: Techniques and Applications.* Ph.D. Thesis, Columbia University, 1988.

[25] Impagliazzo, Russell and Moti Yung, "Direct Minimum Knowledge Computations," Proceedings, *Advances in Cryptology,* Crypto 1987.

[26] Kilian, Joe, "On The Power of Oblivious Transfer," *Proceedings of the* 20th *STOC*, ACM, 1988, pp. 20-29. Also appeared in *Uses of Randomness In Algorithms and Protocols*, An ACM Distinguished Dissertation 1989.

[27] J. Kilian. S. Micali. P. Rogaway *Security Definitions for Multi Party Protocols.* In Preparation.

[28] Micali Luby Rackoff 83. *The Miraculous Exchange of a Secret bit*, Proc. of *FOCS* 1983.

[29] A. Shamir. How to Share a Secret. *CACM 22*, 612-613, 1979.

[30] Yao, Andrew C. "Protocols for Secure Computations," *Proceedings of the* 23rd *FOCS*, IEEE, 1982, 160–164.

[31] Yao, Andrew C. "How to Generate and Exchange Secrets," *Proceedings of the* 27th *FOCS*, IEEE, 1986, 162–167.

One-Way Group Actions

Gilles Brassard *

Département d'informatique et de R.O.
Université de Montréal
C.P. 6128, succ. "A"
Montréal, Québec CANADA H3C 3J7

Moti Yung

IBM T. J. Watson Research Center
Yorktown Heights
NY 10598, U.S.A.

Abstract

Bit commitment schemes are central to all zero-knowledge protocols [GMR89] for NP–complete problems [GMW86, BC86a, BC86b, BCC88, BCY89, FS89, etc.]. One-way group actions is a natural and powerful primitive for the implementation of bit commitment schemes. It is a generalization of the one-way group homomorphism [IY88], which was not powerful enough to capture the bit commitment scheme based on graph isomorphism [BC86b]. It provides a unified theory for all the known bit commitment schemes that offer unconditional protection for the originator of the commitments, and for many of those that offer her statistical protection. (Unconditional protection means that the value of the bit committed to is always perfectly concealed. Statistical protection either means that this is almost always the case, or that only an arbitrarily small probabilistic bias about this bit can leak; in either cases, statistical protection must hold even against unlimited computing power.)

Bit commitment schemes based on one-way group actions automatically have the chameleon property [BCC88] (also called trap–door [FS89]), which is useful for the parallelization of zero-knowledge protocols [BCY89, FS89]. Moreover, these bit commitment schemes allow the originator of two commitments to convince the receiver that they are commitments to the same bit, provided that this is so, without disclosing any information about which bit this is.

In addition, one-way group actions are also a natural primitive for the implementation of claw–free pairs of functions [GMRi88].

1 Bit commitment schemes

Central to all zero-knowledge interactive protocols [GMR89] for NP–complete statements [GMW86, BC86a, BC86b, BCC88, BCY89, FS89, etc.] is the notion of *bit commitment scheme*. The purpose of a bit commitment scheme is to allow one party, the *originator*, to commit to the value of a bit in a way that prevents the other party,

---

*Supported in part by Canada NSERC grant A4107.

the *receiver*, from learning it without the first party's help, but also in a way that prevents the first party from changing its value. At any time after she[1] has committed to a bit, the originator can show the receiver which bit she had committed to, a process known as *opening* the bit commitment. Of course, she should not be able to cheat by "changing her mind", i.e. not showing the genuine bit that she had in mind when she committed.

Bit commitment schemes can be implemented in a great many ways (see [BCC88] for several examples). When they are based on cryptography and computational complexity (rather than being implemented through physical protection, such as using quantum cryptography [BB84, BC90] or sealed envelopes), they are necessarily imperfect. This imperfection can take place in two very different ways. If it is impossible for the originator to change her commitments in the receiver's back, then it can be at best infeasible (i.e. within a reasonable amount of time) for the receiver to determine the bits committed to without the originator's help. Such bit commitment schemes are called *unconditionally binding*, or *unconditionally secure for the receiver*. Conversely, if it is impossible for the receiver to determine the bits committed to by the originator, or even to obtain partial or probabilistic information about them, then it can be at best infeasible for the originator to cheat and change her mind about a bit she had committed to when (and if) she subsequently decides to open the commitment. Such commitments are called *unconditionally concealing*, or *unconditionally secure for the originator*.

If the impossibility in the above definition is replaced by a near impossibility, the scheme is *statistically* (rather than unconditionally) binding or concealing, whichever the case may be. By "nearly impossible", we mean an event that can occur only with arbitrarily small probability, regardless of the computing power of the parties under consideration. A bit commitment scheme can be statistically concealing in two different ways. It could be that the receiver is expected to learn an arbitrarily small fraction of one bit of information about the bit committed to [IN89], or it could be that he has an arbitrarily small probability of learning the bit with certainty [Cha86, BC86b, NOVY90, etc.]. Statistically concealing bit commitment schemes that fall in the second category usually require a cheating receiver to be *daring* in the sense that he is guaranteed to learn nothing unless he is willing to risk being caught cheating by the originator with near certainty.

All the known perfect zero-knowledge interactive protocols for statements about NP–complete problems[2] are based on unconditionally concealing bit commitment schemes [BCC88, BCY89]. Similarly, statistically zero-knowledge interactive protocols can be obtained from statistically concealing bit commitment schemes [Cha86, BC86b]. In this paper, we are concerned exclusively with unconditionally and statistically concealing bit commitment schemes. We also restrict our attention to bit commitment schemes that can be implemented in practice by probabilistic

---

[1] We shall refer to the originator as a "she" and to the receiver as a "he".

[2] These perfect zero-knowledge protocols are *not* interactive proof–systems in the sense of [GMR89] because they allow a prover with unlimited computing power to cheat by changing her commitments. Hence, they are merely *computationally convincing*.

polynomial-time originator and receiver. In particular, we require of an unconditionally concealing bit commitment scheme that it be impossible for the receiver to learn anything about the bits committed to even if he had unlimited computing power, yet probabilistic polynomial-time computing power must be sufficient in order to carry out the honest protocol. Read [Bra91] for a comprehensive survey of bit commitment schemes, including those that require one of the players to be unreasonably powerful.

As long as we do not consider bit commitment schemes that cannot be implemented in practice, it is known that unconditionally binding bit commitment schemes exist if [ILL89, Nao89, Hås90] and only if [IL89] one-way functions exist. It was recently shown that one-way *permutations* (or even one-way functions with known entropy) are sufficient to implement *statistically* concealing bit commitment schemes [NOVY90]. It would be very nice if *unconditionally* concealing bit commitment schemes could be designed under the mere assumption that one-way *functions* exist. Although we are not able to do this, here we show that it is sufficient to assume the existence of one-way certified group actions, which is the main new notion introduced in this paper. This is a generalization of the *one-way group homomorphism* introduced in [IY88] and used in [BCY89] for the purpose of implementing bit commitment schemes. One-way certified group actions are sufficiently general to capture all the known unconditionally concealing bit commitment schemes. Moreover, one-way *uncertified* group actions capture many of the statistically concealing bit commitment schemes, but not the schemes of [IN89, NOVY90]. Also, we wish to emphasize that bit commitment schemes based on one-way group actions are truly practical.

Beyond their primary purpose, some bit commitment schemes also offer additional capabilities. For instance, a bit commitment scheme has the *equality property* if, given two different commitments to the same bit, the originator can easily convince the receiver that these commitments are indeed both to the same bit, without disclosing anything about whether this bit is a 0 or a 1 (by "easily", we mean that interaction is not needed; otherwise all bit commitment schemes would have the equality property). The *unequality property* is defined similarly. Bit commitment schemes based on one-way group actions automatically have the equality property, but not necessarily the unequality property.

Another useful additional property that some bit commitment schemes have was first put forward by Brassard, Chaum and Crépeau under the name of "chameleon property" [BCC88]. After reading [BCC88], Shamir proposed to call it the "trap-door property" [FS89], and we agree that this is a more self-explanatory terminology, albeit less poetic. A bit commitment scheme has the *trap-door property* if, in addition to the usual requirements of bit commitment schemes, there exists a secret, known as the *key* to the trap-door, that would allow the originator to cheat her commitments any time she wanted if only she knew this key. More precisely, knowledge of this key would make it possible for her to offer fake "commitments" that she could subsequently "open" either way at her choice of the moment, and these fake commitments are information-theoretically indistinguishable from genuine ones. Bit commitment schemes that have the trap-door property are interesting because they make it possible to implement zero-knowledge interactive protocols in a constant number of rounds [BCY89, FS89]. Clearly, the trap-door property cannot exist for bit commitment schemes that are unconditionally (or even statistically) binding. Bit commitment schemes based on one-way group actions automatically have the trap-door property.

The first unconditionally concealing bit commitment scheme ever proposed is reviewed in the Appendix. It possesses the equality, unequality and trap-door properties. We encourage readers unfamiliar with the notion of bit commitment schemes to read the Appendix before proceeding with the next section.

2 One-way group actions

Let us recall what a *group action* is. Let G be a finite group whose operation is simply denoted by juxtaposition and let ε denote the identity element of G. Let S be any finite set. We say that G *acts* on S if each element of G induces a permutation of S such that the permutation induced by gh is the composition of the permutations induced by g and by h, where g and h are any elements of G. More formally, we have a function $T : G \to (S \to S)$ such that

(1) $(\forall g \in G)(\forall h \in G)(\forall s \in S)[(T(gh))(s) = (T(g))((T(h))(s))]$, and

(2) $(\forall g \in G)(\forall t \in S)(\exists! s \in S)[(T(g))(s) = t]$.
    It is an easy exercise to show that this unique s is $(T(g^{-1}))(t)$.

Given condition (1), it is elementary to prove that condition (2) is equivalent to saying that the function induced by the group identity element is the identity function. In other words, G act on S through T if and only if conditions (1) above and (3) below are satisfied.

(3) $(\forall s \in S)[(T(\varepsilon))(s) = s]$.

To avoid cluttering the text with parentheses, it is customary (but sometimes confusing — see section 6.2) to denote $(T(g))(s)$ simply by gs. Therefore, condition (1) can be restated simply as $(gh)s = g(hs)$. (Despite the appearance of this formula, it does not really have anything to do with associativity!)

Let us now suppose that G acts on S. Let s_0 be a fixed element of S. The group action is $s_0-one\text{-}way$ if

- Membership in G and S can be tested efficiently.

- It is feasible to draw randomly within G with uniform distribution (this condition can be relaxed somewhat). By $g \in_R G$, we mean that g is chosen randomly within G with uniform distribution.

- The group operation, the group inversion, and the group action can be computed efficiently. In other words, given any $g \in G$, $h \in G$ and $s \in S$, it is easy to compute gh, g^{-1}, and gs.

- Consider $g \in_R G$ and let $t = gs_0$. Given s_0 and t, it is infeasible to compute any $\hat{g}$ such that $\hat{g}s_0 = t$, except with negligible probability, where the probability is taken over all choices of g and possibly over the random choices taken by the efficient algorithm trying to defeat this property. Note that the problem is *not* to find some $\hat{g} \neq g$, which may or may not exist.

A group action is *one-way* if it is feasible to find an $s_0 \in S$ such that the group action is s_0–one-way. Such an s_0 will be referred to as the *source* of the action. Given any $s \in S$, let $Q(s)$ denote the orbit $\{t \in S \mid (\exists g \in G)[t = gs]\}$. A one-way group action whose source is s_0 is *certified* if

- Given any $t \in S$, it is easy to decide whether or not $t \in Q(s_0)$. Of course, the easy thing is to decide on the *existence* of a $g \in G$ such that $t = gs_0$, not to actually *discover* any such g.

3   Commitments with certified group actions

Let G be a group and S be a set, and consider a one-way certified group action.

- In order to set up a bit commitment scheme, the receiver chooses a source s_0 for the action and a $g_0 \in_R G$. He computes $s_1 = g_0 s_0$ and he gives s_0 and s_1 to the originator. The originator checks that $s_0 \in S$, $s_1 \in S$, and $s_1 \in Q(s_0)$.

- In order to commit to bit $x \in \{0, 1\}$, the originator chooses $g \in_R G$ and computes $b = gs_x$. She keeps g as her witness to the effect that b is a commitment to bit x.

- In order to open a commitment b as bit x, the originator shows the corresponding witness g. The receiver checks that $b = gs_x$.

Commitments to 0 are produced by computing gs_0 whereas commitments to 1 are produced by computing $gs_1 = g(g_0 s_0) = (gg_0)s_0$, where $g \in_R G$. Therefore, such commitments are unconditionally concealing because the effect of computing gg_0 for a fixed $g_0 \in G$ and a g chosen randomly with uniform distribution within G is in fact to choose randomly an element of G with uniform distribution. In other words, nothing distinguishes commitments to 0 from commitments to 1, except for the witness known by the originator alone. The condition that the one-way group action should be certified is *crucial* here: if the receiver were able to get away with giving the originator some $s_1 \notin Q(s_0)$, the set of commitments to 0 would be *disjoint* from the set of commitments to 1.

On the other hand, assume for a contradiction that the originator is able to open a given commitment b both as a 0 and as a 1. In order to do this, she must know x_0 and x_1 in G such that $b = x_i s_i$. But then $x_1^{-1} x_0 s_0 = x_1^{-1} x_1 s_1 = s_1$. If the originator computes $g = x_1^{-1} x_0$, she will have found a $g \in G$ such that $g s_0 = s_1$, which is precisely what was assumed to be infeasible by the one-wayness of the action.

Bit commitment schemes based on one-way certified group actions automatically have the trap-door and equality properties. The trap-door property is obvious, with g_0 as key. To see the equality property, let b_1 and b_2 be commitments to the same bit, and let g_1 and g_2 be the originator's witnesses for b_1 and b_2, respectively. If the originator provides the receiver with $h = g_2 g_1^{-1}$, the receiver can check that $h b_1 = b_2$. We leave it for the reader to verify that the only way the originator can provide an $h \in G$ that transforms b_1 into b_2 is if she can open both commitments to show the same bit (unless she can open neither one of them!). We also leave it for the reader to verify that no additional information about which way these commitments can be opened leaks when the originator gives h to the receiver.

Curiously, bit commitment schemes based on one-way certified group actions do not seem to feature the unequality property in general, whereas the bit commitment scheme based on the more specific certified discrete logarithm assumption does (see the Appendix).

4 Commitments with uncertified group actions

Even though it is crucial that the one-way group action be certified if it is to be used to implement an *unconditionally* concealing bit commitment scheme, this is not necessary if one is satisfied with a *statistically* concealing bit commitment scheme. Therefore, even a one-way group action that is not certified can be used to implement a computationally convincing statistically zero-knowledge interactive protocol for an arbitrary **NP** statement. This is obvious if one is not concerned much about practical considerations. Indeed, the fact that $s_1 \in Q(s_0)$ is an **NP**–statement whose witness g_0 is known of the receiver (where g_0, s_0 and s_1 are as in the first step of the unconditionally concealing commitment described is section 3). Therefore, the receiver can use a general computationally zero-knowledge interactive proof–system [GMW86, BCC88] in order to convince the originator beyond any reasonable doubt that $s_1 \in Q(s_0)$. In this sub-protocol, the receiver will need to originate unconditionally binding bit commitments, which is possible by the work of [ILL89, Nao89, Hås90] since the assumed existence of a one-way group action clearly implies that of a one-way function.

A moment's thought allows us to do much better. The key observation is that the problem of deciding membership in $Q(s_0)$ is necessarily random self-reducible [AL83, AFK89, TW87]. This is sufficient for using the general constant–round *perfect* zero-knowledge interactive proof–system of [BMO90], which allows the receiver (without any need for an unproved assumption) to convince the originator that $s_1 \in Q(s_0)$.

This approach is vastly more efficient for practical purposes than that suggested in the previous paragraph. Moreover, it is carried out in a constant number of rounds, which is crucial if the resulting trap-door statistically concealing bit commitment scheme is to be used as main building block for a constant-round computationally convincing statistically zero-knowledge interactive protocol for an arbitrary **NP** statement [BCY89, FS89].

5   Claw free pairs of functions

One-way group actions can also be used in order to implement *claw free* pairs of functions [GMRi88], which is not surprising because there is an obvious direct connection between such pairs and bit commitment schemes (implicit in [IY88]). Let G be a group and S be a set, and consider a one-way group action. Let s_0 be a source for the action and let g_o be a random element of G. Consider the functions $f_1, f_2 : G \to S$ defined by $f_1(g) = gs_0$ and $f_2(g) = gg_0s_0$. Clearly, finding a "claw" $g_1, g_2 \in G$ such that $f_1(g_1) = f_2(g_2)$ is as hard as finding a $g \in G$ such that $gs_0 = g_0s_0$ (possibly $g = g_0$). Hence, finding such a claw is infeasible for anyone who knows s_0 and g_0s_0 (which is necessary to compute f_1 and f_2), but who does not know g_0. The action should moreover be certified if it is important that the party unable to find a claw should nonetheless be certain that such claws exist.

6   Examples of one-way group actions

6.1   Based on the discrete logarithm [CDG88, BKK90]

Assuming the certified discrete logarithm assumption (see the Appendix), a one-way certified group action can be built as follows. Let p be a prime for which the factorization of $p - 1$ is known and let α be a generator for $\mathbf{Z}_p^*$. Let G be $\mathbf{Z}_{p-1}$, let S be $\mathbf{Z}_p^*$, and let s_0 be 1. Given $g \in G$ and $s \in S$, the group action is defined as $gs = s\alpha^g$. It is easy to see that all the requirements for a one-way certified group action are satisfied. In this case, the one-wayness of the group action follows directly from the certified discrete logarithm assumption and the one-way group action is certified because recognizing elements of $Q(s_0)$ is trivial since $S = Q(s_0)$ follows from the fact that α is a certified generator.

6.2   Based on factoring [BC86b]

Assuming that factoring large RSA integers is infeasible, a one-way group action can be built as follows. Let n be the product of two large distinct primes (in practice, n would be chosen by the receiver, unless an authority can be trusted for choosing n and never disclosing its factors). Let both G and S be $\mathbf{Z}_n^*$, the multiplicative group of invertible integers modulo n. Let s_0 be 1. Given any $g \in G$ and $s \in S$, the group action is defined as $gs = g^2 s$ (please do not allow this mixed notation to confuse you ... the gs on the left of the equation means "the result of group element g acting on set element s", whereas the $g^2 s$ on the right refers to one squaring and one multiplication in $\mathbf{Z}_n^*$). Once again, it is easy to see that all the requirements for a one-way group action are satisfied. The one-wayness of the action comes from the fact that extracting square roots modulo n is as hard as factoring n, which we assumed to be infeasible.

Although this group action is probably not certified, it has a significant advantage in practice over the group action based on the discrete logarithm: it is much more efficient to compute two modular multiplications than one exponentiation.

6.3 Based on group homomorphism [BCY89]

Consider any one-way group homomorphism $h : X \to Y$ (see ICALP version of [BCY89] for a definition) such that membership in X and Y can be tested efficiently (an important condition forgotten in [BCY89]). Let G be X, S be Y, and s_0 be the identity element of Y. Given $g \in G$ and $s \in S$, the group action is defined as $gs = s * h(g)$. Details that this defines a one-way certified group action are left for the reader.

6.4 Based on graph isomorphism [BC86b]

The notion of one-way group homomorphism described in [BCY89] provides a generalization of the bit commitment scheme based on the certified discrete logarithm assumption, but it is probably not as general as one-way certified group actions. Indeed, we now describe a one-way group action that does not correspond to a one-way group homomorphism. The one-wayness of our group action depends on a cryptographic assumption introduced in [BC86b]. Unfortunately, this group action does not seem to be certified.

Let n be a fixed large integer. Let G be the group of permutations of $X_n = \{1, 2, \ldots, n\}$ under composition (where $(gh)(i) = h(g(i))$). Let S be the set of all graphs with X_n as vertex set. Let us assume the existence of a *hard graph* in the sense of [BC86b]: a graph is hard if it is infeasible to figure out an isomorphism between it and a random isomorphic copy of it, except with negligible probability. Let $s_0 \in S$ be such a hard graph. Given $g \in G$ and $s = (X_n, E) \in S$, the group action is defined as $gs = (X_n, \hat{E})$, where $(u, v) \in \hat{E}$ if and only if $(g(u), g(v)) \in E$. This group action is one-way by assumption. Intuitively, the reason why it cannot be recast as a group homomorphism is that there is no natural group operation that one could put on S.

7 Unifying perfect zero-knowledge proof–systems

When the notion of zero-knowledge proof–systems was presented and examples of languages were given, an intriguing fact was observed by many. That is, the proof–systems used to prove that membership in various languages can be proved in perfect zero-knowledge are very "similar". These languages are in two groups, which may be called "positive examples" and "negative examples". For instance, some positive examples are quadratic residuosity [GMR89], graph isomorphism [GMW86] and proving an element to be a generator, i.e., primitivity [TW87]. The corresponding negative examples (in the same works, respectively) are: quadratic non-residuosity, graph non-isomorphism and not-generated (by a), i.e., the language $\mathbf{Z}_p^* - <a>_p$.

Viewing all these problems as group actions[3], we can show that indeed the perfect zero-knowledge proof–systems are instances of two basic protocol schemes; one scheme for the positive examples and another scheme for the negative ones. This shows that the similarity of the original protocols is not just a matter of coincidence. This observation is not new for the positive examples: Burmester, Desmedt, Piper and Walker have developed an algebraic framework that unifies a large number of zero-knowledge proof systems (in which the use of group actions is but a special case) [BDPW89]. A similar observation was also made by Blum and Kannan with respect to program checkers [BK89]. In this section, we review the use of group actions to unify the positive examples, and we extend it to the negative examples.

The protocol scheme which gives as instances the positive examples demonstrates that an element (or a set of elements) can be in the range of a group action acting on a given source. Showing an element to be a quadratic residue is showing that the group of residues acting on the unity ($s = 1$) includes that element, namely that the group of quadratic residues acting on the input element gives us back the group of quadratic residues. The case of graph isomorphism is showing that the group of permutation acting on the first input graph includes the second input graph (or its automorphism group). Finally, showing primitivity is demonstrating that the claimed generator's group $<g>_p$ acting on 1 gives the entire $\mathbf{Z}_p^*$. These positive examples have been previously characterized as "random self-reducible" problems [AL83, AFK89, TW87]. Independently from our work, the notion of group action has been used by several other researchers to implement random self-reducibility [FKN90, SI90].

Using group action, one can show that the proof–systems for the so-called negative examples are instances of a protocol scheme which demonstrates that one input element from a set S_1 cannot be in the range of the group action by a group G acting on an element from a set S_2 as a source (where actions by G on both sets are defined and the underlying assumption is that telling apart the two sets S_1 and S_2 is hard). Notice that there is an information-theoretic difference between these two inputs: two non-isomorphic graphs, a quadratic non-residue (which is different from the quadratic

---

[3] This section deals with group actions in general, not necessarily those that are one-way, but the problem of membership in the set(s) they act upon must be assumed to be hard for the corresponding protocols to be interesting.

residue $s = 1$ modulo n), or an element b not generated by another element a in $\mathbf{Z}_p^*$ (which means that b is not an element in the range of the group generated by a acting on $s = 1$). This difference can be detected by the powerful prover, a fact used in the various instances of this proof–system.

In summary, the group action abstraction helps in generalizing many of the known protocols for perfect zero-knowledge proof–systems.

Open questions

How general is the notion of one-way group action? Andy Klapper has suggested that this notion might extend to that of one-way *monoid* action. Is there any unconditionally concealing bit commitment scheme that could be obtained from a one-way monoid action but not a one-way group action? Better yet, can one design an unconditionally concealing bit commitment scheme under the only assumption that one-way functions exist? If not, what about a statistically concealing bit commitment scheme? Recall that one-way permutations or even one-way functions with known entropy are sufficient to build a statistically concealing bit commitment scheme [NOVY90]. Note that if one does not insist that the scheme be usable by probabilistic polynomial-time players, it is known that one-way functions are sufficient to implement statistically (but not unconditionally) concealing bit commitment schemes [OVY90].

Conversely, is it possible to design a one-way certified group action (or perhaps monoid action) under the sole assumption that unconditionally concealing bit commitment schemes exist? Notice that a positive answer to this question would imply that all unconditionally concealing bit commitment schemes can be made to have the trapdoor and the equality properties, which would be surprising since this does not seem to be the case for statistically concealing bit commitment schemes [IN89, NOVY90].

Finally, are one-way *certified* group actions really more general than one-way group homomorphisms? Recall that our only example of a one-way group action that did not correspond to a one-way group homomorphism (section 6.4) was probably not certified.

Appendix:
Concrete example of a bit commitment scheme

The first unconditionally concealing bit commitment scheme ever proposed was designed independently by Damgård [CDG88] and by Boyar, Krentel and Kurtz [BKK90]. We describe it here to provide a concrete example of the type of bit commitment scheme that can be obtained by one-way certified group actions (see Section 6.1).

Let us first review some elementary number theory [Kra86]. If p is a prime number, let us denote by $\mathbf{Z}_p^*$ the multiplicative group of non-zero integers modulo p, i.e. $\{1, 2, \ldots, p-1\}$ under multiplication modulo p. Similarly, let us denote by $\mathbf{Z}_{p-1}$ the additive group of integers modulo $p-1$, i.e. $\{0, 1, \ldots, p-2\}$ under addition modulo $p-1$. Notice that $\mathbf{Z}_p^*$ and $\mathbf{Z}_{p-1}$ contain the same number of elements. For any integers a, b and c such that $a \not\equiv 0 \pmod{p}$ and $b \equiv c \pmod{p-1}$, we have by Fermat's theorem that $a^b \equiv a^c \pmod{p}$. Therefore, it makes sense to speak of x^i for $x \in \mathbf{Z}_p^*$ and $i \in \mathbf{Z}_{p-1}$. An element α of $\mathbf{Z}_p^*$ is called a *generator* of $\mathbf{Z}_p^*$ if each element of $\mathbf{Z}_p^*$ can be obtained as a power of α. Thus, α is a generator if and only if the function $exp_\alpha : \mathbf{Z}_{p-1} \to \mathbf{Z}_p^*$ defined by $exp_\alpha(i) = \alpha^i$ establishes a one-one correspondence.

In order to set up the bit commitment scheme, the originator and receiver initially agree on a large prime p for which they both know the factorization of $p-1$ (finding large primes p with known factorization of $p-1$ can be done efficiently in practice [Mau89]). They also agree on a generator α of $\mathbf{Z}_p^*$. Thanks to their knowledge of the factors of $p-1$, they can both verify with certainty that p is a prime and that α is a generator of $\mathbf{Z}_p^*$. Moreover, the density of generators is high enough that one can be found reasonably efficiently by random trial and error. Actually, the parameters p and α need not be changed each time a bit commitment scheme has to be set up. Rather, they could be in the public domain (together with the factorization of $p-1$) after having been selected once and for all by an authority that does not need to be trusted. Given any $i \in \mathbf{Z}_{p-1}$, it is easy to compute α^i efficiently by a divide-and-conquer approach, but no efficient algorithm is known to invert this process (even if the factors of $p-1$ are known, provided they are not too small [PH78]), an operation known as *extracting the discrete logarithm*.

Once the parameters p and α have been agreed upon, the receiver chooses a random $s \in \mathbf{Z}_p^*$ and gives it to the originator. We assume the *certified discrete logarithm assumption*, namely that the originator is not capable of computing the discrete logarithm of s while the protocol is in progress ("certified" because the factors of $p-1$ are known to all parties in order that α be a certified generator — since this could make computing the discrete logarithm easier, this assumption is stronger than the usual discrete logarithm assumption of Blum and Micali [BM84]; nevertheless, the usual assumption is good enough to implement a bit commitment scheme statistically secure for the originator).

In order to commit to bit $x \in \{0, 1\}$, the originator selects a random $r \in \mathbf{Z}_{p-1}$ and she computes $b = \alpha^r s^x$. She gives b to the receiver but she keeps r as her secret *witness*. Subsequently, if the originator wishes to convince the receiver that b was a commitment to bit x, she simply shows him the corresponding witness r. The receiver can then check that indeed $b = \alpha^r s^x$.

Because the function exp_α is a one-one correspondence, any element of $\mathbf{Z}_p^*$ can be used by the originator as commitment to 0 just as well as to 1, depending only on which witness she knows. Moreover, all commitments are randomly and independently distributed according to the uniform distribution over $\mathbf{Z}_p^*$. Therefore, it is information-theoretically impossible for the receiver to distinguish a commitment to 0 from a commitment to 1, regardless of his computing power. On the other hand, the originator is able to cheat and open a given commitment both ways if and only if she knows (or can efficiently compute) the discrete logarithm of s, which we assumed to be infeasible for her.

A moment's thought suffices to see that this bit commitment scheme is trap-door, and that its key is the discrete logarithm of s. Moreover, it is easy to see that this bit commitment scheme has both the equality and the unequality properties.

Acknowledgements

It is a pleasure to acknowledge fruitful discussions with Claude Crépeau, Yvo Desmedt, Russel Impagliazzo, Andy Klapper, Moni Naor, Rafail Ostrovsky, and Hiroki Shizuya. The terms "concealing" and "computationally convincing" are due to David Chaum. We also acknowledge the referees for their suggestions.

References

[AFK89]   Abadi, M., J. Feigenbaum, and J. Kilian, "On hiding information from an oracle", *Journal of Computer and System Sciences*, Vol. 39, 1989, pp. 21–50.

[AL83]   Angluin, D. and D. Lichtenstein, "Provable security of cryptosystems: A survey", Technical Report YALEU/DCS/TR–288, Department of Computer Science, Yale University, 1983.

[BMO90]   Bellare, M., S. Micali, and R. Ostrovsky, "Perfect zero-knowledge in constant rounds", *Proceedings of the 22nd ACM Symposium on Theory of Computing*, 1990, pp. 482–493.

[BB84]   Bennett, C.H. and G. Brassard, "Quantum cryptography: Public key distribution and coin tossing", *Proceedings of IEEE International Conference on Computers, Systems, and Signal Processing*, Bangalore, India, December 1984, pp. 175–179.

[BK89]   Blum, M. and S. Kannan, "Designing programs that check their work", *Proceedings of the 21st ACM Symposium on Theory of Computing*, 1989, pp. 86–97.

[BM84]   Blum, M. and S. Micali, "How to generate cryptographically strong sequences of pseudo-random bits", *SIAM Journal on Computing*, Vol. 13, 1984, pp. 850–864.

[BKK90]   Boyar, J.F., M.W. Krentel, and S.A. Kurtz, "A discrete logarithm implementation of zero-knowledge blobs", *Journal of Cryptology*, Vol. 2, no. 2, 1990.

[Bra91]   Brassard, G., "Cryptology column — Bit commitment schemes", *Sigact News*, in preparation, 1991.

[BCC88]   Brassard, G., D. Chaum, and C. Crépeau, "Minimum disclosure proofs of knowledge", *Journal of Computer and System Sciences*, Vol. 37, no. 2, 1988, pp. 156–189.

[BC86a] Brassard, G. and C. Crépeau, "Zero-knowledge simulation of Boolean circuits", *Advances in Cryptology: CRYPTO '86 Proceedings*, Springer–Verlag, 1987, pp. 224–233.

[BC86b] Brassard, G. and C. Crépeau, "Non-transitive transfer of confidence: A *perfect* zero-knowledge interactive protocol for SAT and beyond", *Proceedings of the 27th IEEE Symposium on Foundations of Computer Science*, 1986, pp. 188–195.

[BC90] Brassard, G. and C. Crépeau, "Quantum bit commitment and coin tossing protocols", *Advances in Cryptology:* these *CRYPTO '90 Proceedings*, Springer–Verlag.

[BCY89] Brassard, G., C. Crépeau, and M. Yung, "Everything in **NP** can be argued in *perfect* zero-knowledge in a *bounded* number of rounds", *Proceedings of the 16th International Colloquium on Automata, Languages and Programming*, Springer–Verlag, 1989, pp. 123–136. Final paper to appear in *Theoretical Computer Science* under the title of "Constant-round perfect zero-knowledge computationally convincing protocols".

[BDPW89] Burmester, M. V. D., Y. G. Desmedt, F. Piper, and M. Walker, "A meta zero-knowledge scheme", *Proceedings of CO89 Combinatorial Optimization Conference*, University of Leeds, July 1989. Submitted for journal publication.

[Cha86] Chaum, D., "Demonstrating that a public predicate can be satisfied without revealing any information about how", *Advances in Cryptology: CRYPTO '86 Proceedings*, Springer–Verlag, 1987, pp. 195–199.

[CDG88] Chaum, D., I. B. Damgård, and J. van de Graaf, "Multiparty computations ensuring privacy of each party's input and correctness of the result", *Advances in Cryptology: CRYPTO '87 Proceedings*, Springer–Verlag, 1988, pp. 87–119.

[FS89] Feige, U. and A. Shamir, "Zero knowledge proofs of knowledge in two rounds", *Advances in Cryptology: CRYPTO '89 Proceedings*, Springer–Verlag, 1990, pp. 526–544.

[FKN90] Feigenbaum, J., S. Kannan, and N. Nisan, "Lower bounds on random self-reducibility", *Proceedings of the 5th IEEE Structure in Complexity Theory Conference*, 1990.

[GMW86] Goldreich, O., S. Micali, and A. Wigderson, "Proofs that yield nothing but their validity and a methodology of cryptographic protocol design", *Proceedings of the 27th IEEE Symposium on Foundations of Computer Science*, 1986, pp. 174–187.

[GMR89] Goldwasser, S., S. Micali, and C. Rackoff, "The knowledge complexity of interactive proof systems", *SIAM Journal on Computing*, Vol. 18, no. 1, 1989, pp. 186–208.

[GMRi88] Goldwasser, S., S. Micali, and R. Rivest, "A secure digital signature scheme", *SIAM Journal on Computing*, Vol. 17, no. 2, 1988, pp. 281–308.

[Hås90] Håstad, J., "Pseudo-random generators under uniform assumptions", *Proceedings of the 22nd ACM Symposium on Theory of Computing*, 1990, pp. 395–404.

[ILL89]   Impagliazzo, R., L. Levin, and M. Luby, "Pseudo-random generation from one-way functions", *Proceedings of the 21st ACM Symposium on Theory of Computing*, 1989, pp. 12–24.

[IL89]   Impagliazzo, R. and M. Luby, "One-way functions are essential for complexity based cryptography", *Proceedings of the 30th IEEE Symposium on Foundations of Computer Science*, 1989, pp. 230–235.

[IN89]   Impagliazzo, R. and M. Naor, "Efficient cryptographic schemes provably as secure as subset sum", *Proceedings of the 30th IEEE Symposium on Foundations of Computer Science*, 1989, pp. 236–241.

[IY88]   Impagliazzo, R. and M. Yung, "Direct minimum-knowledge computations", *Advances in Cryptology: CRYPTO '87 Proceedings*, Springer–Verlag, 1988, pp. 40–51.

[Kra86]   Kranakis, E., *Primality and Cryptography*, Wiley–Teubner Series in Computer Science, 1986.

[Mau89]   Maurer, U. M., "Fast generation of secure RSA–moduli with almost maximal diversity", *Advances in Cryptology: EUROCRYPT '89 Proceedings*, Springer–Verlag, to appear.

[Nao89]   Naor, M., "Bit commitment using pseudo-randomness", *Advances in Cryptology: CRYPTO '89 Proceedings*, Springer–Verlag, 1990, pp. 128–136.

[NOVY90]   Naor, M., R. Ostrovsky, R. Venkatesan, and M. Yung, manuscript, 1990.

[OVY90]   Ostrovsky, R., R. Venkatesan, and M. Yung, manuscript, 1990.

[PH78]   Pohlig, S. and M. E. Hellman, "An improved algorithm for computing logarithms over $GF(p)$ and its cryptographic significance", *IEEE Transactions on Information Theory*, Vol. IT-24, 1978, pp. 106–110.

[SI90]   Shizuya, H. and T. Itoh, "A group-theoretic interface to random self-reducibility", *Transactions of the Institute of Electronics, Information and Communication Engineers (IEICE) of Japan*, Section E, Vol. E73, no. 7, July 25, 1990.

[TW87]   Tompa, M. and H. Woll, "Random self-reducibility and zero-knowledge proofs of possession of knowledge", *Proceedings of the 28th IEEE Symposium on Foundations of Computer Science*, 1987, pp. 472–482.

Session 3
Algebra and Number Theory
Chair: H. Williams, University of Manitoba

Solving Large Sparse Linear Systems Over Finite Fields

B. A. LaMacchia *
A. M. Odlyzko

AT&T Bell Laboratories
Murray Hill, New Jersey 07974

ABSTRACT

Many of the fast methods for factoring integers and computing discrete logarithms require the solution of large sparse linear systems of equations over finite fields. This paper presents the results of implementations of several linear algebra algorithms. It shows that very large sparse systems can be solved efficiently by using combinations of structured Gaussian elimination and the conjugate gradient, Lanczos, and Wiedemann methods.

1. Introduction

Factoring integers and computing discrete logarithms often requires solving large systems of linear equations over finite fields. General surveys of these areas are presented in [14, 17, 19]. So far there have been few implementations of discrete logarithm algorithms, but many of integer factoring methods. Some of the published results have involved solving systems of over 6×10^4 equations in more than 6×10^4 variables [12]. In factoring, equations have had to be solved over the field $GF(2)$. In that situation, ordinary Gaussian elimination can be used effectively, since many coefficients (either 32 or 64 depending on machine word size) can be packed into a single machine word, and addition can be implemented as the exclusive-or operation. Even so, the large size of the systems to be solved has often caused storage problems (a 6×10^4 by 6×10^4 system requires approximately 110 million words of storage on a 32-bit machine), and it has often been difficult to obtain a correspondingly large amount of computer time. In many cases, the linear systems were purposefully kept

---

*Present address: MIT, Cambridge, MA 02139

smaller than would have been optimal from the standpoint of other parts of the factoring algorithm, just to avoid the linear algebra difficulties.

Clearly we cannot hope to be able to solve future systems (even in $GF(2)$) using only ordinary Gaussian elimination. As the size of integers being factored increases, so does the size of the system of equations which must be solved. In addition, the recently discovered number field sieve currently requires (when applied to factoring general integers) the solution of equations over the integers, not just modulo 2. (The best way to obtain such a solution appears to be either to solve the system modulo many small or moderate primes and then apply the Chinese remainder theorem, or else to solve it modulo a particular prime, and then lift that solution to one modulo a power of that prime.) In the case of the number field sieve applied to general integers, the linear algebra problem is currently one of the critical bottlenecks that keep it impractical.

Even in cases where the equations have to be solved modulo 2, linear algebra difficulties are becoming a serious bottleneck. As an example, the very recent factorization of $F_9 = 2^{2^9} + 1 = 2^{512} + 1$ (using a special form of the number field sieve for integers of this form) by A. Lenstra and M. Manasse involved solving a system with dimension $n \approx 2 \times 10^5$. The attack on the RSA challenge cipher (which will require factoring a 129 decimal digit integer) that is currently planned using the quadratic sieve might require solving a system with $n \approx 4 \times 10^5$.

For discrete logarithm algorithms, the linear algebra problem has always seemed to be even more important than in factoring, since the equations have to be solved modulo large primes. The largest system that has been solved was of size about 1.6×10^4 by 1.6×10^4, modulo $2^{127} - 1$, which arose in connection with discrete logarithms in $GF(2^{127})$ [3, 17].

For an $n \times n$ system with $n \approx 10^5$, ordinary Gaussian elimination takes about $n^3 \approx 10^{15}$ operations. Modern supercomputers are capable of between 10^8 and 10^9 integer operations per second, so 10^{15} operations might take a few weeks to a few months on such a machine, if one matrix operation took one machine instruction. In practice, since up to 64 matrix operations are performed in a single supercomputer operation, the required time decreases substantially. However, for those without access to supercomputers, time can easily be a barrier. It is possible to obtain 10^{15} machine operations for free, as that is the approximate amount of work that the recent integer factorization achieved by A. Lenstra and M. Manasse [12] required. However, that effort involved a very decentralized and only loosely coordinated computation on hundreds of workstations. This is acceptable for the sieving stage of the quadratic sieve algorithm, but it causes problems when one tries to solve a system of linear equations; solving such systems requires very close coordination and errors propagate quickly, destroying the validity of the final result. Thus the linear algebra phase requires the use of a single machine (although it can be a massively parallel computer), and it can often be hard to obtain access to one that is fast enough. Memory requirements also present serious difficulties. If the problem is to find a solution modulo 2, the full matrix has 10^{10} bits, or 1,250 megabytes. Only a few supercomputers have this much main memory. On all other machines, one has to work on the matrix in blocks, which slows down the operation considerably.

Both the time and space requirements become much more serious when solving equations modulo a "moderate size" prime p. If $p \approx 2^{100}$, the operation count goes up from 10^{15} to 10^{19}, which is prohibitive even for a supercomputer. The storage requirements increase to 10^{12} bits, which is 125 gigabytes, considerably more than any existing machine has.

Fast matrix multiplication algorithms do not offer much hope. The Strassen $n^{2.81}$ method [21] is practical for n on the order of several hundred, but does not save enough. Later methods, of which the Coppersmith-Winograd $n^{2.376}$ algorithm [8] is currently the fastest, are impractical.

If the equations that arise in factoring and discrete log algorithms were totally random, there would be little hope of solving large systems. However, these equations, while they appear fairly random in many respects, are extremely sparse, with usually no more than 50 non-zero coefficients per equation. Moreover, they are relatively dense in some parts, and very sparse in others. Previous Gaussian elimination implementations, as is mentioned below, already take advantage of some of these features. In addition, several special systematic methods have been developed to take advantage of this sparsity. They are:

1. structured Gaussian elimination (also called intelligent Gaussian elimination) [17],

2. the conjugate gradient and Lanczos algorithms [7, 17],

3. the Wiedemann algorithm [22].

Structured Gaussian elimination was designed to reduce a problem to a much smaller one that could then be solved by other methods. The other methods have running times that are expected to be of order not much bigger than n^2 for a sparse $n \times n$ system. Theoretically, the Wiedemann algorithm is the most attractive of all these techniques, since it can be rigorously proved to work with high probability (if one randomizes certain choices in the initial stages of the algorithm), while the other methods are only heuristic. Asymptotically, it was thought for a long time that the problem of solving large linear systems was the crucial bottleneck determining how algorithms such as the quadratic size performed [18].

This view then changed, as the Wiedemann algorithm showed that linear algebra was only about as important in determining the asymptotic complexity of algorithms such as the quadratic sieve as other steps.

To the authors' knowledge, the Wiedemann algorithm has never been tested on a large system. The conjugate gradient and Lanczos methods have been tested [7, 17], but only on fairly small systems. Structured Gaussian elimination was tested on some very large systems in [17], but those tests used simulated data, while the runs on real data derived from a factoring project solved only fairly small systems. More recently, this method was implemented and used to solve some fairly large binary systems by Pomerance and Smith [20]. Even more recently, a version of this method was used by A. Lenstra and M. Manasse in their factorization of F_9.

This paper reports on the performance of some of these algorithms on several very large sparse systems derived from factoring and discrete logarithm computations. The largest of the systems that were solved had about 3×10^5 equations in about 10^5 unknown, modulo a prime of 191 bits; this system arose in the computation of discrete logarithms in a certain prime field [10]. The basic conclusion is that the conjugate gradient and Lanczos algorithms have essentially the same performance and are very effective in finite fields. One of their advantages is that they use relatively little space. However, even these algorithms are too slow to tackle very large problems. The Wiedemann algorithm (which was not implemented) has modest space requirements, almost exactly the same as those of the conjugate gradient and Lanczos methods. Its running time is likely to be comparable to those of the conjugate gradient and Lanczos algorithms, with the precise comparison depending on the architecture of the computer and implementation details.

We have also found that structured Gaussian elimination is very effective in reducing a large, sparse problem to a much smaller one. Structured Gaussian elimination takes very little time, and can be implemented so as to take very little space. When dealing with a large sparse system modulo a prime, it appears that the best procedure is to first apply structured Gaussian elimination to obtain a smaller system that is still sparse, and then to solve the smaller system with one of the conjugate gradient, Lanczos, or Wiedemann algorithms. When working with equations modulo 2, it is probably better to use ordinary Gaussian elimination for the final step, or else one can use conjugate gradient, Lanczos, or Wiedemann for the entire problem.

Section 2 describes the data sets that were used in the computations, as well as the machine on which the algorithms were run. We describe in Section 3 the Lanczos and conjugate gradient algorithms, and their performance. Section 4 briefly discusses the

Wiedemann algorithm. Structured Gaussian elimination is detailed in Section 5

2. Machines and data

All computations reported in this paper were carried out on a Silicon Graphics 4D-220 computer. It has 4 R3000 MIPS Computers, Inc., 25 MHz processors, each rated at about 18 mips, or 18 times the speed of a DEC VAX 11/780 computer (and about 1.3 times the speed of a DECstation 3100). The parallel processing capability of this system was not used; all times reported here are for a single processor. This machine has 128 Mbytes of main memory.

All programs were written in C or Fortran. They were not carefully optimized, since the aim of the project was only to obtain rough performance figures. Substantial performance improvements can be made fairly easily, even without using assembly language.

Table 1 describes the linear systems that were used in testing the algorithms. Data sets A through J were kindly provided by A. Lenstra and M. Manasse, and come from their work on factoring integers [12]. Sets A, B and C result from runs of the multiple polynomial quadratic sieve (*mpqs*) with the single large prime variation, but have had the large primes eliminated. Set D also comes from a run of *mpqs*, but this time the large primes were still in the data (except that equations with a large prime that does not occur elsewhere were dropped). Set E comes from a factorization that used the new number field sieve, and set $E1$ was derived from set E by deleting 5000 columns at the sparse end of the matrix. (Set $E1$ was created to simulate a system that has more extra equations than E does, but has comparable density.) Sets F and G derive from runs of *ppmpqs*, the two large prime variation of *mpqs* [13]. Both sets arose during the factorization of the same integer; set G was obtained by running the sieving operation longer. Sets H and I come from other runs of *ppmpqs* (set I was produced during the factorization of the 111 decimal digit composite cofactor of $7^{146} + 1$). Set J was produced by the number field sieve factorization of F_9. All of these data sets (A-J) were tested modulo 2 only.

Data set K was obtained in the process of computing discrete logarithms modulo a prime p of 192 bits [10], and had to be solved modulo $\frac{p-1}{2}$ (a prime of 191 bits) and modulo 2. Set K was tested modulo both numbers. Sets $K0$ through $K6$ and L were derived from set K. Set $K2$ was derived by deleting the 144,000 equations from F that had the highest number of non-zero entries (*weight*). Set $K4$ was derived from K by deleting the 144,000 equations that had the lowest weights. Sets $K0$, $K1$, $K3$, $K5$, and $K6$ were obtained by deleting randomly chosen equations from K. (The reason the number of unknowns

Table 1: Large sparse sets of equations

Name	Number of Equations	Number of Unknowns	Average Number of Non-zeros per Equation
A	35,987	35,000	20.4
B	52,254	50,001	21.0
C	65,518	65,500	20.4
D	123,019	106,121	11.0
E	82,470	80,015	47.1
E1	82,470	75,015	46.6
F	25,201	25,001	46.7
G	30,268	25,001	47.9
H	61,343	30,001	49.3
I	102,815	80,001	43.2
J	226,688	199,203	48.8
K	288,017	96,321	15.5
K0	216,105	95,216	15.5
K1	165,245	93,540	15.5
K2	144,017	94,395	13.8
K3	144,432	92,344	15.5
K4	144,017	89,003	17.1
K5	115,659	90,019	15.5
K6	101,057	88,291	15.5
L	7,262	6,006	80.5
M	164,841	94,398	16.9

varies in these sets is that in sets $K, K0, \ldots, K6$, only the unknowns that actually appear in the equations are counted.) Set L was derived from set K by using structured Gaussian elimination. Finally, data set M was produced while computing discrete logarithms modulo a prime p of 224 bits [10].

3. Lanczos and conjugate gradient methods

We first describe the Lanczos algorithm. Suppose that we have to solve the system

$$Ax = w \tag{3.1}$$

for a column n-vector x, where A is a symmetric $n \times n$ matrix, and w is a given column n-vector. Let

$$w_0 = w, \tag{3.2}$$
$$v_1 = Aw_0, \tag{3.3}$$
$$w_1 = v_1 - \frac{(v_1, v_1)}{(w_0, v_1)} w_0, \tag{3.4}$$

and then, for $i \geq 1$, define

$$v_{i+1} = Aw_i, \tag{3.5}$$
$$w_{i+1} = v_{i+1} - \frac{(v_{i+1}, v_{i+1})}{(w_i, v_{i+1})} w_i - \frac{(v_{i+1}, v_i)}{(w_{i-1}, v_i)} w_{i-1}. \tag{3.6}$$

The algorithm stops when it finds a w_j that is conjugate to itself, i.e. such that $(w_j, Aw_j) = 0$. This happens for some $j \leq n$. If $w_j = 0$, then

$$x = \sum_{i=0}^{j-1} b_i w_i \tag{3.7}$$

is a solution to Equation 3.1, where

$$b_i = \frac{(w_i, w)}{(w_i, v_{i+1})}. \tag{3.8}$$

(If $w_j \neq 0$, the algorithm fails.)

The Lanczos algorithm was invented to solve systems with real coefficients [11]. To solve systems over finite fields, we simply take Equations 3.3 to 3.8 and apply them to a finite field situation. This causes possible problems, since over a finite field one can have a non-zero vector that is conjugate to itself. However, this difficulty, as well as some other ones that arise, can be overcome in practice.

In addition to dealing with self-conjugacy, we have to cope with the fact that the systems we need to solve are in general not symmetric, but rather are of the form

$$Bx = u, \tag{3.9}$$

where B is $m \times n$, $m \geq n$, x is an unknown column n-vector, and u is a given column m-vector. (We assume that B has rank n, or at least that u is in the space generated by the columns of B.) We first embed the field over which we have to solve the equations in a possibly larger field F with $|F|$ considerably larger than n. We then let D be an $m \times m$ diagonal matrix with the diagonal elements selected at random from $F \backslash \{0\}$, and we let

$$A = B^T D^2 B,$$
$$w = B^T D^2 u. \tag{3.10}$$

A solution to Equation 3.9 is then a solution to Equation 3.1, and we expect that with high probability a solution to Equation 3.1 will be a solution to Equation 3.9. The random choice of D ought to ensure that the rank of A will be the same as the rank of B (this is not always true), and that we will not run into a self-conjugate w_i in the Lanczos algorithm. Experience has shown that this is indeed what happens.

The Lanczos algorithm is not restricted to dealing with sparse matrices, but that is where it is most useful. At iteration i, we need to compute the vector $v_{i+1} = Aw_i$ ($v_i = Aw_{i-1}$ is already known from the previous iteration), the vector inner products (v_{i+1}, v_{i+1}), (w_i, v_{i+1}), and (v_{i+1}, v_i), and then form w_{i+1} using Equation 3.6. The matrix A will in general be dense, even when B is sparse. However, we do not need to form A, since to compute Aw_i we use Equation 3.10 and compute

$$B^T(D^2(Bw_i)), \tag{3.11}$$

Suppose that B has b non-zero entries. We will further assume, as is the case for the matrices arising in factorization and discrete logarithm computations, that almost all these b entries are ± 1. Let c_1 be the cost of an addition or subtraction in F, and c_2 the cost of a multiplication. Then computing Bw_i costs approximately

$$b \, c_1,$$

multiplying that by D^2 costs

$$n \, c_2,$$

and multiplying $D^2 B w_i$ by B^T costs approximately

$$b c_1,$$

for a total cost of about

$$2 b c_1 + n c_2$$

for each evaluation of $A w_i$. The computation of each vector inner product costs about $nc_1 + nc_2$, and so the cost of each iteration is about

$$2 b c_1 + 4 n c_1 + 5 n c_2, \tag{3.12}$$

so that the total cost of obtaining a solution is about

$$2 n b c_1 + 4 n^2 c_1 + 5 n^2 c_2. \tag{3.13}$$

In this rough accounting we do not charge for the cost of accessing elements of arrays or lists, which will often be the dominant factor, especially when dealing with binary data. On the other hand, on some machines one can perform additions and multiplications in parallel. Therefore one should treat the estimate given by Equation 3.13 as a very rough approximation.

In practice, B will usually be stored with rows represented by lists of positions where that row has a non-zero entry, and (in the case of non-binary problems) by lists of non-zero coefficients. Thus we need about b pointers and (for non-binary data) about b bits to indicate whether that coefficient is $+1$ or -1. (Non-zero coefficients that are not ± 1 are relatively rare and can be treated separately.) The pointers normally have to be of at least $\lceil \log_2 n \rceil$ bits, but one can reduce that by taking advantage of the fact that most indices of positions where the coefficient is non-zero are very small. In any case, storage is not a problem even for very large systems. In the implementations described below, full 32-bit words were used for all pointers and coefficients. The largest of the systems in Table 1 had $b \lesssim 10^7$, so this did not cause any problems on the machine that was used. In fact, our algorithm had separate representations for both B and B^T, which is wasteful.

In a typical situation, we expect that the Lanczos method will be applied to a system that was processed first by structured Gaussian elimination, and so it will not be too sparse. As a result, the cost of the vector inner products ought to be dominated by the cost of the matrix-vector products, $2nbc_1$. As we will describe later, memory access times will often be the dominant factor in determining the efficiency of the matrix-vector product.

In discrete logarithm applications, the system given by Equation 3.9 is usually overdetermined, and so the aim is to find the unique x that solves it. In applications to factoring, though, one is looking for linear dependencies in a set of vectors, and it is necessary to find several such dependencies. This can be stated as the problem of solving the system in Equation 3.9 with B fixed, but for several vectors u, so that we need $x_1, x_2, \ldots, x_r$ such that

$$Bx_j = u_j, \quad 1 \leq j \leq r. \tag{3.14}$$

It is possible to solve all these systems at once, without rerunning the Lanczos algorithm r times. Let $z_j = B^T D^2 u_j$. Apply the algorithm as presented above with $w = z_1$. This produces the vectors $w_0, w_1, \ldots, w_{n-1}$ which are conjugate to each other; i.e. $(w_i, Aw_j) = 0$ for $i \neq j$. Now if

$$x_k = \sum_{j=0}^{n-1} c_{k,j} w_j, \tag{3.15}$$

then

$$(w_i, Ax_k) = \sum_{j=0}^{n-1} c_{k,j}(w_i, Aw_j) = c_{k,i}(w_i, Aw_i). \tag{3.16}$$

On the other hand, since $Ax_k = z_k$, this gives

$$c_{k,i} = \frac{(w_i, z_k)}{(w_i, Aw_i)}. \tag{3.17}$$

Since the terms on the right side above can be computed during the ith iteration of the algorithm, the only substantial extra space that is needed is that for storing the partial sums x_k, which at the end of the ith iteration equal

$$x_k = \sum_{j=0}^{i} c_{k,j} w_j. \tag{3.18}$$

Although the above analysis was based on the Lanczos algorithm, the derived complexity bounds also serve as rough approximations for the conjugate gradient (CG) method [9]. The CG and Lanczos algorithms are very similar. The iterations for the two algorithms are slightly different, but the operation count is almost exactly the same.

Both the Lanczos and the CG algorithms were implemented, Lanczos for solving equations modulo a large prime, CG for solving equations modulo 2. Both worked effectively, as will be described below. Both usually required n iterations to solve a system of size n. One unexpected problem was encountered, though. In the standard Lanczos and CG algorithms, it is not necessary that the matrix A in Equation 3.1 be non-singular. As long as w is in the linear span of the columns of A, the algorithms will converge. In the case of equations over finite fields, however, we observed that a system of less than full rank often gave rise to a self-conjugate vector, and thus to an abort of the algorithm. This phenomenon has not been explored carefully. It was not very important in the cases where these algorithms were tried (computing discrete logarithms), since there the systems of linear equations are overdetermined. This issue might be much more important in the case of factoring algorithms, since in that case one needs to find many linear dependencies modulo 2.

The CG implementation uses auxiliary storage to carry out field operations fast. The field F is chosen to be $GF(2^r)$, with $r = 19, 20$, or 21. F is defined as polynomials of degree $\leq r - 1$ over $GF(2)$ modulo a fixed irreducible polynomial of degree r. Elements $\alpha \in F$ are represented by a full word, $\overline{\alpha}$, with the digits in the binary representation of $\overline{\alpha}$ corresponding to the coefficients of α. This means that $\alpha + \beta$ is represented by the exclusive-or of $\overline{\alpha}$ and $\overline{\beta}$, and this operation is fast. Multiplication is carried out with the aid of an auxiliary array. Some primitive element $\gamma \in F$ is chosen, and then an array $w(j)$, $0 \leq j \leq 2^r - 1$ is generated, with $w(\overline{\alpha})$ for $\alpha \neq 0$ equal to the discrete logarithm of α to base γ. Thus for $\alpha \neq 0$

$$\alpha = \gamma^{w(\overline{\alpha})}, \ 0 \leq w(\overline{\alpha}) \leq 2^r - 2. \tag{3.19}$$

For $\alpha = 0$, $w(\overline{\alpha}) = w(0) = 2^{r+1} - 3$. Another auxiliary array $t(j), 0 \leq j \leq 2^{r+2} - 6$, is formed, with

$$t(j) \ = \ \overline{\gamma^j}, \ 0 \leq j \leq 2^{r+1} - 4, \tag{3.20}$$

$$t(j) \ = \ 0, \ 2^{r+1} - 3 \leq j \leq 2^{r+2} - 6. \tag{3.21}$$

As a result,

$$\overline{\alpha\beta} = t(w(\overline{\alpha}) + w(\overline{\beta})) \tag{3.22}$$

for all $\alpha, \beta \in F$, and thus each product in F can be computed using one integer addition, which on the machine that was used takes about as much time as an exclusive-or. The total cost of a multiplication in F is still higher than that of addition, though, because of the extra table lookups. Given the large size of the tables that are required which will not fit in the cache memory, on many machines it is likely to be faster to implement an algorithm that uses more operations but smaller tables. In practice, the time devoted to multiplication of elements of F is so small that it does not matter what algorithm one uses.

The implementation of the Lanczos algorithm is less efficient than that of CG. The very portable, and reasonably fast, multiprecision code that A. Lenstra and M. Manasse distribute with their factoring package [12] was used. When the non-zero entry in the matrix was ± 1 or ± 2, addition or subtraction routines were invoked; approximately 90% of the non-zero entries in matrix B were $\pm 1, \pm 2$ in data set L. In the other rare cases, multiprecision multiplication was invoked, even when it would have been more efficient to perform several additions.

The implementation of the Lanczos algorithm solved system L modulo a prime of 191 bits in 44 hours. The CG algorithm solved that system modulo 2 in 1.9 hours. Timings of about 100 iterations of the CG algorithm on system E indicate that this system would require about 190 hours to solve.

While quite large systems can be solved with the CG algorithm, the timings reported above are rather slow. For system L, Equation 3.13 indicates that the total cost ought to be around

$$7 \times 10^9 c_1 + 1.8 \times 10^8 c_2$$

If each of c_1 and c_2 were around 1 machine instruction, the total run time would be about 6 minutes. What causes the 1.9 hour run time is the fact that on the computer that was used c_1 and c_2 are much more expensive. This is due to problems of memory access, with the cache size too small to contain the full arrays. On different machines the performance would be quite different. Even on the SGI computer that was used, it is quite likely that one could obtain substantial speedups by arranging the data flow so that the caches are utilized more efficiently.

4. The Wiedemann algorithm

This algorithm is described carefully in [22]. As was pointed out by E. Kaltofen, the basic idea of this algorithm has been known in numerical analysis for a long time in Krylov subspace methods [23]. (It is rather interesting to note that the Lanczos algorithm is also a Krylov subspace method.) The main innovation in the Wiedemann algorithm is the use of the Berlekamp-Massey algorithm [15, 16], which in a finite field setting allows one to determine linear recurrence coefficients very fast, even for huge systems. Here we present only an outline of the method which will enable us to estimate its efficiency. Let us assume that we need to solve

$$Bx = u, \tag{4.1}$$

where B is a sparse non-singular $n \times n$ matrix. (See [22] for methods of dealing with non-square and singular matrices.) B is not required to be symmetric in this algorithm. Suppose that the minimal polynomial of B is given by

$$\sum_{j=0}^{N} c_j B^j = 0, \quad N \le n, \quad c_0 \ne 0. \tag{4.2}$$

Then for any n-vector v, we have

$$\sum_{j=0}^{N} c_j B^{j+k} v = 0, \quad \forall k \geq 0. \tag{4.3}$$

If we let $v_k = B^k v$, then Equation 4.3 says that any one of the coordinates of $v_0, v_1, \ldots, v_{2n}$ satisfies the linear recurrence with coefficients $c_0, c_1, \ldots, c_N$. Given any $2n$ terms of a linear recurrent sequence of order $\leq n$, the Berlekamp-Massey algorithm will find the minimal polynomial of that sequence in $O(n^2)$ operations. (There are even faster variants of the algorithm [1, 2, 4] which are likely to be practical for very large systems.) Hence if we apply the Berlekamp-Massey algorithm to each of the first K coordinates of the vectors $v_0, \ldots, v_{2n}$, in $O(Kn^2)$ steps we will obtain the K polynomials whose least common multiple is likely to be the minimal polynomial of B. Once we find $c_0, \ldots, c_N$, we can obtain the solution to Equation 4.1 from

$$\begin{aligned} u &= -c_0^{-1} \sum_{j=1}^{N} c_j B^j u \\ &= B \left[-c_0^{-1} \sum_{j=1}^{N} c_j B^{j-1} u \right]. \end{aligned} \tag{4.4}$$

If B has b non-zero coefficients, most of them ± 1, and c_1 is again the cost of an addition or subtraction in the field we work with, then computation of $v_0, \ldots, v_{2n}$ costs about

$$a\, n\, b\, c_1. \tag{4.5}$$

This is just about the cost of the Lanczos and CG algorithms. Wiedemann's method saves a factor of 2 by not having to multiply by both B and B^T, but loses a factor of 2 by having to compute $B^j v$ for $0 \leq j \leq 2n$. (In the case of binary data, when all the non-zero coefficients are 1, the cost drops to nbc_1, a reduction similar to that in the Lanczos and CG algorithms.) The Berlekamp-Massey algorithm is expected to be very fast, with a cost of cn^2 for some small constant c, and this ought to be much less than Equation 4.5. Finally, obtaining u through Equation 4.4 will cost about

$$n\, b\, c_1 + n^2\, c_2. \tag{4.6}$$

Thus if c_2 is not too large compared to c_1, or if the matrix is dense enough, the total cost of obtaining a solution using the Wiedemann algorithm is expected to be about 1.5 times as large as through the CG and Lanczos methods, even if $K = 1$ suffices to determine the minimal polynomial of B.

It is possible to cut down on the cost of the Wiedemann algorithm if one uses additional storage. If one uses $v = u$, and stores $v_0, \ldots, v_n$, then the computation of x in Equation 4.4 will only cost $O(n^2)$. In general, however, storing $v_0, \ldots, v_n$ in main memory is likely to be impossible, as that involves n^2 storage of n^2 field elements. On the other hand, since each of the v_j is only needed once during the computation of x, the v_j can be stored on a disk. If disk access is sufficiently rapid, this method could be used to avoid the additional cost, and thus make the Wiedemann method perform just about as fast as the CG and Lanczos algorithms.

Another way to eliminate the need for the extra n matrix-vector products in the Wiedemann algorithm (and thus reduce its cost so that it is no more than that of the CG and Lanczos methods) is to carry out the Berlekamp-Massey computation at the same time that the v_k are computed. At the cost of keeping around several additional vectors, this should allow one to construct the solution vector right away.

The assumption made above that taking $K = 1$ will suffice does not seem unreasonable for large fields. In the binary case, one can use an approach similar to that in the CG implementation described in Section 3 to generate as many sequences as the word size of the computer being used by taking the vector v to be over $GF(2^r)$. This approach would also make it possible to obtain several solutions at once (as in Equation 3.14), once the c_j are determined.

Most of the large systems that are likely to be solved in the near future are binary. In those cases, the discussion above implies that on a true random access machine, the Wiedemann algorithm is likely to be slower than CG or Lanczos by a factor of $3/2$, and could approach their speed only by using substantial additional storage. However, on most machines data access is likely to be the main factor determining the efficiency of the algorithm. In the CG and Lanczos algorithms, the vectors w_i that are multiplied by A have to be on the order of 20 bits, and for all foreseeable problems longer than 16 bits. In the Wiedemann algorithm, it is conceivable that it would suffice to work with 3 or 4 bit vectors. (This is a point that needs testing.) Therefore it is possible that one could utilize the cache much more efficiently.

The general conclusion is that the Wiedemann algorithm is of about the same efficiency as the CG and Lanczos algorithms. However, it is quite a bit more complicated to program, and some crucial steps, such as the randomization procedures described in [22] for dealing with non-square and highly singular cases, have apparently never been tested. (Our analysis above assumes that they would not cause any problems.) It would be desirable to implement the Wiedemann algorithm and test it on some large systems.

5. Structured Gaussian elimination

This method is an adaptation and systematization of some of the standard techniques used in numerical analysis to minimize fill-in during Gaussian elimination, with some additional steps designed to take advantage of the special structure present in matrices arising from integer factorization and discrete logarithm algorithms. The part of the matrix corresponding to the very small primes is actually quite dense, while that corresponding to the large primes is extremely sparse. (In all cases that the authors have looked at, there are even variables corresponding to some large primes that do not appear in any equation.) This fact was taken advantage of in all previous solutions to large systems, in that Gaussian elimination was always performed starting at the sparse end. Had it been performed starting at the dense end, fill-in would have been immediately catastrophic.

By starting at the sparse end, substantial savings have been achieved. No precise measurements are available, but based on some data provided by R. Silverman (personal communication) it appears that about half the time was spent reducing n by n systems to about $n/3$ by $n/3$ systems, which were very dense. This indicates a factor of more than 10 savings over ordinary Gaussian elimination that starts at the dense end. A. Lenstra has indicated that similar results occurred in his work with M. Manasse.

The basic idea of structured Gaussian elimination is to declare some columns (those with the largest number of non-zero elements) as *heavy*, and to work only on preserving the sparsity of the remaining *light* columns. As was suggested by Pomerance and Smith [20], the set of heavy columns is allowed to grow as the algorithm progresses, instead of being chosen once, as was originally proposed [17]. In practice, the matrix would be stored in a sparse encoding, with rows represented by lists of positions where the coefficients are non-zero and with lists of the corresponding coefficients. To visualize the operation of the algorithm, it is easiest to think of the full matrix, though. The algorithm consists of a sequence of steps chosen from the following:

Step 1 Delete all columns that have a single non-zero coefficient and the rows in which those columns have non-zero coefficients.

Step 2 Declare some additional light columns to be heavy, choosing the heaviest ones.

Step 3 Delete some of the rows, selecting those which have the largest number of non-zero elements in the light columns.

Step 4 For any row which has only a single non-zero coefficient equal to ± 1 in the light column, subtract appropriate multiples of that row from all other rows that have non-zero coefficients on that column so as to make those coefficients 0.

As long as only these steps are taken, the number of non-zero coefficients in the light part of the matrix will never increase. In the original description in [17], it was suggested that one might need to take further steps, involving subtracting multiples of rows that have ≥ 2 non-zero elements in the light part of the matrix. However, experiments (some already mentioned in [17]) suggest that this is not only unnecessary, but also leads to rapidly increasing storage and time requirements, and so it is better to avoid such steps.

Experiments mentioned in [17] used a pseudo-random number generator to create data sets that had the statistics of very large discrete logarithm problems over fields of characteristic 2. Those experiments indicated that structured Gaussian elimination ought to be very successful, and that to achieve big reductions in the size of the matrix that has to be solved, the original matrix ought to be kept very sparse, which has implications for the choices of parameters in factorization and discrete logarithm algorithms. Those experiments indicated that if the matrix was sparse enough (either because one started with a sparse data set, or else because enough columns were declared heavy), one could expect a very rapid collapse of the system to a much smaller one. The results of the experiments that we performed on real data confirm these findings. Furthermore, they show that excess equations are a very important factor in the performance of the algorithm. If there are many more equations than unknowns, one can obtain much smaller final systems.

Two versions of the program were implemented, one for solving equations modulo 2, the other for all other systems. (In the second version, coefficients were never reduced modulo anything.) Their performances on data set K were very similar, with the mod 2 version producing a slightly smaller final system. The general versions never produced coefficients larger than 40 in that case. This situation would probably change if the matrix were not so sparse.

The matrix is stored in a single linear array, with several smaller arrays being used to hold information about the status of rows and columns (whether a given column is heavy, for example). Each *active* row (i.e., row that has not been eliminated, was not dropped as unnecessary, and has some non-zero entries in the sparse part) is stored as two adjacent lists, one for the indices of columns in the sparse part of the matrix that have non-zero entries, and one for the indices of the rows of the original matrix that make up the current row. (In the case of the general version, there are also corresponding lists of the coefficients of the matrix entries and of the rows.) When row j is subtracted from row i, a new entry for the modified row, still called i, is created at the end of the linear array, and the space previously occupied by rows i and j is freed up. When available space is exhausted, the large linear array is compacted by invoking a garbage collection routine. If this measure does not free up enough space, then Step 2 is invoked.

Many variations on the above approach are possible. Note that the number of non-zero entries in the light part of the matrix never increases. The only storage requirement that does grow is that for the lists of ancestor rows. Those, however, do not have to be kept in core. If one stores the history of what the algorithm does in a file, the ancestor lists can be reconstructed later. This is the approach used by Pomerance and Smith [20], for example, as well as by A. Lenstra and M. Manasse. Our implementation was motivated by the availability of substantial memory on our machine and the fact that when the ancestor lists get large, the heavy part of the matrix gets quite dense, which is undesirable, and so (as will be described later) it seems better to thin out the matrix by using Step 2.

One advantage of the algorithm as described here is that it can be implemented in very little space. Our implementation keeps all the arrays in core, and is very wasteful in that it uses full 32-bit words for all pointers and coefficients. Since only a modest number of passes through the data were performed, one could keep the rows stored on a disk, and use core storage only for the more frequently accessed arrays that store information about row and column sums.

In our implementation, Step 1 is applied repeatedly until no more columns of weight 1 (i.e., with a single non-zero coefficient) exist, then Step 2 is used. The number of columns that are declared heavy affects the performance of the algorithm to some extent. We usually applied this step to about $c/30$ columns, where c is the number of currently light columns that have weight > 0. For matrices that were expected to reduce to very small size, such as data set K and sets derived from it, values around $c/100$ were used. Generally speaking, the smaller the number of columns that are put into the heavy part at a single time, the better the final result, but also more work is required. (Pomerance and Smith [20] use values of about $c/1000$, for example.) The columns that are declared heavy are those of highest weight. Step 2 is followed by Step 4, which is applied repeatedly. When Step 4 cannot be applied any longer, Step 2 (followed by Step 4) is applied again, and so on. At a certain stage, when the number of heavy columns is a substantial fraction of the expected size of the final dense matrix, Step 3 (followed by Step 1) is invoked. The selection of the point at which to apply Step 3 is very important, and will be discussed later.

Very often, especially if the initial matrix is fairly dense, or there are not many more equations than unknowns, the final stages of structured Gaussian elimination produce rows that have many ancestors, and so the heavy parts of those rows are quite dense. What was done to counteract this tendency was to first run the algorithm as described above, and then rerun it with two parameters c_1 and c_2 that were set based on the experience of the first run. When the number of heavy columns exceeded c_1, Step 2 was invoked so as to bring this number all the way up to c_2. After this application of Step 2, the sparse part of the matrix usually collapsed very quickly. The results of this step are described below and in Table 3.

The description above is not very precise. The reason is that the various elements of the algorithm can be, and often were, applied in different sequences and with different parameters. The output is fairly sensitive to the choices that are made. No clear guidelines exist as to what the optimal choices are, since it was hard to explore all the possible variations. However, even very suboptimal choices usually lead to small final systems.

The output of the structured Gaussian elimination program is a smaller matrix, which then has to be solved by another method. In our experience (primarily based on data set K), substitution of the results of solving the dense system into the original one gives values for almost all of the original variables in a small number of passes, each of which looks for equations in which only one variable is not yet determined.

Table 2: Structured Gaussian elimination performance – factoring data

Data Set	Number of Equations	Number of Unknowns	No. Equations / No. Unknowns	Size of Dense Matrix	Percent Reduction
A	35,987	35,000	1.03	9,222	73.7
B	52,254	50,001	1.05	12,003	76.0
C	65,518	65,500	1.00	17,251	73.7
D	123,019	106,121	1.16	12,700	88.0
E	82,470	80,015	1.03	36,810	54.0
E1	82,470	75,015	1.10	31,285	58.3
F	25,201	25,001	1.01	11,461	54.2
G	30,268	25,001	1.21	10,835	56.7
H	61,343	30,001	2.04	19,011	36.6
I	102,815	80,001	1.29	32,303	59.6
J	226,688	199,203	1.14	90,979	54.3

Structured Gaussian elimination was very successful on data set K, since it reduced it to set L very quickly (in about 20 minutes for reading the data, roughly the same amount of time for the basic run, and then under an hour to produce the dense set of equations that form set L). It also worked well on the other systems. Table 2 summarizes the performance of structured Gaussian elimination on data sets A through J, and Table 4 does this for sets $K, K0, \ldots, K6$, and M. The size of the dense matrix is the number of unknowns in the reduced system. In each reduced data set, the number of equations exceeded the number of unknowns by 20.

Table 3: Density of heavy matrix resulting from structured Gaussian elimination

Data Set	c_1	c_2	Average Weight of Dense Row
B	–	–	$\geq 2,000$
B	8,000	16,000	456
B	6,000	16,000	486
B	6,000	20,000	149
E	–	–	6,620
E	20,000	50,000	260
E	20,000	60,000	115
$E1$	–	–	6,172
$E1$	20,000	35,000	1,366
$E1$	25,000	40,000	499
K	–	–	1,393
K	3,000	3,400	883
K	3,000	4,000	346
K	2,500	4,000	230
K	2,000	4,500	140
M	–	–	2,602
M	6,750	9,750	295
M	6,750	10,500	212
M	6,750	11,000	177

Obtaining a small set of equations is not satisfactory by itself in many cases, since the new system might be so dense as to be hard to solve. Table 3 presents some data on this point. For example, while set B was reduced to about 12,000 equations, the resulting set was very dense, with each row having on average $\geq 2,000$ non-zero entries. When the number of heavy columns was increased to 20,000 as soon as it exceeded 6,000, the resulting dense matrix had only 149 non-zero entries per row. Similarly, for set E, the standard algorithm produces 36,810 equations, with 6,620 non-zeros each on average. If we only reduce the system to 60,000 equations, the resulting matrix has average row weight of only 115.

Table 3 also shows how the density of final systems derived from discrete logarithm data could be improved. Data set K was reduced to a system in 3,215 unknowns, but that system had, on average, 1,393 non-zero entries per equation. By invoking Step 2 early, before the number of heavy columns reached 3,215, less dense final systems were obtained. Increasing the number of unknowns to 4,500 as soon as 2,000 heavy columns are obtained reduced the density of the smaller system to only 140 non-zero entries per equation. For data set M, a similar order of magnitude decrease in the density of the smaller system was obtained with less than a factor of two increase in the number of unknowns.

Table 4: Structured Gaussian elimination performance – discrete logarithm data

Data Set	Number of Equations	Number of Unknowns	No. Equations / No. Unknowns	Size of Dense Matrix	Percent Reduction
K	288,017	96,321	2.99	3,215	96.7
$K0$	216,105	95,216	2.27	3,850	96.0
$K1$	165,245	93,540	1.77	4,625	95.1
$K2$	144,017	94,395	1.53	9,158	90.3
$K3$	144,432	92,344	1.56	5,534	94.0
$K4$	144,017	89,003	1.62	3,544	96.0
$K5$	115,659	90,019	1.28	6,251	93.1
$K6$	101,057	88,291	1.14	7,298	91.7
M	164,841	94,398	1.75	9,508	90.0

Table 4 presents the results of some experiments that show the influence of extra equations and variations in matrix density. All the runs were performed with the same algorithm on data sets derived from data set K and solved the system modulo 2. The performance of the algorithm on set K that is reported in Table 4 is better than that mentioned before (which reduced it to set L, which has 6,006 unknowns). This is partially due to working modulo 2, but mostly it results from use of somewhat different parameters in the algorithm, and not caring about the density of the final dense matrix.

The results for sets $K2$, $K3$, and $K4$ might seem very counterintuitive, since the densest set $(K4)$ was reduced the most, while the sparsest one $(K2)$, was reduced the least. This appears to be due to the fact that heavy rows tend to have few entries in the sparse part of the matrix. (This has been checked to be the case in the data, and is to be expected, since in the discrete logarithm scheme that was used to derive set K [10], equations come from factoring integers of roughly equal size, so that if there are many prime factors, few of them can be large.) Thus, by selecting the heaviest rows, one makes it easier for structured Gaussian elimination to take advantage of the extreme sparsity of the sparse end of the matrix.

The results obtained with set K may not be entirely characteristic of what one might encounter in other situations because this data set is much larger in the number of unknowns (as well as in the number of equations) than would be optimal for solving the discrete logarithm problem of [10]. If one selected only equations out of K that had roughly the 25,000 unknowns corresponding to the smallest primes and prime elements of smallest norms, set K would have yielded a solution to it. The existence of all the extraneous variables and equations may enable structured Gaussian elimination to yield a better result than it would obtain in more realistic situations.

The results for systems A to J were derived in a non-systematic manner; it is quite likely that much better results can be obtained by different choices of parameters. In the case of system K, and to some extent also systems $K0$ through $K6$, more extensive tests were performed. They were all done with a linear array of length 1.6×10^7 for storage, and with variations only in the applications of Steps 2 and 3. The number of columns to which Step 2 was applied did not seem to have a major influence on the size of the final matrix. On the other hand, the decision of when to apply Step 3 was very important. In all the experiments that were carried out, essentially all the excess rows were dropped at the same time; the effect of spreading out this procedure was not studied. It appeared that the best time to apply Step 3, if one is simply trying to minimize the size of the final system, is when the number of heavy columns reaches the size of the final matrix, since in that case the system tends to collapse very quickly after the application of Step 3. In practice, what this means is that one has to experiment with several different thresholds for when to apply Step 3. Since the generation of the dense equations usually takes several times (and when the dense system is large, many times) longer than structured Gaussian elimination, this does not effect the total running time very much.

On the basis of the experiments that have been performed so far, it appears that the best results are achieved if the point at which Step 3 is applied is chosen so that the steps that follow reduce the matrix very rapidly, without any additional applications of Step 2. For example, the entry for set K in Table 4 was obtained by specifying that Step 3 be applied as soon as the number of heavy columns exceeded 3,200. The resulting matrix collapsed right afterwards. On the other hand, when the excess rows were deleted as soon as the number of heavy columns exceeded 3,150, the algorithm took a lot longer to terminate, resulted in a final matrix with 3,425 columns (but with the density of the final matrix lower than in the other case). At an extreme, set $K2$ (which corresponds to dropping 144,000 rows right at the beginning of the algorithm) resulted in a final matrix of size 9,158. In the case of systems with fewer excess equations (such as set A), some results indicate that it is preferable to apply Step 3 somewhat earlier.

The results reported here are very specific to our implementation. One of the essential features of the program was that it kept the lists of ancestor rows in core memory. Thus the algorithm was constrained most severely by the size of the big linear array, which essentially limited the total number of ancestor rows of the active rows. This had the desirable indirect benefit of producing a relatively sparse final matrix, but it undoubtedly made the algorithm behave quite differently than it would have otherwise. In particular, it must have skewed the comparisons between different data sets (since initially smaller data sets in effect could have more ancestor rows). It might be worthwhile to experiment with various variations of this method.

In the case of data set J (which came from the factorization of F_9), our version of structured Gaussian elimination reduced 199,203 equations to 90,979. A. Lenstra and M. Manasse used their version of the program to reduce set J to about 72,000 equations. Their program did not maintain ancestor lists, but the final matrix was almost completely dense, with about 36,000 non-zero coefficients per equation. Our program produced equations that on average had 7,000 non-zero coefficients. Looking at the output of the program, it appears that as soon as the number of heavy columns exceeded about 70,000, catastrophic collapse of the sparse part of the matrix began. The increase in the size of the heavy part was caused by space restrictions which bounded the size of the ancestor lists. In the F_9 case, since the final matrix was solved using ordinary Gaussian elimination, the decrease in the density of the final matrix that our program gave was probably not worth the increase in size. In other applications, especially when dealing with solving equations modulo large primes, and with sparser initial systems, our strategy is likely to be preferable.

The main conclusion that can be drawn from the results of these experiments is that sparse systems produce much smaller final systems than do denser ones. What is perhaps even more important, however, is that excess equations substantially improve the performance of the algorithm. When one has access to a distributed network of machines with a lot of available computing time, but where solving the matrix might be a bottleneck (due to a need to perform the calculations on a single processor) one can simplify the task substantially by choosing a larger factor base and obtaining more equations. In extreme cases, when using the quadratic sieve, for example, and when only small machines are available, it might even be worthwhile not to use the two large primes variation of A. Lenstra and M. Manasse [13] (which in any case only appears to be useful for integers $> 10^{100}$), or possibly not even the old single large prime variation.

It appears that structured Gaussian elimination should be used as a preliminary step in all linear systems arising from integer factorization and discrete logarithm algorithms. It takes very little time to run, and produces smaller systems, in many cases dramatically smaller. For this method to work best, linear systems ought to be sparse, and, perhaps most important, there should be considerably more equations than unknowns. Producing the extra equations requires more effort, but it does simplify the linear algebra steps.

6. Acknowledgements

The authors thank E. Kaltofen, L. Kaufman, A. Lenstra, M. Manasse, C. Pomerance, and R. Silverman for their comments.

References

[1] G. S. Ammar and W. G. Gragg, Superfast solution of real positive definite Toeplitz systems, *SIAM J. Matrix Anal. Appl.*, **9** (1988), 61-76.

[2] R. R. Bitmead and B. D. O. Anderson, Asymptotically fast solution of Toeplitz and related systems of linear equations, *Lin. Alg. Appl.* **34** (1980), 103-116.

[3] I. F. Blake, R. Fuji-Hara, R. C. Mullin, and S. A. Vanstone, Computing logarithms in fields of characteristic two, *SIAM J. Alg. Disc. Methods* **5** (1984), 276-285.

[4] R. P. Brent, F. G. Gustavson, and D. Y. Y. Yun, Fast solution of Toeplitz systems of equations and computation of Padé approximants, *J. Algorithms* **1** (1980), 259-295.

[5] D. Coppersmith, Fast evaluation of discrete logarithms in fields of characteristic two, *IEEE Trans. on Information Theory* **30** (1984), 587-594.

[6] D. Coppersmith and J. H. Davenport, An application of factoring, *J. Symbolic Computation* **1** (1985), 241-243.

[7] D. Coppersmith, A. Odlyzko, and R. Schroeppel, Discrete logarithms in $GF(p)$, *Algorithmica* **1** (1986), 1-15.

[8] D. Coppersmith and S. Winograd, Matrix multiplication via arithmetic progressions, *Proc. 19th ACM Symp. Theory Comp.* (1987), 1-6.

[9] M. R. Hestenes and E. Stiefel, Methods of conjugate gradients for solving linear systems, *J. Res. Nat. Bureau of Standards* **49** (1952), 409-436.

[10] B. A. LaMacchia and A. M. Odlyzko, Computation of discrete logarithms in prime fields, *Designs, Codes, and Cryptography* **1** (1991), to appear.

[11] C. Lanczos, Solution of systems of linear equations by minimized iterations, *J. Res. Nat. Bureau of Standards* **49** (1952), 33-53.

[12] A. K. Lenstra and M. S. Manasse, Factoring by electronic mail, *Advances in Cryptology: Proceedings of Eurocrypt '89*, J.-J. Quisquater, ed., to be published.

[13] A. K. Lenstra and M. S. Manasse, Factoring with two large primes, *Advances in Cryptology: Proceedings of Eurocrypt '90*, I. Damgard, ed., to be published.

[14] K. S. McCurley, The discrete logarithm problem, in *Cryptography and Computational Number Theory*, C. Pomerance, ed., *Proc. Symp. Appl. Math.*, Amer. Math. Soc., 1990, to appear.

[15] J. L. Massey, Shift-register synthesis and BCH decoding, *IEEE Trans. Information Theory* **IT-15** (1969), 122-127.

[16] W. H. Mills, Continued fractions and linear recurrences, *Math. Comp.* **29** (1975), 173-180.

[17] A. M. Odlyzko, Discrete logarithms in finite fields and their cryptographic significance, *Advances in Cryptology: Proceedings of Eurocrypt '84*, T. Beth, N. Cot, I. Ingemarsson, eds., *Lecture Notes in Computer Science* **209**, Springer-Verlag, NY (1985), 224-314.

[18] C. Pomerance, Analysis and comparison of some integer factoring algorithms, *Computational Methods in Number Theory: Part 1*, H. W. Lenstra, Jr., and R. Tijdeman, eds., *Math. Centre Tract* **154** (1982), Math. Centre Amsterdam, 89-139.

[19] C. Pomerance, Factoring, in *Cryptography and Computational Number Theory*, C. Pomerance, ed., *Proc. Symp. Appl. Math.*, Amer. Math. Soc., 1990, to appear.

[20] C. Pomerance and J. W. Smith, Reduction of large, sparse matrices over a finite field via created catastrophes, manuscript in preparation.

[21] V. Strassen, Gaussian elimination is not optimal, *Numerische Math.* **13** (1969), 354-356.

[22] D. H. Wiedemann, Solving sparse linear equations over finite fields, *IEEE Trans. Information Theory* **IT-32** (1986), 54-62.

[23] J. H. Wilkinson, *The Algebraic Eigenvalue Problem*, Oxford Univ. Press, 1965.

On the Computation of Discrete Logarithms in Class Groups

Extended Abstract

Johannes Buchmann
Stephan Düllmann
FB14-Informatik
Universität des Saarlandes
D-6600 Saarbrücken
West Germany

1 Introduction

In [3] and [1] a new key exchange system was introduced whose security is related to the difficulty of solving the discrete logarithm problem in the class group of imaginary quadratic orders. Subsequently, in [5] and [4] a subexponential algorithm for computing those class groups was presented and it was shown how to use this algorithm and the index-calculus method to calculate discrete logarithms.

In this paper we show how the output of the class group algorithm can be used to simplify the index-calculus algorithm in class groups considerably. This simplification enables us to use a slight modification of our implementation [2] of the algorithm of Hafner and McCurley to calculate discrete logarithms in fairly large class groups. At the end of the paper we will present the results of some experiments which show that the computation of discrete logarithms in class groups is very easy once the class group has been computed by the subexponential algorithm.

2   The idea

Let G be a finite abelian group. Let

$$G = <\gamma_1> \times \ldots \times <\gamma_l> \qquad (1)$$

be a presentation of G as a direct product of cyclic groups. Suppose for $\alpha, \beta \in G$ we wish to find $x \in Z$ with

$$\alpha^x = \beta. \qquad (2)$$

The method we suggest is very simple: Calculate the representations

$$\alpha = \prod_{i=1}^{l} \gamma_i^{a_i} , \beta = \prod_{i=1}^{l} \gamma_i^{b_i}.$$

Then (2) implies

$$\prod_{i=1}^{l} \gamma_i^{x \cdot a_i} = \prod_{i=1}^{l} \gamma_i^{b_i}$$

which is solvable if and only if the system of simultaneous congruences

$$x a_i \equiv b_i \mod g_i \qquad (1 \leq i \leq l) \qquad (3)$$

where $g_i = |<\gamma_i>| \ (1 \leq i \leq l)$ has a solution. This system can be solved by means of the generalized chinese remainder theorem.

3   Application to class groups

Let Cl be the class group of an imaginary quadratic order of discriminant D. The algorithm of Hafner and McCurley starts from a generating set $\{\mathcal{P}_1, \ldots, \mathcal{P}_k\}$ for Cl and subsequently calculates a basis $\{\underline{b}_1, \ldots, \underline{b}_k\} \subseteq Z^k$ for the relation lattice

$$L = \left\{ \underline{e} = (e_1, \ldots, e_k) \in Z^k : \prod_{i=1}^{k} \mathcal{P}_i^{e_i} = 1 \right\}.$$

Then the Smith normal form

$$S = \text{diag}\,(g_1,\ldots,g_l,1,\ldots,1) \in \mathcal{Z}^{k \times k}$$

of $B = (\underline{b}_1,\ldots,\underline{b}_k)$ is calculated, $(g_l > 1)$,

$$S = U^{-1}BV$$

with $U,V \in \text{GL}\,(k,\mathcal{Z})$. The transformation matrices U and U^{-1} are also output of the algorithm. If we put $U = (u_{ij})_{k \times k}$ and

$$G_i = \prod_{j=1}^{k} \mathcal{P}_j^{u_{ij}} \qquad (1 \le i \le l) \tag{4}$$

then

$$Cl =< G_1 > \times \ldots \times < G_l >$$

and

$$|< G_i >| = g_i \qquad (1 \le i \le l).$$

Conversely, if we let $U^{-1} = (u'_{i,j})_{k \times k}$ then we have

$$\mathcal{P}_i = \prod_{j=1}^{l} G_j^{u'_{i,j}} \qquad (1 \le i \le k) \tag{5}$$

Moreover, if we are given a representation of an element in the class group on the generating system $\{\mathcal{P}_1,\ldots,\mathcal{P}_k\}$, then we can use (5) to come up with a representation of that element on the generating system $\{G_1 \ldots,G_l\}$.

Now suppose that we want to solve

$$A^x = B$$

in Cl. In order to apply the ideas of the previous section it is sufficient to determine representations

$$A = \prod_{i=1}^{k} \mathcal{P}_i^{a'_i}, \ B = \prod_{i=1}^{k} \mathcal{P}_i^{b'_i} \tag{6}$$

since those can be transformed into presentations

$$A = \prod_{i=1}^{l} G_i^{a_i} \, , \ B = \prod_{i=1}^{l} G_i^{b_i} . \tag{7}$$

But those presentations are computed as follows: Let $\wp_1, \ldots, \wp_k$ be first degree prime ideals such that $\mathcal{P}_i$ is the equivalence class of $\wp_i$ ($1 \leq i \leq k$) and let $\mathcal{A}$ be the reduced ideal in the class of A. For random exponent vectors $\underline{v} = (v_1, \ldots, v_k) \in [0, \ldots D-1]^k$ we calculate the reduced ideal $\mathcal{A}'$ in the class of $\mathcal{A} \prod_{i=1}^{k} \wp_i^{v_i}$ until we find such an $\mathcal{A}'$ which can be written as $\mathcal{A}' = \prod_{i=1}^{k} \wp_i^{v'_i}$. Then

$$A = \prod_{i=1}^{k} \wp_i^{v'_i - v_i}$$

is the presentation we were looking for. Analogeously, we can find such a representation for a reduced ideal $\mathcal{B}$ in the class of B. If we use all the prime ideals whose norm is bounded by $L[\beta]$ where for $\beta > 0$ we use the notation

$$L[\beta] = \left(\exp \sqrt{\log D \log \log D} \right)^{\beta + o(1)}$$

as usual then each trial takes time $L[0]$ and the probability for being able to factor $\mathcal{A}'$ is $L\left[-\frac{1}{4\beta}\right]$. So the expected running time of the procedure that finds the representation on the original generating system takes time $L[\frac{1}{4\beta}]$. The computation of the representation on the generating system $\{G_1, \ldots, G_l\}$ can be carried out in time $L[\beta]$. The optimal value for β is $\beta = \frac{1}{2}$. Hence the expected running time for each new discrete logarithm problem is $L\left[\frac{1}{2}\right]$.

4 Numerical results

In the tables below we present the results of some experiments concerning the computation of discrete logarithms in class groups of imaginary quadratic fields. In the first table we give the following data:

- discriminant D,

- size k of the generating set $\{\mathcal{P}_1, \ldots, \mathcal{P}_k\}$,

- size l of the generating system $\{G_i, \ldots G_l\}$,

- values of g_i $(1 \leq i \leq l)$,

- class number h.

D	k	l	h	$g_i (1 \leq i \leq l)$
$-(4 \cdot 10^{24} + 4)$	1404	3	1 154 987 161 920	2, 4,
				144 373 395 240
$-(4 \cdot 10^{29} + 4)$	1902	3	436 605 442 139 682	2, 2,
				109 151 360 534 920
$-(4 \cdot 10^{34} + 4)$	2609	4	189 652 590 177 168 096	2, 2, 2,
				23 706 573 772 146 012
$-4 \cdot F_7$	3257	2	17 787 144 930 223 461 408	2,
				8 893 572 465 111 730 704

$(4 \cdot F_7 = 4 \cdot (2^{2^7} + 1) = 1\ 361\ 129\ 467\ 683\ 753\ 853\ 853\ 498\ 429\ 727\ 072\ 845\ 828)$

In the second table we present the running times for the several stages of the algorithm. All timings given here are seconds CPU-time on a Sun 4/60-Sparc Station 1.

- time t_1 to compute the sets $\{G_1, \ldots, G_l\}, \{g_1, \ldots, g_l\}$, the transformation matrices U and V and the class number h using our implementation [2].

- time t_2 to determine the representations (6) for given A and B,

- time t_3 to transform the representation (6) for given A and B into the presentation (7).

- time t_4 to solve the simultaneous congruences (3).

Note that t_2, t_3 and t_4 are very small compared to t_1 and so the effort for each new discrete logarithm problem in the same field is quite small.

D	t_1	t_2	t_3	t_4
$-(4 \cdot 10^{24} + 4)$	3418	5	4	< 1
$-(4 \cdot 10^{29} + 4)$	18 587	21	5	< 1
$-(4 \cdot 10^{34} + 4)$	123 404	37	10	< 1
$-4 \cdot F_7$	511 978	96	18	< 1

References

[1] J. Buchmann, S. Düllmann, H.C. Williams, *On the complexity and efficiency of a new key exchange system*, Proceedings EUROCRYPT'89, to appear.

[2] J. Buchmann, S. Düllmann, *A probabilistic class group and regulator algorithm and its implementation*, Proceedings Colloquium on Computational Number Theory, Debrecen 1989, to appear.

[3] J. Buchmann, H.C. Williams, *A key exchange system based on imaginary quadratic fields*, J. Cryptology 1 (1988), 107-118.

[4] J.L. Hafner, K.S. McCurley, *A rigorous subexponential algorithm for computation of class groups*, Journal AMS, to appear.

[5] K.S. McCurley, *Cryptographic key distribution and computation in class groups*, Proceeding of NATO ASI Number Theory and Applications, Kluwer Academic Publishers 1989, 459-479.

Matrix Extensions of the RSA Algorithm

Chih-Chwen Chuang and James George Dunham
Department of Electrical Engineering
Southern Methodist University
Dallas, TX 75275

Abstract

A new matrix extension of the RSA algorithm is proposed which is based on the Cayley-Hamilton theorem and a one-way function. The security of this algorithm rests upon both that of the RSA algorithm and the one-way function. The computational efficiency of the new algorithm depends on the dimension of the matrix. The most efficient implementation is the 2×2 case in which both encryption and decryption use a single modulo arithmetic multiplication and single evaluation of the one-way function.

1. Introduction

The Rivest-Shamir-Adleman (RSA) [8] algorithm is the best known public-key cryptosystem. Although many papers have discussed efficient implementations of discrete exponentiation algorithms [5-7,9,11], the RSA runs substantially slower than many secret-key cryptosystems such as the Data Encryption Standard (DES) algorithm. V. Varadharajan and R. Odoni [10] proposed a matrix extension of the RSA algorithm, but did not carefully address security issues.

A new matrix extension is proposed that is based upon the Cayley-Hamilton theorem and a one-way function. Under a chosen plaintext attack on the key, the security of the new algorithm is equivalent to that of the RSA algorithm. Under a known plaintext attack on the message, the security of the system rests upon that of the one-way function.

The computational efficiency of the new algorithm depends upon the dimension of the matrix. The most efficient implementation is the 2×2 case in which, both encryption and decryption use a single modulo arithmetic multiplication and single evaluation of the one-way function. Thus these public-key cryptosystems have the potential of a fast implementation.

2. Background

The main tool in computing the matrix RSA scheme will be the Cayley-Hamilton theorem. Let $\mathbf{A}$ be an $n \times n$ matrix. Define

$$P_{\mathbf{A}}(\lambda) \triangleq \det(\lambda \mathbf{I} - \mathbf{A}) = \lambda^n + a_{n-1}\lambda^{n-1} + \cdots + a_0$$

to be the characteristic polynomial of $\mathbf{A}$. Then the Cayley-Hamilton theorem states that

$$P_{\mathbf{A}} = \mathbf{A}^n + a_{n-1}\mathbf{A}^{n-1} + \cdots + a_0\mathbf{I} = 0.$$

One important use of the Cayley-Hamilton theorem is to evaluate powers of $\mathbf{A}$ as

$$\mathbf{A}^k = c_{n-1}\mathbf{A}^{n-1} + \cdots + c_0\mathbf{I} \ . \tag{1}$$

The Cayley-Hamilton theorem holds for matrices whose entries are from any commutative ring such as arithmetic modulo R [3].

The eigenvalues are needed to calculate the coefficients c_i, $i = 0, 1, \cdots, n-1$, in Eq. (1). To simplify the calculation, a triangular matrix is chosen to construct the matrix RSA scheme because the diagonal entries are the eigenvalues of the matrix.

3. Construction of the Cryptosystem

With the above background, the matrix form of the RSA scheme is constructed as follow:

(1) Choose two large strong primes p and q as proposed by Gordon [2] and calculate $R = p \cdot q$;

(2) Choose a large integer e as a public key such that $0 < e < (p-1)(q-1)$ and it is relatively prime to $(p-1)(q-1)$;

(3) Calculate d as a private key from $d \cdot e \equiv 1(mod(p-1)(q-1))$;

(4) Construct an $n \times n$ triangular matrix $\mathbf{A}$ whose diagonal entries are all distinct and the differences between diagonal entries are relatively prime to R;

(5) The entries above (upper triangular matrix) or below (lower triangular matrix) the diagonal are reserved for messages (The details will be described later).

4. Encryption

The encryption algorithm is as follow:

(1) Choose diagonal entries at random subject to the constraints in step (4) stated above;

(2) The number r is a function $g(\cdot)$ computed from the diagonal entries and the function $r \equiv (a_{11}+a_{22}+\cdots+a_{nn})\, mod\ R$ is suggested;

(3) Set up the following equations, calculate the coefficients c_i^e, $i = 0, 1, \cdots, n-1$, and store them in a safe place;

$$a_{11}^e \equiv c_{n-1}^e a_{11}^{n-1} + c_{n-2}^e a_{11}^{n-2} + \cdots + c_0^e$$
$$a_{22}^e \equiv c_{n-1}^e a_{22}^{n-1} + c_{n-2}^e a_{22}^{n-2} + \cdots + c_0^e$$

$$\vdots \tag{2}$$

$$a_{nn}^e \equiv c_{n-1}^e a_{nn}^{n-1} + c_{n-2}^e a_{nn}^{n-2} + \cdots + c_0^e$$

where a_{ii}, $i = 1, 2, \cdots, n$, denotes the ith diagonal entry.

(4) (a) Let $i = 1$ and $j = 2$;

   (b) Calculate $f(r)$ using the number r;

   (c) Calculate $f(r) \oplus m_{ij}$ where m_{ij} is the message and place the result in the $(i, j)^{th}$ entry of the matrix where $\oplus$ denotes bit-by-bit exclusive OR;

   (d) Update $r \equiv r + 1\ mod\ R$ and $j = j + 1$. Repeat steps (b) and (c) until $j = n$;

   (e) Let $i = i + 1$ and $j = i + 1$. Repeat steps (b), (c), and (d) until $i = n - 1$;

(5) Use the calculated coefficients in step (3) and Cayley-Hamilton theorem to encrypt the matrix. Send the ecrypted matrix to the recipients;

(6) Let $r \equiv r+1\ (mod\ R)$ and repeat steps (4) and (5) until all encrypted messages are sent out.

5. Decryption

After the legitimate recipients receive the matrices, the message is decrypted as follow:

(1) Set up the following equations, calculate the coefficients c_i^d, $i = 0, 1, \cdots, n-1$, and store them in a safe place;

$$a_{11}^{ed} \equiv c_{n-1}^{d} a_{11}^{e(n-1)} + c_{n-2}^{d} a_{11}^{e(n-2)} + \cdots + c_{0}^{d}$$
$$a_{22}^{ed} \equiv c_{n-1}^{d} a_{22}^{e(n-1)} + c_{n-2}^{d} a_{22}^{e(n-2)} + \cdots + c_{0}^{d}$$

$$\vdots \qquad\qquad\qquad\qquad\qquad\qquad (3)$$

$$a_{nn}^{ed} \equiv c_{n-1}^{d} a_{nn}^{e(n-1)} + c_{n-2}^{d} a_{nn}^{e(n-2)} + \cdots + c_{0}^{d}$$

where a_{ii}^{e}, $i = 1, 2, \cdots, n$, denotes the ith diagonal entry from the received matrix.

(2) Use the coefficients calculated in step (1) and apply the Cayley-Hamilton theorem to decrypt the matrix;

(3) Calculate $r \equiv (a_{11}+a_{22}+ \cdots +a_{nn}) \bmod R$ and store it in a safe place;

(4) (a) Let $i = 1$ and $j = 2$;

   (b) Calculate $f(r)$ using the number r;

   (c) Calculate the message from

$$f(r) \oplus a_{ij} \equiv f(r) \oplus [f(r) \oplus m_{ij}] \equiv m_{ij} \bmod R$$

   where a_{ij} is the $(i, j)^{th}$ superdiagonal entry of the received matrix;

   (d) Update $r \equiv r + 1 \bmod R$ and $j = j + 1$. Repeat steps (b) and (c) until $j = n$;

   (e) Let $i = i + 1$ and $j = i + 1$. Repeat steps (b), (c), and (d) until $i = n - 1$;

(5) Let $r \equiv r+1 \ (\bmod R)$ and repeat steps (2) and (4) until all messages are received.

Only e, R, and the function $f(\cdot)$ and $g(\cdot)$ are revealed to the public. Knowledge of d, r, a_{ii}, $i = 1, 2, \cdots, n$, and the primes p and q remain secret. The a_{ii}'s may be discarded.

Example 1:

Assume that e, d, and R are 47, 3983, and 7663, respectively and the message are 124 and 150.

A. Encryption

(1) Construct a 2×2 matrix by choosing $a_{11} = 53$ and $a_{22} = 59$.

(2) Set up the system of equations according to Eq. (2) as follow:

$$53^{47} \equiv 2824 \equiv c_0^e + 53\,c_1^e \; mod \; 7663$$

$$59^{47} \equiv 4194 \equiv c_0^e + 59\,c_1^e \; mod \; 7663$$

and solve this system of equations. The answer to c_0^e and c_1^e is 3494 and 5337, respectively.

(3) This step depends on $f(r)$, and we did not specifically define this function. So let us assume that the sequence generated by $f(r)$ is 47 and 1447.

(4) First calculate $f(r) \oplus m$ and fill the result in a_{12}. For example, $47 \oplus 124 = 83$. Then encrypt the first block of message by calculating

$$\mathbf{A}^e \equiv \mathbf{A}^{47} \equiv \begin{bmatrix} 3494 & 0 \\ 0 & 3494 \end{bmatrix} + 5337 \cdot \begin{bmatrix} 53 & 83 \\ 0 & 59 \end{bmatrix} \; mod \; 7663$$

$$\equiv \begin{bmatrix} 2824 & 6180 \\ 0 & 4194 \end{bmatrix} \; mod \; 7663 \; .$$

(5) Encrypt the rest of the message in the same manner as step (4). The encrypted sequence is 6180 and 4194.

B. Decryption

(1) Set up the system of equations according to Eq. (3) as follows:

$$2824^{3983} \equiv 53 \equiv c_0^d + 2824\,c_1\,mod \; 7663$$

$$4194^{3983} \equiv 59 \equiv c_0^d + 4194\,c_1^d \; mod \; 7663$$

and solve this set of equations. The answer to c_0^d and c_1^d is 1260 and 6645, respectively.

(2) Decrypt the first message by calculating the following equation

$$(\mathbf{A}^e)^{3983} \equiv \begin{bmatrix} 1260 & 0 \\ 0 & 1260 \end{bmatrix} + 6645 \cdot \begin{bmatrix} 2824 & 6180 \\ 0 & 4194 \end{bmatrix} \; mod \; 7663$$

$$\equiv \begin{bmatrix} 53 & 83 \\ 0 & 59 \end{bmatrix} \; mod \; 7663 \; .$$

(3) Recover the first message by calculating $f(r) \oplus a_{12}$, while in this case is $m = 47 \oplus 83 = 124$.

(4) Repeat steps (2) and (3), except calculating the sequence of $f(r)$, to recover whole the message as 124 and 150. □

6. Security

The security of the matrix extension scheme is different from that of the original RSA scheme. We have to carefully analyze the structure of matrix $\mathbf{A}$ when $\mathbf{A}$ is raised to the eth power. The structure of $\mathbf{A}^e$ can be formally stated in the following theorem.

Theorem 1: Let $\mathbf{A}$ be an $n \times n$ upper triangular matrix. Denote $a_{i,i+j}$ and $a_{i,i+j}^{(e)}$ as the $(i,i+j)^{th}$ entry and the $(i,i+j)^{th}$ entry after matrix $\mathbf{A}$ raised to the eth power, respectively. Then $a_{i,i+j}^{(e)}$, $1 \le i \le n, 0 \le j \le n-i$, can be represented as

$$a_{i,i+j}^{(e)} = a_{i,i+j} \sum_{i_1=1}^{e} a_{ii}^{e-i_1} a_{i+j,i+j}^{i_1-1}$$

$$+ \sum_{l_1=1}^{j-1} a_{i,i+l_1} a_{i+l_1,i+j} \sum_{i_1=1}^{e-1} \sum_{i_2=i_1}^{e-1} a_{ii}^{e-1-i_2} a_{i+l_1,i+l_1}^{i_2-i_1} a_{i+j,i+j}^{i_1-1}$$

$$+ \sum_{l_1=1}^{j-2} \sum_{l_2=l_1+1}^{j-1} a_{i,i+l_1} a_{i+l_1,i+l_2} a_{i+l_2,i+j} \sum_{i_1=1}^{e-2} \sum_{i_2=i_1}^{e-2} \sum_{i_3=i_2}^{e-2} a_{ii}^{e-2-i_3} a_{i+l_1,i+l_1}^{i_3-i_2} a_{i+l_2,i+l_2}^{i_2-i_1} a_{i+j,i+j}^{i_1-1}$$

$$\vdots$$

$$\qquad\qquad (4)$$

$$+ a_{i,i+1} a_{i+1,i+2} \cdots a_{i+j-1,i+j} \sum_{i_1=1}^{e-j+1} \sum_{i_2=i_1}^{e-j+1} \cdots \sum_{i_j=i_{j-1}}^{e-j+1} a_{ii}^{e-j-i_j+1} a_{i+1,i+1}^{i_j-i_{j-1}} \cdots a_{i+j,i+j}^{i_1-1}$$

where each term

$$\sum_{i_1=1}^{e-k} \sum_{i_2=i_1}^{e-k} \cdots \sum_{i_k=i_{k-1}}^{e-k} \sum_{i_{k+1}=i_k}^{e-k} a_{ii}^{e-k-i_{k+1}+1} a_{i+l_1,i+l_1}^{i_{k+1}-i_k} \cdots a_{i+l_k,i+l_k}^{i_2-i_1} a_{i+j,i+j}^{i_1-1}$$

$$= \frac{\displaystyle\sum_{m=i,i+l_1,i+l_2,\dots,i+l_k,i+j} (-1)^{\delta} a_{mm}^e \prod_{\substack{m_1,m_2=i,i+l_1,i+l_2,\dots,i+l_k,i+j \\ m_1,m_2 \ne m \\ i \le m_1 < m_2 \le i+j}} (a_{m_2 m_2} - a_{m_1 m_1})}{\displaystyle\prod_{\substack{m_1,m_2=i,i+l_1,i+l_2,\dots,i+l_k,i+j \\ i \le m_1 < m_2 \le i+j}} (a_{m_2 m_2} - a_{m_1 m_1})} . \qquad (5)$$

where $k = 1, 2, \cdots, j-1$, and

$$s = \begin{cases} k+1, & m = i \\ k+1+subscript\,(l_{k_i}), & m = i+l_{k_1}, k_1 = 1, 2, \cdots, k \\ 2k+2, & m = i+j \end{cases}.$$

Proof: This can be proved by induction by repeatedly multiplying the matrix by itself or with the aid of Cayley-Hamilton theorem. □

Note that in order to recover the original matrix after it being raised to the eth power, the denominator of Eq. (5) has to be relatively prime to R. The constraint of a 2×2 matrix is that the difference between diagonal entries is relatively prime to R (a 2×2 matrix is computational the most efficient case).

The general form of the numerator of Eq. (5) can be decomposed and rewritten in a different form. This statement can be formally summarized in the following lemma.

Lemma 1: The general form of the numerator of Eq. (5) can be written as the nonlinear combination of the lower order equations with the same form, i.e.

$$\sum_{m=1}^{n} (-1)^S a_{mm}^{ed} \prod_{\substack{m_1,m_2 \\ m_1,m_2 \neq m \\ 1 \leq m_1 < m_2 \leq n}} (a_{m_2 m_2} - a_{m_1 m_1}) \; , \; s = n+m$$

$$= \sum_{m=1}^{n} (-1)^{S_1} a_{mm}^{n-2} [\sum_{\substack{m_1=1 \\ m_1 \neq m}}^{n} (-1)^{s_2} a_{m_1 m_1}^{ed} \prod_{\substack{m_2,m_3=1 \\ m_2,m_3 \neq m_1 \\ 1 \leq m_2 < m_3 \leq n}}^{n} (a_{m_3 m_3} - a_{m_2 m_2})] \tag{6}$$

where $s_1 = n+m-1$ and

$$s_2 = \begin{cases} n+m_1, & m_1 < m \\ n+m_1-1, & m_1 > m \end{cases}.$$

Proof: The proof can be found in [1]. □

In general, cryptosystems are most vulnerable to a chosen-plaintext attack. There is no exception in our case because under a chosen-plaintext attack all the superdiagonal entries of the matrices can be carefully selected by the attacker. The diagonal entries, however, are fixed for a particular set of messages only and are chosen by the sender. So the diagonal entries are secret to everyone except the sender. In this case, the best way of breaking the extension scheme is finding the decryption key d. This can be formally stated in the following theorem.

Theorem 2: Consider a chosen-plaintext attack on the secret key d. If there is a polynomial time algorithm which can find the decryption key d and break the RSA algorithm, then one can find the value of the diagonal and superdiagonal entries and break the extension scheme. Conversely, if there is a polynomial time algorithm which can solve d from the equations which are set up according to Theorem 1 given $0 \equiv a_{ii}^{ed} - a_{ii} \bmod R$, one can break the RSA scheme using the same method.

Proof: The encrypted diagonal entries have exactly the same form as that of the RSA algorithm. So if there exists a polynomial time algorithm which can find the decryption key d and break the RSA algorithm, then this algorithm can also be employed to break the extension scheme. The proof of the first part of the theorem is done.

First define a function $f\left(i,\, i+l_1,\, i+l_2,\, \cdots,\, i+l_k,\, i+j\right)$ as

$$
f\left(i,\, i+l_1,\, i+l_2,\, \cdots,\, i+l_k,\, i+j\right)
$$

$$
\triangleq \frac{\displaystyle\sum_{m=i,i+l_1,\ldots,i+l_k,i+j} (-1)^s\, a_{mm}^{ed} \prod_{\substack{m_1,m_2=i,i+l_1,\cdots,i+l_k,i+j \\ m_1,m_2 \neq m \\ m_1 < m_2}} \left(a_{m_2 m_2} - a_{m_1 m_1}\right)}{\displaystyle\prod_{\substack{m_1,m_2=i,i+l_1,\cdots,i+l_k,i+j \\ i \le m_1 < m_2 \le i+j}} \left(a_{m_2 m_2} - a_{m_1 m_1}\right)}, \tag{7}
$$

where $k = 1, 2, \cdots, j-1$, and

$$
s = \begin{cases} k+1, & m=i \\ k+1+subscript(l_k), & m=i+l_k,\ l_k = 1, 2, \cdots, j-1 \\ 2k+2, & m=i+j \end{cases}.
$$

The difference between Eqs. (4) and (7) is that the encryption key e in Eq. (4) is substituted by ed. Now substitute Eq. (7) into Eq. (7) and rewrite Eq. (4) as

$$a_{i,i+j}^{(ed)} \equiv a_{i,i+j}$$

$$\equiv [a_{i,i+j} f_1(i,i+j)$$

$$+\sum_{l_1=1}^{j-1} a_{i,i+l_1} a_{i+l_1,i+j} \ f_2(i,i+l_1,i+j)$$

$$+\sum_{l_1=1}^{j-2}\sum_{l_2=l_1}^{j-1} a_{i,i+l_1} a_{i+l_1,i+l_2} a_{i+l_2,i+j} \times$$

$$f_3(i,i+l_1,i+l_2,i+j)$$

$$\vdots \tag{8}$$

$$+a_{i,i+1} a_{i+1,i+2} \cdots a_{i+j-1,i+j} \times$$

$$f_j(i,i+1,\cdots,i+j)] \ mod \ R \ .$$

It is clear that if Eq. (8) holds, then $f_1(i, i+j) \equiv 1 \ mod \ R$ and $f_k(i, i+l_1, \cdots, i+l_k, i+j) \equiv 0 \ mod \ R$, $k = 1, 2, \cdots, j$. Under this condition, $f_1(i, i+j) \equiv 1 \ mod \ R$ can be explicitly written as:

$$0 \equiv (a_{i+j,i+j}^{ed} - a_{i+j,i+j}) - (a_{ii}^{ed} - a_{ii}) \ mod \ R \ . \tag{9}$$

The trivial solution to Eq. (9) is that d satisfies both

$$0 \equiv a_{ii}^{ed} - a_{ii} \ mod \ R \tag{10}$$

and

$$0 \equiv a_{i+j,i+j}^{ed} - a_{i+j,i+j} \ mod \ R \ . \tag{11}$$

Eqs. (10) and (11) have exactly the same form as that of the RSA algorithm. As discussed earlier, the solution to Eqs. (10) and (11) is a subset of the solution of Eq. (9). So if there exists a polynomial time algorithm which can find solutions to d given Eqs. (10) and (11) by solving Eq. (9), then this algorithm can also be employed to find the decryption key d of the RSA algorithm in the same manner.

If $f_k(i, i+l_1, \cdots, i+j) \equiv 0 \bmod R$ holds, Lemma 4.1 can be employed several times until the right hand side of Eq. (8) has the following form:

$$\sum_{m=0,l_1,\ldots,j} sgn_1\, a_{mm}^{k-2} \cdots \sum_{\substack{m_{k-2}=0,l_1,\ldots,j \\ m_{k-2}\neq m,m_1,\ldots,m_{k-3}}} sgn_{k-1}\, a_{m_{k-2}m_{k-2}} \times$$

$$\sum_{\substack{m_{k-1},m_{k-1},l_1,\ldots,j \\ m_{k-1},m_k\neq m,m_1,\ldots,m_{k-2} \\ m_k > m_{k-1}}} \left(a_{m_k m_k}^{ed} - a_{m_{k-1}m_{k-1}}^{ed} \right). \tag{12}$$

where sgn_i, $i = 1, 2, \cdots, k$ denotes the sign with respect to each coefficient. The last summation term of Eq. (12) can be rewritten as:

$$\sum_{\substack{m_{k-1},m_{k-1},l_1,\ldots,j \\ m_{k-1},m_k\neq m,m_1,\ldots,m_{k-2} \\ m_k > m_{k-1}}} \left(a_{m_k m_k}^{ed} - a_{m_{k-1}m_{k-1}}^{ed} \right)$$

$$= \sum_{\substack{m_{k-1},m_{k-1},l_1,\ldots,j \\ m_{k-1},m_k\neq m,m_1,\ldots,m_{k-2} \\ m_k > m_{k-1}}} \left(a_{m_k m_k}^{ed} - a_{m_k m_k} \right) - \left(a_{m_{k-1}m_{k-1}}^{ed} - a_{m_{k-1}m_{k-1}} \right) \tag{13}$$

Eq. (13) is similar to Eq. (9), so the solution of d subject to $a_{m_k m_k}^{ed} \equiv a_{m_k m_k} \bmod R$ and $a_{m_{k-1}m_{k-1}}^{ed} \equiv a_{m_{k-1}m_{k-1}} \bmod R$ is a subset solution to Eq. (13). If there is a polynomial time algorithm which can solve Eq. (13) given Eqs. (10) and (11) to find solutions to d, then the same algorithm can be employed to break the RSA algorithm by finding its decryption key as in the proof of Theorem 2. This concludes the second part of the theorem. □

Clearly, from Theorem 2, finding the encryption key d from the extension scheme is as hard as finding it from the RSA scheme. Up to this point, it was assumed that all the information except the decryption key d is known to the attacker. Now assume that the attacker chooses his own messages and sends them to his partner. After receiving the message, his partner chooses the diagonal entries and extra messages and then sends the encrypted messages back to the attacker. Under this condition, the attacker has control only part of the messages and he tries to determine the remaining messages. The security of this scheme under a chosen-plaintext attack on the message can be summarized in the following theorem.

Theorem 3: Under a chosen-plaintext attack on the message, the extension scheme is secure when $f(\cdot)$ is a one-way function and satisfies the following property:

(P1) Let $r \equiv \sum_{i=1}^{n} a_{ii} \ mod \ R$. It is infeasible to compute $f(r + I \ mod \ R)$ given $f(r + i \ mod \ R), 0 \leq i < I$.

Proof: In order to analyze this problem, let us first set up two equations:

$$a_{11}^{e} \equiv c_0 + c_1 a_{11} + \cdots + c_{n-1} a_{11}^{n-1} \ mod \ R$$
$$a_{22}^{e} \equiv c_0 + c_1 a_{22} + \cdots + c_{n-1} a_{22}^{n-1} \ mod \ R$$

$$\vdots \tag{14}$$

$$a_{nn}^{e} \equiv c_0 + c_1 a_{nn} + \cdots + c_{n-1} a_{nn}^{n-1} \ mod \ R$$

and

$$a_{i,i+j}^{(e)} \equiv a_{i,i+j} \cdot g(i, i+j) + \sum_{l=1}^{j-1} a_{i,i+l} a_{i+l,i+j} \cdot g(i, i+l, i+j)$$

$$+ \sum_{l_1=1}^{j-2} \sum_{l_2=l_1+1}^{j-1} a_{i,i+l_1} a_{i+l_1,i+l_2} a_{i+l_2,i+j} \cdot g(i, i+l_1, i+l_2, i+j)$$

$$\vdots \tag{15}$$

$$+ \sum_{l_1=1}^{1} \sum_{l_2=l_1+1}^{2} \cdots \sum_{l_{j-1}=l_{j-2}+1}^{j-1} a_{i,i+l_1} a_{i+l_1,i+l_2} \cdots a_{i+l_{j-1},i+j} \times$$

$$g(i, i+l_1, \cdots, i+l_{j-1}, i+j) \quad , j=1,2,...,n-i .$$

According to Theorem 1, $g(\cdot)$ is a function of diagonal entries which are constant for a particular set of messages and $a_{i+k_1,i+k_2}$ can be represented as:

$$a_{i+k_1,i+k_2} \equiv f(\sum_{i=1}^{n} a_{ii} + L \ mod \ R) \oplus m_{i+k_1,i+k_2}, \tag{16}$$

where

$$L = i+k_2 - 1 + \frac{2n(i+k_1) - 2n - (i+k_1)^2 + (i+k_1)}{2} + \frac{n(n-1)}{2} \cdot (k-1)$$

for the kth matrix.

Suppose there exists a polynomial time algorithm that can solve Eq. (15) given $m_{i+k_1, i+k_2}$ and uniquely determine the value of $g(\cdot)$. Consequently, the value of $f(\cdot)$ can be calculated. Since $f(\cdot)$ is a one-way function, it is infeasible to compute $\sum_{i=1}^{n} a_{ii} \bmod R$ from $f(\cdot)$. Without knowing $\sum_{i=1}^{n} a_{ii} \bmod R$, it is impossible to calculate the value of subsequent $f(\cdot)$'s. Thus, the enemy still cannot compute the remaining messages. In general, there is more than one block of known message available. In order to prevent this scheme from being broken under this condition, $f(\cdot)$ has to satisfy a tighter restriction, i.e., Property (P1).

System of equations of Eq. (14) can be added up and represented as

$$\sum_{i=1}^{n} a_{ii} \equiv c_1^{-1} \sum_{i=1}^{n} a_{ii}^{e} - (n \cdot c_0 + c_2 \sum_{i=1}^{n} a_{ii}^2 + \cdots + c_{n-1} \sum_{i=1}^{n} a_{ii}^{n-1}) c_1^{-1} \bmod R \qquad (17)$$

One can break the scheme under this condition if $\sum_{i=1}^{n} a_{ii} \bmod R$ is known. So $\sum_{i=1}^{n} a_{ii} \bmod R$ can be considered as one variable and Eq. (17) can be rewritten as

$$r \equiv c_1^{-1} \sum_{i=1}^{n} a_{ii}^{e} - c_1^{-1} \cdot k \bmod R \qquad (18)$$

There are three unknowns r, k, and c_1 in Eqs. (16) and (18). It is practically impossible to enumerate the value of r for testing given $\sum_{i=1}^{n} a_{ii}^{e}$ is fixed and known because there are too many possible combinations. So it is impossible to uniquely determine r from both Eqs. (16) and (18) simultaneously. Thus the scheme is still secure even if there exists a polynomial time algorithm that can uniquely solve for $g(\cdot)$ and $a_{i+k_1, i+k_2}$ from Eq. (16). This concludes the proof of this theorem. $\square$

7. Computational Complexity

The main issue of this section is to show that this scheme has much faster encryption and decryption algorithms than that of the RSA scheme. The encryption and decryption algorithms were discussed in sections 3, 4, and 5. Now the speed with which one can raise the matrix $\mathbf{A}$ to the eth (for encryption) or to the dth (for decryption) power is considered. The encryption and decryption algorithms include two parts. The first part is to set up the Eq. (2) or Eq. (3) and calculate the coefficients c_i^{e} and c_i^{d}. The second part of the algorithm is to calculate the matrix raised to the high power.

A. Precalculation of Coefficients

The decryption algorithm has exactly the same computational complexity as that of the encryption algorithm, so here we only discuss the computational complexity of encryption algorithm. Raising a_{ii} to the eth power requires at most $2\left\lfloor \log_2 e \right\rfloor$ multiplications [4]. Thus, to set up Eq. (2) requires at most

$$2n\left\lfloor \log_2 e \right\rfloor + n(n-2) \tag{19}$$

multiplications. There are two ways to solve Eq. (2). One is using the Cramer's rule and the other is using the Vandermonde algorithm. If Cramer's rule is used to calculate the coefficient c_{ii}^{ℓ}, then this stage needs at most

$$2n\left\lfloor \log_2 e \right\rfloor + n(n-2) + (n+1)\sum_{i=1}^{n-1}(\prod_{j=n-i+1}^{n} j) + 15\left\lfloor \log_{10} R \right\rfloor \tag{20}$$

multiplications and

$$(n+1)\sum_{i=1}^{n-1}[(\prod_{j=n-i}^{n} j)/(n-i+1)] + 10\left\lfloor \log_{10} R \right\rfloor \tag{21}$$

additions. If one observes Eq. (2) carefully, one notices that it is a Vandermonde system, hence the Vandermonde algorithm can be used to calculate the coefficients. This algorithm has a distinct computational advantage when the size of the matrix is large (e.g. $n \geq 7$). This stage needs at most

$$2n\left\lfloor \log_2 e \right\rfloor + n(n-2) + \frac{n(n-1)}{2}(15\left\lfloor \log_{10} R \right\rfloor + 3) \tag{22}$$

multiplications and

$$\frac{n(n-1)}{2}(10\left\lfloor \log_{10} R \right\rfloor + 3) \tag{23}$$

additions.

B. Encryption and Decryption

Eq. (1) shows that one only has to calculate $\mathbf{A}^2, \mathbf{A}^3, \cdots, \mathbf{A}^{n-1}$ and multiply them with the corresponding coefficients and add them together. This stage takes

$$\frac{n(n+1)(n+2)(n-2)}{6} + \frac{n(n+1)(n-1)}{2} \tag{24}$$

multiplications and

$$\frac{n(n+1)(n-1)(n-2)}{6} + \frac{n(n+1)(n-2)}{2} \tag{25}$$

additions. In fact the diagonal entries are fixed for a particular set of messages and the encrypted diagonal entries are not functions of the superdiagonal entries. So only the superdiagonal entries from the second matrix on need to be calculated. Thus this stage can speed up the encryption and decryption even more. In this case, we can reduce the computational complexity to

$$\frac{n(n+1)(n+2)(n-2)}{6} + \frac{n(n-1)^2}{2} \tag{26}$$

multiplications and

$$\frac{n(n+1)(n-1)(n-2)}{6} + \frac{n(n-1)(n-2)}{2} \tag{27}$$

additions.

We now give an example to illustrate the computational advantage of this scheme.

Example 2: Suppose one chooses two large primes p and q such that $R = p \cdot q$ is a 200-digit number, i.e. $\lfloor \log_{10} R \rfloor = 200$. We assume that the block lengths of each message are the same in both the RSA scheme and the extension scheme. The RSA scheme needs at most $2 \lceil \log_2 e \rceil$ multiplications for encryption. The RSA algorithm and the 2×2 matrix can encrypt or decrypt one block of message, and the 3×3 matrix can encrypt 3 blocks of messages each time, respectively. In this example, we compare how efficiently one can encrypt 1 block of message using the RSA algorithm, 2×2 matrix, and 3×3 matrix. The results of the comparison are listed in the following table.

The results show that the extension scheme has more computational advantage with a smaller size and large encryption key over the RSA scheme. □

Table 1. The computational complexity comparison
of RSA, 2×2 matrix, and 3×3 matrix.

	RSA	Pre-computation				Post-computation			
		2×2 matrix		3×3 matrix		2×2 matrix		3×3 matrix	
	×	×	+	×	+	×	+	×	+
$\left\lfloor \log_2 e \right\rfloor = 50$	100	3205	2003	3390	2020	1	0	$\dfrac{16}{3}$	$\dfrac{7}{3}$
$\left\lfloor \log_2 e \right\rfloor = 100$	200	3405	2003	3690	2020	1	0	$\dfrac{16}{3}$	$\dfrac{7}{3}$
$\left\lfloor \log_2 e \right\rfloor = 150$	300	3605	2003	3990	2020	1	0	$\dfrac{16}{3}$	$\dfrac{7}{3}$
$\left\lfloor \log_2 e \right\rfloor = 200$	400	3805	2003	4210	2020	1	0	$\dfrac{16}{3}$	$\dfrac{7}{3}$

8. Conclusion

A new way of extending the RSA algorithm using a triangular matrix and a
one-way function was proposed. The security of this scheme has been shown to
be equivalent to that of the RSA algorithm under a chosen plaintext attack on
the key and a ciphertext only attack. Under a known plaintext attack on the
message, the security of this scheme rests on the security of the RSA algorithm as
well as the one-way function $f(\cdot)$. The fast encryption and decryption algorithms
of this scheme are based on the Cayley-Hamilton theorem. The speed of this algorithm depends on both the dimension of the matrix and the capability of evaluating the one-way function. The most efficient implementation is the 2×2 case in
which both encryption and decryption use a single modulo arithmetic multiplication and single evaluation of the one-way function.

In practice, the first block of the message can be transmitted using the RSA
scheme and then the remaining message can be encrypted by calculating
$f(m_i) \oplus m_{i+1}$. The extension scheme of the RSA algorithm was developed
independently from the above system. However, the matrix version of the RSA
algorithm turned out to have a similar form as that of the above system.

The criteria for choosing the one-way function is the efficiency of evaluating
this function. A question remains as to which one-way function should be chosen.

155

Does this function has to be a one-way function in order to keep this scheme secure. This topic requires further investigation.

Acknowledgements

We would like to express our sincere gratitude and appreciation to Dr. Don Coppersmith at IBM Thomas J. Watson Laboratory and Dr. Andrew Odlyzko at AT&T Bell Laboratory for their invaluable suggestions during our research.

References

[1] C.C. Chuang, *Matrix Extension of the RSA Algorithm, Ph.D. Dissertation*, SMU, Dallas, Texas, 1990.

[2] J. Gordon, "Strong primes are easy to find," *Proceedings of Crypto'87*, pp. 216-223.

[3] R. A. Horn, and C. A. Johnson, *Matrix Analysis*, Cambridge University Press, NY, 1985.

[4] D. E. Knuth, *The Art of Computer Programming, Vol. 2: Seminumerical Algorithms*, Addison-Wesley, Reading, 2nd ed., 1981.

[5] R.F. Rieden, J.B. Snyder, R.J. Widman, and W.J. Barnard, "A two-chip implementation of the RSA public-key encryption algorithm," *GOMAC* (Government Microcircuit Applications Conference), (Orlando, FL), pp. 24-27 Nov. 1982.

[6] R.L. Rivest, "A description of a single-chip implementation of the RSA cipher," *Lambda*, vol.1, no. 3, pp. 14-18, Fall 1980.

[7] R.L. Rivest, "RSA chips (past/present/future)," *Eurocrypt'84*, pp. 159-165.

[8] R.L. Rivest, A. Shamir, and L. Adleman, "A method for obtaining digital signatures and public-key cryptosystems," *Comm. ACM*, vol. 21, pp. 120-126, 1978.

[9] G.J Simmons, "High speed arithmetic utilizing redundant number systems," *National Telecommunications Conf.* (Houston,TX), pp. 49.3.1-2, Nov.30-Dec. 4, 1980.

[10] V. Varadharajan, and R. Odoni, "Extension of RSA cryptosystems to matrix rings," *Cryptologia*, vol. 9, no. 2, pp. 140-153, April, 1985.

[11] K. Yiu and K. Peterson, "A single-chip VLSI implementation of the discrete exponential public key distribution system," *GOMAC* (Government Microcircuit Applications Conference), (Orlando, FL), pp. 18-23, Nov. 1982.

Constructing Elliptic Curve Cryptosystems
in Characteristic 2

Neal Koblitz

Dept. of Mathematics, Univ. of Washington, Seattle WA 98195

1. Introduction

Since the group of an elliptic curve defined over a finite field $\mathbf{F}_q$ was proposed for Diffie–Hellman type cryptosystems in [7] and [15], some work on implementation has been done using special types of elliptic curves for which the order of the group is trivial to compute ([2], [13]). A consideration which discourages the use of an arbitrary elliptic curve is that one needs Schoof's algorithm [16] to count the order of the corresponding group, and this algorithm, in addition to being rather complicated, has running time $O(\log^9 q)$ for an elliptic curve defined over $\mathbf{F}_q$. Thus, in applications of elliptic curves where one needs extremely large q — for example, the original version of the elliptic curve primality test ([4], [11]) — this algorithm is too time-consuming.

However, elliptic curve cryptosystems seem to be secure at present provided only that the order of the group has a prime factor of about 40 digits, and in this range Schoof's algorithm is feasible. The purpose of this paper is to describe how one can search for suitable elliptic curves with random coefficients using Schoof's algorithm. We treat the important special case of characteristic 2, where one has certain simplifications in some of the algorithms.

Acknowledgments. I wish to thank Scott Vanstone, Gordon Agnew, Alfred Menezes, and Joe Buhler for valuable discussions.

2. Motivation for constructing elliptic curve cryptosystems with variable coefficients

At present no subexponential algorithm is known for the discrete logarithm problem on a general elliptic curve: the "baby step – giant step" algorithm (which applies in any group) requires time fully exponential in the length of the largest prime factor of the order of the group. In other words, suppose that we have a nonsupersingular elliptic curve E defined over a finite field whose order $|E|$ is divisible, say, by a 40-digit prime l; you give me a point P on E (whose order is divisible by l); and I multiply P by a secret integer k and give you the result $Q = kP$. Then, with our present level of theoretical knowledge and technology, you will be unable to find k from Q. This is because no algorithm faster than the baby step – giant step algorithm is known for such an elliptic curve.

This situation is in stark contrast with that of the classical discrete logarithm problem in the multiplicative group of a finite field. There, "index calculus" type subexponential probabilistic algorithms have been known for some time, and work by D. Coppersmith (in small characteristic) and D. Gordon (over a prime field, using the number field sieve) make it reasonable to expect that the time to solve the discrete log in $\mathbf{F}_q^\times$ is bounded by $L_q[1/3, c] = \exp\left((c+o(1))((\log q)^{1/3}(\log\log q)^{2/3})\right)$ for a fairly small constant c.

For this reason, it seems that discrete log cryptosystems based on the group of an elliptic curve are secure over much smaller fields than those based on the multiplicative group of the field. We also note that there is much more choice available when working with elliptic curves: for fixed q one has only one group $\mathbf{F}_q^\times$, but one obtains many groups E by varying the coefficients of the defining equation of the elliptic curve.

Recently, S. A. Vanstone's group at the University of Waterloo implemented a cryptosystem using the elliptic curve $y^2 + y = x^3$ over $\mathbf{F}_q$ with $q = 2^{593}$ [13]. This elliptic curve has very special properties — complex multiplication by cube roots of unity, and supersingularity — and this means that for $q \equiv 2 \pmod 3$ one has the simple formula $|E| = q + 1$. In the present paper we discuss using a variable elliptic curve, i.e., taking advantage of the availability of many different E over a fixed field $\mathbf{F}_q$, $q = 2^n$.

From a practical point of view, there are both pros and cons in using random elliptic curves over $\mathbf{F}_{2^n}$ rather than the special one in [13]. On the positive side, we obtain the added security of being able to change the curve periodically. Moreover, in order to break the cipher one would need an algorithm for solving the discrete log problem on an arbitrary elliptic curve, rather than just on a particular elliptic curve with special structure (complex multiplication by cube roots of unity and supersingularity). Very recently, this advantage has become especially significant because of [14], in which Menezes, Okamoto and Vanstone obtained a reduction of the discrete logarithm on an elliptic curve to the discrete logarithm in a finite field, a reduction which leads to a subexponential algorithm for the discrete log on a supersingular elliptic curve but not on a nonsupersingular curve (which is the general case).

(It should be noted, however, that to avoid the Menezes–Okamoto–Vanstone reduction one does not have to use random curves and Schoof's algorithm. There are families of nonsupersingular curves whose orders are easy to compute, for example:

(1) the curve $y^2 + xy = x^3 + x^2 + 1$ over $\mathbf{F}_{2^n}$ for variable n has $|E| = \left| \left(\frac{1+\sqrt{-7}}{2} \right)^n - 1 \right|^2$;

(2) the curve $y^2 + y = x^3$ over $\mathbf{F}_p$ for variable $p \equiv 1 \pmod 3$ has $|E| = p + 1 + a$, where a is given by $a^2 + 3b^2 = 4p$ with integers $a \equiv 1 \pmod 3$ and $b \equiv 0 \pmod 3$.)

On the negative side, when using a random curve, in addition to the burden of having to apply Schoof's algorithm to find a case when the number of points is divisible by a ≥ 40-digit prime, the actual computations on a random curve are somewhat slower than on the special curve $y^2 + y = x^3$ used in [13]. Suppose we want to compute the multiple of a point by an integer that contains $n + 1$ bits, of which $m + 1$ bits are 1. In the case of the curve $y^2 + y = x^3$, this computation takes only $9m$ multiplications in the field. But in the case of the curve $y^2 + xy = x^3 + a_2 x^2 + a_6$ (see §3 below for details on the notation), we need $16m + 4n$ multiplications. A second annoyance is that in the general case one always has to carry along both the x- and y-coordinates of points, whereas in the case of the special curve one can simply keep track of one bit of y, and at any time reconstruct y from that bit and the corresponding x, without performing any multiplications (see [13]).

An implementation of a random–curve cryptosystem might work as follows. A special–purpose chip is set up which does arithmetic in a fixed large extension of $\mathbf{F}_2$ and which can compute on an elliptic curve over the field once the coefficients are given to it. Once a week, a computer generates a new random coefficient a_6 such that the order of either the curve $y^2 + xy = x^3 + a_6$ or the "twisted" curve $y^2 + xy = x^3 + a_2 x^2 + a_6$, where a_2 is any element of the field having trace 1 ($a_2 = 1$ will do if the field has odd degree over $\mathbf{F}_2$), is divisible by a large prime. This involves finding the t from Schoof's algorithm (see §4 below) for the first curve — then the first curve has $2^n + 1 - t$ points and the twisted curve has $2^n + 1 + t$ points — and verifying (perhaps by the elliptic curve factorization algorithm) that one of these two numbers does not factor completely into primes of fewer than 40 digits. Then for the week that follows the coefficient pair (a_2, a_6) becomes part of everyone's public key, i.e., it is read into each of the special–purpose chips that are programmed to perform key exchanges, signatures, message transmission, etc., using computations on a given elliptic curve.

3. Elliptic curves in characteristic 2

An elliptic curve E over an arbitrary field K can be defined as the set of solutions of an equation

$$y^2 + a_1 xy + a_3 y = x^3 + a_2 x^2 + a_4 x + a_6 \qquad (1)$$

(where $a_i \in K$ and the curve has no singularities), together with the "point at infinity O," which is the identity element of the abelian group E. Here the subscripts of the coefficients indicate their "weights" when they are regarded as indeterminates; the weights are chosen so that the equation (1) is homogeneous if x and y are given weights 2 and 3, respectively.

If char $K \neq 2$, one can use a linear change of variables to reduce the equation to a form in which $a_1 = a_3 = 0$. However, we shall be interested in the case char $K = 2$. In that case it is easy to see that E has a nontrivial point of order 2 (i.e., $|E|$ is even) if and only if $a_1 \neq 0$: in fact, the point with x-coordinate $x = a_3/a_1$ is the point of order 2. Such a curve is called "nonsupersingular" (equivalently, its j-invariant is nonzero). In that case, using a linear change of variables, without loss of generality we may assume that the equation of E is in the form

$$y^2 + xy = x^3 + a_2 x^2 + a_6. \qquad (2a)$$

The other possibility is that E is "supersingular," i.e., any of the following equivalent conditions holds: (i) $a_1 = 0$, (ii) $|E|$ is odd, (iii) the j-invariant of E is zero. In this case, using a linear change of variables, without loss of generality we may suppose that the equation of E is in the form

$$y^2 + a_3 y = x^3 + a_4 x + a_6. \qquad (2b)$$

In characteristic 2, the addition law $P_{x_3,y_3} = P_{x_1,y_1} \oplus P_{x_2,y_2}$ is given by the following rules in the nonsupersingular case (equation (2a)) and the supersingular case (equation (2b)), respectively: (1) the additive inverse of $P_{x,y}$ is $-P_{x,y} = P_{x,y+x}$ (respectively, $-P_{x,y} = P_{x,y+a_3}$); (2) if $P_{x_1,y_1} \neq \pm P_{x_2,y_2}$, then

$$x_3 = x_1 + x_2 + a_2 + (y_1 + y_2)/(x_1 + x_2) + (y_1^2 + y_2^2)/(x_1^2 + x_2^2),$$
$$y_3 = y_1 + x_3 + (x_1 + x_3)(y_1 + y_2)/(x_1 + x_2); \qquad (3a)$$

(respectively,

$$x_3 = x_1 + x_2 + (y_1^2 + y_2^2)/(x_1^2 + x_2^2),$$

$$y_3 = y_1 + a_3 + (x_1 + x_3)(y_1 + y_2)/(x_1 + x_2);)$$ (3b)

and (3) if $P_{x_1,y_1} = P_{x_2,y_2}$, then

$$x_3 = (x_1^4 + a_6)/x_1^2, \qquad y_3 = y_1 + x_3 + (x_1^2 + y)(x_1 + x_3)/x_1; \qquad (4a)$$

(respectively,

$$x_3 = (x_1^4 + a_4^2)/a_3^2, \qquad y_3 = y_1 + a_3 + (x_1^2 + a_4)(x_1 + x_3)/a_3.) \qquad (4b)$$

4. Schoof's algorithm

A detailed description of the algorithm is in [16]. Here we shall give only an outline. By Hasse's theorem, the number of points on an elliptic curve E over the field of $q = 2^n$ elements is of the form $N = q + 1 - t$, where $|t| \leq 2\sqrt{q}$. Schoof's algorithm determines N modulo l for a bunch of small primes l. If we run through enough l so that $\prod l > 4\sqrt{q}$, then N can be uniquely determined by the Chinese Remainder Theorem.

For $l > 2$ one determines N modulo l by looking at the points of order l with coordinates in field extensions of $\mathbf{F}_q$. It turns out that N modulo l is determined by the action of the map $(x, y) \mapsto (x^q, y^q)$ on the set of points of order l. For example, suppose that the map $(x, y) \mapsto (x^q, y^q)$ leaves some such point fixed. Then this means that there is a point of order l whose coordinates are in $\mathbf{F}_q$, i.e., our original group of points with $\mathbf{F}_q$ coordinates has a nontrivial element of order l. In that case $N \equiv 0 \pmod{l}$. More generally, the value of N modulo l is determined by how the q-th power map permutes the points of order l.

Thus, a basic role in Schoof's algorithm is played by the so-called "division polynomials," which characterize the points P (with coordinates in extensions of $\mathbf{F}_q$) for which lP is the identity.

5. Division polynomials in characteristic 2

Before specializing to characteristic 2, we recall that in the general case of an elliptic curve given by (1), the division polynomial $f_n \in \mathbf{Z}[x, y, a_1, a_2, a_3, a_4, a_6]$ is a nonzero homogeneous polynomial of total weight $n^2 - 1$ (recall that x has weight 2, y has weight 3, a_i has weight i) such that for a nonzero point $P_{x,y}$ on the elliptic curve one has $nP_{x,y} = O$ ("$P_{x,y}$ is a point of order n") if and only if $f_n(x, y) = 0$ (where for fixed $a_i \in K$ we consider f_n as a polynomial in $K[x, y]$). These polynomials satisfy the following fundamental relations:

Proposition 1. *For* $m > n \geq 2$

$$f_{m+1}f_{m-1}f_n^2 - f_{n+1}f_{n-1}f_m^2 = f_{m+n}f_{m-n}. \tag{5}_{m,n}$$

For the proof, see [10].

Proposition 2. *For* $n \geq 1$,

$$f_{2n} = (f_2 \circ n)f_n^4, \tag{6}$$

where $f_2 \circ n$ *denotes the function* f_2 *applied to the* x- *and* y-*coordinates of* $nP_{x,y}$.

The **proof** follows the same method as the proof of $(5)_{m,n}$ in [10]. That is, (6) will hold as a formal identity in $\mathbf{Z}[x, y, a_1, a_2, a_3, a_4, a_6]$ — and hence will hold over any field and with any stipulated values of the a_i — provided that it holds over the complex numbers. To prove (6) as an identity over $\mathbf{C}$, one observes that f_{2n} has a simple zero at all non-lattice points of order $2n$ and a pole of order $4n^2 - 1$ at the lattice points; f_n^4 has a zero of order 4 at all non-lattice points of order n and a pole of order $4n^2 - 4$ at the lattice points; and $f_2 \circ n$ has a simple zero at all points of order $2n$ which are not of order n and a triple pole at all points of order n. Thus, both sides of (6) have the same zeros and poles, and so are equal up to a constant factor, which is easily checked to be 1. This completes the proof.

In the case when char $K = 2$ and E has the equation (2a), the first few f_n are:

$$f_1 = 1, \quad f_2 = x, \quad f_3 = x^4 + x^3 + a_6, \quad f_4 = x^6 + x^2 a_6. \tag{7a}$$

In the supersingular case (2b), the first few f_n are:

$$f_1 = 1, \quad f_2 = a_3, \quad f_3 = x^4 + a_3^2 x + a_4^2, \quad f_4 = a_3^5. \tag{7b}$$

Remark. Using the expression for f_4 in (7a), we see that the number of points on the elliptic curve (2a) is divisible by 4 if and only if the trace of a_2 from $K = \mathbf{F}_{2^n}$ to $\mathbf{F}_2$ is zero. Namely, since $f_4 = x^2(x^4 + a_6)$, the two nontrivial points of order 4 are those with x-coordinate $x = a_6^{2^{n-2}}$. Their y-coordinates are in K if and only if (2a) can be solved for y with this value of x. Using the change of variables $y \mapsto xy$, we see that the y-coordinates are in K if and only if $x + a_2 + a_6 x^{-2}$ with $x = a_6^{2^{n-2}}$

has zero trace. But $a_6 x^{-2} = a_6^{2^{n-1}}$ is a conjugate of x, and so the first and third terms in the trinomial have the same trace. Thus, we have a nontrivial point of order 4 if and only if the trace of a_2 is zero.

Returning to the general case of arbitrary characteristic, we see that for $n \geq 5$ the following special cases of Proposition 1 can be used to compute f_n recursively:

$$f_{2n+1} = f_{n+2}f_n^3 - f_{n-1}f_{n+1}^3; \qquad (5)_{n+1,n}$$

$$f_2 f_{2n} = f_{n+2}f_n f_{n-1}^2 - f_{n-2}f_n f_{n+1}^2. \qquad (5)_{n+1,n-1}$$

From this it is easy to see that f_n can be expressed as a homogeneous polynomial in f_2, f_3 and f_4 of total weight $n^2 - 1$, where f_2, f_3 and f_4 are assigned weights 3, 8 and 15, respectively.

Remark. In the case of a nonsupersingular curve in characteristic 2 with equation (2a), it is not hard to show by induction that the f_n are monic as polynomials in x.

In the case of a supersingular elliptic curve in characteristic 2 with equation (2b), the division polynomials have a particularly simple form. For simplicity, we take $a_3 = 1$.

Proposition 3. *If $a_3 = 1$ in (2a), then*

(i) *for n even, $f_n = f_{n/2}^4$;*

(ii) *for n odd, if one sets $z = f_3 = x^4 + x + a_4^2$, then there exists a polynomial $P_n \in \mathbf{F}_2[u]$ of degree $[(n^2 - 1)/24]$ such that $f_n = P_n(z^3)$ if $3 \nmid n$ and $f_n = zP_n(z^3)$ if $3 \mid n$.*

6. Multiples of a point in characteristic 2

Because the formulas in the literature (e.g., [10]) do not apply in characteristic 2, we shall give a proof of modified formulas that apply over $\mathbf{F}_{2^n}$.

Let h_4 denote the partial derivative with respect to x of the defining equation of E, i.e.,

$$h_4 = \begin{cases} x^2 + y, & \text{in the nonsupersingular case (2a);} \\ \\ x^2 + a_4, & \text{in the supersingular case (2b).} \end{cases} \qquad (8)$$

(h is assigned the subscript 4 to indicate its weight).

Proposition 4. *Let $P = (x, y)$ be a point on an elliptic curve E over a field K of characteristic 2 having equation (2a) (resp. (2b)). For $n \geq 1$ let $f_n \in$*

$F_2[x, y, a_2, a_6]$ (resp. $f_n \in F_2[x, y, a_3, a_4]$) be the division polynomials, and set $f_0 = 0$. Then for $n \geq 2$ the coordinates of nP are

$$\left(x + \frac{f_{n+1}f_{n-1}}{f_n^2}, \; y + (f_2 \circ n) + \frac{f_{n+1}^2 f_{n-2}}{f_2 f_n^3} + h_4 \frac{f_{n+1}f_{n-1}}{f_2 f_n^2}\right), \tag{9}$$

where h_4 is as in (8) and $f_2 \circ n$ has the same meaning as in Proposition 2, i.e.,

$$f_2 \circ n = \begin{cases} x + f_{n-1}f_{n+1}/f_n^2, & \text{in the nonsupersingular case (2a);} \\ a_3, & \text{in the supersingular case (2b).} \end{cases}$$

Proof. The formula for the x-coordinate of nP is the same as in [10] and [16], and the proof in the general case is valid in characteristic 2. However, the formula for the y-coordinate is quite different (because in [10] and [16] one has to divide by 2). We prove the formula for the y-coordinate in (9) by induction on n. For $n = 2$ it follows immediately from (4a) and (4b). Now for $n \geq 2$ we suppose that nP is given by (9), and we prove the formula for the y-coordinate of $(n+1)P$.

For the duration of this proof we introduce the notation x_n and y_n for the x- and y-coordinates of $nP_{x,y}$, and we set

$$\tilde{x}_n = x_n + x = f_{n+1}f_{n-1}/f_n^2; \qquad \tilde{y}_n = y_n + y + (f_2 \circ n).$$

Thus, our induction assumption is that $\tilde{y}_n = f_{n+1}^2 f_{n-2}/(f_2 f_n^3) + (h_4/f_2)\tilde{x}_n$, and we must prove the analogous formula with n replaced by $n+1$. Applying the addition formulas (3a) and (3b) to compute the y-coordinate of $P_{x,y} \oplus nP_{x,y}$, in both the supersingular and nonsupersingular cases we have

$$\tilde{y}_{n+1} = \frac{\tilde{x}_{n+1}}{\tilde{x}_n}\left(\tilde{y}_n + (f_2 \circ n)\right)$$

$$= \frac{f_{n+2}f_n^3}{f_{n-1}f_{n+1}^3}\left(\frac{f_{n+1}^2 f_{n-2}}{f_2 f_n^3} + \frac{f_{2n}}{f_n^4}\right) + \frac{h_4}{f_2}\tilde{x}_{n+1},$$

by the induction assumption and Proposition 2. After clearing denominators, we find that the desired formula for $\tilde{y}_{n+1}$ reduces to $(5)_{n+1,n-1}$. This completes the proof.

7. Curves of almost-prime order

For applications to discrete log cryptosystems ([7], [15]), one needs elliptic curves over $\mathbf{F}_{2^n}$ whose order N is either prime or "almost prime." If B is some constant, we shall use the term "B-almost prime" to mean that N is divisible by a prime factor $\geq N/B$.

In practice, apparently such elliptic curves occur with reasonable frequency, even when n is fairly large. However, from a theoretical point of view, the situation is not satisfactory. In fact, at present one cannot prove (for any fixed B) that there are infinitely many elliptic curves over $\mathbf{F}_{2^n}$ (as n and the coefficients a_i vary) of B-almost prime order. Because of results of Deuring [3], Waterhouse [19] and Schoof [17] on the distribution of this order (see also Lenstra's Proposition 1.7 in [11]), we know that for large n the orders of the elliptic curves over $\mathbf{F}_{2^n}$ are close to being uniformly distributed among the even numbers N which satisfy $|N - 2^n - 1| \leq 2\sqrt{2^n} = 2^{n/2+1}$ (more precisely, to be sure there is an E with a given N, one must take N closer to $2^n + 1$, i.e., $|N - 2^n - 1| \leq 2^{n/2}$). Thus, the conjecture that there are infinitely many elliptic curves of 2-almost prime order over $\mathbf{F}_{2^n}$ as n varies would follow from the following conjecture: There are infinitely many primes in the set $S = \cup_n \left(2^n - 2^{(n-1)/2}, 2^n + 2^{(n-1)/2}\right)$. More generally, one would expect that the probability of an integer in S being B-almost prime is similar to the probability that an arbitrary integer of the same order of magnitude is B-almost prime. But such a conjecture has not been proved.

One could resolve this theoretical difficulty by constructing cryptosystems from the jacobians of genus 2 curves, as described in [9]. Then from a result of Iwaniec and Juttila on the number of primes between $2^{2n} - 2^{1.5n}$ and 2^{2n} (see Theorem 5 in [1]) and a result of Adleman and Huang [1] on the distribution of the orders of such jacobians it follows that for any n one can find a genus 2 curve over $\mathbf{F}_{2^n}$ of prime order in probabilistic polynomial time in n. However, the analog of Schoof's algorithm for genus 2 curves seems to be prohibitively complicated; in any case, no one has yet implemented a polynomial time algorithm to determine the number of points on a random genus 2 curve.

In what follows, let us assume that as the coefficients vary in (2a) the probability of B-almost primality of $N = |E|$ is the same as that of a random even integer of the same order of magnitude. Since $N \approx q = 2^n$, for fixed B and large q the latter probability is asymptotic to $\sum_{j=1}^{B/2} \frac{1}{j \log(q/2j)} \approx \frac{1}{n} \log_2(B/2)$. Thus, if we want a ≥ 40-digit (i.e., ≥ 134-bit) prime factor of N, so that we can take $B = 2^{n-134}$, then we expect to have to try $n/(n-135)$ curves before finding E with $|E|$ divisible by a $\geq$40-digit prime. For example, if we choose $n = 148$, then we expect to have to apply Schoof's algorithm about 6 times (since each time we are actually determining the order of a curve and its twist simultaneously).

Alternatively, we could set $B = 2$, i.e., insist that $|E|$ be twice a prime. Recall that $|E|/2$ is odd if and only if a_2 has trace 1 in (2a). Although we must apply Schoof's algorithm more times (≈ 46 if $n = 135$), we can shorten the process in the following way. In Schoof's algorithm, when we compute t (mod l) for the first few values of $l = 3, 5, 7, \ldots$, we first determine whether $t \equiv q + 1$ (mod l); in that case our curve has order $q + 1 - t$ divisible by l, and so we immediately move on to another random choice of a_6. For instance, with $q = 2^{135}$, after quickly ruling out E for which 3, 5 or 7 divides $|E|$, the expected number of curves we must go through before finding E with $|E|/2$ prime is $\frac{1}{2} \cdot \frac{2}{3} \cdot \frac{4}{5} \cdot \frac{6}{7} \cdot \log 2^{134} \approx 21$.

8. Running time of the search for a suitable curve

To fix ideas, suppose that we want to find a curve $E : y^2 + xy = x^3 + x^2 + a_6$ over $\mathbf{F}_q$ with $q = 2^{135}$, such that $|E| = q + 1 - t$ is twice a prime. We shall give a rough estimate of the number of field multiplications required to determine t. In comparison, testing $(q + 1 - t)/2$ for primality is extremely fast. As explained at the end of the last section, we expect to have to go through this procedure about 21 times with different random $a_6 \in \mathbf{F}_q$ before we find the desired E.

As explained in §4, Schoof's algorithm proceeds by computing t modulo l for all odd primes $l \leq L$, where L is the smallest prime such that $\prod_{l \leq L} l > \sqrt{q} = 2^{67.5}$, i.e., $L = 59$. (Here we have $\sqrt{q}$ rather than $4\sqrt{q}$ because we already know that $|E|$ (mod 4) is 2.) For each l, one runs through the possible τ, $0 \leq \tau < l$, testing whether or not $t \equiv \tau$ (mod l). On the average one expects to find the value of τ which is t (mod l) after testing about $l/2$ values of τ. Given l and τ, the testing procedure (except for one or two exceptional values of τ, which we shall neglect in our time estimate) consists in determining whether a certain polynomial is zero modulo $f_l(x)$. Part of that polynomial does not depend on τ, and so can be computed once and for all modulo $f_l(x)$. It turns out that the most time-consuming part of the algorithm is computing f_τ^{2q}, $f_{\tau-1}^q$, and $f_{\tau+1}^q$ modulo f_l. For $\tau \geq 2$ the first two of these will be available from the computations for $\tau - 2$ and $\tau - 1$, and so the heart of the computation is to find $f_{\tau+1}^q$ modulo f_l. Note that $f_l \in \mathbf{F}_q[x]$ is monic of degree $(l^2 - 1)/2$. Thus, 135 times we must successively square a polynomial of degree $< l^2/2$ and divide the result by f_l. The division requires about $(l^2/2)^2 = l^4/4$

field multiplications. Putting this all together, we find the following estimate for the number of field multiplications in the most time-consuming part of Schoof's algorithm for a given elliptic curve:

$$135 \cdot \sum_{3 \leq l \leq 59,\ l \text{ prime}} l^5/8 \approx 3 \cdot 10^{10}.$$

In [13] the authors describe a special–purpose chip that performs about 15000 multiplications per second in $\mathbf{F}_{2^{593}}$, using an optimal normal basis. Since the time is roughly linear in the extension degree, a similar chip for $\mathbf{F}_{2^{135}}$ would perform about 66000 multiplications per second; hence, the length of time to find $|E|$ is about

$$3 \cdot 10^{10}/66000 = 4.5 \cdot 10^5 \text{ sec} \approx 5 \text{ days}.$$

Thus, if we have more than 21 computers working in parallel, each with a different a_6, then within a week we are likely to find a new elliptic curve E such that $|E|/2$ is a 40-digit prime.

Remark. The above time estimate is too big, perhaps, for complete practicality. However, the improved versions of Schoof's algorithm that are being developed (by A. O. L. Atkin, N. Elkies, V. Miller, and others) should soon decrease this time estimate, thereby making the random–curve method a practical choice of public key cryptosystem.

References

1. Adleman L. M. and Huang M. A., "Recognizing primes in random polynomial time," *Proc. 19th Annual ACM Symp. on Theory of Computing*, 1987, 462-469.

2. Bender A. and Guy Castagloni, "On the implementation of elliptic curve cryptosystems," *Advances in Cryptology – Crypto '89*, Springer-Verlag, 1990, 186-192.

3. Deuring M., "Die Typen der Multiplikatorenringe elliptischer Funktionenkörper," *Abh. Math. Sem. Hansischen Univ.* 14 (1941), 197-272.

4. Goldwasser S. and Kilian J., "Almost all primes can be quickly certified," *Proc. 18th Annual ACM Symp. on Theory of Computing*, 1986, 316-329.

5. Koblitz N., *Introduction to Elliptic Curves and Modular Forms*, Springer-Verlag, 1984.

6. Koblitz N., *A Course in Number Theory and Cryptography*, Springer-Verlag, 1987.

7. Koblitz N., "Elliptic curve cryptosystems," *Math. Comp.* **48** (1987), 203-209.

8. Koblitz N., "Primality of the number of points on an elliptic curve over a finite field," *Pacific J. Math.* **131** (1988), 157-165.

9. Koblitz N., "Hyperelliptic cryptosystems," *J. Cryptology* **1** (1989), 139-150.

10. Lang S., *Elliptic Curves Diophantine Analysis*, Springer-Verlag, 1978.

11. Lenstra A. K. and Lenstra H. W., Jr., "Algorithms in number theory," Technical Report 87-008, Univ. Chicago, 1987.

12. Menezes A. and S. A. Vanstone, "Isomorphism classes of elliptic curves over finite fields," *Research Report 90-01*, University of Waterloo, 1990.

13. Menezes A. and S. A. Vanstone, "The implementation of elliptic curve cryptosystems," preprint.

14. Menezes A., T. Okamoto, and S. A. Vanstone, "Reducing elliptic curve logarithms to logarithms in a finite field," preprint.

15. Miller V., "Use of elliptic curves in cryptography," *Advances in Cryptology – Crypto '85*, Springer-Verlag, 1986, 417-426.

16. Schoof R. J., "Elliptic curves over finite fields and the computation of square roots mod p," *Math. Comp.* **44** (1985), 483-494.

17. Schoof R. J., "Nonsingular plane cubic curves over finite fields," *J. Combinatorial Theory* **46** (1987), 183-211.

18. Silverman J., *The Arithmetic of Elliptic Curves*, Springer-Verlag, 1986.

19. Waterhouse W. C., "Abelian varieties over finite fields," *Ann. Sci. École Norm. Sup.*, 4e sér. **2** (1969), 521-560.

Session 4

Signatures and Authentication

Chair: D. Stinson, University of Nebraska

Identification Tokens — or:
Solving The Chess Grandmaster Problem

Thomas Beth
Fakultät für Informatik
Universität Karlsruhe
Germany

*Yvo Desmedt**
Dept. EE & CS
Univ. of Wisconsin –
Milwaukee, U.S.A.

Abstract. *Fiat and Shamir have proposed to use zero-knowledge interactive proofs to obtain secure identification mechanisms. Real time attacks in which active eavesdroppers relay questions and answers or in which the prover helps deliberately an impersonator have been described [4]. In this paper a solution against such frauds is given and (based on some physical assumptions) it is proved that the solution protects against the real-time attacks.*

1 Introduction

The use of zero-knowledge interactive proof systems for identification purposes was proposed by Fiat and Shamir [7]. Later Fiat and Shamir [8] have extended this idea to the process of identification *without* having to rely on physical description (see also [6]).

In this paper we will describe interactive proof systems and the process of identification from a game theoretic viewpoint. The game model is an essential tool in this paper. It will allow us to formalize the concept of the so called *mafia* and *terrorist* fraud [4] based on the idea of simultaneous display [2]. The *purpose* of this paper is to present a model which allows to *solve* the "Chess Grandmaster" problem, into which the identification problem will be converted. Such a model enables us to present an identification scheme which is provably secure against the aforementioned real-time attacks. This scheme does not rely on physical description of the individual who is identifying himself. We are not concerned about the rental fraud [4], but we will discuss it briefly at the end.

---

*Work done while visiting the EISS, University of Karlsruhe, West Germany.

2 Interactive proofs: a formal game theoretic viewpoint

2.1 THE LOGICAL LINK

Interactive proofs [9] are probabilistic games in a formal sense as we now explain.

We define games following [2, p. 71], via the notion of a game tree. An interactive proof of membership [9] consists of a prover A and a verifier B, who formally correspond to probabilistic Turing machines communicating with each other according to a protocol (A, B). On their common input tape is a binary string x for which A proves that x is an element of a given set L (a "language"). The execution tree of the protocol can be interpreted as a game tree and we call A and B players. We now assume that the verifier B follows the described protocol (which in the literature is noted as B being the honest verifier. But the reader is warned to attach too much interpretation to the word "honest"). For the prover there is not such a restriction. When the game starts the prover basically has two options, which are:

- to input an $x \in L$ and to follow A's protocol.

- to input an $x \notin L$ and to follow any protocol.

(In the formal definition of interactive proof the input is written on the common input tape, to let this fit with our purposes we have followed the above approach). Let ϵ and γ respectively be the failure and the cheating probabilities, which are related to completeness and soundness. We now say that if the verifier accepts (x) then the prover wins the game, else the verifier wins. This game aspect of zero-knowledge is the only property of this concept we will need in this paper. (An almost identical reasoning is valid for proofs of knowledge.) Due to the completeness and soundness properties we obtain the following transitions:

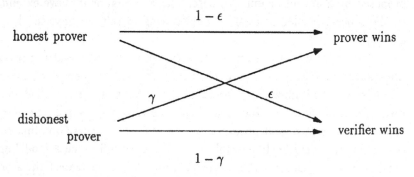

2.2 THE IMPACT

In game theory there is [2, p. 75]:

> *a famous story of the little girl who played ... against two Chess Grandmasters ... How was it that she managed to win one of the games? Anne-Louise played Black against Spassky. White against Fisher. Spassky moved*

first, and Anne-Louise just copied his move as the first move of her game against Fisher, then copied Fisher's reply as her own reply to Spassky's first move, and so on.

We will refer to the above as the *Chess Grandmaster problem* and call the fraud the *little girl's fraud*. It is clear that two games are played which we call: game 1 and game 2. Because zero-knowledge can be described as a game, the above scenario is valid in the context of Fiat-Shamir like identification. The *main purpose of this paper* is to find solutions for this Chess Grandmaster problem and to apply these solutions to cryptography.

Observe that when the little girl plays against the Right player, she is copying (mimicking) the Left player and when she plays against the Left player she is copying (mimicking) the Right player.

2.3 RELATION WITH IDENTIFICATION

Related to identification, the Chess Grandmaster problem corresponds to the mafia fraud [4]. The mafia fraud uses a pair of two cooperative persons in the middle, resembling the little girl in the Chess Grandmaster problem.

One can wonder to what the so called "terrorist fraud" [4] corresponds in game theory, which in short reads as follows: a citizen of α-land is helping deliberately a terrorist enter α-land. Hereto the citizen helps the terrorist answer questions asked by the immigration officer. From a game theoretic point of view, the difference between the mafia fraud and the terrorist fraud vanishes, when carefully analyzed.

These analogies imply the following very important conclusions:

Observation 1 *Secure identification cannot be solved based on techniques which can properly be modeled using game theory.*

Therefore, to *make secure identification schemes one has to rely on a different model.*

Observation 2 *Each time a solution is presented against the mafia fraud, then this solution can, in theory, be extended to protect against the terrorist fraud.*

Hereto it is sufficient that the prover's part of the secure protocol is embedded into a tamperfree system which enforces the prover to follow the protocol, for so far it is technically feasible to enforce it.

3 A new practical solution against the Chess Grandmaster problem

Suppose that Grandmasters want to make sure that they are not fooled by the little girl. In other words they want to be sure that if the little girl wins the chess game, it was her brain that allowed her to win, without having to tap the brain of another

Chess Grandmaster. To solve this problem all chess players will from now on follow the following protocol:

Step 1 Before the two players start the chess "game"[1] they agree on a certain t, where t is a time period expressed in seconds. (As usual they then agree who should start the "game".) We prefer to call the one who starts the "game" F (for first or Fisher) and the other player S (for second or Spassky).

Step 2 F opens the "game" and at the same time he resets his clock and sets $z := 0$.

Step 3 S resets his clock. (S thinks about his first move.) S makes his move at *precisely* time t and sets $y := t$.

Step 4 F reads from the clock the time e. *If* $e - z \neq t$,
    then F stops playing and the protocol terminates (F assumes that he was fooled)
    else if S won the "game"
        then F stops playing and the protocol terminates
        else (F thinks and) at *precisely* time $e + t$ he makes his move and sets $z := e + t$.

Step 5 S reads from the clock the time f. *If* $f - y \neq t$,
    then S stops playing and the protocol terminates (S assumes that he was fooled)
    else if F won the "game"
        then S stops playing and the protocol terminates
        else (S thinks and) at *precisely* time $f + t$ he makes his move and sets $y := f + t$.

Step 6 Goto Step 4.

Observe that we have used two symbols e and f to indicate elapsed time respectively of F and of S. This means that both have their own clock and do not trust outside clocks.

Theorem 1 *If the little girl G needs at least a time $l > 0$ to communicate the moves between "game 1" and "game 2" and F and S follow the protocol, and the number of moves m in the game is more than 2 (so $m \geq 3$), then the little girl's fraud is detected by F or S.*

Proof. When a little girl G is present, "game 1" is played by F against G and "game 2" is played by G against S and G copies moves as described earlier. Suppose that in Step 1 of the protocol of "game 1" F and G agree on time t_1 and in "game 2" G and S agree on time t_2 (t_1 and t_2 are not necessarily identical). F makes his first move at moment 0 for "game 1" and sets $z := 0$. (Starting at another moment than 0

---

[1] We have used quotation marks because what we have described is no longer a formal game.

would only make the notations heavier for no reason.) To copy this move to "game 2", G needs the time $l_1 \geq l > 0$. So the move arrives there at the moment l_1 and at that moment S resets *his* clock. Then S makes his move (still on "game 2") at time $l_1 + t_2$ and sets $y := t_2$. To copy this move to "game 1", G needs the time $l_2 \geq l > 0$ (there is no need that $l_1 = l_2$). So the move arrives in "game 1" at the moment $l_1 + t_2 + l_2$. F now reads the time e and checks that $e - z \neq t_1$. Now $e = l_1 + t_2 + l_2$ and $z = 0$. So, *at this point* F will not always detect the fraud. Indeed if $t_1 = l_1 + t_2 + l_2$ it will not be detected *at this point*. So if F has detected the fraud the proof of the theorem ends at this stage.

So we now assume that the fraud was not yet detected, implying that:

$$t_1 = l_1 + t_2 + l_2. \tag{1}$$

F will now make his move at time $l_1 + t_2 + l_2 + t_1$. To copy this move to "game 2", G needs the time $l_3 \geq l > 0$. So the move arrives there at the moment $l_1 + t_2 + l_2 + t_1 + l_3$. S now reads the time f on *his* clock. *His* clock reads: $f = t_2 + l_2 + t_1 + l_3$ and $y := t_2$. So $f - y = l_2 + t_1 + l_3$ and S checks if $f - y \neq t_2$. In order that the fraud would not be detected one needs that:

$$t_2 = l_2 + t_1 + l_3. \tag{2}$$

However combining equations (1) and (2) we obtain $l_1 + 2l_2 + l_3 = 0$ but because all $l_i \geq l > 0$ this is impossible. So S will detect the fraud. □

Remarks:

1. We emphasize that according to the above theorem F or S will detect the fraud. This could imply that one of the two remains in the dark about it. Rivest pointed out that when the little girl plays chess against *many* (deterministic) robots, she could win of one robot and the loosing robot will not detect the fraud. Hereto she will *abort* some games, start new games and copy the moves of older games. When the robots' games are influenced by random and are sufficiently independent, it is unlikely that this fraud will work. Indeed moves of old games will be useless. Zero-knowledge based identification scheme are in fact such random games, so in this context the above problem is nil. A more formal discussion of this multi-game problem will be given in the final paper.

2. In some informal discussions some scientists had the intuition that the above theorem could easily be generalized by systems they proposed us. All those turned out to be insecure. Let us just describe one variation. In it, F and G agree in Step 1 on two times t and t'. F will use as response time t and S's response time will be t'. When the little girl is in the middle we obtain t_1 as F's response time, and t'_1, t_2 as G's response times in game 1 and respectively game 2, and t'_2 as S's response time. By reading the last observation in Section 2.2 one can check that when $t'_1 \geq t'_2 + 2l$ and $t_2 \geq t_1 + 2l$, then the little girl can always defraud the system.

3. It may appear that the above mathematical solution is physically unfeasible as to question of precision. The next section will address this problem.

4 Converting the solution into a secure identification scheme

4.1 SOLVING THE MAFIA FRAUD

Before adapting our solution to identification, observe that the speed of light is not infinite. So when F sends a signal to S (makes his move) the communication time is l/c, where c is the speed of light and l is the distance between F and S.

Cryptosystems [1] have been proposed which security depends on physical assumptions. We follow a similar approach. Beside some computational complexity assumption, we need the following physical assumptions:

- The speed of light is constant [5] and cannot be influenced (by an opponent).

- An opponent cannot slow down or speed up an individual's time, taking into account that time is a relative concept to speed of F vice versa S and the gravitational field.

and the following engineering assumptions:

- One cannot influence the *clock* of an opponent, and all other aspects of time used inside a secure device.

- One cannot be made invisible.

Let us now explain the identification scheme[2].

In the identification scheme prover and verifier measure independently the *relative* distance between themselves. The required accuracy depends on the crowdedness of their environment. In some applications (such as identification in banks) it is easy to guarantee that the area is not too crowded and in such circumstances the verifier can organize himself that he knows the distance. The above protocol is then followed, in which the "game" is a zero-knowledge proof[3].

Inexpensive quartz technology gives a sufficient precision [11] for our purposes as will be fully explained in the final paper.

---

[2] For simplicity we assume in this abstract that prover and verifier are on this planet (time is relative to the gravity field) and that they do not move relative to each other (in the final paper we will explain that excluding rocket technology the speeds which can be obtained by individuals with modern technology on this planet is too small to be significant).

[3] Because $P \subset ZKIP$ we evidently have to assume that it is hard for an opponent to check membership and/or to calculate the knowledge.

4.2 SOLVING THE TERRORIST FRAUD

To adapt the above to make it secure against the mafia fraud, we rely on a trusted center who makes and distributes electronic identity cards (credit cards, etc.). The devices made by the center are *tamperfree*. Moreover it are those devices *themselves* (and not the carriers of those) which will execute the protocol (it is measure the relative distance and so on). In many circumstances it is very realistic to assume that small automatic devices can perform the above (as will be explained in the full paper).

5 Final observations and conclusions

5.1 OBSERVATIONS

Earlier a method [3] has been proposed to avoid the mafia fraud. In that solution a prover signs as message the exact, *absolute* location he is standing on earth. To identifying himself he proves to the verifier in zero-knowledge the knowledge of this signature. This method does not protect against the terrorist fraud. Using our Observation 2, one can solve that problem when the identification device itself measures this location (cf. the final paper).

As said in the introduction we have not been concerned about the rental fraud in which some prover borrows his identity device to somebody else. It seems that solutions need to take the physical description of the individual into consideration. However when one relies on this description, it is easier that the center just signs the individual's description [4, 10, 12]. A solution which doesn't require physical description is that the identification device is attached to the individual and that taking the device off will be detected by the device itself, which then deactivates itself. Under some circumstances it is only required that this device remains attached for a few hours (see final paper).

5.2 CONCLUSION

Because the speed of light is finite and constant we have provided a practical solution to the mafia and terrorist fraud. Its applications go beyond identification.

ACKNOWLEDGEMENT

The authors thank Louis Guillou and Shimon Even for having observed that the mafia fraud is similar to the little girl who played simultaneously chess against two Chess Grandmasters. This inspired the game approach followed in this paper. The authors thank Gilles Brassard, Jim Massey, Ron Rivest, and Rainer Rueppel for discussions related to this paper.

6 REFERENCES

[1] C. H. Bennett and G. Brassard. An update on quantum cryptography. In *Advances in Cryptology. Proc. of Crypto'84 (Lecture Notes in Computer Science 196)*, pp. 475–480. Springer-Verlag, New York, 1985. Santa Barbara, August 1984.

[2] J. H. Conway. *On numbers and games.* Academic Press Inc., London,U.K., 1976.

[3] Y. Desmedt. Major security problems with the "unforgeable" (Feige-)Fiat-Shamir proofs of identity and how to overcome them. In *Securicom 88, 6th worldwide congress on computer and communications security and protection*, pp. 147–159. SEDEP Paris France, March 15–17, 1988.

[4] Y. Desmedt, C. Goutier, and S. Bengio. Special uses and abuses of the Fiat-Shamir passport protocol. In C. Pomerance, editor, *Advances in Cryptology, Proc. of Crypto '87 (Lecture Notes in Computer Science 293)*, pp. 21–39. Springer-Verlag, 1988. Santa Barbara, California, U.S.A., August 16–20.

[5] A. Einstein. *Relativitätstheorie.* Friedr. Vieweg, Braunschwig, 1916.

[6] U. Feige, A. Fiat, and A. Shamir. Zero knowledge proofs of identity. *Journal of Cryptology*, 1(2), pp. 77–94, 1988.

[7] A. Fiat and A. Shamir. How to prove yourself: Practical solutions to identification and signature problems. In A. Odlyzko, editor, *Advances in Cryptology, Proc. of Crypto'86 (Lecture Notes in Computer Science 263)*, pp. 186–194. Springer-Verlag, 1987. Santa Barbara, California, U. S. A., August 11–15.

[8] A. Fiat and A. Shamir. Unforgeable proofs of identity. In *Securicom 87*, pp. 147–153, March 4–6, 1987. Paris, France.

[9] S. Goldwasser, S. Micali, and C. Rackoff. The knowledge complexity of interactive proof systems. *Siam J. Comput.*, 18(1), pp. 186–208, February 1989.

[10] P. D. Merillat. Secure stand-alone positive personnel identity verification system (ssa-ppiv). Technical Report SAND79-0070, Sandia National Laboratories, March 1979.

[11] N. F. Ramsey. Precise measurement of time. *American Scientist*, 76, pp. 42–49, January–February 1988.

[12] G. J. Simmons. A system for verifying user identity and authorization at the point-of sale or access. *Cryptologia*, 8(1), pp. 1–21, January 1984.

Arbitrated Unconditionally Secure Authentication Can Be Unconditionally Protected against Arbiter's Attacks

(Extended Abstract)

Yvo Desmedt
Dept. of EE & CS
Univ. of Wisconsin –
Milwaukee
WI 53201, U.S.A.

Moti Yung
IBM
T. J. Watson Research Center
Yorktown Heights
NY 10598, U.S.A.

Abstract. *Given an arbiter whose arbitrage is trusted, an authentication scheme is presented which is unconditionally secure against impersonation and/or substitution attacks performed by the arbiter, whereas previous scheme did not protect against such attacks. Furthermore, the scheme protects unconditionally against: impersonation/substitution attacks done by an outsider, against disavowal of a message by the sender, and against the receiver forging a message which was never sent. A practical scheme based on finite geometry is presented. Adaptations of the scheme realize an asymmetric conventional authentication scheme, and the set-up of an unconditionally secure oblivious transfer system.*

1 Introduction

When Sandy sends a message to Russ, Russ wants to be certain that the message is authentic, *i.e.*, it originates from Sandy and the message has not been substituted (altered). Authentication codes protect against such attacks [16].

While authentication systems protect against attacks by outsiders, they do not necessarily protect against disputes between sender and receiver. In such disputes, Sandy could deny having sent an embarrassing message that Russ claims she did, or Russ could modify, to his own advantage, a message that he received. The first schemes protecting against disputes are signature schemes [6]. The most known one is the RSA scheme [13]. Although RSA is somewhat unsuited for certain situations [4, 2, 3], some provably secure signature systems (as secure as inverting hard functions) are around [8, 11, 14].

Signatures schemes have unfortunately to rely on some unproven assumptions [9]. In contrast, no such reliance is required by unconditionally secure authentication codes [7, 19, 16].

The first unconditionally secure authentication scheme dealing with disputes has been proposed by Simmons [15, 18]. It is based on trust in the arbiter. *Simmons' scheme, however, suffers from a major disadvantage: Arby can impersonate Sandy, and Russ will not observe it.* Simmons mentions the disadvantage of his scheme and a natural question to ask is whether it can be reduced. In [1] a system with multi arbiters was suggested by Brickell and Stinson in order to somewhat reduce the attacking power of arbitration agents, by adding assumptions and active participants. *The purpose of this paper* is to come up with a scheme which *does not suffer from this disadvantage.* To compare with Brickell and Stinson's work we only need *one* arbiter as in Simmons' original scheme.

We remark that an arbiter may be a trusted party as far as arbitration between the parties is concerned. However, even such a participant may have an interest in impersonating a party, thus influencing the course of events. An "imaginary" scenario of arbiter cheating is when a boss-of-an-agency is playing the role of an arbiter between two of his employees, an operation officer, and a field agent. The arbiter in this case may impersonate the officer to send illegal instructions for some covert operation. Because the field agent believes that the message is authentic (originates from the officer) it will be executed. In case the operation fails, it is the officer who will be blamed for it, as he was actually set up as a "fall-guy"!

We note that such cases of cheating are especially very tempting when it is known that they will go undetected. A provision of a scheme which deters the arbiter from attempting impersonation seems to be necessary in such delicate scenarios.

In Simmons' solution [15, 18] we distinguish three stages (the description of which can easily be formalized later on). Let us call S the sender, R the receiver, A the arbiter, and O the outside opponent. The three stages are:

The key initialization phase in which S, R and A interact to come up with the necessary keys.

The transmission phase in which R receives a message and wants to ascertain that the message is authentic. A does *not* interact in this stage.

The dispute phase in which A is requested to resolve a dispute between S and R, based on information gathered by A during the initialization phase.

Our scheme contains these three stages as well. This allows a fair comparison of our solution with Simmons'. We observe that the *arbiter is* not *involved in the transmission phase*. This is contrary to the classical notion of arbitered signatures [10, p. 409].

The threats that we are faced with can originate from the outside opponent O, a dishonest $\tilde{S}$, a dishonest $\tilde{R}$, and a dishonest $\tilde{A}$. We follow Simmons' description of such threats. For the first three threats see [18].

The arbiter's threat. A dishonest $\tilde{A}$ can send a message to R which R will accept as authentic. As in the case of the opponent's attack the arbiter can either choose an impersonation or a substitution attack.

The attack is successful if and only if the message originating at $\tilde{A}$ will be accepted by R.

Let us now describe an observation which is the driving force behind our solution.

It is *extremely important* to observe that the scenario we now describe is *not* considered to be a fraud! In this scenario, $\tilde{S}$ sends a message to a honest R who rejects it as being *not* authentic. However, when $\tilde{S}$ hands over this message to A, A decides that the message is authentic. If $\tilde{S}$ succeeds in sending such messages, we do *not* say that $\tilde{S}$ has performed a (successful) attack. This makes perfect sense and one should not confuse on-line authentication and contract schemes which are binding in court (practically forever). We only consider this problem and its solution in Section 5.)

In Section 2 we give an example of a scheme which achieves our goal. In Section 3 we formalize the requirements. Practical schemes are presented in Section 4. Extensions and adaptations of these schemes are discussed in Section 5. One of the adaptations allows the set-up of asymmetric conventional authentication to allow unconditionally secure authentication in network environments. In Section 5 we discuss the relation between oblivious transfer and arbitrage and we then conclude in Section 6.

2 An elementary example

To keep the example simple we will momentarily only worry about impersonation attacks. It means that S wants to send *one fixed* message at some beforehand unknown moment; so our message space $\mathcal{M} = \{h\}$. We also do not yet intend to achieve schemes for which the cheating probabilities are very small. In these schemes, as well as in all our schemes, the key initialization phase contains three parts. First, R and S agree on some common information, $X_{(S,R)}$, secret to A. Secondly, R will choose some key, $X_{(R,A)}$, and communicate it to A. This $X_{(R,A)}$ identifies some subset of codewords. Thirdly, A selects out of this a subsubset and sends the key, $X_{(S,A)}$ to S to identify the selected subsubset. The scheme relies on random decisions by the parties: when b is chosen out of the set $\mathcal{B}$ with uniform probability distribution, we denote the event $b \in_R \mathcal{B}$.

In our first example let the set of *all* codewords (valid or non-valid) be $\mathcal{C} = \{0, 1, \ldots, 7\}$. To simplify our discussion let us organize those codewords in the following matrix:

$$T = \begin{pmatrix} 0 & 2 & 4 & 6 \\ 1 & 3 & 5 & 7 \end{pmatrix}$$

The set of codewords, $\mathcal{C}$ is public. Using the key initialization phase the private sets: $\mathcal{C}_R, \mathcal{C}_A$, and $\mathcal{C}_S$ will be set up. $\mathcal{C}_R$ is the set of codewords that R accepts as authentic. $\mathcal{C}_A$ is the set of codewords for which A will certify that they originate from R (this certification is not necessarily correct). And finally, $\mathcal{C}_S$ is the set of codewords that S will actually use to communicate authentic messages. To build up these sets, S, R, and A are involved in the following protocol in which keys are interchanged during the key initialization phase:

Step 1 S and R agree on one bit $X_{(S,R)}$ ($X_{(S,R)} \in_R \mathcal{X}_{(S,R)} = \{0,1\}$), which identifies a row in T.

Step 2 R and A agree on the pair $X_{(R,A)} = (m,n)$, where $m \neq n$, $m, n \in \{0,1,2,3\}$. The numbers m and n indicate the codewords $2m, 2m+1, 2n, 2n+1$, which correspond to two different columns in T. In other words $X_{(R,A)} \in_R \mathcal{X}_{(R,A)} = \{(0,1),(0,2),\ldots,(2,3)\}$.

Step 3 A selects one of these columns and gives the selection to S. Hereto A sends to S: $X_{(S,A)} \in_R \{m,n\}$.

The keys $X_{(S,R)}$ and $X_{(S,A)}$ specify uniquely the set of codewords, $\mathcal{C}_S$, that S will use. When S wants to send R her message h, she will send him the codeword: $2 \cdot X_{(S,A)} + X_{(S,R)}$ (so here $\mathcal{C}_S = \{2 \cdot X_{(S,A)} + X_{(S,R)}\}$). R will accept as authentic the codewords: $\mathcal{C}_R = \{2m + X_{(S,R)}, 2n + X_{(S,R)}\}$. (So here also $X_{(S,R)}$ and $X_{(R,A)}$ determine uniquely $\mathcal{C}_R$.) A will certify as being authentic (as being a codeword which originates from S) the codewords belonging to $\mathcal{C}_A = \{2X_{(S,A)}, 2X_{(S,A)}+1\}$. So $\mathcal{C}_A$ consists of one column of the matrix T.

Let us now discuss informally the security, against several attacks, of the above scheme. A cheating $\tilde{A}$ must guess the correct $X_{(S,R)}$, so the probability of a successful attack is $1/2$. When $\tilde{R}$ wants to cheat he could come up with $2m$, $2m+1$, $2n$, or $2n+1$. But A will only accept two of those as authentic, and because $\tilde{R}$ does not know $X_{(S,A)}$ his probability of a successful attack is $1/2$. When $\tilde{S}$ wants to perform her attack, she has to guess the other column that R has sent to A; her probability of success is $1/3$. Indeed, $\tilde{S}$ knows that 4 pairs are possible, but that the $X_{(S,A)}$'s column (which corresponds to $(2X_{(S,A)}, 2X_{(S,A)}+1)$) is impossible because A would certify it as originating from S. Thus, three columns are left over to choose from, but there is only one other column of codewords that R will accept as being authentic. Finally the outside opponent's probability of success is $1/4$, because the receiver will only accept two out of eight codewords of T as being authentic. Notice that the example above relies on the decisions made bilaterally and individually.

Observe that in this example the set $\mathcal{X}_{(S,A)} = \{0,1,2,3\}$. The probability that a particular key $X_{(S,A)}$ has been chosen depends on the actual value of $X_{(R,A)}$. Although S and A share $X_{(S,A)}$ the choice of it has only been made by A.

3 Formalizing the problem and theoretical results

Let us first formalize what our objectives are. To be general we will allow each participant (S, R and A) to make their subset of codewords using shared keys and using private information.

Definition 1 Let $\mathcal{M}$ be a non-empty message space (sometimes called the set of source states). Let $\mathcal{C}$ be the set of codewords. Let $G = (\mathcal{V}, \mathcal{E})$ be a complete graph with vertex set $\mathcal{V} = \{S, R, A\}$. Let $\mathcal{X}$ and $\mathcal{Y}$ be respectively the collection of all $\mathcal{X}_{(i,j)}$ $((i,j) \in \mathcal{E})$ and the collection of all $\mathcal{Y}_k$ $(k \in \mathcal{V})$, where $\mathcal{X}_{i,j}$ and $\mathcal{Y}_k$ are non-empty *key* sets. These sets are associated with edges and vertices, respectively. Each set of keys has a probability distribution associated with. We call the collection of these distributions $\mathcal{D}$. Let $\mathcal{F}$ be a set of functions associating a subset of codewords to keys such that $\mathcal{F} = \{f_{l,M} \mid l \in \mathcal{V} \text{ and } M \in \mathcal{M} \text{ and } f_{l,M} : \mathcal{B}_l \to \mathcal{P}(\mathcal{C})\}$ where $\mathcal{B}_S \subset \mathcal{X}_{(S,R)} \times \mathcal{X}_{(S,A)} \times \mathcal{Y}_S$, $\mathcal{B}_R \subset \mathcal{X}_{(S,R)} \times \mathcal{X}_{(R,A)} \times \mathcal{Y}_R$, and $\mathcal{B}_A \subset \mathcal{X}_{(S,A)} \times \mathcal{X}_{(R,A)} \times \mathcal{Y}_A$, and $\mathcal{P}(\mathcal{C})$ is the power set of C. We call $\mathcal{B}$ the collection of $\mathcal{B}_l$ (where $l \in \mathcal{V}$). We say that $(G, \mathcal{M}, \mathcal{C}, \mathcal{X}, \mathcal{Y}, \mathcal{D}, \mathcal{B}, \mathcal{F})$ is a *communication scheme with sender S, receiver R, and arbiter A*, or shortly: a *communication scheme* when there is no ambiguity what S, R and A are.

In this text we will assume that there is no ambiguity when we speak about a communication scheme. In our initial example no Y_R was used. So $\mathcal{Y}_R$ contains only one element. From this viewpoint Simmons' scheme has the property that $|\mathcal{X}_{(S,R)}| = 1$.

Definition 2 In the key initialization phase each $(i,j) \in \mathcal{E}$ agrees securely on an $X_{(i,j)} \in \mathcal{X}_{(i,j)}$ and each $i \in \mathcal{V}$ chooses an $Y_i \in \mathcal{Y}_i$, which is done accordingly to distributions $\mathcal{D}_{(i,j)}$ and $\mathcal{D}_i$ respectively.

Let $C_{S,M} = f_{S,M}(X_{(S,R)}, X_{(S,A)}, Y_S)$, $C_{R,M} = f_{R,M}(X_{(S,R)}, X_{(R,A)}, Y_R)$, and $C_{A,M} = f_{A,M}(X_{(S,A)}, X_{(R,A)}, Y_A)$. We call: $C_S = \bigcup_{M \in \mathcal{M}} C_{S,M}$, $C_R = \bigcup_{M \in \mathcal{M}} C_{R,M}$, and $C_A = \bigcup_{M \in \mathcal{M}} C_{A,M}$ the set of codewords that respectively S, R, and A accept.

The probability distributions $\mathcal{D}_{(R,A)}$, $\mathcal{D}_{(S,R)}$ and $\mathcal{D}_R$ can be inter dependent. Similarly the probability distributions $\mathcal{D}_{(S,A)}$ and $\mathcal{D}_A$ can be inter dependent and could be a function of $X_{(R,A)}$. Finally $\mathcal{D}_S$ can be a function of $X_{(S,R)}$ and $X_{(S,A)}$.

A communication scheme is well defined when the above probability distributions guarantee that:

$$\forall(X_{(S,R)}, X_{(S,A)}, Y_S) \in (\mathcal{X}_{(S,R)} \times \mathcal{X}_{(S,A)} \times \mathcal{Y}_S) \setminus \mathcal{B}_S : \quad \Pr(X_{(S,R)}, X_{(S,A)}, Y_S) = 0$$
$$\forall(X_{(S,R)}, X_{(R,A)}, Y_R) \in (\mathcal{X}_{(S,R)} \times \mathcal{X}_{(R,A)} \times \mathcal{Y}_R) \setminus \mathcal{B}_R : \quad \Pr(X_{(S,R)}, X_{(R,A)}, Y_R) = 0$$
$$\forall(X_{(S,A)}, X_{(R,A)}, Y_A) \in (\mathcal{X}_{(S,A)} \times \mathcal{X}_{(R,A)} \times \mathcal{Y}_A) \setminus \mathcal{B}_A : \quad \Pr(X_{(S,A)}, X_{(R,A)}, Y_A) = 0.$$

We say that *the number of interactions* in the key initialization phase is:

$$3 - \sum_{i \in \mathcal{E}}(\text{if } \{|\mathcal{X}_i| = 1\} \text{ then } 1 \text{ else } 0).$$

All the above distributions can be public or secret. The subsets $\mathcal{B}_l$ are however all public.

Let us now define what a secure authentication scheme is.

Definition 3 A well defined communication scheme $(G, \mathcal{M}, \mathcal{C}, \mathcal{X}, \mathcal{Y}, \mathcal{D}, \mathcal{B}, \mathcal{F})$ with arbiter A is *uniquely decodable* when simultaneously $\forall M \in \mathcal{M} : C_{S,M} \subset C_{R,M}, C_{S,M} \neq$

$\emptyset$, and also: $C_S \subset C_A$, and that $\{C_{R,M} \mid M \in \mathcal{M}\}$ forms a partition of C_R. This partition naturally defines the function $m_S : C_S \to \mathcal{M}$ and its extension $m_R : C_R \to \mathcal{M}$. We will speak about m in both cases. When $\{C_{A,M} \mid M \in \mathcal{M}\}$ forms a partition of C_A such that $\forall M \in \mathcal{M} : C_{S,M} \subset C_{A,M}$ we say that there is *no privacy protection relative to A*.

Remark 1 The subsets $\mathcal{B}_S$, $\mathcal{B}_R$ and $\mathcal{B}_A$ can now be motivated. The exclusion of some undesired choices helps guarantee that a communication scheme is uniquely decodable. Our first example illustrates this. Indeed given $X_{(R,A)}$ not all choices of $X_{(S,A)}$ are possible, otherwise we could not guarantee a particular scheme to be uniquely decodable.

In the final paper [5] we formally define $P_O, P_{\tilde{S}}, P_{\tilde{R}}, P_{\tilde{A}}$ and require that they are all less than 2^{-k}, where k is the security parameter. An informal definition can be found in [18]. When $P_{O_0} = P_{O_1} = P_{\tilde{S}} = P_{\tilde{R}_0} = P_{\tilde{R}_1} = P_{\tilde{A}_0} = P_{\tilde{A}_1} < 1$, we say that the scheme is *super-equitable*, which is motivated by Simmons' definition [18].

Our definitions are quite general. No restrictions whatsoever were imposed on the sets of keys ($X_{(S,R)}$, etc.) that can be communicated between the participants S, R, and A.

In the final paper [5] we prove the following theorems.

Theorem 1 *Super-equitable schemes for which the number of iterations is 2 do exist.*

Theorem 2 *Let $k > 0$. For a k-secure authentication scheme (with arbiter) which uses a 2-interaction key initialization phase, holds that $k \leq 1$. So P_O or $P_{\tilde{S}}$ or $P_{\tilde{R}}$ or $P_{\tilde{A}}$ is larger or equal to $1/2$.*

So, to obtain a decent security one needs 3 interactions in the key initialization phase. Practical schemes exist, in the next section we will discuss some practical schemes based on geometry.

4 Practical secure authentication schemes with arbiter

In this section we will use many sets. Hereto we first define the functions f_S, f_R, and f_A. These have the same domains and co-domains as the functions $f_{S,M}$, $f_{R,M}$, and $f_{A,M}$ respectively (see Definition 1) such that:

$$f_S(X_{(S,R)}, X_{(S,A)}, Y_S) = \bigcup_M f_{S,M}(X_{(S,R)}, X_{(S,A)}, Y_S)$$

$$f_R(X_{(S,R)}, X_{(R,A)}, Y_R) = \bigcup_M f_{R,M}(X_{(S,R)}, X_{(R,A)}, Y_R)$$

$$f_A(X_{(S,A)}, X_{(R,A)}, Y_A) = \bigcup_M f_{A,M}(X_{(S,A)}, X_{(R,A)}, Y_A)$$

and this holds for all possible inputs. So all those functions have as co-domain $\mathcal{P}(\mathcal{C})$. Using this terminology, for example, $\mathcal{C}_R = f_R(X_{(S,R)}, X_{(R,A)}, Y_R)$, which clarifies the above. The sets we define next give S some specific information about $\mathcal{C}_A$. S receives $X_{(S,A)}$ from A and this allows S to calculate the sets:

$$\mathcal{I}_A^{X_{(S,A)}} \quad = \bigcap_{\substack{(X_{(R,A)}, Y_A) \in \mathcal{X}_{(R,A)} \times \mathcal{Y}_A \\ (X_{(S,A)}, X_{(R,A)}, Y_A) \in \mathcal{B}_A}} f_A(X_{(S,A)}, X_{(R,A)}, Y_A) \tag{1}$$

$$\mathcal{U}_A^{X_{(S,A)}} \quad = \bigcup_{\substack{(X_{(R,A)}, Y_A) \in \mathcal{X}_{(R,A)} \times \mathcal{Y}_A \\ (X_{(S,A)}, X_{(R,A)}, Y_A) \in \mathcal{B}_A}} f_A(X_{(S,A)}, X_{(R,A)}, Y_A) \tag{2}$$

The notation of these sets is easy to read when the following mnemonics is used. The above sets give information about $\mathcal{C}_A$, and $\mathcal{I}_A^{X_{(S,A)}}$ and $\mathcal{U}_A^{X_{(S,A)}}$ can be computed starting only from $X_{(S,A)}$, that is, when $X_{(S,A)}$ is known. The symbol $\mathcal{I}$ indicates intersection and we use the symbol $\mathcal{U}$ when the union of sets is involved.

All sets defined in the sequel are denoted similarly, these are:

$$\mathcal{I}_A^{X_{(R,A)}} \quad = \bigcap_{\substack{(X_{(S,A)}, Y_A) \in \mathcal{X}_{(S,A)} \times \mathcal{Y}_A \\ (X_{(S,A)}, X_{(R,A)}, Y_A) \in \mathcal{B}_A}} f_A(X_{(S,A)}, X_{(R,A)}, Y_A) \tag{3}$$

$$\mathcal{I}_R^{X_{(R,A)}} \quad = \bigcap_{\substack{(X_{(S,R)}, Y_R) \in \mathcal{X}_{(S,R)} \times \mathcal{Y}_R \\ (X_{(S,R)}, X_{(R,A)}, Y_R) \in \mathcal{B}_R}} f_R(X_{(S,R)}, X_{(R,A)}, Y_R) \tag{4}$$

$$\mathcal{I}_R^{X_{(S,R)}} \quad = \bigcap_{\substack{(X_{(R,A)}, Y_R) \in \mathcal{X}_{(R,A)} \times \mathcal{Y}_R \\ (X_{(S,R)}, X_{(R,A)}, Y_R) \in \mathcal{B}_R}} f_R(X_{(S,R)}, X_{(R,A)}, Y_R) \tag{5}$$

and similarly we define $\mathcal{U}_A^{X_{(R,A)}}$, $\mathcal{U}_R^{X_{(R,A)}}$, and $\mathcal{U}_R^{X_{(S,R)}}$ by replacing the intersection symbols by union symbols in respectively (3), (4), and (5).

In this section $|\mathcal{Y}_S| = 1$, $|\mathcal{Y}_R| = 1$ and $|\mathcal{Y}_A| = 1$. In order to facilitate reading, we will often, in this section, use the symbols $\mathcal{U}_R^{X_{(S,R)}}$, $\mathcal{U}_R^{X_{(R,A)}}$, etc. without proving immediately that this notation is compatible with our definitions.

Before explaining our general practical scheme (any $\mathcal{M}$) we now explain a very similar scheme for which $|\mathcal{M}| = 1$ which will facilitate the grasping of our general scheme. In this scheme p is a public prime, and $|p| \geq k$. $\mathcal{C}$ corresponds with the *three* dimensional space: $Z_p \times Z_p \times Z_p$, which co-ordinates are denoted by (x, y, z).

The key initialization phase

Step 1 R chooses $X_{(S,R)} \in_R Z_p$, $X_{(R,A)}^1 \in_R Z_p$, and $X_{(R,A)}^2 \in_R Z_p$. Then R sends S the number $X_{(S,R)}$ and A the pair: $X_{(R,A)} = (X_{(R,A)}^1, X_{(R,A)}^2)$ to which respectively correspond the 2-dimensional planes:

$$\mathcal{U}_R^{X_{(S,R)}}: \qquad\qquad y \;=\; X_{(S,R)}$$

$$\mathcal{U}_A^{X_{(R,A)}} = \mathcal{U}_R^{X_{(R,A)}}: \qquad x + X_{(R,A)}^1 \cdot z \;=\; X_{(R,A)}^2 .$$

$\mathcal{C}_R = \mathcal{U}_R^{X_{(S,R)}} \cap \mathcal{U}_A^{X_{(R,A)}}$, which is always a 1-dimensional line.

Step 2 A chooses $X^1_{(S,A)} \in_R Z_p$ and calculates: $X^2_{(S,A)} = X^2_{(R,A)} - X^1_{(S,A)} \cdot X^1_{(R,A)}$ sends S the pair: $X_{(S,A)} = (X^1_{(S,A)}, X^2_{(S,A)})$. C_A corresponds with the 1-dimensional line:

$$\begin{cases} x = X^2_{(S,A)} \\ z = X^1_{(S,A)} \, . \end{cases}$$

Step 3 The set $C_S = \mathcal{U}_R^{X_{(S,R)}} \cap C_A = \{(X^2_{(S,A)}, X_{(S,R)}, X^1_{(S,A)})\}$.

When S wants to send her message (in the transmission phase), she sends R the following codeword: $(X^2_{(S,A)}, X_{(S,R)}, X^1_{(S,A)})$. Observe that S knows C_A and that C_A is the intersection of $\mathcal{U}_A^{X_{(R,A)}}$ with the 2-dimensional plane: $z = X^1_{(S,A)}$.

It is not too difficult to analyze that $P_{O_0} = 1/p^2$, $P_{\bar{A}_0} = 1/p$ and that $P_{\bar{R}_0} = 1/p$. In the final paper we will explain why $P_{\bar{S}} = 1/p$.

Let us now explain the general scheme. In this scheme p is a public prime, and $|p| \geq k$ and $p = |\mathcal{M}|$. C corresponds to the *four* dimensional space: $Z_p \times Z_p \times Z_p \times Z_p$, which coordinates are denoted by (x, y, z, u). We denote this four dimensional space as: Z_p^4.

The key initialization phase

Step 1 R sends S the tuple $X_{(S,R)} = (X^1_{(S,R)}, X^2_{(S,R)}) \in_R Z_p^2$ and R sends A the tuple: $X_{(R,A)} = (X^1_{(R,A)}, X^2_{(R,A)}, X^3_{(R,A)}) \in_R Z_p^3$ to which respectively correspond the 3-dimensional planes:

$$\mathcal{U}_R^{X_{(S,R)}} : \qquad y = X^1_{(S,R)} \cdot u + X^2_{(S,R)} \qquad (6)$$

$$\mathcal{U}_A^{X_{(R,A)}} = \mathcal{U}_R^{X_{(R,A)}} : \qquad x + X^1_{(R,A)} \cdot z = X^2_{(R,A)} \cdot u + X^3_{(R,A)}. \qquad (7)$$

$C_R = \mathcal{U}_R^{X_{(S,R)}} \cap \mathcal{U}_A^{X_{(R,A)}}$, which is always a 2-dimensional plane.

Step 2 A chooses and/or calculates:

$$X^1_{(S,A)} \in_R Z_p$$
$$X^2_{(S,A)} \in_R Z_p$$
$$X^3_{(S,A)} = X^2_{(R,A)} - X^1_{(S,A)} \cdot X^1_{(R,A)} \qquad (8)$$
$$X^4_{(S,A)} = X^3_{(R,A)} - X^2_{(S,A)} \cdot X^1_{(R,A)} \qquad (9)$$

and sends S the tuple: $X_{(S,A)} = (X^1_{(S,A)}, X^2_{(S,A)}, X^3_{(S,A)}, X^4_{(S,A)})$. C_A corresponds with the 2-dimensional plane:

$$\begin{cases} z = X^1_{(S,A)} \cdot u + X^2_{(S,A)} \\ x = X^3_{(S,A)} \cdot u + X^4_{(S,A)} \, . \end{cases} \qquad (10)$$

Step 3 The set $C_S = \mathcal{U}_R^{X_{(S,R)}} \cap C_A$, which is always a 1-dimensional line.

When S wants to send the message $M \in \mathcal{M}$, she calculates the codeword:

$$(x_0, y_0, z_0, M) = (X^3_{(S,A)} \cdot M + X^4_{(S,A)}, X^1_{(S,R)} \cdot M + X^2_{(S,R)}, X^1_{(S,A)} \cdot M + X^2_{(S,A)}, M)$$

and she sends it to R. Observe that S knows C_A and that C_A is the intersection of $\mathcal{U}_A^{X(R,A)}$ with the 3-dimensional plane: $z = X^1_{(S,A)} \cdot u + X^2_{(S,A)}$.

Theorem 3 *When $|p| \geq k$ and $p = |\mathcal{M}|$ then the general scheme is a k-secure authentication scheme with arbiter. The length of the key is proportional to k and when $|\mathcal{M}| \leq 2^k$ the length of the key is independent of k. The length of the codewords (when $p = |\mathcal{M}|$) is $4|p|$.*

When $|\mathcal{M}| > 2^k$ the scheme can easily be adapted, however the scheme is then no more so optimal. Observe that in the Wegman-Carter (no-arbiter) scheme [19] the length of the codewords is dramatically shorter.

5 Extensions

Here we introduce the ideas, in the final paper [5] we will formalize the problem and describe in more detail the solutions.

A new fraud in arbitrated authentication is a *jamming* type fraud. Indeed when during the key initialization phase of the previous scheme $\tilde{A}$ gives S an C'_A which is *not* a subset of $U_R^{X(R,A)}$, then R will reject all S's codewords! By using a similar idea as in [17] an extensions of the geometry based scheme protects probabilisticly against such frauds. Another extension gives a family of super-equitable authentication schemes with arbiter.

We now discuss asymmetric conventional authentication. Suppose that a sender S wants to send (broadcast) the *same* message to n (*e.g.* two) individuals $R_1, R_2, \ldots, R_n$ and authenticate it with an unconditionally secure scheme. The first solution would be that S gives the *same* key to all R_i, however each R_i could impersonate S. To avoid this fraud, the obvious solution is to use n keys and to send n authenticated messages (each authenticated with a different key). This transmission procedure is slow and no real broadcast can be used. The apparent ideal solution would be a signature scheme, but as said in the introduction, this requires a one-way function and the solution is no longer unconditional secure. We now discuss a situation in which a compromise solution is quite acceptable.

Suppose that Sandy, a new president of an investment company, gives each of her n brokers a different key K_i and keeps the "master key": K. In an emergency, such as a stock exchange crash, she will use K to authenticate M giving *one* codeword C, which she will broadcast. Ideally the length of C is independent of n. By adapting our geometrical scheme, such scheme can be constructed. This is formalized and a solution is presented in [5].

A major observation is that *each family of authentication schemes with arbiter A is a 1-out-of-2 family of secure asymmetric authentication schemes.* Indeed choose

$R_1 = R$ and $R_2 = A$. However, in the key initialization phase of an asymmetric authentication scheme there is no longer a secure communication channel between R_1 and R_2, so the scheme must be adapted. To solve this let us make a very important observation (see also [18, p. 101]). The schemes of Section 4 remains functional when S chooses $X_{(S,R)}$ (i.e. the plane $\mathcal{U}_R^{X_{(S,R)}}$) and $X_{(S,A)}$ (i.e. the set $\mathcal{C}_A$) and sends those securely to respectively R and A. Then A chooses some $X_{(R,A)}$ (i.e. a plane containing $\mathcal{C}_A$) and sends it securely to R. As before, $\mathcal{C}_R = \mathcal{U}_R^{X_{(S,R)}} \cap \mathcal{U}_A^{X_{(R,A)}}$. In the asymmetric authentication scheme there is no need for the communication of $X_{(R,A)}$. This remark is the driving force behind the scheme which was only introduced here; we will describe the scheme in the final paper. Another feature of the system which enhances its applicability is the fact that it may be used in such a way so that only one receiver (say, R_1) will accept the message.

Another extension allows oblivious transfer [12]. In an oblivious transfer system Bob sends a codeword to Cleo. The probability that this codeword is meaningful is $1/2$. In oblivious transfer Cleo knows when she received the message, however Bob does not, thus the transfer is indeed oblivious. We now prove that this can be achieved using secure authentication systems with arbiter. Let Bob correspond to R and Cleo with S and suppose that we have an authentication system with arbiter such that: $|\mathcal{C}_R| = 2 \cdot |\mathcal{C}_S|$. Observe that the sender corresponds to R now and the potential receiver to S! In the final paper we will prove that this system is an oblivious transfer system. Our goal, of course, was not to suggest an oblivious transfer with three parties as a major discovery, but rather to draw the analogy of the requirements of the authentication scheme protected against attacks by all participants and such an oblivious transfer scheme, which actually shows the strength of the authentication scheme.

6 Conclusions

While Simmons scheme does not protect against impersonation and substitution by the arbiter, the schemes presented here do protect against such frauds. Compared with Simmons solution our schemes use one interaction more in the key initialization phase than Simmons schemes. However we have demonstrated that 3 interactions are necessary (in the key initialization phase) to come up with a decent security.

We have presented a practical scheme for which the length of the key is only proportional to $\log_2(|\mathcal{M}|)$, which is better than in Simmons scheme. And, we have shown that a scheme with an arbiter allows us to come up with an oblivious transfer system.

The paper introduces many open problems. First, can arbitrated authentication schemes be obtained which are optimal as the Wegman-Carter scheme. Do other examples exist of asymmetric conventional cryptosystems. What is the relation between sharing and authentication?

Acknowledgments

The lecture of Gus Simmons at the Monte Verita workshop (October 15–21, 1989, Ascona, Switzerland) arouse the first author's interest in the topic of arbitrage. He thanks Gus Simmons for his enlightening explanations. The second author wishes to thank the U. of Wisconsin at Milwaukee for his visit where part of this work was done.

7 REFERENCES

[1] E. F. Brickell and D. R. Stinson. Authentication codes with multiple arbiters. In C. G. Günther, editor, *Advances in Cryptology, Proc. of Eurocrypt '88 (Lecture Notes in Computer Science 330)*, pp. 51–55. Springer-Verlag, May 1988. Davos, Switzerland.

[2] W. de Jonge and D. Chaum. Attacks on some RSA signatures. In *Advances in Cryptology. Proc. of Crypto '85 (Lecture Notes in Computer Science 218)*, pp. 18–27. Springer-Verlag, New York, 1986. Santa Barbara, California, U.S.A., August 18–22, 1985.

[3] W. de Jonge and D. Chaum. Some variations on RSA signatures & their security. In A. Odlyzko, editor, *Advances in Cryptology, Proc. of Crypto '86 (Lecture Notes in Computer Science 263)*, pp. 49–59. Springer-Verlag, 1987. Santa Barbara, California, U. S. A., August 11–15.

[4] D. E. R. Denning. Digital signatures with RSA and other public-key cryptosystems. *Comm. ACM 27*, pp. 388–392, 1984.

[5] Y. Desmedt and M. Yung. Arbitrated unconditionally secure authentication can be unconditionally protected against arbiter's attacks. Full paper, available from authors, 1990.

[6] W. Diffie and M. E. Hellman. New directions in cryptography. *IEEE Trans. Inform. Theory*, IT-22(6), pp. 644–654, November 1976.

[7] E. Gilbert, F. MacWilliams, and N. Sloane. Codes which detect deception. *The BELL System Technical Journal*, 53(3), pp. 405–424, March 1974.

[8] S. Goldwasser, S. Micali, and R. Rivest. A digital signature scheme secure against adaptive chosen-message attacks. *Siam J. Comput.*, 17(2), pp. 281–308, April 1988.

[9] R. Impagliazzo and M. Luby. One-way functions are essential for complexity based cryptography. In *30th Annual Symp. on Foundations of Computer Science (FOCS)*, pp. 230–235. IEEE Computer Society Press, October 30–November 1, 1989. Research Triangle Park, NC, U.S.A.

[10] C. H. Meyer and S. M. Matyas. *Cryptography: A New Dimension in Computer Data Security.* J. Wiley, New York, 1982.

[11] M. Naor and M. Yung. Universal one-way hash functions and their cryptographic applications. In *Proceedings of the twenty first annual ACM Symp. Theory of Computing, STOC,* pp. 33–43, May 15–17, 1989.

[12] M. Rabin. How to exchange secrets by oblivious transfer. Technical Memo TR-81, Havard Center for Research in Computer Technology, 1981.

[13] R. L. Rivest, A. Shamir, and L. Adleman. A method for obtaining digital signatures and public key cryptosystems. *Commun. ACM,* 21, pp. 294–299, April 1978.

[14] J. Rompel. One-way functions are necessary and sufficient for secure signatures. In *Proceedings of the twenty second annual ACM Symp. Theory of Computing, STOC,* pp. 387–394, May 14–16, 1990.

[15] G. J. Simmons. Message authentication with arbitration of transmitter/receiver disputes. In D. Chaum and W. L. Price, editors, *Advances in Cryptology — Eurocrypt '87 (Lecture Notes in Computer Science 304),* pp. 151–165. Springer-Verlag, Berlin, 1988. Amsterdam, The Netherlands, April 13–15, 1987, full paper submitted to the Journal of Cryptology.

[16] G. J. Simmons. A survey of information authentication. *Proc. IEEE,* 76(5), pp. 603–620, May 1988.

[17] G. J. Simmons. Robust shared secret schemes. *Congressus Numerantium,* 68, pp. 215–248, 1989.

[18] G. J. Simmons. A Cartesian product construction for unconditionally secure authentication codes that permit arbitration. *Journal of Cryptology,* 2(2), pp. 77–104, 1990.

[19] M. N. Wegman and J. L. Carter. New hash fuctions and their use in authentication and set equality. *Journal of Computer and System Sciences,* 22, pp. 265–279, 1981.

Convertible Undeniable Signatures

Joan Boyar*　　　David Chaum　　　Ivan Damgård
Aarhus University　　　CWI　　　Aarhus University

Torben Pedersen
Aarhus University

Abstract

We introduce a new concept called *convertible undeniable signature schemes*. In these schemes, release of a single bit string by the signer turns all of his signatures, which were originally undeniable signatures, into ordinary digital signatures. We prove that the existence of such schemes is implied by the existence of digital signature schemes. Then, looking at the problem more practically, we present a very efficient convertible undeniable signature scheme. This scheme has the added benefit that signatures can also be selectively converted.

1　Introduction

Undeniable signatures were introduced in [CvA90]. For certain applications, these signatures are preferable to ordinary digital signatures because simply copying a signature does not produce something which can be directly verified. Instead, signatures are verified via a protocol between the signer and verifier, so the cooperation of the signer is necessary. The signer is not, however, allowed to deny a signature simply by refusing to participate in the protocol; there must also be a protocol which the signer can use in order to deny an invalid signature.

If, for example, a software company wanted to certify that they had provided a certain program, they could sign it using an undeniable signature. Only someone who had directly purchased the software from that company could verify the signature and be certain that no viruses had been introduced. However, if the software company sold programs which contained bugs, they should be unable to deny their signatures afterwards.

In addition to the properties of undeniable signatures described above, it could be useful if there were some secret information, which the signer could release at some point after signing, which would turn the undeniable signatures into ordinary digital signatures. Thus these signatures could be verified without the aid of the signer,

---

*Supported in part by the ESPRIT II Basic Research Actions Program of the EC under contract No. 3075 (Project ALCOM).

but they should still be difficult to forge. We will call such signatures *convertible undeniable signatures*.

A first advantage in the software company example of using convertible undeniable signatures is that several employees of the company could be given the ability to verify signatures, without being able to sign messages.[1] This would pose a smaller security risk than if the entire secret key to the system was distributed this way.

Secondly, if the company later goes bankrupt (or dissolves for any reason), it can release the secret information needed to verify signatures, so the software can still be used safely. At this point, the company would no longer be protected against the pirating of its software, but it would no longer care much about it either.

Undeniable signatures could also be useful in any situation in which an individual wishes to sign a document, but does not want the press to be able to prove that he signed that document. Suppose further that this individual must allow some other party to prove later that the signature is valid, without allowing this other party to forge signatures. An example of such a situation is a last will and testament which contains instructions that the signer would not want made public. After the signer's death, it is important that the signer's attorney be capable of validating the signature. The attorney should not, however, be capable of creating a new will and forging the deceased's signature. If a convertible undeniable signature is used, the attorney can be given the secret information which converts the undeniable signature into a digital signature. Then the attorney could act on the signer's behalf, verifying and denying signatures.

To summarize, for each signer there should be a public key K_P and two private keys K_{S1} and K_{S2}. The first private key K_{S1} should never be released; the signer uses it to produce signatures. The second private key K_{S2} may be released to convert the undeniable signatures into ordinary digital signatures.

- There should be an efficient algorithm for producing signatures, using the private keys K_{S1} and K_{S2}.

- There should be efficient protocols (efficient for both the signer and the verifier), one for verifying valid signatures and one for denying invalid signatures. If the signer participates in one of these protocols successfully, the verifier should be convinced that the signer had a negligible probability of cheating.

- After the undeniable signatures have been converted to digital signatures, it should be easy to verify them, so there should be an efficient algorithm which, given K_P and K_{S2}, can be used to verify valid signatures.

In order for a convertible undeniable signature scheme to be secure, it should also have the following three properties:

- The verifier should be unable to forge the signer's signature on any message for which it has not already seen a signature, even though

  1 The verifier may be able to get the signer to sign arbitrary messages.

---

[1]The key which converts the undeniable signatures into digital signatures can be used in verifying and denying protocols which are zero-knowledge proofs based on the circuits for verifying and denying the underlying digital signatures.

2 The verifier may be able to get the signer to enter into the verifying or denying protocol (whichever is appropriate) for arbitrary "signed" messages.

3 The second private key K_{S2} may be available. One may assume, however, that after K_{S2} is available, the prover refuses to participate in any more verifying or denying protocols.

- The verifier should be unable to produce a string for which the signer, with the correct public key K_P, is unable to either verify or deny that the string is a signature, even though

  1 The verifier may be able to get the signer to sign arbitrary messages.

  2 The verifier may be able to get the signer to enter into the verifying or denying protocol (whichever is appropriate) for arbitrary "signed" messages.

- The verifier should be unable to distinguish between valid and invalid signatures, with any significant advantage, without entering into one of these protocols with the signer. See section 3.1 for a formalization of this.

In some applications of convertible undeniable signatures, including that of the last will and testament, mentioned above, one might prefer to convert only selected undeniable signatures into digital signatures. (The signer may not wish everything he ever signed to be public, even after his death.) When a scheme allows this, we will say that it is a *selectively convertible undeniable signature scheme*.

The next section in this paper discusses previous work on undeniable signatures. In section 3, we first present a formal definition for undeniability, and then we present a selectively convertible undeniable signature scheme, based on the sole assumption that a secure digital signature scheme exists. The reader who is more interested in practical than theoretical results could skip that section and continue with section 4, in which we present an efficient selectively convertible undeniable signature scheme based on El Gamal signatures. The final section of the paper is a summary.

2 Related Work

In [CvA90], undeniable signatures were presented for the first time, and an implementation was described, based on the difficulty of computing discrete logarithms in a cyclic group of prime order. In this scheme, the public key has the form (g, g^x), where g is a generator of the group, and x is the secret key. For a message m, the signature has the form m^x.

In [Cha90] zero-knowledge denial and verification protocols were presented for this scheme. Its security and efficiency is based on the fact that the group order is prime and public, and on the assumption that all messages are bit strings representing elements in the group (or there is an easy way of checking that a message is in the group).

These conditions can be met, for example, by using the subgroup of index 2 of $\mathbb{Z}_p^*$, where p is a prime and $p - 1 = 2q$ for q prime. It is natural to try to generalize this scheme to other groups, for example by using a composite modulus, or by using the group on an elliptic curve. Such generalizations could potentially be more secure and could (in the composite modulus case, where one could release x^{-1} without revealing x) produce a convertible scheme.

Such a straightforward generalization, however, immediately runs into problems, most notably the fact that there may be no way (even for the signer) to tell whether a given message represents an element in the cyclic subgroup we are using.

The scheme we present in section 4 avoids these problems, is almost as efficient as the scheme from [CvA90] when used in the same group,[2] and could be generalized to any group in which discrete log is a hard problem.

3 Theoretical Results

3.1 A definition of undeniability

Undeniable signatures differ from ordinary digital signatures in that, given an undeniable signature, the verifier should be unable to distinguish between valid and invalid signatures, with any significant advantage, without entering into either a verifying or denying protocol with the signer. In order to make this more precise, we need to have a simulator which can produce fake signatures which cannot be distinguished from valid signatures. This signature simulator should also be able to produce transcripts of verifying protocols which are indistinguishable from true transcripts so that the existence of a good transcript does not prove that a signature is valid. This is important in some applications such as that of the software company wishing to protect against the piracy of its software. In addition, we must ensure that this task of distinguishing between fake and valid signatures does not become significantly easier if the verifier enters into verifying and denying protocols for other messages and signatures.

Definition 3.1
A *signature simulator, relative to a verifier V,* is a probabilistic polynomial time algorithm, which, when given a message m, outputs a string $Fake(m)$ and a simulated transcript $FakeT(Fake(m), m)$ of a verifying conversation between the signer and V, "proving" that $Fake(m)$ is a valid signature.

Definition 3.2
The *signature oracle O, relative to a verifier V,* receives a message m as input and flips a fair coin to decide whether to

1 run the signature simulator relative to V and give the simulator's output, or

2 output a random valid signature, $Sign(m)$, and a transcript $ValidT(Sign(m), m)$, chosen randomly from the distribution of transcripts from verifying conversations, involving the true signer and the verifier V, proving that $Sign(m)$ is a valid signature.

---

[2]The public keys in the scheme presented here are a little longer than those in [CvA90], and slightly more computation is required

Definition 3.3

The probabilistic polynomial time *distinguisher* D, attempting to distinguish between the fake and valid outputs of the oracle is allowed to:

1. Choose a message m and give that to the signature oracle O.

2. Observe an output (s, T) from O. This pair (s, T) is either from the set FF, which contains forgery-transcript pairs of the form

$$(Fake(m), FakeT(Fake(m), m))$$

or from the set SV, which signature-transcript pairs of the form

$$(Sign(m), ValidT(Sign(m), m)).$$

3. Interact with the true signer, obtaining some valid signatures on messages in a set M', with $m \notin M'$.

4. Interact with the true signer in verifying protocols for messages in the set M' and signatures in the set S', and in denying protocols for messages in the set M'' and strings in a set S'' created by D, with $m \notin M'$, $m \notin M''$, $s \notin S'$, and $s \notin S''$.

Definition 3.4

Let $D(s, T, m)$ denote D's output when its input is the possible signature s, for message m, and possible transcript T. Let n be the security parameter. Then, a signature system is *undeniable* if, for any verifier V, there exists a signature simulator relative to V such that, for any polynomial time distinguisher D, and for any constant c, the following holds for n sufficiently large:

$$|Prob[D(s, T, m) = 1 : (s, T) \in SV] - Prob[D(s, T, m) = 1 : (s, T) \in FF]| < 1/n^c.$$

In some applications it would be useful for the verifying and denying protocols to be more symmetric in that transcripts of denying protocols should not be transferable, just as transcripts for verifying protocols should not be transferable. If this is the case, we have *symmetric undeniable signatures*. To make this more formal, one defines a *denial simulator relative to a verifier* V similarly to the signature simulator in definition 3.1, except that the simulator is either given the message m and a valid signature on m, or it is just given the message m. If the simulator is given m and a valid signature, it should output a fake transcript of a denying conversation between the signer and V "proving" that the signature is a forgery. If the simulator is only given m as input, it should produce a forged signature $Fake(m)$. The *denial oracle* should flip a fair coin to decide whether to

1. give the denial simulator m and a valid signature $Sign(m)$, and output $Sign(m)$ and the fake transcript produced by the denial simulator, or

2. give the denial simulator just the message m, and output the forgery $Fake(m)$ produced by the denial simulator, along with a random valid transcript of an execution of the denial protocol for $Fake(m)$ with the true prover and V.

The distinguisher would be similar to that in definition 3.3, except that the oracle used would be the denial oracle.

All of the signature schemes we present in this paper are, in fact, symmetric undeniable signature schemes, since all of our protocols are zero-knowledge. Since these protocols are zero-knowledge, to show that the schemes are undeniable, it is only necessary to prove that there is a signature simulator S_1 which can produce false signatures $Fake(m)$ that are indistinguishable from real signatures $Sign(m)$. To see this, let S_2 be the simulator guaranteed by the fact that the verifying protocol is zero-knowledge. Thus S_2 produces valid looking transcripts when given $(m, Sign(m))$ as input. But it must also do so when given $(m, Fake(m))$ as input since otherwise we would have a contradiction with the property of S_1. Thus running S_1 and then running S_2 on the output of S_1 will produce the simulator required by Definition 3.1. It is also clear from the zero-knowledge property that entering into verifying or denying protocols concerning other messages or signatures will not help the distinguisher.

Note that if the verifying and denying protocols are zero-knowledge, then protocol transcripts will not help an enemy either to forge a signature on any message for which it has not already seen a signature or to produce a string for which the signer is unable to either verify or deny that the string is signature.

It appears, at first glance, as if the above definition of undeniability requires that the verifying protocol be zero-knowledge. In fact, this does not seem to be the case. The difference is that we allow the signature simulator to create its own forgery, so it is conceivable that, although it can produce transcripts when it creates the forgery, it might be unable to produce good transcripts when it is just given a valid signature.

3.2 Existence of convertible undeniable signature schemes

In this section, we will discuss which assumptions are sufficient for the construction of schemes of the type in which we are interested. If one makes the assumption that a secure digital signature scheme exists, then we will see that it is quite easy to design a convertible undeniable signature scheme. Thus, by the result of [Rom90], it is sufficient to assume the existence of a one-way function.

By a "secure digital signature scheme" we mean one which is "not existentially forgeable under an adaptive chosen plaintext attack", i.e. even if an enemy can get signatures on messages of his choice, he cannot sign any message that has not been signed by the signer (see [GMR88]).

Theorem 3.5
There exists a secure selectively convertible undeniable signature scheme if and only if there exists a secure digital signature scheme.

Proof sketch
First, we remark that if a convertible undeniable signature scheme exists, then we trivially have an ordinary signature scheme by releasing K_{S2} immediately.

Conversely, to set up a digital signature scheme, there must be a polynomial time probabilistic algorithm which on input a random string r, produces a pair (P, S), where P is a public key, and S is the matching secret key. It is intuitively obvious that the mapping from r to P must be a one-way function if the scheme is secure. A formal proof can be derived by using the scheme to build a secure identification protocol and using the result of [IL89].

Thus the existence of a secure digital signature scheme implies the existence of a one-way function, which by [GL89] and [ILL89] in turn implies the existence of pseudorandom generators, and hence by [GGM84] the existence of a pseudorandom function family. This is a parameterized family of functions $\{f_K\}$, where the parameter K can be thought of as a key. To a polynomially bounded enemy who does not know the key, images $f_K(x)$ appear to be totally random values with no correlation to x, even if the enemy gets to choose x.

In addition to pseudorandom functions, we will also need bit commitments. A bit commitment scheme may be thought of as a function BC that takes as input the bit string to be committed to, B, and some random input R. From this, one can compute the commitment $BC(B, R)$. Given only the commitment, it is "hard" to guess B better than at random, but it is also "hard" for the committer to change his mind, i.e. find $R, R', B \neq B'$, such that $BC(B, R) = BC(B', R')$. Given R, however, the commitment can be opened, i.e. B can be computed.

This description is actually a simplification - some commitment schemes require interaction - and commitments of the form just described require the existence of 1-1 one-way functions. We will assume first that bit commitments have this simple form, and describe later how to get rid of the 1-1 assumption.

Let P, S be a user's public and secret key for the signature scheme we are given and let $S(M)$ denote the signature of M using the secret key, S. We establish the undeniable system as follows: the user's public key is $K_P = (P, BC(K, R))$, where K is a key for the pseudorandom function family. The first private key is $K_{S1} = S$, and the second is $K_{S2} = R$. A signature on message M has the following form: $sign(M) = BC(S(M), f_K(M))$.

The protocols for verifying and denying signatures can be constructed from a circuit that works as follows (see figure 1): Using R, it will open the commitment to K, from which it computes $f_K(M)$. With this value, it opens the commitment to $S(M)$, and finally it checks this signature on M using the public key P. The circuit gives three bits $b1, b2, b3$ as output. They are defined to be 1, if the opening of the two commitments and the signature check, respectively, was successful.

By the general protocols of [BCC88] [IY88], the signer can now convince anyone of the value of any boolean function of $b1, b2, b3$ in zero-knowledge, in particular without revealing R. If he wants to verify a signature, he convinces the verifier that $b1 \wedge b2 \wedge b3 = 1$, if he wants to deny a signature, he convinces the verifier that $b1 \wedge ((\neg b2) \vee (\neg b3)) = 1$.

The scheme is secure against forgery because, since the signer chooses R independently of S, any forgery of the undeniable signatures could be used to forge signatures in the original signature scheme.

The scheme is undeniable because the signature simulator need only make a bit commitment to a random string of the correct length. If the bit commitment scheme and the pseudorandom function are secure, it should be impossible to distinguish

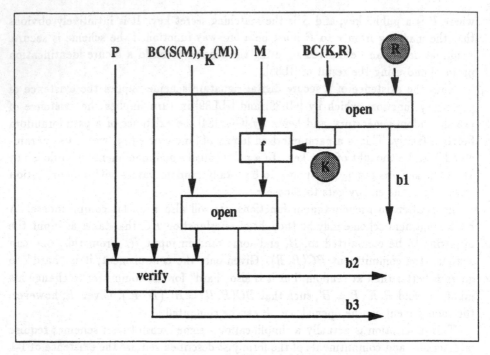

Figure 1: Circuit for verifying or denying signatures.

between this and a valid signature. The existence of this signature simulator, together with the fact that the protocols are zero-knowledge, is sufficient to prove that the scheme is undeniable.

The scheme is convertible, since the release of R enables the computation of K, and therefore all commitments to signatures can be opened. It is also selectively convertible, since for a signed message M, one can release $f_K(M)$. This allows computation of $S(M)$ from $sign(M)$, but by the properties of pseudorandom functions it does not help in computing any other function values.

Finally we address the problem of basing the scheme on *any* one-way function. By the result of Naor, [Nao90], one can build bit commitments from any one-way function, but this requires interaction: the verifier sends a random string R_V, and the signer/prover responds with the commitment. The randomness of R_V is necessary to ensure that the prover is actually committed, but it does not affect the secrecy of the bits committed to. We will use this scheme for the commitment to K; for this commitment, R_V can be supplied by a trusted key-center, which will usually have to exist to guarantee the authenticity of the public keys. But any mutually trusted source of random bits (such as a multiparty coin-flipping protocol) would suffice here. Once K is committed to, we do not need Naor's scheme any more. For the commitments to signatures, we can use the "hard-core" bits of the one-way function (see [GL89]), because the random input is now determined by K. ∎

The conditions needed for the construction of an undeniable signature scheme are no weaker than the necessary conditions for the construction of a convertible undeniable signature scheme as shown in the following corollary.

Corollary 3.6
There exists a secure undeniable signature system if and only if there exists a one-way function.

Proof sketch
If undeniable signatures exist, one can prove the existence of a one-way function in the same way as in the proof of theorem of theorem 3.5.

The converse follows from the previous theorem and the result of [Rom90] that secure digital signatures exist if one-way functions exist. ∎

Independently, this corollary has earlier been proven by Micali ([Mic90]).

4 A Practical Solution

In this section we show how the El Gamal signature scheme [EG85] can be changed into a convertible undeniable signature scheme.

First some notation. Let G be a group and let g be an element in this group. By $<g>$ we denote the subgroup of G generated by g, and by $|H|$ the order of the subgroup H ($|g| = |<g>|$). We use $DL(h, g)$ as shorthand for the discrete logarithm of h with respect to g. Thus $g^{DL(h,g)} = h$.

Let p be a prime such that it is hard to compute discrete logarithms in $\mathbb{Z}_p^*$ and let q be a large prime divisor of $p - 1$ such that everybody knows q. In the following all computations are in $\mathbb{Z}_p^*$ unless otherwise specified.

Let α be a generator of the subgroup of $\mathbb{Z}_p^*$ of order q. The private key in the El Gamal signature scheme is a number x between 1 and q and the public key is $y = \alpha^x$. The signature on a message m ($1 \leq m < q$) is a pair (r, s) satisfying

$$\alpha^m = y^r r^s.$$

This signature is constructed by choosing $k \in [1, q - 1]$ and computing r and s by

$$r = \alpha^k$$

and

$$s = k^{-1}(m - xr) \bmod q.$$

4.1 The Scheme

Using the El Gamal signature scheme, we can construct an undeniable signature scheme as follows. As before let α generate a subgroup of $\mathbb{Z}_p^*$ of prime order q. The private keys are

$$K_{S1} = x \text{ and } K_{S2} = z, \quad 1 < x, z < q$$

and the public key is

$$K_P = (\alpha, y, u), \text{ where } y = \alpha^x \text{ and } u = \alpha^z.$$

When the signer makes public $K_P = (\alpha, y, u)$, the receiver, which could be a key center or a user, should verify that $\alpha^q = y^q = u^q = 1$ and that none of the components of K_P is the identity. By the properties of $\mathbb{Z}_p^*$, this proves that α, y and u generate the same group.

The signature on the message m is $sign(m) = (\alpha^t, r, s)$, where (r, s) is the El Gamal signature on $\alpha^t tzm \bmod q$ (in this product α^t is considered to be a representation of an element in $\mathbb{Z}_q$).

In the El Gamal scheme, it is possible for a forger to construct a signature (r', s') on a message m'. It is very unlikely that m' is meaningful, but this attack implies that the El Gamal scheme must be used together with a hash function. The new scheme also requires a hash function, but we will not mention it when describing the scheme.

The triple (T, r, s) is a legal signature on a message m, if and only if

$$(T^{Tm})^z = y^r r^s$$

(whenever T is in the exponent, it is considered to be an element of $\mathbb{Z}_q$). Throughout this section we will use v to denote $y^r r^s$ and w to denote T^{Tm}. Thus verifying a signature (T, r, s) on m is equivalent to deciding if $DL(v, w)$ equals $DL(u, \alpha)$.

The signer can prove that (T, r, s) is a legal signature on the message m as follows: (S is the signer and V, the verifier)

PROTOCOL VERIFY SIGNATURE

1. S and V compute $w = T^{Tm}$ and $v = y^r r^s$.

2. S proves that $DL(v, w) = DL(u, \alpha)$ using the protocol for simultaneous discrete logarithm shown in figure 2 (see also [Cha90]).

3. V accepts the signature if and only if it accepts the proof.

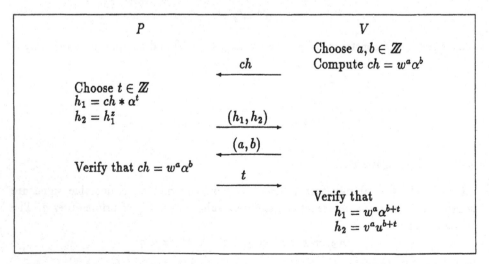

Figure 2: Proof that $DL(v, w)$ equals $DL(u, \alpha)$. The prover knows $z = DL(u, \alpha)$.

Lemma 4.1
If (T, r, s) is a legal signature on m, the following hold

1. The verifier always accepts.

2. PROTOCOL VERIFY SIGNATURE is zero-knowledge.

If (T, r, s) is a false signature, the verifier accepts with negligible probability (in the length of q).

Proof
It is sufficient to prove that the protocol in figure 2 is a zero-knowledge proof system with perfect completeness and negligible probability of the verifier accepting a false claim.

If $v = w^z$, the verifier will always accept.

Now assume that $w^z \neq v$.
If $w \neq 1$, w generates $<\alpha>$. For each value of $a \in \{0, \ldots, q-1\}$, there is exactly one value of b giving the same challenge. Thus ch contains no information about a. Now assume that the prover can find a pair (h_1, h_2) and t_1 and t_2 so that

$$h_1 = w^{a_1} \alpha^{b_1 + t_1} = w^{a_2} \alpha^{b_2 + t_2}$$

and

$$h_2 = v^{a_1} u^{b_1 + t_1} = v^{a_2} u^{b_2 + t_2}$$

where $a_1 \neq a_2$. Then we would have

$$
\begin{aligned}
DL(v, u) &= (a_1 - a_2)^{-1}((b_2 - b_1) + (t_2 - t_1)) \bmod q \\
&= DL(w, \alpha)
\end{aligned}
$$

and therefore $DL(v, w) = DL(u, \alpha)$, which is a contradiction. Hence S has probability at most $1/q$ of finding a pair (h_1, h_2) that V will accept.

The protocol is zero-knowledge, because for any verifier V', it can be simulated as follows

1. Get a challenge, ch, from V'.

2. Choose e and compute $h_1' = \alpha^e$ and $h_2' = u^e$.

3. Get (a, b) from the verifier.
   If $ch \neq w^a \alpha^b$, stop; and otherwise goto 4.

4. Rewind V' to after the challenge is sent.
   Choose t and compute $h_1 = w^a \alpha^{b+t}$ and $h_2 = v^a u^{b+t}$.

5. Get (a', b') from the verifier.
   If $ch = w^{a'} \alpha^{b'}$, send t to the verifier; and otherwise goto 4.

This simulation works because

- The verifier cannot find two different pairs (a_1, b_1) and (a_2, b_2) resulting in the same challenge without finding the discrete logarithm of w with respect to α.

- The first pair (h'_1, h'_2) has the same distribution as a pair (h_1, h_2) from the honest prover.

∎

If (T, r, s) is a false signature, the simulation still works and it is impossible to tell that it is a simulation with a false signature unless one can distinguish legal signatures from invalid signatures. This property ensures that a transcript from an execution of PROTOCOL VERIFY SIGNATURE cannot be used as a proof of the validity of a signature.

Before presenting the protocol for denying false signatures, we consider the general problem of proving that $DL(v, w) \neq DL(u, \alpha)$. Knowing $z = DL(u, \alpha)$, a polynomial time prover can demonstrate that these logarithms are different as shown in figure 3. In this protocol, $BC(\gamma, R)$ denotes a bit commitment to the bit γ using random input R. The blob is opened by revealing R.

Repeat k times:

P		V
		Choose $e \in \mathbb{Z}$ s.t. $1 \leq e \leq q - 1$
		Choose $\beta \in \{0, 1\}$
		Compute $a = \alpha^e$, $b = u^e$ if $\beta = 0$
	$\xleftarrow{\quad (a,b) \quad}$	and $a = w^e$, $b = v^e$ if $\beta = 1$
If $a^z = b$, set $\gamma = 0$		
else $\gamma = 1$		
Let $g = BC(\gamma, R)$	$\xrightarrow{\quad g \quad}$	
	$\xleftarrow{\quad e \quad}$	
If $(a, b) = (\alpha^e, u^e)$		
or $(a, b) = (w^e, v^e)$,		
$\quad ans = R$		
Otherwise $ans = stop$	$\xrightarrow{\quad ans \quad}$	
		If $ans = stop$, stop.
		Otherwise verify that
		$BC(\beta, ans) = g$

Figure 3: Proof that $DL(u, \alpha) \neq DL(v, w)$. The prover knows $z = DL(u, \alpha)$.

Lemma 4.2

If $DL(v, w) \neq DL(u, \alpha) \bmod q$, the verifier will accept with probability 1.

If $DL(v, w) = DL(u, \alpha) \bmod q$, the verifier will accept with probability 2^{-k}.

If the blobs are perfect, the protocol is perfect zero-knowledge even when the k rounds are run in parallel.

Proof

In the case where $DL(v, w) \neq DL(u, \alpha)$, the prover will always find $\gamma = \beta$. If $\beta = 0$,

$$a^z = \alpha^{ez} = u^e = b$$

and thus $\gamma = 0$. If $\beta = 1$ and $a^z = b$, we have

$$w^{ez} = a^z = b = v^e.$$

Since e is relatively prime to q, this implies that $w^z = v$ and thus $DL(v, w) = z = DL(u, \alpha)$. A contradiction.

If $DL(u, \alpha) = DL(v, w)$, the pair (a, b) contains no Shannon information about β, because w generates $<\alpha>$. Therefore, the prover can do no better than trying to guess β.

If the blobs are perfect, the protocol can be simulated using the same technique as in the proof of lemma 4.1. Therefore it is perfect zero-knowledge in this case. In addition, one can use the techniques of [GMW86] (graph non-isomorphism) to show that the protocol is also perfect zero-knowledge when the k rounds are run in parallel.

∎

If the blobs are not perfect in the sense that encryptions of 0 are only computationally indistinguishable from blobs containing 1, a proof such as that in [BDLP89] shows that the protocol is computational zero-knowledge (also when run in parallel).

The above protocol is quite straightforward. An alternate protocol is given in [Cha90]. Chaum's protocol is more efficient in terms of the number of bits exchanged (or the number of rounds if the protocol is executed sequentially), but there is a trade-off requiring more computation on the part of the signer. In order to save a factor of $O(t)$ bits, the signer creates a table of 2^t powers of a specific element, and sorts the table. Extra computation would usually be much less expensive than communicating extra bits, so Chaum's protocol can be a big improvement over the one presented here.

With the proof system from figure 3, it is pretty straightforward to construct

PROTOCOL DENY SIGNATURE

1. S and V both compute $w = T^{Tm}$ and $v = y^r r^s$.

2. S proves that $DL(u, \alpha) \neq DL(v, w)$ using the protocol in figure 3.

3. S accepts the denial if and only if it accepts the proof.

Lemma 4.3

If (T, r, s) is a false signature on m, the verifier will always accept the denial.

If (T, r, s) is a legal signature on m, the verifier will reject the denial with high probability no matter what the signer does.

PROTOCOL DENY SIGNATURE is perfect or computational zero-knowledge depending on whether or not perfect blobs are used.

Proof
Follows from lemma 4.2. ∎

4.2 Conversion of all signatures

As mentioned in the introduction, an undeniable signature is converted to an ordinary signature by releasing K_{S2}. Knowing $K_{S2} = z$ and K_P, everybody can verify a signature (T, r, s) on the message m by computing $(T^{Tm})^z$ and verifying that it equals $y^r r^s$. Thus when z is released, all previous and future signatures are equivalent to El Gamal signatures. Since anyone knowing z could have played the rôle of the prover in the previous executions of the protocols for verifying and denying signatures, the transcripts of these executions cannot help a forger (see also the subsection about security) after z is released.

4.3 Selective conversion

Knowing t such that $T = \alpha^t$, anyone can check that (T, r, s) is a signature on m by verifying that

$$T = \alpha^t \text{ and } u^{tTm} = y^r r^s.$$

Therefore, a single signature can be converted to an ordinary digital signature by releasing t. This method of converting signatures requires that the signer remembers the t used to construct the signature on m. This is most conveniently done by choosing a key k to a pseudorandom function f_k (see [GGM84]) and then computing t as $f_k(m)$. The properties of families of pseudorandom functions guarantee that, given polynomially many pairs $(m_i, f_k(m_i))$, it is infeasible to find $f_k(m)$ for a message $m \neq m_i$. Therefore, conversion of any polynomial number of signatures cannot affect the undeniability of other signatures.

4.4 Security

We will begin by discussing the possibility of creating false signatures. Since the verify and deny protocols are zero-knowledge, the strongest attack in this context is the one in which the enemy can ask for signatures on messages of his choice, and later tries to "sign" a different message. For our scheme, this means that the enemy can get triples of the form (T, r, s), such that

$$T^{Tzm} = y^r r^s,$$

where m is chosen by the enemy, and T is chosen by the signer. In the following, we make the worst case assumption that the enemy knows t, the discrete log of T, and z. This means that the enemy gets El Gamal signatures on numbers of the form $Ttmz$.

The only known consequence for the El Gamal scheme under this attack is that the enemy can construct new "signed" messages from the ones he is given (see [EG85]), but these new messages result from applying a hard-to-invert transformation to the known messages, and therefore they cannot be controlled easily.[3] In the El Gamal scheme, as in ours, this problem is solved by applying a one-way hash function to the messages before signing.

Now suppose that the enemy is somehow able to create a signature (T, r, s) in our scheme on a message m. There are two cases:

1. If he also knows t, such that $T = \alpha^t$, he has created an El Gamal signature on $Ttmz$. So either he has found a completely new way to break the El Gamal system, or he has found a way to write the result of the hard-to-invert transformation mentioned above in the form $Ttmz$. We conjecture that this is a hard problem: m is in fact shorthand for a one-way hashed image of the actual message, the mapping $f(t) = \alpha^t t$ can reasonably be assumed to be one-way, and z is a constant. Thus none of the factors in $(Tt)mz$ can be easily controlled by the enemy.

2. The only remaining possibility is that the enemy can find values satisfying $(T^T)^{mz} = y^r r^s$ *without* knowing the discrete log of T. This problem could only be easier than case 1 if T is computed in some clever way from signatures the enemy got earlier from the signer. As discussed above, these are equivalent to El Gamal signatures on messages of a special form. But these messages cannot be controlled by the enemy, since they all involve a factor of the form $t\alpha^t$, where t is chosen independently by the signer. Hence it is reasonable to claim that these signed messages will be of no more use to the enemy than the ones he can construct himself from scratch. Under this assumption the enemy might as well choose T's for which he knows the discrete log, and hence we are back in case 1.

We now turn to the problem of verifying signatures without the aid of the signer. Again, since the verify and deny protocols are zero-knowledge, we can simply assume that the enemy is given some number of signatures he knows are valid, and is trying to guess whether a given triple (T, r, s) matches a message m, i.e. whether these values satisfy the usual equation $T^{Tmz} = y^r r^s$. The natural way to verify an equation like this is to compute each side and compare. But if the enemy can compute the left side, he can also compute $\alpha^{tz} = (T^{Tmz})^{(Tm)^{-1}}$. This computation of α^{tz} from α^z, which is known from the public key, and $T = \alpha^t$ is the Diffie-Hellman key exchange problem, which we assume is intractable.

When a number of valid signatures (T_i, r_i, s_i) are known to the enemy, we have a situation where $\alpha^{t_i z}, t_i, \alpha^z$ is known for a number of independently chosen t_i's (we make the worst case assumption that the signer releases t_i for each i). The enemy is trying to guess the value of α^{tz} for a t independent of all t_i's. For each i, the values mentioned so far could easily be generated with the same distribution by the enemy himself. The only additional information he has is that each $\alpha^{t_i z}$ can be expressed in a special form, namely as $(y^{r_i} r_i^{s_i})^{(T_i m_i)^{-1}}$. Since this expression involves the independently chosen r_i's, we conjecture that this extra information does not help the enemy.

---

[3] It is also possible to construct "signed" - but still hard to control - messages from scratch. They have the form $m = \alpha^B y^C BC^{-1}$, where B, C can be arbitrary integers. The construction that uses already signed messages is similar, but more complicated.

The definition of undeniability in section 3.1 calls for a signature simulator. As a consequence of the above discussion, we conjecture that the signature simulator need only output three random numbers for the triple (T, r, s).

4.5 Generalizations

This method of constructing undeniable signatures can be used in any group. However, if the group in question $(<\alpha>)$ is not of prime order, one has to apply the more general protocol presented in [CEvdG88] for proving equality between logarithms. The reason for this is that the proof of lemma 4.1 does not work if w (which the signer chooses) generates a small subgroup.

5 Conclusion

We have introduced the concept of convertible undeniable signatures in which release of a single bit string by the signer turns all of his signatures, which were originally undeniable signatures, into ordinary digital signatures. The existence of such schemes is implied by the existence of digital signature schemes which exist if and only if a one-way function exists. We have presented a very efficient selectively convertible undeniable signature scheme.

Acknowledgement

The authors are thankful to Whitfield Diffie for suggesting a problem which motivated the idea of converting undeniable signatures to ordinary digital signatures.

References

[BCC88]   Gilles Brassard, David Chaum, and Claude Crépeau. Minimum disclosure proofs of knowledge. *Journal of Computer and System Sciences*, 37:156–189, 1988.

[BDLP89]   Jørgen Brandt, Ivan Damgård, Peter Landrock, and Torben Pedersen. Zero-knowledge authentication scheme with secret key exchange. Submitted to Journal of Cryptology, 1989.

[CEvdG88] David Chaum, Jan-Hendrik Evertse, and Jeroen van de Graaf. An improved protocol for demonstrating possession of discrete logarithms and some generalizations. In *Advances in Cryptology - proceedings of EUROCRYPT 87*, Lecture Notes in Computer Science. Springer-Verlag, 1988.

[Cha90]   David Chaum. Zero-knowledge undeniable signatures. To appear in the proceedings of EUROCRYPT'90, 1990.

[CvA90]   David Chaum and Hans van Antwerpen. Undeniable signatures. In *Advances in Cryptology - proceedings of CRYPTO 89*, Lecture Notes in Computer Science. Springer Verlag, 1990.

[EG85]   Taher El Gamal. A public key cryptosystem and a signatures scheme based on discrete logarithms. In *Advances in Cryptology - proceedings of CRYPTO 84*, Lecture Notes in Computer Science. Springer-Verlag, 1985.

[GGM84]   Oded Goldreich, Shafi Goldwasser, and Silvio Micali. How to construct random functions. In *Proceedings of the 25th IEEE Symposium on the Foundations of Computer Science*, 1984.

[GL89]   Oded Goldreich and Leonid A. Levin. A hard-core predicate for all one-way functions. In *Proceedings of the 21st Annual ACM Symposium on the Theory of Computing*, 1989.

[GMR88]   S. Goldwasser, S. Micali, and R. L. Rivest. A digital signature scheme secure against adaptive chosen message attack. *SIAM Journal on Computing*, 17(2):281 - 308, April 1988.

[GMW86]   Oded Goldreich, Silvio Micali, and Avi Wigderson. Proofs that yield nothing but their validity and a methodology of cryptographic protocol design. In *Proceedings of the 27th IEEE Symposium on the Foundations of Computer Science*, pages 174–187, 1986.

[IL89]   Russel Impagliazzo and Michael Luby. One-way functions are essential for complexity based cryptography. In *Proceedings of the 28th IEEE Symposium on the Foundations of Computer Science*, 1989.

[ILL89]   Russell Impagliazzo, Leonid A. Levin, and Michael Luby. Pseudo-random generation from one-way functions. In *Proceedings of the 21st Annual ACM Symposium on the Theory of Computing*, 1989.

[IY88]   Russel Impagliazzo and Moti Yung. Direct minimum-knowledge computations. In *Advances in Cryptology - proceedings of CRYPTO 87*, Lecture Notes in Computer Science, pages 40–51. Springer-Verlag, 1988.

[Mic90]   S. Micali, August 1990. Personal communication.

[Nao90]   Moni Naor. Bit commitment using randomness. In *Advances in Cryptology - proceedings of CRYPTO 89*, Lecture Notes in Computer Science, pages 128 –136, 1990.

[Rom90]   John Rompel. One-way functions are necessary and sufficient for secure signatures. In *Proceedings of the 22nd Annual ACM Symposium on the Theory of Computing*, 1990.

Unconditionally-Secure Digital Signatures

David Chaum

Centre for Mathematics and Computer Science (CWI)
Kruislaan 413, 1098 SJ Amsterdam

Sandra Roijakkers

Eindhoven University of Technology (TUE)
Den Dolech 2, 5600 MB Eindhoven (Research conducted at CWI)

Abstract. All known digital signature schemes can be forged by anyone having enough computing power. For a finite set of participants, we can overcome this weakness.

We present a polynomial time protocol in which a participant can convince (with an exponentially small error probability) any other participant that his signature is valid. Moreover, such a convinced participant can convince any other participant of the signature's validity, without interaction with the original signer.

An extension allows, in most cases, a participant who receives a signature from any source to convince each other participant of its validity. If a participant cannot use the signature to convince others, he knows so when he receives it.

1. Introduction

For many purposes digital signatures, as originally proposed in [DH76], are a useful tool: everyone can test the validity of a signature and no one can forge one. Some well-known examples are the RSA-scheme ([RSA78]), the scheme of ElGamal ([ElG85]), and the Fiat-Shamir scheme ([FS87]). They all rely on cryptographic assumptions, which means forgery is, in principle, always possible by someone using enough computing power.

The scheme we present here does not have this disadvantage: even someone with infinite computing power is unable to forge a signature. The price we pay for this is that our scheme has to be set up among a fixed, finite set of participants.

In [RB89], a "non-cryptographic weaker version of digital signatures" was introduced. Their model is essentially the same as ours. Unlike a digital signature, however, their scheme requires each recipient to conduct a protocol with all other participants to test a signature after it has been issued to him. Even so, only a participant who receives a signature directly from the signer can convince another participant. In contrast, our result is a true signature scheme: a signature is a collection of bits which can be verified independently by any recipient and successively transferred to other participants who can do the same (a related work based on cryptographic assumptions is described in [BPW90]).

In establishing the public key in our scheme, the signer receives messages from the other participants by an untraceable sending protocol, like that introduced as "the Dining Cryptographers Problem" ([Cha88]). The signature will contain some of the values that were received. The essential observation is that since the signer does not know who sent what, he will be unable (except with very small probability) to give a signature that one participant will accept that will not similarly be accepted by any participant.

Section 2 describes the model and the assumptions we make, and gives a precise definition of our aim. In Section 3, a known untraceable sending scheme is introduced. Here we also explain how to make it impossible for a disruptive participant to change (one of) the numbers sent by someone else without being caught. Section 4 explains the basic protocol, and shows that it achieves the desired result. In Section 5, we extend the protocol such that a first receiver can convince a second receiver, and that each participant who receives the signature later on knows *a priori* if he can convince a next receiver. In the last section some final remarks will be made.

2. Setting and Objectives

In the first subsection we give the setting we work in; in the second subsection the objectives are given.

2.1. Model and Assumptions

We assume that the "world" consists of a finite set $\mathcal{P}$ of n participants $\{P_1, P_2, ..., P_n\}$.

We assume the following means of communication between participants:
1. *an authenticated broadcast channel*. This enables each participant to send the same message to all other participants, identifies the sender, and is completely reliable. In particular, if any participant receives a message via the broadcast channel, all other participants will receive the same message at the same time.

2. *a private, authenticated channel between each pair of participants.* Such a channel cannot be read or tampered with by other participants, and each of the communicants is absolutely sure of the identity of the other.

2.2. Objectives

We want a participant S to be able to send a bit b to a participant R such that the following conditions hold:
1. only R receives b.
2. R can prevent S from convincing other participants that he sent $b \oplus 1$.
3. R can convince any participant that he got b from S.
4. R cannot convince any participant that he got $b \oplus 1$ from S.

Our aim is to obtain the four conditions, using a protocol that is polynomial time in a security parameter m, but with an error probability that is exponentially small in m, and we do not require any limitations on the computing power available to each participant.

Notice that in models which rely on cryptographic assumptions there is a difference between cheating that can be done offline at home, without risk of detection, and cheating which involves a substantial probability of being detected. Since we have no such assumptions, in our model there is no difference between the two.

3. Background

We make use of an Untraceable Sending protocol as introduced by [Cha88] and further elaborated by [BB89] and [Pfi89].

This protocol allows participants to send messages (elements of the abelian group $(\mathbb{Z}_v, +)$) to a fixed participant S, such that S does not know who sent which message.

The protocol relies on the use of keys. A key is a random group element, known by two participants. One of them uses the key, the other the negative (modulo v) of the key ([BB89], [Pfi89]).

Every participant, except S, broadcasts the sum (mod v) of his message and all keys he shares. Only one participant, who is allowed to send, has a message unequal to 0. Now S computes the sum (mod v) of all sums broadcasted and his own sum. This equals the message, because all keys add up to 0.

It is not necessary that each pair of participants shares a key; even if a particular participant shares only one key that another participant does not know, that participant cannot compute the first participant's message. Let the participants share keys according to a trust graph T on the participants: if (P_i, P_j) is an edge in T, P_i and P_j trust each other, and they share a key.

We start with a completely connected graph T. If a particular round is disrupted (how to detect this will follow from Section 4), this round is entirely opened (i.e. all secret messages and keys are broadcasted), resulting in disagreement about a key or in detection of a participant who disrupted. In the first case, the corresponding edge in T is removed; in the second the corresponding vertex of T is removed.

Thus, opening a disrupted round always results in a reduction of T, and only vertices corresponding to disrupters and edges connected to at least one disrupter are removed.

4. Basic Protocol

We want some participant $S \in \mathcal{P}$ to send a random bit b, with his signature attached to it, to some participant $R \in \mathcal{P}$. To achieve this, all participants initially agree on a security parameter m, such that $\frac{1}{2} m \cdot (0.65)^m$, upper bounding the error probability, is sufficiently small, and they agree on a prime p, $2^m < p < 2^{m+1}$.

First we need a *preparation phase* in which each of the $n-1$ participants unequal to S sends untraceably m pairs of random numbers to S.

Round μ of the preparation phase ($1 \leq \mu \leq m$) looks like:
step 1. The participants start with a subprotocol, called the *reservation phase*, to determine the order in which they have to send their messages. This subprotocol is described in [Cha88].
   If it is not successful, this can be due to collision or to disruption. In the first case the participants just start again with the reservation phase; in the second, T is reduced before doing so.
   After a successful reservation, the only thing each participant unequal to S knows is when he is allowed to send.
step 2. Each participant ($\neq$ S) sends S untraceably and in the defined order a pair of numbers (N^0, N^1) chosen uniformly from $\mathbb{Z}_p \times \mathbb{Z}_p$, and their product $C := N^0 \cdot N^1 \bmod p$. A disrupter can modify the pair by adding (modulo

p) some non-zero pair to it, but since S only accepts pairs $(\widetilde{N}^0, \widetilde{N}^1)$ for which the received $\widetilde{C}$ equals the product modulo p of $\widetilde{N}^0$ and $\widetilde{N}^1$, the probability that S accepts a modified pair is smaller than 2^{-m} (see below). If S does not accept a pair, this round is opened, T is reduced, and the participants start again with step 1.

After the preparation phase we can start with the *signing phase*:

S has obtained the $(n-1) \times m$ matrix $A: A_{ij} = (\widetilde{N}^0{}_{ij}, \widetilde{N}^1{}_{ij}, \widetilde{C}_{ij})$ for $1 \le i \le n-1$, $1 \le j \le m$. S only knows that each participant has sent him one entry of each column, while the participants distinct from S also know which entries of each column are theirs.

S sends his bit b to R by sending him b and the $(n-1) \times m$ matrix A^b: $A^b{}_{ij} = \widetilde{N}^b{}_{ij}$. R accepts this bit b if all the N^b he sent to S are correctly contained in this matrix.

R can convince an other participant P that he got b from S by sending him A^b. P accepts b from R (i.e. he is convinced that R accepted b from S) if he sees at least half of his N^b correctly in this matrix. If the protocol would require P to see all his N^b correctly, it would be rather easy for a disruptive S to convince R, while R could not convince anyone else.

One can compute the following error probabilities:

- $\mathbb{P}$(R has reason to reject a bit b that a non-disrupt S sent him)

  = $\mathbb{P}$(at least one N^b of R is disrupted, but still accepted by S)

  $\le m \cdot \dfrac{1}{p-1}$

  $\le m \cdot 2^{-m}$.

- Since in round μ of the untraceable sending protocol S receives $n-1$ $\widetilde{N}^b$, and sends a subset of them to R (after he received the whole set of $m \cdot (n-1)$ $\widetilde{N}^b$), we find:

  $\mathbb{P}$(R has reason to accept a bit b, which a non-disrupt P does not accept from him)

  $= \displaystyle\sum_{k=0}^{\lfloor \frac{1}{2}m \rfloor} \binom{m}{k} \Big(\mathbb{P}(\text{from a column of } A, \text{ S sends both R's and P's } \widetilde{N}^b \text{ to R}) \Big)^k$

$$\left(\mathbb{P}\,(\text{from a column of } A, \text{ S sends R's } \tilde{N}^b \text{ to R, but not P's } \tilde{N}^b) \right)^{m-k}$$

$$< \sum_{k=1}^{\lfloor \frac{1}{2}m \rfloor} \binom{m+k}{k} \left(\frac{m+k}{2m} \right)^m \left(\frac{m}{2m} \right)^m$$

$$< \tfrac{1}{2}\, m \left(\frac{3\sqrt{3}}{8} \right)^m .$$

- $\mathbb{P}\,$(P has reason to accept $b \oplus 1$ from (a disrupt) R, while R got b from S)

$$= \sum_{k=0}^{\lfloor \frac{1}{2}m \rfloor} \binom{m}{k} \left(\frac{p-1}{p} \right)^k \left(\frac{1}{p} \right)^{m-k}$$

$$< \left(\frac{1}{p} \right)^{\lceil \frac{1}{2}m \rceil} \cdot \tfrac{1}{2} \cdot 2^m$$

$$< 2^{-m}.$$

- $\mathbb{P}\,$(P has reason to reject b, while both S and R were honest)

$$< \binom{m}{\lceil \frac{1}{2}m \rceil} \left(\frac{1}{p} \right)^{\lceil \frac{1}{2}m \rceil}$$

$$< 2^{-m}.$$

As a consequence, an upper bound on the error probability is $\tfrac{1}{2}\, m \cdot (0.65)^m$.

5. Transferability

In this section we will denote the first receiver R by R_1 and the second receiver P by R_2.

At first glance, R_2 can pass the signature to a third receiver R_3, just as R_1 passed it to him. But the problem is that R_2 does not know how many of R_3's numbers in the matrix have been changed.

If only half of R_2's numbers in the matrix were correct, of course an honest R_2 does not want to guarantee that the same fraction (or more) of R_3's numbers are correct. Therefore, each time the signature is passed, the number of correct entries required has to be reduced.

This scheme has two disadvantages; m has to be very large if there are a lot of (potential) receivers, and each receiver has to know his position in the chain.

Therefore we adapt the scheme such that a receiver cannot change any of the $m \cdot (n-1)$ $\widetilde{N}^b$ without being caught by the receiver he passes the signature to.

In the *preparation phase*, instead of sending (N^0, N^1, C), where $C = N^0 \cdot N^1 \bmod p$, each participant sends a set of four numbers (N^0, N^1, K, C), where N^0, N^1 and K are chosen uniformly from $\mathbb{Z}_p$, and C is their product $N^0 \cdot N^1 \cdot K \bmod p$. S only accepts triples $(\widetilde{N}^0, \widetilde{N}^1, \widetilde{K})$ for which the received $\widetilde{C}$ equals their product modulo p, thus the probability that he accepts a modified triple can easily be calculated to be smaller than 2^{-m}.

K is a key that determines a hash function H_K from a universal class of hash functions that map arbitrary large inputs to numbers of $\mathbb{Z}_p$. Given K, each participant knows H_K.

When S has obtained the $(n-1) \times m$ matrix $A: A_{ij} = (\widetilde{N}^0{}_{ij}, \widetilde{N}^1{}_{ij}, \widetilde{K}_{ij}, \widetilde{C}_{ij})$, the *signing phase* can start. To send a bit b to R_1, S sends him b and the $(n-1) \times m$ matrix $A^b: A^b{}_{ij} = (\widetilde{N}^b{}_{ij}, X_{ij})$, where the checksums X_{ij} are defined by the following funtion on ordered sets:

$$X_{ij} := H_{\widetilde{K}_{ij}}(\{\widetilde{N}^b{}_{kl} \mid 1 \leq k < n, 1 \leq l \leq m\} \cup \{X_{kl} \mid 1 \leq k < n, 1 \leq l < j\}) +$$
$$\widetilde{N}^{b \oplus 1}{}_{ij} \bmod p.$$

In words: the X_{ij} are output values of a hash function on all message numbers and all checksums of the previous columns. The random number $\widetilde{N}^{b \oplus 1}{}_{ij}$ is added to make it impossible for a disruptive receiver who was not the sender of A_{ij} to calculate the key $\widetilde{K}_{ij}$. Thus a receiver who modifies one of the $\widetilde{N}^b{}_{ij}$ is unable to change the checksums accordingly. Therefore, a receiver who finds at least one of his checksums correct, knows that all message numbers are as S sent them to the first receiver.

R_1 checks that all the N^b he sent to S are correctly contained in A^b, and that all his checksums are correct. If something is wrong, R_1 knows S is a disrupter and he rejects the signature.

Each of the following receivers R_k ($k \geq 2$) checks if at least half of the N^b he sent to S are correctly contained in A^b. If this is not the case, R_k rejects the signature and knows that R_{k-1} or S has been cheating. Otherwise R_k checks his checksums. If at least one of them is correct, he assumes that all random numbers are as S gave them to R_1, as it is very unlikely that a preceding receiver modified them and guessed correctly a corresponding checksum. In this case R_k *strongly accepts* the signature, which means that he is convinced that receiver R_{k+1} will accept it from him. On the other hand, if none of R_k's checksums is correct, R_k has no idea of how many of an other participants' message numbers have been changed. Therefore he only *weakly accepts* the signature: he is convinced that S gave b to R_1, but he is not sure that he can convince someone else.

A receiver R_k can get additional information from the structure of the received matrix. For example, if R_k does not find all his N^b correctly in A^b, but at least one correct checksum on the values in the matrix, he knows that S has been cheating. The same holds if R_k finds an incorrect checksum that is the input of a correct checksum.

If a receiver would tell the next receiver which prefix of columns he can check that actually originate from S, it is even more often possible to point out a disrupter who is responsible for inconsistencies.

6. Summary and Suggestions for Further Research

We devised a signature scheme that is of polynomial complexity in the number of participants n and the security parameter m, allowing each of the participants to convince each other participant of the validity of his signature. Moreover, this convinced participant can convince every other participant of the signature's validity, without interaction of the original signer.

An extension of this scheme, that is still of polynomial complexity, allows a participant that receives the signature from any source to check *a priori* if he will be able to convince every other participant of the signature's validity (without interaction with the original signer).

For some applications (e.g. multiparty computations), it would be useful if non-acceptance of a signature from the original signer S, would enable the other participants to decide who is disrupting.

It would also be nice if a receiver of the signature, upon noticing inconsistencies, would know who has been cheating.

Finally, the efficiency of the scheme would be significantly improved if it was possible to sign arbitrary messages instead of single bits. Research is currently being done at CWI to use a universal hashing function on a message with the two numbers N^0 and N^1 as keys, instead of just choosing N^b for a single bit message b.

Bibliography

[BB89]   J. Bos, B. den Boer: "Detection of Disrupters in the DC Protocol", *Advances in Cryptology - EUROCRYPT '89 Proceedings*, 1989.

[BPW90] G. Bleumer, B. Pfitzmann, M. Waidner: "A remark on a signature scheme where forgery can be proved", to appear in *Advances in Cryptology - EUROCRYPT '90 Proceedings*, 1990.

[Cha88]   D. Chaum: "The Dining Cryptographers Problem: Unconditional Sender and Recipient Untraceability", *Journal of Cryptology 1/1*, 1988.

[DH76]   W. Diffie, M.E. Hellman: "New Directions in Cryptography", *IEEE Transactions on Information Theory IT-22*, 1976.

[ElG85]   T. ElGamal, "A Public Key Cryptosystem and a Signature Scheme Based on Discrete Logarithms", *IEEE Transactions on Information Theory IT-31*, 1985.

[FS87]   A. Fiat, A. Shamir: "How To Prove Yourself: Practical Solutions to Identification and Signature Problems", *Proceedings of Crypto 86*, Lecture Notes in Computer Science, Vol. 263, Berlin: Springer - Verlag, 1987.

[Pfi89]   A. Pfitzmann: "*Diensteintegrierende Kommunikationsnetze mit Teilnemher-überprüfbarem Datenschutz*", Dissertation Universität Karlsruhe, Fakultät für Informatik, 1989.

[RB89]   Rabin, T., Ben-Or, M.: Verifiable secret sharing and multiparty protocols with honest majority. *Proceedings, 21th Annual ACM Symposium on the Theory of Computing*,1989.

[RSA78] R.L. Rivest, A. Shamir, L. Adleman, "A Method for obtaining digital signatures and public-key cryptosystems", *Communications of the ACM, vol. 21*, 1978.

Session 5

Secret Sharing

Chair: M. De Soete, Philips

Geometric Shared Secret and/or Shared Control Schemes[*]

Gustavus J. Simmons
Sandia National Laboratories
Albuquerque, New Mexico 87185, USA

Introduction

A shared secret scheme is normally specified in terms of a desired security, P_d, and a concurrence scheme, Γ. The concurrence scheme (aka access structure) identifies subsets of participants (also called trustees or shareholders) each of which should be able to cooperatively recover the secret and/or initiate the controlled action. The security requirement is expressed as the maximum acceptable probability, P_d, that the secret can be exposed or the controlled action initiated by a collection of persons that doesn't include at least one of the authorized subsets identified in the concurrence scheme. A concurrence scheme is said to be <u>monotone</u> if every set of participants that includes one or more sets from Γ is also able to recover the secret. The <u>closure of Γ</u>, denoted by $\hat{\Gamma}$, is the collection of all supersets (not necessarily proper) of the sets in Γ, i.e., the collection of all sets of participants that can recover the secret and/or initiate the controlled action. A shared secret scheme implementing a concurrence scheme Γ is said to be <u>perfect</u> if the probability of recovering the secret is the same for every set, $\mathbf{C}$, of participants: $\mathbf{C} \not\subset \hat{\Gamma}$. Since, in particular, $\mathbf{C}$ could consist of only nonparticipants, i.e., of persons with no insider information about the secret, the probability, P, of an unauthorized recovery of the secret in a perfect scheme is just the probability of being able to "guess" the secret using only public information about Γ and the shared secret scheme implementing Γ: $P \leq P_d$. A shared secret scheme is said to be <u>unconditionally secure</u> if P is independent of the computing power or effort that the opponent(s) may be willing to expend in an effort to improperly recover the secret.

---
[*] This work performed at Sandia National Laboratories supported by the U. S. Department of Energy under contract no. DE-AC04-76DP00789.

Our convention will be that the secret is a point, p, in a publicly known space V_d, and that every point in this space is a priori equally likely to be the secret. This says that

$$|V_d| \geq \frac{1}{P_d}$$

i.e., that the minimum cardinality of V_d is determined by the security requirements. V_d is considered to be embedded in another space S, where—except in the degenerate case in which each of the participants can unilaterally initiate the controlled action—S will be of higher dimension than V_d:

$$\dim(S) = n > \dim(V_d) = m \quad .$$

At each point in V_d, there will be the same number of (n-m)-dimensional subspaces of S each of which has only that point in common with V_d. A point p in V_d and one of the (n-m)-dimensional subspaces, V_i, lying on p are chosen randomly and with a uniform probability distribution. The subspace V_i is called the indicator since given it and knowing V_d, p can be easily identified, i.e., V_i indicates or points to the point p in V_d. Conversely, given V_d and any subspace disjoint from V_d, because of the way in which p was chosen, p can only be "guessed" at with a probability of success (on the first try) of

$$P = \frac{1}{|V_d|} \leq P_d \quad .$$

A perfect (monotone) geometric shared secret scheme implementing the concurrence scheme Γ is an assignment of subspaces (algebraic varieties in general) of V_i to the participants in such a way that the collection of subspaces held by any set of participants $\mathbf{C}$, $\mathbf{C} \epsilon \Gamma$, span V_i and hence indicate p, while the space spanned by the collection of subspaces held by a set $\mathbf{D}$, for every $\mathbf{D} \not{\hat{\Gamma}}$, is disjoint from V_d and hence yields no information whatsoever about p. While it may not be obvious, it is at least plausible—and as it happens, true—that the minimum dimension of V_i is determined by the concurrence scheme Γ. Thus, since the security requirement only determines the minimum cardinality of V_d and the concurrence scheme the minimum dimension of V_i, it should be no surprise that the specifications for a shared control scheme do not uniquely define a geometric shared secret scheme.

While it isn't really necessary to exhibit an example to understand the implications of the preceding remark, an example does make it easier to see why the designer of a shared control scheme might choose one realization in preference to others. Consider a simple 2-out-of-4 threshold scheme (also called a (2,4) threshold scheme) for which the specified security is $P_d \leq 10^{-6}$, i.e., for which the chance of an an outsider or any participant alone guessing the secret on their first try will be no greater than one in a million. This says that the subspace in which the secret is concealed must contain at least a million points. Since we wish to work with finite geometries coordinatized by finite fields, a natural choice in this case would be to work with an extension field over GF(2) since $2^{20} = 1,048,576$. The dimension of the indicator subspace must be at least one since the lowest dimensional realization of an indicator for a 2-out-of-4 threshold scheme consists of four distinct points on a line (the minimum dimension of V_i is determined by Γ). Figure 1 shows two possible realizations in this case.

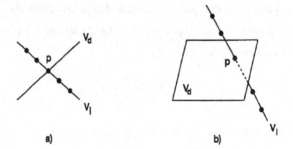

Figure 1.

In (a), since $|V_d| = 2^{20}$, $q = 2^{20}$. Consequently ≈ 40 bits[1] of information will be required to identify a point (the private pieces of information) in the plane, S, containing V_d and V_i. On the other hand, in (b), $q = 2^{10}$ since V_d is 2-dimensional. S is 3-dimensional in this case, so that the private pieces of information need only be ≈ 30 bits in size. V_d could also be chosen to be 5-dimensional (over $GF(2^4)$) in

---

1. If the constructions are in AG(n,q), then the information content of the private pieces of information will be equal to $n\log_2(q)$. If S = PG(n,q) the number of points in the space is $(q^{n+1}-1)/(q-1)$ instead of q^n, so that the number of bits required to specify a point will be larger than $n\log_2(q)$.

which case S would be 6-dimensional and the private pieces of information would consist of $\approx$ 24 bits. This is the most economical construction possible for this example in an affine geometry since if V_d were
made to be 10-dimensional (over $GF(2^2)$) there would only be four points
on a line. On the indicator line V_i, one of these would have to be the
point p. Hence, it would be impossible to assign four distinct points
as the private pieces of information, each of which would also have to
be distinct from p, as required in the specification of the desired
shared control. The scheme could just be fitted into $PG(11,2^2)$ since in
this case there are five points on each line. This would be slightly
more economical of information—saving epsilon more than one bit. However, the first point that we wanted to make with this example should be
clear; namely, that even after the indicator V_i has been chosen, the
designer may still have a choice of V_d to make depending on considerations other than just the specification of P_d and Γ.

A more interesting freedom exists in the choice of V_i in the first
place. Even for this very simple concurrence scheme (Γ a 2-out-of-4
threshold scheme) there are infinitely many choices for V_i. All that is
required is that there be at least four distinct and proper subspaces of
V_i any two of which span V_i and no one of which lies on the specified
point p in V_i. The smallest such example consisted of four distinct
points on a line containing at least five points. Figure 2 shows three
low-dimensional possible choices for V_i.

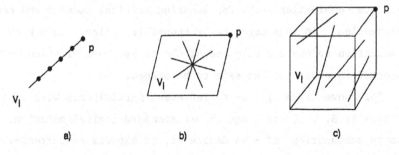

Figure 2.

(a) we have already discussed at length. In (b) the private pieces of
information are four lines in the plane V_i, no one of which lies on the
point p (they need not be concurrent as shown). In (c) the private
pieces of information are four pairwise skew lines in the 3-space V_i, no

one of which lies on the point p. Obviously there are infinitely many
choices for the space V_i and associated spanning set of subspaces—what
isn't obvious is why the designer would ever chose to use anything other
than the minimal dimensional realization of Γ. To illustrate this, one
must consider more complex concurrences than simple threshold schemes.
The treatment of these more general—and complicated—concurrence
schemes is the primary objective of this paper, so we will defer the
discussion of these considerations until later. The second point that
we wanted to make with this example was to illustrate the freedom of
choice for V_i which is also available to the designer of a shared
control scheme.

We should remark at this point, that in this paper we will only be
concerned with unconditionally secure perfect monotone geometric shared
secret schemes.

The Geometry of Concurrence Schemes

When there are only two participants in a shared control scheme,
there are only two types of control possible: either it is possible for
either one of them to initiate the controlled action unilaterally, or
else it requires the concurrence of both of them to do so. The first
situation corresponds to two persons knowing the combination to a conventional safe so that either of them can open it, while the second
corresponds to the U.S. military's common usage of safes with two
separate combination locks for securing critical command and control
information. In this case, two responsible officers each know the
combination to one and only one of the locks, both of which must be
unlocked in order for the safe to be opened.

Our conventions will be to represent participants with capital
letters A, B, ..., etc., and to use standard logical notation, ($\cdot$) to
denote conjunction and + to denote or, to express concurrences. For the
case of two participants, n = 2, we therefore have the pair of concurrence schemes:

$$\Gamma = A + B \qquad \text{and} \qquad \Gamma = AB \ .$$

These may be represented graphically

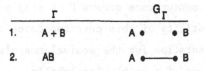

Figure 3.

with the edge AB in the right-hand figure indicating that A and B
(denoted by A · B or AB) must concur in order for the controlled event
to be initiated.

For n = 3, the situation is somewhat more interesting since in this
case there are five possible equivalence classes of concurrence schemes
(up to a permutation of the labels for the participants):

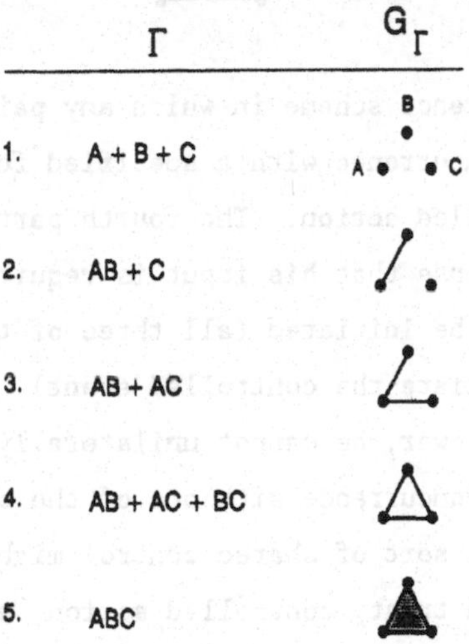

	Γ	G_Γ
1.	A + B + C	A • • C B •
2.	AB + C	
3.	AB + AC	
4.	AB + AC + BC	
5.	ABC	

Figure 4.

The unlabeled graphs in the right-hand column, G_Γ, correspond to
equivalence classes of concurrence schemes. The concurrence schemes
shown in the column, Γ, are the specific member of the class obtained
with the indicated labeling for the participants.

Observation: There is a natural one-to-one correspondence between
the set of isomorphism classes of monotone concurrence schemes involving
n participants and the set of hypergraphs on n vertices; subject to the
condition that no hyperedge properly contains any other edge of the
graph. To see this, label the vertices with the participants and
include as an edge in G any subset, **C**, of participants that appears in
the concurrence scheme Γ, i.e., **C** ε Γ. Conversely, given a hypergraph

G, the associated concurrence scheme Γ is simply an enumeration of the edges of G. The utility of this correspondence is that it provides a convenient representation for the equivalence classes of concurrence schemes, independent of a particular labeling.

represents a 2-out-of-4 threshold scheme which already has a concise description. However

represents a concurrence scheme in which any pair out of a set of three participants, in concurrence with a specified fourth participant, can initiate the controlled action. The fourth participant has a kind of veto power in the sense that his input is required in order for the controlled event to be initiated (all three of the other participants together cannot initiate the controlled event). However in spite of this absolute veto power, he cannot unilaterally initiate the controlled action not even in concurrence with one of the other participants. An application for this sort of shared control might very reasonably arise in connection with a treaty controlled action, say between the U.S. and three of its allies where the U.S. wants to retain the right to veto the action, but the allies wish to be guaranteed that at least two of them must agree before the event can be initiated. The reader can now appreciate the utility of the graphical representation which concisely expresses everything that has been said about this concurrence scheme.

Figure 5 shows the twenty concurrence schemes possible for four participants. The column headed Γ shows a canonical representative of each class corresponding to the labeling of vertices shown in 1. The schemes with concise descriptions are 1, 11, 19 and 20 corresponding to (1,4), (2,4), (3,4) and (4,4) threshold schemes, respectively. Many of the others have no concise description as we have already seen for concurrence scheme number 18.

223

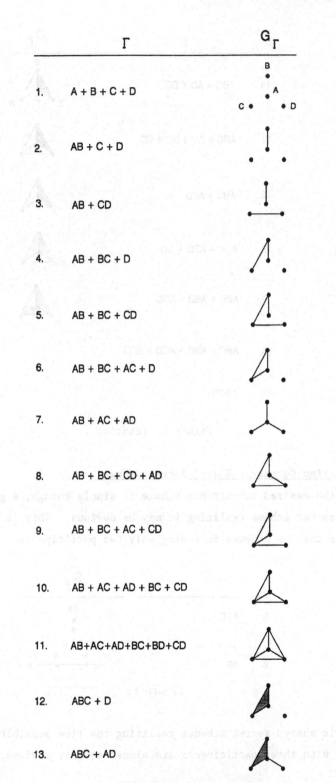

	Γ	G_Γ
1.	A + B + C + D	
2.	AB + C + D	
3.	AB + CD	
4.	AB + BC + D	
5.	AB + BC + CD	
6.	AB + BC + AC + D	
7.	AB + AC + AD	
8.	AB + BC + CD + AD	
9.	AB + BC + AC + CD	
10.	AB + AC + AD + BC + CD	
11.	AB+AC+AD+BC+BD+CD	
12.	ABC + D	
13.	ABC + AD	

Figure 5.

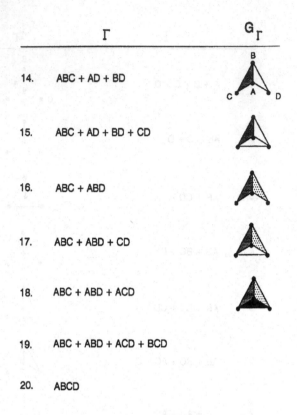

	Γ	G_Γ
14.	ABC + AD + BD	
15.	ABC + AD + BD + CD	
16.	ABC + ABD	
17.	ABC + ABD + CD	
18.	ABC + ABD + ACD	
19.	ABC + ABD + ACD + BCD	
20.	ABCD	

Figure 5. (cont'd)

Constructing Geometric Shared Secret Schemes

If the desired concurrence scheme is simple enough, a geometric shared secret scheme realizing it may be obvious. This is certainly the case for the two schemes involving only two participants:

	Γ	S_Γ
1.	A+B	A,B •p
2.	AB	A B •p

Figure 6.

Geometric shared secret schemes realizing the five possible concurrence schemes with three participants are almost equally obvious:

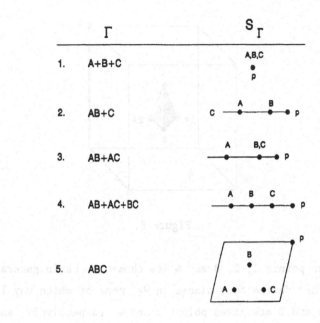

	Γ	S Γ
1.	A+B+C	
2.	AB+C	
3.	AB+AC	
4.	AB+AC+BC	
5.	ABC	

Figure 7.

In general, this will not be the case, though, and formal means for constructing geometric schemes are needed. For example, it is far from obvious how to construct shared secret schemes realizing several of the concurrence schemes shown in Figure 5. To verify this claim, the reader may wish to try to construct schemes realizing concurrences 13, 14 and 17 before reading further.

We will use concurrence scheme #5 from Figure 5 as an example. This scheme was first discussed by Benaloh and Leichter [1] who used it to prove that not every concurrence scheme (which they call an access structure) can be realized by an ideal secret sharing scheme.[2] While it isn't too difficult to devise a geometric shared secret scheme realizing Γ, a construction certainly isn't obvious either. Assume that V_i is 3-dimensional, then one possible scheme is:

---

2. A shared secret scheme is said to be ideal if all of the private pieces of information come from the same domain as the secret; i.e., if they are all points in the same space.

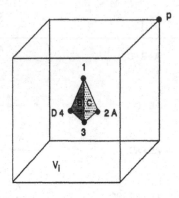

Figure 8.

The four points 1, 2, 3 and 4 are chosen to be in general position and hence they define four planes in V_i, none of which may lie on the point p. A and D are given points 2 and 4, respectively, as their private pieces of information. B and C are given the planes lying on the triples of points 1, 3 and 4 and 1, 2 and 3, respectively. Clearly the subspaces held by A and B or by B and C, or by C and D span V_i. Equally clearly V_i is not spanned by the subspaces held by any other pair of the participants. A's point is in the plane held by C, which by construction does not lie on p. Similarly, D's point is in the plane held by B, etc. Points 2 and 4 (held by A and D) define a line that lies in two planes neither of which lies on p, and hence the line does not lie on p either. Therefore, the configuration shown in Figure 6 is a perfect monotone geometric shared secret scheme realizing the Benaloh-Leichter concurrence.

G_Γ can be redrawn to emphasize its symmetry

It is easy to see that G_Γ and S_Γ have the same symmetry, i.e., they have the same automorphism group. This is also true for the other small examples (of G_Γ, S_Γ pairs) we have seen thus far. It seems plausible, and one might be tempted to conjecture, that for any concurrence scheme Γ, G_Γ and S_Γ will have the same automorphism group. If this were true it would be a powerful tool for the construction of S_Γ. Unfortunately, the statement is not true as the following alternate geometric realization of the Benaloh-Leichter concurrence shows:

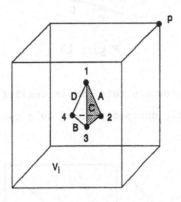

Figure 9.

The assignment of the private pieces of information are: A is given the line defined by points 1 and 2—<1,2>, B the line <3,4>, C the plane <1,2,3> and D the line <1,4>. It is easy to see that this is also a perfect monotone geometric shared secret scheme realizing the Benaloh-Leichter concurrence, but completely lacking the symmetry of G_Γ.

The primary objective in this section is the statement and illustration of several observations about shared secret schemes based on properties of the associated concurrence schemes. We will dignify these—because of their usefulness—by calling them theorems, although their validity is generally self-evident.

Theorem 1. If the hypergraph G_Γ representing the concurrence scheme Γ is disjoint, then a geometric shared secret scheme, S_Γ, can be constructed as the union of independent geometric shared secret schemes realizing each of the components—all indicating the same point p in V_d however.

Theorem 1 can be applied to concurrence scheme 3 in Figure 5:

$$\Gamma = AB + CD \ .$$

Since there are two components to G_Γ, there will be two indicators in a shared secret scheme constructed using Theorem 1; both indicating the

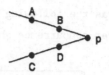

Figure 10.

It is interesting to compare this simple realization to one involving
only a single indicator subspace; i.e., to a construction made without
the aid of Theorem 1.

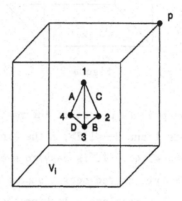

Figure 11.

We know of no simpler realization of Γ using only a single indicator.
The simplification resulting from applying Theorem 1, while illustrated
by this small example, can be dramatic for more complex concurrence
schemes.

It should be remarked at this point that Ito, Saito and Nishizeki
[6] first proved that every concurrence scheme can be realized by a
perfect (nongeometric) shared secret scheme using a construction similar
to those made using Theorem 1. Given a concurrence Γ in disjunctive
normal form (a sum of products of the literals), they construct an
independent shared secret scheme—revealing the same secret, of course—
for each term (product) in Γ. For the example just discussed, they
would also construct the S_Γ shown in Figure 10. However, their constructive technique would apply equally well to the concurrence

$$\Gamma = AB + AC$$

whose hypergraph representation is not disjoint so that our Theorem 1 would not apply. Since concurrence schemes are drawn from the power set of the set of n participants, the cardinality of Γ can be exponential in n, hence Ito, Saito and Nishizeki's construction is more in the nature of an existence proof (for perfect shared secret schemes) than a practical method of construction.

<u>Theorem 2.</u> The geometric realization for a concurrence scheme Γ in which Γ can be factored into the product of disjoint logical expressions is the space spanned by the disjoint geometrical realizations of the factors.

Theorem 2 can be applied to concurrence scheme 13 in Figure 5, which is one of those for which the reader was challenged earlier to construct a shared secret scheme:

$$\Gamma = ABC + AD = A(BC + D) \quad .$$

Applying Theorem 2, we easily construct one such shared secret scheme:

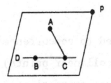

Figure 12.

<u>Theorem 3.</u> The geometric realization for a concurrence scheme in which Γ can be factored into the sum of the products of expressions disjointly partitioning the variables, can be realized as the union of geometric realizations of the form given by Theorems 1 and 2.

Theorem 3 can be applied to concurrence scheme 14 in Figure 5 (the second of the challenge schemes)

$$\Gamma = ABC + AD + BD = (AB)C + (A+B)D \quad .$$

One of the shared secret schemes that can be constructed using Theorem 3 is:

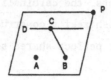

Figure 13.

Theorem 4. The concurrence scheme Γ whose hypergraph representation is $G_\Gamma = K_{k:\ell}$ (the complete hypergraph consisting of all $\binom{k}{\ell}$ k-edges on ℓ vertices) can be realized by a set of ℓ linearly independent points in a (k-1)-dimensional indicator space.

Proof: Γ consists of all of the $\binom{k}{\ell}$ k element subsets of the ℓ participants, i.e., it is a simple (k,ℓ) threshold scheme. Given ℓ linearly independent points in a (k-1)-dimensional space, no subset of j, $2 \leq j \leq k-1$, of the points can lie in a (j-1)-dimensional subspace. Therefore, since V_i is only (k-1)-dimensional, every subset of k of them must span V_i. ∎

Theorem 4 can be applied to concurrences 11 and 19 in Figure 5. The construction of S_{11} (four collinear points) is obvious. The construction of S_{19} is somewhat more interesting, consisting in this special case (n = 4) of four points in general position in a plane, V_i, no pair of which are collinear with the indicated point p.

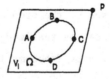

Figure 14.

The curve Ω lying on the four points A, B, C and D is a conic, i.e., for a field of odd characteristics a set of points in V_i no three of which are collinear. The same construction would hold for any $(3,\ell)$ threshold scheme. The maximum value for ℓ would be q if p lies on Ω and $(q+1)/2$ if it doesn't, since each secant of Ω through p can only lie on one point of Ω that can be used as a private piece of information.

Theorem 5. If in the hypergraph representing a concurrence scheme there are two or more independent and isomorphic points, all of these points can be identified in a reduced hypergraph representing the same concurrence scheme.

Theorem 5 is probably the most useful of all of the results given here. It applies to many of the concurrence schemes shown in Figure 5. We will use number 10 to illustrate its utility:

$$\Gamma = AB + AC + AD + BC + CD \quad .$$

Figure 15.

Vertices B and D are independent and isomorphic, and hence by Theorem 5 can be identified. Consequently, G_Γ can be replaced by the simpler

Figure 16.

to which Theorem 4 applies. One of the resulting shared secret schemes is:

Figure 17.

Almost as useful as Theorem 5 itself, is the following Corollary which allows a designer to add new participants to an existing shared secret scheme in those cases where the new participants are intended to have the same capability as one (or more) of the existing participants.

Corollary: Given a realization of a concurrence scheme, any share can be given to as many participants as desired—all of whom will be independent and have isomorphic capabilities.

Figure 18 shows a geometric shared secret scheme realizing each of the concurrence schemes shown in Figure 5. Some of these constructions are obvious a priori, others—constructed with the assistance of various of the theorems just given—are obvious after the fact, while a few may not be obvious at all.

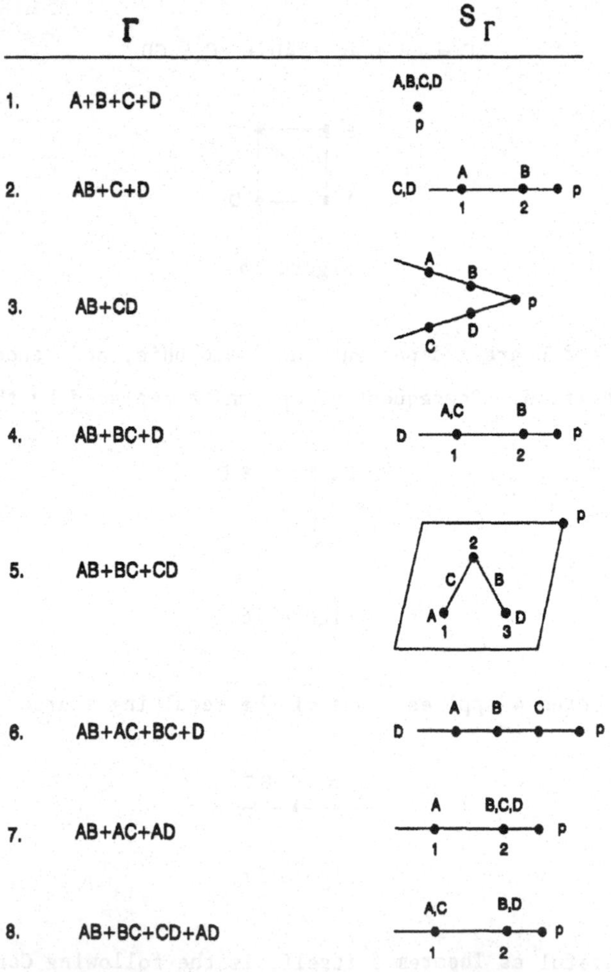

Γ	S_Γ
1. A+B+C+D	
2. AB+C+D	
3. AB+CD	
4. AB+BC+D	
5. AB+BC+CD	
6. AB+AC+BC+D	
7. AB+AC+AD	
8. AB+BC+CD+AD	

Figure 18.

233

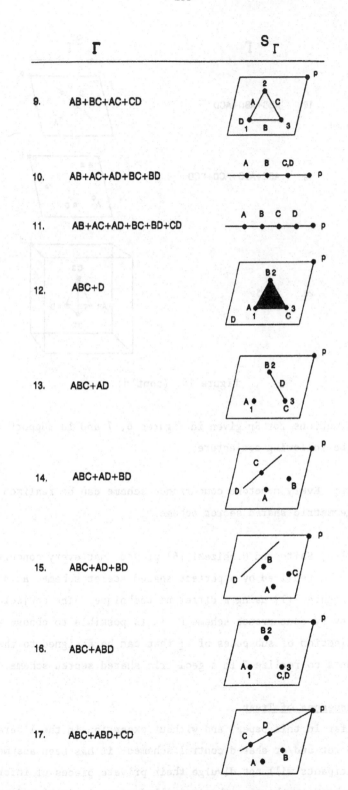

Figure 18. (cont'd)

$$\Gamma \qquad\qquad S_\Gamma$$

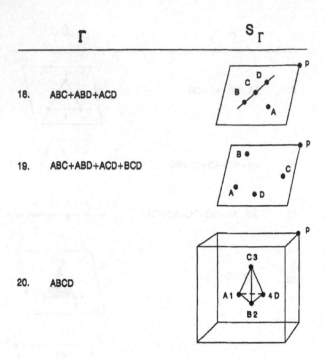

18.	ABC+ABD+ACD
19.	ABC+ABD+ACD+BCD
20.	ABCD

Figure 18. (cont'd)

The constructions for S_Γ given in Figures 6, 7 and 18 support (and prompt) the following conjecture.

Conjecture: Every monotone concurrence scheme can be realized by a perfect geometric shared secret scheme.

Remark: Ito, Saito and Nishizeki [6] proved that every concurrence scheme can be realized by a perfect shared secret scheme, as did Benaloh-Leichter [1] using a different technique. The conjecture is that for every concurrence scheme Γ, it is possible to choose a space V_i and a collection of subspaces of V_i that can be assigned to the participants to realize Γ in a geometric shared secret scheme.

The Consequences of Trust

Thus far in this paper, and without exception in the literature on shared secret and/or shared control schemes, it has been assumed that the participants will not divulge their private pieces of information—except perhaps at the time the controlled event is initiated. This is

not the same as assuming that the participants are unconditionally
trustworthy, and in fact several persons have studied the problem of how
to make the functioning of a shared control scheme be reliable when
(some) participants may not be [2,3,4,5,7,8,9]. Realistically, though,
one must accept the possibility that a participant may share what he
knows with whomever he trusts. The consequences of such sharing may be
surprising (to the key distribution center who set up the secret sharing
scheme with a desired concurrence in mind). For example, in the two
participant scheme to realize Γ = AB (2 in Figure 3) if A trusts B and
tells him his private piece of information, B can thereafter unilaterally initiate the controlled action. This isn't what the key distribution center had in mind, since it was his intention that A and B would
have to concur <u>at the time</u> that the controlled event is to be initiated.
However, there is no notion of simultaneity in the logic of shared control, only a specification of which private pieces of information will
be needed to initiate the controlled action. In the example, A's input
is required and is present—in B's possession. In effect, A has given B
his proxy which B can exercise whenever he chooses. Thus, even though
the resulting control is not what the key distribution center had in
mind, it is also not a logical surprise either.

On the other hand, consider the concurrence scheme Γ = AB + AC + AD
(7 in Figures 5 and 8). The intent of the key distribution center in
this case is that A must concur with at least one of B, C or D in order
for the controlled event to be initiated. We have already discussed a
similar example in the setting of a treaty controlled action where A
(say the U.S.) retains a veto power over the action, but in spite of
this absolute veto capability can't unilaterally initiate the controlled
action. In the present example, this requires the concurrence of at
least one of the three other signatories to the treaty. Now assume that
A trusts B and C together and shares his private piece of information
with them in such a way that they can jointly reconstruct his input to
the shared control scheme. Neither B nor C alone can initiate the controlled action. The unexpected result though is that B, C and D
together could then initiate the controlled action. Γ has been replaced
with a new concurrence scheme

$$\Gamma' = AB + AC + AD + BCD$$

where the three participants B, C and D can act without needing A's
concurrence. This consequence of A's trust of B and C is more surprising than the result in previous example, since there a proxy (trust
relationship) was used to eliminate a participant from an authorized
subset of Γ. Here it is used to replace a participant in an authorized
concurrence with a subset of the other participants. The result is that
new (and unexpected) sets are capable of initiating the controlled
action. In both cases, a literal (A in both of these examples) is
replaced with a trusted subset (BC). In the first case, a participant
is eliminated as a result, while in the second, one participant is
eliminated and two are added:

$$ABC \rightarrow BCBC \rightarrow BC \qquad \text{and} \qquad AD \rightarrow BCD \quad .$$

The basic notion (and problem) should be clear from these two small
examples. If one or more of the participants trust some collections of
the other participants, i.e., if they share their private pieces of
information in such a way that subsets that they trust can jointly act
in their stead the result may be that quite different concurrences than
were originally intended (Γ) may be able to initiate the controlled
action.

When a key distribution center sets up a shared control scheme S_Γ to
realize a concurrence Γ, he must implicitly accept all of the concurrence schemes reachable from Γ as a result of the possible trust relationships between the participants—since he can't know and can't control who trusts whom. Incidentally, there are concurrences that are not
reachable from a given concurrence; for example Γ = AB is not reachable
from Γ = A + B, since if both participants are initially able to unilaterally initiate the controlled action, nothing that can be done by
either participant can lessen the other's capability. Since trust
relationships can only increase the capability of groupings of participants, and can never take capability away from a subset C that previously had it (C ε Γ), a lattice of concurrence schemes can be defined,
in which the nodes are concurrence schemes and the edges are trust relationships. At Crypto'90 in the lecture on which this paper is based we
made a conjecture as to the structure of this lattice—essentially
equating the lattice of concurrence schemes Γ and the geometric lattice

In the case of two participants, AB dominates A + B, and the trust relationship to reach A+B from AB is that A must trust B and vice versa. For three participants the situation is more complex. Obviously ABC dominates all other concurrence schemes and A+B+C is dominated by everything else. The ordering of the other three concurrence schemes however requires some analysis. AB+AC dominates AB+AC+BC since if A trusts B and C jointly (meaning that A can be replaced by BC), we have

$$AB + AC \rightarrow BCB + BCC \rightarrow BC$$

and

$$\Gamma' = AB + AC + BC \quad .$$

Similarly AB + AC + BC dominates AB+C, requiring that A trust C. Three participant concurrence schemes therefore are ordered as shown in Figure 19.

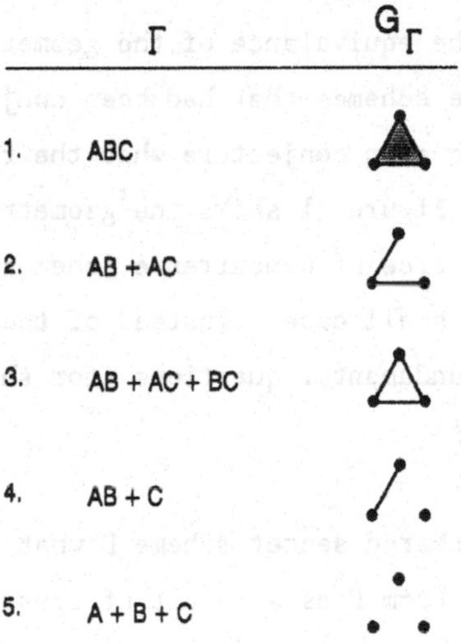

Γ	G_Γ
1. ABC	
2. AB + AC	
3. AB + AC + BC	
4. AB + C	
5. A + B + C	

Figure 19.

The geometric latice (of hypergraphs) in which order is determined by set (edge) inclusion has a different order however:

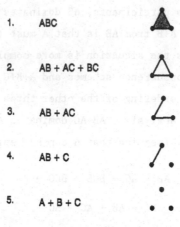

1. ABC

2. AB + AC + BC

3. AB + AC

4. AB + C

5. A + B + C

Figure 20.

The reversal of the order of AB+AC+BC and AB+AC in these two lattices is a counterexample to the equivalence of the geometric lattice and the lattice of concurrence schemes that had been conjectured. At the present, we are unable to even conjecture what the relationship between the two lattices may be. Figure 21 shows the geometric lattice for three participants. The lattice of concurrence schemes is still being investigated for even this small case. Instead of the (refuted) conjecture, we instead, ask the fundamental questions (for shared secret and/or shared control schemes).

Question 1. Given a shared secret scheme Γ what other shared secret schemes are reachable from Γ as a result of trust relationships that may exist among the participants.

The next question is closely related, but not necessarily the same.

Question 2. Characterize the lattice of concurrence schemes for n participants.

239

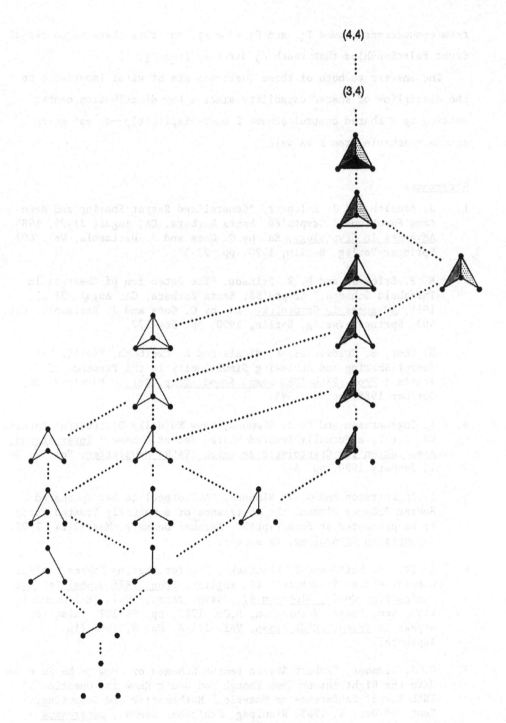

(4,4)

(3,4)

Figure 21.

The reason that we say that Questions 1 and 2 may not be equivalent is that it could be the case that concurrence scheme Γ_2 is reachable from concurrence scheme Γ_1, and Γ_3 from Γ_2, but that there is no set of trust relationships that reach Γ_3 directly from Γ_1.

The answers to both of these questions are of vital importance to the discipline of shared capability since a key distribution center setting up a shared control scheme Γ must—implicitly—accept every scheme reachable from Γ as well.

References

1. J. Benaloh and J. Leichter, "Generalized Secret Sharing and Monotone Functions," Crypto'88, Santa Barbara, CA, August 21-25, 1988, <u>Advances in Cryptology</u>, Ed. by G. Goos and J. Hartmanis, Vol. 403, Springer-Verlag, Berlin, 1990, pp. 27-35.

2. E. F. Brickell and D. R. Stinson, "The Detection of Cheaters in Threshold Schemes," Crypto'88, Santa Barbara, CA, August 21-25, 1988, <u>Advances in Cryptology</u>, Ed. by G. Goos and J. Hartmanis, Vol. 403, Springer-Verlag, Berlin, 1990, pp. 564-577.

3. B. Chor, S. Goldwasser, S. Micali and B. Awerbuch, "Verifiable Secret Sharing and Achieving Simultaneity in the Presence of Faults," <u>Proc. 26th IEEE Symp. Found. Comp. Sci.</u>, Portland, OR, October 1985, pp. 383-395.

4. I. Ingemarsson and G. J. Simmons, "How Mutually Distrustful Parties Can Set Up a Mutually Trusted Shared Secret Scheme," <u>International Association for Cryptologic Research (IACR) Newsletter</u>, Vol. 7, No. 1, January 1990, pp. 4-7.

5. I. Ingemarsson and G. J. Simmons, "A Protocol to Set Up Shared Secret Schemes Without the Assistance of a Mutually Trusted Party," to be presented at Eurocrypt'90, Aarhus, Denmark, May 21-24, 1990, <u>Advances in Cryptology</u>, to appear.

6. M. Ito, A. Saito and T. Nishizeki, "Secret Sharing Scheme Realizing General Access Structure," (in English) <u>Proc. IEEE Global Telecommunications Conf., Globecom'87</u>, Tokyo, Japan, 1987, IEEE Communications Soc. Press, Washington, D.C., 1987, pp. 99-102. Also to appear in <u>Trans. IEICE Japan</u>, Vol. J71-A, No. 8, 1988 (in Japanese).

7. G. J. Simmons, "Robust Shared Secret Schemes or 'How to be Sure You Have the Right Answer Even Though You Don't Know the Question'," 18th Annual Conference on Numerical Mathematics and Computing, Sept. 29-Oct. 1, 1988, Winnipeg, Manitoba, Canada, <u>Congressus Numerantium</u>, Vol. 68, May 1989, pp. 215-248.

8. G. J. Simmons, "Prepositioned Shared Secret and/or Shared Control Schemes," Eurocrypt'89, Houthalen, Belgium, April 11-13, 1989, <u>Advances in Cryptology</u>, to appear.

9.   M. Tompa and H. Woll, "How to Share a Secret with Cheaters,"
     Crypto'86, Santa Barbara, CA, Aug. 19-21, 1986, Advances in
     Cryptology, Vol. 263, Ed. by A. M. Odlyzko, Springer-Verlag,
     Berlin, 1986, pp. 261-265; also Journal of Cryptology, Vol. 1, No.
     2, 1988, pp. 133-138.

Some Improved Bounds on the Information Rate of Perfect Secret Sharing Schemes

(extended abstract)

E. F. Brickell[1]
Sandia National Laboratories
Albuquerque NM 87185

D. R. Stinson[2]
Computer Science and Engineering
University of Nebraska
Lincoln NE 68588

1. Introduction and definitions

Informally, a *secret sharing scheme* is a method of sharing a secret key K among a finite set of participants, in such a way that certain specified subsets of participants can compute a key. Suppose that $\mathbf{P}$ is the set of participants. Denote by Γ the set of subsets of participants which we desire to be able to determine the key; hence $\Gamma \subseteq 2^{\mathbf{P}}$. Γ is called the *access structure* of the secret sharing scheme. It seems reasonable to require that Γ be *monotone*, i.e.

$$\text{if } B \in \Gamma \text{ and } B \subseteq C \subseteq \mathbf{P}, \text{ then } C \in \Gamma.$$

For any $\Gamma_0 \subseteq 2^{\mathbf{P}}$, define the *closure* of Γ_0 to be

$$\text{cl}(\Gamma_0) = \{C : B \in \Gamma \text{ and } B \subseteq C \subseteq \mathbf{P}\}.$$

Note that the closure of any set of subsets is monotone.

Let $\mathbf{K}$ be a set of q elements called *keys*, and let $\mathbf{S}$ be a set of s elements called *shares*. Suppose a dealer D wants to a share the secret key $K \in \mathbf{K}$ among the participants in $\mathbf{P}$ (we will assume

[1] This work performed at Sandia National Laboratories and supported by the U. S. Department of Energy under contract number DE-AC04-76DP00789

[2] Research supported by NSERC operating grant A9287 and by the Center for Communication and Information Science, University of Nebraska

that $D \notin \mathbf{P}$). He does this by giving each participant a share. We say that the scheme is a *perfect* scheme with access structure Γ if the following two properties are satisfied:

1) if a subset B of participants pool their shares, where $B \in \Gamma$, then they can determine the value of K.

2) if a subset B of participants pool their shares, where $B \notin \Gamma$, then they can determine nothing about the value of K (in an information-theoretic sense), even with infinite computational resources.

We will depict a secret sharing scheme as a matrix M, as was done in [5]. There will be $|\mathbf{P}| + 1$ columns. The first column of M will be indexed by D, and the remaining columns are indexed by the members of $\mathbf{P}$. In any row of M, we place a value of the key K in the column D, and a possible list of shares corresponding to K in the remaining columns. When D wants to distribute shares corresponding to a key K, he will choose at random a row of M having K in column D, and distribute the shares in that row to the participants.

With this matrix representation, it is easy to describe conditions 1) and 2) above. Condition 1) becomes the following.

1') if $B \in \Gamma$ and $M(r, b) = M(r', b)$ for all $b \in B$, then $M(r, D) = M(r', D)$.

We will replace Condition 2) by a condition which Brickell and Davenport [5] call "having no probabilistic information regarding the key". This condition is the following:

2') if $B \notin \Gamma$ and $f: B \to \mathbf{S}$ is any function, then there exists a non-negative integer $\lambda(f, B)$ such that

$$|\{r: \{(b, M(r, b)): b \in B\} = \{(b, f(b)): b \in B\} \text{ and } M(r, D) = K\}| = \lambda(f, B),$$

independent of the value of K.

The *information rate* of the secret sharing scheme is defined to be $\rho = \log_2 q / \log_2 s$. It is not difficult to see that $q \leq s$ in a perfect scheme, so the information rate $\rho \leq 1$. If a secret sharing scheme is to be practical, we do not want to have to distribute too much secret information as shares. Consequently, we want to make the information rate as close to 1 as possible. A perfect secret sharing scheme with information rate $\rho = 1$ is called *ideal*. In Example 1.1, we depict an ideal secret sharing scheme.

Example 1.1 Let $\mathbf{P} = \{a, b, c\}$ and let $\Gamma = \left\{ \{a, b\}, \{b, c\}, \{a, b, c\} \right\}$. The following is a PS($\Gamma$, 1, 3}.

D	a	b	c
1	1	2	1
1	2	0	2
1	0	1	0
2	1	0	1
2	2	1	2
2	0	2	0
0	1	1	1
0	2	2	2
0	0	0	0

Note that if a has share s_a and b has share s_b, then they can compute the key as $s_b - s_a$ (modulo 3). Similarly, b and c can compute the key as $s_b - s_c$ (modulo 3). However, a and c together have no information regarding the key, since $s_a = s_c$ in every row.

We will use the notation PS(Γ, ρ, q) to denote a perfect secret sharing scheme with access structure Γ and information rate ρ for a set of q keys.

In the special case where the access structure $\Gamma = \{B \subseteq \mathbf{P}: |B| \geq t\}$, then the secret sharing scheme is called a (t, w)-*threshold scheme*, where $w = |\mathbf{P}|$. Threshold schemes have been extensively studied in the literature; see Simmons [9] for a comprehensive bibliography.

Secret sharing schemes for general access structures were first studied by Ito, Saito and Nishizeki in [6]. They proved that *any* monotone access structure can be realized by a perfect secret sharing scheme. A more efficient construction was given by Beneloh and Leichter in [1]. In both these constructions, however, the information rate is exponentially small as a function of $|\mathbf{P}|$.

Some constructions for ideal schemes were given by Brickell [4]. More recently, ideal schemes were characterized by Brickell and Davenport [5] in terms of matroids.

2. Ideal secret sharing schemes

In this section, we will discuss ideal secret sharing schemes in the case where the access structure consists of the closure of a graph. In this paper, graphs do not have loops or multiple edges; a graph with multiple edges will be termed a *multigraph*. If G is a graph, we denote the vertex set of G by $V(G)$ and the edge set by $E(G)$. G is *connected* if any two vertices are joined by a path. The *complete graph* K_n is the graph on n vertices in which any two vertices are joined by an edge. The *complete multipartite graph* $K_{n_1, n_2, \ldots, n_t}$ is a graph on $\sum_{i=1}^{t} n_i$ vertices, in which the vertex set is partitioned into subsets of size n_i ($1 \leq i \leq t$), such that vw is an edge if and only if v and w are in different subsets of the partition. An alternative way to characterize a complete multipartite graph is to say that the complementary graph is a vertex-disjoint union of cliques.

For a graph G, define $PS(G, \rho, q)$ to be $PS(\Gamma, \rho, q)$, where $\Gamma = cl(E(G))$.

The following result characterizing which graphs admit ideal secret sharing schemes was proved in [5].

Theorem 2.1 [5, Theorems 4 and 5] Suppose G is a connected graph. Then there exists a $PS(G, 1, q)$ for some q if and only if G is a complete multipartite graph.

Theorem 2.1 requires that G be connected. The cases when G is not connected are easily handled by the following easy observation.

Theorem 2.2 Suppose G is a graph having as its connected components G_i, $1 \leq i \leq t$. Suppose that there is a $PS(G_i, \rho, q)$, $1 \leq i \leq t$. Then there is a $PS(G, \rho, q)$.

We can easily prove the constructive half of Theorem 2.1 by using a couple of simple constructions. Suppose G is a graph and $v \in V(G)$. We define a graph $G(v)$ by replacing v by two non-adjacent vertices v_1 and v_2, such that v_iw is an edge of $G(v)$ if and only if vw is an edge of G ($i = 1, 2$). We say that $G(v)$ is constructed from G by *splitting* v.

Theorem 2.3 Suppose G is a graph and there exists a PS(G, ρ, q). Then for any vertex v of G, there exists a PS$(G(v), \rho, q)$.

Proof: Replace column v of the matrix M by two identical columns v_1 and v_2.

The next theorem generalizes the Shamir construction for a $(2, 2)$-threshold scheme [7]. It uses a structure from combinatorial design theory called an orthogonal array. An *orthogonal array* $OA(k, n)$ is an $n^2 \times k$ array, with entries chosen from a symbol set of n elements, such that any pair of columns contains every ordered pair of symbols exactly once.

Theorem 2.4 Suppose t is a positive integer, and there exists an orthogonal array $OA(t + 1, q)$. Then there is a PS$(K_t, 1, q)$.

Proof: We will use the $OA(t + 1, q)$ as the matrix M representing the secret sharing scheme. The first column is indexed by D, and the remaining t columns are indexed by the participants. Let P_i and P_j be two participants. In the two corresponding columns, every ordered pair of shares occurs exactly once. Hence, property 1') is satisfied. If we consider any one participant P_i, any share $s = f(P_i)$, and any key K, there is a unique row of M such that s occurs in column P_i and K occurs in column D. Hence, property 2') is satisfied with $\lambda(f, P_i) = 1$.

Corollary 2.5 Suppose t is a positive integer, q is a prime power, and $q \geq t$. Then there is a PS$(K_t, 1, q)$.

Proof: It is well-known that an $OA(t + 1, q)$ exists if q is a prime power and $q \geq t$ (e.g., see [2]).

We can now prove the constructive half of Theorem 2.1 as a corollary of these constructions.

Corollary 2.6 [5, Theorem 5] Suppose q is a prime power and $q \geq t$. Then there is a PS$(K_{n_1, n_2, ..., n_t}, 1, q)$.

Proof: Start with a PS$(K_t, 1, q)$ and split vertices until $K_{n_1, n_2, ..., n_t}$ is obtained.

If we consider the possible graphs on at most four vertices, we find that all of them admit ideal secret sharing schemes, with two exceptions. We have the following consequence of the Theorems 2.1 and 2.2.

Theorem 2.7 If G is a graph and $|V(G)| \leq 4$, then there exists a PS$(G, 1, q)$ for some q, unless G is isomorphic to one of the following two graphs:

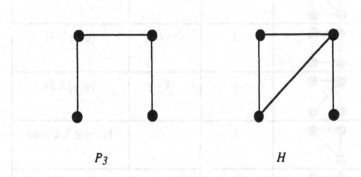

P_3 H

Remark: It was first shown by Beneloh and Leichter [1] that there does not exist a PS$(P_3, 1, q)$, where P_3 is the path of length 3, for any q.

In fact, we can be more precise about the values of q admitted in Theorem 2.7.

Theorem 2.8 If G is a connected graph, $|V(G)| \leq 4$, and G is not isomorphic to P_3 or H, then there exists a PS$(G, 1, q)$ for all integers $q \in Q(G)$, where $Q(G)$ is defined in Table 1.

Proof: It is known that there exists an $OA(5, q)$ if $q \geq 4$, $q \neq 6$, 10; there exists an $OA(4, q)$ if $q \geq 3$, $q \neq 6$; and there exists an $OA(3, q)$ if $q \geq 2$ (see [2] for proofs).

Table 1

G	$|V(G)|$	G^c	$Q(G)$
	4		$\{q:\ q \geq 5, q \neq 6, 10\}$
	4	K_2	$\{q:\ q \geq 3, q \neq 6\}$
	4	$K_2 \cup K_2$	$\{q:\ q \geq 2\}$
	4	K_3	$\{q:\ q \geq 2\}$
	3		$\{q:\ q \geq 3, q \neq 6\}$
	3	K_2	$\{q:\ q \geq 2\}$
	2		$\{q:\ q \geq 2\}$

3. Improved lower bounds on the information rate

We now turn to the construction of perfect secret sharing schemes in the cases where ideal schemes do not exist. First, we give a construction that shows that the existence of a secret sharing scheme $PS(\Gamma, \rho, q)$ for a single value of q implies the existence of an infinite class of schemes with the same information rate.

Theorem 3.1 Suppose there is a $PS(\Gamma, \rho, q_1)$ and a $PS(\Gamma, \rho, q_2)$. Then there is a $PS(\Gamma, \rho, q_1 q_2)$.

Corollary 3.2 Suppose there is a $PS(\Gamma, \rho, q)$. Then, for any positive integer n, there is a $PS(\Gamma, \rho, q^n)$.

If G is a graph, then G_1 is said to be a *subgraph* of G if $V(G) \subseteq V(G_1)$ and $E(G) \subseteq E(G_1)$. If $V_1 \subseteq V(G)$, then we define the graph $G[V_1]$ to have vertex set V_1 and edge set $\{uv \in E(G), u, v \in V_1\}$. We say that $G[V_1]$ is an *induced subgraph* of G. The following theorem is obvious.

Theorem 3.3 Suppose G is a graph and G_1 is an induced subgraph of G. If there is a $PG(G_1, \rho, q)$, then there exists a $PS(G_1, \rho, q)$.

Next, we prove some powerful "decomposition" constructions.

Theorem 3.4 Suppose G is a graph, and G_1 and G_2 are subgraphs of G such that $E(G) = E(G_1) \cup E(G_2)$. Suppose that there is a $PS(G_1, \rho_1, q)$ and a $PS(G_2, \rho_2, q)$. Then there is a $PS(G, \rho, q)$, where

$$\rho = \frac{\rho_1 \rho_2}{\rho_1 + \rho_2}.$$

This theorem can be generalized as follows.

Theorem 3.5 Suppose G is a graph and $G_1, \ldots, G_t$ are all subgraphs of G, such that each edge of G occurs in at least one of the G_i's. For $1 \leq i \leq t$, suppose that there is a $PS(G_i, \rho_i, q)$. For every vertex v, define

$$\rho(v) = \frac{1}{\displaystyle\sum_{\{i: \, v \in G_i\}} \frac{1}{\rho_i}}.$$

Then there is a $PS(G, \rho, q)$, where $\rho = \min\{\rho(v): v \in V(G)\}$.

Corollary 3.6 Suppose G is any graph with maximum degree d, and $q \geq 2$ is any integer. Then there is a $PS(G, 1/d, q)$.

Proof: Define each G_i to be an edge of G, and apply Theorem 3.5.

Remark: Corollary 3.6 can also be proved by the "monotone circuit" construction of Beneloh and Leichter [1].

We can now obtain schemes for the two graphs P_3 and H from the previous constructions.

Corollary 3.7 There exist schemes $PS(P_3, 0.5, q)$ and $PS(H, 0.5, q)$ for all $q \geq 2$.

Proof: Existence of a scheme $PS(P_3, 0.5, q)$ follows from Corollary 3.6. Existence of $PS(H, 0.5, q)$ follows from decomposing H into two edge-disjoint paths of length two, each of which admits an ideal secret sharing scheme, and applying Theorem 3.5.

We now establish a general lower bound improving that of Corollary 3.6.

Theorem 3.8 Suppose G is a graph of maximimum degree d, and denote $e = \lceil d/2 \rceil$. Then there is a constant $\rho \geq 1/(e + 1)$ such that there exists a $PS(G, \rho, q)$ for all $q \geq 2$.

Proof: Let x_i $(1 \leq i \leq 2t)$ be the vertices in $V(G)$ having odd degree (any graph has an even number of vertices of odd degree). Construct G' from G by adding t new edges $x_{2i-1} x_{2i}$ $(1 \leq i \leq t)$. Observe that G' may contain edges of multiplicity two, in which case it is a multigraph. Every vertex of G' has even degree; hence G' is Eulerian. Let C be a (directed) Eulerian tour of G'. For every vertex $v \in V(G)$ define G_v to consist of the edges of $C \cap E(G)$ for which v is the head. Then the subgraphs G_v $(v \in V(G))$ form an edge-decomposition of G. Also, each G_v is isomorphic to a complete bipartite graph K_{1,n_0}, where

$$n_0 = d_0 / 2, \text{ if } v \text{ has degree } d_0 \text{ in } G \text{ and } d_0 \text{ is even}$$
$$n_0 = \lceil d_0 / 2 \rceil \text{ or } \lfloor d_0 / 2 \rfloor, \text{ if } v \text{ has degree } d_0 \text{ in } G \text{ and } d_0 \text{ is odd}.$$

Hence, each G_v admits an ideal secret sharing scheme for any $q \geq 2$ (Corollary 2.6). Now, apply Theorem 3.5. For every vertex $v \in V(G)$, we have

$$\rho(v) = 1/(e_0 + 1), \text{ if } v \text{ has even degree } d_0 \text{ in } G \text{ and } e_0 = d_0 / 2,$$
$$\rho(v) = 1/e_0 \text{ or } 1/(e_0 + 1), \text{ if } v \text{ has odd degree } d_0 \text{ in } G \text{ and } e_0 = \lceil d_0 / 2 \rceil.$$

It follows that the resulting secret sharing scheme has rate $\rho = 1/e$ or $1/(e + 1)$, where G has maximum degree d and $e = \lceil d/2 \rceil$. Such a scheme can be constructed for any $q \geq 2$.

The last topic of this section is a direct construction for a secret sharing scheme for C_6, the cycle of size 6. Note that there is no ideal scheme in this case.

Example 3.1 The following is a $PS(C_6, \log_3 2, 2)$, where $V(C_6) = \{a, b, c, d, e, f\}$ and $E(C_6)$ $= \left\{ \{a, b\}, \{b, c\}, \{c, d\}, \{d, e\}, \{e, f\}, \{f, a\} \right\}$.

D	a	b	c	d	e	f
0	0	0	1	1	2	2
0	0	0	2	2	1	1
0	1	1	2	2	0	0
0	1	1	0	0	2	2
0	2	2	0	0	1	1
0	2	2	1	1	0	0
1	0	1	1	2	2	0
1	0	2	2	1	1	0
1	1	2	2	0	0	1
1	1	0	0	2	2	1
1	2	0	0	1	1	2
1	2	1	1	0	0	2

Note that if a has share s_a and b has share s_b, then they can compute the key to be 0 if $s_b = s_a$, and 1 otherwise. However, a and c together have no information regarding the key, since for every ordered pair (s_b, s_c) that occurs, there is exactly one row where the key is 0 and one row where the key is 1. The analysis for other pairs of participants is similar to these arguments. The information rate $\rho = \log_2 2 / \log_2 3 = \log_3 2 \approx 0.6309298$.

Remark: Example 3.1 also provides us with a $PS(P_3, \log_3 2, 2)$, since P_3 is an induced subgraph of C_6.

References

1.   J. Beneloh and J. Leichter, *Generalized secret sharing and monotone functions*, in "Advances in Cryptology CRYPTO '88 Proceedings", Lecture Notes in Computer Science 403 (1990), 27-35.

2.   Th. Beth, D. Jungnickel and H. Lenz, *Design Theory*, Bibliographisches Institut, Zurich, 1985.

3.   G. R. Blakley, *Safeguarding cryptographic keys*, Proc. National Computer Conference, vol. 48, AFIPS Conference Proceedings 48 (1979), 313-317.

4.   E. F. Brickell, *Some ideal secret sharing schemes* , J. Combin. Math. and Combin. Comput. 6 (1989), 105-113.

5.   E. F. Brickell and D. M. Davenport, *On the classification of ideal secret sharing schemes*, J. Cryptology, to appear.

6.   M. Ito, A. Saito and T. Nishizeki, *Secret sharing scheme realizing general access structure*, Proc. IEEE Globecom '87, Tokyo, Japan, 1987, pp. 99-102.

7.   A. Shamir, *How to share a secret*, Commun. of the ACM 22, (1979), 612-613.

8.   P. J. Schellenberg and D. R. Stinson, *Threshold schemes from combinatorial designs*, J. Combin. Math. and Combin. Comput. 5 (1989), 143-160.

9.   Gustavus J. Simmons, *Robust shared secret schemes or "how to be sure you have the right answer even though you don't know the question"*, Congressus Numer. 68 (1989), 215-248.

10.   D. R. Stinson and S. A. Vanstone, *A combinatorial approach to threshold schemes*, SIAM J. on Discrete Math. 1 (1988), 230-236.

Collective Coin Tossing Without Assumptions nor Broadcasting

Silvio Micali   Tal Rabin

1 Introduction

To obtain security, one needs to utilize many resources. Among these are one-way functions, physically secure communication channels, and —though less well known— *broadcasting*.

We will argue, though, that this resource should not be taken for granted in a cryptographic scenario, and that actually should be removed. We will show that this can be done thanks to some recent developments in the field of distributed computation and actually hope to generate more awareness about this field for our cryptographic work.

We focus on one such a primitive, collective coin flipping. Here a group of players, some of which are dishonest, want to select a common, random and totally unbiased bit. Our desire of having the coin totally unbiased obliges us to dispens with cryptography, since else one would always have a miniscule chance of guessing the relevant secret key and bias the coin. To explain how to get perfect common coins, we need to revisit another protocol: verifiable secret sharing.

As we shall see, along the way, we will provide a very simple proof of a beautiful and unpublished, VSS protocol.

1.1 Verifiable Secret Sharing

Awerbuch, Chor, Goldwasser, and Micali [B.Mi86] introduced and cryptographically implemented the somewhat paradoxical notion of a verifiable secret sharing. This is a protocol involving a distinguished party, called the *dealer*, and additional parties, called the *players*. Any of these parties (including the dealer) may be malicious, and deviate from their prescribed instructions in an arbitrary way. Informally, the protocol consists of two stages. In the first stage the dealer "secretly commits" to a value of its choice. In the second stage this value is recovered. The value is *secret*, at the end of stage 1, in the sense that no subset of players of suitably small size can guess it better than at random, even if they exchange all the information in their possession so far (which good players never do in the first stage.) The value is *committed*, in stage 1, in the sense that a good player can VERIFY that there exists a unique value x such that whenever stage 2 is performed, with or without the help of the dealer, and *no matter what the bad players might do,* all the good players will recover x. Moreover this unique, but unknown, value x is what a good dealer chose it to be.

Applications. Verifiable secret sharing is extremely useful. It is the crucial subroutine of all recent completeness theorems for protocols with honest majority, most notably [GoMiWi86, GaHaYu87, BeGoWi88, ChCrDa88, RaBe89, BeMiRo90].

Below let us point out just two applications that will help us to illustrate some future points.

1. *Delayed Disclosure.* Assume that the president of the United States wants his generals to know the secret password for the Country's nuclear defense system, if he is killed. Then he may execute stage 1 of a VSS protocol when he is still alive and order his generals to execute stage 2 only if he gets killed. As he trusts the majority of his generals to follow his orders, the password will remain secret until he is alive. Should he get killed, again because the majority of his generals will participate in stage 2, the password is guaranteed to be recovered.

2. *Collective Coin Flipping.* Assume n parties want to agree on a common, random bit. Then each party secretly and randomly selects a bit, and commits herself to it using stage 1 of a VSS protocol. Once all have done it, stage two is executed, all the committed bits are recovered and broadcasted, and the common coin is assumed to be the sum modulo 2 of all decommitted bits.

In the first application, the emphasis is on an honest dealer who does not trust any single player, or even any minority of the players; in the second one, on an honest group of players who do not trust the dealer.

1.2   Verifiable vs Simple Secret Sharing

Secret Sharing. The earlier notion of a secret sharing was independently introduced by Blakley [Bla79] and Shamir [Sha79]. In a secret sharing protocol with parameters n and t, a *dealer D* possesses a secret string s. From s the dealer computes n other strings $s_1, ..., s_n$ —called *shares*— such that s is unpredictable given any $\leq t$ of the shares, but s is easily computable given any $t + 1$ of the shares.

For instance, in [Sha79] the dealer randomly chooses a polynomial P of degree t with coefficients in Z_p, p prime, such that $P(0) = s$, and gives to player i the string $P(i)$ as his share.

The limitations of Secret Sharing. Secret sharing does not achieve secret commitment as discussed above. For instance,

- In the case of application 1, some generals may be trahitors and, during the reconstruction of the password, may contribute wrong strings as their shares of the secret. This will avoid that the good general reconstruct the password! Though the password is correctably reconstructed when given $t + 1$ good shares and nothin else, all bets are off when, together with good shares, one is given also bad ones. For instance, in the implementation of [Sha79], $t + 1$ shares uniquely identify a polynomial. Thus if t shares are bad out of —say— $3t + 1$, as soon one chooses t shares, almost surely a bad one would be included and a wrong secret reconstructed. Cycling through all possible subsets of shares of size $t + 1$ (so to identify the $2t + 1$ shares that define the same polynomial) would be impossible since it would require exponential time.

- In case of application 2, every player acts as a dealer. One such dealer, D, may co-operate with the bad players as follows. He gives them good shares to begin with, but during reconstruction he tells them whether they should contribute the good shares or random ones. This allows D to bias the common coin. Assume that he wants the common coin to come up 0. If the sum of all previously decommitted bits and his own bit happens to be 0, he tells the bad players to contribute the original share he gave them. This way the reconstruction of his secret will proceed smoothly, and the common coin will be 0 as he wanted. If the sum modulo 2 of all bits is 1, he tells the bad players to contribute random strings during the reconstruction of his own bit. Thus the good players cannot reconstruct any bit for D. Now they are in trouble no matter what they do. If their strategy is to take the sum modulo 2 of the reconstructed bits, they would easily allow D to bias the coin. In fact D has two chances of having 0: one if the sum of all bits modulo 2 is 0, the other if the sum of all the bits except his own is 0. If their strategy consists of starting again the protocol without D, again D would have two chances of obtaining 0. (This interesting phenomenon was first observed by Broder and Dolev [BrDo84] in the case of 2-people coin flipping.)

Problem 1 could be solved by having the dealer digitally sign the shares he hands out, but problem 2 is of no easy solution. We need verifiable secret sharing.

1.3 Our Solution

Our protocol is the first one to simultaneously enjoy many attractive properties:

1. It cannot be defeated even if 1/3 of the players are malicious and co-operate with each other to disrupt it.

2. It works without one-way functions if the players communicate via safe lines. Thus even if the bad players have infinite computing resources, they cannot defeat it.

3. It has 0 probability of error. Thus there is *absolute certainty* that the dealer's input is committed, is secret, and will later be correctly recovered.

4. It works in constant number of rounds.

5. It works *without broadcasting*. It is enough thatevery pair of players can exchange messages.

Our protocol is in fact the first VSS protocol implementable without broadcasting. Properties 1, 2 alone were achieved by Chaum, Crépeau, and Damgård [ChCrDa88]; properties 1,2 and 3 were —independently— achieved by Ben-Or, Goldwasser, and Wigderson [BeGoWi88]; properties 1, 2, 3, and 4 were later achieved by Feldman in his Ph.D Thesis. His method has not been separately published, but appears without proof in [BeGoWi88], whose authors have also announced to have found an equivalent but much more complicated method. In this paper we also provide a simpler proof of Feldman's protocol.

Let us also say that Cynthia Dwork has told us that she, Dolev, Naor, and Yung have obtained this same result, and that they will not write it up since we have already done it.

Dispensing with Broadcasting. Removing broadcasting is useful, not only from a theoretical point of view —where one wants to know what are the resources necessary to guarantee security— but also from a practical one.

Capability of broadcasting may be obtained among processors imbedded in a special parallel machine. However, the players of cryptographic protocols are physically far away, and do not belong to a special computer hardware. In this scenario, it is hard to believe that they players may want or always can to communicate —say— via radio using established frequencies! Even if they could, this would hardly be considered a secure communication channel, unless cryptography is used. It is a main point here not to use cryptography to understand what security can still be achieved if one-way functions do not exist!

Broadcasting a message may also be simulated by sending the same message to all other players. This, however, only works if all players are honest. In a cryptographic setting, one better not assume that a player really sends the same message to all other players!

We remove broadcast as follows. First we blend Feldman's protocol with graded broadcast (a protocol due to [FeMi90]) thus obtaining a protocol that is implementable in a point-to-point communication network but still presents a degree of ambiguity. This ambiguity is then removed by running the expected constant-round Byzantine agreement of [FeMi90] a constant number of times. In this protocol, however, the players do not terminate simultaneously, but they can be off of one round. Thus some good players may start executing other steps of our protocol ahead of bad players, and, in doing so, they may divulge information before before the bad ones have sent theirs to anyone. Though this is potentially dangerous it will not affect the correctness of our enterprise. This extends also to the point when VSS is used to secretly committing to bits that are later Exclusive-Ored to obtain a common coin. Generating a common coin thus entails running concurrently n Byzantine agreements. Though each one ends in expected constant-rounds, one cannot "expect" that all of them will end in expected constant-rounds! (To see this, let's change game. Assume that an individual flips a fair coin. Then it will get Heads in expected two trials. Assume now that n people flip each a fair coin. Then it is not true that all will get Heads in expected two trials. Rather After one round half will have gotten Heads, in one more round another half will get Heads, and so $\log n$ round will be needed.) Thus we must make use of a recent result of Ben-Or and El-Yaniv [BeEl88] that extends the work of [FeMi90] to many concurrent Byzantine agreements. Though the players may even more seriously be out-of-step, one can argue that security of the coin flip is not affected.

Optimality. In the final paper, we will prove our result to be optimal in all mentioned accounts.

More on Private Channels. Protocols whose security relies on private channels are much preferable to the ones relying on one-way functions. First, because all communication can still be encrypted though private channels are available (thus an enemy must both —say— factor, and have access to physically protected lines (or human couriers). Second, because one-way functions may not exist, but secure channels may. And third, because even if an enemy manages to dig —say— a hole in the ground and tap a channel that was believed to be secure, we can consider this equivalent to having the enemy corrupting the player who owned the channel. Since we can tolerate 1/3 of the players to be corrupted, we may essentially tolerate an enemy to tap quite a few channels without compromising our security.

2   Definitions

Graded Protocol - Let P be a distributed terminating protocol, executed by n players. There is a distinguished player, D, the dealer, who starts with a private value $s \in [0..m-1]$. The protocol P is intended to distribute the value

s to the n players. At the end of the protocol each player P_i outputs a *grade*, $P-confidence_i \in \{0,1,2\}$, and is able to "access" a $P - value_i \in [0..m - 1]$. The meaning of "access" depends on the type of the protocol, P. We say that P is a *graded protocol* if the following properties hold:

1. *Acceptance of good values* - If the dealer D is honest then for each honest player P_i, $P-confidence_i = 2$.

2. *Semi-unanimity* - If any honest player P_i outputs $P-confidence_i = 2$, then $P-confidence_j > 0$ for each honest player P_j.

3. *Verifiability* - There exists a value $s' \in [0..m - 1]$, such that all good players whose $P-confidence_i > 0$, can access s'. If D is honest then $s = s'$.

In this paper we shall need the following definitions of two particular graded-protocols.

Gradecast Protocol - Is a graded protocol. The meaning of "access" in this protocol is that player P_i actually holds $GCST-value_i$ at the end of the Gradecast.

Graded Share/Verify and Recover Protocol - Graded Share/Verify and Recover is a graded protocol. Player P_i "accesses" $GSV-value_i$ by executing the Recover Protocol, of which the output is $GSV-value_i$. An additional property is required for the Graded Share/Verify:

Unpredictability - Let A be an adversary acting on the protocol, who doesn't corrupt the dealer, and who can corrupt up to $t < n/3$ of the players. If A outputs a value τ as his prediction of the dealer's value before the start of *Recover*, then the probability that $\tau = s$ is $1/m$.

Verifiable Secret Sharing Protocol - Is a distributed, two phase, terminating protocol, executed by n players, and a distinguished player D, the dealer. The dealer holds a private input $s \in [0..m - 1]$ which he distributes in some manner in the first phase of the protocol. At the end of the first phase the dealer will either be disqualified, or it will be known that in the second phase, the value s will be known to all honest players.

Interactive Consistency Protocol [PSL]: Is a distributed protocol carried out by n players. Player P_i has a private value v_i. The protocol allows each player to compute a vector $vector_i = b_{i1}b_{i2}...b_{in}$, so that for each honest P_i and P_j we have $vector_i = vector_j$. And for all honest players P_i and P_j we have that $vector_i[j] = v_j$. In different words, this is n Byzantine Agreements executed concurrently.

3   Graded Share/Verify and Recover

Theorem 1 *Graded Share/Verify and Recover with the above properties can be achieved in constant time, where $t < n/3$, without the use of broadcast channels and with no probability of error.*

We shall start by stating our protocol:
Graded Share/Verify Protocol

1. Dealer randomly chooses a_{ij} $\in Z_p$ $0 \leq i,j \leq t$ where $p > n, m$, except $a_{00} = s$, and defines a bivariate polynomial $f(x,y) = \sum_{i,j} a_{ij} x^i y^j$, so that $f(0,0) = s$. He computes $f(i,y)$ and $f(x,i)$ for all i and defines: $g_i(y) = f(i,y)$, $h_i(x) = f(x,i)$. He hands over to player P_i, on the private channel, the polynomials $g_i(y)$ and $h_i(x)$.

2. Player P_i computes $h_i(j)$ for each j and hands the value to player P_j.

3. Player P_i looks at all the values he received in the previous step, $h_1(i), ..., h_n(i)$ (some may have not been received), and checks whether they satisfy

$$g_i(j) = h_j(i)?$$

   For every j that doesn't satisfy the equation, P_i gradecasts "expose $g_i(j)$".

4. The dealer gradecasts the values $g_i(j)$ for all requests that he received with $GCST-confidence_D = 1$ or 2.

5. Player P_i checks for all the values $g_i(j)$ and $g_k(i)$ that were gradecasted by the dealer whether:

   - $GCST-confidence_i = 2$.
   - Does the $GCST-value_i$, gradecasted by the dealer equal the value which he holds.

If either one is not satisfied he gradecasts "expose $g_i(y)$ and $h_i(x)$" and distributes on the private channelles "disqualify dealer".

6. The dealer gradecasts all the polynomials requested in the previous step for requests with $GCST-confidence_D = 1$ or 2.

7. Player P_i checks for all requests, in Step 5, whose $GCST-confidence_i = 2$: if the reply in Step 6 doesn't have $GCST-confidence_i = 2$, or for some gradecasted $g_k(y)$ and $h_k(x)$, $g_k(i) \neq h_i(k)$ or $h_k(i) \neq g_i(k)$ then he distributes "disqualify dealer".

8. Player P_i counts how many "disqualify dealer" votes he got if $count \geq t + 1$ then he distributes "no secret" otherwise he distributes "secret".

9. Player P_i counts how many votes of "secret" he got and sets $GSV-confidence_i$ of the Graded Share/Verify in the following manner:

   - $count\ of\ "secret" \geq 2t + 1$ set $GSV-confidence_i = 2$, else,
   - $count\ of\ "secret" \geq t + 1$ set $GSV-confidence_i = 1$, else,
   - otherwise $GSV-confidence_i = 0$.

Lemma 1.1 *If all honest players' polynomials do not define the same bivariate polynomial then each honest player P_i will set* GSV—confidence$_i = 0$.

Proof of Lemma
If at the end of step 5, $t + 1$ or more honest players distributed "disqualify dealer" then all honest players will set $GSV-confidence_i = 0$. Thus we can assume that the number of satisfied honest players, at the end of Step 5, is $\geq t + 1$. If P_i is satisfied that means that for all j, $g_i(j) = h_j(i)$. Let us assume, w.l.o.g., that $P_1, .., P_r$ $r \geq t + 1$ are satisfied, and that they hold $\{g_1(y)\ h_1(x)\}, ..., \{g_r(y)\ h_r(x)\}$ respectively. Through the polynomials $g_1(y), ..., g_{t+1}(y)$ a single bivariate polynomial $\bar{f}(x, y)$, can be interpolated. From $\bar{f}(x, y)$ we can defin e $\bar{g}_i(y)$ and $\bar{h}_i(x)$ $1 \leq i \leq r$. We need to show that $\bar{g}_i(y) = g_i(y)$ and $\bar{h}_i(x) = h_i(x)$ for $1 \leq i \leq r$. And from this we can deduce that any subset of $t + 1$ polynomials from this set define the same bivariate polynomial $\bar{f}(x, y)$. We immediately have that $\bar{g}_i(y) = g_i(y)$ for $1 \leq i \leq t + 1$, from the definition.

Claim: For $1 \leq i \leq r$, $h_i(x) = \bar{h}_i(x)$.

It is enough to prove for $h_i(x)$ that $h_i(j) = \bar{h}_i(j)$ for $1 \leq j \leq t+1$, (because $h_i(x)$ is a polynomial of degree t, and if it is equal to another polynomial at $t+1$ points, then they are the same polynomial).

Proof of Claim

For $1 \leq j \leq t+1$

$$\bar{h}_i(j) \overset{\text{def of } \bar{h}}{=} \bar{f}(j,i) \overset{\text{def of } \bar{g}}{=} \bar{g}_j(i) \overset{\text{shown before}}{=} g_j(i) \overset{\text{def}}{=} h_i(j)$$

□

From the above we have that $h_1(x), ..., h_r(x)$ define $\bar{f}(x,y)$, and by the same reasoning $g_1(y), ..., g_r(y)$ define $\bar{f}(x,y)$. In other words all satisfied players define the same bivariate polynomial $\bar{f}(x,y)$. If at Step 6 the dealer gradecasts some polynomial $g_k(y)$ and $h_k(x)$ which do not satisfy the equation that $g_k(y) = \bar{g}_k(y)$ (same for h) then this polynomial will match at most t of the previously satisfied players thus increasing the number of unsatisfied players to $\geq t+1$. So either all $2t+1$ polynomials held by honest players define the same $\bar{f}(x,y)$ or they will all set their confidence to 0.

Lemma 1.2 *If the dealer is honest then for all honest players, P_i, we will have GSV–confidence$_i$ = 2.*

Proof of Lemma

This is equivalent to showing that no honest player will ever distribute "disqualify dealer". This can happen only if there is a contradiction between two values handed out by the dealer, which can never happen when the dealer is honest.

Recover Protocol

1. Player P_i distributes the polynomials $g_i(y)$ and $h_i(x)$.

2. Player P_i received w.l.o.g $g_1(y), h_1(x), ..., g_r(y), h_r(x)$ $r \geq 2t+1$. He checks if $g_j(y)$ satisfies the equation

   $$g_j(k_l) = h_{k_l}(j) \quad for \ l \geq 2t+1$$

   If yes then he determines that $g_j(y)$ is in fact $f(j,y)$. He takes a set of $t+1$ good g's and interpolates through them to compute $f(x,y)$, and from that to compute $f(0,0)$.

4 Verifiable Secret Sharing

Theorem 2 *VSS can be achieved in constant expected time where $t < n/3$, with no broadcast channels and with no probability of error.*

We will start by stating our protocol.
VSS Protocol
First Phase:

1. Dealer executes Graded Share/Verify

2. All P_i's execute the expected constant-round [FeMi90] Byzantine Agreement where their input into the BA is as follows for P_i: if $GSV-confidence_i = 2$ then enter "yes" if $GSV-confidence_i = 0$ or 1then enter "no".

3. If result of BA is "yes" determine that there is a secret and that it is recoverable, otherwise the dealer is faulty.

Second Phase:
The Recover Protocol stated above.
Proof of Theorem:
The above protocol achieves Theorem 2.
Honest dealer: At the end of the GSV all honest players have $GSV-confidence_i = 2$, due to the property of "acceptance of good values", so they all enter "yes" into the BA. Because of the meaningfulness property of the BA, which states that if each honest player enters the same value, v, into the BA, then the result of the BA will be v, they will agree on "yes", achieving the desired properties of the VSS.
Dishonest dealer:
If at the end of the GSV the honest players have a $GSV-confidence_i = 0$ or 1 then they will all enter "no" into the BA and as in the above case due to the meaningfulness of the BA the result of the BA will be "no". If the honest players have a $GSV-confidence_i = 1$ or 2 then some will enter "yes" and some "no". But in this case we don't mind what the result of the BA will be. If all honest players have $GSV-confidence_i = 1$ or 2, then due to the *verifiability* property of the GSV protocol they can all reconstruct the same secret. So whether they *all* decide to reconstruct or not they will be able to achieve their goal.

Run time: 15 steps
+ constant expect BA (FM)
O(1).

5 Concurrent VSS

Concurrent VSS Protocol - Is a distributed two phase protocol, executed by n players. Each player P_i holds a private value s_i. In the first phase of the protocol all players, concurrently, distribute their values. At the end of the first phase all honest players will determine for each player P_i whether he is disqualified, and if he is not then they all know that his value s_i can be recoverable in the second phase.

Theorem 3 *Concurrent VSS can be achieved in constant expected time where $t < n/3$, without the use of broadcast channels and with no probability of error.*

Concurrent VSS Protocol

1. Dealer $D_1, ..., D_n$ execute Graded Share/Verify concurrently, for values $s_1, ..., s_n$. Let us denote by $GSV-confidence_{ij}$ the confidence P_i has for the GSV executed by D_j.

2. Execute the expected constant-round Interactive Consistency Protocol of [BeEl88], where the value entered by P_i into the jth BA is: if $GSV-confidence_{ij} = 2$ then enter "yes", otherwise "no".

3. For all j, if $vector_i[j] = yes$ then player P_i determines that D_j's secret is recoverable, otherwise he determines that D_j is faulty.

Correctness: As for single VSS.
Runtime: 15 steps n independent VSS
+ constant expected n parallel BS (BE)
O(1)

6 Common Coin

Definition - A common coin is a coin which is visable to all players.

Main Theorem *A common coin for which $Pr(coin = 1) = 1/2$ can be achieved in constant expected time with no broadcast channels and $t < n/3$.*
Common Coin Protocol

1. All players P_i shares a random bit r_i using the Concurrent VSS Protocol

2. All players reconstruct the secrets which were not disqualified during the VSS. The set of secrets is $r_{i_1}, ..., r_{i_k}$ $k \geq 2t + 1$

3. The coin will be $r_{i_1} \oplus ... \oplus r_{i_k}$

Claim The above protocol achieves our Main Theorem.

Proof The fact that the coin is common to all honest players is easily seen. Due to the BA they all consider the same subset of secrets as correct secrets, and so in step 2 they will all reconstruct the same set of secrets. Each reconstructed secret will be the same for all players because of the VSS properties. To see that the $Pr(coin = 1) = 1/2$ we need only note that there is at least one truly random bit shared by an honest player and that this bit is unknown to the dishonest players at the time when they commit to their value by sharing it using the VSS.

References

[BeEl88]   M. Ben-Or and R. El-Yaniv. Interactive consistency in constant expected time. Inst. of Math. and Comp. Sci., Hebrew University, Jerusalem, 1988.

[BeGoWi88] M. Ben-Or, S. Goldwasser, and A. Wigderson. Completeness theorems for fault-tolerant distributed computing. In *Proc. 20th ACM Symposium on Theory of Computing*, pages 1–10, Chicago, 1988. ACM.

[BeMiRo90] D. Beaver, S. Micali, and P. Rogaway. The round complexity of secure protocols. In *Proc. 22th ACM Symposium on Theory of Computing*, May 1990.

[Bla79]   G. Blakely. Safeguarding cryptographic keys. In *AFIPS*, volume 48, pages 313–317. NCC, June 1979.

[B.Mi86]   S. Goldwasser B. Awerbuch, B. Chor and S. Micali. Verifiable secret sharing in the presence of faults. In *Proc. of the 27th Annual IEEE Symposium on Foundations of Computer Science*, 1986.

266

[BrDo84]   A.Z. Broder and D. Dolev. Flipping coins in many pockets
              (byzantine agreement on uniformly random values. In *Proc. of
              the 25th Annual IEEE Symposium on Foundations of Computer
              Science*, pages 157–170. IEEE Computer Society Press, October
              1984.

[ChCrDa88]   D. Chaum, C. Crepeau, and I. Damgård. Multi-party uncon-
              ditionally secure protocols. In *Proc. 20th ACM Symposium on
              Theory of Computing*, Chicago, 1988. ACM.

[FeMi90]   P. Feldman and S. Micali. An optimal algorithm for synchronous
              byzantine agreement. Technical Report LCS/TM-425, MIT,
              June 1990. (Submitted for publication in SIAM J. on Comput-
              ing.).

[GaHaYu87]   Z. Galil, S. Haber, and M. Yung. Cryptographic computation:
              Secure falt-tolerant protocols and public-key model. In *Proc.
              CRYPTO 87*, pages 135–155. Springer Verlag, 1987.

[GoMiWi86]   O. Goldreich, S. Micali, and A. Wigderson. Proofs that yield
              nothing but their validity and a methodology of cryptographic
              protocol design. In *Proc. of the 27th Annual IEEE Symposium
              on Foundations of Computer Science*, pages 174–187, Toronto,
              1986. IEEE.

[RaBe89]   T. Rabin and M. Ben-Or. Verifiable secret sharing and mul-
              tiparty protocoles with honest majority. In *Proc. 21th ACM
              Symposium on Theory of Computing*, 1989.

[Sha79]   A. Shamir. How to share a secret. *Communcations of the ACM*,
              22:612–613, November 1979.

Key Distribution

Chair: T. Berson, Anagram Laboratories

A Key Distribution "Paradox"

Yacov Yacobi

Bellcore

445 South St.

Morristown, NJ 07960

Abstract

The so called, Rabin "paradox" is a proof that a given signature system, which is secure under ciphertext only attack is insecure under chosen message attack. The construction that is used to prove the first clause is also used to prove the second. For several years it was believed to be inherent to public key signature systems. A similar problem existed for public key cryptosystems (under chosen ciphertext attack). Trap-door functions were inherent in the construction of the "paradox."

In 1984 Goldwasser, Micali and Rivest constructively showed that one can overcome the "paradox." Naor and Yung (1989) resolved the similar problem for public key cryptosystems. Both solution actually solve two problems. They resolve the "paradox," with the strictest definition of security (for a cryptosystem it amounts to the demand that for a given cryptogram c and two messages m_0, m_1 it should be infeasible to decide whether c resulted from m_0 or m_1 with probability significantly greater than half). Both solutions are very complicated.

We show that a similar "paradox" exists for many key distribution systems, even if non-trapdoor one way functions are used (like in the Diffie-Hellman variations). Using the simple basic definition of security (given the messages exchanged during the protocol it should be impossible to find the resulting session key in probabilistic polynomial time) we show a simple and practical key distribution system which is provably free of the paradox.

1 Introduction

Consider 2-party Key Distribution Systems (KDS) with one transmission in each direction (party i transmits r_i); these transmissions are independent of the private secret keys (and therefore, these systems are zero-knowledge as far as the private secret keys are concerned). The transmissions may be the results of computations $r_i = F_i(e_i)$, where the functions F_i may be one-way, and e_i is randomly chosen. S_i, P_i are party i's secret and public keys respectively.

Let A be a "reference point" (believed to be a) hard problem, like factorization, or equivalently, Composite Diffie-Hellman (CDH) ([S],[M],

A: **Input:** I; **Output:** $O = A(I)$.

Let B_{cop} denote the cracking problem of a given KDS, under Ciphertext-Only attack, by a Passive adversary, i.e.

B_{cop}: **Input:** X, r_1, r_2 (X is the public data); **Output:** $k = g(X, r_1, r_2)$.

Let B_{kkp} denote the cracking problem (of the same system), under Know (old session) Key Attack, by a Passive adversary, i.e.

B_{kkp}: **Input:** $X, r_1, r_2, r'_1, r'_2, k' = g(X, r'_1, r'_2)$; **Output:** $k = g(X, r_1, r_2)$.

Throughout **efficient computation** means "computable in probabilistic polynomial time." If a cracking problem is efficiently solvable then a system is *insecure* for that attack. We show that if B_{kkp} is reducible to A in probabilistic polynomial time, and A is reducible to B_{cop} in probabilistic polynomial time, s.t. the second reduction holds for every [1] r_1, r_2, and such that the reductions maintain certain parameters, and the functions F_i^{-1} are efficiently computable. then B_{kkp} has efficient solution. The crux of the proof is combining the two reductions into one reduction from B_{kkp} to B_{cop}, and then using k', taken from B_{kkp}'s input to replace oracle B_{cop}. The above dichotomy (hard B_{cop}, and easy B_{kkp}) does not hold for systems s.t. triples (r'_1, r'_2, k') are efficiently computable given only the public data X. Using this we present a simple, secure, non "paradoxical" KDS. This system, and several of our "paradoxical" systems appeared in [MTI]. However, they do not mention the "paradox," and no formal definition of security is given.

2 The main results

Let problems A, B_{cop}, B_{kkp} be as defined above.

Theorem 1: If B_{kkp} is reducible in probabilistic polynomial time to A, and A is reducible in probabilistic polynomial time to B_{cop}, s.t.

(i) The second reduction holds for every r_1, r_2, in the targets of F_1, and F_2, respectively, and

(ii) The public data, X, of B_{kkp} is identical to that of A ($I = X$) and B_{cop}, and

(iii) F_1, F_2 are not one-way functions (i.e. F_i^{-1} are efficiently computable),

then B_{kkp} is efficiently solvable.

Proof: The reduction from B_{kkp} to A together with $I = X$ imply the existence of efficiently computable function G_1, s.t. $k = G_1(X, r_1, r_2, r'_1, r'_2, k', A(X))$. The reduction from A to B_{cop} together with (i) imply the existence of efficiently computable

---

[1]The demand that the reduction holds for every r_1, r_2 is used to substantiate uniform hardness claims.

function G_2, s.t. $A(X) = G_2(X, e_1', e_2', k')$. Hence B_{kkp} is efficiently solvable using $k = G_1(X, r_1, r_2, r_1', r_2', k', G_2(X, F_1^{-1}(r_1'), F_2^{-1}(r_2'), k'))$.

Q.E.D.

if given X, arbitrary triples (r_1', r_2', k') are polynomially computable, then B_{kkp} and B_{cop} are of the same complexity. A system with the above property does not have the "paradox." We later show such a KDS.

3 Example of a "paradoxical" system

The system is a slight modification of a system shown in [YS]. It belongs to the Diffie-Hellman family of KDS, which relies on the difficulty of the discrete-log problem. Let p and q be two large primes, and let $m = pq$. Let α be an element of high order in Z_m^*. Each participant i has a pair of public and secret keys (p_i, s_i), where $p_i \equiv \alpha^{-s_i} \bmod m$. The protocol is completely symmetric, and therefore we describe just one side, i. The other side j mirrors i's actions.

  begin

  1. Party i chooses a random $r_i \in_R (1, m)$ with uniform distribution, and the parties exchange these values.

  2. Party i computes $k_{ij} \equiv (\alpha^{r_j} p_j)^{r_i - s_i} \bmod m$.

  end

Clearly, $k_{ij} \equiv k_{ji} \equiv \alpha^{(r_i - s_i)(r_j - s_j)} \bmod m$

The initial cracking problem (before any communication) is not solvable, since there isn't enough information to determine even one bit of the key. The communication is completely independent of the secrets, so it does not provide any additional information on the secret keys (s_i and s_j). This proves Lemma 1.

Lemma 1: In the above KDS no information on the identification secrets leaks, under ciphertext only attack.

Shmuely [S] (and later McCurley [M]) analyzed a composite DH scheme, in which the public and secret keys are as in this scheme, and the session key is $k_{ij} \equiv \alpha^{s_i s_j} \bmod m$. We henceforth refer to this system as CDH (Composite Diffie-Hellman). Shmuely and McCurley gave evidence that for suitably chosen α and m the cracking problem of CDH is hard on the average. We summarize the CDH cracking problem (A), and the cracking problem of the new system (B_{cop}).

A: Input: $\alpha^x, \alpha^y, \alpha, m$; Output: $\alpha^{xy} \bmod m$.
B_{cop}: Input: $r_i, r_j, \alpha^{-s_i}, \alpha^{-s_j}, \alpha, m$; Output: $\alpha^{(r_i - s_i)(r_j - s_j)} \bmod m$.

Lemma 2: $\forall r_i, r_j$ A is reducible in polynomial time to B_{cop}.

Proof: For any $r_i, r_j \in [0, m)$, set $\alpha^{-s_i} = \alpha^x$, $\alpha^{-s_j} = \alpha^y$. The oracle outputs $\alpha^{(r_i - s_i)(r_j - s_j)} = \alpha^{r_i r_j} \cdot (\alpha^{-s_i})^{r_j} \cdot (\alpha^{-s_j})^{r_i} \cdot \alpha^{s_i s_j}$. The first three multiplicands are known, hence from the oracle's answer one can compute the fourth multiplicand, which equals the desired answer to problem A.

Q.E.D.

Remark: In [YS] a similar reduction is presented, for malicious adversary (impersonator), under ciphertext only attack.

Lemma 3: For this KDS B_{kkp} has efficient solution.

Proof: The proof is almost identical to that of Lemma 2 only now a given old key, k', plays the role of the oracle's answer (and the corresponding r'_i, r'_j are known). Once $\alpha^{s_i s_j} \bmod m$ is computed from the old key, one can easily compute the new key $\alpha^{(r_i - s_i)(r_j - s_j)} \bmod m$.

Q.E.D.

4 Example of a non "paradoxical" system

Transmissions: $r_i \equiv \alpha^{e_i} \bmod m$,

Session key (as computed by 1): $k \equiv (\alpha^{s_2})^{e_1} \cdot (\alpha^{e_2})^{s_1} \equiv \alpha^{s_1 e_2 + s_2 e_1} \bmod m$

Secrecy: A is reducible in polynomial time to B_{cop}, by the assignments $\alpha^{s_1} = \alpha^x, \alpha^{e_2} = \alpha^y$, with arbitrarily chosen s_2, e_1. Also, a reduction in reverse direction exists (with two oracle calls), hence B_{cop} is as hard as A.

Triples $(r'_1, r'_2, k' \equiv (\alpha^{s_2})^{e_1} \cdot (\alpha^{s_1})^{e_2} \bmod m)$, can be easily computed, hence they don't contribute any new knowledge, and B_{kkp} is as hard to solve as B_{cop}, for this system.

Resilience:

In general a protocol is assumed resilient if a disruptive adversary cannot bring the honest participants to assume a wrong outcome after executing the protocol. To end up with a practical protocol we have to impose some reasonable restrictions on this definition. Therefore, we address the following disruptive adversary: The adversary is an impersonator, playing in the middle, between i and j, pretending to be j when talking to i, and vice-versa. He tries to establish a session-key with each of the legitimate parties (not necessarily the same key). In doing so he may deviate from the original protocol by sending messages, computed entirely different from the intended computations (as long as his computations are done in probabilistic polynomial time). However, he must conform with the basic structure of the protocol, i.e. send messages of the right structure and size, when expected.

We can reduce the basic Diffie-Hellman problem to the cracking problem under impersonation attack, with known old session's information. Since old information can be reproduced by anybody easily, we can remove this obstacle and concentrate on a reduction to the cracking problem without that history. Again, the DH problem is **Input:** $\alpha, \alpha^x, \alpha^y, N$; **Output:** $\alpha^{xy} \bmod N$.

The cracking problem for impersonator who plays in the middle, trying to impersonate j when talking to i (for example) should be defined in general terms, that is, we cannot assume that all he does is choosing some $\tilde{R}_j$ instead of R_j, but otherwise participates in the protocol as originally designed. We assume that the impersonator picks some $\tilde{R}_j$, and sends $h(\alpha, \tilde{R}_j)$ to i, where $h(.,.)$ is any probabilistic polynomial time function. This function may have more inputs; Any public information can be part of its input. So the cracking problem of the impersonator is defined as follows:

Input: $\alpha, N, \alpha^{R_i}, P_i \equiv \alpha^{S_i} \bmod N, P_j \equiv \alpha^{S_j}, h(\alpha, \tilde{R}_j)$;
Output: $h(\alpha, \tilde{R}_j)^{S_i} \cdot (\alpha^{S_j})^{R_i} \bmod N$.

The randomized reduction from the DH problem to this one goes as follows: Set $\alpha^{R_i} \leftarrow \alpha^y; P_j \leftarrow \alpha^x; N \leftarrow N$, and pick S_i and $h(\alpha, \tilde{R}_j)$ from the appropriate domains with homogeneous distribution. Compute $P_i \equiv \alpha^{S_i} \bmod N$. Given the oracles answer $h(\alpha, \tilde{R}_j)^{S_i} \cdot (\alpha^{S_j})^{R_i} \bmod N$ one can easily compute now $\alpha^{xy} \bmod N$.

Acknowledgment:
I wish to thank Shimon Even for many insightful discussions.

5 References

BCGL Ben-David, S., Chor, B., Goldreich, O., Luby, M.: "On the Theory of Average Case Complexity," *STOC*, 1989, pp. 204-216.

BM Bellare, M., and Micali, S.: "How to Sign Given Any Trap-Door Function", *STOC, 1988*, pp. 32-34.

DEK Dolev, D., Even, S., Karp, R.: "On the Security of Ping-Pong Protocols," *Advances in Cryptology: Proc. of Crypto'82*, Plenum Press, pp. 177-186, 1983.

DH Diffie, W.,, Hellman, M.: "New Directions In Cryptography," *IEEE Trans. on Inf. Theory*, 1976, IT-22, pp. 644-654.

GMR Goldwasser, S., Micali, S., Rivest, R.L.: "A Digital Signature Scheme Secure Against Chosen Message Attacks," *SIAM J. On Comput.*, Vol. 17, No. 2, 1988, pp. 281-308.

M McCurley, K.S.: "A Key Distribution System Equivalent to Factoring," *J. of Cryptology*, Vol. 1, No. 2, 1988, pp. 95-106.

MTI Matsumoto, T., Takashima, Y., Imai, H.: "On Seeking Smart Public-Key-Distribution Systems," *The Transactions of the IECE of Japan*, Vol. E69, No. 2, February 1986, pp. 99-106.

NY89 Naor, M., Yung, M.: "Universal One-Way Hash Functions and their Cryptographic Applications," *STOC*, 1989, pp. 33-43, 1989.

NY90 Naor, M., Yung, M.: "Public-Key cryptosystems provably secure against chosen ciphertext attacks," to appear.

R Rabin, M.O.: "Digital Signature and Public Key Functions as Intractable as Factoring," Technical Memo TM-212, Lab for Computer Science, MIT, 1979.

RSA Rivest, R.L., Shamir, A., and Adelman, L.: "A Method for Obtaining Digital Signatures and Public-Key Cryptosystems," *Commun. ACM* 1978, 21, pp. 120-126.

S Shmuely, Z.: "Composite Diffie-Hellman Public-Key Generating Systems Are Hard to Break," TR. No. 356, *Computer Science Dept. Technion, IIT* , Feb. 1985.

YS Yacobi, Y., Shmuely, Z.: "On Key Distribution Systems," Proc. *Crypto'89*.

A Modular Approach to Key Distribution

Walter Fumy and Michael Munzert

Siemens AG, Germany

Abstract. *The purpose of key management is to provide procedures for handling cryptographic keying material to be used in symmetric or asymmetric cryptographic mechanisms. As a result of varied design decisions appropriate to different conditions, a large variety of key distribution protocols exist. There is a need to explicate key distribution protocols in a way that allows to understand which results they achieve and on which assumptions they depend. We define a modular system that can be used to transform cryptographic protocols into a generic form and that has proven to be useful in the analysis and the construction of such protocols.*

1. Introduction

The purpose of key management is to provide procedures for handling cryptographic keying material to be used in symmetric or asymmetric cryptographic mechanisms. Key management includes user registration, key generation, key distribution, key storage, and key deletion. A fundamental problem of key management is to establish keying material whose origin, integrity, and - in the case of secret keys - confidentiality can be guaranteed. Most of the important properties of key management protocols do not depend on the underlying cryptographic algorithms, but rather on the structure of the messages exchanged. Bugs in such protocols therefore usually do not come from weak cryptographic algorithms, but from mistakes in higher levels of the design.

A large variety of mechanisms for key distribution and especially for key agreement can be found in the literature. [Diff 76] and [Ruep 88] e.g. describe procedures which allow the establishment of a common secret key for two users and which only require the communication of public messages. [Okam 86] proposes similar schemes that utilize each user's identification information to authenticate the exchanged messages. [Günt 89] and [Baus 89] use data exchanged during an authentication protocol to construct a session key. [Koya 87] shows how to generate a common secret conference key for two or more users that are connected in a ring, a complete graph, or a star network.

Key management has also been addressed by different standardization bodies which led to several national and international standards, in particular in the area of banking [ANSI 85], [CCIT 87]. Standards for other application areas as well as base standards dealing with generic issues of key management can be expected to follow [ANSI 89], [ISO 90c], [ISO 90d]. Until now, standardization bodies focus on key distribution in contrast to key agreement.

Key management schemes generally depend on the type of keys to be distributed, on the given facilities (e.g. the properties of the specific environment) and on the specific application. The most important considerations are the threats to be protected against, and the physical and architectural structure of the system.

This paper addresses the problem of key distribution by an approach that is modular, open, and generic, such that additional requirements, building blocks, and composition rules can be added if desired. It allows the construction of a large variety of individual key distribution schemes with desired properties. Such a modular approach is advocated within IEC/ISO/JTC1/SC27 for its standards on key management currently under development [ISO 90c], [ISO 90d]. The following section will describe generic security requirements for key distribution protocols. Section 3 gives some examples for building blocks and composition rules. Section 4 finally shows the analysis and construction of typical key distribution mechanisms.

2. Generic Requirements for Key Distribution

The fundamental problem of key distribution is to establish keying material to be used in symmetric or asymmetric cryptographic mechanisms whose origin, integrity, and - in the case of secret keys - confidentiality can be guaranteed. A key may be distributed either manually or automatically. Manually distributed keys are exchanged between parties by use of a courier or some other physical means. When using only symmetric cryptographic techniques at least the first key has to be manually exchanged between two parties in order to allow secure communications.

An automatic distribution of keys typically employs different types of messages. A transaction usually is initiated by requesting a key from some central facility (e.g. a Key Distribution Centre), or from the entity a key is to be exchanged with. Cryptographic Service Messages (CSMs) are exchanged between communicating parties for the transmission of keying material, or for authentication purposes. CSMs may contain keys, or other keying material, such as the distinguished names of entities, key identities, count or random values. CSMs have to be protected depending on their contents and on the security requirements which for their part depend on several parameters, and especially on the given facilities. Generic requirements include:

(a) **Data Confidentiality**: Secret keys and possibly other data are to be kept confidential while being transmitted or stored.

(b) Modification Detection is to counter the active threat of unauthorized modification of data items. In most environments cryptographic service messages have to be protected against modification.

(c) Replay Detection / Timeliness: Replay detection is to counter unauthorized duplication of data items. Timeliness requires that the response to a challenge message is prompt and does not allow for play-back of some authentic response message by an impersonator.

(d) Authentication is to corroborate that an entity is the one claimed. This is part of data origin authentication (see below). The general problem of authentication is to establish a message whose origin, uniqueness and timeliness can be verified.

(e) Data Origin Authentication is to corroborate that the source of a message is the one claimed. As defined in [ISO 88] it does not provide protection against duplication or modification of the message. In practice, however, data origin authentication often is a combination of sender authentication and modification detection.

(f) Proof of Delivery shows the sender of a message that the message has been received by its legitimate receiver correctly.

3. Building Blocks and Composition Rules

As a result of varied design decisions appropriate to different circumstances, a large variety of key distribution protocols exist (see e.g. [Mill 87], [Need 78], [Otwa 87]). Therefore, there is a need to explicate key distribution protocols in a way that allows to understand which results the different protocols achieve and on which assumptions they depend. We define a modular system that can be used to transform cryptographic protocols into a generic form and that has proven to be useful in the analysis and the construction of such protocols. Formal methods devoted to the analysis of (authentication) protocols have recently been developed by M.Burrows, M.Abadi and R.Needham [Burr 90].

The basic elements of cryptographic service messages can be classified in several ways. There are building blocks that append data to a message which is independent of the message itself, building blocks that append data which is dependent on the message, and building blocks that transform a message in a certain way. Note that in the first case the original message may be empty. Each of the building blocks described below addresses one or more of the requirements given in section 2.

(a) Encipherment: The confidentiality of a data item D can be ensured by enciphering D with an appropriate key K. Depending on whether a secret key algorithm or a public key algorithm is used for the enciphering process, D will be enciphered with a secret key K shared between the sender and the legitimate recipient of the message (building block a1), or with the legitimate recipient B's public key K_{Bp} (a2). Encipherment with the sender A's private key K_{As} provides a digital signature which may be used to authenticate the origin of data item D, or to identify A (a3). Encipherment with a secret key (a1, a3) provides modification detection if B has some means to check the validity of D (e.g. if B knows D beforehand, or if D contains suitable redundancy).

generic:		**$eK(D)$**	
(a1)	A $\rightarrow$ B:	$eK_{AB}(D)$	
(a2)	X $\rightarrow$ B:	$eK_{Bp}(D)$	
(a3)	A $\rightarrow$ X:	$eK_{As}(D)$	

(b) Modification Detection Codes: To detect a modification of a data item D one can add some redundancy that has to be calculated using a collision-free function, i.e. it must be computationally infeasible to find two different values of D that render the same result. Moreover, this process has to involve a secret parameter K in order to prevent forgery. Appropriate combination of K and D also allows for data origin authentication. Examples of suitable building blocks are message authentication codes as defined in [ISO 89] (see b1), or hash-functions, often combined with encipherment (b2 through b5).

generic:		**$D \parallel mdcK(D)$**	
(b1)	A $\rightarrow$ B:	$D \parallel macK_{AB}(D)$	
(b2)	A $\rightarrow$ B:	$D \parallel eK_{AB}(h(D))$	
(b3)	A $\rightarrow$ X:	$D \parallel eK_{As}(h(D))$	
(b4)	A $\rightarrow$ B:	$D \parallel h(K_{AB} \parallel D)$	
(b5)	A $\rightarrow$ B:	$eK_{AB}(D \parallel h(D))$	

These building blocks enable the legitimate recipient to detect unauthorized modification of the transmitted data immediately after receipt. The correctness of distributed keying material can also be checked if the sender confirms his knowledge of the key in a second step (see section (d) below).

(c) Replay Detection Codes: To detect the replay of a message and to check its timeliness, some explicit or implicit challenge and response mechanism has to be used, since the recipient has to be able to decide on the acceptance. This paragraph only deals with implicit mechanisms; explicit challenge and response mechanisms are being dealt with in section (d) (see below). In most applications the inclusion of a replay detection code (e.g. a timestamp TD, a counter CT, or a random number R) will only make sense if it is protected by modification detection. If modification detection of the data item D is required, the concatenation of D and the rdc also has to be protected against separation.

(c1)	$D := D \parallel rdc$	$rdc \in \{CT, TD\}$

With symmetric cryptographic mechanisms key modification can be used to detect the replay of a message. Building block c2 combines (e.g. XORs) the secret key with an rdc (e.g. a counter CT, or a random number R). Key offsetting used to protect data enciphered for distribution is a special case of building block c2. In this process the key used for encipherment is XORed with a count value [ANSI 85].

$$\text{(c2)} \qquad K_{AB} := f(K_{AB}, rdc) \qquad\qquad rdc \in \{R, CT\}$$

(d) Proof of Knowledge of a Key: Authentication can be implemented by showing knowledge of a secret (e.g. a secret key). Nevertheless, a building block that proves the knowledge of a key K can also be useful, when K is public. There are several ways for A to prove to B the knowledge of a key that are all based on the principle of challenge and response in order to prevent a replay attack. Depending on the challenge which may be a data item in cleartext or in ciphertext, A has to process the key K and the rdc in an appropriate way (e.g. by encipherment (see d1), or by calculating a message authentication code (see d2)), or A has to perform a deciphering operation (d4).

The challenge may explicitly be provided by B (e.g. a random number R) or implicitly be given by a synchronized parameter (e.g. a timestamp TD, or a counter CT). For some building blocks the latter case requires only one pass to proof knowledge of K; its tradeoff is the necessary synchronization. If B provides a challenge enciphered with a key K^*, A has to apply the corresponding deciphering key K. In these cases the enciphered data item has to be unpredictable (e.g. a random number R, or a key K^{**}).

generic:		**authK(A to B)**	
(d1)	A ← B:	rdc	obsolete if rdc ∈ {CT, TD}
	A → B:	eK(rdc)	
(d2)	A ← B:	rdc	obsolete if rdc ∈ {CT, TD}
	A → B:	rdc ‖ macK(rdc)	
(d3)	A ← B:	rdc	obsolete if rdc ∈ {CT, TD}
	A → B:	rdc ‖ h(K ‖ rdc)	
(d4)	A ← B:	eK*(rdc)	rdc random value
	A → B:	rdc	
(d5)	A ← B:	eK*(K**) ‖ rdc	rdc arbitrary
	A → B:	eK**(rdc)	
(d6)	A ← B:	eK*(K**) ‖ rdc	rdc arbitrary
	A → B:	macK**(rdc)	
(d7)	A ← B:	eK*(K**) ‖ rdc	rdc arbitrary
	A → B:	h(K** ‖ rdc)	

Building blocks d5 through d7 of course also confirm that A knows K^{**} in addition to the deciphering key K.

(e) **Composition Rules**: Some composition rules extracted from the description of the above building blocks and their effects on different security requirements are summarized in table 1 below.

Building Block	Requirement			
	Confidentiality	Modification Detection	Replay Detection	Data Origin Authentication
$A \rightarrow B$: $eK_{AB}(D)$	yes	only if recipient can check validity of D	$D := D \parallel rdc$	only if recipient can check validity of D
$X \rightarrow B$: $eK_{Bp}(D)$	yes	no	$D := D \parallel rdc$	no
$A \rightarrow X$: $eK_{As}(D)$	no	only if recipient can check validity of D	$D := D \parallel rdc$	only if recipient can check validity of D
$A \rightarrow B$: $D \parallel macK_{AB}(D)$	no	yes	$D := D \parallel rdc$ or $K_{AB} := f(K_{AB}, rdc)$	yes
$A \rightarrow B$: $D \parallel eK_{AB}(h(D))$	no	yes	$D := D \parallel rdc$ or $K_{AB} := f(K_{AB}, rdc)$	yes
$A \rightarrow X$: $D \parallel eK_{As}(h(D))$	no	yes	$D := D \parallel rdc$	yes
$A \rightarrow B$: $D \parallel h(K_{AB} \parallel D)$	no	yes	$D := D \parallel rdc$ or $K_{AB} := f(K_{AB}, rdc)$	yes
$A \rightarrow B$: $eK_{AB}(D \parallel h(D))$	yes	yes	$D := D \parallel rdc$ or $K_{AB} := f(K_{AB}, rdc)$	yes

The building blocks (cx) have to be applied first, so that the combination of (c1) with (a1) e.g. results in

$$A \rightarrow B: \qquad eK_{AB}(D \parallel rdc)$$

Besides the above composition rules one also can give several general rules:

(e1) A secret key shall not be used for both encipherment and authentication of the same data item.

(e2) Two consecutive transmissions from A to B may be replaced by one transmission of concatenated messages.

(e3) $D1 \parallel D2$ may be replaced by $D2 \parallel D1$.

(e4) $eK(D1) \parallel eK(D2)$ may be replaced by $eK(D1 \parallel D2)$.

4. Examples for Point-to-Point Key Distribution Protocols

The basic mechanism of every key distribution scheme is point-to-point key distribution. If based on symmetric cryptographic techniques point-to-point key distribution requires that the two parties involved already share a key that can be used to protect the keying material to be distributed. In this section we discuss protocols for point-to-point distribution of a secret key that are derived from [ISO 90a], [ANSI 85], and [ISO 90b], respectively. The first example is to illustrate the construction of a key distribution protocol out of building blocks. Generic descriptions are used to exhibit similarities and differences between the discussed protocols.

General assumptions are:

- The initiator A is able to generate or otherwise acquire a secret key K^*.
- Security requirements are confidentiality of K^*, modification and replay detection, mutual authentication of A and B, and a proof of delivery for K^*.

For point-to-point key distribution protocols based on symmetric cryptographic techniques we additionally assume:

- A key K_{AB} is already shared by A and B.

The first two security requirements can be met by an appropriate combination of building blocks a1 through c2 (see table 1), whereas for the other two requirements one can choose from building blocks d1 through d7. As a first example we show a protocol built up from building blocks a1 and c1 (step 1: confidentiality of K^*, modification and replay detection), d1 and d5 (steps 2 to 4: mutual proof of knowledge of K_{AB} that includes B's proof of knowledge of K^*), and d4 (steps 5 and 6: A's proof of knowledge of K^*).

A	Protocol 1: Point-to-Point Key Distribution	B
$(1) \rightarrow$	$eK_{AB}(K^* \parallel rdc_1)$	
$(2) \rightarrow$	$eK_{AB}(rdc_2)$	
$(3) \rightarrow$	$eK_{AB}(K^*) \parallel rdc_3$	
	$eK^*(rdc_3)$	$\leftarrow (4)$
	$eK^*(rdc_4)$	$\leftarrow (5)$
$(6) \rightarrow$	rdc_4	

The above protocol can be greatly simplified by identifying the parameters rdc_2 and rdc_3 with rdc_1 ($= N$ which can be chosen to be a counter CT or a timestamp TD), and by applying composition rules e2 and e4 to steps 4 and 5. The resulting point-to-point key distribution protocol is one proposed in [ISO 90c].

A	Protocol 1': Point-to-Point Key Distribution (ISO/IEC CD 9798-2)	B
(1) →	$eK_{AB}(K^* \parallel N)$	
	$eK^*(N \parallel R)$	← (2)
(3) →	R	

In generic form this protocol can be desribed as follows:

A	Protocol 1': Generic Form	B
(1) →	$eK(K^* \parallel rdc)$	
(2) →	$authK^*(A \text{ to } B)$	
	$authK^*(B \text{ to } A)$	← (3)

A point-to-point key distribution protocol proposed in [ANSI 85] takes a somewhat different approach. To achieve replay and modification detection protocol 2 (see below) makes use of building blocks c1 and b1 (see also table 1). A proves to B its knowledge of K^* (and thus the knowledge of K_{AB}) using building block d2, whereas B proves its knowledge of K_{AB} with building block d6 which also confirms the correct receipt of K^*.

A	Protocol 2: Point-to-Point Key Distribution (ANSI X9.17)	B
(1) →	$D \parallel eK_{AB}(K^*) \parallel N \parallel macK^*(\ldots)$	
	$macK^*(D)$	← (2)

The generic form of protocol 2 exhibits the essential differences between the two protocols.

A	Protocol 2: Generic Form	B
(1) →	$eK(K^*) \parallel rdc \parallel mdcK^*(\ldots)$	
	$authK^*(B \text{ to } A)$	← (2)

Finally we give an example for a point-to-point key distribution protocol based on public key techniques. We make the following supplementary assumptions:

- There is no shared key known to A and B before the key exchange process starts.

- There is a trusted third party C, where A can receive a certificate that contains the distinguished names of A and C, A's public key K_{Ap}, and the certificate's expiration date TE. The integrity of the certificate is protected by C's signature. As an example A's certificate is shown below:

$$ID_C \parallel ID_A \parallel K_{Ap} \parallel TE \parallel eK_{Cs}(h(ID_C \parallel ID_A \parallel K_{Ap} \parallel TE))$$

The exchange of certificates can be performed off-line and is not shown in the following protocol. In this protocol A sends a message (often refered to as *token*) to B that consists of a secret key K* enciphered with B's public key (building block a2) and an appended rdc. The integrity of the token is protected by A's signature (building block b3 combined with c1). This guarantees modification and replay detection, as well as data origin authentication. B responds with the enciphered rdc thereby acknowledging that it has received the key K* (building block d3).

A	Protocol 3: Point-to-Point Key Distribution (ISO/IEC CD 9798-3)	B
(1) →	$eK_{Bp}(K^*) \parallel rdc \parallel eK_{As}(h(eK_{Bp}(K^*) \parallel rdc))$	
	$eK^*(rdc)$	← (2)

The generic form of protocol 3 shows its similarity with protocol 2.

A	Protocol 3: Generic Form	B
(1) →	$eK(K^*) \parallel rdc \parallel mdcK'(...)$	
	$authK^*(B \text{ to } A)$	← (2)

Acknowledgements

We would like to thank Thomas Berson and Peter Landrock for helpful suggestions and stimulating discussions on the subject.

References:

[ANSI 85] ANSI X9.17-1985: *Financial Institution Key Management (Wholesale)*, 1985.

[ANSI 89] ANSI X12.42-198x: *EDI Security Structures and Cryptographic Service Message Transaction Set*, 1989.

[Baus 89] Bauspieß, F.; Knobloch, H.-J.: "How to Keep Authenticity Alive in a Computer Network", Proceedings of Eurocrypt'89, Springer LNCS **434** (1990), 38-46.

[Burr 90]   Burrows, M.; Abadi, M.; Needham, R.: *A Logic of Authentication*, DEC
              System Research Center Report **39**, 1990.

[CCIT 87]   CCITT Draft Recommendation X.509: *The Directory - Authentication
              Framework*, 1987.

[Diff 76]   Diffie, W.; Hellman, M.E.: "New Directions in Cryptography", IEEE
              Transactions on Information Theory, **22** (1976), 644-654.

[Günt 89]   Günther, Ch.G.: "An Identity-Based Key-Exchange Protocol", Proceedings
              of Eurocrypt'89, Springer LNCS **434** (1990), 29-37.

[ISO 88]   ISO 7498-2: *Open Systems Interconnections - Part 2: Security Architecture*,
              1988.

[ISO 89]   IEC/ISO 9797: *Data Integrity Mechanism Using a Cryptographic Check
              Function Employing a Block Cipher Algorithm*, 1989.

[ISO 90a]   IEC/ISO Committee Draft 9798-2: *Entity Authentication Mechanisms - Part
              2: Entity Authentication Using Symmetric Techniques, 1990*.

[ISO 90b]   IEC/ISO Committee Draft 9798-3: *Entity Authentication Mechanisms - Part
              3: Entity Authentication Using a Public-Key Algorithm, 1990*.

[ISO 90c]   IEC/ISO/JTC1/SC27/WG2 Working Draft: *Key Management Part 2: Key
              Management Using Symmetric Cryptographic Techniques*, 1990.

[ISO 90d]   IEC/ISO/JTC1/SC27/WG2 Working Draft: *Key Management Part 3: Key
              Management Using Public Key Techniques*, 1990.

[Koya 87]   Koyama K.; Ohta, K.: "Identity-Based Conference Key Distribution
              Systems", Proceedings of Crypto'87, Springer LNCS **293** (1988),
              175-184.

[Mill 87]   Miller, S.P.; Neuman, C.; Schiller, J.I.; Saltzer, J.H.: *Kerberos Authentication
              and Authorization System*, Project Athena Technical Plan, MIT, 1987.

[Need 78]   Needham, R.M.; Schroeder, M.D.: "Using Encryption for Authentication in
              Large Networks of Computers", Communications of the ACM, **21**
              (1978), 993-999.

[Okam 86]   Okamoto, E.: "Proposal for Identity-Based Key Distribution Systems",
              Electronic Letters, **22** (1986), 1283-1284.

[Otwa 87]   Otway, D.; Rees, O.: "Efficient and Timely Mutual Authentication",
              Operating Systems Review, **21** (1987), 8-10.

[Ruep 88]   Rueppel, R.A.: "Key Agreements Based on Function Composition",
              Proceedings of Eurocrypt'88, Springer LNCS **330** (1988), 3-10.

Session 7

Hash Functions

Chair: R. Rueppel, Crypto AG

Structural Properties of One-Way Hash Functions

Yuliang Zheng

Tsutomu Matsumoto

Hideki Imai

Division of Electrical and Computer Engineering
Yokohama National University
156 Tokiwadai, Hodogaya, Yokohama, 240 JAPAN

Abstract

We study the following two kinds of one-way hash functions: *universal one-way hash functions* (UOHs) and *collision intractable hash functions* (CIHs). The main property of the former is that *given an initial-string* x, it is computationally difficult to find a different string y that collides with x. And the main property of the latter is that it is computationally difficult to find a pair $x \neq y$ of strings such that x collides with y. Our main results are as follows. First we prove that UOHs with respect to initial-strings chosen *arbitrarily* exist if and only if UOHs with respect to initial-strings chosen *uniformly at random* exist. Then, as an application of the result, we show that UOHs with respect to initial-strings chosen arbitrarily can be constructed under a weaker assumption, the existence of one-way *quasi*-injections. Finally, we investigate relationships among various versions of one-way hash functions. We prove that some versions of one-way hash functions are strictly included in others by explicitly constructing hash functions that are one-way in the sense of the former but not in the sense of the latter.

1 Introduction

One-way hash functions are a principal primitive in cryptography. There are roughly two kinds of one-way hash functions: *universal one-way hash functions* (UOHs) and *collision intractable hash functions* (CIHs). The main property of the former is that *given an initial-string* x, it is computationally difficult to find a different string y

that collides with x. And the main property of the latter is that it is computationally difficult to find a pair $x \neq y$ of strings such that x collides with y. Naor and Yung constructed UOHs under the assumption of the existence of one-way injections (i.e., one-way one-to-one functions) [NY89], and Damgård constructed CIHs under a stronger assumption, the existence of *claw-free pairs of permutations* [Dam89]. In [NY89], Naor and Yung also presented a general method for transforming any UOH into a secure digital signature scheme. We are interested both in constructing UOHs under weaker assumptions and in relationships among various versions of one-way hash functions. Our main results are summarized as follows.

First, we prove that UOHs with respect to initial-strings chosen *uniformly at random* can be transformed into UOHs with respect to initial-strings chosen *arbitrarily*. Thus UOHs with respect to initial-strings chosen arbitrarily exist if and only if UOHs with respect to initial-strings chosen uniformly at random exist. The proof is constructive, and may significantly simplify the construction of UOHs with respect to initial-strings chosen arbitrarily, under the assumption of the existence of one-way functions. Then, as an application of the transformation result, we prove that UOHs with respect to initial-strings chosen arbitrarily can be constructed under a weaker assumption, the existence of one-way quasi-injections (whose definition is to be given in Section 5). Next, we investigate relationships among various versions of one-way hash functions. We show that some versions of one-way hash functions are strictly included in others by explicitly constructing hash functions that are one-way in the sense of the former but not in the sense of the latter. A simple method, which appears in [ZMI90], for constructing UOHs from one-way permutations whose (simultaneously) hard bits have been identified is described in Appendix.

2 Notation and Definitions

The set of all positive integers is denoted by N. Let $\Sigma = \{0, 1\}$ be the alphabet we consider. For $n \in N$, denote by Σ^n the set of all strings over Σ with length n, by Σ^* that of all finite length strings including the empty string, denoted by λ, over Σ, and by Σ^+ the set $\Sigma^* - \{\lambda\}$. The concatenation of two strings x, y is denoted by $x \diamond y$, or simply by xy if no confusion arises. The length of a string x is denoted by $|x|$, and the number of elements in a set S is denoted by $\sharp S$.

Let ℓ be a monotone increasing function from N to N, and f a (total) function from D to R, where $D = \bigcup_n D_n, D_n \subseteq \Sigma^n$, and $R = \bigcup_n R_n, R_n \subseteq \Sigma^{\ell(n)}$. D is called the *domain*, and R the *range* of f. For simplicity of presentation, in this paper we always assume that $D_n = \Sigma^n$ and $R_n = \Sigma^{\ell(n)}$. Denote by f_n the restriction of f on Σ^n. We are concerned only with the case when the range of f_n is $\Sigma^{\ell(n)}$, i.e., f_n is a function from Σ^n to $\Sigma^{\ell(n)}$. f is an *injection* if each f_n is a one-to-one function, and is a *permutation* if each f_n is a one-to-one and onto function. f is (deterministic/probabilistic) *polynomial time computable* if there is a (deterministic/probabilistic) polynomial (in $|x|$) time algorithm (Turing machine) computing $f(x)$ for all $x \in D$. The composition of two functions f and g is defined as $f \circ g(x) = f(g(x))$. In particular, the i-fold composition of f is denoted by $f^{(i)}$.

A (probability) *ensemble* E with length $\ell(n)$ is a family of *probability distributions* $\{E_n | E_n : \Sigma^{\ell(n)} \to [0,1], n \in \mathbb{N}\}$. The *uniform ensemble* U with length $\ell(n)$ is the family of *uniform probability distributions* U_n, where each U_n is defined as $U_n(x) = 1/2^{\ell(n)}$ for all $x \in \Sigma^{\ell(n)}$. By $x \in_E \Sigma^{\ell(n)}$ we mean that x is randomly chosen from $\Sigma^{\ell(n)}$ according to E_n, and in particular, by $x \in_R S$ we mean that x is chosen from the set S uniformly at random. E is *samplable* if there is a (probabilistic) algorithm M that on input n outputs an $x \in_E \Sigma^{\ell(n)}$, and *polynomially samplable* if furthermore, the running time of M is polynomially bounded.

Now we introduce the notion for *one-way functions*, a topic that has received extensive research (see for examples [Yao82] [Wa88] [ILL89]).

Definition 1 *Let* $f : D \to R$, *where* $D = \bigcup_n \Sigma^n$ *and* $R = \bigcup_n \Sigma^{\ell(n)}$, *be a polynomial time computable function, and let* E *be an ensemble with length* n. *(1)* f *is* one-way *with respect to* E *if for each probabilistic polynomial time algorithm* M, *for each polynomial* Q *and for all sufficiently large* n, $\Pr\{f_n(x) = f_n(M(f_n(x)))\} < 1/Q(n)$, *when* $x \in_E \Sigma^n$. *(2)* f *is* one-way *if it is one-way with respect to the uniform ensemble* U *with length* n.

There are two basic computation models: Turing machines and combinational circuits (see for examples [Pip79] [KL82] [BDG88]). The above definition for one-way functions is with respect to the Turing machine model. A stronger version of one-way functions that is with respect to the circuit model can be obtained by changing algorithms M in the above definition to families $M = \{M_n \mid n \in \mathbb{N}\}$ of polynomial size circuits.

3 Universal One-Way Hash Functions

The central concept treated in this paper is *one-way hash functions*. Two kinds of one-way hash functions have been considered in the literature: *universal one-way hash functions* and *collision-intractable hash functions* (or shortly UOHs and CIHs, respectively). In [Mer89] the former is called *weakly* and the latter *strongly*, one-way hash functions respectively. Naor and Yung gave a formal definition for UOH [NY89], and Damgård gave for CIH [Dam89]. In this section, a formal definition for UOH that is more general than that of [NY89] is given. We feel our formulation more reasonable. This will be explained after the formulation is introduced. CIH will be treated in later sections.

Let ℓ be a polynomial with $\ell(n) > n$, H be a family of functions defined by $H = \bigcup_n H_n$ where H_n is a (possibly multi-)set of functions from $\Sigma^{\ell(n)}$ to Σ^n. Call H a *hash function* compressing $\ell(n)$-bit input into n-bit output strings. For two strings $x, y \in \Sigma^{\ell(n)}$ with $x \neq y$, we say that x and y collide with each other under $h \in H_n$, or (x, y) is a collision pair for h, if $h(x) = h(y)$.

H is *polynomial time computable* if there is a polynomial (in n) time algorithm computing all $h \in H$, and *accessible* if there is a probabilistic polynomial time algorithm that on input $n \in N$ outputs uniformly at random a description of $h \in H_n$. It is assumed that all hash functions considered in this paper are both polynomial time computable and accessible.

Let H be a hash function compressing $\ell(n)$-bit input into n-bit output strings, and E an ensemble with length $\ell(n)$. The definition for UOH is best described as a three-party game. The three parties are S (an *initial-string supplier*), G (a *hash function instance generator*) and F (a *collision-string finder*). S is an oracle whose power is un-limited, and both G and F are probabilistic polynomial time algorithms. The first move is taken by S, who outputs an *initial-string* $x \in_E \Sigma^{\ell(n)}$ and sends it to both G and F. The second move is taken by G, who chooses, independently of x, an $h \in_R H_n$ and sends it to F. The third and also final (null) move is taken by F, who on input $x \in \Sigma^{\ell(n)}$ and $h \in H_n$ outputs either "?" (I don't know) or a string $y \in \Sigma^{\ell(n)}$ such that $x \neq y$ and $h(x) = h(y)$. F wins a game iff his/her output is *not* equal to "?". Informally, H is a universal one-way hash function with respect to E if for any collision-string finder F, the probability that F wins a game is negligible. More precisely:

Definition 2 *Let H be a hash function compressing $\ell(n)$-bit input into n-bit output strings, P a collection of ensembles with length $\ell(n)$, and F a collision-string finder. H is a universal one-way hash function with respect to P, denoted by UOH/P, if for each $E \in P$, for each F, for each polynomial Q, and for all sufficiently large n, $\Pr\{F(x, h) \neq ?\} < 1/Q(n)$, where x and h are independently chosen from $\Sigma^{\ell(n)}$ and H_n according to E_n and to the uniform distribution over H_n respectively, and the probability $\Pr\{F(x, h) \neq ?\}$ is computed over $\Sigma^{\ell(n)}$, H_n and the sample space of all finite strings of coin flips that F could have tossed.*

If P consists of a single ensemble E (i.e., $P = \{E\}$), UOH/E is synonymous with UOH/P. Of particular interest are the following versions of UOH: (1) UOH/$EN[\ell]$, where $EN[\ell]$ is the collection of all ensembles with length $\ell(n)$. (2) UOH/$PSE[\ell]$, where $PSE[\ell]$ is the collection of all polynomially samplable ensembles with length $\ell(n)$. (3) UOH/U, where U is the uniform ensemble with length $\ell(n)$.

In [NY89], Naor and Yung gave a definition for UOH. They did not separate initial-string ensembles from collision-string finders. Instead, they introduced a probabilistic *polynomial* time algorithm $A(\cdot, \cdot)$, called a *collision adversary* that works in two stages: At the first stage, the algorithm A, on input (λ, λ) where λ denotes the empty string, outputs an *initial value* (corresponding to our *initial-string*) $x = A(\lambda, \lambda) \in \Sigma^{\ell(n)}$. At the second stage, it, when given an $h \in H_n$, attempts to find a string $y = A(x, h) \in \Sigma^{\ell(n)}$ such that $x \neq y$ and $h(x) = h(y)$.

Thus Naor and Yung defined, in our terms, *universal one-way hash function with respect to polynomially samplable ensembles with length* $\ell(n)$, i.e., UOH/$PSE[\ell]$. Naor and Yung constructed one-way hash functions in the sense of UOH/$PSE[\ell]$ under the assumption of the existence of one-way injections [NY89]. Note that they actually obtained a construction for one-way hash functions in the sense of UOH/$EN[\ell]$. In [ZMI90] we construct, in a different approach, one-way hash functions in the sense of UOH/$EN[\ell]$ under the assumption of the existence of one-way permutations. See Appendix for the description of the construction.

Separating initial-string ensembles from collision-string finders is conceptually much clearer, and enables us to reduce the problem of constructing one-way hash functions in the sense of UOH/$EN[\ell]$ (the "strongest" UOHs) to that of constructing one-way hash functions in the sense of UOH/U (the "weakest" UOHs). This topic is treated in Section 4.

The above definition for UOH is with respect to the Turing machine model. As a natural counterpart of UOH/P, where P is a set of ensembles with length $\ell(n)$, we have UOH$_C$/P, whose definition is obtained simply by changing probabilistic polynomial time algorithms F in Definition 2 to families $F = \{F_n \mid n \in \mathbf{N}\}$ of polynomial size circuits.

The definition for UOH can also be generalized in another direction: In addition to $x \in \Sigma^{\ell(n)}$ and $h \in H_n$, a collision-string finder F is allowed to receive an extra *advice* string a. As before, the output of F is either "?" or a string $y \in \Sigma^{\ell(n)}$ such that $x \neq y$ and $h(x) = h(y)$.

Definition 3 *Let H be a hash function compressing $\ell(n)$-bit input into n-bit output strings. H is a* universal one-way hash function with respect to polynomial length advice, *denoted by* UOH/$EN[poly]$, *if for each pair (Q_1, Q_2) of polynomials with $Q_1(n) \geq \ell(n)$, for each ensemble E with length $Q_1(n)$, for each collision-string finder F, and for all sufficiently large n, $\Pr\{F(x, a, h) \neq ?\} < 1/Q_2(n)$, where $x \in \Sigma^{\ell(n)}$, $a \in \Sigma^{Q_1(n) - \ell(n)}$, $x \diamond a$ and h are independently chosen from $\Sigma^{Q_1(n)}$ and H_n according to E_n and to the uniform distribution over H_n respectively, and the probability $\Pr\{F(x, a, h) \neq ?\}$ is computed over $\Sigma^{Q_1(n)}$, H_n and the sample space of all finite strings of coin flips that F could have tossed.*

Notice the difference between *Turing machines taking advice* discussed in [Pip79] [KL82] and collision-string finders in our Definition 3. In the former case, advice strings are uniquely determined for each $n \in \mathbf{N}$. While in the latter case, they are generated probabilistically. In Section 7, we will discuss relationships among various versions of one-way hash functions including UOH/U, UOH/$PSE[\ell]$, UOH/$EN[\ell]$, UOH$_C$/$EN[\ell]$, and UOH/$EN[poly]$.

4 Transforming UOH/U into UOH/$EN[\ell]$

Let P_1, P_2 be collections of ensembles with length $\ell(n)$. We say that UOH/P_1 is *transformable* into UOH/P_2 iff given a one-way hash function H in the sense of UOH/P_1, we can construct from H a one-way hash function H' in the sense of UOH/P_2. The main result of this section is Theorem 1 to be proved below, which states that UOH/U is transformable into UOH/$EN[\ell]$. Thus constructing one-way hash functions in the sense of UOH/$EN[\ell]$ under certain assumptions can be fulfilled in two steps: At the first step, we construct one-way hash functions in the sense of UOH/U. This would be easier, since a uniform ensemble would be easier to handle than arbitrary ones. Then at the second step, we apply the proof technique for Theorem 1 to obtain one-way hash functions in the sense of UOH/$EN[\ell]$.

To prove Theorem 1, we require a function family called *an invertible uniformizer*. Let T_n be a set of permutations over $\Sigma^{\ell(n)}$, and let $T = \bigcup_n T_n$. T is a *uniformizer* with length $\ell(n)$ if it has the following properties 1, 2 and 3. Furthermore, F is *invertible* if it also has the following property 4.

1. For each n, for each pair of strings $x, y \in \Sigma^{\ell(n)}$, there are exactly $\sharp T_n/2^{\ell(n)}$ permutations in T_n that map x to y.

2. There is a probabilistic polynomial time algorithm that on input n outputs a $t \in_R T_n$.

3. There is a polynomial time algorithm that computes all $t \in T$.

4. There is a polynomial time algorithm that computes t^{-1} for all $t \in T$.

The first property implies that for any $n \in \mathbf{N}$ and any $x \in \Sigma^{\ell(n)}$, when t is chosen randomly and uniformly from T_n, the probability that $t(x)$ coincides with a particular $y \in \Sigma^{\ell(n)}$ is $(\sharp T_n/2^{\ell(n)})/\sharp T_n = 1/2^{\ell(n)}$, i.e., $t(x)$ is distributed randomly and uniformly over $\Sigma^{\ell(n)}$.

Now we give a concrete invertible uniformizer with length $\ell(n)$. Note that there is a natural one-to-one correspondence between strings of $\Sigma^{\ell(n)}$ and elements of $GF(2^{\ell(n)})$. So we will not distinguish $GF(2^{\ell(n)})$ from $\Sigma^{\ell(n)}$. Let a and b be elements of $GF(2^{\ell(n)})$ with $a \neq 0$. Then the affine transformation t defined by $t(x) = a \cdot x + b$ is a permutation over $GF(2^{\ell(n)})$, where $\cdot$ and $+$ are multiplication and addition over $GF(2^{\ell(n)})$ respectively. Denote by T_n the set of all the affine transformations on $GF(2^{\ell(n)})$ defined as above. Clearly, $\sharp T_n = 2^{\ell(n)}(2^{\ell(n)} - 1)$, and for any elements $x, y \in GF(2^{\ell(n)})$, there are exactly $(2^{\ell(n)} - 1) = \sharp T_n/2^{\ell(n)}$ affine transformations in T_n that map x to y. In addition, generating $t \in_R T_n$ is easy, and for all $t \in T$, computing t and t^{-1} are simple tasks. Thus $T = \bigcup_n T_n$ is an invertible uniformizer with length $\ell(n)$. In section 5, T will once again play a crucial role in constructing one-way hash functions in the sense of UOH/$EN[\ell]$ from one-way quasi-injections. Now we are ready to prove the following:

Theorem 1 *UOH/U is transformable into UOH/EN[ℓ].* [1]

Proof : Assume that H is a one-way hash function in the sense of UOH/U, where U is the uniform ensemble with length $\ell(n)$. We show how to construct from H a hash function H' that is one-way in the sense of UOH/$EN[\ell]$.

Let $T = \bigcup_n T_n$ be an invertible uniformizer with length $\ell(n)$. Given H and $T = \bigcup_n T_n$, we construct H' as follows: $H' = \bigcup_n H'_n$, where $H'_n = \{h' \mid h' = h \circ t, h \in H_n, t \in T_n\}$. We claim that H' is one-way in the sense of UOH/$EN[\ell]$.

Assume for contradiction that H' is not one-way in the sense of UOH/$EN[\ell]$. Then there are a polynomial Q, an infinite subset $\mathbf{N}' \subseteq \mathbf{N}$, an ensemble E' with length $\ell(n)$ and a probabilistic polynomial time algorithm F' such that for all $n \in \mathbf{N}'$, the algorithm F', on input $x' \in_{E'} \Sigma^{\ell(n)}$ and $h' \in_R H'_n$, finds with probability $1/Q(n)$ a string $y' \in \Sigma^{\ell(n)}$ with $x' \neq y'$ and $h'(x') = h'(y')$. Now we show how to derive from F' a collision-string finder F that for all $n \in \mathbf{N}'$, on input $x \in_R \Sigma^{\ell(n)}$ and $h \in_R H_n$ where x is produced in a particular way to be described below, outputs with the same probability $1/Q(n)$ a string $y \in \Sigma^{\ell(n)}$ with $x \neq y$ and $h(x) = h(y)$.

Let M be a probabilistic Turing machine *with an oracle O that on input n outputs an $x' \in_{E'} \Sigma^{\ell(n)}$*. M produces $x \in_R \Sigma^{\ell(n)}$ in the following particular way:

1. Query the oracle O with n. Denote by x' the string answered by O. (Note that the oracle O is indispensable, as E' may be not samplable.)

2. Generate an $s \in_R T_n$ using its random tape.

3. Output $x = s(x')$.

From the first property of the uniformizer $T = \bigcup_n T_n$, we know that the ensemble E_M defined by the output of M is the uniform ensemble with length $\ell(n)$.

Let F be a probabilistic Turing machine. F uses the *same* random tape as M's and its read-only head for the random tape is in the same position as M's at the outset. On input $x \in_{E_M} \Sigma^{\ell(n)}$ and $h \in_R H_n$, (important note: since E_M is the uniform ensemble with length $\ell(n)$, $x \in_{E_M} \Sigma^{\ell(n)}$ is equivalent to $x \in_R \Sigma^{\ell(n)}$), F works as follows:

1. Generate a $t \in_R T_n$ using the random tape and in the same way as M does. Since M shares the random tape with F, we have $t = s$.

2. Calculate $z = t^{-1}(x)$. Since $t = s$, we have $z = x' \in_{E'} \Sigma^{\ell(n)}$.

---

[1]De Santis and Yung obtained, independently, this theorem too [DY90].

3. Call F' with input (z, h'), where $h' = h \circ t$. Note that $h' \in_R H_n'$, since $h \in_R H_n$ and $t \in_R T_n$.

4. Let $y' = F'(z, h')$. Output $y = y'$ whenever $y' = ?$, and $y = t(y')$ otherwise.

Since F' is polynomial time bounded, F is also polynomial time bounded. Furthermore, since t is a permutation over $\Sigma^{\ell(n)}$, we have $y \neq ?$ (i.e. $x \neq y$ and $h(x) = h(y)$) iff $y' \neq ?$ (i.e. $x' \neq y'$ and $h'(x') = h'(y')$). Thus for all $n \in \mathbf{N}'$, F outputs, with the same probability $1/Q(n)$, a string y such that $x \neq y$ and $h(x) = h(y)$, which implies that H is *not* a one-way hash function in the sense of UOH/U, a contradiction.

From the above discussions we know that H' is indeed a one-way hash function in the sense of UOH/$EN[\ell]$. This completes the proof. $\qquad\qquad\square$

A significant corollary of Theorem 1 is:

Corollary 1 *One-way hash functions in the sense of UOH/EN[ℓ] exist iff those in the sense of UOH/U exist.*

5 UOHs Based on a Weakened Assumption

As an application of Theorem 1, in this section we construct one-way hash functions in the sense of UOH/$EN[\ell]$ under a weaker assumption — the existence of one-way *quasi*-injections. Main ingredients of our construction include (1) one-way quasi-injections, (2) universal hash functions with the collision accessibility property, (3) pair-wise independent uniformizers and, (4) invertible uniformizers. Our construction is partially inspired by [NY89].

5.1 Preliminaries

Assume that f is a one-way function from $\bigcup_n \Sigma^n$ to $\bigcup_n \Sigma^{\ell(n)}$. A string $x \in \Sigma^n$ is said to *have a brother* if there is a string $y \in \Sigma^n$ such that $f_n(x) = f_n(y)$.

Definition 4 *A one-way function f is a one-way quasi-injection iff for any polynomial Q and for all sufficiently large $n \in \mathbf{N}$, $\sharp B_n/2^n < 1/Q(n)$ where B_n is the collection of all strings in Σ^n that have brothers.*

Let ℓ be a polynomial with $\ell(n) > n$, $S = \bigcup_n S_n$ be a hash function compressing $\ell(n)$-bit input into n-bit output strings. S is a *strongly universal₂* hash function [CW79] [WC81] if for each n, for each pairs (x_1, x_2) and (y_1, y_2) with $x_1 \neq x_2$, $x_1, x_2 \in \Sigma^{\ell(n)}$ and $y_1, y_2 \in \Sigma^n$, there are $\sharp S_n/(\sharp \Sigma^n)^2$ functions in S_n that map x_1 to y_1 and x_2 to y_2. S is said to have the *collision accessibility property* [NY89] if given a pair (x, y) of strings in $\Sigma^{\ell(n)}$ with $x \neq y$ and a requirement that $s(x) = s(y)$, it is possible to generate in polynomial time a function $s \in S_n$ such that $s(x) = s(y)$ with equal probability over all functions in S_n which obey the requirement. Note that strongly universal$_2$ hash functions with collision accessibility property are available without any assumption [NY89].

Let V_n be a set of permutations over $\Sigma^{\ell(n)}$, and $V = \bigcup_n V_n$. V is a *pair-wise independent uniformizer* with length $\ell(n)$ if it has the following three properties.

1. For each n, for any pairs of strings (x_1, x_2) and (y_1, y_2), there are exactly $\sharp V_n / [2^{\ell(n)}(2^{\ell(n)} - 1)]$ permutations in V_n that map x_1 to y_1 and x_2 to y_2, where $x_1, x_2, y_1, y_2 \in \Sigma^{\ell(n)}$, $x_1 \neq x_2$, $y_1 \neq y_2$, and $2^{\ell(n)}(2^{\ell(n)} - 1)$ is the total number of ordered pairs (x, y) with $x \neq y$ and $x, y \in \Sigma^{\ell(n)}$.

2. There is a probabilistic polynomial time algorithm that on input n outputs a $v \in_R V_n$.

3. There is a polynomial time algorithm that computes all $v \in V$.

Similar to uniformizers defined in Section 4, the first property implies that for any $n \in \mathbf{N}$ and any (x_1, x_2) with $x_1 \neq x_2$ and $x_1, x_2 \in \Sigma^{\ell(n)}$, when v is chosen randomly and uniformly from V_n, $(v(x_1), v(x_2))$ is distributed randomly and uniformly over all ordered pairs (y_1, y_2) with $y_1 \neq y_2$ and $y_1, y_2 \in \Sigma^{\ell(n)}$.

Recall the invertible uniformizer $T = \bigcup_n T_n$ constructed in Section 4. For any $x_1, x_2, y_1, y_2 \in \Sigma^{\ell(n)}$ with $x_1 \neq x_2$ and $y_1 \neq y_2$, there is exactly one permutation in T_n that maps x_1 to y_1 and x_2 to y_2. Note that $1 = 2^{\ell(n)}(2^{\ell(n)} - 1)/2^{\ell(n)}(2^{\ell(n)} - 1) = \sharp T_n / [2^{\ell(n)}(2^{\ell(n)} - 1)]$, which implies that T is a pair-wise independent uniformizer.

5.2   UOHs from One-Way Quasi-Injections

Assume that we are given a one-way quasi-injection f from D to R where $D = \bigcup_n \Sigma^n$, $R = \bigcup_n \Sigma^{m(n)}$ and m is a polynomial with $m(n) \geq n$. Let $V = \bigcup_n V_n$ be a pair-wise independent uniformizer with length $m(n)$, and $S = \bigcup_n S_n$ be a strongly universal$_2$ hash function that compresses $m(n)$-bit input into $(n-1)$-bit output strings and has the collision accessibility property.

Lemma 1 *let* $H_n = \{h \mid h = s \circ v \circ f_{n+1}, s \in S_{n+1}, v \in V_{n+1}\}$, *and* $H = \bigcup_n H_n$. *Then H is a one-way hash function in the sense of UOH/U compressing $(n+1)$-bit input into n-bit output strings, under the assumption that f is a one-way quasi-injection.*

Proof :   Assume for contradiction that H is not one-way in the sense of UOH/U. Then there are a polynomial Q_1, an infinite subset $\mathbf{N'} \subseteq \mathbf{N}$ and a collision-string finder F such that for all $n \in \mathbf{N'}$, the finder F, on input $x \in_R \Sigma^{n+1}$ and $h \in_R H_n$, outputs with probability at least $1/Q_1(n)$ a string $y \in \Sigma^{n+1}$ with $x \neq y$ and $h(x) = h(y)$. We show that F can be used to construct an algorithm M that for all sufficiently large $n \in \mathbf{N'}$, inverts f_{n+1} with probability greater than $1/2Q_1(n)$.

Assume that $w \in_R \Sigma^{n+1}$ and $z = f_{n+1}(w)$. On input z, the algorithm M runs as follows in trying to compute a y such that $z = f_{n+1}(y)$:

Algorithm M:

1. Generate an $x \in_R \Sigma^{n+1}$. If $z = f_{n+1}(x)$ then output $y = x$ and halt. Otherwise execute the following steps.

2. Generate a $v \in_R V_{n+1}$.

3. Let $u_1 = v \circ f_{n+1}(x)$ and $u_2 = v(z)$. Choose a random $s \in S_{n+1}$ such that $s(u_1) = s(u_2)$. This is possible according to the collision accessibility property of S.

4. Let $h = s \circ v \circ f_{n+1}$. Call F with input h and x, and output $y = F(x, h)$.

First we show that h produced by M is a random element in H_n. At Step 2, a $v \in_R V_{n+1}$ is generated. Since $f_{n+1}(x) \neq z$, from the first property of V we know that $(v \circ f_{n+1}(x), v(z))$ is distributed randomly and uniformly over all pairs (x_1, x_2) with $x_1 \neq x_2$ and $x_1, x_2 \in \Sigma^{m(n+1)}$. At Step 3, s is chosen uniformly at random from all those functions in S_{n+1} that map u_1 and u_2 to the same string. Consequently, $h = s \circ v \circ f_{n+1}$ is a random element in H_n.

The running time of M is clearly polynomial in n. Next we estimate the probability that M outputs y such that $z = f_{n+1}(y)$. Denote by $\mathrm{Inv}(z)$ the set $\{e \mid z = f_{n+1}(e), e \in \Sigma^{n+1}\}$. Then M halts at Step 1 iff $x \in \mathrm{Inv}(z)$.

First we note that

$$\Pr\{z = f_{n+1}(y)\} \geq \Pr\{x \in \Sigma^{n+1} - \mathrm{Inv}(z), x \text{ has no brother}, z = f_{n+1}(y)\},$$

where $\Pr\{z = f_{n+1}(y)\}$ is computed over Σ^{n+1}, Σ^{n+1}, V_{n+1}, S_{n+1} and the sample space of all finite strings of coin flips that F could have tossed. Note that the two compound events " $x \in \Sigma^{n+1} - \mathrm{Inv}(z)$, x has no brother, $z = f_{n+1}(y)$" and " $x \in \Sigma^{n+1} - \mathrm{Inv}(z)$, x has no brother, $y \neq ?$" are in fact the same. So the probability $\Pr\{z = f_{n+1}(y)\}$ can be estimated via the probability $\Pr\{x \in \Sigma^{n+1} - \mathrm{Inv}(z), x \text{ has no brother}, y \neq ?\}$. Now we focus on the latter. By assumption, we have $\Pr\{y \neq ?\} \geq 1/Q_1(n)$ for all $n \in N'$, where $\Pr\{y \neq ?\}$ is computed over Σ^{n+1}, V_{n+1}, S_{n+1} and the sample space of all finite strings of coin flips that F could have tossed. On the other hand,

$$
\begin{aligned}
\Pr\{y \neq ?\} &= \Pr\{x \in \mathrm{Inv}(z), y \neq ?\} + \Pr\{x \in \Sigma^{n+1} - \mathrm{Inv}(z), y \neq ?\} \\
&= \Pr\{x \in \mathrm{Inv}(z), y \neq ?\} + \\
&\quad \Pr\{x \in \Sigma^{n+1} - \mathrm{Inv}(z), x \text{ has a brother}, y \neq ?\} + \\
&\quad \Pr\{x \in \Sigma^{n+1} - \mathrm{Inv}(z), x \text{ has no brother}, y \neq ?\}.
\end{aligned}
$$

Recall that f is one-way. So for all sufficiently large $n \in \mathbb{N}$, we have

$$\Pr\{x \in \mathrm{Inv}(z), y \neq?\} \leq \Pr\{x \in \mathrm{Inv}(z)\} < 1/4Q_1(n).$$

Furthermore, for all sufficiently n we have

$$\Pr\{x \in \Sigma^{n+1} - \mathrm{Inv}(z), x \text{ has a brother}, y \neq?\} \leq \Pr\{x \text{ has a brother}\} < 1/4Q_1(n),$$

since f is a one-way quasi-injection. Thus for all sufficiently large $n \in \mathbb{N}'$,

$$
\begin{aligned}
\Pr\{z = f_{n+1}(y)\} \ &\geq\ \Pr\{x \in \Sigma^{n+1} - \mathrm{Inv}(z), x \text{ has no brother}, z = f_{n+1}(y)\} \\
&=\ \Pr\{x \in \Sigma^{n+1} - \mathrm{Inv}(z), x \text{ has no brother}, y \neq?\} \\
&\geq\ 1/Q_1(n) - [\Pr\{x \in \mathrm{Inv}(z), y \neq?\} + \\
&\qquad \Pr\{x \in \Sigma^{n+1} - \mathrm{Inv}(z), x \text{ has a brother}, y \neq?\}] \\
&\geq\ 1/Q_1(n) - [1/4Q_1(n) + 1/4Q_1(n)] \\
&\geq\ 1/2Q_1(n).
\end{aligned}
$$

This contradicts our assumption that f is a one-way quasi-injection, and hence the theorem follows. □

Combining Theorem 1 and Lemma 1, we have the following result: *A one-way hash function H' in the sense of UOH/EN$[\ell']$, where ℓ' is defined by $\ell'(n) = n + 1$, can be constructed under the assumption that f is a one-way quasi-injection.* By an argument analogous to that of Theorem 3.1 of [Dam89], it can be proved that for any polynomial ℓ, we can construct from H' a one-way hash function H'' in the sense of UOH/$EN[\ell]$. Thus:

Theorem 2 *One-way hash functions in the sense of UOH/$EN[\ell]$ can be constructed assuming the existence of one-way quasi-injections.*

Similarly, we can construct one-way hash functions in the sense of UOH$_C$/$EN[\ell]$ assuming the existence of one-way quasi-injections *with respect to the circuit model.*

6   Collision Intractable Hash Functions

This section gives formal definitions for collision intractable hash functions. Let $H = \bigcup_n H_n$ be a hash function compressing $\ell(n)$-bit input into n-bit output strings. Let A, a *collision-pair finder*, be a probabilistic polynomial time algorithm that on input $h \in H_n$ outputs either "?" or a pair of strings $x, y \in \Sigma^{\ell(n)}$ with $x \neq y$ and $h(x) = h(y)$.

Definition 5 *H is called a* collision-intractable hash function (CIH) *if for each A, for each polynomial Q, and for all sufficiently large n, $\Pr\{A(h) \neq?\} < 1/Q(n)$, where $h \in_R H_n$, and the probability $\Pr\{A(h) \neq?\}$ is computed over H_n and the sample space of all finite strings of coin flips that A could have tossed.*

In [Dam89] (see also [Dam87]) CIH is called *collision free function family*. Damgård obtained CIHs under the assumption of the existence of claw-free pairs of permutations. In [ZMI90], we show that CIHs can be constructed from *distinction-intractable permutations*. We also propose *practical* CIHs, the fastest of which compress nearly $2n$-bit long input into n-bit long output strings by applying only *twice* a one-way function.

CIH defined above are with respect to the Turing machine model. So as in the case for UOH, we have CIH_C with respect to the circuit model. The definition for CIH_C is similar to Definition 5, except that probabilistic polynomial time algorithms A are replaced by families $A = \{A_n \mid n \in \mathbf{N}\}$ of polynomial size circuits.

In addition, analogous to Definition 3, we have the following generalization for CIH. Let $H = \bigcup_n H_n$ be a hash function compressing $\ell(n)$-bit input into n-bit output strings, Q_1 a polynomial, and $a \in \Sigma^{Q_1(n)}$. a is called an *advice* string of length $Q_1(n)$. Let A, a collision-pair finder, be a probabilistic polynomial time algorithm that on input $a \in \Sigma^{Q_1(n)}$ and $h \in H_n$ outputs either "?" or a pair of strings $x, y \in \Sigma^{\ell(n)}$ with $x \neq y$ and $h(x) = h(y)$.

Definition 6 *H is called a* collision intractable hash function with respect to polynomial length advice, *denoted by CIH/EN[poly], if for each pair (Q_1, Q_2) of polynomials, for each ensemble E with length $Q_1(n)$, for each A, and for all sufficiently large n, $\Pr\{A(a, h) \neq ?\} < 1/Q_2(n)$, where a and h are independently chosen from $\Sigma^{Q_1(n)}$ and H_n according to E_n and to the uniform distribution over H_n respectively, and the probability $\Pr\{A(a, h) \neq ?\}$ is computed over $\Sigma^{Q_1(n)}$, H_n and the sample space of all finite strings of coin flips that A could have tossed.*

7 A Hierarchy of One-Way Hash Functions

In this section, we discuss relationships among various versions of one-way hash functions: UOH/U, UOH/PSE[ℓ], UOH/EN[ℓ], UOH$_C$/EN[ℓ], UOH/EN[poly], CIH, CIH$_C$ and CIH/EN[poly].

First we define a relation between two versions, Ver_1 and Ver_2, of one-way hash functions. We say that

1. Ver_1 is *included in* Ver_2, denoted by $Ver_1 \subseteq Ver_2$, if all one-way hash functions in the sense of Ver_1 are also one-way hash functions in the sense of Ver_2.

2. Ver_1 is *strictly* included in Ver_2, denoted by $Ver_1 \subset Ver_2$, if $Ver_1 \subseteq Ver_2$ and there is a one-way hash function in the sense of Ver_2 but not in the sense of Ver_1.

3. Ver_1 and Ver_2 are *equivalent*, denoted by $Ver_1 = Ver_2$, if $Ver_1 \subseteq Ver_2$ and $Ver_2 \subseteq Ver_1$.

Lemma 2 *The following statements hold:*

(1) $CIH_C = CIH/EN[poly]$.

(2) $UOH_C/EN[\ell] = UOH/EN[poly]$.

(3) $UOH/EN[poly] \subseteq UOH/EN[\ell] \subseteq UOH/PSE[\ell] \subseteq UOH/U$.

(4) $CIH/EN[poly] \subseteq CIH$.

(5) $CIH \subseteq UOH/PSE[\ell]$.

(6) $CIH/EN[poly] \subseteq UOH/EN[poly]$.

Proof : Proofs for (1) and (2) are analogous to that for "polynomial size circuits vs. P/poly" [Pip79]. (3),(4), (5) and (6) are obvious. Here we give a detailed description for the proof of (1). Proof for (2) is similar, and is omitted.

The "$\subseteq$" part: Assume that H is a one-way hash function in the sense of CIH_C. If H is not one-way in the sense of $CIH/EN[poly]$, then there are polynomials Q_1 and Q_2, an infinite subset $N' \subseteq N$, an ensemble E with length $Q_2(n)$, and a collision-pair finder F, such that for all $n \in N'$, the finder F, on input $z \in_E \Sigma^{Q_2(n)}$ and $h \in_R H_n$, outputs a collision-pair with probability $1/Q_1(n)$. Note that for each $n \in N$ and $h \in_R H_n$, the probability that F successfully outputs a collision-pair is computed over $\Sigma^{Q_2(n)}$ and the sample space of all finite strings of coin flips that F could have tossed. Let z_{max} be the first string according to the lexicographic order in $\Sigma^{Q_2(n)}$ such that for $h \in_R H_n$, F outputs a collision-pair with the maximum probability, which is certainly at least $1/Q_1(n)$. F can be converted into a family $A = \{A_n \mid n \in N\}$ of probabilistic polynomial size circuits with z_{max} being "embedded in" A_n. Thus for each $n \in N'$, A_n on input $h \in_R H_n$ outputs a collision-pair with probability at least $1/Q_1(n)$. In other words, H is not one-way in the sense of CIH_C, which is a contradiction.

The "$\supseteq$" part: Assume that H is a one-way hash function in the sense of $CIH/EN[poly]$. If H is not one-way in the sense of CIH_C, then there are a polynomial Q_1, an infinite subset $N' \subseteq N$, and a collision-pair finder $A = \{A_n \mid n \in N\}$, such that for all $n \in N'$, A_n outputs a collision-pair with probability $1/Q_1(n)$. Since the size of A is polynomially bounded, there is a polynomial Q_2 such that the description of A_n is not longer than $Q_2(n)$ for all $n \in N$. Without loss of generality, assume that the description of A_n is exactly $Q_2(n)$ bits long. Let E be the ensemble with length $Q_2(n)$ defined by $E_n(x) = 1$ whenever x is the description of A_n, and $E_n(x) = 0$ otherwise. Note that E may be not samplable.

Recall that the (probabilistic) *circuit value problem* is (probabilistic) polynomial time computable (see [BDG88], p.110). So there is a (probabilistic) polynomial time algorithm F that on input $z \in_E \Sigma^{Q_2(n)}$ and $h \in_R H_n$, (Note: By the definition of E, we have z=the description of A_n), output a collision-pair with probability $1/Q(n)$.

This implies that H is not one-way in the sense of CIH/$EN[poly]$, which contradicts our assumption. □

Theorem 3 *The following statements hold:*

(1) *UOH/PSE[ℓ] $\subset$ UOH/U.*

(2) *There are one-way hash functions in the sense of UOH/EN[poly] but not in the sense of CIH.*

(3) *CIH $\subset$ UOH/PSE[ℓ].*

(4) *CIH/EN[poly] $\subset$ UOH/EN[poly].*

Proof : (1) We show that given a one-way hash function H in the sense of UOH/U, we can construct from H a hash function H' that is still one-way in the sense of UOH/U but not in the sense of UOH/$PSE[\ell]$.

H' is constructed as follows: Denote by $0^{\ell(n)}$ ($1^{\ell(n)}$, respectively) the all-0 (all-1, respectively) string of length $\ell(n)$. For each $h \in H_n$, define a function $h' : \Sigma^{\ell(n)} \to \Sigma^n$ by $h'(x) = h(0^{\ell(n)})$ whenever $x = 1^{\ell(n)}$ and $h'(x) = h(x)$ otherwise. Thus the only difference between h and h' is the images of $1^{\ell(n)}$. Let H'_n be the collection of all h', and let $H' = \bigcup_n H'_n$. We claim that H' is still one-way in the sense of UOH/U but not in the sense of UOH/$PSE[\ell]$.

Let M be a polynomial time algorithm that on input n outputs $1^{\ell(n)}$. By definition, the ensemble E defined by the output of M is polynomially samplable. Let F be a collision-string finder that on input x and h' outputs the string $0^{\ell(n)}$ whenever $x = 1^{\ell(n)}$ and "?" otherwise. Clearly, for all n, $x \in_E \Sigma^{\ell(n)}$ and $h' \in H'_n$, F always finds a string y that collides with x. Therefore H' is not one-way in the sense of UOH/$PSE[\ell]$.

Now we prove that H' is one-way in the sense of UOH/U. Assume for contradiction that H' is not one-way in the sense of UOH/U. Then there are an infinite subset $N' \subseteq N$ and a collision-string finder F such that for some polynomial Q and for all $n \in N'$, $\Pr\{F(x,h') \neq ?\} \geq 1/Q(n)$, when $x \in_R \Sigma^{\ell(n)}$ and $h' \in_R H'_n$.

Note that

$$\Pr\{F(x,h') \neq ?\}$$
$$= \Pr\{F(x,h') \neq ? \mid h'(x) = h'(0^{\ell(n)})\} \cdot \Pr\{h'(x) = h'(0^{\ell(n)})\} +$$
$$\Pr\{F(x,h') \neq ? \mid h'(x) \neq h'(0^{\ell(n)})\} \cdot \Pr\{h'(x) \neq h'(0^{\ell(n)})\}$$
$$\geq 1/Q(n),$$

and that

$$\Pr\{F(x,h') \neq? \mid h'(x) = h'(0^{\ell(n)})\} \cdot \Pr\{h'(x) = h'(0^{\ell(n)})\}$$
$$\leq \Pr\{h'(x) = h'(0^{\ell(n)})\}$$
$$\leq \Pr\{h(x) = h(0^{\ell(n)})\} + 1/2^{\ell(n)}$$
$$\leq 2\Pr\{h(x) = h(0^{\ell(n)})\}.$$

Since H is one-way in the sense of UOH/U, we have $\Pr\{h(x) = h(0^{\ell(n)})\} < 1/4Q(n)$ for all sufficiently large n. Thus for all sufficiently large $n \in \mathbf{N}'$,

$$\Pr\{F(x,h') \neq? \mid h'(x) \neq h'(0^{\ell(n)})\}$$
$$\geq \Pr\{F(x,h') \neq? \mid h'(x) \neq h'(0^{\ell(n)})\} \cdot \Pr\{h'(x) \neq h'(0^{\ell(n)})\}$$
$$\geq 1/Q(n) - \Pr\{F(x,h') \neq? \mid h'(x) = h'(0^{\ell(n)})\} \cdot \Pr\{h'(x) = h'(0^{\ell(n)})\}$$
$$> 1/2Q(n).$$

By definition, when $h'(x) \neq h'(0^{\ell(n)})$, a string $y \in \Sigma^{\ell(n)}$ with $x \neq y$ collides with x under h' iff it does under h. Consequently, the collision-string finder F can be used to "break" H, this implies that H is not one-way in the sense of UOH/U, a contradiction.

(2) The proof is very similar to that for (1). Given H, a one-way hash function in the sense of UOH/$EN[poly]$, we construct a hash function H' that is still one-way in the sense of UOH/$EN[poly]$ but not in the sense of CIH.

Without loss of generality, assume that the length of the description of $h \in H_n$ is greater than $n/2$, and for any distinct $h_1, h_2 \in H_n$ the first $n/2$ bits of h_1 is different from that of h_2. For each $h \in H_n$, we associate with it a particular $\ell(n)$-bit string x_h that is obtained by repeatedly concatenating the first $n/2$ bits of the description of h until the length of the resulting string becomes $\ell(n)$.

For each $h \in H_n$, define a function $h' : \Sigma^{\ell(n)} \to \Sigma^n$ by $h'(x) = h(x_h)$ whenever $x = \overline{x}_h$ and $h'(x) = h(x)$ otherwise, where $\overline{x}_h$ is the complement of x_h. Thus the only difference between h and h' is the images of $\overline{x}_h$. Let H'_n be the collection of all h', and let $H' = \bigcup_n H'_n$. By analyses similar to (1), one can verify that H' is still one-way in the sense of UOH/$EN[poly]$ but not in the sense of CIH.

(3) follows from (2) and $CIH \subseteq$ UOH/$PSE[\ell]$. (4) follows from (2) and the facts that CIH/$EN[poly] \subseteq CIH$ and that CIH/$EN[poly] \subseteq$ UOH/$EN[poly]$. $\quad\square$

From Lemma 2 and Theorem 3, we have the following hierarchical structure for one-way hash functions (see Figure 1.)

$$\text{UOH}/U$$
$$\cup$$

$$\text{CIH} \quad \subset \quad \text{UOH}/PSE[\ell]$$

$$|\cup$$

$$\text{UOH}/EN[\ell]$$

$$|\cup \qquad\qquad |\cup$$

$$\text{CIH}/EN[poly] \quad \subset \quad \text{UOH}/EN[poly]$$

$$\| \qquad\qquad\qquad \|$$

$$\text{CIH}_C \qquad\qquad \text{UOH}_C/EN[\ell]$$

Figure 1. Hierarchical Structure of One-Way Hash Functions

By Theorem 3, there are one-way hash functions in the sense of $\text{UOH}/EN[poly]$ but not in the sense of CIH. However, it is not clear whether or not $\text{CIH} \subseteq \text{UOH}/EN[poly]$. So it is worth while examining such problems as whether or not CIH is *strictly* included in $\text{UOH}/EN[poly]$.

8 Conclusions

We have proved that UOHs with respect to initial-strings chosen uniformly at random can be transformed into UOHs with respect to initial-strings chosen arbitrarily, and that UOHs with respect to initial-strings chosen arbitrarily can be constructed under a weaker assumption, the existence of one-way quasi-injections. We have also investigated relationships among various versions of one-way hash functions. In particular, we have shown that $\text{UOH}/PSE[\ell]$, CIH and $\text{CIH}/EN[poly]$ are strictly included in UOH/U, $\text{UOH}/PSE[\ell]$ and $\text{UOH}/EN[poly]$ respectively, and that there are one-way hash functions in the sense of $\text{UOH}/EN[poly]$ but not in the sense of CIH.

Recently, substantial progress on the *construction* of UOHs has been made by De Santis and Yung [DY90], and especially, by Rompel [Rom90] who finally solved the problem of constructing UOHs under the sole assumption of the existence of one-way functions.

Acknowledgments　　We would like to thank J. Leo, M. Ogiwara, K. Ohta and K. Sakurai for their fruitful discussions.

References

[BDG88] J. Balcázar, J. Díaz and J. Gabarró: *Structural Complexity I*, EATCS Monographs on Theoretical Computer Science, Springer-Verlag, Berlin, 1988.

[CW79]   J. Carter and M. Wegman: "Universal classes of hash functions", *Journal of Computer and System Sciences*, Vol.18, 1979, pp.143-154.

[Dam87] I. Damgård: "Collision free hash functions and public key signature schemes", *Proceedings of EuroCrypt'87*, 1987, pp.203-216.

[Dam89] I. Damgård: "A design principle for hash functions", *Presented at Crypto'89*, 1989.

[DY90]   A. De Santis and M. Yung: "On the design of provably-secure cryptographic hash functions", *Presented at EuroCrypt'90*, 1990.

[ILL89] R. Impagliazzo, L. Levin and M. Luby: "Pseudo-random generation from one-way functions", *Proceedings of the 21-th ACM Symposium on Theory of Computing*, 1989, pp.12-24.

[KL82]   R. Karp and R. Lipton: "Turing machines that take advice", *L'enseigment Mathematique*, Vol.28, 1982, pp.191-209.

[Mer89] R. Merkle: "One way hash functions and DES", *Presented at Crypto'89*, 1989.

[NY89]   M. Naor and M. Yung: "Universal one-way hash functions and their cryptographic applications", *Proceedings of the 21-th ACM Symposium on Theory of Computing*, 1989, pp.33-43.

[Pip79] N. Pippenger: "On simultaneous resource bounds", *Proceedings of the 20-th IEEE Symposium on the Foundations of Computer Science*, 1979, pp.307-311.

[Rom90] J. Rompel: "One-way functions are necessary and sufficient for secure signatures", *Proceedings of the 22-nd ACM Symposium on Theory of Computing*, 1990, pp.387-394.

[Wa88]   O. Watanabe: "On one-way functions", Presented at *the International Symposium on Combinatorial Optimization*, Tianjin, China, 1988.

[WC81]   M. Wegman and J. Carter: "New hash functions and their use in authentication and set equality", *Journal of Computer and System Sciences*, Vol.22, 1981, pp.265-279.

[Yao82] A. Yao: "Theory and applications of trapdoor functions", *Proceedings of the 23-rd IEEE Symposium on the Foundations of Computer Science*, 1982, pp.80-91.

[ZMI90] Y. Zheng, T. Matsumoto and H. Imai: "Duality between two cryptographic primitives", To be presented at *8-th International Conference on Applied Algebra, Algebraic Algorithms and Error Correcting Codes (AAECC-8)*, Tokyo, August 1990. A preliminary version appears in *IEICE Technical Reports on Information Security*, TG ISEC89-46, March 16, 1990.

A   Appendix — UOHs from One-Way Permutations

In this appendix we sketch a simple method, which appears in [ZMI90], for constructing UOHs from one-way permutations whose (simutaneously) hard bits have been identified. An interesting feature of our construction is that *it does not apply universal hash functions*, and hence is extremely compact, in comparison with most of the currently known constructions.

Assume that f is a one-way permutation on $D = \bigcup_n \Sigma^n$, and that i has been proved to be a hard bit of f. For $b \in \Sigma$, $x \in \Sigma^{n-1}$ and $y \in \Sigma^n$, define $\text{ins}(x, b) = x_{n-1}x_{i-2}\cdots x_i b x_{i-1}\cdots x_2 x_1$, and denote by $\text{drop}(y)$ a function dropping the i-th bit of y. Then we have the following theorem.

Theorem 4 *Let ℓ be a polynomial with $\ell(n) > n$, $\alpha \in \Sigma^{n-1}$ and $x = x_{\ell(n)}\cdots x_2 x_1$ where $x_i \in \Sigma$ for each $1 \le i \le \ell(n)$. Let h_α be the function from $\Sigma^{\ell(n)}$ to Σ^n defined by:*

$$
\begin{aligned}
y_0 &= \alpha, \\
y_1 &= \text{drop}(f_n(\text{ins}(y_0, x_{\ell(n)}))), \\
&\cdots \\
y_j &= \text{drop}(f_n(\text{ins}(y_{j-1}, x_{\ell(n)-j+1}))), \\
&\cdots \\
h_\alpha(x) &= f_n(\text{ins}(y_{\ell(n)-1}, x_1)).
\end{aligned}
$$

Let $H_n = \{h_\alpha \mid \alpha \in \Sigma^{n-1}\}$ and $H = \bigcup_n H_n$. Then under the assumption that f is a one-way permutation, H is a UOH/EN[ℓ] compressing $\ell(n)$-bit input into n-bit output strings.

The efficiency of the above constructed UOHs can be improved by a factor of β, for any $\beta = O(\log n)$, if β simultaneously hard bits of f have been identified.

The MD4 Message Digest Algorithm

Ronald L. Rivest*

Laboratory for Computer Science

Massachusetts Institute of Technology

Cambridge, MA 02139

Abstract

The MD4 message digest algorithm takes an input message of arbitrary length and produces an output 128-bit "fingerprint" or "message digest", in such a way that it is (hopefully) computationally infeasible to produce two messages having the same message digest, or to produce any message having a given prespecified target message digest. The MD4 algorithm is thus ideal for digital signature applications: a large file can be securely "compressed" with MD4 before being signed with (say) the RSA public-key cryptosystem.

The MD4 algorithm is designed to be quite fast on 32-bit machines. For example, on a SUN Sparc station, MD4 runs at 1,450,000 bytes/second (11.6 Mbit/sec). In addition, the MD4 algorithm does not require any large substitution tables; the algorithm can be coded quite compactly.

The MD4 algorithm is being placed in the public domain for review and possible adoption as a standard.

1   Introduction

One-way functions were first described in the mid-1970's, as a means to avoid having to store passwords in a time-shared computer system. (This idea is due to Needham (see Wilkes [10, page 91]) and Evans, Kantrowitz, and Weiss [4].)

In 1976, Diffie and Hellman [3] began the exploration of the relationship between one-way functions and other kinds of cryptographic operations, a theme that continues to the present day. They also propose the operation of exponentiating modulo a prime as a candidate one-way function, attributing this idea to John Gill.

A major application of one-way functions was given by Davies and Price in 1980 [2]. They introduce the idea of signing a message M by signing $h(M)$ with a public-key cryptosystem, where h is a one-way function. This procedure has the advantage of permitting considerable improvement in efficiency if M is long, since computing

*Supported by RSA Data Security (Redwood City, California, 94065).   email address: rivest@theory.lcs.mit.edu

$h(M)$ and signing the result can take much less time than directly signing all of M—note that h can be fast to compute and $h(M)$ can be short (say 128 bits). The value $h(M)$ is often called the "message digest" of the message M. This application is the motivation for the development of the MD4 algorithm.

The theoretical importance of one-way functions as a foundation for cryptography is becoming increasingly clear. Although there has been much work in this area, I'll cite only a couple of references, since the present paper is oriented more towards the practical utilization of one-way functions than towards their theoretical importance. First, Impagliazzo, Levin, and Luby [5] have recently shown that the existence of one-way functions is necessary and sufficient for the existence of secure pseudo-random generators. Using known results, this implies that secure private-key encryption and secure zero-knowledge protocols can be based on any one-way function. Second, Rompel [9] has recently shown (building on the work of Naor and Yung [8]) that the existence of one-way functions is necessary and sufficient for the existence of secure digital signature schemes.

Turning to the practical utilization of one-way functions, it is clear that high speed is a major design criterion. It is desirable to be able to sign very large files (e.g., megabytes in length) very quickly, and to verify these signatures very quickly as well. In one application, for example, it is desired to check the signature on an executable code module before loading and executing it, in order to verify the authenticity of the code module.

There have been many concrete proposals for efficient one-way functions; I don't attempt to survey these proposals here, but merely to give a couple of examples. One approach is to base the one-way function on an efficient conventional encryption scheme. For example, Merkle [7] shows how to construct a secure one-way function if DES is a good random block cipher. However, even his fastest method only hashes 18 bits of message per application of DES. As a second example, Damgård [1] studies the design of one-way functions, proves some theorems regarding the security of one-way functions that work in a "block by block" manner, and proposes a fast one-way function based on the knapsack problem. The design of MD4 was influenced by Damgård's work.

2 Overview and Design Goals

The first design goal is, of course, *security*: it should be computationally infeasible to find two messages M_1 and M_2 that have the same message digest. Here we define a task to be "computationally infeasible" if it requires more than 2^{64} operations.

The goal of security is to be achieved *directly*, without assumptions. That is, we do not wish to design a hash function that is secure if, say, factoring is difficult. While much of cryptography is based on such reductions, "the buck stops" at one-way functions—these need to be designed to be difficult to invert without any further assumptions.

The second design goal is *speed*: the algorithm should be as fast as possible. Here we are interested in speed in *software*; designs that require special-purpose hardware are of limited interest. In particular, we are interested in algorithms that are fast on 32-bit architectures, since that is becoming the dominant standard processor architecture. Thus, the algorithm should be based on a simple set of primitive operations on 32-bit words.

The third design goal is *simplicity and compactness*: the algorithm should be simple to describe and simple to program, without requiring large programs or substitution tables. This is not only desirable from an engineering standpoint, but also desirable from a security viewpoint, since a simple algorithm is more likely to receive the necessary critical review.

A fourth design goal was to *favor little-endian architectures*. Some processor architectures (such as the Intel 80xxx line) are "little endian": they store the least-significant byte of a word in the low-address byte position. Others (such as a SUN Sparcstation) are "big-endian": the most-significant byte of a word goes in the low-address byte position. This distinction is significant when treating a message as a sequence of 32-bit words, since one architecture or the other will have to byte-reverse each word before processing. Since the big-endian processors are generally faster (it seems), it was decided to let them do the reversing. This incurs a performance penalty of about 25%.

3 Terminology and Notation

In this note a *word* is a 32-bit quantity and a byte is an 8-bit quantity. A sequence of bits can be interpreted in a natural manner as a sequence of bytes, where each consecutive group of 8 bits is interpreted as a byte with the high-order (most significant) bit of each byte listed first. Similarly, a sequence of bytes can be interpreted as a sequence of 32-bit words, where each consecutive group of 4 bytes is interpreted as a word with the low-order (least significant) byte given first.

Let the symbol "+" denote addition of words (i.e., modulo-2^{32} addition). Let $(X <<< s)$ denote the 32-bit value obtained by circularly shifting (rotating) X left by s bit positions. Let $\neg X$ denote the bit-wise complement of X, and let $X \vee Y$ denote the bit-wise OR of X and Y. Let $X \oplus Y$ denote the bit-wise XOR of X and Y, and let XY denote the bit-wise AND of X and Y.

4 MD4 Algorithm Description

We begin by supposing that we have a b-bit message as input, and that we wish to find its message digest. Here b is an arbitrary nonnegative integer; b may be zero, it need not be a multiple of 8, and it may be arbitrarily large. We imagine the bits of the message written down as follows:

$$m_0 m_1 \ldots m_{b-1}.$$

The following five steps are performed to compute the message digest of the message.

Step 1. Append padding bits

The message is padded (extended) so that its length (in bits) is congruent to 448, modulo 512. That is, the message is extended so that it is just 64 bits shy of being a multiple of 512 bits long. Padding is always performed, even if the length of the message is already congruent to 448, modulo 512 (in which case 512 bits of padding are added).

Padding is performed as follows: a single "1" bit is appended to the message, and then enough zero bits are appended so that the length in bits of the padded message becomes congruent to 448, modulo 512. (This padding operation is invertible, so that different inputs yield different outputs—this would not be true if we merely padded with 0's.)

Step 2. Append length

A 64-bit representation of b (the length of the message before the padding bits were added) is appended to the result of the previous step. These bits are appended as two 32-bit words and appended low-order word first in accordance with the previous conventions. In the unlikely event that b is greater than 2^{64}, then only the low-order 64 bits of b are used.

At this point the resulting message (after padding with bits and with b) has a length that is an exact multiple of 512 bits. Equivalently, this message has a length that is an exact multiple of 16 (32-bit) words. Let $M[0 \ldots N-1]$ denote the words of the resulting message, where N is a multiple of 16.

Step 3. Initialize MD buffer

A 4-word buffer (A, B, C, D) is used to compute the message digest. Here each of A, B, C, D is a 32-bit register. These registers are initialized to the following values (in hexadecimal, low-order bytes first):

$$
\begin{aligned}
&\text{word } A: \quad \texttt{01 23 45 67} \\
&\text{word } B: \quad \texttt{89 ab cd ef} \\
&\text{word } C: \quad \texttt{fe dc ba 98} \\
&\text{word } D: \quad \texttt{76 54 32 10}
\end{aligned}
$$

Step 4. Process message in 16-word blocks

We first define three auxiliary functions that each take as input three 32-bit words and produce as output one 32-bit word.

$$
\begin{aligned}
f(X, Y, Z) &= XY \vee (\neg X)Z \\
g(X, Y, Z) &= XY \vee XZ \vee YZ \\
h(X, Y, Z) &= X \oplus Y \oplus Z
\end{aligned}
$$

In each bit position f acts as a conditional: if x then y else z. In each bit position g acts as a majority function: if at least two of x, y, z are one, then g has a one in that position. The function h is the bit-wise *xor* or *parity* function. It is interesting to note that if the bits of X, Y, and Z are independent and unbiased, the each bit of $f(X, Y, Z)$ is independent and unbiased, and similarly for $g(X, Y, Z)$ and $h(X, Y, Z)$.

MD4 utilizes two "magic constants" in rounds two and three. The round two constant is $\sqrt{2}$ and the round 3 constant is $\sqrt{3}$. (See Knuth [6, page 660].) Here are their values in octal and hex (with high-order digits given first).

	Octal	Hex
Round 2 constant ($\sqrt{2}$):	013240474631	5A827999
Round 3 constant ($\sqrt{3}$):	015666365641	6ED9EBA1

Do the following:

```
For i = 0 to N/16-1 do          /* process each 16-word block */
    Set X[j] to M[i*16+j], for j = 0, 1, ..., 15.
    Save A as AA, B as BB, C as CC, and D as DD.

    [Round 1]
        Let [A B C D i s] denote the operation
            A = (A + f(B,C,D) + X[i]) <<< s  .
        Do the following 16 operations:
            [A B C D 0  3]
            [D A B C 1  7]
            [C D A B 2  11]
            [B C D A 3  19]
            [A B C D 4  3]
            [D A B C 5  7]
            [C D A B 6  11]
            [B C D A 7  19]
            [A B C D 8  3]
            [D A B C 9  7]
            [C D A B 10 11]
            [B C D A 11 19]
            [A B C D 12 3]
            [D A B C 13 7]
            [C D A B 14 11]
            [B C D A 15 19]

    [Round 2]
        Let [A B C D i s] denote the operation
            A = (A + g(B,C,D) + X[i] + 5A827999) <<< s  .
        Do the following 16 operations:
            [A B C D 0  3]
            [D A B C 4  5]
            [C D A B 8  9]
            [B C D A 12 13]
            [A B C D 1  3]
```

```
[D A B C 5  5]
[C D A B 9  9]
[B C D A 13 13]
[A B C D 2  3]
[D A B C 6  5]
[C D A B 10 9]
[B C D A 14 13]
[A B C D 3  3]
[D A B C 7  5]
[C D A B 11 9]
[B C D A 15 13]
```

[Round 3]

Let [A B C D i s] denote the operation

$$A = (A + h(B,C,D) + X[i] + 6ED9EBA1) \lll s .$$

Do the following 16 operations:

```
[A B C D 0  3]
[D A B C 8  9]
[C D A B 4  11]
[B C D A 12 15]
[A B C D 2  3]
[D A B C 10 9]
[C D A B 6  11]
[B C D A 14 15]
[A B C D 1  3]
[D A B C 9  9]
[C D A B 5  11]
[B C D A 13 15]
[A B C D 3  3]
[D A B C 11 9]
[C D A B 7  11]
[B C D A 15 15]
```

Then perform the following additions:

```
A = A + AA
B = B + BB
C = C + CC
D = D + DD
```

(That is, each of the four registers is incremented by the value
it had before this block was started.)

end /* of loop on i */

Step 5. Output

The message digest produced as output is A, B, C, D. That is, we begin with the low-order byte of A, and end with the high-order byte of D.

This completes the description of MD4.

5 Extensions

If more than 128 bits of output are required, then the following procedure is recommended to obtain a 256-bit output. No provision is made for obtaining more than 256 bits.

Two copies of MD4 are run in parallel over the input. The first copy is standard as described above. The second copy is modified as follows.

The initial state of the second copy is:

$$
\begin{array}{ll}
\text{word } A: & \text{00 11 22 33} \\
\text{word } B: & \text{44 55 66 77} \\
\text{word } C: & \text{88 99 aa bb} \\
\text{word } D: & \text{cc dd ee ff}
\end{array}
$$

The magic constants in rounds 2 and 3 for the second copy of MD4 are changed from $\sqrt{2}$ and $\sqrt{3}$ to $\sqrt[3]{2}$ and $\sqrt[3]{3}$:

	Octal	Hex
Round 2 constant ($\sqrt[3]{2}$):	012050505746	50a28be6
Round 3 constant ($\sqrt[3]{3}$):	013423350444	5c4dd124

Finally, after every 16-word block is processed (including the last block), the values of the A registers in the two copies are exchanged.

The final message digest is obtaining by appending the result of the second copy of MD4 to the end of the result of the first copy of MD4.

6 Implementation

The MD4 algorithm has been implemented in C and run on many different workstations. Here is a sampling of the running times achieved. (These running times include all processing, including byte-reversing the input words, but does not include file I/O time.) Assembly language implementations would of course be even faster.

Processor	Speed (Bytes/second)
SUN Sparc station	1,450,000
DEC MicroVax II	70,000
20MHz 80286	32,000

A reference implementation of MD4 in C is available as file md4.doc by anonymous ftp from theory.lcs.mit.edu and rsa.com, or from *RSA Data Security, 10 Twin Dolphin Drive, Redwood City, California 94065, phone: 1-800-PUBLIKEY.*

If you implement MD4 based on the description in this paper rather than the reference implementation, you may wish to check the following input-output values for MD4.

Input	Output
""	31d6cfe0d16ae931b73c59d7e0c089c0
"a"	bde52cb31de33e46245e05fbdbd6fb24
"abc"	a448017aaf21d8525fc10ae87aa6729d
"message digest"	d9130a8164549fe818874806e1c7014b
"abcdefghijklmnopqrstuvwxyz"	d79e1c308aa5bbcdeea8ed63df412da9

7 Summary

The MD4 message digest algorithm is simple to implement, and provides a "fingerprint" or message digest of a message of arbitrary length.

It is conjectured that the difficulty of coming up with two messages having the same message digest is on the order of 2^{64} operations, and that the difficulty of coming up with any message having a given message digest is on the order of 2^{128} operations. The MD4 algorithm has been carefully scrutinized for weaknesses. It is, however, a relatively new algorithm and further security analysis is of course justified, as is the case with any new proposal of this sort.[1] The level of security provided by MD4 should be sufficient for implementing very high security hybrid digital signature schemes based on MD4 and the RSA public-key cryptosystem.

8 Acknowledgments

I'd like to thank Don Coppersmith, Burt Kaliski, Ralph Merkle, and Noam Nisan for numerous helpful comments and suggestions.

References

[1] Ivan Bjerre Damgård. A design principle for hash functions. In G. Brassard, editor, *Proceedings CRYPTO 89*, pages 416–427. Springer, 1990. Lecture Notes in Computer Science No. 435.

[2] D. W. Davies and W. L. Price. The application of digital signatures based on public-key cryptosystems. In *Proc. Fifth Intl. Computer Communications Conference*, pages 525–530, October 1980.

---

[1]Ralph Merkle has recently shown how to find two messages that collide in a modified form of MD4 that omits the third round. This technique does not seem to generalize to handle the full MD4 method, or even one in which the first or second round is omitted instead of the third.

[3] W. Diffie and M. E. Hellman. New directions in cryptography. *IEEE Trans. Inform. Theory*, IT-22:644–654, November 1976.

[4] A. Evans, W. Kantrowitz, and E. Weiss. A user authentication scheme not requiring secrecy in the computer. *CACM*, 17:437–442, August 1974.

[5] Russell Impagliazzo, Leonid A. Levin, and Michael Luby. Pseudo-random generation from one-way functions. In *Proc. 21th ACM Symposium on Theory of Computing*, pages 12–24, Seattle, 1989. ACM.

[6] Donald E. Knuth. *Seminumerical Algorithms*, volume 2 of *The Art of Computer Programming*. Addison-Wesley, 1969. Second edition, 1981.

[7] Ralph C. Merkle. One way hash functions and DES. In G. Brassard, editor, *Proceedings CRYPTO 89*, pages 428–446. Springer, 1990. Lecture Notes in Computer Science No. 435.

[8] M. Naor and M. Yung. Universal one-way hash functions and their cryptographic applications. In *Proc. 21th ACM Symposium on Theory of Computing*, pages 33–43, Seattle, 1989. ACM.

[9] John Rompel. One-way functions are necessary and sufficient for secure signatures. In *Proc. 22nd ACM Symposium on Theory of Computing*, pages 387–394, Baltimore, Maryland, 1990. ACM.

[10] M. V. Wilkes. *Time-sharing computer systems*. Elsevier, 1975. Third edition.

Session 8
Zero-Knowledge
Chair: A. Fiat, Tel-Aviv University

Achieving Zero-Knowledge Robustly

J. Kilian*

Abstract

We introduce the notion of *robust transformations* of interactive proof systems. A robust transformation takes an interactive proof system (P, V), and produces a new interactive proof system, (P^*, V^*), such that the power of P^* is within a polynomial factor of that of P. We show that, given an ideal protocol for secure circuit evaluation, there exists a robust transformation that converts interactive proof systems to zero-knowledge interactive proof systems.

1 Introduction.

1.1 Background and Motivation.

There exist many general transformations that take an interactive proof system (P, V) for a language L, and produce a new interactive proof system (P^*, V^*) for L, that has some additional desired property. To give a simple example, one may wish to decrease the error probability of the proof system from $\frac{1}{3}$ to $2^{-|x|}$, on input x. In the new protocol, (P^*, V^*) runs (P, V) many times, and then V^* takes a majority vote. To give some slightly more complicated examples, one can,

1. Transform (P, V) into (P^*, V^*), such that V^* never rejects on a valid input [2],

2. Transform (P, V) into (P^*, V^*), such that V^* only uses public coins [3], and,

3. Given a secure cryptographic committal scheme, transform (P, V) into (P^*, V^*), such that (P^*, V^*) achieves zero-knowledge [5].

This paper is motivated by a consideration of how powerful the new prover, P^*, must be in the transformed proof system. In the error reduction transformation, P^* makes a polynomial number of calls to P, and otherwise runs in polynomial time. However, in

---

*Harvard University and MIT Laboratory for Computer Science, 545 Technology Square, Cambridge, MA 02139 USA, joek@theory.lcs.mit.edu. Supported by an NSF Postdoctoral Fellowship. Some of the writing up of these results supported by Bell Communications.

all of the other transformations given above, there is no obvious relationship between the power of P and P^*. While much progress has been made in finding simple transformations with the above properties, all known techniques involve a possibly exponential time overhead, even if calls to P are for unit cost. In some sense, then, these transformations are nonconstructive.

To capture a more constructive notion of a protocol transformation, we introduce the notion of a *robust transformation*, as follows.

Definition 1 Let $\phi : (P, V) \rightarrow (P^*, V^*)$ be a transformation from interactive proof systems to interactive proof systems. We say that ϕ is robust if,

1. For all (P, V), $\phi(P, V) = (P^*, V^*)$ accepts the same language as (P, V), and,

2. P^* can be evaluated by a probabilistic polynomial-time Turing machine M with access to a black-box evaluator for P.

By a black-box evaluator for P, we mean a function that takes as input a partial conversation, and outputs a distribution equal to that of P, given the partial conversation so far.

1.2 Our result.

Thus far, no robust transformation is known for converting interactive proof systems into Arthur-Merlin form (i.e., turning a private-coin proof into a public coin proof). However, all of the transformations for converting arbitrary interactive proof systems into zero-knowledge interactive proof systems first transform the protocol into Arthur-Merlin form. This remains true even if ideal, information theoretically secure envelopes are allowed.

The contribution of this paper is to show that a stronger cryptographic primitive can indeed allow for a robust transformation of proofs into zero-knowledge proofs. Our theorem is as follows.

Theorem: Suppose we have ideal secure circuit evaluation as a cryptographic primitive. Then there exists a robust transformation that converts interactive proofs to statistically zero-knowledge interactive proofs.

By secure circuit evaluation, we mean the following: Consider a polynomial-sized circuit, $C(i, j)$. Suppose that P has an input i, and V has an input j. We say that P and V securely evaluate C if they achieve the following state of knowledge (ignorance).

1. V learn the value of $C(i, j)$, but gains no additional information about the value of i.

2. P learns nothing about j.

In the ideal, information theoretic scenario, we can imagine a trusted third party, M, who has private communication lines with P and V. P and V send i and j respectively to M. M computes $C(i,j)$, and sends this value to V. As a simple generalization of this, we can make C a probabilistic circuit; this case may be easily reduced to the case where C is deterministic.

1.3 Reducing our theorem to other assumptions.

Our theorem may be compared to the better known result that IP is in zero-knowledge if one has a bit committal primitive. It seems that the primitive required by our theorem is more powerful than simple bit committal. It is worth considering what other assumptions we should be able to reduce our theorem to. There exist information-theoretic reduction from secure circuit computation to oblivious transfer [6]. Along a more standard vein of research, it should be possible to prove an analog to our theorem that relies on a complexity theoretic assumption. Such a theorem follows, with many details, from the existence of a secure circuit evaluation protocol that is,

1. Information theoretically secure against one of the parties (the prover),

2. Simulatable in a cryptographically secure fashion against the other party, using the auxiliary input model for security,[1] and,

3. Playable by two polynomial-time bounded players.

The circuit evaluation protocols of currently in the literature do not achieve this property. However, it seems that one can implement such a protocol based on either,

1. The Diffie and Hellman assumption for discrete logs,[2] or

2. The existence of trapdoor permutations and families of claw free permutations.

Both of these assumptions seem to be much stronger than that required to make cryptographic analogs of envelopes [4, 7]. Working these techniques out in full, one should be able to get the following theorem.

Future Theorem: There exist a robust transformation from interactive proof systems to cryptographically zero-knowledge interactive proof systems, based on either of the above intractability assumptions.

---

[1] We refer the reader to an upcoming paper of Rogaway and Micali, which gives a very detailed description of what a good simulation should entail.

[2] This assumption is as follows. Suppose one picks a random k bit prime p, a generator g of Z_p^*, and random $x, y \in Z_p^*$. Then it is hard to compute g^{xy}, knowing only p, g, g^x, g^y

There are no foreseen technical difficulties to proving such a theorem. However, a rigorous proof will most likely prove very lengthy and unwieldy. This paper is part of a two or three pronged attack. In addition to this paper, we require a rigorous write up of the various new implementations of secure circuit evaluation, and some more formalisms on using cryptographically secure protocols in place of their ideal protocols. Much of this theory has been sketched out; essentially, this is an exercise in formalizing and writing up a number of "folk theorems."

Another reasonable approach to constructing a cryptographic protocol is to use the blob techniques of Chaum, Damgard, and van de Graaf [1]. By using cryptographically (but not informationally) secure blobs, many of the problems with chaining together computations in a secure way can be avoided. Again, this approach requires that a large body of simulation machinery be developed or rigorously written up. It is also quite possible that their secure circuit evaluation protocol can be shown to have the necessary properties, outlined above.

1.4   Outline of the paper.

In Section 2, we give an overview of the proof of our theorem. In Section 3 we give the construction of our robust zero-knowledge transformation. In Section 4, we show that the transformed protocol remains a proof system, and achieves zero-knowledge.

2   Overview of the proof.

We wish to take an ordinary proof system, (P, V) for a language L, and robustly transform it into a zero-knowledge proof system, (P^*, V^*). To do this, we must deal with the many ways that a malicious or even an honest verifier may obtain information from the original protocol. One easily dealt with difficulty is that the probability with which V accepts a string $x \in L$ may leak additional information about x. This problem is solved by robustly transforming the protocol so as to achieve an exponentially small error probability. In this case, for all $x \in L$, V will accept with probability indistinguishable from 1, thus yielding no extra information about x.[3]

More serious is the fact that the verifier receives vast amounts of potential information from simply being able to see the transcript of its conversation with the prover. The standard trick, first proposed by Ben-Or, is to encrypt the entire conversation, thus concealing it from the verifier. However, it is then unclear how the prover and the verifier can figure out the verifier's questions to the prover. The verifier can't compute them, since it can't see what is going on, and the prover can't compute them, since they may depend on the verifier's private coin tosses. An elegant way around this impasse, also first proposed by

---

[3]Note that we cannot use any of the known transformations that make this probability equal to 1, since these transformations are not robust.

Ben-Or, is to transform the original interactive proof system into an Arthur-Merlin game. Then, the verifier's questions may be simulated by a straightforward application of bit comitment and coin-tossing protocols. All the known rigorous proofs that IP is in zero-knowledge (modulo complexity assumptions or the existence of ideal encryption schemes) use this general approach. Unfortunately, we know of no provably robust transformation from IP to AM (or even one that is conjectured to be robust), and so must use a different approach.

Instead, we use standard techniques of secure circuit evaluation to get around this impasse in another way. First, we break up the verifier's private information into shares, one held by the prover, and one held by the verifier. Neither share is enough to give any information about the private data, but when both are input to a secure circuit, the shares may be combined and used to simulate the computations that would have been made by the verifier in the original protocol. The answers that the prover would normally give to the verifier are also fed into the secure circuit, thus hiding this other source of information from the verifier. At the end of the protocol, the prover and the verifier can perform a final circuit computation to see if the verifier should have accepted given the simulated conversation thus far.

There are a few technical issues to be addressed. Most important of these is that we must guarantee that neither party can manipulate the protocol by altering their shares of the verifier's history. To make this guarantee, we set up a system of consistency checks, ensuring that any such cheating will with high probability result in the protocol effectively aborting.

3 Construction of the zero-knowledge proof system.

3.1 Breaking the proof up into a series of circuits.

We can view an interactive proof system as follows. Initially, V computes a private history, h_0, that consists solely of a sequence of $|x|^{c_1}$ uniformly distributed bits, for some constant $c_2 1$. Given h_0, V computes its first question q_1. In Step i, V sends question q_i to P, and P sends back an answer, a_i. V computes a new history and a new question, $h_i, q_{i+1} = H_i(h_{i-1}, a_i)$, where H_i is computed by a polynomial size circuit. At the end of $m = |x|^{c_2}$ steps, for some constant c_2, V computes ACCEPT(h_m), where ACCEPT is computed by a polynomial size circuit, which outputs either a 0 (for reject) or a 1 (for accept). We assume for convenience that all of the inputs and outputs of H_i can be encoded as $n = |x|^{c_3}$ bit strings, for some constant c_3. Thus, for instance, the string R or h_5 can be padded to make it the proper length if it is not long enough. Since x is known to both parties, we may hardwire it into the circuit, and thus we do not explicitly include it as an input.

For our initial construction, we want to only trust V in a very limited way. We do not trust him to flip coins at random, or to correctly perform any computations on his own. Instead, P and V will perform the initialization step, the computations of q_i, h_i, and the decision to accept or reject via secure circuit computations. We will, however, trust V to give the output of one circuit as the input to another circuit, or as a message to P.

The construction of an initial history h_0 and the first question q_1, can be performed by a secure circuit evaluation, as follows. Let circuit $H_0(R_1, R_2)$ take an $|x|^{c_1}$-bit string, R_1, from P, and an $|x|^{c_1}$-bit string, R_2, from V. $H_0(R_1, R_2)$ computes h_0, q_1, where h_0 is the pairwise exclusive-or of R_1 and R_2, and q_1 is the first question V would ask on input x, with random bits h_0. H_0 outputs h_0, q_1 with enough additional padding bits to make these outputs of length n. If either P or V is honest, then h_0 will be distributed uniformly. Also, if V is honest, then P will get no information about h_0.

Similarly, in order to compute h_i, q_{i+1}, V first sends q_i to P, who then computes a_i. P and V then securely evaluate H_i, where P inputs a_i, and V inputs h_{i-1}. In order to compute $\text{ACCEPT}(h_i)$, P and V securely evaluate ACCEPT, where P inputs nothing, and V inputs the output of circuit H_m.

This sequence of circuit evaluations mirrors the original interactive proof system. V will accept iff she would have accepted in the original protocol, given the provers answers to her queries. However, the protocol also gives V essentially the same knowledge as does the original protocol. The values of a_i are hidden from direct view by the secure circuit evaluation, but will almost certainly be recoverable from h_i.

3.2 Randomizing the values of the intermediate circuits.

To achieve zero-knowledge, it is imperative that we hide the values of $h_0, \ldots, h_m$ and $q_1, \ldots, q_m$ from the verifier. We accomplish this by a simple exclusive-or trick. The resulting protocol is not a proof system in the normal sense, but can be considered a proof system subject to P obeying certain constraints on his behavior. In particular, we will require equality between certain inputs from the prover to the various circuits.

Our technique is quite simple. First, we modify our circuits to allow for n-bit masking vectors. We define $H_0'(R_1, R_2, M)$ as the circuit that outputs $h_0' = H_0(R_1, R_2) \oplus M$, where $\oplus$ denotes bitwise exclusive-or. Similarly, we define $H_i'(h, a, M_1, M_2, M_3)$ as the circuit that outputs $h_i' = h_i \oplus M_2$, and $q_i' = q_i \oplus M_3$, where $h_i, q_i = H_i(h \oplus M_1, a)$. Finally, we define $\text{ACCEPT}'(h, M)$ as the circuit that outputs $\text{ACCEPT}(h \oplus M)$. Here, the M_i's are input by P. Our new protocol now proceeds as follows.

Step 0: First, P' uniformly chooses n-bit masks, $M_0^H, \ldots, M_m^H, M_1^Q, \ldots, M_m^Q$, and R_1. Then V' randomly selects R_2. The two then securely evaluate $H_0'(R_1, R_2, M_0^H, M_1^Q)$, which outputs $h_0' = h_0 \oplus M_0^H$ and $q_1' = q_1 \oplus M_1^Q$ to V'.

Step i: V' sends q_i' to P', who then recovers $q_i = q_i' \oplus M_i^Q$, and computes his answer, a_i. P' and V' securely compute

$$H_i'(h_{i-1}', a, M_{i-1}^H, M_i^H, M_i^Q),$$

which will output $h_i' = h_i \oplus M_i^H$ and $q_i' = q_i \oplus M_i^Q$ to V'.

Final Step: P' and V' compute $accept'(h'_m, M^H_m)$, and V' accepts iff the output is 1.

The protocol, as stated above, is not a proof, nor is it zero-knowledge against an active adversary. It will be a proof if P' could be guaranteed to be consistent in his input values for M^H_i. That is, if P' was guaranteed to always input the same string in all both circuit evaluations where M^H_i is supposed to be input, then the protocol would essentially mirror the original one. Similarly, the protocol would hide everything but the final accept/reject verdict if V' was guaranteed to always give as input to each circuit the output of the prescribed earlier circuit computation.

3.3 Constraining the prover and the verifier's behavior.

We now describe a simple technique to constrain the prover and the verifier's behavior as required. To explain our technique, we introduce the notion of *triple blobs*. These blobs will be used to enforce consistency for P' and V'. Essentially, we use the exclusive-or tricks that have been used in countless other papers.

3.3.1 Triple Blobs.

We now define triple blobs (blobs, for short), and give some elementary facts about them.

Definition 2 Let $b \in \{0,1\}$, and let

$$B = (b_{1,1}, b_{1,2}, b_{1,3}), \dots, (b_{k,1}, b_{k,2}, b_{k,3}),$$

where $b_{i,j} \in \{0,1\}$. We say that B is a *triple blob*, with value b, and security parameter k, if for all $1 \le i \le k$, $b = b_{i,1} \oplus b_{i,2} \oplus b_{i,3}$. If there is an i and j such that,

$$b_{i,1} \oplus b_{i,2} \oplus b_{i,3} \ne b_{j,1} \oplus b_{j,2} \oplus b_{j,3},$$

we say that B is inconsistent.

For our application, the prover and the verifier need to experiment on a blob in order to verify equality. This is done by evaluating the function E, defined below.

Definition 3 Let $B = \{b_{i,j}\}$ be a triple blob with security parameter k. For $Y = y_1, \dots, y_k \in \{1, 2, 3\}$, we define

$$E(B, Y) = b_{1,y_1}, \dots, b_{k,y_k}.$$

We say that (B, Y, Z) is inconsistent if B is inconsistent or if $E(B, Y) \ne Z$.

Lemmas 1 and 2 follow from a simple probability argument.

Lemma 1 For $b \in \{0,1\}$, let B_b be chosen uniformly from triple blobs with value b. Then for all Y_1 and Y_2, $(E(B_0, Y_1), E(B_0, Y_2))$ and $(E(B_1, Y_1), E(B_1, Y_2))$ will have identical distributions. ∎

Lemma 2 Let B_0 and B_1 be any two triple blobs for 0 and 1 respectively. If Y is chosen at random, then

$$prob(E(B_0, Y) = E(B_1, Y)) \leq \left(\frac{2}{3}\right)^k . \quad ∎$$

Finally, it is useful to define the construction of a random blob that is consistent with a given Y and Z.

Definition 4 For $y \in \{1,2,3\}$ and $b, z \in \{0,1\}$, define distribution $c(b, y, z)$ to be uniform over all triples (b_1, b_2, b_3) such that,

1. $b = b_1 \oplus b_2 \oplus b_3$, and,

2. $b_y = z$.

For $Y = y_1, \ldots, y_k$ and $Z = z_1, \ldots, z_k$, we define distribution $C(b, Y, Z)$ by

$$C(b, Y, Z) = c(b, y_1, z_1), \ldots, c(b, y_k, z_k).$$

The following lemma follows virtually by definition.

Lemma 3 Let B be chosen from $C(b, Y, Z)$. Then B will be distributed uniformly over all triple blobs of value b, subject to $E(B, Y) = Z$. If in addition, Z is chosen uniformly, then B will be distributed uniformly over all triple blobs for b. ∎

Instead of working with single bits, we will typically work with strings of length n. For notational convenience, we will write $\vec{B}$ to denote an n vector of triple blobs. Similarly, we will use $\vec{Y}$ and $\vec{Z}$ to denote n vectors of their usual type. For $w \in \{0,1\}^n$, we will also write $C(w, \vec{Y}, \vec{Z})$, and $E(\vec{B}, \vec{Y})$, where all operations are done componentwise.

To give some intuition about what is going on, we can think of evaluating $E(\vec{B}, \vec{Y})$ as obtaining a shadow of blob $\vec{B}$. If $\vec{B}_{w_0}$ is a blob for a string w_0 and $\vec{B}_{w_1}$ is a blob for a string $w_1 \neq w_0$, and $\vec{Y}$ is chosen at random, then with high probability, $E(\vec{B}_{w_0}, \vec{Y}) \neq E(\vec{B}_{w_1}, \vec{Y})$ (Lemma 2). This allows one to make sure that someone is using the same string in two different locations. However, if $\vec{B}$ is uniformly generated, with value w, then seeing $E(\vec{B}, \vec{Y})$, for two different values of $\vec{Y}$ will still not give any information about w (Lemma 2).

3.3.2 Using triple blobs to enforce consistency.

We now augment our circuits in order to handle blobs. For ease of exposition, we will allow our circuits to flip coins. This can be simulated by a deterministic circuit that takes random bits from both parties and computes pairwise exclusive or's, much as in the design of H_0. We will denote objects which are in "blob" form by putting them in brackets. Thus, $[w]$ denotes a blob representation of w.

We define

$$H_0^*(R_1, R_2, [M_0^H], \vec{Y}_0^M, \vec{Y}_0^h, \vec{Z}_0^h, \vec{Y}_1^q, \vec{Z}_1^q, M_1^Q)$$

to be the circuit that,

1. Outputs "abort" if $[M_0^H]$ is inconsistent,

2. Computes $h_0', q_1' = H_0'(R_1, R_2, M_0^H, M_1^Q)$.

3. Outputs $[h_0'] \leftarrow C(h_0', \vec{Y}_0^h, \vec{Z}_0^h)$, $[q_1'] \leftarrow C(q_1', \vec{Y}_1^q, \vec{Z}_1^q)$, and $\vec{Z}_0^M = E([M_0^H], \vec{Y}_0^M)$ to V.

We define

$$H_i^*([h_{i-1}'], \vec{Y}_{i-1}^h, \vec{Z}_{i-1}^h, a, [M_{i-1}^H], \vec{Y}_{i-1}^M, \vec{Z}_{i-1}^M, [M_i^H], \vec{Y}_i^M, M_{i+1}^Q, \vec{Y}_{i+1}^q, \vec{Z}_{i+1}^q, \vec{Y}_i^h, \vec{Z}_i^h)$$

to be the circuit that,

1. Outputs "abort" if either $([h_{i-1}'], \vec{Y}_{i-1}^h, \vec{Z}_{i-1}^h)$, $([M_{i-1}^H], \vec{Y}_{i-1}^M, \vec{Z}_{i-1}^M)$, or $[M_i^H]$ are inconsistent.

2. Computes $h_i', q_{i+1}' = H_i'(h_{i-1}, a, M_{i-1}^H, M_i^H, M_{i+1}^Q)$.

3. Outputs $[h_i'] \leftarrow C(h_i', \vec{Y}_i^h, \vec{Z}_i^h)$, $[q_{i+1}'] = C(q_{i+1}', \vec{Y}_{i+1}^q, \vec{Z}_{i+1}^q)$, and $\vec{Z}_i^M = E([M_i^H], \vec{Y}_i^M)$ to V.

Finally, we define

$$\text{ACCEPT}^*([h_m'], \vec{Y}_m^h, \vec{Z}_m^h, [M_m^H], \vec{Y}_m^M, \vec{Z}_m^M)$$

to be the circuit that,

1. Outputs "abort" if either $(h_m'], \vec{Y}_m^h, \vec{Z}_m^h,)$ or $([M_m^H], \vec{Y}_m^M, \vec{Z}_m^M)$ is inconsistent.

2. Outputs $\text{ACCEPT}'(h_m', M_m^H)$.

3.4 The final protocol.

Using the circuits defined above, we now specify our protocol (P^*, V^*).

Step 0: P^* uniformly selects masks, $M_0^H, \ldots, M_m^H$ and $M_1^Q, \ldots, M_m^Q$, and uniformly chooses blob representations, $[M_0^H], \ldots, [M_m^H]$. P^* uniformly chooses,

$$(\vec{Y}_0^h, \vec{Z}_0^h), \ldots, (\vec{Y}_m^h, \vec{Z}_m^h), (\vec{Y}_1^q, \vec{Z}_1^q), \ldots, (\vec{Y}_m^q, \vec{Z}_m^q),$$

and R_1. V^* uniformly chooses $\vec{Y}_0^M, \ldots, \vec{Y}_m^M$, and R_2.

P^* and V^* securely evaluate,

$$H_0^*(R_1, R_2, [M_0^H], \vec{Y}_0^M, \vec{Y}_0^h, \vec{Z}_0^h).$$

If this circuit, or any other circuit ever outputs "abort," then V^* immediately aborts the protocol and rejects. Otherwise, V^* recovers $[h_0'], [q_1']$, and $\vec{Z}_0^M$. Note that $h_0' = h_0 \oplus M_0^H$.

Step i: First, V^* sends $[q_i']$ to P^*, who aborts immediately if $([q_i'], \vec{Y}_i^q, \vec{Z}_i^q)$ is inconsistent. P^* and V^* securely evaluate,

$$H_i^*([h_{i-1}'], \vec{Y}_{i-1}^h, \vec{Z}_{i-1}^h, a, [M_{i-1}^H], \vec{Y}_{i-1}^M, \vec{Z}_{i-1}^M, [M_i^H], \vec{Y}_i^M, M_{i+1}^Q, \vec{Y}_{i+1}^q, \vec{Z}_{i+1}^q, \vec{Y}_i^h, \vec{Z}_i^h),$$

and V^* recovers $[h_i'], [q_{i+1}']$, and $\vec{Z}_i^M$. Note that $h_i' = h_i \oplus M_i^H$ and $q_{i+1}' = q_{i+1} \oplus M_{i+1}^Q$.

Final Step: P^* and V^* securely evaluate

$$\text{ACCEPT}^*([h_m'], \vec{Y}_m^h, \vec{Z}_m^h, [M_m^H], \vec{Y}_m^M, \vec{Z}_m^M),$$

and V^* accepts iff the circuit outputs a 1.

4 The protocol is a zero-knowledge proof system.

We now sketch the argument that our final protocol is a zero-knowledge proof system. First, we argue that it will remain a proof system. That is, if (P, V) accepts with high probability on input x, then so will (P^*, V^*), and similarly, if (P, V) rejects x with high probability, then so will (P^*, V^*).

4.1 (P^*, V^*) is a proof system.

First, we note that if (P, V) accept x with probability at least $p(x)$, then so will (P^*, V^*). If P^* abides by the consistency constraints, then the distribution on $h_0, \ldots, h_m, q_1, \ldots, q_m$, and $a_0, \ldots, a_1$ will be identical to that produced by (P, V). By inspection of the protocol, we see that V^* will accept, given a setting of the above variables if V would have as well. The point is that if P^* behaves properly, then (P^*, V^*) will essentially run the original protocol, merely coded up in a strange way.

We now wish to show that for any malicious prover, $\hat{P}$, the probability that $(\hat{P}, V^*)$ accepts x is nonnegligible, then there must be a prover P' such that (P', V) accepts x with nonnegligible probability. P' essentially runs $\hat{P}$ on input x, encodes V's queries into the same form as V^* would use, and then decodes P^*'s answers into a acceptable to V.

Step 0: P' starts running P^*, continuing the run through the point where P^* makes his inputs to circuit H_0^*. In particular, P' learns the values of M_i^Q, $\vec{Y}_i^q$ and $\vec{Z}_i^q$.

Step i: V makes query q_i to P'. P' computes,

$$[q_i'] \leftarrow C(q_i \oplus M_i^Q, \vec{Y}_i^q, \vec{Z}_i^q),$$

and sends $[q_i']$ to P^*. P' continues the run of P^*, through the point where P^* makes his inputs to circuit H_i^*. In particular, P' learns the values of a_i, which he sends to V, and also the values of M_{i+1}^Q, $\vec{Y}_{i+1}^q$ and $\vec{Z}_{i+1}^q$.

Aside from his choice of answers, P^*'s can cheat in two general ways. First, he can violate a consistency constraint, i.e. use a different value for M_i^H in two different places in the protocol. however, if he ever attempts to do this, then by Lemma 2, V^* will immediately reject with probability $1 - \left(\frac{2}{3}\right)^{|x|}$. If V^* doesn't reject though, we can make no guarantees about his chance of finally accepting x. Second, he can give inconsistent values for some experiment, (Y, Z), or give slightly inconsistent blob representations of M_i^H in two different places. This latter form of cheating will only increase the probability that the circuit will abort, without changing its output if it doesn't abort, so we can assume without loss of of generality that this form of cheating doesn't occur.

By a routine probabilistic analysis, we see that, subject to P^* not violating any of his consistency constraints (CC's), having P' supply $[q_i']$ will be essentially indistinguishable from actually running the protocol and having V^*'s send $[q_i']$ to P^*. From this fact, we obtain

$$prob((P', V) \text{ accepts}) \geq prob((\hat{P}, V^*) \text{ accepts \& } P^* \text{ didn't violate his CC's}).$$

However, using the security of the blob consistency checks, we have,

$$prob((\hat{P}, V^*) \text{ accepts \& } P^* \text{ violates a CC}) \leq \left(\frac{2}{3}\right)^k.$$

Hence, we obtain,

$$prob((\hat{P}, V^*) \text{ accepts}) - prob((P', V) \text{ accepts}) \leq \left(\frac{2}{3}\right)^k,$$

which implies our claim.

4.2 (P^*, V^*) is a zero-knowledge protocol.

We now produce a simulator S for (P^*, V^*). Given a possibly malicious $\hat{V}$, S must take $\hat{V}$'s queries, $[q_0'], \ldots, [q_m']$, and $\hat{V}$'s inputs to the various circuits, and simulate the circuits' outputs. Furthermore, S must also correctly simulate situations in which P^* aborts the protocol. S works as follows.

Step 0: S uniformly chooses

- $[M_0^H], \ldots, [M_m^H]$,

- $[h_0'], \ldots [h_m']$ and $\vec{Y}_0^h, \ldots, \vec{Y}_m^h$,

- $[q_1'], \ldots, [q_m']$ and $\vec{Y}_0^q, \ldots, \vec{Y}_m^q$,

For $0 \leq i \leq m$, S computes $\vec{Z}_i^h = E([h_i'], \vec{Y}_i^h)$, and for $1 \leq i \leq m$, S computes $\vec{Z}_i^q = E([q_i'], \vec{Y}_i^q)$.

S simulates the secure evaluation of H_0^* as follows. S takes R_2 and $\vec{Y}_0^M$ as input from $\hat{V}$. S gives $\hat{V}$ the values of $[h_0']$, $[q_1']$ and $E([M_0^H], \vec{Y}_0^M)$ as output.

Step i: $\hat{V}$ will then send a string $[q_i^{\hat{V}}]$ to S. S simulates P^*, aborting the protocol if $[q_i^{\hat{V}}]$ is not a valid blob, or if $([q_i^{\hat{V}}], \vec{Y}_i^q, \vec{Z}_i^q)$ is inconsistent. S simulates the secure evaluation of H_i^* as follows. S takes $[h_{i-1}']$, $\vec{Y}_{i-1}^M$, $\vec{Z}_{i-1}^M$, and $\vec{Y}_i^M$ as input from $\hat{V}$. S now executes the following procedure:

1. Output "abort" if $([h_{i-1}'], \vec{Y}_{i-1}^h, \vec{Z}_{i-1}^h)$ or $([M_{i-1}^H], \vec{Y}_{i-1}^M, \vec{Z}_{i-1}^M)$ is inconsistent.

2. Otherwise, output $[h_i']$, $[q_i']$, and $E([M_i^H], \vec{Y}_i^M)$.

Final Step: S simulates the running of ACCEPT* as follows. S accepts $[h_m]$, $\vec{Y}_m^M$, and $\vec{Z}_m^M$ from $\hat{V}$ as input. S then follows the following procedure.

1. Output "abort" if $([h_m'], \vec{Y}_m^h, \vec{Z}_m^h)$ or $([M_m^H], \vec{Y}_m^M, \vec{Z}_m^M)$ is inconsistent.

2. Otherwise, output 1 (accept).

Now, we claim that the distribution on $\hat{V}$'s view that is generated by running S with $\hat{V}$ will be statistically indistinguishable from the view generated by running $(P^*, \hat{V})$. First, observe that up to the point where ACCEPT* gives a 0 or a 1 as output, the two distributions are identical. In both cases, the distribution on $[h_0'], \ldots, [h_m']$ and $[q_1'], \ldots, [q_m']$ will be identical. This follows from the uniform choice of the mask vectors, and in fact holds regardless of $\hat{V}$'s choice of inputs to the circuits. Furthermore, Lemma 1 implies that for any Y_1 and Y_2, and any blob $[B]$ chosen by the simulator, the distribution on the values of $(E([B], Y_1), E([B], Y_2))$ will be independent of the actual values of B. For this reason, all of the consistency checks and the $\vec{Z}$ vectors sent to $\hat{V}$ will be distributed identically with the the the checks and $\vec{Z}$ vectors output by the actual protocol.

Thus, one can show that until ACCEPT* outputs a 0 or a 1, the simulation and the view from the actual protocol are identical. The only difference in the behavior of the simulation is that the output of ACCEPT* is, when not "abort," always equal to 1. In the actual protocol, ACCEPT* may sometimes output a 0. However, we can show that this event will occur with probability exponentially small in $|x|$.

As with a malicious prover, we can classify a malicious verifier's cheating to be in two forms. We say that an input $[q_i^{\hat{V}}]$ $\{[h_i^{\hat{V}}]\}$ to a circuit or to P^* is *legitimate* if it is a well formed blob and its contents are equal to q_i' $\{h_i'\}$. Otherwise, we say that the input is illegitimate.

Now, if $\hat{V}$ never gives an illegitimate input, then the distribution on $h_i = h_i' \oplus M_i^H$ will be identical to that produced by (P, V), and thus ACCEPT* will be equal to 0 with probability at most $2^{-|x|}$. On the other hand, if $\hat{V}$ ever gives an illegitimate input, then with probability $1 - (2/3)^{|x|}$, (by Lemma 2), the circuit will output "abort," or the prover will abort. From then on, $\hat{V}$'s next such input will be illegitimate with probability $1 - (2/3)^{|x|}$. By a simple probability analysis, ACCEPT* will output "abort" with probability at least $1 - m(2/3)^{|x|}$.

References

[1] D. Chaum, I. Damgard, and J. van de Graaf. Multiparty Computations Ensuring Secrecy of Each Party's Input and Correctness of the Output, Proc. CRYPTO85, Springer-Verlag, 1986, 477–488.

[2] O. Goldreich, Y. Mansour, and M. Sipser. Interactive Proof Systems: Provers that never fail and random selection. Proc. FOCS87.

[3] S. Goldwasser and M. Sipser. On public versus private coins in interactive proof systems. Proc. STOC86.

[4] R. Impagliazzo, L. Levin, and M. Luby. Pseudo-random Generation from One-Way Functions, Proc. STOC89

[5] R. Impagliazzo and M. Yung. Direct Minimum-Knowledge Computation, Proc. of CRYPTO87.

[6] J. Kilian. Founding Cryptography on Oblivious Transfer, Proc. of STOC88. Personal Communication.

[7] M. Naor Pseudorandomnesss and Bit Commitment, Proc. of Crypto89.

Hiding Instances in Zero-Knowledge Proof Systems

(Extended Abstract)

Donald Beaver*   Joan Feigenbaum†   Victor Shoup‡

Abstract

Informally speaking, an *instance-hiding proof system* for the function f is
a protocol in which a polynomial-time verifier is convinced of the value of
$f(x)$ but does not reveal the input x to the provers. We show here that a
boolean function f has an instance-hiding proof system if and only if it is the
characteristic function of a language in NEXP ∩ coNEXP. We formalize the
notion of zero-knowledge for instance-hiding proof systems with several provers
and show that all such systems can be made perfect zero-knowledge.

1   Introduction

In this paper, we show that every function that has a multiprover interactive proof
system in fact has one in which the verifier does not learn the proof, and the provers
do not learn what they are proving.

Consider interactive protocols involving a computationally limited verifier V and
$m \geq 1$ powerful provers $P_1, \ldots, P_m$ in which the provers are allowed to communicate
with V, but not with each other.

In an *interactive proof system* for a language L (cf. [12, 7, 10]) the input x is
on a shared tape, accessible to the verifier and provers. If x is in L, the protocol
allows V to obtain convincing evidence of this fact. Because it obtains this evidence,
V need not trust the provers to behave correctly. One can also consider interactive
proof systems for functions f in which the verifier learns $f(x)$ and obtains convincing
evidence of the correctness of this value (cf. [11]).

---

*AT&T Bell Laboratories, Room 2C324, 600 Mountain Avenue, Murray Hill, NJ 07974 USA,
beaver@research.att.com. Work done at Harvard University, supported in part by NSF grant CCR-
870-4513.

†AT&T Bell Laboratories, Room 2C473, 600 Mountain Avenue, Murray Hill, NJ 07974 USA,
jf@research.att.com.

‡University of Toronto, Computer Science Department, Toronto, Ontario M5S 1A4, CANADA,
shoup@theory.toronto.edu. Work done at AT&T Bell Laboratories as a Postdoctoral Fellow in
Theoretical Computer Science.

It is known (cf. [14, 16]) that the class IP of languages recognized by 1-prover interactive proof systems is equal to the complexity class PSPACE. Furthermore, it is shown in [2] that the class MIP of languages recognized by multi-prover interactive proof systems is equal to the complexity class NEXP = NTIME(2^{poly}).

In an *instance-hiding scheme* for a function f (cf. [1, 4, 5]), the input x is on a private tape, accessible only to the querier V. The protocol allows V to obtain the value of $f(x)$ without revealing to any prover any information about x (other than its length); however, V does not necessarily obtain any evidence of the the correctness of this value (because of this, the powerful players are referred to as "oracles" in [1, 4, 5]). In this model, V does not entrust any information about x to the provers, but it does have to trust the provers to behave correctly.

Beaver and Feigenbaum [4] have shown that *all* functions f have multi-prover instance-hiding schemes, thus settling a question of Rivest [15].

In this paper, we introduce the notion of an *instance-hiding proof system* for a function f and characterize the functions that have such systems. An instance-hiding proof system is similar to an instance-hiding scheme, except that along with the value of $f(x)$, the protocol allows V to obtain convincing evidence of the correctness of this value. Thus, the verifier need not entrust any information about x to the provers, nor need it trust the provers to behave correctly.

Let fNEXP denote the class of total functions computable by nondeterministic exponential time Turing machine transducers. The restriction of fNEXP to Boolean functions consists of the characteristic functions of languages in NEXP $\cap$ coNEXP. We prove the following.

Theorem 1 *Every Boolean function $f \in$ fNEXP has an instance-hiding proof system.*

The fact that MIP = NEXP implies that Theorem 1 is the best possible, since if the function f has an instance-hiding proof system, then clearly f is the characteristic function of a language in MIP $\cap$ coMIP, and hence f is in fNEXP.

We also define in a natural way the notion of zero-knowledge for instance-hiding proof systems and show that any instance-hiding proof system can be made zero-knowledge. In any type of proof system, the definition of zero-knowledge should capture the intuitive idea that the provers do not trust the verifier to behave correctly and that the verifier is not to be entrusted with any information other than the fact being proved. The definition of zero-knowledge for interactive proof systems for a function f on input x captures the intuitive idea that the verifier—even a misbehaving one—learns the value of $f(x)$ and nothing else. In an instance-hiding proof system for a function f, the provers do not know the input x, nor can they infer anything about x (except its size) from the messages they receive from the verifier. Thus they cannot hope to prevent a verifier from learning, say, $f(x')$ instead of $f(x)$, where $|x'| = |x|$. Our definition of a zero-knowledge instance-hiding proof system captures the intuitive idea that the verifier—even a misbehaving one—learns the value of f at exactly one input of length n and nothing else. Thus, in a zero-knowledge instance-hiding proof system, the verifier and the provers do not trust each other to behave correctly, nor do they entrust each other with any non-essential information: The provers learn nothing about x, and the verifier learns nothing but the value of $f(x)$.

For the purpose of constructing zero-knowledge protocols, it is convenient to assume, as in [7], that the provers have access to a shared random tape that is not accessible to V. In [7], it is shown that every language in MIP has a zero-knowledge interactive proof system.

We prove the following.

Theorem 2 *Every Boolean function $f \in fNEXP$ has a perfect zero-knowledge instance-hiding proof system.*

The protocols that we construct in order to prove Theorems 1 and 2 involve multiple provers. Feigenbaum and Ostrovsky have recently shown that a function has a one-prover instance-hiding proof system if and only if it has a one-oracle instance-hiding scheme and it is in fPSPACE. They have also shown that the existence of a one-way function implies that all one-prover instance-hiding proof systems can be made (computational) zero-knowledge.

We remark that the notion of *private/adaptive checker*, which was introduced by Blum, Luby and Rubinfeld [9], can be viewed as a restricted form of instance-hiding proof system in which the provers are only asked questions of the form "what is $f(y)$."

The rest of this paper is organized as follows. In Section 2 we give the formal definitions of "instance-hiding proof system" and "zero-knowledge." In Section 3 we prove Theorem 1. In Section 4 we prove Theorem 2, along the way giving a new and simple perfect zero-knowledge protocol for languages in MIP. In Section 5 we state an open problem.

Most of these results first appeared in our Technical Memorandum [6].

2 Definitions

We now formally define instance-hiding proof systems and the corresponding notion of zero-knowledge. The intuition behind these definitions can be found in Section 1. Let V, P_1, ..., P_m be a set of interactive Turing Machines. As in ordinary MIP, the verifier V is a probabilistic polynomial-time Turing Machine, the provers $P_1, \ldots, P_m$ are computationally unbounded, and the verifier can communicate reliably and privately during the protocol with each of the provers, but the provers cannot communicate with each other. Also as in ordinary MIP, the provers have a shared random tape to which the verifier does not have access; however, this random tape is only required in the construction of zero-knowledge instance-hiding proof systems. Unlike ordinary MIP, the input x in an instance-hiding proof system is known only to the verifier. The output produced by V after interacting with a set $\{P_i^*\}$ of (possibly misbehaving) provers is an element of the set $\{0, 1, reject\}$ and is denoted by $(V(x), P_1^*, \ldots, P_m^*)$.

For each prover P_i, the transcript $T(V, P_i, x)$ of messages sent between V and P_i on input x is a random variable, and its distribution is induced by the random coin-tosses of the verifier and provers.

Definition 2.1 *The protocol* $(V, P_1, \ldots, P_m)$ *is an* **instance-hiding proof system** *for the function* f *if it satisfies the following properties.*

(i) For all constants $c > 0$, *for all sufficiently large* x,

$$\text{Prob}((V(x), P_1, \ldots, P_m) = f(x)) > 1 - 1/|x|^c.$$

(ii) For all constants $c > 0$, *for all sufficiently large* x, *for all* $P_1^*, \ldots, P_m^*$,

$$\text{Prob}((V(x), P_1^*, \ldots, P_m^*) \notin \{f(x), reject\}) < 1/|x|^c.$$

(iii) For all $P_1^*, \ldots, P_m^*$, *for all inputs* x *and* x' *with* $|x| = |x'|$, *for* $1 \leq i \leq m$, *the distribution of the transcripts* $T(V, P_i^*, x)$ *and* $T(V, P_i^*, x')$ *are the same.*

Conditions (i) and (ii) capture the notion of a proof system for a function. Condition (iii) captures the notion of instance-hiding—the protocol leaks no more than the length of x to any individual, isolated prover. However, pairs of transcripts, say $T(V, P_i, x)$ and $T(V, P_j, x)$ may be dependent. Thus pairs of provers must be kept physically separated for two reasons: As in ordinary multiprover systems, colluding provers could cause the verifier to accept a wrong value for $f(x)$; as in ordinary instance-hiding schemes, colluding provers could compute more information about x than its size. A more general definition of instance-hiding is given in [1]; if we restrict attention to the case in which at most the length of the instance is leaked to the provers, then condition (iii) is equivalent to the definition in [1].

Definition 2.2 *An instance-hiding proof system* $(V, P_1, \ldots, P_m)$ *for the function* f *is* **computational** *(resp.* **statistical, perfect***) zero-knowledge if, for any probabilistic polynomial-time verifier* V^*, *there is a probabilistic, expected-polynomial-time oracle machine* M_{V^*} *(called the* **simulator***) with the following property. During its execution on input* x, M_{V^*} *may make exactly one query to an* f-*oracle, and the query must have length* $|x|$. *The distribution of the simulator's output* $M_{V^*}(x)$ *is* **computationally indistinguishable from** *(resp.* **statistically indistinguishable from, the same as***) the transcripts* $\langle T(V^*, P_1, x), \ldots, T(V^*, P_m, x) \rangle$.

3 Proof of Theorem 1

3.1 Arithmetization of Boolean Functions

Let $f : \{0,1\}^* \to \{0,1\}$ be any Boolean function.

For any $n \geq 1$, we denote by K a fixed finite field such that $n + 2 \leq |K| = O(n)$. Such a field can be constructed deterministically in polynomial time. In what follows, $\alpha_1, \ldots, \alpha_{n+1}$ will denote fixed nonzero elements in K.

We consider the restriction of f to inputs of length n. We define a polynomial $g \in K[X_1, \ldots, X_n]$ in the following way. For each $A = (a_1, \cdots, a_n) \in \{0,1\}^n$, let

$$\delta_A(X_1, \ldots, X_n) = \prod_{i=1}^{n} (X_i - \overline{a_i})(-1)^{\overline{a_i}} \in K[X_1, \ldots, X_n].$$

So, for each $(x_1, \cdots, x_n) \in \{0,1\}^n$, $\delta_A(x_1, \ldots, x_n)$ is 1 if $x_i = a_i$, for $1 \leq i \leq n$, and it is 0 otherwise. Next, let

$$g(X_1, \ldots, X_n) = \sum_{A \in \{0,1\}^n} f(A)\delta_A(X_1, \ldots, X_n).$$

We can of course view g as a function mapping K^n into K in the usual way. We make the following simple observations.

Proposition 3.1

(i) $g(x_1, \ldots, x_n) = f(x_1, \ldots, x_n)$ for all $(x_1, \ldots, x_n) \in \{0,1\}^n$.

(ii) $\deg g \leq n$.

(iii) If $f \in fNEXP$, then $g \in fNEXP$.

A polynomial such as g which extends f to a larger arithmetic domain is sometimes referred to as an "arithmetization" of f. Arithmetizations were first used in the context of interactive protocols by Beaver and Feigenbaum [4].

3.2 An Instance-Hiding Proof System

Now suppose that $f \in fNEXP$, and let g be its arithmetization. Let $x = (x_1, \ldots, x_n)$ be the input. Define the language L_g as follows. For u_1, ..., u_n, and v in K, $(u_1, \ldots, u_n, v) \in L_g$ if and only if $g(u_1, \ldots, u_n) = v$. Our instance-hiding proof system for f requires $2(n+1)$ provers on inputs of length n; we call the provers $P_1, P_1', \ldots, P_{n+1}, P_{n+1}'$.

Protocol A.

A1. V picks $r_1, \ldots, r_n \in K$ at random, and computes $y(i,j) := r_j \alpha_i + x_j$ for $i = 1 \ldots n+1$ and $j = 1 \ldots n$. For $i = 1 \ldots n+1$, V sends $(y(i,1), \ldots, y(i,n))$ to provers P_i, P_i'.

A2. For $i = 1 \ldots n+1$: prover P_i computes $z_i := g(y(i,1), \ldots, y(i,n))$; P_i sends z_i to V.

A3. For $i = 1 \ldots n+1$: P_i, P_i' prove to V that $(y(i,1), \ldots, y(i,n), z_i) \in L_g$.

A4. V interpolates the points (α_i, z_i) $(i = 1 \ldots n+1)$ to obtain a polynomial $w(X) \in K[X]$. The constant term of $w(X)$ is equal to $f(x)$.

One must verify that (1) Protocol A is a proof system, and (2) Protocol A is instance-hiding. To prove (1), observe that statements (i) and (ii) of Proposition 3.1 guarantee that the constant term of $w(X)$ in step A4 is indeed equal to $f(x)$. Also, observe that statement (iii) of Proposition 3.1 implies that $L_g \in NEXP$; therefore, the result of [2] that NEXP = MIP allows us to implement step A3 with one-sided, exponentially small error probability. If the provers follow the protocol, the output of the verifier is always $f(x_1, \ldots, x_n)$; otherwise, the verifier will accept a wrong answer with exponentially small probability. Claim (2) can be proved using the line of reasoning found in [4]—the essential point is that each $y(i, j)$ is distributed uniformly over K (although pairs $y(i, j)$ and $y(k, j)$ are correlated); these random elements of K leak only the size of the input.

4 Proof of Theorem 2

The basic steps required to convert Protocol A in Section 3 to a zero-knowledge, instance-hiding proof system are the following.

1. We replace step A3 by a zero-knowledge simulation protocol.

2. In step A2, V learns the value of z_i, which it certainly could not compute on its own. We solve this problem by having P_i send instead $z_i' := z_i + h(\alpha_i)$, where $h(X)$ is a random polynomial over K of degree $\leq n$ and constant term zero. V then interpolates the points (α_i, z_i') in step A4; the constant term of the resulting polynomial has the correct value. As long as the verifier follows the protocol in step A1, z_i' is just the value of a random polynomial of degree $\leq n$ with constant term $f(x_1, \ldots, x_n)$, evaluated at α_i.

3. In step A1, a cheating verifier may not follow the protocol, and may send $y(i, j)$ values that do not correspond in a legitimate way to some point in $\{0, 1\}^n$. In particular, this would invalidate our fix to A2, and could also allow a cheating verifier to learn the value of g at any point in K^n, which we do not want to allow. We prevent this by using a distributed function evaluation protocol that will reveal the true values of $z_1', \ldots, z_n'$ to V only if the $y(i, j)$ values correspond to some input value in $\{0, 1\}^n$.

The remainder of this section supplies the details of these steps.

4.1 Building Blocks

We describe here the subprotocols that are used in our zero-knowledge proof system. These are building blocks that appear elsewhere in the literature or slight variations thereof.

4.1.1 Bit Commitment

Using the shared random tape, simple bit commitment can be implemented in a very simple way as in [7]. In the bit commitment scheme, there are two protocols: a *bit commit protocol* and a *bit reveal protocol*. In order to ensure that the scheme works properly, the prover that executes the bit reveal protocol must not have any knowledge of random bits sent by the verifier during the bit commit protocol. One way to guarantee this is simply to dedicate one prover to the task of executing bit reveal protocols.

4.1.2 Committing Shared Random Bits

Several provers can easily commit to the same random bit by simply taking that bit from the shared random tape. Only one of the provers actually executes the bit commit protocol. A group of provers can commit to a set of shared random bits in this fashion, and there is no need to "prove" to the verifier that they committed to the same ones—the ordinary reveal protocol will prevent any cheating.

4.1.3 Multiple-use Notarized Envelopes

In [8] it is shown how to construct a *notarized envelope scheme* from a protocol for simple bit commitment. There are two protocols: a *notarized bit commit protocol* and a *prove protocol*. The notarized bit commit protocol allows a prover to commit a bit. If a is a bit string, we will use the phrase "put a in a notarized envelope" to mean "perform the notarized bit commit protocol for each bit in a." The prove protocol allows a prover to prove one NC^1 predicate[1] involving bits in notarized envelopes in such a way that no information about these bits is revealed (other than that implied by the truth of the predicate), and if the predicate is not true the verifier can catch a cheating prover with probability at least 1/poly.

The restriction that a notarized envelope can be used in only one proof is just an artifact of the implementation that can easily be lifted. Instead of representing a bit b as the sum $c_1 \oplus c_2$, where c_1 and c_2 are committed using an ordinary bit commitment protocol (as done in [8]), we can represent b as the sum $c_1 \oplus \cdots \oplus c_m$. Using the same techniques as in [8], which involve Barrington's result on bounded-width branching programs [3], this representation allows b to be involved in $m-1$ proofs, as each proof reveals at most one of the c_i's. This modification has the effect of decreasing slightly the verifier's chances of catching a cheating prover, but the probability is still 1/poly.

4.1.4 Distributed Function Evaluation

We will need a protocol for the following simple version of distributed function evaluation. Let $F(u_1, \ldots, u_m)$ be an NC^1 function, where the u_i's are bit strings. We have provers $P_1, \ldots, P_m$ and verifier V. Initially, each P_i knows u_i; some of the u_i may be known to V, whereas others may be in notarized envelopes and unknown to V. At the end of the protocol, V should learn nothing but the value of $F(u_1, \ldots, u_m)$, rejecting a wrong answer with probability at least 1/poly, and each of the P_i's should learn nothing.

The statement that V learns nothing but the value of F means that (1) during the protocol, V learns the value of F, and (2) there is a simulation procedure that, when given the value of F, will simulate the conversations that take place during the protocol. The statement that each prover learns nothing means that each prover receives messages that consist of uncorrelated random bits.

We briefly sketch an implementation of the protocol using a variant of Kilian's oblivious NC^1 circuit evaluation protocol [13]. Without loss of generality, we can

---

[1]In this paper, NC^1 means P-uniform NC^1.

assume that F is a Boolean-valued function. Since $F \in NC^1$, there is a (polynomial-time constructible) branching program M that realizes F [3]. On a given input, M determines a sequence of permutations in S_5, $\sigma_1, \ldots, \sigma_m$, where each σ_j is determined by the value of a single input bit; moreover, the product $\prod_j \sigma_j$ is equal to the identity in S_5 if $F = 0$, and it is equal to some fixed nonidentity element in S_5 otherwise.

Let $\rho_1, \ldots, \rho_{m-1}$ be random permutations in S_5, and let ρ_0 and ρ_m be the identity permutation. Let $\tau_j = \rho_{j-1}^{-1} \sigma_j \rho_j$ for $j = 1, \ldots, m$. Then $\prod_j \tau_j = \prod_j \sigma_j$, and the list of τ_j's are uniformly distributed apart from satisfying this equality; therefore, nothing can be inferred from the values of τ_j other than the value of F.

The function evaluation protocol runs as follows. The provers put shared random permutations $\rho_1, \ldots, \rho_{m-1}$ in notarized envelopes. Each prover P_i computes and sends to V the permutations τ_j corresponding to each input bit of u_i. For each such τ_j, prover P_i proves to V that τ_j was computed correctly. This correctness predicate is an NC^1 predicate involving τ_j, the pair of permutations ρ_{j-1} and ρ_j (which are in notarized envelopes), and the corresponding input bit (which may be in a notarized envelope); therefore, the prove protocol for notarized envelopes described above may be used. Once V has received all such permutations, V can multiply them together to obtain the value of F.

4.2 A Zero-Knowledge MIP Protocol

We now describe a perfect zero-knowledge proof system for any language L in MIP. Our protocol is simpler than that in [7], and it will be easy to see that ours can be embedded as a subprotocol in an instance-hiding proof system in which the input bits to the subprotocol are not on a shared input tape, but are in notarized envelopes, or are known initially only to the verifier. Our protocol does not require oblivious transfer or general oblivious circuit evaluation.

4.2.1 A Normal Form

We begin with a normal form for MIP protocols in which the verifier's role is extremely limited.

Proposition 4.1 *Any language in $L \in MIP$ has a 2-prover protocol with the following structure.*

Protocol N.

N1. *V sends a random string r to P_1, who sends a response a_1.*

N2. *V sends a random string r' to P_1, who sends a response a_2.*

N3. *V sends a_2 to P_2, who sends a response a_3.*

N4. *V computes an NC^1 acceptance predicate $accept(x, r, r', a_1, a_2, a_3)$.*

On inputs $x \in L$, V accepts with probability 1. On inputs $x \notin L$, V rejects with probability at least $1/poly$.

Proof (sketch): By the "completeness theorem" of [7] and the "probabilistic oracle machine" characterization of [10], we can assume that there is a poly-time deterministic oracle machine $\phi(x, r)$ such that

1. for all $x \in L$, there exists an oracle E such that for all r, $\phi^E(x, r) = 1$;

2. for all $x \notin L$, for all oracles E, the probability that $\phi^E(x, r) = 1$ for randomly chosen r is at most $1/3$.

The provers choose an oracle E. The verifier V selects a random string r and sends it to P_1. Then P_1 computes a response a_1 which encodes the entire computation of $\phi^E(x, r)$, including all the oracle queries $q_i, i = 1 \ldots m$ and oracle answers $s_i :=$ $E(q_i), i = 1 \ldots m$. V sends a random string r' to P_1, which represents a random number $i(r')$ between 1 and m. P_1 sends a response $a_2 := q_{i(r')}$ to the verifier. Now V sends a_2 to P_2. P_2 sends a response $a_3 := E(a_2)$. The acceptance predicate $accept(x, r, r', a_1, a_2, a_3)$ just checks that (1) a_1 encodes a valid accepting computation (imposing no constraints on the oracle responses), (2) $a_2 = q_{i(r')}$, and (3) $a_3 = s_{i(r')}$.

The argument that this protocol has the desired properties is similar to that found in [10]. ∎

4.2.2 Zero-Knowledge Simulation

Now we show how to simulate Protocol N in zero-knowledge. The basic idea is the following. The provers will put their responses in notarized envelopes, and the verifier will use the distributed function evaluation protocol to evaluate the acceptance predicate. However, difficulties arise in step N3—the response a_2 must somehow be passed to P_2, (1) without letting V know the value of a_2, and (2) without relying on V to follow the protocol. The first problem is solved by having P_1 send $a_2' := a_2 \oplus e$ to V, where e is a shared random string (of length equal to that of a_2) that is put in a notarized envelope at the beginning of the protocol. The second problem is solved by modifying the acceptance predicate so that if V sends anything other than a_2' to P_2, the acceptance predicate becomes trivially true, and hence V can not possibly gain any information by trying to cheat in this way. Since P_2 knows a_2' and e, it can recover a_2 and compute its response a_3.

Here are the details. Let

$$accept'(x, r, r', a_1, a_2', e; c, a_3) = (a_2' \neq c) \vee accept(x, r, r', a_1, a_2' \oplus e, a_3).$$

The distributed function evaluation protocol will be used in the following protocol to evaluate $accept'$, with P_1 supplying the arguments x, r, r', a_1, a_2', e and P_2 supplying the arguments c, a_3.

Protocol Z.

Z1. The provers put a shared random string e in a notarized envelope.

Z2. V sends r to P_1; P_1 puts the response a_1 in a notarized envelope.

Z3. V sends r' to P_1; P_1 sends $a'_2 := a_2 \oplus e$ to V.

Z4. V sends $c := a'_2$ to P_2; P_2 puts the response a_3 in a notarized envelope.

Z5. Evaluate the predicate $accept'(x, r, r', a_1, a'_2, e; c, a_3)$ using the distributed function evaluation protocol.

If $x \in L$, the verifier will always accept; otherwise, the verifier will reject with probability at least $1/poly$. To reduce the error probability, the protocol can be repeated.

To show that this protocol is perfect zero-knowledge, we describe a simulation program M. In steps Z1–Z4, the messages received by the verifier will just consist of random bits, which M can easily simulate. Since M knows that $accept'$ will be true no matter what the verifier does in steps Z1–Z4, M can simulate the conversations that occur during the distributed function evaluation protocol in step Z5.

Clearly, this protocol can be embedded in a larger protocol in which some of the input bits are in notarized envelopes. Furthermore, if an input bit b is initially known only to V, V can send $b_1 := b$ to P_1 and $b_2 := b$ to P_2, and the provers can effectively guarantee that $b_1 = b_2$ by replacing the acceptance predicate $\phi(\cdots b \cdots)$ with $(b_1 \neq b_2) \vee \phi(\cdots b_1 \cdots)$. Both of these modifications will be utilized in what follows.

Up to now it has been implicitly assumed that a third prover is dedicated to the bit reveal protocol. This assumption simplifies the protocol, but those researchers whose budget will allow them to purchase only two provers will be happy to know that two provers will suffice. Very briefly, we can't safely use prover P_2 for revealing committed bits after it has received the message c from V in step Z4. However, P_1 can execute its part of the distributed function evaluation protocol before this occurs, allowing P_2 to be used to reveal bits committed by P_1 during this process. We leave the rest of the details to the interested reader.

4.3   A Zero-Knowledge Instance-Hiding Proof System

We now have everything we need to modify Protocol A to obtain a perfect zero-knowledge instance-hiding proof system. We shall the use notation introduced in Section 3.

Let L'_g be the language defined as follows. For $u_1, \ldots, u_n, v, \alpha \in K$, and $h \in K[X]$ a polynomial of degree n with constant term zero (represented as a list of coefficients), $(u_1, \ldots, u_n, v, \alpha, h) \in L'_g$ if and only if $g(u_1, \ldots, u_n) + h(\alpha) = v$.

Let $[y(i, j)]$ $(i = 1 \ldots n+1, j = 1 \ldots n)$ be a collection of elements in K. We shall say that the $y(i, j)$ satisfy the *linearity condition* if there exist (necessarily unique) elements $r'_1, \ldots, r'_n \in K$ and $x'_1, \ldots, x'_n \in \{0, 1\}$ such that $y(i, j) = r'_j \alpha_i + x'_j$ for each $y(i, j)$. It is easy to show that the linearity condition is an NC^1 predicate, and that, if this condition is satisfied, the r'_j and x'_j can be recovered in polynomial time.

Let $[z'_i]$ $(i = 1 \ldots n+1)$ be a collection of elements in K. Let the function

$$F([y(i, j)]; [z'_i])$$

be defined as follows. If the $y(i,j)$ satisfy the linearity condition, then $F = (z'_1, \ldots, z'_{n+1})$; otherwise, $F = (0, \ldots, 0)$. It is easy to verify that F can be computed in NC^1.

Protocol B.

B1. V picks $r_1, \ldots, r_n \in K$ at random, and computes $y(i,j) := r_j \alpha_i + x_j$ for $i = 1 \ldots n + 1$ and $j = 1 \ldots n$. For $i = 1 \ldots n + 1$, V sends $(y(i,1), \ldots, y(i,n))$ to provers P_i, P'_i.

B2. The provers put the coefficients of a shared random polynomial h over K of degree $\leq n$ with constant term zero in notarized envelopes.

B3. For $i = 1 \ldots n + 1$: prover P_i computes $z'_i := g(y(i,1), \ldots, y(i,n)) + h(\alpha_i)$; P_i puts z'_i in a notarized envelope.

B4. For $i = 1 \ldots n + 1$: P_i, P'_i prove in zero-knowledge to V that

$$(y(i,1), \ldots, y(i,n), z'_i, \alpha_i, h) \in L'_g.$$

B5. Using the distributed function evaluation protocol, V evaluates

$$F([y(i,j)]; [z'_i]),$$

obtaining $z'_1, \ldots, z'_{n+1}$.

B6. V interpolates the points (α_i, z'_i) $(i = 1 \ldots n + 1)$ to obtain a polynomial $w'(X) \in K[X]$. The constant term of $w'(X)$ is the final result.

We must show that (1) Protocol B is a proof system, (2) Protocol B is instance-hiding, and (3) Protocol B is zero-knowledge.

To prove (1), one can easily show that if the provers follow the protocol, the verifier will always learn the correct value of $f(x_1, \ldots, x_n)$; otherwise, the verifier will accept the wrong answer with probability at most $1 - 1/\text{poly}$. The error probability can be decreased by iterating steps B2–B6 of the protocol.

Property (2) is proven as in Theorem 1.

To prove (3), we describe a simulation program M interacting with an arbitrary verifier V^*. We only discuss the simulation of the distributed function evaluation protocol in step B5; the other parts of the protocol can be easily simulated by virtue of the zero-knowledge properties of the various building blocks.

It will suffice to show how M can obtain the value of F, since this will allow it to then simulate the conversations that occur in the distributed function evaluation protocol. If the $y(i,j)$ values given by V^* in step B1 do not satisfy the linearity condition, the value of F is $(0, \ldots, 0)$. Otherwise, M can easily recover the corresponding values $x'_1, \ldots, x'_n$ and $r'_1, \ldots, r'_n$. M can then consult an f-oracle to obtain $f(x'_1, \ldots, x'_n)$. Notice that the polynomial $w'(X)$ can be written as

$$w'(X) = g(r'_1 X + x'_1, \ldots, r'_n X + x'_n) + h(X),$$

and so we see that $w'(X)$ is just a random polynomial of degree $\leq n$ over K with constant term equal to $f(x'_1, \ldots, x'_n)$. M can generate such a $w'(X)$ at random, and then generate the z'_i values using the formula $z'_i = w'(\alpha_i)$ $(i = 1 \ldots n+1)$. The value of F is $(z'_1, \ldots, z'_{n+1})$.

5 Open Problem

Our protocols require a polynomial number of provers. One can ask whether some fixed number (perhaps 2) of provers would suffice for all instance-hiding proof systems. Note that it is not even known whether a constant number of provers suffice for the construction of instance-hiding *schemes* (in which no proof is required that the provers' answers are right) for boolean functions in fNEXP—the best known upper bound for the number of provers is $n/\log n$ and is given by the generic construction in [5]. Thus obtaining general instance-hiding proof systems with a constant number of provers may be impossible and, in any case, seems to require a wholely new technique.

References

[1] M. Abadi, J. Feigenbaum, and J. Kilian. On Hiding Information from an Oracle, *J. Comput. System Sci.* 39 (1989), 21–50.

[2] L. Babai, L. Fortnow, and C. Lund. Nondeterministic Exponential Time has Two-Prover Interactive Protocols, *Proc. of the 31st FOCS* (1990), IEEE.

[3] D. Barrington. Bounded-Width Polynomial-Size Branching Programs Recognize Exactly Those Languages in NC^1, *J. Comput. System Sci.* 38 (1989), 150–164.

[4] D. Beaver and J. Feigenbaum. Hiding Instances in Multioracle Queries, *Proc. of the 7th STACS* (1990), Springer Verlag LNCS 415, 37–48.

[5] D. Beaver, J. Feigenbaum, J. Kilian, and P. Rogaway. Security with Low Communication Overhead, *these proceedings.*

[6] D. Beaver, J. Feigenbaum, and V. Shoup. Hiding Instances in Zero-Knowledge Proof Systems, AT&T Bell Laboratories Technical Memorandum, April 12, 1990.

[7] M. Ben-Or, S. Goldwasser, J. Kilian, and A. Wigderson. Multiprover Interactive Proof Systems: How to Remove Intractability Assumptions, *Proc. of the 20th STOC* (1988), ACM, 113–131.

[8] M. Ben-Or, O. Goldreich, S. Goldwasser, J. Håstad, J. Kilian, S. Micali, and P. Rogaway. Everything Provable is Provable in Zero-Knowledge, *Proc. of the 8th CRYPTO* (1988), Springer Verlag LNCS 403, 37–56.

[9] M. Blum, M. Luby, and R. Rubinfeld. Program Result Checking Against Adaptive Programs and in Cryptographic Settings, *Proc. of the DIMACS Workshop on Distributed Computing and Cryptography* (1989), AMS.

[10] L. Fortnow, J. Rompel, and M. Sipser. On the Power of Multiprover Interactive Protocols, *Proc. of the 3rd Structure in Complexity Theory Conference* (1988), IEEE, 156–161.

[11] Z. Galil, S. Haber, and M. Yung. Minimum-Knowledge Interactive Proofs for Decision Problems, *SIAM J. Comput.* 18 (1989), 711–739.

338

[12] S. Goldwasser, S. Micali, and C. Rackoff. The Knowledge Complexity of Interactive Proof Systems, *SIAM J. Comput.* 18 (1989), 186–208.

[13] J. Kilian. Founding Cryptography on Oblivious Transfer, *Proc. of 20th STOC* (1988), ACM, 20–31.

[14] C. Lund, L. Fortnow, H. Karloff, and N. Nisan. Algebraic Methods for Interactive Proof Systems, *Proc. of the 31st FOCS* (1990), IEEE.

[15] R. Rivest. Workshop on Communication and Computing, MIT, October, 1986.

[16] A. Shamir. IP = PSPACE, *Proc. of the 31st FOCS* (1990), IEEE.

Multi-Language Zero Knowledge Interactive Proof Systems

Kaoru KUROSAWA   Shigeo TSUJII

Department of Electrical and Electronic Engineering,

Faculty of Engineering,

Tokyo Institute of Technology

2-12-1, Ookayama, Meguro-ku, Tokyo 152, JAPAN

Tel.   +81-3-726-1111(Ext. 2577)

Fax   +81-3-729-0685

E-mail   kkurosaw@ss.titech.ac.jp or

kkurosaw%ss.titech.ac.jp@relay.cs.net

Abstract

Suppose that two ZKIPs are given for language L_1 and L_2. The total number of bits communicated is the sum of the two. This paper shows that it is possible to get the same effect in less amount of communication. We call such protocols "multi-language zero knowledge interactive proof systems".

1 Introduction

In zero knowledge interactive proof systems (ZKIPs) [GMR89], a large amount of communication is the bottleneck. Suppose that Alice wants to convince Bob of two theorems in zero knowledge, such as z is a quadratic residue mod N and G is Hamiltonian. The easiest way is to concatenate the two ZKIPs. The total number of bits communicated is the sum of the two. It will be nice if Alice can do that in shorter conversation.

This paper shows that it is possible. Alice can convince Bob in zero knowledge that $x_1 \in L_1$ and $x_2 \in L_2$ independently, and the total number of bits communicated is less than the sum of the two. We call such protocols "multi-language zero knowledge interactive proof systems (MZKIP)".

The paper is organized in the following way: In section 2, the definition of ZKIP is reviewed. In subsection 3.1, Kurosawa's cryptosystem is shown. (This cryptosystem itself is interesting.) In subsection 3.2, we define conditioned QNR and present a ZKIP for that by using Kurosawa's cryptosystem. In section 4, the definition of MZKIP is given. In section 5, we show an example of MZKIP for conditioned QNR and Hamilton problem.

2 ZKIP

For the definition of ZKIP, we refer the reader to [GMR89].
(Definition)

(A, B) is an interactive proof system for L if we have the following.
(1) Completeness

For each k, for sufficiently large x in L, B accepts with probability at least $1 - |x|^{-k}$.
(2) Soundness

For each k, for sufficiently large x not in L, for any A', on input x to

(A', B), B accepts x with probability at most $|x|^{-k}$. (The probabilities here are taken over the coin tosses of A' and B)

Let P(U, C, x) be the probability that a poly-size circuit C_x outputs 1 on input a random string distributed according to U(x).

(Definition)

(A, B) is zero-knowledge on L for B' if there exists a probabilistic turing machine $M_{B'}$, running in expected polynomial time, such that, for all poly-size family of circuits C, for all constant $c > 0$ and all sufficiently long strings $x \in L$,

$$|P(View_{AB'}, C, (x, H)) - P(M_{B'}, C, (x, H))| < |x|^{-c}$$

where H is an extra input tape to B'.

(A, B) is zero-knowledge on L if it is zero-knowledge on L for all B'.

(Definition)

(A, B) is a zero-knowledge proof system for L if it is an interactive proof system for L and zero-knowledge protocol on L.

3 Kurosawa's cryptosystem

3.1 Proposed public key cryptosystem [KIT87]

RSA is not know to be as hard as factorization. Rabin's cryptosystem is as hard as factorization. However, it is not uniquely deciphered because four different plaintexts produce the same ciphertext. Williams showed that this disadvantage can be overcome if the secret two prime numbers, p and q, are chosen such that p=q=3 mod 4. In Kurosawa's cryptosystem,

(1) p and q are arbitrary.

(2) It is as hard as factorization.

(3) It is uniquely deciphered.

The cryptosystem is as follows.

(Secret key) Two prime numbers, p and q.

(Public key) R(=pq) and c, where

$$(c/p) = (c/q) = -1 \tag{1}$$

(Plaintext) M

(Ciphertext) (E, s, t), where

$$E = M + (c/M) \bmod R \tag{2}$$

$$s = \begin{cases} 0 & \text{if } (M/R) = 1 \\ 1 & \text{if } (M/R) = -1 \end{cases} \tag{3}$$

$$t = \begin{cases} 0 & \text{if } M < (c/M \bmod R) \\ 1 & \text{if } M > (c/M \bmod R) \end{cases} \tag{4}$$

(Decryption)

From eq.(2), we obtain

$$M^2 - EM + c = 0 \tag{5}$$

Let a_1 and a_2 be the roots of eq.(5) mod p, and b_1 and b_2 be the roots of eq.(5) mod q. ([R80] shows how to find them.) Then, eq.(5) mod R has the following four roots.

$$M_1 = [a_1, b_1], \quad M_2 = [a_2, b_2]$$
$$M_3 = [a_1, b_2], \quad M_4 = [a_2, b_1]$$

where $M_1 = [a_1, b_1]$ means

$$M_1 = a_1 \bmod p, \quad M_1 = b_1 \bmod q$$

The original plaintext M is one of the four roots. "s" and "t" tell which one the plaintext M is, as we will see.

From eq.(5) and eq.(1), we obtain

$$(a_1/p)(a_2/p) = (c/p) = -1$$

We thus set

$$(a_1/p) = 1, \quad (a_2/p) = -1 \tag{6}$$

Similarly, we set

$$(b_1/q) = 1, \quad (b_2/q) = -1 \tag{7}$$

We then obtain

$$(M_1/R) = (M_1/p)(M_1/q) = (a_1/p)(b_1/q) = 1$$

Similarly, we obtain

$$(M_2/R) = 1$$

$$(M_3/R) = (M_4/R) = -1$$

Therefore, the receiver sees that

$$M = \begin{cases} M_1 & \text{or} & M_2 & \text{if } s = 0 \\ M_3 & \text{or} & M_4 & \text{if } s = 1 \end{cases} \tag{8}$$

Now, suppose that s=0. From eq.(5), we get

$$M_1 M_2 = [a_1 a_2, b_1 b_2] = [c, c] = c \bmod R$$

Hence

$$M_2 = c/M_1 \bmod R$$

Therefore, the receiver sees that

$$M = \begin{cases} min(M_1, M_2) & \text{if } t = 0 \\ max(M_1, M_2) & \text{if } t = 1 \end{cases} \tag{9}$$

When s=1,

$$M = \begin{cases} min(M_3, M_4) & \text{if } t = 0 \\ max(M_3, M_4) & \text{if } t = 1 \end{cases} \tag{10}$$

Thus, any ciphertext is uniquely deciphered.

It is clear that the cryptosystem is broken if one can factor R=pq. We will prove the converse.

[Lemma 1]

$$a_1 \neq a_2 \bmod p, \quad b_1 \neq b_2 \bmod q$$

(Proof)

It is clear from eq.(6) and eq.(7).

Q.E.D.

[Theorem 1]

Suppose that there exists a probabilistic polynomial time algorithm finding a plaintext from any ciphertext. Then, there exists a probabilistic polynomial time algorithm factoring R=pq.

(Proof)

Choose at random c such that (c/R)=1. Such c satisfies eq.(1) with probability 1/2. Let (R, c) be a public key of the cryptosystem.

Choose M randomly and compute M' as follows.

$$
\begin{aligned}
M \quad &\rightarrow \quad (E, s, t) \quad \text{(encryption)} \\
&\rightarrow \quad (E, s', t) \\
&\rightarrow \quad M' \qquad \text{(decryption)}
\end{aligned}
\tag{11}
$$

where $s' = s + 1 \bmod 2$. Let $M = [f_1, g_1]$. Since $s' = s + 1 \bmod 2$,

$$M' = [f_1, g_2] \quad or \quad [f_2, g_1]$$

First, consider the case of $M' = [f_1, g_2]$. Then,

$$M - M' = [f_1, g_1] - [f_1, g_2] = [0, g_1 - g_2]$$

From lemma 1,

$$M - M' = 0 \bmod p, \quad M - M' \neq 0 \bmod q$$

Therefore,

$$gcd(M - M', R) = p.$$

The case of $[f_2, g_1]$ is similar.

Q.E.D.

[Theorem 2]

Suppose that there exists a probabilistic polynomial time algorithm finding a plaintext from 1/poly(n) of all ciphertexts, where $n = |R|$. Then, there exists a probabilistic polynomial time algorithm factoring R=pq.

3.2 Conditioned QNR

QNR (quadratic non-residue) is defined as follows.

$$QNR = \{(c, N)|(c/N) = 1, \quad N = \prod_i p_i^{e_i}, \quad (c/p_j) = -1 \text{ for some j.}\}$$

We define "conditioned QNR" as follows.

$$\text{conditioned QNR} = \{(c, N)|(c/N) = 1, \quad N = \prod_i p_i^{e_i},$$

$$(c/p_j^{e_j}) = -1 \text{ for some j.}\}$$

We present a ZKIP for conditioned QNR below.

Without loss of generality, let $(c/p_1^{e_1}) = -1$ and set $Q = N/p_1^{e_1}$. $x = [a, b]$ denotes

$$x = a \bmod Q, \quad x = b \bmod p_1^{e_1}$$

Repeat step 1-4 n times, where $n = |N|$.

(step 1)

A chooses a random number r and computes

$$y = r + (c/r) \bmod N$$

A sends y to B.

(step 2)

B sends randomly e=1 or -1 to A.

(step 3)

A computes

$$x = \begin{cases} r & \text{if } (r/N) = e \\ [r, c/r] & \text{if } (r/N) = -e \end{cases} \tag{12}$$

A sends x to B.

(step 4)

B checks that

$$(x/N) = e$$

(Remarks)

1. The validity of the above protocol is proved by using the same discussion of 3.1.

2. The number of bits communicated is $1/n$ of [GMR89].

3. The above ZKIP is also an Arthur-Merlin game.

4 Multi-language zero knowledge interactive proof systems

4.1 Probabilities and bit complexity

ZKIPs require a large amount of bits communicated so that the probabilities of soundness and zero-knowledgeness get sufficiently small. In other words, such probabilities are functions of the number of bits communicated.

Let $F(=(A, B))$ be a ZKIP for L. Let x be an input to F.

(Definition)

Let a_i (and b_i) be the i-th message of A(and B) Let

$$H_n \triangleq \{x | x \in \{0, 1\}^*, |x| = n\}$$

Then, we define

$$t(F, n) \triangleq \max |b_1| + |a_1| + \dots$$

where the maximum is taken over all $x \in H_n$ and the coin tosses of A and B.

(Definition)

$$P_s(F, x) \triangleq \max \ \Pr \ (B \ accepts \ x)$$

where the maximum is taken over all A' and the coin tosses of A' and B.

(Definition)

$$P_z(F, x) \triangleq \max_{B'} \min_{M_{B'}} \max_C |P(View_{AB'}, C, (x, H)) - P(M_{B'}, C, (x, H))|$$

4.2 Multi-language zero knowledge interactive proof systems

Suppose that two languages are given, $L_1 \subseteq \{0,1\}^*$ and $L_2 \subseteq \{0,1\}^*$. Let $K(=(A, B))$ be an interactive protocol with an input $x = (x_1, x_2)$, where $|x_1| = |x_2|$. B accepts nothing, x_1, x_2 or both x_1 and x_2.

(Definition)

We say that K is a concatenatable ZKIP (CZKIP) for L_1 and L_2 if we have the following.

(1) Completeness

If $x_i \in L_i$, B accepts x_i with probability at least $1 - |x_i|^{-k}$ for all k and x_i large enough, where i=1, 2.

(2) Soundness

If $x_i \notin L_i$, then for any A', B accepts x_i with probability at most $|x_i|^{-k}$ for all k and x_i large enough, where i=1, 2.

(3) Zero-knowledgeness

K is zero-knowledge on L, where $L \triangleq \{(x_1, x_2) | x_1 \in L_1 \text{ and } x_2 \in L_2\}$.

(Remarks)

1. The completeness is independent of the other x_i. The soundness is also.

2. Therefore, CZKIP is different from a ZKIP for

$L = \{(x_1, x_2) | x_1 \in L_1 \text{ and } x_2 \in L_2\}$ or $L = \{(x_1, x_2) | x_1 \in L_1 \text{ or } x_2 \in L_2\}$

Let $K(=(A, B))$ be a CZKIP for L_1 and L_2. Let $x(= (x_1, x_2))$ be an input to K.

(Definition)

Let a_i (and b_i) be the i-th message of A(and B). Let

$$H'_n \triangleq \{(x_1, x_2)|x_i \in \{0,1\}^*, |x_1| = |x_2| = n\}$$

Then, we define

$$t'(K,n) \triangleq \max |b_1| + |a_1| + \dots$$

where the maximum is taken over all $(x_1, x_2) \in H'_n$ and the coin tosses of A and B.

(Definition)

$$P'_s(K,x) \triangleq \max \Pr \text{ (B accepts } x_i)$$

where the maximum is taken over all A' and the coin tosses of A' and B.

(Definition)

$$P'_z(K,x) = \max_{B'} \min_{M_{B'}} \max_C |P(View_{AB'}, C, (x, H)) - P(M_{B'}, C, (x, H))|$$

Let K be a CZKIP for L_1 and L_2. Let F_i be a ZKIP for L_i, i=1, 2.

(Definition)

We say that K is a multi-language ZKIP (MZKIP) for F_1 and F_2 if we have the following. Let $x = (x_1, x_2)$, $|x_1| = |x_2| = n$. Then, for sufficiently long n,

1. $t'(K,n) < t(F_1, n) + t(F_2, n)$ for any n.

2. $P'_s(K, x_i) < P_s(F_i, x_i)$ if $x_i \notin L_i$

3. $P'_z(K,x) \leq \max(P_z(F_1, x_1), P_z(F_2, x_2))$
   if $x_i \in L_i$ for i=1, 2.

(Remark)

MZKIPs for more than two languages are defined in a similar way.

5

(step 4)

A computes

$$x_{ij} = \begin{cases} r_{ij} & \text{if } (r_{ij}/N) = e_1 \\ [r_{ij}, \ c/r_{ij}] & \text{if } (r_{ij}/N) = -e_1 \end{cases}$$

If $e_2 = 0$, A sends π and $\{x_{ij}\}$ to B.

If $e_2 = 1$, A sends $\pi(S)$ and those x_{ij} such that edge ij is in $\pi(S)$.

(step 5)

B checks what he received.

(Remarks)

1. It is easily verified that the above protocol satisfies the conditions of MZKIP.

2. The number of bits communicated is nearly the same as that of $ZKIP_2$. That of $ZKIP_1$ is saved.

3. e_i is a question for L_i, i=1, 2.

4. If $(c, \ N) \notin L_1$ and $G \in L_2$, B accepts only G with overwhelming probability, and vice versa.

5.2 Other examples

The following ZKIPs are known.

$ZKIP_3$: $L_3 = \{(z, N)|z$ is a quadratic residue mod N $\}$ [GMR89]

$ZKIP_4$: $L_4 = \{(z, a, p)|z = a^z \bmod p\}$[TW87]

$ZKIP_5$: $L_5 = \{N|p^i$ divides N and p^{i+1} does not,

where $p = 3 \bmod 4$ is prime and i is odd $\}$ [B82]

$ZKIP_6$: $L_6 = \{$3-colorable graph $\}$ [GMW87]

$ZKIP_7$: $L_7 = \{$SAT$\}$ [BCC88]

A MZKIP is obtained for any one of $(ZKIP_1, ZKIP_3, ZKIP_4, ZKIP_5)$ and any one of $(ZKIP_2, ZKIP_6, ZKIP_7)$. A MZKIP for $ZKIP_3$ and $ZKIP5$ is also possible.

6 Summary

This paper proposed the notion of "multi-language zero-knowledge interactive proof systems". Some examples were given.

It will be a further work to clarify what kinds of ZKIPs can be combined so that the MZKIP is obtained.

References

[B82]   Blum: " Coin flipping by telephone", IEEE, COMPCON, pp.133-137 (1982)

[B86]   Blum: " How to prove a theorem so no one else can claim it Proc. International Congress of Mathematics, pp.1444-1451 (1986)

[BCC88] Brassard, Chaum and Crepeau: " Minimum disclosure proofs of knowledge", JCSS, pp.156-166 (1988)

[GMR89] Goldwasser, Micali and Rackoff: " The knowledge complexity of interactive proof systems", SIAM J. on Comp. vol.18, No.1, pp.186-208 (1989)

[GMW86] Goldreich, Micali and Wigderson: " How to prove all NP-statements in zero knowledge, and a methodology of cryptographic protocol design", Crypt'86, pp.171-185 (1986)

[KIT87]   Kurosawa, Itoh and Takeuchi: " Public key cryptosystem using a reciprocal number with the same intractability as factoring a large number", Electronics Letters, vol.23, No.15, pp.809-810 (1987), CRYPTOLOGIA, vol.XII, No.4, pp.225-233 (1988)

[R80]   Rabin: " Probabilistic algorithms in finite fields", SIAM J. Comput. 9, pp.273-280 (1980)

[TW87]   Tompa and Woll: " Random self reducibility and zero knowledge interactive proofs of possession of information", FOCS, pp.472-482 (1987)

Publicly Verifiable Non-Interactive Zero-Knowledge Proofs

Dror Lapidot   Adi Shamir

Department of Applied Mathematics

The Weizmann Institute of Science

Rehovot, Israel

Abstract

In this paper we construct the first publicly verifiable non-interactive zero-knowledge proof for any NP statement under the general assumption that one way permutations exist. If the prover is polynomially bounded then our scheme is based on the stronger assumption that trapdoor permutations exist. In both cases we assume that P and V have a common random string, and use it to prove a single theorem (which may be chosen as a function of the known string).

1 Introduction

The notion of a non-interactive zero-knowledge (NIZK) proof was introduced by [BlFeMi]. It allows a prover to prove in writing (without interaction) any NP-theorem to a polynomially bounded verifier, without revealing any knowledge besides the validity of the theorem, provided that they possess a common random string (such as the $1,000,000$ random digits published by the RAND corporation). These NIZK proofs should be *publicly verifiable* (i.e. checkable by anyone rather than directed at a particular verifier) and zero-knowledge to any coalition of verifiers. Such proofs have important cryptographic applications, such as digital signatures, message authentication (see [BeGo]), and protection of public key cryptosystems against chosen ciphertext attacks (see[NaYu]).

[BlFeMi] and [DeMiPe] describe concrete implementations of this model based on the difficulty of specific computational problems (distinguishing products of two primes from products of three primes or distinguishing quadratic residues from quadratic non residues). Under the assumption that Oblivious Transfer protocols exist, [KiMiOs] and [BeMi] show how after an initial preprocessing stage, the prover can noninteractively prove polynomially many NP-statements, but these proofs are not publicly verifiable and all of them are directed to a particular verifier.

Finally the scheme of [DeMiPe1] and the preliminary scheme we present in section 2 are based on a model in which the prover proves a random theorem in an interactive preprocessing stage and then uses it to prove the actual theorem noninteractively. These two schemes can be implemented using any one-way function.

Our main result in this paper is a publicly verifiable NIZK proof with a common random string, for any NP-theorem, under the general assumption that one-way permutations exist. The protocol remains zero-knowledge even when the theorem is chosen as a function of the random string. If the prover is polynomial time bounded, then our scheme is based on the stronger assumption that trapdoor permutations exist. This is the first known protocol of this type which is not based on the difficulty of specific computational problems.

Our result together with the result of [NaYu] imply that under the general assumption that trapdoor permutations exist, there exists a public key cryptosystem which is provably secure against chosen ciphertext attacks.

The paper is organized in the following way: In Section 2 we present a new construction of NIZK proofs with preprocessing which are as efficient as their interactive counterparts. In Section 3 we describe our main result and in Section 4 we prove its correctness. Section 5 is devoted to several extensions and applications of the main result.

2   A NIZK proof with preprocessing

Consider a prover who wants to prove the Hamiltonicity of an arbitrary graph G with n nodes. We assume that the prover and the verifier can execute a preliminary interactive stage which is independent of G (i.e. at this stage they know that in the non-interactive stage the prover will prove the Hamiltonicity of an n node G, but they don't know which graph it will be). Only after the termination of this interactive stage, they get G and execute the non-interactive move in which the prover sends a written message to the verifier in order to convince him in zero-knowledge that G is Hamiltonian. The verifier is not allowed to ask the prover any questions and should be convinced just by reading this message.

The Basic Step

Let H be a randomly chosen Hamiltonian cycle on n nodes. The adjacency matrix of H is a permutation matrix with a single 1 in each row and column, and a single cycle. Let S be such an adjacency matrix in which each entry is replaced by a string which hides it (for example: by the hard bit construction of [GoLe] or by a probabilistic encryption), so that a polynomially bounded observer cannot determine the locations of the 1's.

Assume now that S is given to P and V, and that P wants to prove to V the Hamiltonicity of some graph G with n nodes. Since P is infinitely powerful, he can recover the original Hamiltonian cycle H from S and determine the permutation π that maps H onto the Hamiltonian cycle of G (i.e., $\pi(H) \subseteq G$). To convince V that G is Hamiltonian, P just sends him (in writing) the permutation π and the original values of all the entries in $\pi(S)$ which do not correspond to edges in G. V accepts the proof iff all the revealed entries are 0, since this implies that the n 1's that remain in $\pi(S)$ correspond to edges of G . The proof is zero knowledge since all the verifier gets is a random permutation and a collection of encryptions of 0's, which can be easily simulated.

The resulting NIZK proof with preprocessing (regardless of whether P is polynomially bounded or not) is executed as follows: In the preliminary interactive stage P sequentially sends k (=security parameter) such random matrices $S_1, S_2, \ldots, S_k$ to V and receives k random bits $b_1, b_2, \ldots, b_k$ from V. In the non-interactive move he reveals all the entries of those S_i's for which $b_i = 0$, and executes the basic step for those S_i for which $b_i = 1$. If all the S_i with $b_i = 0$ are of the appropriate form, V can conclude with high probability that at least one of the other S_i is also proper, in which case G is guaranteed to be Hamiltonian.

In order to compare this protocol to Blum's protocol for Hamiltonicity [Bl], lets recall that in the first move of Blum's scheme P randomly permutes G and sends V the encrypted adjacency matrix of this isomorphic copy. V then sends a random bit to P and according to that bit P either reveals all the entries in the matrix and the permutation, or reveals only the entries which correspond to the edges of the Hamiltonian cycle. Our protocol resembles Blum's protocol, with one major difference: In Blum's protocol all the moves depend on G, while in our protocol only the last move depends on G. As a result, Blum's protocol cannot be split into a preprocessing stage and a non-interactive proof as we did in our protocol.

Remark:

The NIZK proof with preprocessing can be extended to a variety of graph theoretic problems which are satisfied by a single minimal graph (under isomorphism). This family includes: Clique, Graph partition into triangles, Graph partition into cliques (and therefore also Graph coloring), 3-Dimensional Matching etc.

3 A NIZK Proof with A Common Random String

In this section we show that under the assumption that oneway permutations exist, if the prover and the verifier initially share a common random string then the initial preprocessing stage of our protocol can be discarded, yielding a NIZK proof for any NP statement in the original noninteractive model of Blum, Feldman and Micali.

3.1 Definitions

Definition: For any NP language L, Let R_L be the relation which contains all the pairs (x, ω) such that $x \in L$ and ω is a witness for that. $\diamond$

The input of P is a pair of words (x, ω) and the common random string σ whose length is polynomial in the size of x and in the security parameter k.

Notation: $A(x, y, z)$ denotes the output of a probabilistic algorithm A on input (x, y, z).

Definition: A non interactive proof system for an NP language L is a pair of probabilistic algorithms (P, V) (where V is polynomially bounded) satisfying:

1. *Completeness:* $\forall (x, \omega) \in R_L$, $\forall \sigma$ $V(x, \sigma, P(x, \omega, \sigma)) = accept$.

2. *Soundness :* If σ is a random string then the probability of succeeding in proving a false statement is negligible, even if the theorem is chosen by P after seeing σ. Formally:

$$\exists b \ \exists c \ \forall d \ \exists N \ s.t. \ \forall k > N$$

at least $(1 - \frac{1}{k^d})$ of the strings σ of length $|x|^b k^c$ satisfy:

$$\forall x' \notin L \ \forall y \quad V(x', \sigma, y) = reject.$$

Definition: A non-interactive proof system for an NP-language L is zero-knowledge if there exists a random polynomial time simulator M such that for any $(x, \omega) \in R_L$, the two ensembles $(\sigma, P(x, \omega, \sigma))$ and $M(x)$ are polynomially indistinguishable (by nonuniform distinguishers). Formally:

$$\exists M \ s.t. \ \forall D \ \forall (x, \omega) \in R_L \ \forall d$$

$$|Pr(D(M(x)) = 1) - Pr(D(\sigma, P(x, \omega, \sigma)) = 1)| < \frac{1}{k^d}$$

for all sufficiently large k.

The probabilities are taken over the choices of σ and over the coin tosses of P and M.

3.2 Informal Description

Assume that P and V possess a common random string (CRS) and P wants to send V a non-interactive zero-knowledge proof based on the CRS, (rather than on an interactive preprocessing stage) that an arbitrary n node graph G is Hamiltonian. We do this by mapping the CRS into an appropriate sequence of matrices which contain with high probability at least one Hamiltonian matrix. P can then proceed exactly as in the final non-interactive step of the protocol described in Section 2.

How can P construct such matrices? It is possible to get a sequence of hidden random bits from the CRS by calculating an appropriate hard bit of a one-way permutation with respect to each segment of it. But if we naively pack such a block of n^2 hidden random bits into a $n \times n$ 0/1 matrix, the probability that this is a Hamiltonian matrix is exponentially small. Therefore in order to solve this problem we have to transform the CRS into a matrix in a more complicated way.

Assume that the CRS defines a $n^2 \times n^2$ matrix B of zeroes and ones, such that $Pr\{B_{i,j} = 1\} = 1/n^3$ for each (i, j) and this matrix has the same security properties as S. In order to construct a matrix such as S from a given matrix B and to prove that G is Hamiltonian P has to execute the following:

1. If the number of 1's in B is different from n or there exists a row or a column which contains at least two 1's, then P proves this fact by revealing all the entries in B.

2. Otherwise (i.e. B contains a $n \times n$ permutation submatrix), P reveals to V all the entries in the $n^2 - n$ rows and the $n^2 - n$ columns which contain only zeroes, and removes them from B. If the resulting $n \times n$ matrix does not represent a single cycle, P proves this fact to V by revealing all the entries of the remaining matrix.

3. Otherwise (i.e. the remaining matrix represents a single cycle), the original matrix B is called good and P must use the resulting $n \times n$ matrix in the execution of the protocol described in the previous section.

What's left is to show how to transform the CRS into B and to prove that such a matrix is good with sufficiently high probability.

Consider the CRS as a concatenation of polynomially many blocks of k random bits. Let f be a one way permutation that both P and V can evaluate but only P can invert. [GoLe] prove the existence of a hard bit in any one way function. Therefore if we associate such a hard bit with each block of the CRS, we get a new hidden random string (HRS). More precisely, let r' and r'' be two consecutive blocks of k bits in the CRS, let $x = f^{-1}(r')$ and $y = r''$ and let s be the hidden random bit defined by the scalar product of the boolean vectors x, y. This process transforms the sequence of blocks in the CRS into a sequence of hidden random bits.

All we have to show is how to transform the HRS into a sequence of matrices such as B. Consider the HRS as a concatenation of polynomially many consecutive blocks of m bits where $m = log(n^3)$ (w.l.g. we can assume that it is an integer). We interpret a block as 1 if all its m bits are 1 and 0 otherwise, and thus we can pack each consecutive segment of $n^4 m$ hidden random bits into the desired $n^2 \times n^2$ 0/1 matrix B discussed above. In Section 4.2 we prove that the probability that such a matrix is good is $\frac{1}{poly(n)}$, and therefore if the length of the CRS is large enough (polynomial in k and n) then with high probability at least one of the segments defines a Hamiltonian matrix for which P must executes the basic step described in section 2.

In order to formally describe the scheme (which is slightly more efficient than the informal scheme described above) and prove its correctness we introduce some notations and definitions.

3.3 Notations and Definitions

Let $r_1 \circ r_2 \circ \ldots \circ r_{poly(k,n)}$ (where $r_l \in_R \{0,1\}$ for each l, and $\circ$ denotes concatenation) be the common random string (CRS), shared by P and V. Let f be a one-way permutation whose definition is known to both of them. Let $u_1 \circ u_2 \circ \ldots \circ u_{poly(k,n)}$ (where $u_i \in \{0,1\}$ for each i) be an intermediate random string (IRS) which is defined as follows: For each $j \geq 1$,

$$f(x_{j,1}) = y_{j,1} \quad and \quad x_{j,2} = y_{j,2}$$

where:

$$x_{j,1} = u_{2k(j-1)+1} \circ u_{2k(j-1)+2} \circ \ldots \circ u_{2k(j-1)+k}$$

$$x_{j,2} = u_{2k(j-1)+k+1} \circ u_{2k(j-1)+k+2} \circ \ldots \circ u_{2kj}$$

$$y_{j,1} = r_{2k(j-1)+1} \circ r_{2k(j-1)+2} \circ \ldots \circ r_{2k(j-1)+k}$$

$$y_{j,2} = r_{2k(j-1)+k+1} \circ r_{2k(j-1)+k+2} \circ \ldots \circ r_{2kj}.$$

Let $s_1 \circ s_2 \circ \ldots \circ s_{poly(k,n)/2k}$ be the hidden random string (HRS) which is defined as follows: for each $j \geq 1$, s_j is the scalar product of the boolean vectors $x_{j,1}$ and $x_{j,2}$. This construction is based the theorem of [GoLe] which says that, according to these notations, given random $y_{j,1}$ and $y_{j,2}$, s_j is a hard bit.

For each $i \geq 1$ let a_i be such that its binary representation is $s_{(i-1)m+1} \circ s_{(i-1)m+2} \circ \ldots \circ s_{im}$. Lets define for each i:

$$b_i = \begin{cases} 1 & \text{if } a_i = 2^m - 1 \\ 0 & \text{otherwise} \end{cases}$$

Let B_i be a $n^2 \times n^2$ matrix which is defined as follows: $B_i(j,l) = b_{(i-1)n^4+(j-1)n^2+l}$ for every $1 \leq i,j,l$.

Definition: We say that B_i is a *proper* matrix if it contains exactly n ones and each column and row contains at most a single one.

If B_i is a proper matrix let N_i be the $n \times n$ matrix obtained by removing all the $n^2 - n$ columns and $n^2 - n$ rows which contain only zeroes. Otherwise N_i is undefined.

Definition: We say that N_i is a Hamiltonian matrix if there is a permutation $\psi \in S_n$ with a single cycle such that for each $N_i(l,j)$ which is equal to 1 $j = \psi(l)$. In this case we say that B_i is a good matrix.

3.4 The Scheme

Assume that P and V have a CRS with $2n^7 km$ bits and a common one-way permutation f.

P's protocol:

For each $1 \leq i \leq n^3$ do the following:

1. If B_i contains more than n ones then reveal $n+1$ of them.

2. If B_i contains fewer than n ones then reveal all the entries.

3. If there is a column or row which contains two ones then reveal the two entries.

4. (B_i is a proper matrix) Reveal and remove all the $n^2 - n$ columns and all the $n^2 - n$ rows which contain only zeroes. If N_i is not a Hamiltonian matrix then reveal the n ones. Otherwise use N_i in the execution of the protocol described in section 2.

V's protocol:

For each $1 \leq i \leq n^3$ do the following:

1. If P reveals $n + 1$ entries then check that all of them are 1.

2. If P reveals all the entries then check that B_i contains fewer than n ones.

3. If P reveals two entries then check that both of them are 1 and in the same column or row.

4. If P reveals $n^2 - n$ columns and $n^2 - n$ rows then check that all the entries in these rows and columns are zeroes.

5. If P reveals n entries then check that all of them are 1 and N_i is not a Hamiltonian matrix.

6. Otherwise check that the protocol described in Section 2 is carried out correctly.

Accept the proof iff for each $1 \leq i \leq n^3$ one of these checks is successful.

3.5   NIZK Proof for Some Other NP-Statements

The same technique can be used (without reductions) to prove other NP-Complete statements. Consider for example the 3-Dimensional Matching ($3DM$) problem. Each instance of the problem is a 3-dimensional 0/1 matrix M ($n \times n \times n$) and P's goal is to prove that there are n ones in M such that no two of them agree in any coordinate.

Consider each block in the CRS as a hidden random 3-dimensional 0/1 matrix whose size is $n^2 \times n^2 \times n^2$ and set the probability of 1 at each entry to $1/n^5$. The same proof technique implies that with high probability there is a block in the CRS which hides a good matrix B, namely a matrix with exactly n ones such that no two of them agree in any coordinate. P reveals all the 2-dimensional submatrices of B which contain only zeroes so that the remaining $n \times n \times n$ hidden matrix N forms a random minimal example for 3-dimensional matching.

To prove that a given M contains a 3D matching, P sends to V the permutation that moves the n ones in N to the locations of the matching in M, and then proves that every 0 in M corresponds to a zero in the permuted N.

4   Correctness

4.1   Completeness

The non-interactive proof of Hamiltonicity is complete because in every $n^2 \times n^2$ matrix that does not yield a Hamiltonian matrix, all P has to do is to open some of its entries, and V will accept his proof as valid.

4.2 Soundness

Lemma : The probability that B_i contains exactly n 1's is $\geq 1/3n$, for every i.
Proof : The bits of the HRS are unbiased and independent, and for each j the probability that $b_j = 1$ is $1/n^3$. Therefore the expected number of 1's in B_i is n. If x denotes the number of 1's then Chebyshev's Inequality implies that

$$Pr\{|x - n| > n\} < \frac{Var(x)}{n^2} = \frac{n^4 n^{-3}(1 - n^{-3})}{n^2} < n^{-1}$$

therefore

$$\sum_{i=0}^{2n} Pr\{x = i\} > 1 - n^{-1}.$$

Since the maximal probability is at $x = n$

$$Pr\{x = n\} > \frac{1 - n^{-1}}{2n + 1} > 1/3n \quad \square$$

The size of B_i is $n^2 \times n^2$ and therefore by the birthday paradox if B_i contains exactly n 1's then the probability that each row and each column contains at most one 1, is a constant.
The number of permutations in S_n which consist of a single cycle (of length n) is $(n - 1)!$, therefore the probability that N_i is a Hamiltonian matrix, given that it is a permutation matrix, is n^{-1}.
We conclude that, for every i, the probability that B_i yields a Hamiltonian matrix N_i is $\geq dn^{-2}$, where d is a constant. Thus if the length of the CRS is $O(n^7 km)$ bits then with probability $(1 - e^{-n})$ at least one of the B_i's yields a Hamiltonian matrix. Any such matrix will expose a cheating P.
Remark: If $log(n^3)$ is not an integer, we have to set $m = \lceil log(n^3) \rceil$ and choose B_i as a $\lceil bn^2 \rceil \times n^2$ matrix where $b = \frac{2^m}{n^3}$ $(1 < b < 2)$.

4.3 Zero-Knowledge

In order to simplify the proof of zero-knowledge we refer only to the informal scheme described in (3.1). We construct a random polynomial time simulator M which generates a "random string" and a "proof" of Hamiltonicity which are polynomially indistinguishable (by nonuniform distinguishers) from those generated by a real execution of the protocol.
We use the transitivity of the property of indistinguishability: First we construct a random polynomial time algorithm P' (with access to the Hamiltonian cycle of G) whose output is indistinguishable from a truly random string appended to a proof of the real prover, and then we construct a random polynomial time simulator M (who does not know the Hamiltonian cycle) whose output is polynomially indistinguishable from that of P'. Therefore these constructions imply that our scheme is zero-knowledge.

Let P' be the random polynomial time algorithm which executes the real protocol with the following exception: it chooses a sequence of truly random bits (IRS), and then gets the CRS by applying the one-way permutation f in the forward direction. Clearly the output of P' is indistinguishable from that of the real prover.

The simulator M accepts G and the security parameter k as inputs, and outputs a string σ_k of length $2n^7km$ bits and a "proof" in the following way:

1. M randomly chooses a sequence of $2n^7km$ truly random bits and uses them as the intermediate random string (IRS). In every segment that yields a Hamiltonian matrix it randomly changes the interpretation of all the ones to zeroes. More precisely: For each i for which N_i is a Hamiltonian matrix and for each j, l such that $N_i(j, l) = 1$, M randomly and independently chooses $2km$ bits instead of: $u_{((i-1)n^4+(j-1)n^2+(l-1))m2k+1} \cdots u_{((i-1)n^4+(j-1)n^2+l)m2k}$ until $N_i(j, l) = 0$ (the probability of success is $1 - \frac{1}{n^3}$).

2. M transforms the modified IRS into a common random string (CRS) σ_k by applying f in the forward direction and computes the [GoLe] hidden random string (HRS) as the dot product of consecutive pairs of blocks in the IRS.

3. For each i such that B_i has not changed in the first step M reveals all the entries of B_i. For each of the other B_i's it randomly reveals $n^2 - n$ rows and $n^2 - n$ columns. Since the resulting $n \times n$ matrix contains only zeroes, M can easily simulate the basic step by choosing a random permutation $\psi \in_R S_n$ and revealing every $B_i(j, l)$ such that there is no edge between j and l in $\psi(G)$.

The output of M is denoted by $(\sigma_k, proof'(\sigma_k, G))$ where the second component includes all the revealed bits and permutations. Let τ_k be a string of length $2n^7km$ bit, and denote by $proof(\tau_k, G)$ a proof of P' based on G and τ_k.

For any nonuniform distinguisher D, let $D(x)$ denote the 0/1 output of D on input x. Let

$$P_{P,k} = Pr\{D((\tau_k, proof(\tau_k, G)), G) = 1\}$$

$$P_{M,k} = Pr\{D((\sigma_k, proof'(\sigma_k, G)), G) = 1\}.$$

The probabilities are taken over the choices of τ_k and over the coin tosses of P' and M.

Theorem: For any Hamiltonian graph G, for any nonuniform random polynomial time distinguisher D and for any polynomial Q:

$$|P_{P,k} - P_{M,k}| < \frac{1}{Q(k)}$$

for all sufficiently large k.

Proof: Assume that there exists an efficient distinguisher D, a polynomial Q and an infinite subset $\mathcal{I} \subset \mathcal{N}$ such that for every $k \in \mathcal{I}$:

$$(*) \quad |P_{P,k} - P_{M,k}| \geq \frac{1}{Q(k)}.$$

Let k be an element in $\mathcal{I}$. Let $\alpha = (i_1, \ldots, i_t, \psi_1, \ldots, \psi_u)$ $(1 \leq i_1 < \ldots < i_t \leq n^7 m$ and for each $1 \leq i \leq u$ $\psi_i \in S_n$) and let $P_{\alpha,k}$ $(P'_{\alpha,k})$ be the probability that $s_{i_1}, \ldots, s_{i_t}$ are the hidden bits revealed by P' (M) and $\psi_1, \ldots, \psi_u$ are the permutations given by P' (M) (each one associated with a Hamiltonian matrix). Since τ_k is a truly random string, M simulates P' and all the choices of M are random we conclude that for any α:

$$P_{\alpha,k} = P'_{\alpha,k}.$$

Let $proof(\tau_k, G, \alpha)$ and $proof'(\sigma_k, G, \alpha)$ denote proofs of P' and M based on τ_k and σ_k respectively, in which the revealed bits and the random permutations are according to α. It is obvious that in the case of P', once τ is chosen, α is fixed. Denote by $P_{P,\alpha,k}$ the probability that D outputs 1 on the input $(\tau_k, proof(\tau_k, G, \alpha))$ (while τ is a truly random string) and by $P_{M,\alpha,k}$ the probability that D outputs 1 on input $(\sigma_k, proof'(\sigma_k, G, \alpha))$.
It is obvious that

$$(**) \quad P_{P,k} = \sum_\alpha P_{\alpha,k} P_{P,\alpha,k}$$

and

$$(***) \quad P_{M,k} = \sum_\alpha P_{\alpha,k} P_{M,\alpha,k}.$$

The following Lemma claims that for any α, D is unable to distinguish between $(\tau_k, proof(\tau_k, G, \alpha))$ and $(\sigma_k, proof'(\sigma_k, G, \alpha))$.

Lemma: For every α

$$|P_{P,\alpha,k} - P_{M,\alpha,k}| < \frac{1}{Q(k)}.$$

Proof: Assume that this is not true, namely there is α for which w.l.g.

$$P_{P,\alpha,k} - P_{M,\alpha,k} \geq \frac{1}{Q(k)}.$$

For every $1 \leq j \leq n^7 m$, $P^j_{P/M,\alpha,k}$ denotes the probability that D outputs 1 on the following (string, proof): The first $2k(j-1)$ bits in the string are randomly chosen (a prefix of a real CRS) and associated with a proof of P' until that point, while all the other bits and the rest of the proof are generated by M and both of these parts follow the vector α. Following the well known Hybrid argument of [GoMi] we conclude that there is $1 \leq i \leq n^7 m$ for which :

$$P^{i+1}_{P/M,\alpha,k} - P^i_{P/M,\alpha,k} \geq \frac{1}{Q(k)n^7 m} \ .$$

From the description of P' and M we conclude that i is the index of one of the hidden bits of one of the appearances of $\underbrace{1, 1, \ldots, 1}_{m}$ in a segment which defines a Hamiltonian matrix in the simulation of P'. We'll construct a random polynomial time nonuniform algorithm C_k whose auxiliary input is the graph G, including the definition of a Hamiltonian cycle, α and i which on input $(f(x), y)$ (x, y are randomly chosen) outputs a bit b which is the hard bit of $(f(x),y)$ with probability $\geq \frac{1}{2}+\frac{1}{poly(k)}$. This is a contradiction to the assumption that f is one-way. This algorithm uses P', M and D as subroutines and executes the following steps:

1. Run P' so that the indices of the hidden bits which are revealed and the permutations associated with the Hamiltonian matrices are according to α.

2. Run M according to the same rule.

3. Erase from the output of P' all the bits coming after the $(i-1)$'th block, namely remain with the first $2(i-1)k$ bits of the string appending the revealed bits and the permutations associated with the Hamiltonian matrices (call this prefix S_P).

4. Erase from the output of M the first i blocks, namely remain with the last $2n^7km - 2ik$ bits of the string appending the revealed bits and the permutations associated with the Hamiltonian matrices (call this suffix S_M).

5. Feed D with $S_P \circ f(x) \circ y \circ S_M$.

6. If $D(S_P \circ f(x) \circ y \circ S_M) = 1$ then $b = 1$ else $b = 0$.

It is easy to verify that with probability $\geq \frac{1}{2} + \frac{1}{poly(k)}$, b is the hard bit of $(f(x),y)$ and this is a contradiction to the assumption that f is one-way. $\square$

This lemma together with $(**)$ and $(***)$ contradicts $(*)$ which completes the proof of the theorem. $\square$

Remark: Consider an NP-statement which is polynomially chosen as a function of the random string namely, there is a nonuniform random polynomial time algorithm which gets a random string and outputs an NP-statement (which is a function of it) including an appropriate witness.

The simulator generates the "random string" independently of the NP-theorem. Therefore considering the construction of the appropriate C_k, we conclude that:

Corollary: Our non-interactive proof remains zero-knowledge even if the NP-statement (of size n) is polynomially chosen as a function of the common random string.

5 Extensions and Applications

5.1 A Polynomial Time Prover

If the prover is polynomial time bounded then our scheme is based on the stronger assumption that trapdoor permutations exist. In fact, we assume that for every security parameter there exists an exponentially large family of trapdoor permutations whose indices are n^c bit strings (c is constant). The only difference from the scheme described in section 3 is that now P randomly chooses a trapdoor permutation f from that family, sends its index to V and keeps the trapdoor information secret. Now the ability of P to invert f is implied by his knowledge of the trapdoor. The proof of completeness remains unchanged, but there might be a problem with the soundness: In contrast to the scheme described in section 3 in which the (unbounded) prover does not choose the one-way permutation, in this scheme a cheating prover may choose a particularly useful trapdoor permutation after seeing the CRS. To overcome this difficulty, we only have to extend the CRS: If the number of bits in it is $O(n^{6+c}km)$ then the probability of cheating in our scheme is at most $O(\frac{2n^c}{e^{n^c}})$ since this is an upper bound on the fraction of random strings which can be bad for any trapdoor permutation.

The proof of the zero-knowledge property resembles its counterpart for the original scheme, except that we have to consider all the choices of trapdoor permutations.

5.2 Public-Key Cryptosystems Secure against Chosen Ciphertext Attacks

The existence of public-key cryptosystems which are secure against passive eavesdropping under the assumption that trapdoor permutations exist is well known. [NaYu] show how to construct a public-key cryptosystem which is provably secure against chosen ciphertext attacks (CCS-PKC), given a public-key cryptosystem which is secure against passive eavesdropping and a non-interactive zero-knowledge proof system in the shared string model. Using their result together with our construction (for polynomial time provers) we have:

Corollary: CCS-PKC exist under the general assumption that trapdoor permutations exist.

This is the first known CCS-PKC which is not based on the difficulty of specific computational problems.

5.3 Multiple NIZK Proofs

We have to emphasize that our scheme is a bounded NIZK proof system in the sense that using a random string, the prover can prove in zero-knowledge only a single theorem. Recently, Feige, Lapidot and Shamir [FeLaSh] have shown how to transform any bounded NIZK proof system with polynomial time provers into a general NIZK proof system in which polynomially many independent provers can share the same random string and use it to prove polynomially many statements of polynomial length in a completely memoryless way.

References

[BeGo]   M. Bellare, and S. Goldwasser, *New Paradigms for Digital Signatures and Message Authentication Based on Non-Interactive Zero-Knowledge Proofs.* CRYPTO 89.

[BeMi]   M. Bellare, and S. Micali, *Non-Interactive Oblivious Transfer and Applications*. CRYPTO 89.

[Bl]   M. Blum, a presentation in the 1986 International Congress of Mathematics.

[BDMP]   M.Blum, A. De Santis, S. Micali and G. Persiano, *Non-Interactive Zero-Knowledge* , Manuscript, December 1989.

[BlFeMi] M. Blum, P. Feldman, and S. Micali, *Non-Interactive Zero-Knowledge Proof Systems and Applications*, Proceedings of the 20th Annual ACM Symposium on Theory of Computing, 1988.

[DeMiPe] A. De Santis, S. Micali, and G. Persiano, *Non-Interactive Zero-Knowledge Proof Systems*, CRYPTO 87.

[DeMiPe1] A. De Santis, S. Micali, and G. Persiano, *Non-Interactive Zero-Knowledge with Preprocessing*, CRYPTO 88.

[FeLaSh] U. Feige, D. Lapidot and A. Shamir, *Multiple Non-Interactive Zero Knowledge Proofs Based on a Single Random String.* FOCS 90.

[FeSh]   U. Feige, and A. Shamir, *Zero-Knowledge Proofs of Knowledge in Two Rounds.* CRYPTO 89.

[GoLe]   O. Goldreich, L.A. Levin, *A Hard-Core Predicate for all One-Way Functions.* STOC 89.

[GoMiWi] O. Goldreich, S. Micali, and A. Wigderson, *Proofs that Yield Nothing But Their Validity and a Methodology of Cryptographic Protocol Design .* Proc. 27th FOCS, 1986.

[GoMi]   S. Goldwasser, and S. Micali *Probabilistic Encryption*, Journal of Computer and System Sciences 28, 1984

[GoMiRa] S. Goldwasser, S. Micali, and C. Rackoff, *The Knowledge Complexity of Interactive Proofs.* STOC 85.

[KiMiOs] J. Kilian, S. Micali, and R. Ostrovsky, *Minimum Resource Zero-Knowledge Proofs.*, FOCS 89.

[NaYu]   M. Naor, M.Yung, *Public-key Cryptosystems Provably Secure Against Chosen Ciphertext Attacks* , Proc. of STOC 90.

Cryptographic Applications of the Non-Interactive Metaproof and Many-prover Systems

Alfredo De Santis*

Dipartimento di Informatica ed Applicazioni

Università di Salerno

84081 Baronissi (Salerno), Italy

Moti Yung

IBM Research Division

T. J. Watson Research Center

Yorktown Heights, NY 10598

Preliminary Version

Abstract

In a companion paper [DeYu] we have developed the tool of non-interactive proof-system we call "Metaproof" (μ-NIZK proof system); this provides a proof of "the existence of a proof to a statement". Using a reduction of the theorem to a set of claims about encrypted values, enabled us to develop a crucial proof-system property which we called "on-line simulatable NIZK proof-system". This was used to implement the "Many-Prover Non-Interactive Proof-System" where independent users can send proofs (which was not known in the original system and was open), and a "Self-Referential NIZK proof system" where the random reference string is available to the polynomial-time opponent who chooses the theorem to prove, (this was an intriguing question regarding such systems).

In this abstract we present an introduction to the basic tools and their possible applications. The subject of this paper is a variety of cryptographic applications provided by the new tools. We demonstrate its applicability in enhancing security and properties of a methodology for signature and authentication developed by Bellare and Goldwasser [BeGo] (by using the Metaproof system to solve the open problem of many-prover NIZK system). We also show, among other things, how the tools can be used to provide security mechanisms such as an "Oblivious Warden" which translates non-interactive proofs to random ones independently of the proof itself, and the notion of "Gradual opening of a zero-knowledge computation" which is first demonstrated to be correct using a non-interactive proof, and then is opened gradually and fast (i.e., without further proofs).

---

*Part of this work was done while the author was visiting IBM Research Division, T. J. Watson Research Ctr, Yorktown Heights, NY 10598.

1 Introduction

The development of zero-knowledge proof-systems introduced by Goldwasser, Micali, and Rackoff [GoMiRa] has revolutionized the field of cryptographic primitives and protocols design. Designing of basic primitives was made possible and proving security was made easy.

Two very useful notions of zero-knowledge proofs were given: interactive proofs (ZKIP) [GoMiRa, GoMiWi1, ImYu] and non-interactive proofs (NIZK) (introduced by Blum, Feldman, and Micali) [BlFeMi, DeMiPe1, BlDeMiPe]. Next we evaluate the current relative advantages and shortcomings of the two notions.

In the non-interactive model indeed interaction was shown not to be a necessary ingredient of zero-knowledge proofs. It was replaced by a shared public (short) string of random bits. The motivation for such a model is the availability of public random sources. For instance, a community in which everyone possess (in the local library) a copy of the same tables of random numbers prepared by RAND corporation, the RAND tables. NIZK is a new tool which is not well-understood yet and many more questions regarding the possibility of NIZK proof-systems are intriguing questions, we have recently solved some of them [DeYu]. In this work we present applications of the new tools.

Our results:

In [DeYu], we have introduced two new non-interactive tools. The first one is a "Metaproof system". A meta-proof in terms of proof-theory is *a proof that there is a proof for a theorem*. Indeed the development of deductive systems and the notion of system which proves theorem and then another logical metasystem which proves theorems about theorems, is one of the major development of foundations of mathematics in the last century. However, for a language in $\mathcal{NP}$, in the usual sense a proof of an existence of a proof is just another way (possibly a weird one) to claim that the original theorem is in the language by claiming that there is a proof for it. Nevertheless, in the context of the theory of zero-knowledge proofs, we will show that this way of proving the existence of a proof is a very useful tool. One implication of the tool is an implementation of the Many-prover NIZK (MP-NIZK), an extension of NIZK to many users, which was an open question.

This work presents a variety of applications of μ-NIZK and MP-NIZK in typical cryptographic settings. We present applications to encryption and signature schemes, and numerous cryptographic protocols and other primitives.

Among our applications are extensions and improvements of the very nice set of cryptographic applications suggested by the paradigm of Bellare and Goldwasser [BeGo], who showed how combining pseudo-random functions, encryptions, and zero-knowledge proofs gives signature and similar primitives. We show how to implement such notions as history-independent signature schemes, and ID distribution in the context of identification schemes, with security as high as the encryption functions and the non-interactive zero-knowledge proofs involved.

Another application is in the domain of resource abuse prevention. An *Oblivious Warden* whose task is to eliminate abuses of a channel [De]. Our tool eliminates additional (illegal) information embedded in a messages which is sent as non-interactive proofs. The warden changes the message while maintaining the semantics of the proof.

Meta-proofs can be nested. We note that the Meta-proof sequencing and nesting property shows that the metaproof is more than just an indirect proof of a theorem, a property which helps in achieving the MP-NIZK (in this sense this is similar to [FeLaSh]). However, the Meta-proof notion is also a tool for combining proofs and enables the forwarding of a proof based on a zero-knowledge witness rather than the "real" witness itself which gives the flexibility which is the strength behind some of our applications. In this paper we mainly present these applications.

2 Preliminaries

Next, we present the necessary background: the basic definitions, bounded NIZK, and encryption functions.

2.1 Basic definitions.

A sequence of probabilistic Turing machines $\{T_n\}_{n \in \mathcal{N}}$ is an *efficient non-uniform algorithm* if there exists a positive constant c such that, for all sufficiently large n, T_n halts in expected n^c and the size of its program is $\leq n^c$. We use efficient non-uniform algorithms to gain the power of using different Turing machines for different input lengths. For instance, T_n can be used for inputs of length n. The power of non-uniformity lies in the fact that each Turing machine in the sequence may have "wired-in" (i.e. properly encoded in its program) a small amount of special information about its own input length.

If $A(\cdot)$ is a probabilistic algorithm, then for any input x, the notation $A(x)$ refers to the probability space that assigns to the string σ the probability that A, on input x, outputs σ. Notice that we do not mention explicitly the random coins used by probabilistic algorithms.

If $p(\cdot, \cdot, \cdots)$ is a predicate, the notation $Pr(x \xleftarrow{R} S; y \xleftarrow{R} T; \ldots : p(x, y, \cdots))$ denotes the probability that $p(x, y, \cdots)$ will be true after the ordered execution of the algorithms $x \xleftarrow{R} S$, $y \xleftarrow{R} T$, ...

The notation $\{x \xleftarrow{R} S; y \xleftarrow{R} T; \cdots : (x, y, \cdots)\}$ denotes the probability space over $\{(x, y, \cdots)\}$ generated by the ordered execution of the algorithms $x \xleftarrow{R} S$, $y \xleftarrow{R} T$, $\cdots$.

A notion which is important in our context is *"a history-insensitive algorithm"*. A probabilistic Turing machine R has *one-way input tape, one-way output tape, one-way random tape*, and a regular *work tape*. A one-way tape is a tape in which after each read/write operation the head moves, always from left to right. R is called a history-insensitive algorithm if it works as follows. First, after copying the input to its work tape, R produces the output and writes it on the output tape. Then, R erases its work tape and returns to its initial state, without backtracking the one-way heads.

2.2 Bounded Non-Interactive Zero-knowledge Proof Systems

Bounded NIZK proof systems were conceived by Blum, Feldman, and Micali, and were presented in [BlFeMi], [DeMiPe1], and [BlDeMiPe]. The term "Bounded" refers to the fact that the proof system is defined for a single theorem or a few "short" theorems. Without loss of generality we use a complete language in $\mathcal{NP}$: $3SAT$ [Co].

Definition 2.1 Let A_1 and A_2 be Turing Machines. We say that (A_1, A_2) is a *sender-receiver* pair if their computation on a *common input* x works as follows. First, algorithm A_1, on input x, outputs a string (message) m_x. Then, algorithm A_2, computes on inputs x and m_x and outputs ACCEPT or REJECT. A_1 is called the sender and A_2 the receiver. The running times of both machines is calculated in terms of the common input.

Definition 2.2 Let $(Prover, Verifier)$ be a sender-receiver pair, where *Prover* is history-insensitive and *Verifier* is polynomial-time. We say that $(Prover, Verifier)$, is a Bounded Non-Interactive Zero-Knowledge Proof System (Bounded NIZK proof system) for $3SAT$ if there exists a positive constant c such that:

1. *Completeness.* $\forall \Phi \in 3SAT$ and satisfying assignments t,

$$Pr(\sigma \xleftarrow{R} \{0,1\}^{n^c}; Proof \xleftarrow{R} Prover(\sigma, \Phi, t) : Verifier(\sigma, \Phi. Proof) = 1) = 1.$$

2. *Soundness.* For all probabilistic algorithms *Adversary* outputting pairs $(\Phi, Proof)$, where $\Phi \notin 3SAT_n$, $\forall d > 0$, and all sufficiently large n,

$$Pr(\sigma \xleftarrow{R} \{0,1\}^{n^c}; (\Phi, Proof) \xleftarrow{R} Adversary(\sigma) : Verifier(\sigma, \Phi, Proof) = 1) < n^{-d}.$$

3. *Zero-Knowledge.* There exists an efficient algorithm S such that $\forall \Phi \in 3SAT_n$, for all satisfying assignments t for Φ, for all efficient non-uniform (distinguishing) algorithms D, $\forall d > 0$, and all sufficiently large n,

$$\left| Pr(s \xleftarrow{R} View(n, \Phi, t) : D_n(s) = 1) - Pr(s \xleftarrow{R} S(1^n, \Phi) : D_n(s) = 1) \right| < n^{-d},$$

where

$$View(n, \Phi, t) = \{\sigma \xleftarrow{R} \{0,1\}^{n^c}; Proof \xleftarrow{R} Prover(\sigma, \Phi, t) : (\sigma, Proof)\}.$$

We call algorithm S the *Simulator*.

A sender–receiver pair (*Prover*, *Verifier*) is a Bounded Non-Interactive Proof System for $3SAT$ if there exists a positive constant c such that completeness and soundness hold (such a c will be referred as the *constant* of (*Prover*, *Verifier*)).
We call the "common" random string σ, input to both *Prover* and *Verifier*, the *reference string*. (Above σ and Φ are the common input.)
In the above definition, there is no limitation on the running time of *Prover*. In cryptographic applications it is required that the prover be expected polynomial time. A Bounded NIZK proof system (*Prover*, *Verifier*) with an efficient prover is a Bounded NIZK proof system where *Prover* on any common input (i.e. a reference string and a formula) runs in expected polynomial time. Recently, it was shown how to base bounded non-interactive system on any one-way permutation [LaSh, FeLaSh].

2.3 Non-Interactive Encryption Tools

We have developed two encryption tools. First, we have shown that *secure probabilistic encryption scheme* exists in the non-interactive model, based on any one way function. (We use Naor's bit-commitment protocol [Na]). Next, an *ambiguous encryption* is possible in the model, based on a one-way function; it is a good bit encryption method in the model which can be simulated to be opened as both bits!

3 Review: New Non-Interactive Proof Systems

We next describe the recent non-interactive systems we have designed.

3.1 Metaproofs

Roughly speaking, the "metaproof of a theorem T" is a NIZK proof that "there is a NIZK proof of T". Assume that, for a formula Φ, there is a NIZK proof pf computed using a reference string σ_1. The *metaprover* μP on input a formula Φ and pf, computes a NIZK proof *Metaproof* using a different reference string σ_2, that there is indeed a string pf such that *Verifier* would accept as proof of Φ. The *metaverifier* μV checks that *Metaproof* has been correctly computed, but has no access whatsoever to pf.

More formally, let (*Prover, Verifier*) be a Bounded NIZK proof system for $3SAT$. Next, let $Prover(\sigma, \Phi, t)$ be an efficient *Prover*'s program that uses σ as its reference string and the satisfying assignment t to prove $\Phi \in 3SAT_n$. Thus, there is a constant $c > 0$ such that on input $r \in \{0,1\}^{n^c}$, $\Phi \in 3SAT_n$, and a satisfying assignment t, *Prover* computes a string pf, $|pf| \leq n^c$, such that $Verifier(r, \Phi, pf) = 1$. Let $L = \bigcup_n L(n)$ be the language where

$$L(n) = \{(r, \Phi) : |r| = n^c,\ \Phi \in 3SAT_n,\ \text{and } \exists pf, |pf| \leq n^c \text{ such that } Verifier(r, \Phi, pf) = 1\}.$$

Then $\Phi \in 3SAT_n$ iff $(r, \Phi) \in L(n)$ for all strings r. Moreover $L \in \mathcal{NP}$ and thus there is a fixed polynomial-time computable reduction $REDUCE$ such that

$$(r, \Phi) \in L(n) \iff \Psi = REDUCE(r, \Phi) \in 3SAT_{n^b},$$

where $b > 0$ is a fixed constant depending only on the reduction $REDUCE$. More precisely, the formula Ψ is obtained by encoding the computation of *Verifier* on input r, Φ, pf as in Cook's Theorem, and then reducing it to a 3-satisfiable formula, as in [Co]. A well known property of this reduction is that to each "witness" pf one can associate in polynomial-time a satisfying assignment α for Ψ. We call $Witness(r, \Phi, pf)$ the poly-time procedure that returns the satisfying assignment α for $\Psi = REDUCE(r, \Phi)$.

Now, we describe the programs for the metaprover $\mu P(\cdot, \cdot, \cdot)$ and the metaverifier $\mu V(\cdot, \cdot)$.

The sender–receiver pair $(\mu P, \mu V)$

Input to μP and μV:

- A random string $\sigma_1 \circ \sigma_2$, where $|\sigma_1| = n^c$ and $|\sigma_2| = n^{bc}$.

- $\Phi \in 3SAT_n$.

Instructions for μP

Private Input: a string pf such that $Verifier(\sigma_1, \Phi, pf) = 1$.

$\mu P.1$ Compute $\Psi = REDUCE(\sigma_1, \Phi)$ and $\alpha = Witness(\sigma_1, \Phi, pf)$.

$\mu P.2$ Run $Prover(\sigma_2, \Psi, \alpha)$. Call *Metaproof* the output and send it to μV.

Instructions for μV

Input from μP: a string *Metaproof.*

$\mu V.0$ Compute n from $\sigma_1 \circ \sigma_2$.

Verify that Φ has at most n clauses with 3 literals each. If not, REJECT.

$\mu V.1$ Compute the formula $\Psi = REDUCE(\sigma_1, \Phi)$.

$\mu V.2$ If $Verifier(\sigma_2, \Psi, Metaproof) = 1$ then ACCEPT. Else, REJECT.

We formally prove in [DeYu] that the metaproof system $(\mu P, \mu V)$ above is a Bounded NIZK proof system for $3SAT$. Indeed, the tool does not seem to help, especially since the meta-prover need not be more than an efficient program. However, this intuition is wrong.

3.2 Theorem Translation and On-line Simulation

The original notion of Bounded-NIZK was defined to be zero-knowledge by exhibiting a simulator which generates transcripts of reference strings and proofs which a polynomial machine cannot tell apart from real proofs. The simulator was defined as a machine which first gets the theorem to be proved and then starts the computation. Next we define and implement a simulator which works in a different mode. In a preprocessing stage the processor prepares a prefix of a simulation (the reference string); when given a theorem, the simulated proof with respect to the reference string is generated.

This fashion of simulation resembles ideas presented in simulations in [DeMiPe2, ImYu]. It is not clear that it is a stronger definition, however, this simulation mode will be instrumental in constructing a many-provers NIZK proof system using metaproofs.

Definition 3.1 Let $(Prover, Verifier)$ be a Bounded NIZK proof system for $3SAT$. A simulator $M(\cdot, \cdot)$ for $(Prover, Verifier)$ is an *on-line simulator* if it consists of a pair of efficient algorithms $M = (M_1, M_2)$ that work as follows: First it gets as input 1^n and it compute: $(\sigma, state) \xleftarrow{R} M_1(1^n)$. Then it gets as second input: $x \in 3SAT_n$ and it computes $Proof \xleftarrow{R} M_2(state, x)$. It outputs: $(\sigma, Proof)$.

A Bounded NIZK proof system for $3SAT$ is *on-line simulatable* if it has an on-line simulator.

Theorem Translation: an overview of the construction.

The idea is to prepare a machinery for the proof based on ciphertexts of an encryption function in an off line fashion, independently of the proof. That is, the statement of the proof is reduced to claims about certain encrypted values. In the simulation the public string can therefore be prepared independently of the theorem to be proved. This enables the on-line simulatable proof-system as the public string is independent of the proof itself. The idea can be viewed as a bootstrapping method on the usual method of hiding part of the proof using encryption which is usually done in ZKIP and NIZK systems which rely on encryption (e.g., [GoMiWi1]). More details are given in [DeYu]

3.3 Many-provers Non-Interactive Zero-knowledge Proof Systems

Consider a scenario in which we have many independent provers, using the same random string σ to prove different theorems. For instance, a scientific community in which all libraries possess copies of the same tables of random numbers prepared by RAND corporation, the RAND tables. This is essentially a short string *shared* by the scientific community. Can they use the RAND tables to give one another Non-Interactive Zero-Knowledge Proofs? (see [DeMiPe1]) A many-provers NIZK proof system is a solution to this problem.

Definition 3.2 Let (*Prover, Verifier*) be a sender–receiver pair, where *Prover* is history-insensitive and *Verifier* is polynomial time. We say that (*Prover, Verifier*) is a Many-provers Non-Interactive Zero-Knowledge Proof System (MP-NIZK proof system) if the following 3 conditions hold.

1. *Completeness.* $\forall \Phi \in 3SAT$, and for all satisfying assignments t for Φ,

$$Pr\left(\sigma \xleftarrow{R} \{0,1\}^n; Proof \xleftarrow{R} Prover(\sigma, \Phi, t) : Verifier(\sigma, \Phi, Proof) = 1\right) = 1.$$

2. *Soundness.* For all probabilistic algorithms *Adversary* outputting pairs $(\Phi', Proof')$, where $\Phi' \notin 3SAT$, $\forall d > 0$, and all sufficiently large n,

$$Pr\left(\sigma \xleftarrow{R} \{0,1\}^n; (\Phi', Proof') \xleftarrow{R} Adversary(\sigma) : Verifier(\sigma, \Phi', Proof') = 1\right) < n^{-d}.$$

3. *Zero-Knowledge.* There exists an efficient algorithm S such that $\forall \Phi_1, \Phi_2, \ldots \in 3SAT$, for all satisfying assignments $t_1, t_2, \ldots$, for all efficient non-uniform algorithms D, $\forall d > 0$, and all sufficiently large n,

$$\left| Pr(s \xleftarrow{R} View(n, \Phi_1, t_1, \Phi_2, t_2, \ldots) : D_n(s) = 1) - Pr(s \xleftarrow{R} S(1^n, \Phi_1, \Phi_2, \ldots) : D_n(s) = 1) \right| < n^{-d}$$

where

$$View(n, \Phi_1, t_1, \Phi_2, t_2, \ldots) = \Big\{ \sigma \xleftarrow{R} \{0,1\}^n; \quad Proof_1 \xleftarrow{R} Prover(\sigma, \Phi_1, t_1);$$
$$Proof_2 \xleftarrow{R} Prover(\sigma, \Phi_2, t_2);$$
$$\vdots$$
$$: (\sigma, Proof_1, Proof_2, \ldots) \Big\}.$$

We call *Simulator* the algorithm S.

A sender–receiver pair (*Prover, Verifier*) is a Non-Interactive Proof System for $3SAT$ if Completeness and Soundness hold. An alternative definition of the zero-knowledge property is that there are several independent provers, each using the same algorithm and the same reference string, but its own private random string. Since the prover is history-insensitive these two definitions are equivalent. When the metaproofs are combined with an on-line simulatable bounded NIZK proof system, they give a protocol for many-provers NIZK proof systems.

In [DeYu], we describe a sender–receiver pair (P, V). P can prove in zero-knowledge the 3-satisfiability of any number of 3-satisfiable formulae with n clauses each. We then employ a technique of [BlDeMiPe] to extend this by showing how to use the same protocol to prove any number of formulae, each of arbitrary size.

3.4 Self-Referential NIZK

Another important intriguing problem is that the non-interactive model is shown zero-knowledge based on random reference string which is available on-line, and not off-line, in advance. On the other hand the motivation for such a tool is the availability of random public sources "the Rand books". This has been bothering researchers and, for example, Bellare and Goldwasser [BeGo] presented a definition of a strong non-interactive system which allows on-line randomness (maybe after a stage of preprocessing). They did not have (and actually did not need) such a system.

Based on the meta-proof system we can finally have an "on-line" system, where the polynomial-time theorem chooser is getting access to the random reference string. (The theorem can rely on this string and thus the system can be self-referential in the sense that the same string will be used to prove the correctness of the theorem). This increases the applicability of the NIZK systems to many more scenarios and protocols.

4   Applications to Identification and Signature

The goal of this paper is to show how to use the above notions. The primitives above can be applied by efficient (polynomial-time) users of a cryptographic system and thus can be applied in cryptographic settings. They give a variety of applications and new tools for secure systems. The applications use a few facts. First, the fact that the metaproof system gives a proof in an indirect fashion, covered by additional encryption mechanism. Second, the in the metaproof the metaprover possesses a zero-knowledge witness and does not have to have a real knowledge about the witness of the proof itself. Third fact, is that metaproof can be applied recursively.

We start with applications related to a new methodology suggested recently by Bellare and Goldwasser.

4.1   Signatures without history

Based on secure probabilistic encryption schemes and NIZK, Bellare and Goldwasser [BeGo] have suggested a signature scheme which relies on the two tools. More specifically, they use a NIZK proof systems which is publicly verifiable and a pseudo-random functions collection. Their method uses an encryption of a seed of a pseudorandom function, and uses non-interactive proofs to show that certain activity related to the message and the encryption is performed correctly; only the signer is able to perform the task. (For more details see [BeGo]). They construct a scheme which is secure against a random message attack.

Even, Goldreich, and Micali [EvGoMi] proved that any scheme secure against random message attack (and memoryless) can be transformed into one secure against adaptive chosen message attack (and memoryless).

The scheme using NIZK is not memory-less since for the original NIZK, a proof depends on previously given proofs. To prevent history-dependence Bellare and Goldwasser suggest a NIZK which involves initial preprocessing or reliance on a trusted center. Then, Feige and Shamir [FeSh] by relaxing the security requirement to Witness-Hiding rather than Zero-Knowledge can apply the protocol without initial interaction.

By using MP-NIZK rather than NIZK (which is history dependent) we finally achieve a signature system secure against adaptive chosen plaintext attack in the paradigm of [BeGo], which is history-free, preprocessing-free (no trusted server as well), and *without* relaxation of the original security definition.

The signature schemes based on Universal One-way hash functions (UOWHF), an approach initiated in [NaYu] which proved that a trapdoor-less provably-secure signature is possible, has all its implementations history-dependent.

4.2 Hierarchical identification.

Another application mentioned in [BeGo] is identification schemes. We extend the notion (using the metaproof system) to enable hierarchical distribution of identification information. The original system enables a center to distribute unforgeable ID numbers. With the metaproof system we can implement a hierarchical system in which a center can issue ID's to sub-centers (officers), later the local center can transfer the ID's on. Based on metaproofs level (metaproof, metametaproof, etc.), the user can verify the authenticity of ID's and the level of the officer which is giving the ID. This hierarchical center structure is typical to large organizations.

5 Applications to Encryption, Non-Interactive Proofs, and Resource Protection

5.1 Enhancing security by sequencing proofs

An immediate application of the Metaproof is cascading a constant number of metaproof systems to enhance security of zero-knowledge schemes. Using a metaproof, one can hide the previous proof applying a different encryption key (we view the proofs as nested). In each level one can use a key and even if only one of the keys is secure, the entire proof is secure (zero-knowledge). It is important to notice that even if certain outer-most levels are insecure, the system is still secure. The outer-most secure claim has the zero-knowledge property and when the opponent decrypts the claims he obtains a claim which is actually encrypted securely.

The level of a meta-proof may be used to trace the proof (given with a signature) back to its origin if a proof is passed among users.

5.2 Abuse-freeness: the oblivious warden

Desmedt [De] has introduced the notion of protecting against the abuse of channels used for cryptographic tasks. This is a classical problem of prevention of abuse of resources and prevention of violations by users. His example is an authentication channel whose users do not care about the authentication, but try to convey extra information in the process of authenticating themselves. Desmedt suggests to protect channels by assigning wardens to monitor and modify information passing through the channel. He gives a nice set of techniques which enable abuse-freeness of protocols. He also suggests to use NIZK by which the sender proves to the warden that it follows the protocol correctly with respect to some initial interactive commitment.

Using the notion of the metaproof, a different idea can be developed. A NIZK system used by the sender can be made abuse-free by having an oblivious warden (whose task is to prevent violations). The warden simply gets a proof of a theorem, verifies it and forward to the receiver the metaproof, rather then the original proof. He is able to convince the receiver just as well as the original sender, but by sending a proof which is based on his own random bits. The warden's task is independent of the actual proof or NIZK system in use so it can be a general procedure which obliviously translates NIZK proofs and thus assures they are abuse-free.

5.3 Gradual NIZK result-opening

In [ImYu] it was shown how an adaptive verifier can open a result of a computation which was proven to him (encrypted computation performed in zero-knowledge) by the prover. The opening of the result is requested bit by bit by the verifier, and the prover opens the result (fast— without further proofs– for efficiency reasons), each time the verifier can decide which question to ask next. This implies that the simulator in the zero-knowledge proof (which does not know the result but gets it bit by bit as well) should also be able to open result bits of its proof. The difficulty is that the simulator has to open the result bits in an on-line fashion, (after he committed to the proof of the computing circuit). The simulator, on the other hand, should not use more knowledge than the on-line already opened bits and the current result to be opened (which it gets from a "result oracle"). How can this be done without performing the opening stages themselves in a zero-knowledge fashion (which requires further proofs!)?

This can be achieved in the NIZK scenario as well, using the tool of ambiguous non-interactive encryption which we developed, thus closing another gap between the interactive and the non-interactive scenarios.

5.4 Combination Transferable/Non-Transferable (IZK-NIZK)

Another remark which may be useful in applications, is that we can forward non-interactive proofs to propagate an (authentication) capability in the system, using (up to a constant number) of metaproof levels (if needed) or directly transfer the proof itself. Then, at a certain level, we reach the boundary and then the authentication may be needed but should not be transferred. Thus it is the right point to switch to an interactive proof. proving the possession of a NIZK based on the NIZK's and the statement. Recall that the possession of a metaproof is an elegant way to have a "zero-knowledge witness" of a statement.

5.5 Non-interactive witness-hiding equivalent to zero-knowledge.

The notion of Witness-hiding was originally suggested as a relaxation of the notion of zero-knowledge [FeSh]. In the non-interactive scenario, based on the existence of one-way function we can show, using the meta-proof system, that the notions are equivalent. Thus, our constructions can all be based on bounded non-interactive witness-hiding protocol (maybe such can be implemented based on any one-way function

6 Conclusions

We have presented a few applications in various cryptographic scenarios based on recent Non-interactive Zero-Knowledge Proof-Systems we developed. The new tools can also be applied to produce Secure Distributed Computation tools and protocols, which we describe in [DeYu]. Details and full proofs will be provided in [DeYu] as well.

References

[BaMo]   L. Babai and S. Moran, *Arthur–Merlin Games: A Randomized Proof System and a Hierarchy of Complexity Classes*, Journal of Computer and System Sciences, vol. 36, 1988, pp. 254–276.

[BeGo]   M. Bellare and S. Goldwasser, *New Paradigms for Digital Signatures and Message Authentication based on Non-interactive Zero-knowledge Proofs*, Crypto 1989.

[BeMi]   M. Bellare and S. Micali, *Non-interactive Oblivious Transfer and Applications*, Crypto 1989.

[BlDeMiPe] M. Blum, A. De Santis, S. Micali, and G. Persiano, *Non-Interactive Zero-Knowledge Proof Systems*, preprint.

[BlFeMi] M. Blum, P. Feldman, and S. Micali, *Non-Interactive Zero-Knowledge Proof Systems and Applications*, Proceedings of the 20th Annual ACM Symposium on Theory of Computing, Chicago, Illinois, 1988.

[Bl]   M. Blum, *How to Prove a Theorem So No One Else Can Claim It*, Proceedings of the International Congress of Mathematicians, Berkeley, California, 1986, pp. 1444–1451.

[Co]   S. A. Cook, *The Complexity of Theorem-Proving Procedures*, Proc. 3rd Ann. ACM Symp. on Theory of Computing, New York, pp. 151–158.

[De]   Y. Desmeth, *Abuse-free Cryptosystems: Particularly Subliminal-Free Authentication and Signature*, preprint.

[DiHe]   W. Diffie and M. E. Hellman, *New Directions in Cryptography*, IEEE Transactions on Information Theory, vol. IT-22, no. 6, Nov. 1976, pp. 644–654.

[DePe]   A. De Santis and G. Persiano, *Public-Randomness in Public-key Cryptosystems*, Eurocrypt-90.

[DeMiPe1] A. De Santis, S. Micali, and G. Persiano, *Non-Interactive Zero-Knowledge Proof-Systems*, in "Advances in Cryptology – CRYPTO 87", vol. 293 of "Lecture Notes in Computer Science", Springer Verlag.

[DeMiPe2] A. De Santis, S. Micali, and G. Persiano, *Non-Interactive Zero-Knowledge Proof-Systems with Preprocessing*, Crypto 1988.

[DeYu]   A. De Santis and M. Yung, *Non-Interactive Metaproofs and Non-Interactive Protocols*, Manuscript.

[EvGoMi] S. Even, O. Goldreich, and S. Micali, *On-line/Off-line Digital Signatures*, Crypto 1989.

[FeLaSh] U. Feige, D. Lapidot and A. Shamir, *Multiple Non-Interactive Zero Knowledge Proofs Based on a Single Random String*, Focs 90.

[FeSh]   U. Feige, and A. Shamir, *Witness-Hiding Protocols*, Proceedings of the 22th Annual ACM Symposium on Theory of Computing, 1990, announcement in Crypto-89.

[GaJo]   M. Garey and D. Johnson, *Computers and Intractability: a Guide to the Theory of NP-Completeness*, W. H. Freeman & Co., New York, 1979.

[Go]   O. Goldreich, *A Uniform-Complexity Treatment of Encryption and Zero-Knowledge*, Technical Report no. 568, Technion, June 1989.

[GoGoMi] O. Goldreich, S. Goldwasser, and S. Micali, *How to Construct Random Functions*, Journal of the Association for Computing Machinery, vol. 33, no. 4, 1986, pp. 792–807.

[GoMi1]   S. Goldwasser and S. Micali, *Probabilistic Encryption*, Journal of Computer and System Science, vol. 28, n. 2, 1984, pp. 270–299.

[GoMiRa] S. Goldwasser, S. Micali, and C. Rackoff, *The Knowledge Complexity of Interactive Proof-Systems*, SIAM Journal on Computing, vol. 18, n. 1, February 1989.

[GoMiRi] S. Goldwasser, S. Micali, and R. Rivest, *A Digital Signature Scheme Secure Against Adaptive Chosen-Message Attack*, SIAM Journal of Computing, vol. 17, n. 2, April 1988, pp. 281–308.

[GoMiWi1] O. Goldreich, S. Micali, and A. Wigderson, *Proofs that Yield Nothing but their Validity and a Methodology of Cryptographic Design*, Proceedings of 27th Annual Symposium on Foundations of Computer Science, 1986, pp. 174–187.

[GoMiWi2] O. Goldreich, S. Micali, and A. Wigderson, *How to Play Any Mental Game*, Proceedings of the 19th Annual ACM Symposium on Theory of Computing, New York, pp. 218–229.

[Ha]   J. Håstad, *Pseudorandom Generation under Uniform Assumptions*, Proceedings of the 22th Annual ACM Symposium on Theory of Computing, 1990.

[ImLeLu] R. Impagliazzo, L. Levin, and M. Luby, *Pseudo-Random Generation from One-way Functions*, Proceedings of 21st STOC, May 1989.

[ImNa]   R. Impagliazzo and M. Naor, *Efficient Cryptographic Schemes Provably Secure as Subset Sum*, Proceedings of 30th FOCS, 1989.

[ImYu]   R. Impagliazzo and M. Yung, *Direct Minimum Knowledge Computations*, in "Advances in Cryptology – CRYPTO 87", vol. 293 of "Lecture Notes in Computer Science", Springer Verlag pp. 40–51.

[LaSh]   D. Lapidot and A. Shamir, These Proceedings.

[Na]   M. Naor, *Bit Commitment using Pseudo-randomness*, Crypto 1989.

[NaYu]   M. Naor and M. Yung, *Public-key Cryptosystems Probably Secure Against Chosen Ciphertext Attacks*, Proceedings of the 22th Annual ACM Symposium on Theory of Computing, 1990.

[Ro]   J. Rompel, *One-way functions are Necessary and Sufficient for Secure Signatures*, STOC 90.

[Ya]   A. Yao, *Theory and Applications of Trapdoor Functions*, Proc. 23rd IEEE Symp. on Foundations of Computer Science, 1982, pp. 80–91.

Interactive Proofs with Provable Security against Honest Verifiers

J. Kilian*

Abstract

Nearly all of the work on constructing zero-knowledge proof systems relies on very strong complexity theoretic assumptions. We consider a form of "no use" zero-knowledge, and show that every language in PSPACE has an interactive proof system that provably achieves "no-use" zero-knowledge against honest verifiers.

1 Introduction.

1.1 Difficulties with proving zero-knowledge.

There are at least two neat things about interactive proof systems [10]. First, they allow one to prove PSPACE hard assertions [19]. Second, they *seem* to allow us to divorce the transfer of confidence from the transfer of knowledge, through the elegant notion of *zero-knowledge interactive proof systems* [10]. Unfortunately, there are few nontrivial languages (e.g., graph nonisomorphism [12]) that are known to have zero-knowledge proof systems. The only way known to show that a language has a zero-knowledge proof system is to show that it has a statistically zero-knowledge proof system. However, such an approach can not give very much generality: Results of Fortnow [7] and Boppana-Håstad-Zachos [5] imply that if NP has statistically zero-knowledge proofs, then the polynomial-time hierarchy collapses[1]

Such negativism stands in sharp contrast to the bright potential of computational zero-knowledge proof systems. All of IP (and hence all of PSPACE) has zero-knowledge proofs provided that a secure cryptographic bit-committal scheme exists [15]. Secure cryptographic bit-committal schemes can be based on pseudorandom bit generators [17], which in turn can be based on one-way functions [14, 13]. However, we may never be able to prove

*Harvard University and MIT Laboratory for Computer Science, 545 Technology Square, Cambridge, MA 02139 USA, joek@theory.lcs.mit.edu. Supported by an NSF Postdoctoral Fellowship. Some of the writing up of these results supported by Bell Communications.

[1]See also [1] for more structural theorems about statistical zero-knowledge.

the existence of one-way functions. How much security can we actually prove, here and now, without any conjectures? Recent techniques allow us to prove some not completely trivial positive theorems about secure proof systems.

1.2 "No-use" zero-knowledge against honest verifiers.

A massive simplifying assumption one can make is that the verifier obeys the protocol, and only later attempts to obtain extra information. However, even in the honest verifier model, there are no interesting language classes that have zero-knowledge proof systems. Indeed, the negative results of [7, 5, 1] hold for the honest verifier model.

In this paper, we consider a slightly weaker form of security, which is a form of "no-use" zero-knowledge against nonuniform honest verifiers. Various definitions of "no-use" zero-knowledge have been proposed [20, 6]. Our basic intuition is as follows: Seeing a proof that $x \in L$, should not enable one to compute any predicates on x that one could not compute before. This intuition motivates the following definition.

Definition 1 Let (P, V) be an interactive proof system for a language L, and let $(P, V)(x)$ denote the distribution on transcripts produced by running (P, V) on input x. For S an arbitrary subset of L, define $S_k = \{x : x \in S, |x| = k\}$. We say that (P, V) is "no-use" zero-knowledge against honest verifiers if for all $S \subseteq L$, and all predicates Q, the following holds: Suppose there exists a (possibly nonuniform) circuit family $\{C_k\}$ such that $|C_k| \leq k^{c_1}$, and

$$prob(C_k(x, (P, V)(x)) = Q(x)) > \frac{1}{2} + \frac{1}{k^{c_2}},$$

for all $k \in S_k$, where c_1 and c_2 are constants (independent of k). Then there exists a (possibly nonuniform) circuit family $\{C_k'\}$ such that $|C_k'| \leq k^{c_3}$, for some constant c_3 (depending only on c_1, c_2 and L), and $C_k'(x) = Q(x)$ for $x \in S_k$.

The above definitions arguably captures some of our basic intuition about security with respect to an honest verifier. It is certainly far from ideal, but has the vitue of provability. In this extended abstract, we sketch a proof of the following theorem.

Theorem: Any language that has an interactive proof system (P, V) (i.e. any language in PSPACE) has an interactive proof system (P^*, V^*) that is "no-use" zero-knowledge against honest verifiers.

This theorem also allows us to show that other natural notions of security may be achieved. For instance, one may wish to see a proof that $x \in L$, and use this to compute some predicate Q on y, for some other string y. However, for y of length that is some fixed polynomial in x, one can construct a new language L' such that $(x, y) \in L'$ iff $x \in L$, a new predicate $Q'(x, y) = Q(y)$, and apply our theorem.

Our proof uses many fashionable techniques, including

1. Methods for constructing functions that are locally self reducible [2, 16],

2. Shamir's theorem that $IP = \text{PSPACE}$ [19],

3. Results on universal hard-core predicates [8], and

4. Zero-knowledge proofs based on ideal bit-commitment [4].

1.3 Outline of the paper

In Section 2, we give the intuition behind our proof. In Section 3, we discuss bit committal based on a PSPACE hard language (QBF for explicitness). In Section 4, we outline the construction of our secure proof system. In Section 5, we outline the argument that the protocol is secure.

2 Overview of the proof.

The essence of our proof is as follows. Suppose one augments the standard model for interactive proof system with an abstract ideal committal scheme, colloquially known as an envelope. Then for any language $L \in IP$ (aka PSPACE), there exists a provably zero-knowledge interactive proof system for L [4]. A reasonable approach is to implement envelopes with a cryptographic protocol that still preserves some of the security properties of abstract envelopes.

A difficulty with this approach is that we must base our commitment scheme on some complexity assumption. However, this assumption will be beyond our ability to prove correct, and so we must allow for the possibility of it being completely wrong! Our approach is to make our committal scheme hard to break relative to the difficulty of simulating the prover. Roughly, if there is a small circuit that can distinguish a committed 0 from a committed 1, then there is a small circuit that can perform the most vital functions of the prover.

How do we make such a committal protocol? We first construct a function F that is computable in PSPACE, and very hard to compute on average. Any circuit that can compute F with nonnegligible probability on a random input of size k^c, for some constant c, can be transformed into a circuit for computing QBF (the set of true quantified boolean formulas) on inputs of size k.[2] We construct such a function by using the techniques of Beaver-Feigenbaum, Lipton, and Yao [2, 16, 21]. We can then use a lemma of Goldreich-Levin [8] to argue that if x and y are chosen at random, then it is hard to compute $b = F(x) \cdot y$, where $F(x)$ and y are treated as boolean vectors. Thus, a random x and y serves to commit a random bit b. This bit may be revealed later by giving an interactive proof that $b = F(x) \cdot y$, using Shamir's protocol [19].

---

[2]We do not use anything special about QBF - just that it is PSPACE complete.

Given a perfect zero-knowledge proof with envelopes, we now simply replace the envelopes with out commitment scheme. The resulting protocol can be perfectly simulated by a polynomial-time simulator, S^{perf}, that has access to the following two pieces of magic:

1. An oracle that computes QBF on inputs of size $|x|^c$, where c depends on l.

2. An advice distribution that outputs a set of sufficiently many random committals and decommittals for $b = 0$ and $b = 1$, using the appropriate security parameter (based on the size of x).

Unfortunately, this simulation uses too much magic to be immediately useful. Using the simulator for the envelope protocol, we construct a "simulator," S^*, that has access to the advice distribution, but does not have access to the QBF oracle.

We can't prove that the simulation performed by S^* is indistinguishable from the actual protocol. If we are lucky, it will be as good as the real thing insofar as computing predicates is concerned. However, if this is not the case, we can construct a circuit that, using only the advice distribution, can compute QBF on inputs of size $|x|^c$. Using this circuit, we can then perfectly simulate the protocol with just the advice distribution. Finally, we can easily show that in the circuit model of computation access to such an advice distribution does not allow one to compute any new predicates. This is accomplished by a simple "hardwiring" argument, and the fact that the advice distribution depends only on the size of x.

3 Committing bits using our PSPACE hard problem.

In this section, we describe our new bit-committal protocol. The novel feature of our bit is that a small circuit that is able to distinguish a committed 0 from a committed 1 can be transformed into a small circuit to solve bounded sized instances of QBF (quantified boolean formulas). We first show the existence of a function

$$F_k' : \{0,1\}^{k^{c_1}} \to \{0,1\}^{k^{c_1}},$$

for some constant c_1, such that if for nearly all random x, one can compute $F_k'(x)$ correctly, then one can efficiently decide QBF on problems of size k. Using a construction due Yao [21], we then create a function F_k such that computing F_k with nonnegligible probability on a random input allows one to solve QBF. Finally, we use a result by Goldreich-Levin [8], to create a bit committal scheme with the required properties.

For an additional look at using average-case hard problems to achieve bit-committal (as well as numerous other results in this area), we refer the reader to a forthcoming manuscript by Ostrovsky, Venkatesan, and Yung [18]. Interestingly, they have a completely different way of constructing problem that is PSPACE hard on average, using the more traditional tools of average-case completeness.

3.1 Creating a hard function.

Our construction follows immediately from the methods of Beaver-Feigenbaum and Lipton [2, 16]. Let ι be such that $2^\iota > k+1$, and define the field $\mathcal{F} = GF(2^\iota)$. Note that $\mathcal{F}$ has at least $k+1$ nonzero elements. Let $QBF_k : \{0,1\}^k \rightarrow \{0,1\}$ be the characteristic function of QBF, restricted to k-bit inputs.

First, we define $p_0[x_i] = 1 - x_i$ and $p_1[x_i] = x_i$. Given a boolean k-vector, $\vec{A} = a_1, \ldots, a_k$, we define $\delta_{\vec{A}} : \mathcal{F}^k \rightarrow \mathcal{F}^k$ by

$$\delta_{\vec{A}}(x_1, \ldots, x_k) = \prod_{1 \leq i \leq k} p_{a_i}[x_i].$$

Note that $\delta_{\vec{A}}$ is a multivariate polynomial of degree k. Furthermore, it is not hard to show that for $x_1, \ldots, x_k \in \{0,1\}$, we have

$$\delta_{\vec{A}}(x_1, \ldots, x_k) = \begin{cases} 1 & \text{if } x_i = a_i \text{ for } 1 \leq i \leq k, \text{ or,} \\ 0 & \text{if } x_i \neq a_i \text{ for some } 1 \leq i \leq k. \end{cases}$$

We define $F'_k : \mathcal{F}^k \rightarrow \mathcal{F}$ by

$$F'_k(x_1, \ldots, x_k) = \sum_{\vec{A} \in \{0,1\}^k} QBF_k(\vec{A}) \delta_{\vec{A}}(x_1, \ldots, x_k).$$

Note that F'_k is also a multi-variate polynomial of degree at most k. Furthermore, for $x_1, \ldots, x_k \in \{0,1\}$, we have

$$F'_k(x_1, \ldots, x_k) = QBF_k(x_1, \ldots, x_k).$$

Also, note that F'_k can be uniformly computed in PSPACE.

Now, since F' is a multivariate polynomial of degree k over a field with at least $k+1$ nonzero elements, we can randomly reduce the problem of computing $F'(\vec{X})$ to that of computing

$$F(\vec{Y_0}), \ldots, F(\vec{Y_k}),$$

where each individual Y_i is distributed uniformly over $\mathcal{F}^k$ (implicitly in [2], more explicitly in [3]). Using an argument of Lipton [16], we have the following lemma.

Lemma 1 Suppose there exists a circuit C of size s such that if $x_1, \ldots, x_k \in \mathcal{F}$ is uniformly distributed,

$$prob(C(x_1, \ldots, x_k) = F'_k(x_1, \ldots, x_k)) > 1 - \frac{1}{3k}.$$

Then there exists a circuit C' of size $(sk)^c$ that computes F'_k (and thus QBF_k). Here, c is some global constant. Furthermore, for k sufficently large, F'_k will be nonzero on at least $1/3k$ of its inputs.

Proof: (Sketch) Our proof works the same way as does Lipton's proof of the average case complexity of the permanent. One can compute $QBF_k(x)$ by a locally random reduction to $F'(y_0), \ldots, F'_k(y_k)$, where for each i, y_i is distributed uniformly. Now, for any i, there is at most a $1/3k$ chance that $C(y_i)$ will be different from $F'_k(y_i)$, and thus there is at most a $(k+1)/3k$ chance that $C(y_i)$ deviates from $F'_k(y_i)$ for any $i \in [0, k]$. Hence, if one performs a locally random reduction to from QBF_k to F'_k, and substitutes the output of C' for that of F'_k, one will obtain the correct answer with probability $> \frac{1}{2}$. The probabilistic circuit one obtains can be easily changed into a deterministic circuit with only polynomial blow up.

To see that F'_k must be nonzero with probability at least $1/3k$ (for suitably large k), we note the following fact, which follows straightforwardly from the definition of the Beaver-Feigenbaum reduction: If $F'_k(y_i) = 0$ for all $i \in [0, k]$, then $QBF_k(x)$ must be 0. Since for k sufficently large, there always exists some x such that $QBF_k(x)$ is nonzero, the proof follows from the same argument of Lipton's. ∎

Untuitively, it should be hard to compute F' on a large (but polynomial-sized) set of random inputs, since one of them is bound to be in the hard set. Using an amplification lemma due to Yao, we can create a new function F_k that runs F'_k on several inputs in parallel. Using Yao's technique, and the previous lemma, we can prove the following lemma.

Lemma 2 For $k > 1$, there exists a function, $F_k : k^{c_2} \to k^{c_2}$, where c_2 is some global constant, with the following property. Suppose there existed a circuit C of size s such that if $x_1, \ldots, x_{k^{c_2}} \in \mathcal{F}$ is uniformly distributed,

$$prob(C(x_1, \ldots, x_{k^{c_2}}) = F'_k(x_1, \ldots, x_{k^{c_2}})) > \epsilon,$$

and $\epsilon > 2^{-k}$. Then there exists a circuit C' of size $(sk/\epsilon)^{c_3}$, where c_3 is some global constant, that computes QBF_k. Furthermore, for k sufficiently large, $F_k(x_1, \ldots, x_{k^{c_2}})$ is nonzero with probability at least $1 - 2^{-k}$. ∎

Clearly, F_k can be computed in PSPACE. It may seem odd that Lemma 2 can allow ϵ to become superpolynomially small. However, in such cases, the bound on the circuit size also becomes superpolynomial.

3.2 Using F_k to commit a bit.

For our protocol, we need to commit and decommit a bit b. In the following protocols, the committor runs in probabilistic PSPACE, and the verifier runs in probabilistic polynomial time.

Protocol COMMIT(b,k) The committor uniformly chooses $X, Y \in \{0,1\}^{k^{c_2}}$ such that $b = F_k(X) \cdot Y$.[3] The committor sends X, Y to the verifier.

Protocol DECOMMIT(b,k,X,Y) The decommittor output b and, using Shamir's protocol, interactively proves to the verifier that $b = F_k(X) \cdot Y$. Shamir's protocol is run many times so as to achieve a maximum error probability of 2^{-k}.

The above protocols form a committal system, if not necessarily a secure one. Once X and Y are announced, $b = F_k(X) \cdot Y$ is completely specified. Thus, the only way a committor can break a decommittal is to give an interactive proof for a false theorem, in which case he will be caught with probability $1 - 2^{-k}$.

We can't show without any assumptions that our bit commitment scheme is secure. However, using the proof of Goldreich-Levin theorem on hard-core bits, and our previous lemmas, we can relate the circuit complexity of breaking our commitment scheme, with security parameter k, and the circuit complexity of computing QBF_k. Crucial to the proof of this lemma was an additional, very powerful proof technique developed at MIT, known as *asking Yishay for help*.

Lemma 3 Let $k > 1$. Suppose there exists a circuit C of size s such that

$$|prob(C(\text{COMMIT}(0,k)) = 1) - prob(C(\text{COMMIT}(1,k)) = 1)| > \epsilon,$$

and $\epsilon > 2^{-k/4}$. Then there exists a circuit C' of size $(sk/\epsilon)^{c_5}$, where c_5 is some global constant, that computes QBF_k. ∎

Proof: (Sketch) We follow the proof of the existence of hardcore predicates for one-way functions [8]. Consider the following problem: Let X be a boolean n-vector, and let $G_X(Y)$ be a function such that

$$prob(G_X(Y) = X \cdot Y) > \frac{1}{2} + \epsilon,$$

for Y chosen uniformly from the set of boolean n-vectors. Let distribution D be equal to $(Y, G_X(Y))$, where Y is uniformly distributed over boolean n-vectors. Given access to D, how well can one guess X? Goldreich and Levin [8] show how, in expected time polynomial in n and $\frac{1}{\epsilon}$, to construct a list of $O(1/\epsilon^2)$ vectors, such that with high probability X is on the list. Thus, one can guess the correct value of X with probability at least $\Omega(\epsilon^2)$.

We now show how to use C to produce a good guessing function $G_{F_k(X)}$ for a nonnegligible fraction of the X's. First, consider the game where b is chosen uniformly, and X and Y are chosen uniformly subject to $b = F_k(X) \cdot Y$. By a simple probability argument it follows that either

$$prob(C(X,Y) = F_k(X) \cdot Y) > \frac{1}{2} + \frac{\epsilon}{2}, \text{ or,}$$

$$prob(C(X,Y) = F_k(X) \cdot Y) < \frac{1}{2} - \frac{\epsilon}{2}.$$

---

[3]Here, the · operator denotes the dot product.

We now consider the similar case where X and Y are chosen uniformly. Using the fact that $F_k(X)$ is almost always nonzero, we can show that $F_k(X) \cdot Y$ has only a very small bias. Using this fact, and our bound on epsilon, we can then show that either

$$prob(C(X,Y) = F_k(X) \cdot Y) > \frac{1}{2} + \frac{\epsilon}{3}, \text{ or,}$$

$$prob(C(X,Y) = F_k(X) \cdot Y) < \frac{1}{2} - \frac{\epsilon}{3}.$$

Assume without loss of generality that the former case holds (if the latter case holds, simply negate the output of C). Then by a straightforward analysis, with probability at least $\epsilon/2$, a randomly chosen X will have the property that

$$prob(C(X,Y) = F_k(X) \cdot Y) > \frac{1}{2} + \frac{\epsilon}{6},$$

for a uniformly chosen Y. For such X, we can use the Goldreich-Levin algorithm to guess the value of $F_k(X)$ with probability $\Omega(\epsilon^2)$, by using the guessing function,

$$G_{F_k(X)}(Y) = C(X,Y).$$

Even assuming that we fail on all of the other values of X, we can still guess $F_k(x)$ with probability $c\epsilon^3$, for some global constant $c > 0$. This procedure can be hardwired into a circuit of the required size. Finally, for $\epsilon > 2^{-k/4}$, $c\epsilon^3 > 2^{-k}$ for k sufficiently large (constant values of k can be wired in), and we can apply Lemma 2 to give the desired result. ∎

We can use the now standard techniques of Goldwasser-Micali [9] to analyze the security of committing a set of m bits.

Lemma 4 Let $k > 1$, and let B denote some distribution on $\{0,1\}^m$. Given a circuit C (with appropriately many inputs), define $\rho(C, B, k)$ to be the induced distribution on

$$prob(C(\text{COMMIT}(b_1, k), \ldots, \text{COMMIT}(b_m, k)) = 1).$$

Then, if for any $B \in \{0,1\}^m$, there exists a circuit C of size s such that

$$|\rho(C, B, k) - \rho(C, 0^m, k)| > \epsilon,$$

and $\epsilon > m2^{-k/4}$. Then there exists a circuit C' of size $(skm/\epsilon)^{c_6}$, where c_6 is some global constant, that computes QBF_k. ∎

4 Converting an interactive proof system into a secure interactive proof system.

In this section, we show that if a proof system (P, V) exists for a language L, then a proof system (P^*, V^*) exists that is "no use" zero-knowledge against honest verifiers. We first review some elementary facts about achieving zero-knowledge with ideal committal schemes (envelopes). We then give our final protocol, along with a "simulator" that will prove crucial to our proof of security.

4.1 Achieving zero-knowledge with envelopes.

Let us review some known results on making protocols one-sided [11] and implementing zero-knowledge with envelopes [4]. Suppose there exists an interactive proof system (P, V) for a language L. If one is given an ideal, information-theoretically secure bit committal protocol (i.e. envelopes), one can convert (P, V) into a new interactive proof system (P', V'), with the following properties.

1. V' runs in probabilistic polynomial time, and P' runs in probabilistic polynomial time, given access to an oracle for $QBF_{|x|^{c_7}}$, for some constant c_7 that depends only on L.

2. For $x \in L$, (P', V') will accept x with probability 1.

3. For $x \notin L$, and all $\hat{P}$, $(\hat{P}, V')$ will accept with probability less than $2^{-|x|}$.

4. For $x \in L$, V''s view of (P', V') is perfectly simulatable in probabilistic polynomial time.

Furthermore, we can construct (P', V') so that a proof proceeds according to the following general format:

Step 1: P' uniformly chooses $b_1, \ldots, b_n \in \{0, 1\}$, where $n = |x|^{c_8}$, and c_8 is a constant depending only on L. P' commits to $b_1, \ldots, b_n$ using the ideal committal system.

Step 2: P' and V' talk back and forth, generating some conversation transcript, T. Both P' and V' are allowed to flip coins during this phase. We can require that V' immediately reveals to P' all of his coin flips (i.e. that the protocol is Arthur-Merlin).

Step 3: P' sends a set $I \subseteq [1, n]$, and for $i \in I$ ideally decommits b_i. V' computes some predicate,

$$accept(x, T, I, \bigcup_{i \in I} b_i).$$

Remark: In our normal form, bits are committed only in the first stage and decommitted only in the third stage. The prover can effectively commit to a new bit, b, in the second phase by revealing its exclusive-or with a random bit, b_i. Decommitting b_i is then equivalent to decommitting b. Furthermore, the prover can simply state the value of B_i in the second stage, and defer its actual decommittal until Step 3. Note that the verifier has nothing to lose by deferring his abortion of the protocol until Step 3.

We say that a probabilistic circuit S perfectly simulates V''s view of (P', V') if it generates a distribution on

$$(T, I, \bigcup_{i \in I} b_i)$$

that is equal to that induced by (P', V'). Note that S is not required to generate $b_1, \ldots, b_n$ along with T and I. The intuition is that with an ideal commitment scheme, the values of uncommitted bits have nothing to do with V''s view. Note also that S^* implicitly generates V''s coin tosses, since they appear in T.[4]

4.2 Defining our secure protocol.

We now define our secure protocol (P^*, V^*). On input x, (P^*, V^*) execute the following protocol.

Step 1: P^* and V^* start running copies of P' and V'. P' outputs $b_1, \ldots, b_n$. For $1 \leq i \leq n$, P^* runs protocol COMMIT($b_i, |x|^{c_7}$), generating $(X_1, Y_1), \ldots, (X_n, Y_n)$.

Step 2: P^* and V^* run P' and V' through Step 2 of the original protocol, generating some conversation transcript, T.

Step 3: P' will output a set $I \subseteq [1, n]$. For $i \in I$, P^* and V^* perform protocol DECOMMIT($b, |x|^{c_7}, X_i, Y_i$). V^* accepts iff she accepts all of the decommittals and V' accepts on input $(x, T, I, \cup_{i \in I} b_i)$.

4.3 Simulators for our protocol.

The protocol given above is a proof system, since the committal scheme given in Section 3 can only be broken with negligible probability. In order to show that this protocol has some nontrivial security properties, we will construct two simulators. The first simulator gives a perfect simulation, but requires a great deal of outside help. The second simulator requires less help, but gives an imperfect simulation that may be distinguishable from the actual protocol. However, we can show that if one is able to distinguish the second simulation from the actual protocol, then one can implement the first simulation with only a small amount of outside help.

First, we will define our two forms of outside help. The first form of outside help is a $QBF_{|x|^{c_7}}$ oracle. The second form of outside help is an advice distribution $\mathcal{O}(|x|)$. We

---

[4]In fact, one can produce a simulator $S_{\hat{V}}^*$ that will simulate the (possibly hidden) coin flips of a malicious verifier, $\hat{V}$. However, since we only consider security against an honest verifier, we do not need to worry about such considerations.

define $\mathcal{O}(|x|)$ as the distribution that, for $1 \leq i \leq |x|^{c_8}$ and $b \in \{0, 1\}$, outputs (X_i^b, Y_i^b, T_i^b), where

1. X_i^b are Y_i^b are chosen independently from the set of $|x|^{c_2 c_7}$-bit vectors, subject to $b = F_{|x|^{c_7}}(X_i^b) \cdot Y_i^b$, and,

2. T_i^b is chosen from the distribution on transcripts of $\text{DECOMMIT}(b, |x|^{c_7}, X_i^b, Y_i^b)$.

Informally, $\mathcal{O}(|x|)$ gives transcripts of the committals and decommittals of $|x|^{c_8}$ 0's and $|x|^{c_8}$ 1's, with security parameter $|x|^{c_7}$.

Our first simulator, denoted $S^{perf}(x)$, proceeds as follows. First, S^{perf} obtains a sample from $\mathcal{O}(|x|)$, then essentially runs the protocol for P^* and V^*. When it is necessary to simulate P', S^{perf} runs the program for P', using the $QBF_{|x|^{c_7}}$ oracle. However, instead of running the protocol for committing bit b_i, S^{perf} simply outputs the values of (X^{b_i}, Y^{b_i}) provided by $\mathcal{O}$. Similarly, instead of simulating the decommittal of b_i, S^{perf} simply outputs the value of $T_i^{b_i}$ given by $\mathcal{O}$. It is straightforward to verify that $S^{perf}(x)$ gives a perfect simulation for (P^*, V^*) on input $x \in L$.

Our next simulator, $S^*(x)$ works as follows. First, $S_{|x|}^*$ obtains a set of triples (X_i^b, Y_i^b, T_i^b) from $\mathcal{O}(|x|)$. $S_{|x|}^*$ then runs S to obtain $(T, I, \cup_{i \in I} b_i)$. For $i \notin I$, $S_{|x|}^*$ sets $b_i = 0$. $S_{|x|}^*$ then outputs

1. (Step 1) $(X_i^{b_i}, Y_i^{b_i})$, for $1 \leq i \leq |x|^{c_8}$,

2. (Step 2) T, and

3. (Step 3) I, $\bigcup_{i \in I} b_i$, and $\bigcup_{i \in I} T_i^{b_i}$.

Remark: It may seem odd at first that $S_{|x|}^*$ is not necessarily computable by a small probabilistic circuit, but rather needs access to a distribution that may in fact be very hard to generate. However, this doesn't really matter as far as proving no-use zero-knowledge is concerned. Suppose that, when given a sample from some arbitrary but fixed distribution D, a probabilistic circuit C can compute a predicate on a set $\{x_i\}, |x_i| = k$ with an error probability of less than 2^{-k} (taken over D and C's coin tosses). Then we can hardwire C's coin tosses and the output given by D so as to produce a deterministic circuit of the same size that correctly computes the predicate on $\{x_i\}$ with no error.

5 Proving security for our protocol.

We now outline the proof of the main theorem. We first use Lemma 4 to prove the following key lemma.

Lemma 5 Let $x \in L$. Suppose there exists a circuit C of size s such that

$$|prob(C(x, (P^*, V^*)(x)) = 1) - prob(C(x, S^*(x)) = 1)| > \epsilon,$$

where $\epsilon > |x|^{c_8} 2^{-|x|^{c_7}/4}$. Then there exists a circuit of size $(s|x|/\epsilon)^{c_{12}}$ that computes $QBF_{|x|^{c_7}}$. Here, c_{12} is a constant that depends only on L. ∎

Proof: (Sketch) First, we note that S^* correctly outputs many components of the simulation with the correct distribution. By the properties of the simulator for the ideal envelope protocol, it follows that $S^*(x)$ generates the correct distribution for T, I and $\bigcup_{i \in I} b_i$. The definition of $\mathcal{O}$ implies that for $i \in I$, (X_i, Y_i) and T_i will be distributed correctly as well. Let Q represent the set of this correctly simulated material, i.e.,

$$Q = \left(T, I, \bigcup_{i \in I} (b_i, (X_i, Y_i), T_i) \right).$$

We can view $S^*(x)$ and $(P^*, V^*)(x)$ as outputting

$$\left(Q, \bigcup_{i \notin I} (X_i, Y_i) \right),$$

according to (possibly) different distributions. We can further imagine that S^* and (P^*, V^*) first generate Q, and then generate the second component of the output distribution based on Q. This conceptual view is not in accord with the procedures we have specified for generating the distributions in question, but can be justified using conditional probabilities. We denote the distributions induced on the second component by $S^*(x, Q)$ and $(P^*, V^*)(x, Q)$.

When we project onto the first coordinate (looking at the value of Q), the distributions of S^* and $(P^*, V^*)(x)$ are identical. By a straightforward probabilistic argument, it follows that there is some value of Q such that

$$|prob(C(x, (Q, (P^*, V^*)(x, Q))) = 1) - prob(C(x, (Q, S^*(x, Q)) = 1))| > \epsilon.$$

We can hardwire Q into C to obtain a circuit C' that distinguishes $(P^*, V^*)(x, Q)$ from $S^*(x, Q)$. To complete the proof, is suffices to show that a circuit that distinguishing between these two distributions on $\bigcup_{i \notin I}(X_i, Y_i)$ can be transformed into a small circuit for $QBF_{|x|^{c_7}}$.

Given x and Q, $(P^*, V^*)(x, Q)$ can be generated by choosing b_i, for $i \notin I$, according to some (conditional) distribution, and then choosing (X_i, Y_i) according to b_i and the bit committal procedure.[5] $S^*(x, Q)$ can be generated by choosing $b_i = 0$ for $i \notin I$ and then

---

[5] This is one of the points in our proof where the honesty of the verifier is required. We implicitly assume that V^* does not look at the X_i, Y_i vectors; otherwise, this last claim would be false.

choosing (X_i, Y_i) according to b_i and the bit committal procedure. The only difference is in the distribution on the b_i's (for $i \notin I$). Thus, we can let B be the distribution on b_i, $i \notin I$, generated by $(P^*, V^*)(x)$, and apply Lemma 4 to complete the proof. ∎

Using Lemma 5, it is relatively straightforward to complete the proof of our main theorem.

Theorem 1 Let (P^*, V^*) be the interactive proof system for L described above. Then (P^*, V^*) is no-use zero-knowledge against honest verifiers.

Proof: (Sketch) Suppose there existed a set $S \subseteq L$, a predicate Q, a constant c, and a circuit family $\{C_k\}$, such that for $x \in S$,

$$prob(C_{|x|}(x, (P^*, V^*)(x)) = Q(x)) > \frac{1}{2} + \frac{1}{|x|^c}.$$

First, we only consider the case where $1/4|x|^c > |x|^{c_4} 2^{-|x|^{c_7}/3}$. For any value of c, the set of possible x that violate this constraint is finite, and can thus be handled by a look-up table.

We construct a circuit family $\{C_k'\}$ for Q as follows. For each k, we consider the probabilistic circuit $C_k^{sim}(x)$, that has access to a random output of $\mathcal{O}(k)$. $C_k^{sim}(x)$ simply runs $C_k(x, S_k^*(x))$. Now, one of the following cases must hold,

1. For all $x \in S, |x| = k$, we have

$$prob(C_k^{sim}(x) = Q(x)) > \frac{1}{2} + \frac{1}{2k^c}, \text{ or,}$$

2. For some $x_0 \in S, |x_0| = k$, we have

$$|prob(C_k(x_0, (P^*, V^*)(x_0)) = 1) - prob(C_k(x_0, S_k^*(x_0)) = 1)| > \frac{1}{4k^c}.$$

In the first case, we can perform standard amplification on $C_k^{sim}(x)$ to construct a circuit $C_k'(x)$ of size $|x|^{c_{10}}$, where c_{10} is a constant depending only on L and c, such that,

1. $C_k'(x)$ has access to (perhaps many) outputs from $\mathcal{O}(k)$.

2. For all $x \in S, |x| = k$, we have,

$$prob(C_k'(x) \neq Q(x)) < 2^{-k}.$$

We can then hardwire the random and auxiliary inputs (from $\mathcal{O}$) of C', so as to ensure that $C'_k(x) = Q(x)$ for all $x \in S, |x| = k$.

In the second case, we can use Lemma 5 to produce a circuit for $QBF_{k^{c_7}}$ of size $k^{c_{11}}$, where c_{11} is a constant depending only on L and c. Using these small circuits, we can then construct a circuit that simulates S_k^{perf} (S^{perf} restricted to inputs of size k), which is of size $k^{c_{12}}$ (where c_{12} is a constant depending only on L and c), and which only uses an output from $\mathcal{O}(k)$ (since all of the calls to the $QBF_{k^{c_7}}$ oracle are replaced by the actual small circuit). We can then construct a circuit $C_k^*(x)$ that simply runs $C_k(x, S_k^{perf}(x))$, which is in fact equivalent to running $C_k(x, (P^*, V^*)(x))$. We have, for all $x \in S, |x| = k$,

$$prob(C_k^*(x) = Q(x)) > \frac{1}{2} + \frac{1}{k^c}.$$

Then, by the same construction by which we generated a small C'_k from C_k^{sim}, we can construct a circuit C'_k from C_k^*, of size $k^{c_{13}}$, where c_{13} is a constant depending only on c and L. ∎

6 Acknowledgments.

I would like to acknowledge substantial technical help from Yishay Mansour, and some very useful comments on our definition of security by Shafi Goldwasser.

References

[1] B. Aeillo and J. Håstad. Perfect zero-knowledge languages can be recognized in two rounds. Proc. FOCS87.

[2] D. Beaver and J. Feigenbaum. Hiding Instances in Multioracle Queries, *Proc. of the 7th STACS* (1990), Springer Verlag LNCS 415, 37–48.

[3] D. Beaver, J. Feigenbaum, J. Kilian, and P. Rogaway. Cryptographic Applications of Locally Random Reductions, AT&T Bell Laboratories Technical Memorandum, November 15, 1989.

[4] M. Ben-Or, O. Goldreich, S. Goldwasser, J. Hastad, J. Kilian, S. Micali, and P. Rogaway. Everything Provable is Provable in Zero-Knowledge, Proc. of CRYPTO88.

[5] R. Boppana, J. Håstad, and S. Zachos. Does CoNP Have Short Interactive Proofs? IPL, 25, May 1987, P'. 127-132.

[6] C. Dwork and L. Stockmeyer, Interactive Proof Systems with Finite-State Verifiers, Proc. CRYPTO88.

[7] L. Fortnow. The Complexity of Perfect Zero-Knowledge. Proc. STOC87.

[8] O. Goldreich and L. Levin, Hardcore predicates from all one-way functions. Proc. STOC89

[9] S. Goldwasser and S. Micali. Probabilistic Encryption, *J. Comput. System Sci.* **28** (1984), 270–299.

[10] S. Goldwasser, S. Micali, and C. Rackoff. The Knowledge Complexity of Interactive Proof Systems, *SIAM J. Comput.* **18** (1989), 186–208.

[11] O. Goldreich, Y. Mansour, and M. Sipser. Interactive Proof Systems: Provers that never fail and random selection. Proc. FOCS87.

[12] O. Goldreich, S. Micali, and A. Wigderson. Proofs that Yield Nothing but Their Validity and a Methodology of Cryptographic Protocol Design, Proc. of FOCS86.

[13] Johan Håstad. Manuscript.

[14] R. Impagliazzo, L. Levin, and M. Luby. Pseudo-random Generation from One-Way Fynctions, Proc. STOC89

[15] R. Impagliazzo and M. Yung. Direct Minimum-Knowledge Computation, Proc. of CRYPTO87.

[16] R. Lipton. New Directions in Testing, manuscript, October, 1989.

[17] M. Naor Pseudorandomnesss and Bit Commitment, Proc. of Crypto89.

[18] R. Ostrovsky, Venkatesan and M. Yung. Manuscript (Submitted to STOC91)

[19] A. Shamir. IP = PSPACE, manuscript, December 26, 1989.

[20] A. Shamir. CRYPTO Rump Session.

[21] A. C. Yao. Protocols for Secure Computations, Proc. of FOCS82.

Randomness

Chair: R. Rivest, MIT

On the Universality of the Next Bit Test

A.W. Schrift and A. Shamir

Department of Applied Mathematics and Computer Science
The Weizmann Institute of Science
Rehovot 76100, Israel

Abstract

The next bit test was shown by Yao to be a universal test for sources of unbiased independent bits. The aim of this paper is to provide a rigorous methodology of how to test other properties of sources whose output distribution is not necessarily uniform. We prove the surprising result that the natural extension of the next bit test, even in the simplest case of biased independent bits, is no longer universal: We construct a source of biased bits, whose bits are obviously dependent and yet none of these bits can be predicted with probability of success greater than the bias. To overcome this difficulty, we develop new universal tests for arbitrary models of (potentially imperfect) sources of randomness.

1   Introduction

Randomness is an essential resource in many scientific areas, and pseudo-randomness is a good substitute in many applications. In his seminal paper Yao [11] formally defines the notion of perfect pseudo-random bits, i.e. bits that are indistinguishable from truly random bits by any probabilistic polynomial-time observer. He shows that the ability to predict some bit of a given source (the *next bit test*) serves as a universal test for randomness: A natural or pseudo-random source is perfect iff no probabilistic polynomial-time algorithm can, given any prefix of bits, predict the next bit of the source with probability of success significantly greater than $1/2$. The next bit test has proved to be a useful tool for constructing perfect pseudo-random bit generators ([3],[2]) and for proving the imperfectness of other generators ([2],[6]).

Several models of natural sources of randomness have been suggested and investigated in [9], [1], [7] and [4]. In all the models the output distribution of natural sources is not uniform: In [9] a natural source outputs biased independent bits, in [1] a source is modeled by a Markov chain and in [7] and [4] the outcomes of the source are controlled by a powerful adversary. Non-uniform distributions appear also in some applications which require sources of randomness with independent yet biased bits (see for example [10],[5]). Nevertheless no rigorous methodology of how to verify the correspondence between a source of randomness with a non-uniform output distribution and its assumed properties has been given. The aim of our paper is to provide such a formalization.

Consider, for example, the roulette in your favorite Casino, where you are in the habit of placing a variety of bets on 17 with a 1/37 probability of winning each time. However after an unfortunate series of losses you begin to suspect that the roulette has been tampered with. You can easily check that the overall probability of 17 is close to 1/37, but that does not rule out the possibility that the outcomes of the roulette are artificially determined in a way that maintains the overall bias but inhibits 17 from appearing whenever the bets are high. How can you verify that indeed the outcomes of the roulette are independent, and that it is only your bad luck that brought you to the edge of bankruptcy? Clearly the next bit test cannot be employed here since you deal with a biased event.

Using the known notion of polynomial indistiguishability we define the notions of *perfect independence* and in general *perfect simulation* of a source by a mathematical model. We then move to the question of specifying the universal tests for these notions, which will declare a source to be perfect if and only if it passes the universal test. Surprisingly, the natural extension of Yao's work fails, even for the simplest case of independent biased bits. In other words the extended next bit test for biased bits which requires that no observer succeeds in predicting the bits of the source with probability greater than the bias, is no longer a universal test for independence. We introduce the correct test of independence, which we call the *weighted success rate (WSR) test* and prove its universality. We also discuss several alternative tests, and in particular the test we call *the predict or pass (POP) test*.

For general sources of randomness we present the universal test that determines whether a certain mathematical model perfectly simulates a given source. This test is the *comparative version* of the next bit test. The standard next bit test as well as the WSR and POP tests emerge from the comparative next bit test as special cases. Our proof of the universality of the test is the generalization of Yao's original proof, even though the original techniques cannot be implemented directly.

2 Definitions and Notations

Our definitions follow the original definitions of Yao [11]. The notions of a probability distribution, independence etc. are the standard notions from probability theory. All our results are stated in terms of probabilistic polynomial-time algorithms but can be restated in terms of polynomial-size Boolean circuits.

Let Σ^n denote the set of all binary strings of length n. A binary string of length n will be denoted s_1^n. The i-th bit of the string will be denoted by s_i. The substring starting with the j-th bit and ending with the l-th bit $(1 \leq j < l \leq n)$ will be denoted by s_j^l. We use the notation $f < O(\nu(n))$ for any function that vanishes faster than any polynomial, i.e. $\forall$constant k $\exists N$ such that $\forall n > N$: $f < 1/n^k$.

Definition: A *source ensemble* S is a sequence $\{S_n\}$ where S_n is a probability distribution on Σ^n.

Definition: A source S is *biased towards 1* with a fixed bias $1/2 < b < 1$ if for every i: $\Pr_S(s_i = 1) = b$.

Note that by our restriction on the bias the output bits of a biased source have a non-zero probability of being both 0 and 1. This ensures that the definitions of dependency, conditional probabilities etc. remain meaningful.

Let $B = \{B_n\}$ denote the *independent biased ensemble* where the source is biased towards 1 and all the bits are independent. $R = \{R_n\}$ denotes the *truly random ensemble* producing independent unbiased bits. Dealing with arbitrary models, we use $M = \{M_n\}$ for the mathematical model ensemble. We denote by $\Pr_S(E)$ the probability of an event E taking place when the probability distribution is defined by the source ensemble S. Whenever we refer to events that involve a probabilistic algorithm, we explicitly denote only the source ensemble, S, and implicitly assume the probability of the event to be induced by S and by the independent unbiased coin flips of the algorithm.

Definition: A probabilistic polynomial-time algorithm is *constant* if for some value v, $\Pr(\text{algorithm} = v) > 1 - O(\nu(n))$.

To simplify the presentation of our results we require algorithms to be non-constant even when it suffices to require only that for every value v: $\Pr(\text{algorithm} = v) \neq 0$.

Definition: A *distinguisher* is a probabilistic polynomial-time algorithm $D : \{0,1\}^n \to \{0,1\}$.

Definition: A biased source S outputs *perfect independent* bits if for every distinguisher D: $|\Pr_S(D = 1) - \Pr_B(D = 1)| < O(\nu(n))$.

Definition: A model M is *a perfect simulation* of a source S if for every distinguisher D: $|\Pr_S(D = 1) - \Pr_M(D = 1)| < O(\nu(n))$.

3 Universal Tests of Independence

In this section we construct what seems to be the natural extension of Yao's next bit test. We then show that there exist imperfect sources of randomness that pass the extended next bit test, thus disproving its universality. Our proof is based on the following intuition: Dependencies between the bits of an imperfect source will result in 1 having in some cases probability greater than the bias and in other cases probability smaller than the bias. It is possible, however, for the biased source to be imperfect with 1 remaining always more probable than 0. Hence deterministically predicting 1 is the optimal prediction strategy but has a poor probability of success. Following the same intuition we suggest the weighted success rate test that is better suited to detect deviations from the bias. In the WSR test we separately compute the probabilities of success in predicting the 0 and 1 values of a next bit, and compose the two terms with appropriate weights into a single measure.

In the following we assume without loss of generality that all our sources to be biased towards 1 with some fixed bias b. It is easy to extend our results to the case where each bit has a different bias. It is worthwhile to emphasize that since we are interested in detecting dependencies among bits that have a particular bias, our basic WSR test may fail to detect imperfectness that results simply from a different overall bias. Testing the condition that the bits of a source have a certain bias can be done easily in polynomial time and with high accuracy using the law of large numbers. We give an alternative universal test, the POP test, with the additional feature that any deviation from the a-priori known bias is automatically detected.

3.1 The Extended Next Bit Test

Trying to extend the definition of Yao's next bit test to biased sources we must take into consideration the fact that the bits of an independent biased source can be trivially predicted with probability of success b, simply by always predicting 1.

Definition: A biased source S *passes the extended next bit test* if for every $1 \leq i \leq n$ and for every probabilistic polynomial-time algorithm A:

$$\text{Pr}_S(A = s_i) < b + O(\nu(n))$$

Theorem 1:

The extended next bit test is not a universal test for independence.

Proof:

Fix a bias b: $1/2 < b \leq 1 - 1/n^t$, for some constant t. We construct a source which is biased towards 1 with bias b. We show that it is imperfect and yet it passes the extended next bit test. The source is the following:

$$\text{Pr}_S(s_i = 1) = \begin{cases} b & \text{for } 1 \leq i \leq n-1 \\ b+\delta & \text{for } i = n \text{ and } s_1^2 = 01 \\ b-\delta & \text{for } i = n \text{ and } s_1^2 = 10 \\ b & \text{for } i = n \text{ and } s_1^2 = 00 \text{ or } 11 \end{cases}$$

Where $\frac{1}{n^q} \leq \delta < \min(b - \frac{1}{2}, 1 - b)$, for some constant q.

Let the distinguisher D be defined by: D=1 iff $s_1^2 = 01$ and $s_n = 1$. Clearly, $\text{Pr}_S(D = 1) = c \cdot (b + \delta)$, while $\text{Pr}_B(D = 1) = c \cdot b$, where $c = b \cdot (1 - b) \geq 1/2n^t$. Therefore, $\text{Pr}_S(D = 1) - \text{Pr}_B(D = 1) = c \cdot \delta \geq 1/2n^{q+t}$, and by definition the source is imperfect. Nevertheless the source passes the extended next bit test: The n-th bit is always biased towards 1, so the best prediction strategy is to deterministically predict 1 regardless of the known values of the first two bits. It is easy to check that the probability of success of this optimal strategy remains b. $\qquad\square$

3.2 The Weighted Success Rate Test

Definition: Fix $1 \leq i \leq n$. The *weighted success rate* of any non-constant probabilistic polynomial-time algorithm A: $\{0,1\}^{i-1} \rightarrow \{0,1\}$ in predicting the i-th bit of a biased source S is:

$$
\begin{aligned}
ws(A, S, i) &= \frac{\Pr_S(A = s_i | s_i = 1)}{\Pr_S(A = 1)} + \frac{\Pr_S(A = s_i | s_i = 0)}{\Pr_S(A = 0)} = \\
&= \frac{1}{b} \cdot \Pr_S(A = s_i | A = 1) + \frac{1}{1-b} \cdot \Pr_S(A = s_i | A = 0)
\end{aligned}
$$

Definition: A biased source S *passes the weighted success rate test* if for every $1 \leq i \leq n$ and every non-constant probabilistic polynomial-time algorithm A: $\{0,1\}^{i-1} \rightarrow \{0,1\}$:

$$
ws(A, S, i) < 2 + O(\nu(n))
$$

Remark: The above definitions do not allow constant prediction algorithms. Remember that we assume that indeed all the tested sources of randomness have a bias b. Since constant algorithms can only detect that the overall bias is other than b, which is not the case, it is possible without loss of the generality to ignore them.

Theorem 2:

A biased source produces perfect independent bits iff it passes the weighted success rate test.

Sketch of Proof:

If a given source fails the weighted success rate test, it is easy to construct a distinguisher which tells the source apart from a truly independent biased source by using the predictions of the WSR test.

To prove the other direction, we show how to construct a weighted success rate test using any distinguisher D for an imperfect source. Following our intuition that imperfect sources can be recognized using the events where the probability of an i-th bit being 1 significantly differs from the bias, we use the distinguisher to single out these events. We prove that one of the following cases always exists:

1. The probability that the distinguisher outputs 1 on the input sequence $s_1^{i-1} 1 s_{i+1}^n$ with $s_1^{i-1} \in S$ and $s_{i+1}^n \in B$ is significantly changed when $s_i = 1$ is taken out of S or B.

2. The probability that the distinguisher outputs 1 on the input sequence $s_1^{i-1} 0 s_{i+1}^n$ with $s_1^{i-1} \in S$ and $s_{i+1}^n \in B$ is significantly changed when $s_i = 0$ is taken out of S or B.

We construct a different test for each case, and use the corresponding condition on D to prove that in each case one of the terms in the weighted success rate of the corresponding test is significantly greater than 1. We conclude the proof with the following useful lemma:

Prediction Lemma: For any biased source and any non-constant probabilistic polynomial-time algorithm $A : \{0,1\}^{i-1} \to \{0,1\}$: $\mathrm{Pr}_S(A = s_i | A = 1) \geq b + 1/n^{k_1}$ iff $\mathrm{Pr}_S(A = s_i | A = 0) \geq 1 - b + 1/n^{k_2}$, for some constants k_1 and k_2.

The full proofs of the theorem and the lemma are given in the appendix.

3.3 Alternative Versions

In the following we present three tests, that are all equivalent to the WSR test, but emphasize different aspects of detecting dependencies. The first two definitions are closely related to the WSR test. The last test presents an entirely different approach, which stems from the fact that if a source is imperfect it is possible to detect the event in which 1 is more probable than the given bias and ignore all other events.

Definition: A biased source S passes the modified WSR test if for every $1 \leq i \leq n$ and every non-constant probabilistic polynomial-time algorithm A: $\{0,1\}^{i-1} \to \{0,1\}$:

$$\max \left\{ \frac{\mathrm{Pr}_S(A = s_i | s_i = 1)}{\mathrm{Pr}_S(A = 1)}, \frac{\mathrm{Pr}_S(A = s_i | s_i = 0)}{\mathrm{Pr}_S(A = 0)} \right\} =$$

$$= \max \left\{ \frac{1}{b} \mathrm{Pr}_S(A = s_i | A = 1), \frac{1}{1-b} \mathrm{Pr}_S(A = s_i | A = 0) \right\} < 1 + O(\nu(n))$$

Definition: A biased source S passes the behavior test if for every $1 \leq i \leq n$ and every non-constant probabilistic polynomial-time algorithm A: $\{0,1\}^{i-1} \to \{0,1\}$:

$$|\mathrm{Pr}_S(A = 1 | s_i = 1) - \mathrm{Pr}_S(A = 1 | s_i = 0)| < O(\nu(n))$$

Definition: A biased source S passes the predict or pass (POP) test if for every $1 \leq i \leq n$ and every probabilistic polynomial-time algorithm A: $\{0,1\}^{i-1} \to \{0,1,*\}$ the following condition holds:

If $\mathrm{Pr}_S(A \neq *) \geq 1/n^l$ for some constant l, then $|\mathrm{Pr}_S(A = s_i | A \neq *) - b| < O(\nu(n))$.

Using similar techniques to those introduced in Theorem 2 we can prove that the above defined tests are universal. The proofs appear in the appendix.

Theorem 3:

The following conditions are equivalent:
1. A biased source outputs perfect independent bits.
2. A biased source passes the modified WSR test.
3. A biased source passes the behavior test.
4. A biased source passes the POP test.

Remark: The above equivalence holds only for biased sources that were a-priori tested to have a certain bias. Otherwise, the POP test behaves differently from the other tests. Its definition allows constant as well as non-constant prediction algorithms. More important is the fact that unlike the WSR test, the POP test succeeds in detecting imperfectness that results merely from a different overall bias.

The POP test introduces what seems to be a new notion of allowing a predictor to be successful only on some non-negligible fraction of its inputs. Despite the fact that this formal definition is novel (as far as we know), known constructions of pseudo-random bit generators often prove their perfectness by showing that they pass what is essentially a POP test (i.e. it is impossible to predict the output bits of the generator even on a non-negligible fraction of the output strings). Indeed, the POP test is particularly useful for constructing perfect generators for biased independent bits.

3.4   Comparison with the Next Bit Test

For unbiased ($b = 1/2$) independent bits the WSR test and its variations all serve as alternative universal tests to the next bit test. We can, however, show an even stronger equivalence between the tests, namely that the same algorithm that succeeds in the prediction of a certain bit with probability significantly greater than $1/2$ (thus proving the source of the bits to be imperfect by the next bit test) have a weighted success rate that is significantly greater than 2 (thus proving the source to be imperfect by the WSR test).

Proposition 4:

For any unbiased source ($b = 1/2$) and any non-constant probabilistic polynomial-time algorithm $A : \{0,1\}^{i-1} \rightarrow \{0,1\}$: $\Pr_S(A = s_i) \geq 1/2 + 1/n^{k_1}$ iff $ws(A, S, i) \geq 2 + 1/n^{k_2}$, for some constants k_1 and k_2.

In terms of the probability of successful prediction for unbiased sources our new definitions are superior:

Proposition 5:

For any unbiased source and any next bit test T there exists a POP test A, such that for every $1 \leq i \leq n$:

$$\Pr_S(A = s_i \mid A \neq *) \geq \Pr_S(T = s_i)$$

The proofs of the two propositions are given in the appendix.

4   Perfectness with Respect to Arbitrary Models

In this section we consider an arbitrary source S, which we believe to have a certain distribution described by a mathematical model M. As for randomness and independence we search for a convenient universal test, based on the probability of correct predictions:

Definition: A source S *passes the comparative next bit test* with respect to a model M if for every $1 \leq i \leq n$ and every probabilistic polynomial-time algorithm A: $\{0,1\}^{i-1} \rightarrow \{0,1\}$:

$$|\mathrm{Pr}_S(A = s_i) - \mathrm{Pr}_M(A = s_i)| < O(\nu(n))$$

Note that the comparative next bit test enables us to avoid performing any a-priori tests on either sources. The test is easiest to implement when the model is described in such a way that the probability of correct bit predictions for the model can be efficiently computed. Yet we can perform the test even when the model is completely unknown and given to us as a black box. In that case the test simply involves a comparison between two boxes: one containing the tested source and the other containing the model black box.

It is instructive to examine simple examples of the comparative next bit test, where the model source is explicitly known:

1. $M = R$, i.e. the model is a source of unbiased independent bits. In that case we know that no matter which algorithm is used $\mathrm{Pr}_R(A = s_i) = 1/2$ and we can immediately derive the next bit test.

2. $M = B$, i.e. the model is a source of biased independent bits. Here we know that for any non-constant algorithm $\mathrm{Pr}_B(A = s_i | A = 1) = b$ and that $\mathrm{Pr}_B(A = s_i | A = 0) = 1 - b$ so that the predictions must be evaluated according to the value that is being predicted. This gives rise to the WSR test.

3. $M=$ a source with a one-bit memory, in which the probability of the i-th bit is determined according to the outcome of the $(i-1)$-th bit. Let $b_i(0) = \mathrm{Pr}(s_i = 1 | s_{i-1} = 0)$ and $b_i(1) = \mathrm{Pr}(s_i = 1 | s_{i-1} = 1)$. Then it is easy to see that the performance of any algorithm must be evaluated not only according to the value of s_i but also according to the value of s_{i-1}. We therefore get that M is a perfect simulation of a source S if for every $1 \leq i \leq n$ and every probabilistic polynomial-time algorithm A: $\{0,1\}^{i-1} \rightarrow \{0,1,*\}$ such that $\mathrm{Pr}_S(A \neq * | s_{i-1} = 0) \geq 1/n^{l_1}$ and $\mathrm{Pr}_S(A \neq * | s_{i-1} = 1) \geq 1/n^{l_2}$ for some constants l_1, l_2:

$$\max \ \{ \ |\mathrm{Pr}_S(A = s_i | A \neq *, s_{i-1} = 0) - b_i(0)|,$$
$$|\mathrm{Pr}_S(A = s_i | A \neq *, s_{i-1} = 1) - b_i(1)| \ \} < O(\nu(n))$$

It is easy to see that similar analysis holds for any $M=$ Markov chain [1], where predictions must be evaluated according to the output value and to the state (which determines the bias).

Theorem 6:

A model M is a perfect simulation of a source S iff S passes the comparative next bit test with respect to M.

Proof:

It is easy to see that if a source S fails the comparative next bit test it is distinguishable from the model source M. Assume now that we are given that S and M are distinguishable and need to prove that S fails the comparative next bit test w.r.t. M. We cannot implement previous proof techniques directly since they inherently assume independence in concatenating a random prefix of bits taken out of the tested source with a random suffix of bits generated according to the desired distribution. We overcome the problem by using an additional truly random source for the concatenation.

Let $D : \{0,1\}^n \to \{0,1\}$ be the distinguisher for which $|\Pr_S(D = 1) - \Pr_M(D = 1)| \geq 1/n^k$ for some constant k. Let p_i^S (p_i^M) denote the probability that D outputs 1 when the first i bits of its input are taken out of S (M) and the rest are independent unbiased coin flips. Note that $p_n^S = \Pr_S(D = 1)$, $p_n^M = \Pr_M(D = 1)$ and $p_0^S = p_0^M = \Pr_R(D = 1)$. Since $|p_n^S - p_n^M| \geq 1/n^k$, by the pigeonhole principle there exists an i which is the first for which p_i^S and p_i^M significantly differ, i.e.:

1. $|p_i^S - p_i^M| \geq 1/n^{k+1}$, and

2. For all $j \leq i - 1$, $|p_j^S - p_j^M| < O(\nu(n))$.

We can assume w.l.o.g. $p_i^S - p_i^M > 0$. The comparative next bit test A submits to D the string $s = s_1^{i-1} s_i^n$, where $s_1^{i-1} \in S$ or M and $s_i^n \in R$. If $D(s) = 1$ then A outputs s_i, else A outputs $1 - s_i$. It is easy to see that:

$$\Pr_S(A = s_i) = \frac{1}{2} + p_i^S - p_{i-1}^S$$

While:

$$\Pr_M(A = s_i) = \frac{1}{2} + p_i^M - p_{i-1}^M$$

Hence:

$$\Pr_S(A = s_i) - \Pr_M(A = s_i) \geq \frac{1}{n^{k+1}}$$

$\square$

5 Discussion

In this paper we develop a formal theory for the universal testing of non-uniform probability distributions. Our definitions rely on Yao's pioneering work, but evolve from it in a non-obvious way. In addition to its theoretical significance our results have several practical applications:

1. An important property of one-way functions is the existence of hard bits in the argument that are as hard to compute from a given random value of the function as the entire argument. In a recent work [8] the individual security of every bit of the discrete logarithm modulo a composite was proven. The known definitions of unpredictability could not be applied to the most significant bits, since they are biased towards 0 by definition. For those bits it was necessary to use our new definitions in order to define and prove their security.

2. It is possible to apply the universal test of independence to every biased predicate and use a hard biased predicate to construct a generator of independent biased bits. Consider for example the following construction that is based on the intractability of the discrete logarithm modulo a prime. Let $f_{g,p}(x) = g^x \pmod{p}$, where p is a randomly chosen n-bit prime and g is a random generator of Z_p^*. Let b be the desired bias towards 1 and k the desired output length.

$$\forall i \geq 1: \quad f_{p,g}^i(z) = f_{p,g}\left(f_{p,g}^{i-1}(z)\right) \quad \text{with} \quad f_{p,g}^0(z) = z.$$

$$\text{Let} \quad G(z) = \begin{cases} 0 & \text{if } z < \lfloor (1-b) \cdot (p-1) \rfloor \\ 1 & \text{otherwise} \end{cases}$$

For a randomly chosen seed x we shall produce k bits $\{s_1^k\}$ by: $s_m = G\left(f_{p,g}^{m-1}(x)\right)$, and use the universal tests of independence to prove that $\{s_1^k\}$ are perfect independent bits with bias b. For constant output lengths the above is a more efficient construction of independent biased bits than the obvious construction of biased bits from pseudo-random (unbiased) bits.

Acknowledgements

We would like to thank Uriel Feige and Rafi Heiman for many stimulating discussions.

References

[1] Blum, M., "Independent Coin Flips From a Correlated Biased Source: a Finite State Markov Chain", *Proc. 25th FOCS, 1984, pp. 425-433.*

[2] Blum, L., Blum, M., Shub, M., "A Simple Secure Pseudo-Random Generator", *SIAM J. of Computing, Vol. 15, No. 2, 1986, pp. 364-383.*

[3] Blum, M., Micali, S., "How to Generate Cryptographically Strong Sequences of Pseudo-Random Bits", *Proc. 26th FOCS, 1982, pp. 112-117.*

[4] Chor, B., Goldreich, O., "Unbiased Bits from Sources of Weak Randomness and Probabilistic Communication Complexity", *Proc. 26th FOCS, 1985, pp. 429-442.*

[5] Feldman, D., Impagliazzo, R., Naor, M., Nisan, N., Rudich, S., Shamir, A., "On Dice and Coins", *ICALP 1989*.

[6] Plumstead, J., "Inferring a Sequence Generated by a Linear Congruence", *Proc. 23rd FOCS, 1982, pp. 153-159*.

[7] Santha, M., Vazirani, U.V., "Generating Quasi-Random Sequences from Slightly-Random Sources", *Proc. 25th FOCS, 1984, pp. 434-440*.

[8] Schrift, A.W., Shamir, A., "The Discrete Log is Very Discreet", *Proc. 22nd STOC, 1990, pp. 405-415*.

[9] von Neumann, J., "Various Techniques Used in Connection with Random Digits", *Notes by G.E. Forsythe, 1951, Reprinted in von Neumann's Collected Works, Vol. 5, Pergamon Press, 1963, pp. 768-770*.

[10] Vazirani, U.V., Vazirani, V.V., "Trapdoor Pseudo-Random Number Generator with Applications to Protocol Design", *Proc. 24th FOCS, 1983, pp. 23-30*.

[11] Yao, A.C., "Theory and Applications of Trapdoor Functions", *Proc. 23rd FOCS, 1982, pp. 80-91*.

Appendix: Full Proofs

Proof of Theorem 2

Given that a source fails the weighted success rate test, it is easy to construct a distinguisher between the source S and a truly independent biased source B by examining the predictions of the test. Formally assume that we are given a non-constant probabilistic polynomial-time algorithm A: $\{0,1\}^{i-1} \rightarrow \{0,1\}$ for the i-th bit of a source S such that $ws(A,S,i) \geq 2+1/n^k$ for some constant k. We shall use A to construct two possible distinguishers and show that for one of them $|\Pr_S(D=1) - \Pr_B(D=1)| \geq 1/n^{k'}$ for some constant k'. Given s_1^n, both D's submits s_1^{i-1} to A and examine A's output. $D_1 = 1$ iff $A = s_i = 1$. $D_2 = 1$ iff $A = 1$. If the overall behavior of A is the same for S and for B, i.e. $|\Pr_S(A=1) - \Pr_B(A=1)| < O(\nu(n))$, then D_1 distinguishes the source. Otherwise D_2 distinguishes. Hence S is imperfect.

To prove the other direction, we show how to construct a weighted success rate test using any distinguisher D for an imperfect source. Let p_i denote the probability that D=1 when the first i input bits are taken out of S and the rest are independent biased coin flips. Note that $p_n = \Pr_S(D = 1)$, while $p_0 = \Pr_B(D = 1)$. Since D distinguishes between the source and a biased coin, $|p_0 - p_n| \geq 1/n^k$ for some k. By the pigeonhole principle there exists a bit i for which: $|p_i - p_{i-1}| \geq 1/n^{k+1}$. We shall assume w.l.o.g.

that $p_i - p_{i-1} > 0$.

Explicitly:

$$p_i = \sum_{s_1^n} \Pr(D(s_1^n) = 1) \cdot \Pr_S(s_1^i) \cdot \Pr_B(s_{i+1}^n) =$$

$$= \sum_{s_1^{i-1}, s_{i+1}^n} \left[\Pr(D(s_1^{i-1} 1 s_{i+1}^n) = 1) \cdot \Pr_S(s_1^{i-1}) \cdot \Pr_S(s_i = 1 | s_1^{i-1}) \cdot \Pr_B(s_{i+1}^n) + \right.$$

$$\left. + \Pr(D(s_1^{i-1} 0 s_{i+1}^n) = 1) \cdot \Pr_S(s_1^{i-1}) \cdot \Pr_S(s_i = 0 | s_1^{i-1}) \cdot \Pr_B(s_{i+1}^n) \right]$$

$$p_{i-1} = \sum_{s_1^n} \Pr(D(s_1^n) = 1) \cdot \Pr_S(s_1^{i-1}) \cdot \Pr_B(s_i^n) =$$

$$= \sum_{s_1^{i-1}, s_{i+1}^n} \left[\Pr\left(D(s_1^{i-1} 1 s_{i+1}^n) = 1 \right) \cdot \Pr_S(s_1^{i-1}) \cdot \Pr_B(s_i = 1) \cdot \Pr_B(s_{i+1}^n) + \right.$$

$$\left. + \Pr\left(D(s_1^{i-1} 0 s_{i+1}^n) = 1 \right) \cdot \Pr_S(s_1^{i-1}) \cdot \Pr_B(s_i = 0) \cdot \Pr_B(s_{i+1}^n) \right]$$

Since $p_i - p_{i-1} \geq \frac{1}{n^{k+1}}$, then one of the following two equations hold.

(1) $\displaystyle \sum_{s_1^{i-1}, s_{i+1}^n} \left[\Pr\left(D(s_1^{i-1} 1 s_{i+1}^n) = 1 \right) \cdot \Pr_S(s_1^{i-1}) \cdot \Pr_S(s_i = 1 | s_1^{i-1}) \cdot \Pr_B(s_{i+1}^n) - \right.$

$$\left. - \Pr\left(D(s_1^{i-1} 1 s_{i+1}^n) = 1 \right) \cdot \Pr_S(s_1^{i-1}) \cdot \Pr_B(s_i = 1) \cdot \Pr_B(s_{i+1}^n) \right] \geq \frac{1}{2n^{k+1}}$$

(2) $\displaystyle \sum_{s_1^{i-1}, s_{i+1}^n} \left[\Pr\left(D(s_1^{i-1} 0 s_{i+1}^n) = 1 \right) \cdot \Pr_S(s_1^{i-1}) \cdot \Pr_S(s_i = 0 | s_1^{i-1}) \cdot \Pr_B(s_{i+1}^n) - \right.$

$$\left. - \Pr\left(D(s_1^{i-1} 0 s_{i+1}^n) = 1 \right) \cdot \Pr_S(s_1^{i-1}) \cdot \Pr_B(s_i = 0) \cdot \Pr_B(s_{i+1}^n) \right] \geq \frac{1}{2n^{k+1}}$$

By examining D it is possible to decide which of the two holds and construct a WSR test A_i accordingly. Otherwise by constructing the following two tests A_1 and A_2 you are guaranteed that one of them will be successful.

A_1 submits as input to D the string $s_1^{i-1} 1 s_{i+1}^n$, where $s_1^{i-1} \in S$ and $s_{i+1}^n \in B$. If D=1 then $A_1 = 1$; else $A_1 = 0$. A_2 submits as input to D the string $s_1^{i-1} 0 s_{i+1}^n$, where $s_1^{i-1} \in S$ and $s_{i+1}^n \in B$. If D=1 then $A_2 = 0$; else $A_2 = 1$. We shall now analyze separately the two terms of $ws(A_1, S, i)$ and $ws(A_2, S, i)$. To make the analysis simple we use the second alternative in the definition of the weighted success rate, which compares the probabilities of successful predictions to b or $1 - b$.

$$\Pr_S(A_1 = s_i \mid A_1 = 1) =$$

$$= \frac{\sum_{s_1^{i-1}, s_{i+1}^n} \Pr_S(s_i = 1 \mid s_1^{i-1}) \cdot \Pr\left(D(s_1^{i-1} 1 s_{i+1}^n) = 1 \right) \cdot \Pr_S(s_1^{i-1}) \cdot \Pr_B(s_{i+1}^n)}{\sum_{s_1^{i-1}, s_{i+1}^n} \Pr\left(D(s_1^{i-1} 1 s_{i+1}^n) = 1 \right) \cdot \Pr_S(s_1^{i-1}) \cdot \Pr_B(s_{i+1}^n)} \geq$$

(by equation 1)

$$\geq \frac{\sum_{s_1^{i-1}, s_{i+1}^n} \mathrm{Pr}_B(s_i = 1) \cdot \mathrm{Pr}\left(D(s_1^{i-1} 1 s_{i+1}^n) = 1\right) \cdot \mathrm{Pr}_S(s_1^{i-1}) \cdot \mathrm{Pr}_B(s_{i+1}^n) + \frac{1}{2n^{k+1}}}{\sum_{s_1^{i-1}, s_{i+1}^n} \mathrm{Pr}\left(D(s_1^{i-1} 1 s_{i+1}^n) = 1\right) \cdot \mathrm{Pr}_S(s_1^{i-1}) \cdot \mathrm{Pr}_B(s_{i+1}^n)} =$$

$(\mathrm{Pr}_B(s_i = 1) = b)$

$$= b + \frac{\frac{1}{2n^{k+1}}}{\sum_{s_1^{i-1}, s_{i+1}^n} \mathrm{Pr}\left(D(s_1^{i-1} 1 s_{i+1}^n) = 1\right) \cdot \mathrm{Pr}_S(s_1^{i-1}) \cdot \mathrm{Pr}_B(s_{i+1}^n)} \geq$$

(the denominator < 1)

$$\geq b + \frac{1}{2n^{k+1}}$$

Similarly for A_2:

$$\mathrm{Pr}_S(A_2 = s_i | A_2 = 0) =$$

$$= \frac{\sum_{s_1^{i-1}, s_{i+1}^n} \mathrm{Pr}_S(s_i = 0 \mid s_1^{i-1}) \cdot \mathrm{Pr}\left(D(s_1^{i-1} 0 s_{i+1}^n) = 1\right) \cdot \mathrm{Pr}_S(s_1^{i-1}) \cdot \mathrm{Pr}_B(s_{i+1}^n)}{\sum_{s_1^{i-1}, s_{i+1}^n} \mathrm{Pr}\left(D(s_1^{i-1} 0 s_{i+1}^n) = 1\right) \cdot \mathrm{Pr}_S(s_1^{i-1}) \cdot \mathrm{Pr}_B(s_{i+1}^n)} \geq$$

$$\geq 1 - b + \frac{1}{2n^{k+1}}$$

To complete the proof we show that for each of $ws(A_1, S, i)$ and $ws(A_2, S, i)$ the remaining term (that does not appear above) is also significantly greater than 1.

Prediction Lemma: For any biased source and any non-constant probabilistic polynomial-time algorithm $A : \{0,1\}^{i-1} \to \{0,1\}$: $\mathrm{Pr}_S(A = s_i | A = 1) \geq b + 1/n^{k_1}$ iff $\mathrm{Pr}_S(A = s_i | A = 0) \geq 1 - b + 1/n^{k_2}$, for some constants k_1 and k_2.

Proof:

Assume that $\mathrm{Pr}_S(A = s_i | A = 1) \geq b + \varepsilon_1$, where $\varepsilon_1 = 1/n^{k_1}$. Note that $\mathrm{Pr}_S(A = s_i | A = 1) = \mathrm{Pr}_S(s_i = 1 | A = 1)$. Since the overall bias of the source is known to be b,

$$\mathrm{Pr}_S(s_i = 1 | A = 1) \cdot \mathrm{Pr}_S(A = 1) + \mathrm{Pr}_S(s_i = 1 | A = 0) \cdot \mathrm{Pr}_S(A = 0) = b.$$

Therefore:

$$\mathrm{Pr}_S(s_i = 1 | A = 0) \leq \frac{b - (b + \varepsilon_1)\mathrm{Pr}_S(A = 1)}{\mathrm{Pr}_S(A = 0)}$$

Simple manipulations give:

$$\mathrm{Pr}_S(A = s_i | A = 0) = \mathrm{Pr}_S(s_i = 0 | A = 0) = 1 - \mathrm{Pr}_S(s_i = 1 | A = 0) \geq$$

$$\geq 1 - b + \varepsilon_1 \cdot \frac{\mathrm{Pr}_S(A = 1)}{\mathrm{Pr}_S(A = 0)}$$

Similarly when $\mathrm{Pr}_S(A = s_i | A = 0) \geq 1 - b + \varepsilon_2$, where $\varepsilon_2 = 1/n^{k_2}$, we get using the same manipulations that:

$$\mathrm{Pr}_S(A = s_i | A = 1) \geq b + \varepsilon_2 \cdot \frac{\mathrm{Pr}_S(A = 0)}{\mathrm{Pr}_S(A = 1)}$$

$\square$

Proof of Theorem 3

The theorem contains three claims, all follow easily from the proof of Theorem 2.

Claim 1: A biased source outputs perfect independent bits iff it passes the modified WSR test.

Proof: If a biased source fails the modified WSR test it is easy to construct a distinguisher between the source and a truly independent biased source in a similar way to the construction in Theorem 2.

If a biased source is imperfect, then by the proof of Theorem 2 there exists a non-constant probabilistic polynomial-time algorithm A: $\{0,1\}^{i-1} \to \{0,1\}$ such that $\Pr(A = s_i|A = 1) \geq b + 1/n^{k_1}$ and $\Pr(A = s_i|A = 0) \geq 1 - b + 1/n^{k_2}$, for some constants k_1 and k_2. By definition this source fails the modified WSR test. $\square$

Claim 2: A biased source outputs perfect independent bits iff it passes the behavior test.

Proof: For notational simplicity let P_1 denote $\Pr(A = 1|s_i = 1)$ and P_0 denote $\Pr(A = 1|s_i = 0)$. We prove that a biased source passes the behavior test iff it passes the WSR test. This follows from the close relation between the two measures: For any biased source and any non-constant probabilistic polynomial-time algorithm A: $\{0,1\}^{i-1} \to \{0,1\}$:

$$ws(A, S, i) = \frac{P_1}{b \cdot P_1 + (1-b) \cdot P_0} + \frac{1 - P_0}{b \cdot (1 - P_1) + (1 - b) \cdot (1 - P_0)}$$

Clearly if S passes the behavior test then it also passes the WSR test. If S fails the behavior test, then for some non-negligible ε: $|P_1 - P_0| \geq \varepsilon$. Assume w.l.o.g. that $P_1 > P_0$. Using the relation between the tests we then get:

$$ws(A, S, i) \geq 2 + \varepsilon \cdot \left\{ \frac{1-b}{P_1 - \varepsilon \cdot (1-b)} + \frac{b}{1 - P_1 + \varepsilon \cdot (1-b)} \right\}$$

Finally note that $\varepsilon \cdot b \leq P_1 - \varepsilon \cdot (1 - b) \leq 1 - \varepsilon \cdot (1 - b)$, so that the term that is added to 2 is indeed non-negligible. $\square$

Calim 3: A source outputs perfect independent bits iff it passes the POP test.

Proof: Given that a source fails the POP test, it is easy to construct a distinguisher between the source and a truly independent biased source by examining the predictions of the test, as is done in the proof of Theorem 2.

To prove the other direction, assume that S is imperfect and there exists a distinguisher D between S and a truly independent biased source B. Then by the proof of Theorem 2 there exists a non-constant probabilistic polynomial-time prediction algorithm T: $\{0,1\}^{i-1} \to \{0,1\}$ for the i-th bit of S such that $\Pr_S(T = s_i|T = 1) \geq b + 1/n^k$, for some constant k. From T we construct the following POP test A: $\{0,1\}^{i-1} \to \{0,1,*\}$: $A = 1$ iff $T = 1$ and $A = *$ iff $T = 0$. Since T is non-constant, then $\Pr_S(T = 1) = \Pr_S(A \neq *) \geq 1/n^l$ for some constant l. We then get that by definition, S fails the POP test A. $\square$

Proof of Proposition 4

Let A be any non-constant probabilistic polynomial-time algorithm: $\{0,1\}^{i-1} \to \{0,1\}$. Clearly:

(1) $\quad \Pr_S(A = s_i) = \Pr_S(A = 1) \cdot \Pr_S(A = s_i | A = 1) + \Pr_S(A = 0) \cdot \Pr_S(A = s_i | A =)$.

The proposition results from the following easily proved two equivalences. We sketch their proofs in brackets:

1. $\Pr_S(A = s_i) \geq 1/2 + 1/n^{k_1}$, for some constant k_1, iff $\Pr_S(A = s_i | A = 1) \geq 1/2 + 1/n^{l_1}$ and $\Pr_S(A = s_i | A = 0) \geq 1/2 + 1/n^{l_2}$ for some constants l_1 and l_2. (If $\Pr_S(A = s_i) \geq 1/2 + 1/n^{k_1}$, then by (1) there exists a value $\alpha \in \{0,1\}$ such that $\Pr_S(A = s_i | A = \alpha) \geq 1/2 + 1/n^{k_1}$. This in turn implies the equivalence according to the Prediction Lemma. The other direction is an immediate consequence of (1).)

2. $ws(A, S, i) \geq 2 + 1/n^{k_2}$ iff $\Pr_S(A = s_i | A = 1) \geq 1/2 + 1/n^{l_1}$ and $\Pr_S(A = s_i | A = 0) \geq 1/2 + 1/n^{l_2}$ for some constants l_1 and l_2. (A direct result from the proof of Theorem 2). $\square$

Proof of Proposition 5

It is obvious that a POP test can always simulate a next bit test (without ever outputting $*$) and therefore for any unbiased source S and any next bit test T there exists a POP test A, such that for every $1 \leq i \leq n$:

$$\Pr_S(A = s_i \mid A \neq *) = \Pr_S(T = s_i)$$

It remains to prove that inequality is also possible. To do so we shall construct an imperfect source S and demonstrate a POP test that does better than any next bit test. The source is the following:

1. The first $i - 1$ bits are independent unbiased coin flips.

2. Fix any $0 \leq \delta \leq \frac{1}{2}$.

$$\Pr_S(s_n = 1) = \begin{cases} \frac{1}{2} + \delta & \text{if } s_1^2 = 00 \\ \frac{1}{2} - \delta & \text{if } s_1^2 = 01 \\ \frac{1}{2} & \text{if } s_1 = 1 \end{cases}$$

Since the next bit test is a global test, for any next bit test T:

$$\Pr_S(T = s_n) \leq \frac{1}{4} \cdot (\frac{1}{2} + \delta) + \frac{1}{4} \cdot (\frac{1}{2} + \delta) + \left(\frac{1}{2}\right)^2 = \frac{1}{2} + \frac{\delta}{2}$$

The POP test A we shall use is: A=1 iff $s_1^2 = 00$; else A=$*$. Clearly

$$\Pr_S(A = s_n \mid A \neq *) = \frac{1}{2} + \delta$$

$\square$

A Universal Statistical Test for Random Bit Generators

Ueli M. Maurer

Institute for Signal and Information Processing
Swiss Federal Institute of Technology
CH-8092 Zurich, Switzerland

Abstract. A new statistical test for random bit generators is presented that is universal in the sense that any significant deviation of the output statistics from the statistics of a perfect random bit generator is detected with high probability when the defective generator can be modeled as an ergodic stationary source with finite memory. This is in contrast to most presently used statistical tests which can detect only one type of non-randomness, for example, a bias in the distribution of 0's and 1's or a correlation between consecutive bits. Moreover, the new test, whose formulation was motivated by considering the universal data compression algorithms of Elias and of Willems, measures the entropy per output bit of a generator. This is shown to be the correct quality measure for a random bit generator in cryptographic applications. A generator is thus rejected with high probability if and only if the cryptographic significance of a statistical defect is above a specified threshold. The test is easy to implement and very fast and thus well-suited for practical applications.

1. Introduction

A random bit generator is a device whose output sequence can be modeled as a sequence of statistically independent and symmetrically distributed binary random variables (both values 0 and 1 are equally probable), i.e., as a so-called binary symmetric source. Random bit generators have many applications in cryptography, VLSI testing, probabilistic algorithms and other fields. Their major application in cryptography is as the secret-key source of a symmetric cipher system, but random bit generators are also required for generating public-key parameters (e.g., RSA-moduli) and for generating the keystream in the well-known one-time pad system. In these applications, the security crucially depends on the randomness of the source. In particular, a symmetric (secret-key) cipher whose security rests on the fact that an exhaustive key search is infeasible may be completely insecure when not all keys are equiprobable. Similarly, the security of the RSA public-key cryptosystem may be strongly reduced when, because of a statistical defect in the random source used in the procedure generating the primes, the two primes are chosen from a small set of primes only.

Randomness is a property of an abstract model. Whether such a model can give an exact description of reality is a philosophical question related to the question of whether the universe is deterministic or not, and seems to be impossible to answer to everyone's satisfaction. However, there do exist chaotic processes in nature, such as radioactive decay and thermal noise in transistors, that allow the construction of a random bit generator that is completely unpredictable for all practical applications. It is a non-trivial engineering task, however, to design an electronic circuit that explores the randomness of such a process in a way that guarantees the statistical independence and symmetrical distribution of the generated bits. It is therefore essential in a cryptographic application that such a device be tested intensively for malfunction after production, and also periodically during operation.

This paper is concerned with the application of random bit generators as the secret-key source of a symmetric cipher system. A new statistical test for random bit generators is presented that offers two major advantages over the presently used statistical tests (including the common frequency test, serial test, poker test, autocorrelation tests and run test which are described in [1] and [4]). First, unlike these tests, the new test is able to detect any one of a very general class of possible defects a generator may have, including all the defects the above mentioned tests are designed to detect. This class of defects consists of those that can be modeled by an ergodic stationary source and contains those that could reasonably be assumed to occur in a practical implementation of a random bit generator. Second, rather than measuring some parameter (like the relative frequency of 1's) of the output of a generator, the new test measures the actual cryptographic significance of a defect. More precisely, the test parameter is very closely related to the running time of the enemy's optimal key-search strategy when he exploits knowledge of the secret-key source's statistical defect, and thus to the effective key size of the cipher system (if there exists no essentially faster way than an exhaustive key search for breaking the system).

The paper is not concerned with tests for pseudo-random bit generators that stretch a short (randomly selected) seed deterministically into a long sequence of pseudo-random bits, i.e., it is not concerned with the security evaluation of practical keystream generators for stream ciphers. However, it is certainly a necessary (but far from sufficient) condition for security that such a generator pass the test presented here. Design criteria for practical keystream generators are discussed in [5].

In section 2, an analysis of the enemy's optimal key-search strategy based on knowledge about the statistical defect of the secret-key source is presented. It is argued that the per-bit entropy of a bit generator is the correct measure of its cryptographic quality. Section 3 introduces the fundamentals of statistical testing and some of the presently used statistical tests are reviewed. The new universal statistical test is introduced in section 4 and the close relation between the test parameter and the per-bit entropy of a generator is established.

2. Reduction of cipher security due to a statistical defect in the secret-key source

Throughout the paper, let $B = \{0,1\}$ and let $R^N = R_1,\ldots,R_N$ denote a sequence of N statistically independent and symmetrically distributed binary random variables. When a random bit generator based on a chaotic physical phenomenon like thermal transistor noise is either defective or not properly designed, then the generated bits may be biased and/or statistically dependent. The simplest example of such a statistical defect is modeled by a binary memoryless source whose output bits are statistically independent and identically (but not necessarily symmetrically) distributed. Let BMS_p denote the binary memoryless source that emits 1's with probability p and 0's with probability $1 - p$. Another type of statistical defect is modeled by a binary source, denoted by ST_p, whose output bits are symmetrically distributed (0's and 1's occur with probability $1/2$) but whose transition probabilities are biased: a binary digit is followed by its complement with probability p and by the same digit with probability $1 - p$. This is an example of a binary stationary source with one bit of memory. In general, the probability distribution of the i-th bit of a generator's output may depend on the previous M output bits where M is the memory of the source. We argue that the statistical behavior of virtually every (even defective or badly designed) random bit generator can well be modeled by such a source with relatively small memory.

Consider a source S that emits a sequence $U_1, U_2, U_3, \ldots$ of binary random variables. If there exists a positive integer M such that for all $n > M$, the conditional probability distribution of U_n, given $U_1,\ldots,U_{n-1}$, depends only on the past M output bits, i.e., such that

$$P_{U_n|U_{n-1}\ldots U_1}\big(u_n|u_{n-1}\ldots u_1\big) = P_{U_n|U_{n-1}\ldots U_{n-M}}\big(u_n|u_{n-1}\ldots u_{n-M}\big) \qquad (1)$$

for $n > M$ and for every binary sequence $(u_1,\ldots,u_n) \in B^n$, then the smallest such M is called the *memory* of the source S and $\Sigma_n = [U_{n-1},\ldots,U_{n-M}]$ denotes its *state* at time n. Let $\Sigma_1 = [U_0,\ldots,U_{-M+1}]$ be the initial state where $U_{-M+1},\ldots,U_0$ are dummy random variables. If in addition to (1) the source satisfies

$$P_{U_n|\Sigma_n}(u|\sigma) = P_{U_1|\Sigma_1}(u|\sigma)$$

for all $n > M$ and for all $u \in B$ and $\sigma \in B^M$, then it is called *stationary*. A stationary source with memory M is thus completely specified by the probability distribution of the initial state, P_{Σ_1}, and the state transition probability distribution $P_{\Sigma_2|\Sigma_1}$. The state sequence forms a Markov chain with the special property that each of the 2^M states has at most 2 successor states with non-zero probability. See [3], chapters XV and XVI, for a treatment of Markov chains. We will denote the 2^M possible states of the source (or the Markov chain) by the integers in the interval $[0, 2^M - 1]$. ($\Sigma_n = j$ means that $U_{n-1}\ldots U_{n-M}$ is the binary representation of j.) For the class of ergodic Markov chains (see [3] for a definition), which includes virtually all cases that are of practical interest, there exists an invariant state probability distribution, i.e.,

$$\lim_{n \to \infty} P_{\Sigma_n}(j) = p_j$$

for $0 \leq j \leq 2^M - 1$, where the p_j's are the solution, satisfying $\sum_{j=0}^{2^M-1} p_j = 1$, of the following system of linear equations

$$p_j = \sum_{k=0}^{2^M-1} P_{\Sigma_2|\Sigma_1}(j|k) \, p_k, \qquad 0 \leq j \leq 2^M - 1. \tag{2}$$

A good practical cipher is designed such that no essentially faster attack is known than an exhaustive key search. The size of the key space is chosen large enough to ensure that to succeed in such an exhaustive search, even with only very small probability of success, requires an infeasible searching effort. If not all possible values of the secret key have equal *a priori* probability, then the enemy's optimal strategy in an exhaustive key search is to start with the most likely key and to continue testing keys in order of decreasing probabilities. Let Z denote the secret key, let n be its length in bits and let $z_1, z_2, \ldots, z_{2^n}$ be a list of the key values satisfying

$$P_Z(z_1) \geq P_Z(z_2) \geq \cdots \geq P_Z(z_{2^n}).$$

For a given source S and for δ satisfying $0 \leq \delta \leq 1$ let $\mu_S(n, \delta)$ denote the minimum number of key values an enemy must test (using the optimal key-searching strategy) in order to find the correct key with probability at least δ when S is used to generate the n-bit key Z, i.e.,

$$\mu_S(n, \delta) = \min \left\{ k : \sum_{i=1}^{k} P_Z(z_i) \geq \delta \right\}. \tag{3}$$

We define the *effective key size* of a cipher system with key source S to be $\log_2 \mu_S(n, \frac{1}{2})$, i.e., the logarithm of the minimum number of keys an enemy must try in order to find the correct key with probability at least 50%. The choice $\delta = 1/2$ in this definition is somewhat arbitrary, but in general, for large enough n, $\log_2 \mu_S(n, \delta)/n$ is almost independent of δ when δ is not extremely close to 0 or 1. Note that when the key is truly random, i.e., when S is a binary symmetric source, then $\log_2 \mu_S(n, \frac{1}{2}) = n - 1$.

We now determine the effective key size of a cipher system whose key source is BMS_p. Without loss of generality assume that $0 < p \leq 1/2$. Note that the source ST_p described above can be modeled by the source BMS_p with a summator at the output (summing modulo 2 the output bits of BMS_p). Therefore the set of probabilities of keys and hence also the effective key size is identical for both sources. The probability distribution of Z is given by

$$P_Z(z) = p^{w(z)}(1-p)^{n-w(z)},$$

where $w(z)$ denotes the Hamming weight of z. In order to succeed with probability approximately $1/2$ the enemy must examine all keys z with Hamming weight $w(z) \leq$

pn. The effective key size is thus well approximated by

$$\log_2 \mu_{\text{BMS}_p}(n, \tfrac{1}{2}) \approx \log_2 \sum_{i=0}^{pn} \binom{n}{i}. \tag{4}$$

It is well-known (e.g., see [8]) that the term on the right side of (4) is well approximated by $nH(p)$, where $H(x)$ is the binary entropy function defined by

$$H(x) = -x \log_2 x - (1-x) \log_2 (1-x) \tag{5}$$

for $0 < x < 1$ and by $H(0) = H(1) = 0$. Note that $H(x) = H(1-x)$ for $0 \le x \le 1$. This approximation is asymptotically precise, i.e.,

$$\lim_{n \to \infty} \frac{\log_2 \mu_{\text{BMS}_p}(n, \delta)}{n} = H(p) \quad \text{for } 0 < \delta < 1.$$

Note that the entropy per output bit of the source BMS_p, $H(p)$, is equal to the factor by which the effective key size is reduced. Shannon proved (see [6], theorem 4) that for a general ergodic stationary source S,

$$\lim_{n \to \infty} \frac{\log_2 \mu_S(n, \delta)}{n} = H_S \quad \text{for } 0 < \delta < 1,$$

where H_S is the per-bit entropy of S defined as

$$H_S = - \sum_{j=0}^{2^M-1} p_j \sum_{k=0}^{2^M-1} P_{\Sigma_2|\Sigma_1}(k|j) \log_2 P_{\Sigma_2|\Sigma_1}(k|j), \tag{6}$$

and where p_j is for $0 \le j \le 2^M - 1$ defined by (2). In other words, for the general class of ergodic stationary sources, the per-bit entropy H_S is the correct measure of their cryptographic quality when they are used as the secret-key source of a cipher system. Conversely, the per-bit redundancy, $1 - H_S$, is the correct measure of the cryptographic weakness of a key source.

3. Fundamentals of statistical tests

Statistical tests are used to detect a possible statistical defect of a random bit generator, i.e., to detect when the statistical model describing the generator's behavior deviates significantly from a binary symmetric source. Such a test examines a sample sequence of a certain length N and rejects the generator when certain properties of the sample sequence indicate a possible non-randomness (e.g. when the number of 0's and 1's differ considerably). A statistical test T is a function $T : B^N \to \{\text{accept, reject}\}$ which divides the set B^N of binary length N sequences into a (small) set

$$S_T = \{s^N : T(s^N) = \text{reject}\} \subseteq B^N$$

of "bad" sequences and the remaining set of "good" sequences. The two main parameters of a statistical test are the length N of the sample sequence and the rejection rate $\rho = |S_T|/2^N$, which is the probability that a binary symmetric source is rejected.

Note that a statistical defect of a random bit generator can only be detected with a certain detection probability, which depends on the seriousness of the defect and on the length N of the sample sequence. As in other detection problems, there exists a trade-off between the detection probability and the false alarm probability ρ. In a practical test, ρ should be small, for example $\rho \approx 0.001 \ldots 0.01$.

For reasons of feasibility, a statistical test for a reasonable sample length N cannot be implemented by listing the set of "bad" sequences. Instead, a statistical test T is typically implemented by specifying an efficiently computable function f_T that maps the binary length N sequences to the real numbers $\mathcal{R}$:

$$f_T : B^N \to \mathcal{R} : s^N \mapsto f_T(s^N).$$

f_T must be such that the probability distribution of the real-valued random variable $f_T(R^N)$ can be determined, where R^N denotes a sequence of N statistically independent and symmetrically distributed binary random variables. A lower and an upper threshold t_1 and t_2, respectively, can then be specified such that

$$\Pr[f_T(R^N) \leq t_1] + \Pr[f_T(R^N) \geq t_2] = \rho.$$

Usually $\Pr[f_T(R^N) \leq t_1] \approx \Pr[f_T(R^N) \geq t_2] \approx \rho/2$. The set S_T of bad sequences with cardinality $|S_T| = \rho 2^N$ is thus defined by

$$S_T = \left\{ s^N \in B^N : f_T(s^N) \leq t_1 \text{ or } f_T(s^N) \geq t_2 \right\}.$$

Usually, f_T is chosen such that $f_T(R^N)$ is distributed (approximately) according to a well-known probability distribution, most often the normal distribution or the χ^2 distribution with d degrees of freedom for some positive integer d. Since extensive numerical tables of these distributions are available, such a choice strongly simplifies the specification of t_1 and t_2 for given ρ and N. The normal distribution results when a large number of independent and identically distributed random variables are summed. The χ^2 distribution with d degrees of freedom results when the squares of d independent and normally distributed random variables with zero mean and variance 1 are summed.

As an example, consider the most popular statistical tests for random bit generators, the *frequency test* T_F. It is used to determine whether a generator is biased. For a sample sequence $s^N = s_1, \ldots, s_N$, $f_{T_F}(s^N)$ is defined as

$$f_{T_F}(s^N) = \frac{2}{\sqrt{N}} \left(\sum_{i=1}^{N} s_i - N/2 \right).$$

The number of 1's in a random sequence $R^N = R_1, \ldots, R_N$ is approximately distributed according to the normal distribution with mean $N/2$ and variance $N/4$ since $E[R_i] = 1/2$ and $\text{Var}[R_i] = 1/4$ for $1 \leq i \leq N$. Thus the probability distribution of $f_{T_F}(R^N)$ is for large enough N well approximated by the normal distribution with zero mean and variance 1, and reasonable values for the rejection thresholds are $t_2 = -t_1 \approx 2.5 \ldots 3$. The *serial test*, *run test* and *autocorrelation tests* can be defined by similar expressions for the corresponding test functions.

4. The universal entropy-related statistical test

The new statistical test T_U proposed in this section offers two main advantages over all the tests discussed in the previous section:

(1) Rather than being tailored to detecting a specific type of statistical defect, the new test is able to detect any one of the very general class of statistical defects that can be modeled by an ergodic stationary source with finite memory, which includes all those detected by the tests discussed in the previous section and all those that could realistically be assumed to occur in a practical implementation of a random bit generator.

(2) The test measures the actual amount by which the security of a cipher system would be reduced if the tested generator G were used as the key source, i.e., it measures the effective key size $\mu_G(n, \frac{1}{2})$ of a cipher system with key source G. Therefore, statistical defects are weighted according to their actual harm in the cryptographic application.

These two advantages are due to the fact that for the general class of binary ergodic stationary sources with finite memory $M \leq L$, where L is a parameter of the test, the resulting test quantity f_{T_U} is closely related to the per-bit entropy H_S of the source. This claim will be justified after the following description of the test.

The test T_U is specified by the three positive integer-valued parameters L, Q and K. To perform the test T_U, the output sequence of the generator is partitioned into adjacent non-overlapping blocks of length L. The total length of the sample sequence s^N is $N = (Q+K)L$, where K is the number of steps of the test and Q is the number of initialization steps. Let $b_n(s^N) = [s_{Ln}, \ldots, s_{Ln+L-1}]$ for $0 \leq n \leq Q+K-1$ denote the n-th block of length L. For $Q \leq n \leq Q+K-1$, the sequence is scanned for the most recent occurrence of block $b_n(s^N)$, i.e., the least positive integer $i \leq n$ is determined such that $b_n(s^N) = b_{n-i}(s^N)$. Let $A_n(s^N) = i$ if such an i exists and else let $A_n(s^N) = n$. $f_{T_U}(s^N)$ is defined as the average of the logarithm (to the base 2) of the K terms $A_Q(s^N), A_{Q+1}(s^N), \ldots, A_{Q+K-1}(s^N)$. More formally, the test function $f_{T_U} : B^N \to \mathcal{R} : s^N \mapsto f_{T_U}(s^N)$ is defined by

$$f_{T_U}(s^N) = \frac{1}{K} \sum_{n=Q}^{Q+K-1} \log_2 A_n(s^N) \tag{7}$$

where for $Q \leq n \leq Q + K - 1$, $A_n(s^N)$ is defined by

$$A_n(s^N) = \begin{cases} n & \text{if there exists no positive } i \leq n \text{ such that} \\ & b_n(s^N) = b_{n-i}(s^N), \\ \min\{i : i \geq 1, b_n(s^N) = b_{n-i}(s^N)\} & \text{else.} \end{cases} \tag{8}$$

The test can be implemented by using a table (denoted below as *Tab*) of size 2^L that stores for each L-bit block the time index of its most recent occurrence. The main part of a program implementing the test is given below in a PASCAL-like notation:

```
FOR i := 0 TO 2^L - 1 DO Tab[i] := 0;
FOR n := 0 TO Q - 1 DO Tab[b_n(s^N)] := n;
sum := 0.0;
FOR n := Q TO Q + K - 1 DO BEGIN
    sum := sum + log_2(n - Tab[b_n(s^N)]);
    Tab[b_n(s^N)] := n;
END;
f_{T_U}(s^N) := sum/K;
```

We recommend to choose L between 8 and 16, inclusive, $Q \geq 5 \cdot 2^L$ and K as large as possible (e.g., $K = 10^4$ or $K = 10^5$). This choice for Q guarantees that with high probability, every L-bit pattern occurs at least once in the first Q blocks of a random sequence, and thus that the table of $E[f_{T_U}(R^N)]$ and $\text{Var}[\log_2 A_n(R^N)]$ given below for $Q \to \infty$ (Table I) are suitable for determining the threshold values t_1 and t_2. We also recommend to choose $\rho \approx 0.001 \ldots 0.01$, $t_1 = E[f_{T_U}(R^N)] - y\sigma$ and $t_2 = E[f_{T_U}(R^N)] + y\sigma$, where $\sigma = \sqrt{\text{Var}[\log_2 A_n(R^N)]/K} \approx \sqrt{\text{Var}[f_{T_U}(R^N)]}$ (see Table I) and where y is chosen such that $\mathcal{N}(-y) = \rho/2$. The function $\mathcal{N}(x)$ is the integral of the normal density function and is defined as

$$\mathcal{N}(x) = \frac{1}{\sqrt{2\pi}} \int_{-\infty}^{x} e^{-\xi^2/2} d\xi.$$

A table of $\mathcal{N}(x)$ can be found in almost every book on statistics or probability theory (e.g., see [3], p. 176). For example, to obtain a rejection rate of $\rho = 0.01$ or $\rho = 0.001$, one must choose $y = 2.58$ or $y = 3.30$, respectively. Note that σ decreases as $1/\sqrt{K}$ when K increases.

The definition of T_U is based on the idea, which has independently been suggested by Ziv [9], that a universal statistical test can be obtained by application of a universal source coding algorithm. A generator should pass the test if and only if its output sequence cannot be compressed significantly. However, instead of actually compressing the sample sequence we only need to compute a quantity that is related to the length of the compressed sequence. The formulation of our test was motivated by considering the universal source coding algorithms of Elias [2] and of Willems [7], which partition the data sequence into adjacent non-overlapping blocks of length L. For $L \to \infty$, these algorithms can be shown to compress the output of every discrete stationary source to its entropy. The universal source coding algorithm due to Ziv and Lempel [10] seems to be less suited for application as a statistical test because it seems to be difficult to define a test function f_T such that the distribution of $f_T(R^N)$ can easily be determined, i.e., to specify a concrete implementation of a statistical test based on [10]. No indication of the suitability of the Ziv-Lempel algorithm for a practical implementation of a statistical test is given in [9].

The expectation of $f_{T_U}(R^N)$ and a good approximation to the variance of $f_{T_U}(R^N)$, which are needed in order to describe a practical implementation of the proposed test, are determined in the following under the admissible assumption that $Q \to \infty$. For a source emitting the sequence of random variables $U^N = U_1, U_2, \ldots, U_N$ we have

$$\Pr[A_n(U^N)=i] =$$

$$\sum_{b \in B^N} \Pr\left[b_n(U^N) = b, \; b_{n-1}(U^N) \neq b, \ldots, b_{n-i+1}(U^N) \neq b, b_{n-i}(U^N) = b\right].$$

for $i \geq 1$. When the blocks $b_n(U^N)$ for $Q \leq n \leq Q + K - 1$ are statistically independent and identically distributed, then the above probability factors:

$$\Pr[A_n(U^N) = i] = \sum_{b \in B^N} (\Pr[b_n(U^N) = b])^2 \cdot (1 - \Pr[b_n(U^N) = b])^{i-1}. \qquad (9)$$

for $i \geq 1$ and $Q \leq n \leq Q + K - 1$. For a binary symmetric source we thus have

$$\Pr[A_n(R^N) = i] = 2^{-L}(1 - 2^{-L})^{i-1}$$

for $i \geq 1$. The expected value of the sum of random variables equals the sum of their expected values. Therefore

$$E[f_{T_U}(R^N)] = E[\log_2 A_n(R^N)] = 2^{-L} \sum_{i=1}^{\infty} (1 - 2^{-L})^{i-1} \log_2 i \qquad (10)$$

For sufficiently large L (i.e., $L \geq 8$), the terms $A_n(R^N)$ are virtually statistically independent and therefore

$$
\begin{aligned}
K \cdot \mathrm{Var}[f_{T_U}(R^N)] &\approx \mathrm{Var}[\log_2 A_n(R^N)] \\
&= E[(\log_2 A_n(R^N))^2] - (E[\log_2 A_n(R^N)])^2 \\
&= 2^{-L} \sum_{i=1}^{\infty} (1 - 2^{-L})^{i-1} (\log_2 i)^2 - (E[f_{T_U}(R^N)])^2. \qquad (11)
\end{aligned}
$$

Table I summarizes $E[f_{T_U}(R^N)]$ and $\mathrm{Var}[\log_2 A_n(R^N)]$ for $1 \leq L \leq 16$. Note that $E[f_{T_U}(R^N)]$ is closely related to the entropy of a block, which is L bits. In fact, it will be shown below that $E[f_{T_U}(R^N)] - L$ converges to the constant -0.8327 as $L \to \infty$.

In order to show that for $L \to \infty$, $E[f_{T_U}(R^N)] - L$ and $\mathrm{Var}[\log_2 A_n(R^N)]$ converge (exponentially fast) to constants, let

$$v(r) \overset{\text{def}}{=} r \sum_{i=1}^{\infty} (1 - r)^{i-1} \log_2 i \qquad (12)$$

$$\text{and} \quad w(r) \overset{\text{def}}{=} r \sum_{i=1}^{\infty} (1 - r)^{i-1} (\log_2 i)^2. \qquad (13)$$

One can show that

L	$E[f_{T_U}(R^N)]$	$\text{Var}[\log_2 A_n(R^N)]$	L	$E[f_{T_U}(R^N)]$	$\text{Var}[\log_2 A_n(R^N)]$
1	0.73264948	0.690	9	8.17642476	3.311
2	1.53743829	1.338	10	9.17232431	3.356
3	2.40160681	1.901	11	10.1700323	3.384
4	3.31122472	2.358	12	11.1687649	3.401
5	4.25342659	2.705	13	12.1680703	3.410
6	5.21770525	2.954	14	13.1676926	3.416
7	6.19625065	3.125	15	14.1674884	3.419
8	7.18366555	3.238	16	15.1673788	3.421

Table I. Expectation of $f_{T_U}(R^N)$ and variance of $\log_2 A_n(R^N)$ for the test T_U with parameters L, Q and K. For $L \geq 8$, $\text{Var}[f_{T_U}(R^N)]$ is very well approximated by $\text{Var}[\log_2 A_n(R^N)]/K$.

$$\lim_{r \to 0} [v(r) + \log_2 r] = \lim_{r \to 0} \int_r^\infty e^{-\xi} \log_2 \xi \, d\xi \stackrel{\text{def}}{=} C = -0.832746 \qquad (14)$$

and

$$\lim_{r \to 0} [w(r) - (\log_2 r)^2 + 2C \log_2 r] = \lim_{r \to 0} \int_r^\infty e^{-\xi} (\log_2 \xi)^2 d\xi$$

$$\stackrel{\text{def}}{=} D = 4.117181. \qquad (15)$$

Equations (10), (12), (13), (14), (11) and (15) imply that

$$\lim_{L \to \infty} \left(E[f_{T_U}(R^N)] - L \right) = C$$

and $$\lim_{L \to \infty} \text{Var}[\log_2 A_n(R^N)] = D - C^2 = 3.423715,$$

which can both be verified numerically by considering Table I.

Let $U_{\text{BMS}_p}^N$ be the output of the binary memoryless source BMS$_p$. The blocks are independent and thus using (9), (14) and the fact that for $L \to \infty$, $\Pr[b_n(U_{\text{BMS}_p}^N) = b] \to 0$ for all $b \in B^N$ one can show that

$$\lim_{L \to \infty} \left(E[f_{T_U}(U_{\text{BMS}_p}^N)] - Lh(p) \right) = C \qquad (16)$$

for $0 < p < 1$. Equation (16) demonstrates that the test T_U measures the entropy of any binary memoryless source. Table II summarizes $E[f_{T_U}(U_{\text{BMS}_p}^N)]$, $Lh(p) + C$ and $\text{Var}[\log_2 A_n(U_{\text{BMS}_p}^N)]$ for $L = 8$ and $L = 16$ and for several values of p. Note that all entries of Tables I and II are computed precisely rather than obtained by simulations.

L	p	$E[f_{T_U}(U_{BMS_p}^N)]$	$Lh(p) + C$	$\mathrm{Var}[\log_2 A_n(U_{BMS_p}^N)]$
8	0.50	7.18367	7.16725	3.239
8	0.45	7.12687	7.10945	3.393
8	0.40	6.95557	6.93486	3.844
8	0.35	6.66617	6.63980	4.561
8	0.30	6.24950	6.21758	5.472
16	0.50	15.16738	15.16725	3.421
16	0.45	15.05179	15.05165	3.753
16	0.40	14.70169	14.70246	4.741
16	0.35	14.09853	14.11234	6.409
16	0.30	13.22556	13.26791	8.614

Table II. Performance of the universal statistical test for the binary memoryless source BMS_p for $L = 8$ and $L = 16$ and for different values of p.

We have devised an algorithm (which is not described here) for computing $E[f_{T_U}(U_S^N)]$ and $\mathrm{Var}[\log_2 A_n(U_S^N)]$ for an arbitrary stationary source S with memory $M \leq L$, where U_S^N is the output sequence of S. For all examples of stationary sources, the very close relation between $E[f_{T_U}(U_S^N)]$ and $LH_S + C$ could be verified, where H_S is the per-bit entropy of S defined by (6). It is possible to prove, by arguments similar to those used in [7], that for every binary ergodic stationary source S,

$$\lim_{L \to \infty} \frac{E[f_{T_U}(U_S^N)]}{L} = H_S.$$

5. Conclusions

A new universal statistical test for random bit generators has been proposed that measures the per-bit entropy of the generator, which has been argued to be the cryptographically significant quality measure for a secret-key source. The test parameter is virtually normally distributed since it is the average of K identically distributed and virtually independent random variables. Its expected value has been shown to be closely related to the per-bit entropy of the generator when it can well be modeled as an ergodic stationary source. For $1 \leq L \leq 16$, expectation and variance of the test parameter have been tabulated for a binary symmetric source. A practical implementation nas been proposed that makes use of these tables to specify the interval of acceptance for the test parameter as the interval between the expected value minus and plus a certain number of standard deviations. An implementation of our statistical test by Omnisec AG for testing random bit generators used in their equipment has confirmed the theoretical results and the practical usefulness.

Acknowledgement

The problem of designing efficient statistical tests for random bit generators was suggested to the author by Omnisec AG, Trockenloostrasse 91, 8105 Regensdorf, Switzerland. In particular, it is a pleasure to thank M. Benninger and P. Schmid for stimulating discussions and for their generous support. I am also grateful to J. Massey for many suggestions improving the presentation of the results, and to H.-A. Loeliger for suggesting an improvement on the original implementation of the presented statistical test.

References

[1] H. Beker and F. Piper, *Cipher Systems*, London: Northwood Books, 1982.

[2] P. Elias, *Interval and recency rank source coding: Two on-line adaptive variable-length schemes*, IEEE Trans. Inform. Theory, vol. IT-33, pp. 3-10, Jan. 1987.

[3] W. Feller, *An Introduction to Probability Theory and its Applications*, third ed., vol. 1, New York, NY: Wiley, 1968.

[4] D.E. Knuth, *The art of computer programming*, vol. 2, 2nd edition, Reading, MA: Addison-Wesley, 1981.

[5] R.A. Rueppel, *Analysis and Design of Stream Ciphers*, New York, NY: Springer, 1986.

[6] C.E. Shannon, *A mathematical theory of communication*, Bell Syst. Tech. J., vol. 27, pp. 379-423, 623-656, Oct. 1948.

[7] F.M.J. Willems, *Universal data compression and repetition times*, IEEE Trans. Inform. Theory, vol. IT-35, pp. 54-58, Jan. 1989.

[8] J.M. Wozencraft and B. Reiffen, *Sequential Decoding*, Cambridge, MA: Techn. Press of the M.I.T., 1960.

[9] J. Ziv, *Compression, tests for randomness and estimating the statistical model of an individual sequence*, in: Sequences (Ed. R.M. Capocelli), New York, NY: Springer Verlag, 1990.

[10] J. Ziv and A. Lempel, *A universal algorithm for sequential data compression*, IEEE Trans. Inform. Theory, vol. IT-23, pp. 337-343, May 1977.

On the Impossibility of Private Key Cryptography with Weakly Random Keys

James L. McInnes*
University of Toronto

Benny Pinkas[†]
Technion — Israel Institue of Technology

Abstract

The properties of weak sources of randomness have been investigated in many contexts and using several models of weakly random behaviour. For two such models, developed by Santha and Vazirani, and Chor and Goldreich, it is known that the output from one such source cannot be "compressed" to produce nearly random bits. At the same time, however, a single source is sufficient to solve problems in the randomized complexity classes BPP and RP. It is natural to ask exactly which tasks can be done using a single, weak source of randomness and which cannot. The present work begins to answer this question by establishing that a single weakly random source of either model cannot be used to obtain a secure "one-time-pad" type of cryptosystem.

1 Introduction

Secret transmission of information over insecure communication lines is a major issue in cryptography. In the classical setting, two parties A and B, share a secret, private key K. A wishes to send a plaintext message M, to B. A encrypts M using K, and sends the resulting ciphertext C, to B. A listener L can eavesdrop on the communication line and find C (but not alter it). In addition L knows the functions employed by A and B. The goal of the cryptosystem is to enable B to correctly decrypt M, while retaining security against the listener.

In order to operate, the parties A and B need an access to a joint source of randomness. Without such a source, L possesses the same information as B does. As L knows B's program, B has no advantage over L, and so such a cryptosystem will not be secure.

If A and B share a perfect source of unbiased independent random bits, then they can use this source to generate the private key K, and use this key as a *one-*

---

*Address: Dept. of Computer Science,University of Toronto, Toronto, Ontario, Canada M5S 1A4
Email: *jimm@theory.toronto.edu*

[†]Address: Dept. of Computer Science, Technion — Israel Institute of Technology, Haifa 32000 Israel.
Email: *bennyp@techunix.bitnet*. Research supported in part by US-Israel BSF grant 88-00282.

time pad, achieving maximum security [S]. In practice, however, it seems unrealistic to expect a source to be perfectly random. Most physical sources, such as Zener diodes or Geiger counters, are imperfect; that is, they do not output a uniform distribution. The question that motivates this work is whether there is a secure private key cryptosystem (analogous to one-time pad) if a weaker, non-perfect source of randomness is shared by A and B.

Two widely investigated general models for weak-sources of randomness have been suggested by Santha and Vazirani [SV], and Chor and Goldreich [CG]. They are known as the *SV-source* and *PRB-source*, respectively. The sources they describe maintain some amount of randomness but allow the value of each bit output to depend on the values of all previous bits. For both models, it has been shown in [SV, CG] that a single SV or PRB source cannot be used to extract "almost" unbiased random bits.

We show that a private key cryptosystem in which both parties share a private key, generated by a weak source of randomness, and have no access to any other source of randomness, is not secure. It should be stressed that this is not an immediate corollary of the fact that random bits cannot be extracted from such sources. We also show a *secure* cryptosystem, where the parties share a slightly-random private key, and have access to a public source of perfect randomness.

The paper is organized as follows: sections 2 and 3 give the needed background and definitions in weak-sources of randomness and cryptography. In sections 4 and 5 it is shown that a crypto-system in which A and B share a private-key generated by a PRB or SV source, and have no additional sources of randomness, is not secure. In section 6 we allow them to use a public source of truly random bits in addition to the slightly-random key, and show that then it is possible to combine these two sources to produce a secure one-time pad.

2　Weak Sources of Randomness

Physical sources of randomness are imperfect, that is, they do not output a uniform distribution. Several mathematical models of such sources have been investigated. Von Neumann [N] considered a source which generates a sequence of independent tosses of a coin with a fixed but unknown bias, and suggested a method to extract perfect random bits from it. Blum [B] modeled weak randomness as a finite state Markov chain (with unknown transition probabilities). This model allows each output bit to depend on the previous c bits (for any fixed c). Blum gave an algorithm to extract perfect random bits from such a source.

Next we describe two more recent models, in which each output bit can depend on all previous bits.

2.1　SV-model

Santha and Vazirani [SV] suggested a model (hereafter referred to as the *SV-model*) where each bit in the output sequence is 0 with a probability of at least δ and not more than $1 - \delta$ (where $0 \le \delta \le \frac{1}{2}$ is fixed). The probability that a given n-bit string is output is hence bounded above by $(1 - \delta)^n$, and below by δ^n (therefore each bit sequence is output with some positive probability). A source with $\delta = \frac{1}{2}$ is a perfect random source, and one with $\delta = 0$ can have no randomness at all. This model allows each bit to depend on all previous bits.

2.2 PRB-model

A different model was suggested by Chor and Goldreich [CG], where instead of bounding the probability of each individual bit, they bound the probability that any given string will appear in any position. Such a source is called a *PRobability-Bounded source*, or a *PRB-source*. It has two parameters, l and b. A source is said to be an *(l,b)-source* if for every prefix $\alpha \in \{0,1\}^*$ of the output sequence, and every l-bit string β, the conditional probability that the next l bits will equal β (given the prefix α) is at most 2^{-b}. Thus an (l,l)-source is a perfect random source, and an $(l,0)$-source can have no randomness at all.

The PRB-model is a strict generalization of the SV-model. Any SV-source with parameter δ is a $(1, \log_2(1 - \delta)^{-1})$ PRB-source. The inclusion is proper since a probability bounded source may output some strings with probability 0. For example, a (2,1) PRB-source which outputs 11 with probability $\frac{1}{2}$ and 10 with probability $\frac{1}{2}$, cannot be modeled by any SV-source.

2.3 Known Results

It was shown in [SV, CG] that a single SV or PRB source cannot be used to extract "almost" unbiased random bits. On the other hand, in both models, two independent sources suffice for this purpose [V, CG]. A more surprising result is that *BPP* and *RP* problems can be efficiently solved using the output of a single SV or PRB source [VV, CG]. This indicates that some useful randomness can be extracted from these sources, and it leads us to ask how useful a slightly random source would be for cryptography.

Given a boolean function $f : \{0,1\}^n \to \{0,1\}$, define the *density of zeroes* of it to be

$$d = \frac{\{y \in \{0,1\}^n | f(y) = 0\}}{2^n}$$

The following technique is due to Gereb and is given in [SV]:

Lemma 1 *for all $f : \{0,1\}^n \to \{0,1\}, 0 \le \delta \le \frac{1}{2}$, and $d \ge \frac{1}{2}$, there is a strategy to set a SV-source with parameter δ, such that if x is an n bit string generated by this source, and the density of zeroes of f is d, then*

$$Prob(f(x) = 1) \ge 2(1 - \delta)(1 - d)$$

Any extraction scheme to extract a random bit from an n-bit string generated by an SV-source, can be viewed as a function $f : \{0,1\}^n \to \{0,1\}$. The lemma implies that no such scheme can extract a bit with less than $1 - \delta$ bias, from a SV-source with parameter δ. (More precisely, for any scheme f there is a δ-source which causes the outcome of the scheme to be at least $1 - \delta$ biased.)

3 Cryptographic Background

3.1 Cryptosystems

A simple cryptographic system *(A,B)* is composed of two communicating parties, A and B, communicating over an insecure channel. Their goal is for A to pass a secret message (or *plaintext*), M, to B. In a *private key cryptosystem*, A and B share a randomly chosen string, K, which is the *private key*. A sends to B a message C (*ciphertext*), which is a deterministic function of M and K. A *listener*, L, is able to examine the communication between A and B. He knows the functions they use, but not the private key K. The listener is passive, he cannot interject anything of his own on the line. The listener attempts to find the plaintext, or at least to extract as much information about it as possible. Figure 1 sums up the scenario described here.

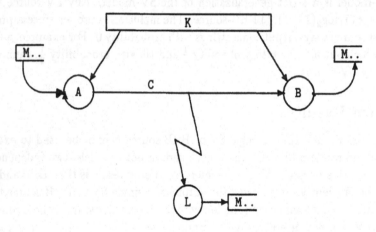

Figure 1: A simple private key cryptographic system.

The simplest scenario is of a one-bit cryptosystem, namely one where the plaintext is composed of a single bit. For a one-bit cryptosystem (A, B), we define the following requirements:

Correctness: (A, B) is *correct* if, given that b is chosen randomly in $\{0,1\}$,

$$\text{Prob}(B \text{ outputs } b \text{ correctly}) \geq 1 - o(1)$$

for all k, and sufficiently large n.

Security: (A, B) is *secure* if, for every listener L, and for a bit b that is chosen randomly in $\{0,1\}$,

$$\text{Prob}(L \text{ outputs the same as } B) \leq \frac{1}{2} + o(1)$$

for all k, and sufficiently large n.

3.2   Cryptographic Setup for Our Problem

Given a source of true randomness, there exists a simple cryptosystem which is secure and correct (the *one-time pad* [S]). In this system an n-bit randomly chosen private key is used to communicate an n-bit plaintext. The ciphertext in this case is just the bitwise exclusive-or of the key with the plaintext. We wish to know whether there is a secure cryptosystem analogous to one-time pad, in which A and B share a key generated by a weak source of randomness. Such a system would be secure regardless of any complexity assumptions we might make, and therefore the computational power of L is not limited (and hence L can be restricted to be deterministic). For convenience we do not limit the power of A and B, as well. (And since we show the impossibility of such a system, these assumptions on A and B do not weaken our results). However, we do not allow A and B to use a source of truly random bits in their computation. Any random bits they need for the computations they make (as probabilistic algorithms) should be taken from the slightly-random key.

For our purposes, we can make the following simplifying assumptions about the cryptosystem (A, B):

- The communication is one-way. Namely, B only receives communication from A, and sends no messages himself. This is possible since A and B share the same source of randomness, and so B does not have any input that A does not have.

- For a given key length n, A always sends the same number m_n of bits to B.

It can be seen that there is no loss of generality incurred in making these assumptions. This reduces a cryptosystem (A, B) to the following:

1. A slightly random key K of length n.

2. An encryption function $f : \{0,1\}^n \times \{0,1\} \rightarrow \{0,1\}^{m_n}$

3. A decryption function $g : \{0,1\}^n \times \{0,1\}^{m_n} \rightarrow \{0,1\}$.

Remarks:

1. The plaintext b is uniformly distributed in $\{0,1\}$.

2. The system operates as follows: A sends the ciphertext $C = f(K, b)$ to B, and B computes $b' = g(K, C)$. As B is allowed to err (with small probability), b' might be different from b.

3. A listener L is specified by an eavesdropping function $h : \{0,1\}^{m_n} \rightarrow \{0,1\}$ that he uses, given the ciphertext, to try and retrieve the plaintext.

4. The listener knows f and g. He also knows the strategy of the weakly random source, namely the a priori probability distribution on the private key K.

5. Other than the weakly random source, there is no other source of randomness in the system.

3.3 A Matrix Representation

We represent the decryption function $g : \{0,1\}^n \times \{0,1\}^{mn} \to \{0,1\}$ by a matrix D having 2^n rows (one for each possible key) and 2^{mn} columns. (one for each possible value of $f(K, b)$). The entries of D are either 0,1 or blank, and each row contains two non-blank entries. Each entry in D is simply $g(K, f(K, b))$ for K and $f(K, b)$ corresponding to that row and column respectively. Two entries need to appear in each row, since, for each K, there are only two possible values of $f(K, b)$ that occur, since A behaves deterministically.

A listener is completely specified by giving an output value in $\{0,1\}$ for each value of $f(K, b)$. In matrix terms this corresponds to giving a $\{0,1\}$-labelling of the columns of D.

We are frequently interested in the extent to which a listener's output matches that of B. This corresponds to asking if a given $\{0,1\}$-labelling of the columns of D (i.e. a given listener) matches the particular row that corresponds to the key K. Since each row has at most two entries there are three possibilities. A row *agrees* with a labelling l if all the entries in the row match the label that l gives for the column in which they appear, and the row disagrees if none of the entries matches l. A row *half-agrees* with l if it has two entries, one which matches l and one which doesn't. Let the *weight* of a row with respect to a particular labelling be the probability (taken over the messages 0 and 1) that L outputs the same as B if that row is chosen. Thus a row which agrees with l has weight 1, a row which half agrees has weight $1/2$, and a row which disagrees has weight 0.

4 Using a PRB-source to Communicate a Single Bit

We first consider the case where A and B share an n-bit slightly-random key generated by a PRB-source. We show that no cryptosystem is secure when its only source of randomness is an $(n, n - c)$ PRB source $(c > 0)$. Theorem 1 establishes this result quantitatively, by showing that for every value of c, there is a listener whose probability of finding the transmitted bit is higher than a constant which depends only on c (and not on n). We also demonstrate a cryptosystem achieving the lower bound of Theorem 1.

Theorem 1 *If* (A, B) *is a cryptosystem such that*

1. *A and B share an n-bit private key K.*

2. *A and B have no additional sources of randomness.*

3. *A sends the encryption of a single bit message b to B, and B tries to decrypt this and find b.*

then for every $0 \leq c \leq n$ there exist an $(n, n - c)$ source S and a listener L such that if K is generated by S then

$$
\text{Prob}(L \text{ outputs the same as } B) \geq
\begin{cases}
1 & \text{for } 2 \leq c \leq n \\[2mm]
\frac{1}{2} + \frac{2^c}{8} & \text{for } 2 - \log_2 3 \leq c \leq 2 \\[2mm]
\frac{2^c}{2} & \text{for } 0 \leq c \leq 2 - \log_2 3
\end{cases}
$$

Proof. We may think of an $(n, n - c)$ source S as selecting a fraction 2^{-c} of the keys, each of which then occurs with probability $1/2^{n-c}$. The remaining keys do not occur. Denote by e the value 2^{-c}. In the combinatorial setting established in the previous section, this corresponds to choosing a set of e of the rows of D. (without loss of generality, assume that $e2^n$ is an integer). From now on we speak of choosing rows of D instead of choosing keys.

Given a labelling l of the columns of D, we say that its rows satisfy $(d_1, 1 - (d_1 + d_0), d_0)$ (where $0 \leq d_0, d_1$ and $d_0 + d_1 \leq 1$), if a fraction d_1 of the rows have weight 1, d_0 of the rows have weight 0, and $1 - (d_1 + d_0)$ of the rows have weight $\frac{1}{2}$.

The strategy of the $(n, n - c)$ source S we use, is to choose exactly a part e of the 2^n rows and give each one the same probability, $\frac{1}{e2^n}$. The source first chooses 1-rows. If there are less than $e2^n$ of these, it also takes $\frac{1}{2}$-rows; and only if there are not enough of these, too, it takes 0-rows. The following observations can be made:

1. Without loss of generality, $d_1 \geq d_0$ (otherwise consider $\bar{l}$, the labelling obtained by reversing the labels of l).

2. $d_1 = d_0$. That is because for any value of e, with a $(d_1, 1 - (d_1 + d_0), d_0)$ matrix (where $d_1 \geq d_0$), the source has more positive weight rows than with a $(d_1, 1 - 2d_1, d_1)$ matrix. Therefore the listener can achieve better success on the former matrix.

3. The following lemma implies that there is a labelling l that satisfies $(d_1, 1 - (d_1 + d_0), d_0)$, with $d_1 \geq \frac{1}{4}$.

Lemma 2 *There is a $\{0,1\}$-labelling of the columns of D which agrees with at least $1/4$ of the rows.*

Proof (of lemma 2). D has 2^n rows and 2^{mn} co $2^{2^{mn}}$ different labellings of the columns of D. Each row agrees with at least $1/4$ of the labellings, since at most two columns have entries, so there are $\frac{2^n \cdot 2^{2^{mn}}}{4} = 2^{2^{mn}+n-2}$ agreements among $2^{2^{mn}}$ labellings. By the Pigeon Hole Principle there is some labelling which agrees with at least

$$
\frac{2^{2^{mn}+n-2}}{2^{2^{mn}}} = 2^{n-2}
$$

of the rows. □

Let us now consider the following cases:

- □▢□▢□▢▢ The source chooses only 1-rows. Therefore the listener has probability 1 of guessing the bit b that is being communicated.

- □▢▢□▢□▢□▢ The source doesn't have to take 0-rows, it has enough positive weight rows to choose from. The average weight achieved is then

$$\frac{d_1 + \frac{1}{2}(e - d_1)}{e} = \frac{1}{2} + \frac{d_1}{2e} \geq \frac{1}{2} + \frac{1}{8e}$$

- □▢□▢□▢▢ There are two possible cases, depending on the value of d_0:

  1. $e \leq 1 - d_0$. As in the former case, the source has enough positive weight rows to choose from. The average weight achieved is then $\frac{1}{2} + \frac{1}{8e}$.

  2. $e > 1 - d_0$. All positive weight rows are used by the source, as well as some 0-weight rows. The success is at least

  $$\frac{d_1 + \frac{1}{2}(1 - 2d_1)}{e} = \frac{1}{2e}$$

  For $e \leq 0.75$, the first bound, $\frac{1}{2} + \frac{1}{8e}$, is lower than the second one, $\frac{1}{2e}$. The resulting lower bound is thus

  $$\frac{1}{2} + \frac{1}{8e}$$

- □▢▢□▢ All positive weight rows, as well as some 0-weight rows, are used, and the value achieved is

$$\frac{d_1 + \frac{1}{2}(1 - 2d_1)}{e} = \frac{1}{2e}$$

This completes the proof of the theorem. □

Interesting cases of the above theorem are for an $(n, n-1)$ source, where we get a lower bound of 0.75, and for $(n, n-c)$ sources $(c \geq 2)$, where the lower bound is 1.

To show that the results of theorem 1 cannot be improved, it is sufficient to exhibit a matrix D for which every labelling agrees with exactly one quarter of the rows. One such matrix is as follows, for a key length of $n = 3$ and with $m_n = 2$.

$$\begin{pmatrix} 1 & 0 & & \\ 1 & 1 & & \\ 0 & 0 & & \\ 0 & 1 & & \\ & 1 & 1 & \\ & 0 & 1 & \\ & & 0 & 0 \\ & & 1 & 0 \end{pmatrix}$$

It can be verified by inspection that every labelling of the columns of D agrees with exactly two rows. It is worth noting that this matrix contains rows which consist of only 0 entries (or 1 entries), and therefore B cannot always decrypt correctly. When one of these rows is selected, B will always output 0 (1), regardless of the value of b, and so will be correct only half of the time. For cryptosystems in which B always decrypts b correctly, we have the following theorem:

Theorem 2 *If (A, B) is as in theorem 1, and in addition B always outputs b correctly, then for every $0 \leq c \leq n$ there exist a $(n, n - c)$ source S and a listener L, such that if the key K is generated by S then*

$$\text{Prob}(L \text{ outputs the same as } B) > \begin{cases} 1 & \text{for } 2 \leq c \leq n \\ \frac{1}{2} + \frac{0.125}{2^{-c}} & \text{for } -\log_2 \frac{3}{4} \leq c \leq 2 \\ \frac{0.5}{2^{-c}} & \text{for } 0 \leq c \leq -\log_2 \frac{3}{4} \end{cases}$$

The only difference from theorem 1 is that here the inequality is strict.

Proof. The proof is the same as in theorem 1, except that in the proof of lemma 2 we now disregard the all-zeroes and all-ones labellings, which here agree with no rows at all. Therefore we get that there is a labelling that agrees with *more* than $\frac{1}{4}$ of the rows. □

Theorem 2 cannot be improved upon. In [M] there is an example of a series of matrices $D_1, D_2, \ldots$ such that D_n represents a cryptosystem in which B always decrypts correctly, and the largest group of rows in agreement with every fixed labelling, is not greater than a $\frac{1}{4} + o(1)$ fraction of the rows.

5 Using an SV-source to Communicate a Single Bit

In this section we show that private key cryptography with private keys generated by an SV-source is not possible. Any correct system (A, B) is not secure. Namely, for any encryption and decryption functions, f and g, there is a δ-source and an eavesdropping function h, such that $\text{Prob}(h(C) = g(K, C)) \geq \frac{1}{2} + p(\delta)$, where p depends on δ (but not on n, the length of the key K, or on m_n, the length of the ciphertext).

We emphasize that this result does not follow from the corresponding one on PRB-sources. The source which was used there to show that correct and secure cryptosystems do not exist, was not a SV-source. On the other hand, the quantitative result here is not as strong: Here we only guarantee an advantage over $\frac{1}{2}$, $p(\delta)$, while there there was a constant advantage of $\frac{1}{4}$ for $(l, l - 1)$-sources, and complete certainty in successful eavesdropping for $(l, l - 2)$-sources.

5.1 Preliminaries

Let us now consider the case where the private key K is an n bit binary string generated by a SV-source with parameter δ. We may think of it as generated by an adversary who chooses, after each bit is output, a probability between δ and $1 - \delta$ that the next bit will be a 0. The adversary strategy can be represented as a complete binary tree of height n, where each left branch corresponds to a 0 being chosen, and a right branch to a 1 being chosen. The leaves correspond to n bit strings, sorted in dictionary order. The adversary chooses at each node, with which probability (between δ and $1 - \delta$) to continue to the left and right branches. This induces a probability distribution on the leaves.

For our purposes, each leaf corresponds to a different key K, of length n, and hence to a different row of D. A $\{0,1\}$-labelling l of the columns of D uniquely assigns a weight to each leaf. This weight is 1 if the leaf *agrees* with l, $\frac{1}{2}$ if it *half-agrees*, and 0 if it *disagrees*. To describe a combination of a matrix D (cryptosystem) and a $\{0,1\}$-labelling l (listener), we define an *adversary tree of height n* as a complete binary tree of height n, the leaves of which are labelled with weights from $\{0, \frac{1}{2}, 1\}$.

Let W_n denote the set of all adversary trees of height n. Each decryption matrix D and labelling l determine a particular tree $T \in W_n$. For this tree, T, the optimal strategy of the adversary is to label the edges of T with probabilities (between δ and $1 - \delta$) such as to maximize the the expected value of the leaf reached.

For a node v, define $val_\delta(v)$ as:

- its weight, if v is a leaf.

- if v has descendants v_1 and v_2, $val_\delta(v) = (1-\delta) \max(val_\delta(v_1),$

  $val_\delta(v_2)) + \delta \min(val_\delta(v_1), val_\delta(v_2))$

For a tree T, define $val_\delta(T)$ as $val_\delta(r)$, where r is the root of T.

Lemma 3 *For a given adversary tree, the source strategy which labels the branch leading to the "heavier" descendant with $1 - \delta$, and the other branch with δ, maximizes the expected value of the leaf reached. The expected value of the leaf reached is then $val_\delta(T)$.*

An adversary tree T is called *balanced* if

- at least one quarter of its leaves are 1-leaves.

- it has the same number of 0-leaves as 1-leaves.

Let Y_n denote the set of all balanced trees of height n.

Lemma 4 *For each decryption matrix D there is a $\{0,1\}$-labelling l, such that for the adversary tree $T \in W_n$, corresponding to D and l, the following holds:*

1. *The sum of the weights of all 2^n leaves is not less than 2^{n-1}.*

2. *At least one quarter of the leaves (2^{n-2} leaves) are 1-leaves.*

Proof: by a counting argument.

Therefore, instead of proving a lower bound on the amount of agreement between a decryption matrix and the optimal $\{0,1\}$-labelling of it (that is, the labelling giving a maximal value to $val_\delta(T)$), it suffices to prove a lower bound for the expected value achieved on a *balanced tree* of height n.

Conjecture 1 *For every balanced tree $T \in Y_n$, it holds that*

$$val_\delta(T) \geq \frac{1}{2} + (\frac{1}{2} - \frac{3}{2}\delta + \delta^2)$$

This lower bound on balanced trees cannot be improved. It equals an upper bound, which is the value achieved on a tree (see figure 2) in which one main subtree (i.e. a subtree descending from the root) has only $\frac{1}{2}$-leaves, while the other main subtree has one subtree the leaves of which are all labeled 1, and another subtree the leaves of which are all labeled 0.

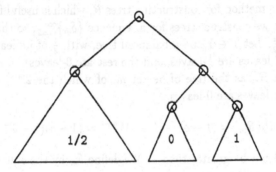

Figure 2: A tree acheiving the lower bound.

Although the lower bound we conjecture here is the best possible bound for adversary trees, it turns out to be difficult to find a cryptosystem for which the maximum success rate a listener can achieve equals this bound. A cryptosystem for which no listener can guess the transmitted bit with more than $1 - \delta$ success, is given in [M].

5.2 Reducing $\{0, \frac{1}{2}, 1\}$-trees to $\{0, 1\}$-trees

We now give a reduction from the problem of finding a lower bound for the value achieved on an adversary tree, to finding a lower bound for the value achieved on a tree that has leaves with weights from $\{0, 1\}$.

Let B_n denote the set of all trees of height n, the leaves of which have weights from $\{0, 1\}$. Define $f_{n,m} : W_n \rightarrow B_{n+m}$ as the transformation which, given an adversary tree $T \in W_n$, does the following:

- replaces each 0-leaf with a subtree of height m, all of its leaves being 0-leaves.

- replaces each 1-leaf with a subtree of height m, all of its leaves being 1-leaves.

- replaces each $\frac{1}{2}$-leaf with a subtree R, such that

  - $R \in B_m$
  - $val_\delta(R) \leq \frac{1}{2}$
  - $val_\delta(R) = \max\{val_\delta(R') | R' \in B_m, val_\delta(R') \, leq\frac{1}{2}\}$

That is, among all trees of B_m that have value not greater than $\frac{1}{2}$, the maximum value is achieved on R. (if there are several trees matching this definition, we take the first in some lexicographical order).

It is clear that for $T \in W_n$, any lower bound on $val_\delta(f_{n,m}(T))$ implies the same lower bound on $val_\delta(T)$.

5.3 Analysis

We now describe a method for constructing trees R, which is useful for values of δ close to $\frac{1}{2}$. Specifically, we construct trees for a sequence $\{\delta_m\}_{m=2}^\infty$, so that $\delta_{m+1} > \delta_m$, and δ_m converges to $\frac{1}{2}$. Let $T \in Y_n$ be a balanced tree, with $\frac{1}{4}$ of its leaves being 1-leaves. (Hence half of its leaves are $\frac{1}{2}$-leaves, and the rest are 0-leaves).

Let us choose R_m as the tree of height m, of which the $2^{m-1} - 1$ left leaves are 1-leaves, all other leaves are 0-leaves.

$$val_\delta(R_m) = (1 - \delta) - (1 - \delta)\delta^{m-1} = (1 - \delta)(1 - \delta^{m-1})$$

This value should not be greater than $\frac{1}{2}$. We define δ_m by the equation

$$val_{\delta_m}(R_m) = (1 - \delta_m)(1 - (\delta_m)^{m-1}) = \frac{1}{2} \tag{1}$$

Let T' denote $f_{n,m}(T)$. The density of 0-s in R_m is $d_{R_m} = \frac{1}{2} + 2^{-m}$, and in T' the density is $d_{T'} = \frac{1}{4} + \frac{1}{2}(\frac{1}{2} + 2^{-m}) = \frac{1}{2} + 2^{-m-1}$. Applying Gereb's bound (Lemma 1), we get the following lower bound for T:

$$val_{\delta_m}(T) \geq 2(1 - \delta_m)(1 - d_{T'}) = (1 - \delta_m)(1 - 2^{-m}) = 1 - \delta_m - (1 - \delta_m)2^{-m} \tag{2}$$

For values of δ in the sequence $\{\delta_m\}$, it is easy, using equation (1), to describe m as a function of δ_m. Thus we get for these values a lower bound of

$$val_{\delta_m}(T) \geq 1 - \delta - \frac{1-\delta}{2}\left(\frac{2-2\delta}{1-2\delta}\right)^{\frac{1}{\log \delta}} = \frac{1}{2} + \left(\frac{1}{2} - \delta - \frac{1-\delta}{2}\left(\frac{2-2\delta}{1-2\delta}\right)^{\frac{1}{\log \delta}}\right) \stackrel{\text{def}}{=} \frac{1}{2} + p(\delta_m)$$

$$\tag{3}$$

$p(m)$ is the advantage over $\frac{1}{2}$, of this lower bound.

5.4

Let $g(\delta)$ be the advantage over $\frac{1}{2}$ stated in conjecture 1, that is, $g(\delta) = \frac{1}{2} - \frac{3}{2}\delta + \delta^2$. The following theorem gives a constant bound for the ratio between the advantages $g(\delta)$ and $p(\delta)$.

Theorem 3 *For a crypto system (A, B), where A and B share an n-bit private key K, which is generated by a SV-source with parameter δ, $\delta \geq 0.45$, there exists a SV-source S and a listener L, such that if K is generated by S then*

$$Prob(\text{ } L \text{ outputs the same as } B) \geq \frac{1}{2} + \frac{g(\delta)}{2.76}$$

Proof: Lemma 4 reduces this problem to finding a lower bound on $val_\delta(T)$, where T is *balanced*, and $\frac{1}{4}$ of its leaves are 1-leaves. The theorem follows from bound (3) and from showing that

$$\frac{g(\delta)}{p(\delta)} \leq 2.76$$

for all δ-s in $[0.45, 0.5]$.

It is easy to show that this ratio is less than 2.60 for all δ_m ($m \geq 3$).

To prove a similar result for all values of δ, note that for $\delta_{m-1} < \delta \leq \delta_m$, a δ_m-source is also a δ-source. Hence lower bound (3) is the same for all δ-s in $(\delta_{m-1}, \delta_m]$.

We should compare the advantages above $\frac{1}{2}$ of the *conjectured* bound with δ_{m-1}, and *our* bound with δ_m. In order to find δ_m, it is needed to solve equation (1). Difficulties arise in solving it analytically (for a general m), and so we needed to solve it using numerical methods. The theorem follows from calculating the ratio between the advantages of the conjectured bound with δ_4, and our bound with δ_5 (this ratio is a little less than 2.76), and showing that for values of δ larger than δ_4, this ratio is not higher than that. The same method can be applied to give a bound for all $\delta \geq \delta_3 = 0.404$ and a ratio of 3.69 instead of 2.76, and for all $\delta \geq \delta_2 = 0.293$ where the ratio is 6.56 instead of 2.76. $\square$

The lower bound we got is not trivial, yet it is not optimal. The technique we employed is rather coarse since it only uses the density of 0-leaves, and not their location. Furthermore, we used a bound for $\{0, 1\}$-trees (in Lemma 1) which is also not optimal.

6 Allowing an Additional Source of Randomness

In the previous two sections we have assumed that the two parties A and B have no additional sources of randomness, public or private. In this section we show to what extent these results depend on this assumption by introducing a public source of truly random bits. By *public* we mean that any truly random bits used by A or B are known to the listener, and in the cryptosystems presented in this section this is made explicit by including any truly random strings used as part of the ciphertext. As a practical matter, a public, truly random source of bits could be something like a satellite using the background radiation left over from the "big bang" as a source of entropy. Mainly, however, this situation is of interest to us from the point of view of investigating the mathematical relationship between weak sources of randomness and cryptography. It seems at first that such a source would not be helpful, but it turns out that in this new situation secure cryptography is possible, and we present a secure system. The complete proofs of the theorems in this section are not given here. The interested reader can find them in [M].

6.1 A Secure System

The following cryptosystem (A, B) is suggested by the construction used initially by Vazirani and Vazirani [VV] and subsequently by Chor and Goldreich [CG] to show that BPP and RP algorithms can be modified to work with just one slightly-random source.

1. (A, B) has a *security parameter* denoted $n \in \mathbf{Z}$.

2. A and B share an n-bit key K generated by an (n, b)-source S, where $K = k_1 \ldots k_n$ for $k_i \in \{0, 1\}$.

3. A wishes to send $m \in \{0, 1\}$ to B.

4. A generates random X such that $|X| = n$.

5. A computes $p \in \{0, 1\}$ (for *pad*) by $p = \vec{X} \cdot \vec{K}$ (the inner product function).

6. A sends $p \oplus m$ and X to B.

7. B is then able to compute $p = \vec{X} \cdot \vec{K}$ and $m = p \oplus (m \oplus p)$.

It is easy to see that this system is correct. It is also secure.

Theorem 4 *Suppose that (A, B) is as above and that the private key K is chosen from an (n, b)-source. If m is randomly chosen in $\{0, 1\}$, then for each listener L which outputs a guess at m,*

$$\text{Prob}(L \text{ outputs } m) \leq 1/2 + 6 \cdot 2^{-b/4}$$

Proof. The proof will appear in the final version. It depends on definitions and results in [CG] in a critical way. See [M] for details. □

Theorem 4 is easily extended to include SV sources.

Corrollary 1 *If (A, B) is modified so that K is generated by an SV source with parameter δ, then Theorem 4 remains true for $b = n \log_2(1 - \delta)^{-1}$.*

There is a natural extension of (A, B) that communicates many bits by running the system many times in parallel. This system can also be proven secure, using an appropriate definition of security for many-bit systems. For details the reader is again referred to [M].

7 Acknowledgments

The authors wish to thank Benny Chor, Michael Luby and Charles Rackoff for many helpful discussions about this work.

References

[B]   M. Blum, "Independent unbiased coin flips from a correlated biased source: A finite state Markov chain", *25th IEEE Sympos. Found. of Comput. Sci.*, pp. 425–433. 1984.

[CG] B. Chor and O. Goldreich, "Unbiased bits from weak sources of randomness and probabilistic communication complexity", *SIAM J. Comput.*, Vol. 17, No. 2, pp. 230–261. April 1988.

[M]   J. L. McInnes, *"Cryptography using weak sources of randomness"*, Technical Report 194/87, Dept. of Computer Science, University of Toronto. 1987.

[N]   J. von Neumann, "Various techniques used in connection with random digits" (notes by G. E. Forsythe), Applied Math Series, Vol. 12, pp.36–38, 1951; National Bureau of Standards, Washington D.C., reprinted in *"Collected Works"*, Vol. 5, pp. 768–770, Pergamon, New York, 1963.

[S]   C. E. Shannon, "Communication theory of secrecy systems", *Bell Sys. Tech. J.*, **28**, pp. 656–715. 1949.

[SV] M. Santha and U. V. Vazirani, "Generating quasi-random sequences from semi-random sources", *J. Comput. System Sci.*, **33**, pp. 75–87. 1986.

[V]   U. V. Vazirani, "Towards a strong communication complexity theory or generating quasi-random sequences from two communicating slightly-random sources",*Proc. 17th Annual Symposium on Theory of Computing*, pp. 366–378. 1985.

[VV] U. V. Vazirani and V. V. Vazirani, "Random polynomial time is equal to slightly random polynomial time", *Proc. 26th Annual Symposium of Foundations of Computer Science*, pp. 417–428. 1985.

Session 10
Applications
Chair: G. Agnew, University of Waterloo

How to Time-Stamp a Digital Document

Stuart Haber
stuart@bellcore.com

W. Scott Stornetta
stornetta@bellcore.com

Bellcore
445 South Street
Morristown, N.J. 07960-1910

Abstract

The prospect of a world in which all text, audio, picture, and video documents are in digital form on easily modifiable media raises the issue of how to certify when a document was created or last changed. The problem is to time-stamp the data, not the medium. We propose computationally practical procedures for digital time-stamping of such documents so that it is infeasible for a user either to back-date or to forward-date his document, even with the collusion of a time-stamping service. Our procedures maintain complete privacy of the documents themselves, and require no record-keeping by the time-stamping service.

Time's glory is to calm contending kings,
To unmask falsehood, and bring truth to light,
To stamp the seal of time in aged things,
To wake the morn, and sentinel the night,
To wrong the wronger till he render right.

The Rape of Lucrece, l. 941

1 Introduction

In many situations there is a need to certify the date a document was created or last modified. For example, in intellectual property matters, it is sometimes crucial to verify the date an inventor first put in writing a patentable idea, in order to establish its precedence over competing claims.

One accepted procedure for time-stamping a scientific idea involves daily notations of one's work in a lab notebook. The dated entries are entered one after another in the notebook, with no pages left blank. The sequentially numbered, sewn-in pages of the notebook make it difficult to tamper with the record without leaving telltale signs. If the notebook is then stamped on a regular basis by a notary public or reviewed and signed by a company manager, the validity of the claim is further enhanced. If the precedence of the inventor's ideas is later challenged, both the physical evidence of the notebook and the established procedure serve to substantiate the inventor's claims of having had the ideas on or before a given date.

There are other methods of time-stamping. For example, one can mail a letter to oneself and leave it unopened. This ensures that the enclosed letter was created before the time postmarked on the envelope. Businesses incorporate more elaborate procedures into their regular order of business to enhance the credibility of their internal documents, should they be challenged at a later date. For example, these methods may ensure that the records are handled by more than one person, so that any tampering with a document by one person will be detected by another. But all these methods rest on two assumptions. First, the records can be examined for telltale signs of tampering. Second, there is another party that views the document whose integrity or impartiality is seen as vouchsafing the claim.

We believe these assumptions are called into serious question for the case of documents created and preserved exclusively in digital form. This is because electronic digital documents are so easy to tamper with, and the change needn't leave any telltale sign on the physical medium. What is needed is a method of time-stamping digital documents with the following two properties. First, one must find a way to time-stamp the data itself, without any reliance on the characteristics of the medium on which the data appears, so that it is impossible to change even one bit of the document without the change being apparent. Second, it should be impossible to stamp a document with a time and date different from the actual one.

The purpose of this paper is to introduce a mathematically sound and computationally practical solution to the time-stamping problem. In the sections that follow, we first consider a naive solution to the problem, the digital safety deposit box. This serves the pedagogical purpose of highlighting additional difficulties associated with digital time-stamping beyond those found in conventional methods of time-stamping. Successive improvements to this naive solution finally lead to practical ways to implement digital time-stamping.

2 The Setting

The setting for our problem is a distributed network of users, perhaps representing individuals, different companies, or divisions within a company; we will refer to the users as *clients*. Each client has a unique identification number.

A solution to the time-stamping problem may have several parts. There is a procedure that is performed immediately when a client desires to have a document time-stamped. There should be a method for the client to verify that this procedure has been correctly performed. There should also be a procedure for meeting a third party's challenge to the validity of a document's time-stamp.

As with any cryptographic problem, it is a delicate matter to characterize precisely the security achieved by a time-stamping scheme. A good solution to the time-stamping problem is one for which, under reasonable assumptions about the computational abilities of the users of the scheme and about the complexity of a computational problem, and possibly about the trustworthiness of the users, it is difficult or impossible to produce false time-stamps. Naturally, the weaker the assumptions needed, the better.

3   A Naive Solution

A naive solution, a "digital safety-deposit box," could work as follows. Whenever a client has a document to be time-stamped, he or she transmits the document to a time-stamping service (TSS). The service records the date and time the document was received and retains a copy of the document for safe-keeping. If the integrity of the client's document is ever challenged, it can be compared to the copy stored by the TSS. If they are identical, this is evidence that the document has not been tampered with after the date contained in the TSS records. This procedure does in fact meet the central requirement for the time-stamping of a digital document.[1] However, this approach raises several concerns:

Privacy This method compromises the privacy of the document in two ways: a third party could eavesdrop while the document is being transmitted, and after transmission it is available indefinitely to the TSS itself. Thus the client has to worry not only about the security of documents it keeps under its direct control, but also about the security of its documents at the TSS.

Bandwidth and storage Both the amount of time required to send a document for time-stamping and the amount of storage required at the TSS depend on the length of the document to be time-stamped. Thus the time and expense required to time-stamp a large document might be prohibitive.

Incompetence The TSS copy of the document could be corrupted in transmission to the TSS, it could be incorrectly time-stamped when it arrives at the TSS, or it could become corrupted or lost altogether at any time while it is stored at the TSS. Any of these occurences would invalidate the client's time-stamping claim.

---

[1]The authors recently learned of a similar proposal sketched by Kanare [14].

Trust The fundamental problem remains: nothing in this scheme prevents the TSS from colluding with a client in order to claim to have time-stamped a document for a date and time different from the actual one.

In the next section we describe a solution that addresses the first three concerns listed above. The final issue, trust, will be handled separately and at greater length in the following section.

4 A Trusted Time-Stamping Service

In this section we assume that the TSS is trusted, and describe two improvements on the naive solution above.

4.1 Hash

Our first simplification is to make use of a family of cryptographically secure *collision-free hash functions*. This is a family of functions $h : \{0,1\}^* \rightarrow \{0,1\}^l$ compressing bit-strings of arbitrary length to bit-strings of a fixed length l, with the following properties:

1. The functions h are easy to compute, and it is easy to pick a member of the family at random.

2. It is computationally infeasible, given one of these functions h, to find a pair of distinct strings x, x' satisfying $h(x) = h(x')$. (Such a pair is called a *collision* for h.)

The practical importance of such functions has been known for some time, and researchers have used them in a number of schemes; see, for example, [7, 15, 16]. Damgård gave the first formal definition, and a constructive proof of their existence, on the assumption that there exist one-way "claw-free" permutations [4]. For this, any "one-way group action" is sufficient [3].

Naor and Yung defined the similar notion of "universal one-way hash functions," which satisfy, in place of the second condition above, the slightly weaker requirement that it be computationally infeasible, given a string x, to compute another string $x' \neq x$ satisfying $h(x) = h(x')$ for a randomly chosen h. They were able to construct such functions on the assumption that there exist one-to-one one-way functions [17]. Rompel has recently shown that such functions exist if there exist one-way functions at all [20]. See §6.3 below for a discussion of the differences between these two sorts of cryptographic hash functions.

There are practical implementations of hash functions, for example that of Rivest [19], which seem to be reasonably secure.

We will use the hash functions as follows. Instead of transmitting his document x to the TSS, a client will send its hash value $h(x) = y$ instead. For the purposes of authentication, time-stamping y is equivalent to time-stamping x. This greatly reduces the bandwidth problem and the storage requirements, and solves the privacy issue as well. Depending on the design goals for an implementation of time-stamping, there may be a single hash function used by everybody, or different hash functions for different users.

For the rest of this paper, we will speak of time-stamping hash values y—random-appearing bit-strings of a fixed length. Part of the procedure for validating a time-stamp will be to produce the pre-image document x that satisfies $h(x) = y$; inability to produce such an x invalidates the putative time-stamp.

4.2 Signature

The second improvement makes use of digital signatures. Informally, a *signature scheme* is an algorithm for a party, the signer, to tag messages in a way that uniquely identifies the signer. Digital signatures were proposed by Rabin and by Diffie and Hellman [18, 7]. After a long sequence of papers by many authors, Rompel [20] showed that the existence of one-way functions can be used in order to design a signature scheme satisfying the very strong notion of security that was first defined by Goldwasser, Micali, and Rivest [10].

With a secure signature scheme available, when the TSS receives the hash value, it appends the date and time, then signs this compound document and sends it to the client. By checking the signature, the client is assured that the TSS actually did process the request, that the hash was correctly received, and that the correct time is included. This takes care of the problem of present and future incompetence on the part of the TSS, and reduces the need for the TSS to store records.

5 Two Time-Stamping Schemes

Sed quis custodiet ipsos Custodes?
Juvenal, c. 100 A.D.
But who will guard the guards themselves?

What we have described so far is, we believe, a practical method for time-stamping digital documents of arbitrary length. However, neither the signature nor the use of hash functions in any way prevents a time-stamping service from issuing a false time-stamp. Ideally, we would like a mechanism which guarantees that no matter how unscrupulous the TSS is, the times it certifies will always be the correct ones, and that it will be unable to issue incorrect time-stamps even if it tries to.

It may seem difficult to specify a time-stamping procedure so as to make it impossible to produce fake time-stamps. After all, if the output of an algorithm A, given as input a document x and some timing information τ, is a bit-string $c = A(x, \tau)$ that stands as a legitimate time-stamp for x, what is to prevent a forger some time later from computing the same timing information τ and then running A to produce the same certificate c? The question is relevant even if A is a probabilistic algorithm.

Our task may be seen as the problem of simulating the action of a trusted TSS, in the absence of generally trusted parties. There are two rather different approaches we might take, and each one leads to a solution. The first approach is to constrain a centralized but possibly untrustworthy TSS to produce genuine time-stamps, in such a way that fake ones are difficult to produce. The second approach is somehow to distribute the required trust among the users of the service. It is not clear that either of these can be done at all.

5.1 Linking

Our first solution begins by observing that the sequence of clients requesting time-stamps and the hashes they submit cannot be known in advance. So if we include bits from the previous sequence of client requests in the signed certificate, then we know that the time-stamp occurred after these requests. But the requirement of including bits from previous documents in the certificate also can be used to solve the problem of constraining the time in the other direction, because the time-stamping company cannot issue later certificates unless it has the current request in hand.

We describe two variants of this linking scheme; the first one, slightly simpler, highlights our main idea, while the second one may be preferable in practice. In both variants, the TSS will make use of a collision-free hash function, to be denoted H. This is in addition to clients' use of hash functions in order to produce the hash value of any documents that they wish to have time-stamped.

To be specific, a time-stamping *request* consists of an l-bit string y (presumably the hash value of the document) and a client identification number ID. We use $\sigma(\cdot)$ to denote the signing procedure used by the TSS. The TSS issues signed, sequentially numbered time-stamp *certificates*. In response to the request (y_n, ID_n) from our client, the nth request in sequence, the TSS does two things:

1. The TSS sends our client the signed certificate $s = \sigma(C_n)$, where the certificate

$$C_n = (n, t_n, \text{ID}_n, y_n; L_n)$$

   consists of the sequence number n, the time t_n, the client number ID_n and the hash value y_n from the request, and certain *linking information*, which comes from the previously issued certificate: $L_n = (t_{n-1}, \text{ID}_{n-1}, y_{n-1}, H(L_{n-1}))$.

2. When the next request has been processed, the TSS sends our client the identification number ID_{n+1} for that next request.

Having received s and ID_{n+1} from the TSS, she checks that s is a valid signature of a good certificate, i.e. one that is of the correct form $(n, t, \text{ID}_n, y_n; L_n)$, containing the correct time t.

If her time-stamped document x is later challenged, the challenger first checks that the time-stamp (s, ID_{n+1}) is of the correct form (with s being a signature of a certificate that indeed contains a hash of x). In order to make sure that our client has not colluded with the TSS, the challenger can call client ID_{n+1} and ask him to produce his time-stamp (s', ID_{n+2}). This includes a signature

$$s' = \sigma(n + 1, t_{n+1}, \text{ID}_{n+1}, y_{n+1}; L_{n+1})$$

of a certificate that contains in its linking information L_{n+1} a copy of her hash value y_n. This linking information is further authenticated by the inclusion of the image $H(L_n)$ of her linking information L_n. An especially suspicious challenger now can call up client ID_{n+2} and verify the next time-stamp in the sequence; this can continue for as long as the challenger wishes. Similarly, the challenger can also follow the chain of time-stamps backward, beginning with client ID_{n-1}.

Why does this constrain the TSS from producing bad time-stamps? First, observe that the use of the signature has the effect that the *only* way to fake a time-stamp is with the collaboration of the TSS. But the TSS cannot forward-date a document, because the certificate must contain bits from requests that immediately preceded the desired time, yet the TSS has not received them. The TSS cannot feasibly back-date a document by preparing a fake time-stamp for an earlier time, because bits from the document in question must be embedded in certificates immediately following that earlier time, yet these certificates have already been issued. Furthermore, correctly embedding a new document into the already-existing stream of time-stamp certificates requires the computation of a collision for the hash function H.

Thus the only possible spoof is to prepare a fake chain of time-stamps, long enough to exhaust the most suspicious challenger that one anticipates.

In the scheme just outlined, clients must keep all their certificates. In order to relax this requirement, in the second variant of this scheme we link each request not just to the next request but to the next k requests. The TSS responds to the nth request as follows:

1. As above, the certificate C_n is of the form $C_n = (n, t_n, \text{ID}_n, y_n; L_n)$, where now

the linking information L_n is of the form

$$L_n = [(t_{n-k}, \text{ID}_{n-k}, y_{n-k}, H(L_{n-k})), \ldots, (t_{n-1}, \text{ID}_{n-1}, y_{n-1}, H(L_{n-1}))].$$

2. After the next k requests have been processed, the TSS sends our client the list $(\text{ID}_{n+1}, \ldots, \text{ID}_{n+k})$.

After checking that this client's time-stamp is of the correct form, a suspicious challenger can ask any one of the next k clients ID_{n+i} to produce his time-stamp. As above, his time-stamp includes a signature of a certificate that contains in its linking information L_{n+i} a copy of the relevant part of the challenged time-stamp certificate C_n, authenticated by the inclusion of the hash by H of the challenged client's linking information L_n. His time-stamp also includes client numbers $(\text{ID}_{n+i+1}, \ldots, \text{ID}_{n+i+k})$, of which the last i are new ones; the challenger can ask these clients for their time-stamps, and this can continue for as long as the challenger wishes.

In addition to easing the requirement that clients save all their certificates, this second variant also has the property that correctly embedding a new document into the already-existing stream of time-stamp certificates requires the computation of a simultaneously k-wise collision for the hash function H, instead of just a pairwise collision.

5.2   Distributed trust

For this scheme, we assume that there is a secure signature scheme so that each user can sign messages, and that a standard secure pseudorandom generator G is available to all users. A *pseudorandom generator* is an algorithm that stretches short input *seeds* to output sequences that are indistinguishable by any feasible algorithm from random sequences; in particular, they are unpredictable. Such generators were first studied by Blum and Micali [2] and by Yao [22]; Impagliazzo, Levin, and Luby have shown that they exist if there exist one-way functions [12].

Once again, we consider a hash value y that our client would like to time-stamp. She uses y as a seed for the pseudorandom generator, whose output can be interpreted in a standard way as a k-tuple of client identification numbers:

$$G(y) = (\text{ID}_1, \text{ID}_2, \ldots, \text{ID}_k).$$

Our client sends her request (y, ID) to each of these clients. She receives in return from client ID_j a signed message $s_j = \sigma_j(t, \text{ID}, y)$ that includes the time t. Her timestamp consists of $[(y, \text{ID}), (s_1, \ldots, s_k)]$. The k signatures s_j can easily be checked by our client or by a would-be challenger. No further communication is required in order to meet a later challenge.

Why should such a list of signatures constitute a believable time-stamp? The reason is that in these circumstances, the only way to produce a time-stamped document with an incorrect time is to use a hash value y so that $G(y)$ names k clients that are willing to cooperate in faking the time-stamp. If at any time there is at most a constant fraction ϵ of possibly dishonest clients, the expected number of seeds y that have to be tried before finding a k-tuple $G(y)$ containing only collaborators from among this fraction is ϵ^{-k}. Furthermore, since we have assumed that G is a secure pseudorandom generator, there is no faster way of finding such a convenient seed y than by choosing it at random. This ignores the adversary's further problem, in most real-world scenarios, of finding a plausible document that hashes to a convenient value y.

The parameter k should be chosen when designing the system so that this is an infeasible computation. Observe that even a highly pessimistic estimate of the percentage of the client population that is corruptible—ϵ could be 90%—does not entail a prohibitively large choice of k. In addition, the list of corruptible clients need not be fixed, as long their fraction of the population never exceeds ϵ.

This scheme need not use a centralized TSS at all. The only requirements are that it be possible to call up other clients at will and receive from them the required signatures, and that there be a public directory of clients so that it is possible to interpret the output of $G(y)$ in a standard way as a k-tuple of clients. A practical implementation of this method would require provisions in the protocol for clients that cannot be contacted at the time of the time-stamping request. For example, for suitable $k' < k$, the system might accept signed responses from any k' of the k clients named by $G(y)$ as a valid time-stamp for y (in which case a greater value for the parameter k would be needed in order to achieve the same low probability of finding a set of collaborators at random).

6 Remarks

6.1 Tradeoffs

There are a number of tradeoffs between the two schemes. The distributed-trust scheme has the advantage that all processing takes place when the request is made. In the linking scheme, on the other hand, the client has a short delay while she waits for the second part of her certificate; and meeting a later challenge may require further communication.

A related disadvantage of the linking scheme is that it depends on at least some parties (clients or, perhaps, the TSS) storing their certificates.

The distributed-trust scheme makes a greater technological demand on the system: the ability to call up and demand a quick signed response at will.

The linking scheme only locates the time of a document between the times of the previous and the next requests, so it is best suited to a setting in which relatively many documents are submitted for time-stamping, compared to the scale at which the timing matters.

It is worth remarking that the time-constraining properties of the linking scheme do not depend on the use of digital signatures.

6.2 Time constraints

We would like to point out that our schemes constrain the event of time-stamping both forward and backward in time. However, if any amount of time may pass between the creation of a document and when it is time-stamped, then no method can do more than forward-constrain the time at which the document itself was created. Thus, in general, time-stamping should only be considered as evidence that a document has not been back-dated.

On the other hand, if the time-stamping event can be made part of the document creation event, then the constraint holds in both directions. For example, consider the sequence of phone conversations that pass through a given switch. In order to process the next call on this switch, one could require that linking information be provided from the previous call. Similarly, at the end of the call, linking information would be passed onto the next call. In this way, the document creation event (the phone call) includes a time-stamping event, and so the time of the phone call can be fixed in both directions. The same idea could apply to sequential financial transactions, such as stock trades or currency exchanges, or any sequence of electronic interactions that take place over a given physical connection.

6.3   Theoretical considerations

Although we will not do it here, we suggest that a precise complexity-theoretic definition of the strongest possible level of time-stamping security could be given along the lines of the definitions given by Goldwasser and Micali [9], Goldwasser, Micali, and Rivest [10], and Galil, Haber, and Yung [8] for various cryptographic tasks. The time-stamping and the verification procedures would all depend on a *security parameter p*. A time-stamp scheme would be *polynomially secure* if the success probability of a polynomially bounded adversary who tries to manufacture a bogus time-stamp is smaller than any given polynomial in $1/p$ for sufficiently large p.

Under the assumption that there exist one-way claw-free permutations, we can prove our linking scheme to be polynomially secure. If we assume that there is always at most a constant fraction of corruptible clients, and assuming as well the existence of one-way functions (and therefore the existence of pseudorandom generators and of a secure signature scheme), we can prove our distributed-trust scheme to be polynomially secure.

In §4.1 above, we mentioned the difference between "collision-free" and "universal one-way" hash functions. The existence of one-way functions is sufficient to give us universal one-way hash functions. However, in order to prove the security of our time-stamping schemes, we apparently need the stronger guarantee of the difficulty of producing hash collisions that is provided by the definition of collision-free hash functions. As far as is currently known, a stronger complexity assumption—namely, the existence of claw-free pairs of permutations—is needed in order to prove the existence of these functions. (See also [5] and [6] for further discussion of the theoretical properties of cryptographic hash functions.)

Universal one-way hash functions were the tool used in order to construct a secure signature scheme. Our apparent need for a stronger assumption suggests a difference, perhaps an essential one, between signatures and time-stamps. It is in the signer's own interest to act correctly in following the instructions of a secure signature scheme (for example, in choosing a hash function at random from a certain set). For time-stamping, on the other hand, a dishonest user or a colluding TSS may find it convenient not to follow the standard instructions (for example, by choosing a hash function so that collisions are easy to find); the time-stamping scheme must be devised so that there is nothing to be gained from such misbehavior.

If it is possible, we would like to reduce the assumptions we require for secure time-stamping to the simple assumption that one-way functions exist. This is the minimum reasonable assumption for us, since all of complexity-based cryptography requires the existence of one-way functions [12, 13]

6.4   Practical considerations

As we move from the realm of complexity theory to that of practical cryptosystems, new questions arise. In one sense, time-stamping places a heavier demand on presumably one-way functions than would some other applications. For example, if an electronic funds transfer system relies on a one-way function for authentication, and that function is broken, then all of the transfers carried out before it was broken are still valid. For time-stamps, however, if the hash function is broken, then all of the time-stamps issued prior to that time are called into question.

A partial answer to this problem is provided by the observation that time-stamps can be renewed. Suppose we have two time-stamping implementations, and that there is reason to believe that the first implementation will soon be broken. Then certificates issued using the old implementation can be renewed using the new implementation. Consider a time-stamp certificate created using the old implementation that is time-stamped with the new implementation before the old one is broken. Prior to the old implementation's breaking, the only way to create a certificate was by legitimate means. Thus, by time-stamping the certificate itself with the new implementation, one has evidence not only that the document existed prior to the time of the new time-stamp, but that it existed at the time stated in the original certificate.

Another issue to consider is that producing hash collisions alone is not sufficient to break the time-stamping scheme. Rather, meaningful documents must be found which lead to collisions. Thus, by specifying the format of a document class, one can complicate the task of finding meaningful collisions. For example, the density of ASCII-only texts among all possible bit-strings of length N bytes is $(2^7/2^8)^N$, or $1/2^N$, simply because the high-order bit of each byte is always 0. Even worse, the density of acceptable English text can be bounded above by an estimate of the entropy of English as judged by native speakers [21]. This value is approximately 1 bit per ASCII character, giving a density of $(2^1/2^8)^N$, or $1/128^N$.

We leave it to future work to determine whether one can formalize the increased difficulty of computing collisions if valid documents are sparsely and perhaps randomly distributed in the input space. Similarly, the fact that a k-way linking scheme requires the would-be adversary to compute k-way collisions rather than collision pairs may be parlayed into relaxing the requirements for the hash function. It may also be worthwhile to explore when there exist hash functions for which there are *no* k-way collisions among strings in a suitably restricted subset of the input space; the security of such a system would no longer depend on a complexity assumption.

7 Applications

Using the theoretically best (cryptographically secure) hash functions, signature schemes, and pseudorandom generators, we have designed time-stamping schemes that possess theoretically desirable properties. However, we would like to emphasize the practical nature of our suggestion: because there are *practical* implementations of these cryptographic tools, both of our time-stamp schemes can be inexpensively implemented as described. Practical hash functions like Rivest's are quite fast, even running on low-end PC's [19].

What kinds of documents would benefit from secure digital time-stamping? For documents that establish the precedence of an invention or idea, time-stamping has a clear value. A particularly desirable feature of digital time-stamping is that it makes it possible to establish precedence of intellectual property without disclosing its contents. This could have a significant effect on copyright and patent law, and could be applied to everything from software to the secret formula for Coca-Cola.

But what about documents where the date is not as significant as simply whether or not the document has been tampered with? These documents can benefit from time-stamping, too, under the following circumstances. Suppose one can establish that either the necessary knowledge or the motivation to tamper with a document did not exist until long after the document's creation. For example, one can imagine a company that deals with large numbers of documents each day, some few of which are later found to be incriminating. If all the company's documents were routinely time-stamped at the time of their creation, then by the time it became apparent which documents were incriminating and how they needed to be modified, it would be too late to tamper with them. We will call such documents *tamper-unpredictable*. It seems clear that many business documents are tamper-unpredictable. Thus, if time-stamping were to be incorporated into the established order of business, the credibility of many documents could be enhanced.

A variation that may be particularly useful for business documents is to time-stamp a log of documents rather than each document individually. For example, each corporate document created in a day could be hashed, and the hash value added to the company's daily log of documents. Then, at the end of the business day, the log alone could be submitted for time-stamping. This would eliminate the expense of time-stamping each document individually, while still making it possible to detect tampering with each document; one could also determine whether any documents had been destroyed altogether.

Of course, digital time-stamping is not limited to text documents. Any string of bits can be time-stamped, including digital audio recordings, photographs, and full-motion videos. Most of these documents are tamper-unpredictable. Therefore, time-stamping can help to distinguish an original photograph from a retouched one, a problem that has received considerable attention of late in the popular press [1, 11]. It is in fact difficult to think of any other algorithmic "fix" that could add more credibility to photographs, videos, or audio recordings than time-stamping.

8 Summary

In this paper, we have shown that the growing use of text, audio and video documents in digital form and the ease with which such documents can be modified creates a new problem: how can one certify when a document was created or last modified? Methods of certification, or time-stamping, must satisfy two criteria. First, they must time-stamp the actual bits of the document, making no assumptions about the physical medium on which the document is recorded. Second, the date and time of the time-stamp must not be forgeable.

We have proposed two solutions to this problem. Both involve the use of one-way hash functions, whose outputs are processed in lieu of the actual documents, and of digital signatures. The solutions differ only in the way that the date and time are made unforgeable. In the first, the hashes of documents submitted to a TSS are linked together, and certificates recording the linking of a given document are distributed to other clients both upstream and downstream from that document. In the second solution, several members of the client pool must time-stamp the hash. The members are chosen by means of a pseudorandom generator that uses the hash of the document itself as seed. This makes it infeasible to deliberately choose which clients should and should not time-stamp a given hash. The second method could be implemented without the need for a centralized TSS at all.

Finally, we have considered whether time-stamping could be extended to enhance the authenticity of documents for which the time of creation itself is not the critical issue. This is the case for a large class of documents which we call "tamper-unpredictable." We further conjecture that no purely algorithmic scheme can add any more credibility to a document than time-stamping provides.

Acknowledgements

We gratefully acknowledge helpful discussions with Don Beaver, Shimon Even, George Furnas, Burt Kaliski, Ralph Merkle, Jeff Shrager, Peter Winkler, Yacov Yacobi, and Moti Yung.

References

[1] J. Alter. When photographs lie. *Newsweek*, pp. 44-45, July 30, 1990.

[2] M. Blum and S. Micali. How to generate cryptographically strong sequences of pseudo-random bits. *SIAM Journal on Computing*, 13(4):850–864, Nov. 1984.

[3] G. Brassard and M. Yung. One-way group actions. In *Advances in Cryptology—Crypto '90*, these proceedings. Lecture Notes in Computer Science, Springer-Verlag, Berlin, 1991.

[4] I. Damgård. Collision-free hash functions and public-key signature schemes. In *Advances in Cryptology—Eurocrypt '87*, pp. 203-217. Lecture Notes in Computer Science, vol. 304, Springer-Verlag, Berlin, 1988.

[5] I. Damgård. A design principle for hash functions. In *Advances in Cryptology—Crypto '89* (ed. G. Brassard), pp. 416-427. Lecture Notes in Computer Science, vol. 435, Springer-Verlag, Berlin, 1990.

[6] A. DeSantis and M. Yung. On the design of provably secure cryptographic hash functions. In *Advances in Cryptology—Eurocrypt '90*. Lecture Notes in Computer Science, Springer-Verlag, Berlin, to appear.

[7] W. Diffie and M.E. Hellman. New directions in cryptography. *IEEE Trans. on Inform. Theory*, vol. IT-22, Nov. 1976, pp. 644-654.

[8] Z. Galil, S. Haber, and M. Yung. Interactive public-key cryptosystems. Submitted for publication, 1990.

[9] S. Goldwasser and S. Micali. Probabilistic encryption. *JCSS*, 28:270–299, April 1984.

[10] S. Goldwasser, S. Micali, and R. Rivest. A secure digital signature scheme. *SIAM Journal on Computing*, 17(2):281–308, 1988.

[11] Andy Grundberg. Ask it no questions: The camera can lie. *The New York Times*, section 2, pp. 1, 29, August 12, 1990.

[12] R. Impagliazzo, L. Levin, and M. Luby. Pseudorandom generation from one-way functions. In *Proc. 21st STOC*, pp. 12-24. ACM, New York, 1989.

[13] R. Impagliazzo and M. Luby. One-way functions are essential for complexity-based cryptography. In *Proc. 30th FOCS*, pp. 230-235. IEEE, New York, 1989.

[14] H. M. Kanare. *Writing the laboratory notebook*, p. 117. American Chemical Society, Washington, D.C., 1985.

[15] R.C. Merkle. Secrecy, authentication, and public-key systems. Ph.D. thesis, Stanford Univeristy, 1979.

[16] R.C. Merkle. One-way hash functions and DES. In *Advances in Cryptology—Crypto '89* (ed. G. Brassard), pp. 428-446. Lecture Notes in Computer Science, vol. 435, Springer-Verlag, Berlin, 1990.

[17] M. Naor and M. Yung. Universal one-way hash functions and their cryptographic applications. In *Proc. 21st STOC*, pp. 33-43. ACM, New York, 1989.

[18] M.O. Rabin. Digitalized signatures. In *Foundations of Secure Computation* (ed. R.A. DeMillo et al.), pp. 155-168. Academic Press, 1978.

[19] R. Rivest. The MD4 message digest algorithm. In *Advances in Cryptology—Crypto '90*, these proceedings. Lecture Notes in Computer Science, Springer-Verlag, Berlin, 1991.

[20] J. Rompel. One-way functions are necessary and sufficient for secure signatures. In *Proc. 22nd STOC*, pp. 387-394. ACM, New York, 1990.

[21] C. Shannon. Prediction and entropy of printed English. *Bell System Technical Journal*, vol. 30 pp. 50-64, 1951.

[22] A.C. Yao. Theory and applications of trapdoor functions. In *Proc. 23rd FOCS*, pp. 80-91. IEEE, New York, 1982.

How to Utilize the Randomness of Zero-Knowledge Proofs

(Extended Abstract)

Tatsuaki Okamoto   Kazuo Ohta

NTT Communications and Information Processing Laboratories
Nippon Telegraph and Telephone Corporation
1-2356, Take, Yokosuka-shi, Kanagawa-ken, 238-03, Japan

Abstract

In zero-knowledge interactive proofs, a lot of randomized information is exchanged between the prover and the verifier, and the randomness of the prover is used in satisfying the zero-knowledge condition. In this paper, we show a new methodology that utilizes the randomness of the prover in a zero-knowledge proof for some positive objectives as well as for zero-knowledge condition. Based on this idea, we propose two types of applications; key distribution, and digital signature. We propose identity-based key distribution schemes that are provably secure against strong active attacks (*chosen-message-known-key active attacks*) assuming the difficulty of factoring a composite number. In addition, we show that *non-transitive* digital signature schemes can be constructed if and only if a one-way function exists. We also show some practical non-transitive digital signature schemes. A new general method of constructing identity-based cryptographic schemes is presented as an application of the identity-based non-transitive digital signature schemes. We also propose a new digital signature scheme based on the (extended) Fiat-Shamir identification scheme.

1. Introduction

In zero-knowledge proofs [GMRa], a lot of randomized information is exchanged between the prover and the verifier. To date, this information has been used just for the zero-knowledge interactive proof. However, many new security applications would become possible if the randomized information could be more effectively utilized.

This was first realized by Desmedt, Goutier and Bengio [DGB] who used the randomized information of the Fiat-Shamir scheme to create a subliminal channel while retaining the zero-knowledge interactive proof property. In another development, Okamoto and Ohta [OkO1] introduced the disposable zero-knowledge authentication protocol in which the provers' randomness (the number of coin flips) is restricted. The most important application of this protocol is an electronic cash system. The subliminal channel of [DGB] is used for *negative purposes* (i.e. abuse), while the protocol of [OkO1] uses randomness in a *negative manner* (i.e. restriction).

This paper propose a new methodology for utilizing randomness in a *positive manner* to achieve several *positive purposes*. Based on this methodology, we create four new cryptographic techniques: identity-based key distribution, non-transitive digital signatures, new digital signature construction using the Fiat-Shamir scheme, and a general technique for constructing identity-based schemes.

The key point of the proposed methodology is that $f(r,a)$ is used instead of the true random number R, where the distributions of $g(f(r,a))$ and $g(R)$ are indistinguishable when r is a true random number, a is a fixed parameter, and $g(R)$ is a message from a prover to a verifier using a zero-knowledge proof. Zero-knowledge proofs are still possible if the distributions of $g(f(r,a))$ and $g(R)$ are indistinguishable. The advantage of using $f(r,a)$ is that it leads to several useful functions. We show that one such function, $a^r \bmod n$, can be used to construct identity-based key distribution schemes, while other functions, $r^a \bmod n$, and bit-commitment functions [N] are appropriate for digital signature schemes.

First, we propose key distribution schemes provably secure against strong active attacks assuming the intractability of factoring. Although the recently advanced key distribution scheme of [YS] is also provably secure against active attacks under the same assumption, and is very simple, the proposed schemes are practically superior because they are identity-based schemes (or they do not need any public-key file), and, moreover, ours are provably secure against stronger active attacks (*chosen-message-known-key active attacks*) than theirs (*plain active attacks*). (Our considered active attacks, *chosen-message-known-key active attacks*, seem to be stronger than any attacks so far considered against key distribution schemes. For example, although Yacobi[Y] has also proposed a key distribution scheme provably secure against stronger passive attacks (*known-key passive attacks*) than primitive passive attacks (*plain passive attacks*), their attacks are still weaker than ours). On the other hand, although some identity-based key distribution schemes have been proposed [Ok, TI, KO, GP], after Shamir explicitly proposed identity-based schemes in 1984 [Sha], no previously published identity-based key distribution scheme has been proven secure against even weaker passive attacks. (Note that our identity-based key distribution schemes can be easily converted to regular (public-key file based) key distribution schemes with the same properties.)

Next, new *non-transitive* digital signature schemes are proposed that utilize the randomness of zero-knowledge proofs. The proposed schemes have the following properties: (we assume that user A sends a message M to user B.)

(1) Only user A can prove the validity of A's message M to any user B by using A's public key or A's identity (validity).

(2) User B cannot prove the origin of message M to another user C (non- transitivity).

With this digital signature scheme, A can validate his message to anyone, while leaving no proof of its origin. That is, the receiver cannot validate the origin of the message to anyone else. The scheme will be useful in many business and political discussions, because messages can be authenticated but they are unattributable. The concept of *non-transitive* digital signature scheme itself is not new, and the approach of using zero-knowledge proofs has been implied by Desmedt [D]. Note that the *undeniable* digital signature scheme has a similar property, but is distinctly different from the *non-transitive* signature scheme (see Section 3 in more detail). In this paper, we show that *non-transitive* digital signature scheme can be constructed if and only if a one-way function exists. We also show some practical (identity-based) non-transitive digital signature schemes.

Using the same technique used in constructing the practical non-transitive digital signature, we construct a digital signature scheme that utilizes the randomness of the (extended) Fiat-Shamir identification scheme. Although Fiat and Shamir [FiS] have already proposed a digital signature scheme based on their identification scheme, we show another construction. The performance (data size, and processing speed) of our scheme is roughly comparable to that of Fiat and Shamir's.

Finally, we show a new general methodology for constructing identity-based cryptographic schemes, using the above-mentioned identity-based non-transitive digital signature scheme.

2. Identity-based key distribution schemes

In this section, we will show a new methodology of constructing provably secure identity-based key distribution schemes utilizing the randomness of zero-knowledge-based identification protocols such as the (extended) Fiat-Shamir scheme [FiS, FFS, GQ, Oh1, OhO].

2.1 Zero-knowledge identification protocols

Here, we introduce some of the typical zero-knowledge-based identification protocols that can be utilized to construct identity-based key distribution schemes.
(1) the Fiat-Shamir scheme [FiS, FFS]
(2) the extended Fiat-Shamir scheme 1 (higher degree version of (1)) [GQ, OhO]
(3) the extended Fiat-Shamir scheme 2 (symmetric version of (2)) [Oh1]
(4) the Beth scheme (discrete log version of (1)) [Be]
Each of the above schemes have three variations:
(a) Sequential version
(b) Parallel version (one round or three moves version)
(c) Non-interactive version
Among these variations, only sequential version (a) is zero-knowledge identification with schemes (1)-(4). The parallel version (b) of scheme (1) has been proven to be secure using no-transferable information [FFS], and the parallel versions (b) of schemes (2)-(3) have been partially proven to be secure by using no-transferable information [OhO, Oh2].

The non-interactive version (c) is constructed based on the parallel version (b) and a one-way function h as follows: Here, we assume that in the parallel version, the prover sends X to the verifier at first, then the verifier sends E to the prover, finally the prover sends Y to the verifier, then the verifier checks the validity of X, Y. In the non-constructive version, the prover generates $E = h(X)$ by himself, then, he generates Y. After generating X, E, Y, he sends them to the verifier. The check by the verifier is the same as in the parallel version. The security of this non-interactive version depends on both the property of the one-way function and the security of the parallel version. The Fiat-Shamir digital signature scheme has the same security as this non-interactive version. If we assume the function is an ideal random function [MS], the non-interactive versions (c) are provably secure when the basic parallel versions are provably secure. Note that these non-interactive versions are different from the framework of non-interactive zero-knowledge proofs [BFM, DMP].

2.2 Identity-based key distribution schemes

In this subsection, we will introduce identity-based key distribution schemes that utilize the randomized information from the identification protocols shown in 2.1. Subsection 2.1 introduced a total of $4 \times 3 = 12$ identification protocols. Because it is tedious to write up 12 key distribution schemes (i.e. for all identification protocols), we will show 4 typical cases here; (1)(a), (2)(b), (2)(c), and (3)(c) (Here, (1)(a) means the sequential version (a) of the Fiat-Shamir scheme (1)).

2.2.1 Construction using the sequential version of the Fiat-Shamir scheme provably secure against active adversary

Key distribution scheme 2.2.1

(1) Preprocessing stage

The unique trusted center in the system generates the Fiat-Shamir scheme secret keys $s_{1,j}$ and $s_{2,j}$ $(j = 1, 2, \ldots, k)$ for user 1 and user 2, respectively. The center's secret key is (p, q), center's public key is (n, g), and $1/s_{i,j} = (f(I_i, j))^{1/2} \bmod n$ $(i = 1, 2, j = 1, 2, \ldots, k)$, where p, q are primes for which $p' = (p-1)/2$ and $q' = (q-1)/2$ are also primes, $n = pq$, the order of $g \in Z_n^*$ is $p'q'$, $|p| = c_1 |n|$, $|q| = c_2 |n|$ $(c_1, c_2$: constant). I_i is the identity of user i.

(2) Key distribution stage

Repeat steps (i) to (v) t times (for $l = 1, 2, \ldots, t$).

(i) User 1 picks a random number $r_1 \in Z_n$ and sends $x_1 = g^{2^{r_1}} \bmod n$ to user 2.

(ii) User 2 sends a random binary vector $(e_{1,1}, \ldots, e_{1,k})$ to user 1. User 2 also picks a random number $r_2 \in Z_n$ and sends $x_2 = g^{2^{r_2}} \bmod n$ to user 1.

(iii) User 1 sends to user 2 y_1 such that $y_1 = g^{r_1} \prod_j s_{1,j}^{e_{1,j}} \bmod n$. User 1 also sends a random binary vector $(e_{2,1}, \ldots, e_{2,k})$ to user 2.

(iv) User 2 checks that $x_1 = y_1^2 \prod_j f(I_1, j)^{e_{1,j}} \pmod{n}$. If the check is valid, he generates K_l such that $K_l = x_1^{r_2} \bmod n$. User 2 also sends to user 1 y_2 such that $y_2 = g^{r_2} \prod_j s_{2,j}^{e_{2,j}} \bmod n$.

(v) User 1 checks that $x_2 = y_2^2 \prod_j f(I_2, j)^{e_{2,j}} \pmod{n}$. If the check is valid, he generates K_l such that $K_l = x_2^{r_1} \bmod n$.

After all t procedure cycles are passed, users 1 and 2 calculate the common key K such that $K = K_1 + K_2 + \ldots + K_t \bmod n$.

Definition 1 Let $(m_1^1, m_2^1, \ldots, m_{k_1}^1)$ and $(m_1^2, m_2^2, \ldots, m_{k_2}^2)$ be the ordered set of messages sent by honest user 1 and user 2, respectively, who follow a key distribution protocol, and finally share a common key $K = h_1(p, s_1, m_1^2, \ldots, m_{k_2}^2, r_1^1, \ldots, r_{l_1}^1)$ $= h_2(p, s_2, m_1^1, \ldots, m_{k_1}^1, r_1^2, \ldots, r_{l_2}^2)$, where h_i $(i = 1, 2)$ is the key generation function for user i, p is public information, s_i is a secret key for user i, r_j^i is a random value employed by user i to generate a message. A *plain active adversary* A interferes with the key distribution protocols between the two honest parties user

1 and user 2 in such a way that A sends a message $\tilde{m}_j^1$ to user 2 after receiving m_j^1 from user 1, and sends $\tilde{m}_j^2$ to user 1. Accordingly, honest user 1 computes $\tilde{K}_1 = h_1(p, s_1, \tilde{m}_1^2, \ldots, \tilde{m}_{k_2}^2, r_1^1, \ldots, r_{l_1}^1)$ instead of K. The *plain active attack* is *successful* if A can finally compute $\tilde{K}_1$.

Remark: Note that A utilizes user 2 to share a key with user 1. A may get two keys, each of which is shared with each honest user. However, this two directional attack is a specific case of the one-directional case in Definition 1.

Definition 2 A *chosen-message-known-key active adversary* A is allowed to play a role of user 2 (i.e., A knows s_2), and to know the value $K = h_1(p, s_1, m_1^2, \ldots, m_{k_2}^2, r_1^1, \ldots, r_{l_1}^1)$ after generating and sending $(m_1^2, m_2^2, \ldots, m_{k_2}^2)$ to user 1. After A is allowed to perform the above attack polynomially many times, A tries the plain active attack shown in Definition 1. The *chosen-message-known-key active attack* is *successful* if A can finally compute $\tilde{K}_1$.

Remark: Definitions 1 and 2 correspond to *malicious adversary* and *amortized security* in [YS], respectively. We can also define two kinds of *passive* attacks; *plain passive attack* and *known-key passive attack*, which correspond to *ciphertext-only attack by a passive adversary* and *known-key attack by a passive adversary* in [Y], respectively. *Chosen-message-known-key active attack* is stronger than the other attacks including the plain active attack, and the two types of passive attacks.

Lemma 1 Let p, q be primes for which $p' = (p-1)/2$ and $q' = (q-1)/2$ are also primes, n be pq, and the order of $g \in Z_n^*$ be $p'q'$. If $r \in Z_{p'q'}$ and $R \in Z_n^*$ are randomly and uniformly selected, then $\{g^{2r} \bmod n\}$ and $\{R^2 \bmod n\}$ are perfectly indistinguishable.

Proof: In order to prove that $g^{2r} \bmod n$ and $R^2 \bmod n$ are perfectly indistinguishable, we will prove that $\{g^{2r} \bmod n\}$ is the set of quadratic residue numbers which are uniformly distributed, if $r \in Z_{p'q'}$ are randomly and uniformly selected. First, we introduce some notations. Any x in Z_n^* can be uniquely expressed as (x_p, x_q), where $x_p = x \bmod p$ and $x_q = x \bmod q$. (Z_p^* is equivalent to $Z_p - 0$.) Any $g^r \bmod n$ can be uniquely expressed as $(g_p^{r_p} \bmod p, g_q^{r_q} \bmod q)$, where $g = (g_p, g_q)$, and $r_p = r \bmod p'$, and $r_q = r \bmod q'$, because the order of g is $p'q'$. We simply write $< r_p, r_q >$ for $g^r \bmod n = (g_p^{r_p} \bmod p, g_q^{r_q} \bmod q)$. Then we show that there exist many g's whose orders are $p'q'$. Let $\bar{g}$ be $(\bar{g}_p, \bar{g}_q)$ such that the order of $\bar{g}_p$ in Z_p^* is $2p'$, and the order of $\bar{g}_q$ in Z_q^* is $2q'$. Then, the order of $\bar{g}$ is $2p'q'$. Any g whose order is $p'q'$ can be expressed as $\bar{g}^a \bmod n$, where $\gcd(a, 2p'q') = 2$. Therefore, the number of g whose order is $p'q'$ is $(p'q' - p' - q' + 1)$. Hence, roughly speaking, about $1/4$ of the elements in Z_n are g with the order of $p'q'$. Here note that g is quadratic residue. Next, any $g^r \bmod n$ can be represented as $< i, j >$ ($i = 0, 1, \ldots, p'-1$; $j = 0, 1, \ldots, q'-1$), because $r(r = 0, 1, \ldots, p'q'-1)$ has a unique solution satisfying $r \equiv i \pmod{p'}$ and $r \equiv j \pmod{q'}$ by the Chinese remainder theorem. Similarly, $g^{2r} \bmod n$ can be represented as $< h, k >$ ($h = 0, 1, \ldots, p'-1$; $k = 0, 1, \ldots, q'-1$), because $r(r = 0, 1, \ldots, p'q'-1)$ has a unique solution satisfying $2r \equiv h \pmod{p'}$ and $2r \equiv k \pmod{q'}$ (since $\gcd(2, p', q') = 1$). Therefore, the numbers of both $\{g^r \bmod n\}$ and $\{g^{2r} \bmod n\}$ are $p'q'$. The number of quadratic residue numbers in Z_n^* is $p'q'$. Hence, any quadratic residue number (or $R^2 \bmod n$) can be expressed by $g^{2r} \bmod n$. Clearly, if $r \in Z_{p'q'}$ is randomly and uniformly selected, then $\{g^{2r} \bmod n\}$ is uniformly distributed. Thus, $\{g^{2r} \bmod n\}$ is the set of quadratic residue numbers which are uniformly distributed, if $r \in Z_{p'q'}$ are randomly and uniformly selected.   **QED**

Lemma 2   Let p, q be primes for which $p' = (p-1)/2$ and $q' = (q-1)/2$ are also primes, n be pq, the order of $g \in Z_n^*$ be $p'q'$, and $|p| = c_1|n|$, $|q| = c_2|n|$ (c_1, c_2: constant). If $r \in Z_n$ and $R \in Z_n$ are randomly and uniformly selected, then $\{g^{2r} \bmod n\}$ and $\{R^2 \bmod n\}$ are statistically indistinguishable.

Proof: Here, we will prove that $\{g^{2r} \bmod n\}$ with $r \in_R Z_n$ is statistically indistinguishable from $\{g^{2r'} \bmod n\}$ with $r' \in_R Z_{p'q'}$, and that $\{R^2 \bmod n\}$ with $R \in_R Z_n$ is statistically indistinguishable from $\{R'^2 \bmod n\}$ with $R' \in_R Z_n^*$. Here, $r \in_R Z_n$ means that r is randomly and uniformly selected from Z_n. By combining the above result and Lemma 1, we can immediately obtain Lemma 2.

Because the order of g is $p'q'$, $g^{2r} \bmod n = g^{2r'} \bmod n$, where $r' = r \bmod p'q'$. The number of the elements of Z_n is $n = (2p' + 1)(2q' + 1) = 4p'q' + 2p' + 2q' + 1$. Then, $n/(p'q') = 4 + (2p' + 2q' + 1)/p'q'$. Therefore, when r' is a value such that $(0 \le r' \le 2p' + 2q')$, and $r \in Z_n$ is randomly and uniformly selected, then

$$Pr(g^{2r} \bmod n = g^{2r'} \bmod n) = 5/n.$$

When r' is a value such that $2p' + 2q' + 1 \le r' \le p'q' - 1$, and $r \in Z_n$ is randomly and uniformly selected, then

$$Pr(g^{2r} \bmod n = g^{2r'} \bmod n) = 4/n.$$

On the other hand, from Lemma 1, $\{g^{2r'} \bmod n\}$ is uniformly distributed on the quadratic residue set modulo n, therefore for a value $\alpha \in \{R^2 \bmod n\}$, if r' is randomly and uniformly selected, then

$$\Pr(g^{2r'} \bmod n = \alpha) = 1/(p'q')$$

Therefore, from the definition of statistical distinguishability [GMRa],

$$\sum_{\alpha \in \{0,1\}^*} |\Pr(g^{2r} \bmod n = \alpha) - \Pr(g^{2r'} \bmod n = \alpha)|$$

$$= \sum_{\alpha \in \{R^2 \bmod n\}} |\Pr(g^{2r} \bmod n = \alpha) - \Pr(g^{2r'} \bmod n = \alpha)|$$

$$= (2p' + 2q' + 1)(5/n - 1/(p'q')) + (p'q' - 2p' - 2q' - 1)(1/(p'q') - 4/n)$$

$$< 2(2p' + 2q' + 1)/n$$

Because $|p'| = c_1|n|$, $|q'| = c_2|n|$ (c_1, c_2: constant), for any constant c,

$$2(2p' + 2q' + 1)/n < 1/|n|^c.$$

Thus, g^{2r} mod n is statistically indistinguishable from $g^{2r'}$ mod n. Similarily, we can prove that R^2 mod n is statistically indistinguishable from R'^2 mod n.   **QED**

Theorem 1   If the factoring assumption is true, then there is no probabilistic polynomial-time *plain active attack* (Definition 1) which is successful with nonnegligible probability against the key distribution scheme 2.2.1.

(Factoring assumption)   There exists no probabilistic polynomial-time algorithm F such that, given n, F computes p with non-negligible probability, where $n = pq$ (p and q are randomly and uniformly selected prime numbers).

Proof sketch: For simplicity, we assume that the Fiat-Shamir scheme's parameter k is 1. By using the technique similar to that in [FFS], we can easily extend our result to the general case that $k \neq 1$.

First, we assume that there exists a probabilistic polynomial-time plain active adversary A (Definition 1) that succeeds in sharing key K with user 1 with non-negligible probability. Here, A utilizes user 2 as a kind of oracle under the protocol condition in order to share key K with user 1. A^{U2} denotes A who utilizes user 2 under the protocol condition. A^{U2} must be verified as user 2 through the Fiat-Shamir Scheme identification t times to obtain final shared key $K = K_1 + .. + K_t$ mod n. Since each K_i is independently determined, A and user 1 must share each K_i to share K.

First, we assume that A generates and sends a message $\widetilde{x}_2$ instead of user 2's valid message x_2 *after* receiving user 1's message x_1. (This assumption is no problem because it is more advantageous than the other assumption such that A generates and sends $\widetilde{x}_2$ *before* receiving x_1.) Because user 1 is a honest party, each K_i must be $\widetilde{x}_2^{r_1}$ mod n at each round. Therefore, A^{U2} must have an algorithm H such that $H : (g, n, g^{2r_1} \bmod n) \rightarrow (\widetilde{x}_2, \widetilde{x}_2^{r_1} \bmod n)$. In addition, A^{U2} must have an algorithm of passing the Fiat-Shamir scheme identification as user 2 with using $\widetilde{x}_2$ instead of x_2. Here, we can assume that A succeeds with nonnegligible probability. Therefore, H must output a correct answer with nonnegligible probability.

Then, we will show that A can construct an algorithm of calculating user 2's secret key by using H. First, A generates a random odd number $t \in Z_n$, and calculates $H : (g, n, g^t \bmod n) \rightarrow (\widetilde{x}_2, \widetilde{x}_2^{t/2} \bmod n)$ with nonnegligible probability, because $\{g^t \bmod n\}$ is statistically indistinguishable from $\{g^{2r_1} \bmod n\}$ (when t is odd and $1 \leq t \leq 2p'q' - 1$, then t mod $p'q'$ has all values from 0 through $p'q' - 1$). Then, A^{U2} follows the protocol with user 1. As mentioned above, A^{U2} has an algorithm to pass the identification protocol as user 2 with using $\widetilde{x}_2$. Here, A can calculate $\widetilde{x}_2^{1/2}$ mod n from $\widetilde{x}_2$ and $\widetilde{x}_2^{t/2}$ mod n, because t is odd. (When we set $X = \widetilde{x}_2^{1/2}$ mod n, then $\widetilde{x}_2 = X^2$ mod n, and $\widetilde{x}_2^{t/2}$ mod $n = X^t$ mod n. Because $\gcd(t, 2) = 1$, A can calculate X from X^2 mod n and X^t mod n.) Therefore, A can calculate one of the solutions $S = 1/f(I_2)^{1/2}$ mod n by $\widetilde{y}_2/\widetilde{x}_2^{1/2}$ mod n with nonnegligible probability.

On the other hand, A interacts with two protocols with user 1 and 2. The interfaces of two protocols are the Fiat-Shamir scheme except that $x_i = \{g^{2r_i} \bmod n\}$ ($i = 1, 2$) is used instead of $\{R^2 \bmod n\}$. As shown in Lemma 2, $x_i = \{g^{2r_i} \bmod n\}$ ($i = 1, 2$) is statistically indistinguishable from $\{R^2 \bmod n\}$. Therefore, the protocols with user 1 and 2 are statistical zero-knowledge proofs, while the original Fiat-Shamir scheme is a perfect zero-knowledge proof. In addition, A interacts with these two protocols in a parallel manner. We can easily prove that any parallel composition of two Fiat-Shamir scheme protocols holds the zero-knowledge property by constructing a simulator for any parallel composition of two protocols (here, note that this property is not guaranteed for general zero-knowledge protocols as shown in Theorem 3.2 in [FeS] and Theorem 7 in [GK]). Therefore, if factoring assumption is true, then A has no chance of obtaining $S = 1/f(I_2)^{1/2} \bmod n$ with nonnegligible probability from the zero-knowledge property unless A is user 2, because factoring is probabilistically polynomial-time reducible to computing S from $f(I)$ [Ra].

However, as above mentioned, if we assume that plain active adversary A succeeds in sharing key K with user 1 with nonnegligible probability, then we can show that A can obtain $S = f(I_2)^{1/2} \bmod n$ with nonnegligible probability. This is a contradiction. **QED**

Remarks: We can obtain the same result even if we replace the factoring assumption by assumption A used in [YS].

(Assumption A) Factorization of n is a one-way function [GL] with super-polynomial security.

2.2.2 Construction using the sequential version of the Fiat-Shamir scheme provably secure against stronger active adversary

In subsection 2.2.1, we have shown that key distribution scheme 2.2.1 is secure against *plain active attack*. However, it is not clear whether the scheme is secure against *chosen-message-known-key active attack* or not. In this subsection, we will propose a modified scheme which is provably secure against *chosen-message-known-key active attack*.

Key distribution scheme 2.2.2

(1) Preprocessing stage

Same as 2.2.1.(1).

(2) Key distribution stage

Repeat steps (i) to (v) t times (for $l = 1, 2, \ldots, t$).

(i) User 1 picks a random number $r_1 \in Z_n$ and sends $x_1 = g^{2r_1} \bmod n$ to user 2. *User 1 proves that s/he knows the value r_1 satisfying $x_1 = g^{2r_1} \bmod n$ using a zero-knowledge proof (see Subprotocol 2.2.2). If this zero-knowledge proof fails, user 2 halts.*

(ii) User 2 sends a random binary vector $(e_{1,1}, \ldots, e_{1,k})$ to user 1. User 2 also picks a random number $r_2 \in Z_n$ and sends $x_2 = g^{2r_2} \bmod n$ to user 1. *User 2 proves that s/he knows the value r_2 satisfying $x_2 = g^{2r_2} \bmod n$ using a zero-knowledge proof. If this zero-knowledge proof fails, user 1 halts.*

(iii) User 1 sends to user 2 y_1 such that $y_1 = g^{r_1} \prod_j s_{1,j}^{e_{1,j}} \bmod n$. User 1 also sends a random binary vector $(e_{2,1}, \ldots, e_{2,k})$ to user 2.

(iv) User 2 checks that $x_1 = y_1^2 \prod_j f(I_1, j)^{e_{1,j}} \pmod{n}$. If the check is valid, he generates K_l such that $K_l = x_1^{r_2} \bmod n$. User 2 also sends to user 1 y_2 such that $y_2 = g^{r_2} \prod_j s_{2,j}^{e_{2,j}} \bmod n$.

(v) User 1 checks that $x_2 = y_2^2 \prod_j f(I_2, j)^{e_{2,j}} \pmod{n}$. If the check is valid, he generates K_l such that $K_l = x_2^{r_1} \bmod n$.

After all t procedure cycles are passed, users 1 and 2 calculate the common key K such that $K = K_1 + K_2 + \ldots + K_t \bmod n$.

Subprotocol 2.2.2 (Zero-knowledge proof of proving that the prover has r satisfying $x = g^{2r} \bmod n$)

(0) First, set $G = g^2 \bmod n$.

(1) Prover (P) selects a random number t in $[0, 2n - 1]$, and sends $X = G^t \bmod n$ to verifier (V).

(2) V sends a random bit e in $\{0, 1\}$.

(3) If $e = 0$, P sends $Y = t$. Otherwise, P calculates $u = r + t$. Then, if u is in the interval $[n, 2n - 1]$, then P sends $Y = u$ to V. If u is out of $[n, 2n - 1]$, then P sends $Y = -1$.

(4) V checks the validity of P's message, if Y is not -1. Then, Y is not valid, P halts. If Y is valid or -1, P continues the procedure.

After repeating the above procedure k times, V accepts P's proof if the procedure does not halt and the number of the rounds in which $Y = -1$ is less than $\lceil (2/3)l \rceil$, where the number of the rounds in which $e = 1$ is l, and $|k| = c_1|n|$, $|l| = c_2|n|$ (C_1, c_2: constant).

Next we show that this protocol is the zero-knowledge proof of proving that the prover has r satisfying $x = G^r \bmod n$.

- (Completeness) The probability that valid P selects bad t such that u is not in $[n, 2n - 1]$ is $1/2$. Therefore the probability that P selects bad t more than $\lceil (2/3)l \rceil$ times through l rounds in which $e = 1$ is l is less than $1/|n|^c$ for any constant c for sufficient large n. Therefore, valid P is accepted with overwhelming probability.

- (Soundness) If invalid P' has an algorithm A that passes the protocol, then P' can construct an algorithm M of computing r in a manner similar to Feige-Fiat-Shamir's algorithm [FFS].

- (Zero-knowledgeness) When M guesses $e = 0$, M generates $(G^Y \bmod n, 0, Y)$, where Y is in $[0, 2n - 1]$. When M guesses $e = 1$, M fips a coin. If it is 0, M generates $(X = G^t \bmod n, e = 1, Y = -1)$. Otherwise, M generates $(G^Y / x \bmod n, 1, Y)$, where Y is in $[n, 2n - 1]$. Then, M uses V as a black-box by checking which value of e is selected after sending X (or checking whether the guess is correct or not), and repeats the procedure.

Theorem 2 If the factoring assumption is true, then there is no probabilistic polynomial-time *chosen-message-known-key active attack* (Definition 2) which is successful with nonnegligible probability against key distribution scheme 2.2.2.

Proof sketch: Let A be a chosen-message-known-key active adversary. Suppose that A is allowed to play the role of user 2 and that A sends $\tilde{x}_2$ instead of x_2. From the soundness condition of the zero-knowledge proof of proving that A knows the value r_2 satisfying $\tilde{x}_2 = g^{2r_2} \bmod n$, A can construct a probabilistic polynomial time algorithm of calculating $K = \tilde{x}_2^{r_1} \bmod n$ by calculating $x_1^{r_2} \bmod n$ with overwhelming probability. On the other hand, we can construct a probabilistic polynomial time algorithm of simulating the total interactive protocol between User 1 (prover) and A (verifier) through (i) to (iv) (This simulation is statistically indistinguishable from the true history of the interaction).

Therefore, in key distribution scheme 2.2.2, A can calculate any knowledge that is given through a chosen-message-known-key attack with overwhelming probability. In other words, in key distribution scheme 2.2.2, any chosen-message-known-key active adversary has the same power as a plain active adversary with overwhelming probability. Thus, because key distribution scheme 2.2.2 is secure against plain active attacks (Theorem 1), this protocol is also secure against chosen-message-known-key active attacks.   **QED**

2.2.3 Construction using the parallel version of the extended Fiat-Shamir scheme 1

Key distribution scheme 2.2.3

(1) Preprocessing stage

The unique trusted center in the system generates the extended Fiat-Shamir scheme secret keys s_1 and s_2 for user 1 and user 2, respectively. Here, the center's secret key is p, q (primes), center's public key is $(n = pq, L, g)$, and $1/s_i = f(I_i)^{1/L} \bmod n$ $(i = 1, 2)$, where $p - 1 = Lp'$, $q - 1 = Lq'$, $(p', q'$: prime), the order of g is $p'q'$, and I_i is an identity of user i.

(2) Key distribution stage

(i) User 1 picks a random number $r_1 \in Z_n$ and sends $x_1 = g^{Lr_1} \bmod n$ to user 2.

(ii) User 2 sends a random number $e_1 \in Z_L^*$ to user 1. User 2 also picks a random number $r_2 \in Z_n$ and sends $x_2 = g^{Lr_2} \bmod n$ to user 1.

(iii) User 1 sends to user 2 y_1 such that $y_1 = g^{r_1} \cdot s_1^{e_1} \bmod n$. User 1 also sends a random number $e_2 \in Z_L^*$ to user 2.

(iv) User 2 checks that $x_1 = y_1^L \cdot f(I_1)^{e_1}$ $(\bmod \; n)$. If the check is valid, he generates the common key K such that $K = x_1^{r_2} \bmod n$. User 2 also sends to user 1 y_2 such that $y_2 = g^{r_2} \cdot s_2^{e_2} \bmod n$.

(v) User 1 checks that $x_2 = y_2^L \cdot f(I_2)^{e_2}$ $(\bmod \; n)$. If the check is valid, he generates the common key K such that $K = x_2^{r_1} \bmod n$.

Remark: The security of the parallel version of the extended Fiat-Shamir scheme where $\gcd(L, p-1) \neq 1$ can be guaranteed by the *no-transferable information* technique [OhO]. Therefore, the security of this identity-based key distribution schemes can be proven in a manner similar to that used in theorem 1. Here, however, note that it is not easy to find $f(I_i)$ that is the L-th residue $\bmod n$. (If we do not use the identity-based system, we do not have this problem, because we can generate s_i randomly and publish $1/s_i^L \bmod n$ instead of $f(I_i)$.) On the other hand, if $\gcd(L, p-1) = \gcd(L, q-1) = 1$, we can always calculate $1/s_i = f(I_i)^{1/L} \bmod n$. However, in this case, the security cannot be guaranteed by the no-transferable information technique [OhO]. A compromise selection for the value L may be $\gcd(L, p-1) = \gcd(L, q-1) = 2$. Although, in this case, the security level for the scheme is 2 (ie., not so secure)[OhO], the security may be proven by the "witness indistinguishable" technique [FeS].

The modification of scheme 2.2.3 which is secure against chosen-message-known-key active attacks can be constructed in a manner similar to scheme 2.2.2. Here, parallel version of subprotocol 2.2.2 can be used.

2.2.4 Construction using the non-interactive version of the extended Fiat-Shamir scheme 1

Key distribution scheme 2.2.4

(1) Preprocessing stage

This stage is the same as the preprocessing stage of 2.2.3.

(2) Key distribution stage

(i) User 1 picks a random number $r_1 \in Z_n$ and generates $x_1 = g^{Lr_1} \bmod n$, $e_1 = h(x_1) \in Z_L$, $y_1 = g^{r_1} \cdot s_1^{e_1} \bmod n$. User 1 sends e_1, y_1 to user 2.

(ii) User 2 picks a random number $r_2 \in Z_n$ and generates $x_2 = g^{Lr_2} \bmod n$, $e_2 = h(x_2) \in Z_L$, $y_2 = g^{r_2} \cdot s_2^{e_2} \bmod n$. User 2 sends e_2, y_2 to user 1.
User 2 calculates $x_1 = y_1^L \cdot f(I_1)^{e_1} \pmod{n}$, and checks that $e_1 = h(x_1)$. If the check is valid, he generates the common key K such that $K = x_1^{r_2} \bmod n$.

(iii) User 1 calculates $x_2 = y_2^L \cdot f(I_2)^{e_2} \pmod{n}$, and checks that $e_2 = h(x_2)$. If the check is valid, he generates the common key K such that $K = x_2^{r_1} \bmod n$.

Remark: If we assume the non-interactive version of the extended Fiat-Shamir scheme 1 is secure, then we can prove the security of this key distribution scheme. The modification of scheme 2.2.4 which may be secure against chosen-message-known-key active attacks can be constructed in a manner similar to scheme 2.2.2. Here, non-interactive version of subprotocol 2.2.2 can be used.

2.2.5 Construction using the non-interactive version of the extended Fiat-Shamir scheme 2

Key distribution scheme 2.2.5

(1) Preprocessing stage

This stage is the same as the preprocessing stage of 2.2.3.

(2) Key distribution stage

(i) User 1 picks a random number $r_1 \in Z_n$ and generates $x_1 = g^{Lr_1} \bmod n$, $e_1 = h(x_1) \in Z_L^*$, $y_1 = g^{r_1 e_1} \cdot s_1 \bmod n$. User 1 sends x_1, y_1 to user 2.

(ii) User 2 picks a random number $r_2 \in Z_n$ and generates $x_2 = g^{Lr_2} \bmod n$, $e_2 = h(x_2) \in Z_L$, $y_2 = g^{r_2 e_2} \cdot s_2 \bmod n$. User 2 sends x_2, y_2 to user 1.
User 2 calculates $e_1 = h(x_1)$, and checks that $x_1^{e_1} = y_1^L \cdot f(I_1) \pmod{n}$. If the check is valid, he generates the common key K such that $K = x_1^{r_2} \bmod n$.

(iii) User 1 calculates $e_2 = h(x_2)$, and checks that $x_2^{e_2} = y_2^L \cdot f(I_2) \pmod{n}$. If the check is valid, he generates the common key K such that $K = x_2^{r_1} \bmod n$.

Remarks:

1. As in the remark given in 2.2.4, if we assume the non-interactive version of the extended Fiat-Shamir scheme 2 is secure, then we can prove the security of

this key distribution scheme. We can also construct the modification of scheme 2.2.4 which may be secure against chosen-message-known-key active attacks can be constructed in a manner similar to scheme 2.2.2.

2. Note that this scheme correponds to the second key distribution scheme proposed by Okamoto [Ok] (although, in his original scheme, e_i was a constant value, he later changed e_i into $h(x_i)$ thus duplicating the above-mentioned scheme). In practice, the scheme given in 2.2.4 is superior to that of 2.2.5 (the Okamoto scheme), because the transmission amount in 2.2.4 is almost half of that required in 2.2.5. That is, in 2.2.4, each user sends e_i and y_i, while in 2.2.5 each user sends x_i and y_i. The sizes of x_i and y_i are almost the size of n, while e_i is much shorter than n. For example, when the size of n is 512 bits and the size of e_i is 20 bits, in 2.2.4 each user sends 532 bits, while in 2.2.5 each user must send 1024 bits.

3. Non-transitive digital signature scheme

3.1 Definition

In this section, we propose new *non-transitive digital signature* schemes through the utilization of the randomness of zero-knowledge proofs. This non-transitive digital signature scheme has the following properties: (we assume that user A sends a message M to user B.)

(1) Only user A can prove the validity of A's message M to any user B (validity).

(2) User B cannot prove the origin of the messgage M to another user C (non-transitivity).

We will compare this non-transitive digital signature with a regular digital signature scheme, a message authentication scheme [I]. We will also show the difference from a *undeniable* digital signature scheme [CA, C] after explaining the application of a non-transitive digital signature.

In a digital signature scheme,

(1) (Same as non-transitive digital signature scheme)(validity)

(2) User B can also prove the origin of the message M to any user C (transitivity).

On the other hand, in a message authentication scheme,

(1) User B can prove the validity of message M to C while pretending to be A. (non-validity).

(2) (Same as non-transitive digital signature scheme) (this is from (1)) (non- transitivity).

Note that message authentication is aimed to prevent message interception and alternation between A and B, not to protect against user B.

We can consider the same security criterion for a non-transitive digital signature as that for a regular digital signature. Therefore, the most hopeful security criterion for a non-transitive digital signature is security against existential forgery under adaptive chosen message attack [GMRi, NY, Ro].

What are some of the applications of this non-transitive digital signature scheme? Many very sensitive negotiations, both political and business, are held every day.

The scheme allows the negotiations to proceed while protecting the privacy (irresponsibility) of all parties. Consider a government officer who is privy to information of public interest but who will unduly suffer if he is identified as the source of the information. The officer can pass the information on to the press unattributively through this non-transitive digital signature. The press can have confidence in the accuracy of the information and its source (from the validity) but the source retains his anonymity (from the non-transitivity). In addition, when we conduct sensitive negotiations for a contract, this kind of privacy (irresponsibility) is often required before concluding the contract. We will also show another application of the non-transitive digital signature in Section 5.

Then, can we use an undeniable digital signature scheme [C, CA] as a non-transitive digital signature? Although it seems that an undeniable digital signature scheme has the property of the non-transitive digital signature scheme, here, we will show that the answer to this question is negative.

In an undeniable signature scheme, the signer issues a signature z (e.g., $z = m^x \bmod n$, where x is his secret key), then he proves the validity of z interactively. Therefore, in this scheme, z can be used as evidence in some situations. The property that z is left with the related message m is an advantage of this scheme in some applications; for example, when a receiver of the undeniable signature wants to be able to confirm the signer's responsibility.

However, suppose that the undeniable digital signature [C, CA] is used for the above-mentioned example, where an officer sends confidential information to the press. After the information is published, the officer may be suspected as the source. In this case, the officer leaves z as well as m. If the goverment obtains z along with m, the goverment can force the officer to reveal his secret key x in order to clear his suspicion. Of course, the officer can refuse to reveal his secret key, but his refusal itself will become an implicit evidence that he is the source. Instead, if the officer uses a disavowal protocol [C], he can prevent his suspicion from falling on him without revealing his secret key. Therefore, the officer has no other reason for refusing a disavowal protocol except that he is the source. Thus, in the undeniable signature scheme, anyone with (m, z) can check whether a suspected signer is the true signer or not. That is, the undeniable signature is not non-transitive.

On the other hand, we can construct a non-transitive digital signature scheme by using the "symmetric public-key encryption" [GHY]. That is, a non-transitive signature signer sends a message encrypted by a symmetric public-key encryption. For the receiver to check the validity of the message, the signer must embed redundant information in the message such as an error correcting code. However, this scheme is an indirect solution of constructing a non-transitive signature scheme, because the security essentially depends on the property of the redundant information. (This scheme corresponds to a message authentication scheme based on the combination of a conventional encryption and redundant information.)

Here we will propose several implementations of the non-transitive digital signature scheme, utilizing the randomness of zero-knowledge proofs. First, we will show a general result about the non-transitive digital signature scheme. That is, we will show that a non-transitive digital signature scheme secure against existential forgery under adaptive chosen message attack can be constructed if and only if a one-way function exists. Next, we will show some practical constructions of non-transitive signature schemes based on the zero-knowledge identification schemes shown in Subsection 2.1, although they have not been proven to be secure. For the same reason as described in Subsection 2.2, we will just show 2 typical cases here; (1)(a) and (2)(b). Here, note that the construction using the non-interactive version of these protocols ((1)-(4)(c)) cannot constitute a non-transitive digital signature; in fact, they are regular (transitive) digital signatures. We will discuss these digital signature protocols in Section 4.

3.2 Construction using one-way function

In this subsection, we show a general result about the existence of a non-transitive digital signature scheme. The key techniques for this result are zero-knowledge proof and bit-commitment.

Theorem 3 A non-transitive digital signature scheme that is secure against existential forgery under adaptive chosen message attack can be constructed if and only if a one-way function exists.

Proof sketch:

The proof of the "only if" part is almost trivial, and can be proven in the same way as shown in [Ro]. Then, we will prove the "if" part. We assume that a one-way function exists. Let signer's secret key be s and its public key be $p = f(s)$, f is a one-way function. Then, we can construct a zero-knowledge proof of proving that the signer has s satisfying $p = f(s)$ because we assume the existence of a one-way function [BCC, Blu, GMW, FFS, ILL, H, N]. In this zero-knowledge proof, we use Naor's construction of bit-commitment using a one-way function (pseudo-random generator) [N]. Here, we use $g(m_i, W)$ instead of S, where S is a random value used for the bit-commitment, g is the bit-commitment function, and W is a random value. If $g(m_i, W)$ is indistinguishable from S, we can use $g(m_i, W)$ instead of S without losing the property of the bit-commitment. Next, we will show the algorithm of the bit-commitment part in more detail. Let $g : b_{<1>}, S_{<n>}, R_{<3n>} \rightarrow d_{<3n>}$ be Naor's bit-commitment function (Section 3 in [N]), where the verifier (Bob) sends $3n$ random bits, $R_{<3n>}$, and the commiter (Alice) generates n random bits, $S_{<n>}$, and sends the bit-commit $d_{<3n>} = g(b_{<1>}, S_{<n>}, R_{<3n>})$ of a bit $b_{<1>}$ to the verifier, and at the reveal stage the commiter opens $S_{<n>}$ to the verifier. Here, the suffix of each parameter means the bit size of the parameter, and a parameter written by a capital letter is true random bits. n is the size of the key.

Let $m_{<1>}^{(l)}$ be the l-th bit of a message to be signed. Hereafter, we simply write $m_{<1>}^{(l)}$ by $m_{<1>}$. In our signature scheme, bit commitment is executed as follows: First, the verifier sends $9n$ random bits $R_{<9n>}$ and $3n$ random bits $T_{<3n>}$ to the signer. The signer generates n random bits, $U_{<n>}$. Then the signer calculates $v_{<3n>} = g((m_{<1>}, U_{<n>}, T_{<3n>})$, and $d_{<9n>} = g(b_{<1>}, v_{<3n>}, R_{<9n>})$. The signer sends $d_{<9n>}$ regarding a bit $b_{<1>}$ and $m_{<1>}$ to the verifier. At the reveal stage, the signer opens $U_{<n>}$ to the verifier.

In the zero-knowledge proof [BCC, Blu, GMW, FFS], the revealed messages are determined by the verifier's message (coin flips). Therefore, the signer embeds his messages in the bit-comitmment dupulicatedly. That is, first the prover sends committed messages X_1 and X_2. Then, the prover reveals either X_1 or X_2 depending on the verifier's message (0 or 1). Here, the prover embeds a message to be signed M into both X_1 and X_2.

This bit-commitment clearly satisfies the criterion of the bit-commitment, because if the verifier can distinguish between $g(b_{<1>}, v_{<3n>}, R_{<9n>})$ and $g(b_{<1>}, V_{<3n>}, R_{<9n>})$ ($V_{<3n>}$ is true random bits) with nonnegligible probability, he must be able to distinguish between true random bits and Naor's bit-commitment sequence. Moreover, from the property of the bit-commitment, message bit $m_{<1>}$ cannot be changed by anyone after sending $d_{<9n>}$.

By this protocol, the signer can sign a message whose size is almost half of the size of committed bits that are necessary for the zero-knowledge proof of proving that the signer has s satisfying $p = f(s)$. Therefore, when the key size is n, $O(n^c)$ bits can be signed as a message, where c is a constant.

From the property of zero-knowldge proof, the above scheme clearly satisfies the non-transitivity, because anyone can make the history of the non-transtive signature (or the interaction between the signer and the verifier). The above scheme also satisfies the security condition from the zero-knowledge property and Naor's bit-commitment's property. **QED**

Remark: More efficient bit-commitment scheme (Section 4 in [N]) can be also used instead of the bit-commitment scheme used in the proof. There are various alternative ways to embed a message to be signed in the bit-commitment scheme.

3.3 Construction using the sequential version of the Fiat-Shamir scheme

Non-transitive digital signature scheme 3.3

(1) Preprocessing stage

The unique trusted center in the system generates Fiat-Shamir scheme's secret key s_j ($j = 1, \ldots, k$) for user A. Here, the center's secret key is p, q (primes), center's public key is $n = pq$, $1/s_j = (f(I_A, j))^{1/2} \bmod n$ ($j = 1, 2, \ldots, k$), and I_A is the identity of user A.

(2) Authentication stage

(0) User A sends A's identity I_A and A's message M to user B.

Repeat steps (i) to (iv) t times.

(i) User A picks a random number $r \in Z_n$ and sends $x = r^{2g(M)} \bmod n$ to user B. Here, function g is a one-way hash function such that $g(m)$ distributes uniformly over Z_n when $m \in dom(h)$ is selected randomly.

(ii) User B sends a random binary vector $(e_1 \ldots, e_k)$ to user A.

(iii) User A sends to user B y such that $y = r \prod_j s_j^{e_j} \bmod n$.

(iv) User B checks that $x = y^{2g(M)} \prod_j f(I_A, j)^{e_j g(M)} \pmod{n}$. If the check is not valid, user B quits the procedure.

After all t rounds procedures are passed, user B recognizes that M is A's valid message.

Remarks:

1. In the above protocol, we showed the *identity-based* version of non-transitive digital signature scheme, because it is well compatible with the original Fiat-Shamir schemes. If each user generates p, q in place of the trusted center, and publishes n, I_A, then the scheme becomes a regular (not identity-based) non-transitive digital signature.

2. In this protocol, $r^{g(M)}$ mod n is used in place of a true random number $R \in Z_n$ in the Fiat-Shamir scheme, where $r \in Z_n$ is a true random number. If $\gcd(g(M), p-1) = \gcd(g(M), q-1) = 1$, $r^{g(M)}$ mod n and R are perfectly indistinguishable. If $g(M)$ distributes uniformly, $g(M)$ satisfies the above condition with overwhelming probability.

3.4 Construction using the parallel version of the extended Fiat-Shamir scheme

Non-transitive digital signature scheme 3.4

(1) Preprocessing stage

The unique trusted center in the system generates a secret key s of the extended Fiat-Shamir scheme for user A. Here, the center's secret key is p, q (primes), center's public key is $n = pq$ and L ($\gcd(L, p-1) = \gcd(L, q-1) = 1$), $1/s = (f(I_A))^{1/L}$ mod n, and I_A is the identity of user A.

(2) Authentication stage

(0) User A sends I_A and message M to user B.

(i) User A picks a random number $r \in Z_n$ and sends $x = r^{Lg(M)}$ mod n to user B. Here, function g is a one-way hash function such that $g(m)$ distributes uniformly over Z_n when $m \in dom(h)$ is selected randomly.

(ii) User B sends a random number $e \in Z_L$ to user A.

(iii) User A sends to user B y such that $y = rs^e$ mod n.

(iv) User B checks that $x = y^{Lg(M)} f(I_A)^{eg(M)}$ (mod n). If the check is valid, user B recognizes that M is A's valid message.

Remark: Same as the remarks in Subsection 3.3.

4. New construction of digital signature schemes using the (extended) Fiat-Shamir scheme

In this section, we will show a construction of the digital signature based on the Fiat-Shamir identification scheme, which is different from the Fiat-Shamir digital signature scheme. This construction uses the technique similar to that used in Section 3. Although we can construct 4 digital signature schemes using non-interactive versions of identification schemes, (1)-(4)(c), shown in Subsection 2.1, we will just one typical case here; (2)(c).

Digital signature scheme 4.

(1) Preprocessing stage

Same as the preprocessing stage in Subsection 3.4.

(2) Authentication stage

(i) User A picks a random number $r \in Z_n$ and calculates $x = r^{Lg(M)} \bmod n$, $e = h(x) \in Z_L$, $y = rs^e \bmod n$. Here, M is a message, and (e, y) is A's signature of M. Function g is a one-way hash function such that $g(M)$ distributes uniformly over Z_n when $M \in dom(h)$ is selected randomly. User A sends I_A, M, and (e, y) to user B.

(ii) User B calculates $x = y^{Lg(M)} f(I_A)^{eg(M)} \pmod{n}$, and checks that $e = h(x)$. If the check is valid, user B recognizes that M is A's valid message.

5. New general method for constructing identity-based schemes

Identity-based cryptographic schemes were explicitly proposed by Shamir [Sha] in 1984 as variants of public-key cryptographic schemes (Okamoto and Shiraishi [OS] also proposed the same idea independently). In the new scheme, we use each user's identity in place of his/her public-key, therefore, we need no public-key file, instead we need a trusted center that generates and distributes each user's secret-key which is based on his/her identity. Preceding Shamir's proposal, Kohnfelder implicitly proposed the identity-based scheme in 1979 [Koh], but his construction is quite different from Shamir's. Thus, there are two types of methods for constructing identity-based cryptographic schemes; one is the *general method* [Koh], and the other is the *individual method* [Sha, OS]. In a general method, we can create an identity-based scheme from any traditional public-key cryptographic scheme, however, the overhead of key length and message length is relatively larger than a well-implemented individual method. On the other hand, in the individual method, each identity-based scheme must be constructed individually. Although only one general method [Koh] has been proposed, many individual identity-based schemes have been proposed such as key distribution schemes [Blo, Ok, MI, KO, TI], and identification and signature schemes [Sha, OS, FiS, GQ, OhO]. (The key distribution schemes shown in Section 2 are also individual identity-based schemes.)

In this section, we will show a new general method that is an application of the identity-based non-transitive digital signature scheme, although this method is similar to that of [Koh]. That is, in our scheme, we use the identity-based non-transitive digital signature scheme shown in Section 3 in place of the digital signature scheme in [Koh].

First, we will introduce the previous general method [Koh]. Trusted center T publishes its public key, P_T, of a public-key digital signature scheme, and holds the corresponding secret key S_T in secret. User U creates his public key E_U and secret key D_U of an arbitrary public-key cryptographic scheme. User U sends his public key E_U to center T with his identity I_U. After checking the validity of user U, T issues the digital signature C_T of U's public key E_U along with U's identity I_U as T's certificate to U's public key and identity. After that, U always uses T's certificate C_T with his public-key E_U and identity I_U. Because anyone can check the validity of T's certificate with T's public key P_T, in this system, without any public key file, anyone can match U's identity I_U with his public key E_U.

Our method, as mentioned above, uses the non-transitive digital signature scheme. The major difference between our method and that of [Koh] is that the certificate is not issued by the trusted center (T) but by each user (U). Our method proceeds as follows. First, the user' secret key S_U is generated as described in 3.3 or 3.4 in a preprocessing operation. The user can select any public key cryptographic scheme that best suits his purpose and create his own private and public keys, D_U and E_U. He can (interactively) generate certificates of his public key E_U at any time using the identity-based non-transitive digital signature scheme described in 3.3 or 3.4. The receiver can cofirm the combination of user's identity I_U and public key E_U by verifying the certificate with the trusted center's public key P_T.

Our method is practically superior to the previous one [Koh], because in our method the user can change or create his own private and public keys, D_U and E_U, without access to the trusted center T, while in the previous method [Koh] the user must always ask the trusted center to issue truted center's certificate C_T when the user change or create his own private and public keys. This property of our method stems from the *identity-based* property of the schemes in 3.3 and 3.4.

Another merit of our method is that the user can often change his own keys, D_U, E_U, and dispose the used keys, in order to prevent abuse of these used keys, while in [Koh] the used keys may be abused by an adversary since the used keys with the certificate can be used by anyone and at any time. This property of our method stems from the *non-transitive* property of the schemes in 3.3 and 3.4.

6. Concluding remarks

In this paper, we have presented a new methodology that utilizes the randomness of the zero-knowledge proof, and have proposed two types of applications: key distribution, and digital signature. It remains a further study to prove the security of the practical schemes shown in Subsections 2.2.3, 2.2.4, 2.2.5, 3.3, 3.4, and 4.

Acknowledgements

We would like to thank David Chaum, Shinichi Kawamura, Kazue Tanaka and anonymous referees for their valuable comments.

References

[Be] T.Beth, "Efficient Zero-Knowledge Identification Scheme For Smart Cards," Eurocrypt'88 (1988)

[BCC] G.Brassard, D.Chaum, and C.Crépeau, "Minimum Disclosure Proofs of Knowledge," Journal of Computer and System Sciences, Vol.37, pp.156-189 (1988)

[Blo] R.Blom, "Non-Public Key Distribution," Crypto'82, pp.231-236 (1982)

[Blu] M.Blum, "How to Prove a Theorem So No One Else Can Claim It," ISO/ TC97/ SC20/ WG2 N73 (1986)

[BFM] M.Blum, P.Feldman and S.Micali, "Non-Interactive Zero-Knowledge and Its Applications," STOC, pp.103-112 (1988)

[C] D.Chaum "Zero-Knowledge Undeniable Signatures," Eurocrypt'90 (1990)

[CA] D.Chaum, and H. van Antwerpen, "Undeniable Signatures," Crypto'89

(1989)

[D] Y.Desmedt, "Subliminal-Free Authentication and Signature," Eurocrypt'88, pp.23-34 (1988)

[DGB] Y.Desmedt, C.Goutier and S.Bengio, "Special Uses and Abuses of the Fiat-Shamir Passport Protocol," Crypto'87 (1987)

[DH] W.Diffie, and M.Hellman, "New Directions in Cryptography," IEEE Transactions on Information Theory, IT-22, 644-654 (1976)

[DMP] A.DeSantis, S.Micali and G.Persiano, "Non-Interactive Zero-Knowledge Proof Systems with Auxiliary Language," Crypto'88 (1988)

[FeS] U.Feige and A.Shamir, "Witness Indistinguishable and Witness Hiding Protocols," STOC, pp.416-426 (1990)

[FFS] U.Feige, A.Fiat and A.Shamir, "Zero Knowledge Proofs of Identity," STOC, pp.210-217 (1987)

[FiS] A.Fiat and A.Shamir, "How to Prove Yourself," Crypto'86 (1986)

[GHY] Z.Galil, S.Harber, and M.Yung "Symmetric Public-Key Encryption," Crypto'85 (1985)

[GK] O.Goldreich, and H.Krawczyk "On the Composition of Zero-Knowledge Proof Systems," Technical Report #570 of Technion (1989)

[GL] O.Goldreich, and A.L.Levin, "A Hard-Core Predicate for All One-Way Functions," STOC'89, pp.25-32 (1989)

[GMRa] S.Goldwasser, S.Micali, and C.Rackoff, "The Knowledge Complexity of Interactive Proofs," SIAM J. Comput., 18, 1, pp.186-208 (1989). Previous version, Proc. STOC, pp291-304 (1985)

[GMRi] S.Goldwasser, S.Micali, and C.Rivest, "A Secure Digital Signature Scheme," SIAM J. Comput., 17, 2, pp.281-308 (1988).

[GMW] O.Goldreich, S.Micali, and A.Wigderson, "Proofs that Yield Nothing But their Validity and a Methodology of Cryptographic Protocol Design," FOCS, pp.174-187 (1986)

[GP] M. Girault, and J.C. Pailles, "An Identity-Based Scheme Providing Zero-Knowledge Authentication and Authenticated Key-Exchange," ISO IEC/ JTC 1/ SC 27/ WG20.2 N200 (1990)

[GQ] L.C.Guillou, and J.J.Quisquater, "A Practical Zero-Knowledge Protocol Fitted to Security Microprocessors Minimizing Both Transmission and Memory," Eurocrypto'88 (1988)

[H] J.Håstad, "Pseudo-Random Generators under Uniform Assumptions," STOC, pp.395-404 (1990)

[I] ISO "Banking- Requirements for Message Authentication (Wholesale)" ISO/ TC68/ SC2/ WG2 N191 (1987 November)

[ILL] R.Impagliazzo, L.Levin, M.Luby "Pseudo-Random Number Generation from One-Way Functions," STOC, pp.12-24 (1989)

[Koh] L.Kohnfelder, "Towards a Practical Public-Key Cryptosystems," B.S.Thesis, MIT (1979)

[KO] K.Koyama, and K.Ohta, "Identity-based Conference Key Distribution Systems," Crypto'87 (1987)

[M] K.S.McCurley, "A Key Distribution System Equivalent Factoring," J. of Cryptology, 1, 2, pp.95-106 (1988)

[MI] T.Matsumoto and H.Imai, "On the Key Distribution Problem," Crypto'87, (1987)

[N] M.Naor, "Bit Commitment Using Pseudo-Randomness," Crypto'89, (1989)

[NY] M.Naor, and M.Yung, "Universal One-Way Hash Functions and Their Cryptographic Applications," STOC, pp.33-43 (1989)

[Oh1] K.Ohta, "Efficient Identification and Signature Scheme," Electronics Letters, 24, 2, pp.115-116 (1988)

[Oh2] K.Ohta, "Encryption and Authentication Techniques for Information Security," Dr.Sci Thesis, Waseda University (1990)

[OhO] K.Ohta, and T.Okamoto, "A Modification of the Fiat-Shamir Scheme," Crypto'88 (1988)

[Ok] E.Okamoto, "Proposal for Identity-based key distribution systems," Electronics Letters, 22, 24, pp.1283-1284 (1986)

[OkO1] T.Okamoto, and K.Ohta "Disposable Zero-Knowledge Authentications and Their Applications to Untraceable Electronic Cash," Crypto'89 (1989)

[OkO2] T.Okamoto, and K.Ohta "Divertible Zero-Knowledge Interactive Proofs and Commutative Random Self-Reducible," Eurocrypt'89 (1989)

[OS] T.Okamoto, and A.Shiraishi "A Single Public-Key Authentication Scheme for Multiple Users," Systems and Computers in Japan, 18, 10, pp.14-24 (1987) Previous version, Technical Report of IECE Japan, IN83-92 (1984)

[Ra] M.Rabin "Digitalized Signatures and Public-Key Cryptosystems," MIT/ LCS/ TR-212, MIT Technical Report (1979)

[Ro] J.Rompel, "One-Way Functions are Sufficient for Secure Signatures," STOC, pp.387-394 (1990)

[Sha] A.Shamir, "Identity-based Cryptosystems and Signature Schemes," Crypto'84 (1984)

[Shm] Z.Shmuely, "Composite Diffie-Hellman Public-Key Generating Systems Are Hard to Break," TR #356, Computer Science Dept. Technion, IIT (1985)

[TI] S.Tsujii, and T.Itoh, "An ID-Based Crypto-system Based on the Discrete Logarithm Problem," IEEE J. Selected Area in Communications, 7, 4 (1989)

[TW] M.Tompa and H.Woll, "Random Self-Reducibility and Zero Knowledge Interactive Proofs of Possession of Information," Proc. FOCS, pp472-482 (1987)

[Y] Y.Yacobi, "A Key Distribution "Paradox"," These Proceedings (1990)

[YS] Y.Yacobi, and Z.Shmuely, "On Key Distribution Systems," Crypto'89 (1989)

Fast Software Encryption Functions

Ralph C. Merkle

Xerox PARC

3333 Coyote Hill Road

Palo Alto, CA 94304

Abstract

Encryption hardware is not available on most computer systems in use today. Despite this fact, there is no well accepted encryption function designed for software implementation -- instead, hardware designs are emulated in software and the resulting performance loss is tolerated. The obvious solution is to design an encryption function for implementation in software. Such an encryption function is presented here -- on a SUN 4/260 it can encrypt at 4 to 8 megabits per second. The combination of modern processor speeds and a faster algorithm make software encryption feasible in applications which previously would have required hardware. This will effectively reduce the cost and increase the availability of cryptographic protection.

Introduction

The computer community has long recognized the need for security and the essential role that encryption must play. Widely adopted, standard encryption functions will make a great contribution to security in the distributed heavily networked environment which is already upon us. IBM recognized the coming need in the 1970's and proposed the Data Encryption

Standard, or DES [19]. Although controversy about its key size has persisted, DES has successfully resisted all public attack and been widely accepted. After some debate its use as a U.S. Federal Standard was reaffirmed until 1992 [14]. However, given the inherent limitations of the 56 bit key size used in DES [16] it seems clear that the standard will at least have to be revised at some point. A recent review of DES by the Office of Technology Assessment [15] quotes Dennis Branstad as saying the "useful lifetime" of DES would be until the late 1990's.

Despite the widespread acceptance of DES the most popular software commercial encryption packages (for, e.g., the IBM PC or the Apple Macintosh) typically offer both DES encryption and their own home-grown encryption function. The reason is simple -- DES is often 50 to 100 times slower than the home-grown alternative. While some of this performance differential is due to a sub-optimal DES implementation or a faster but less secure home-grown encryption function, it seems that DES is inherently 5 to 10 times slower than an equivalent, equally secure encryption function designed for software implementation. This is not to fault DES. One of the design objectives in DES was quite explicitly a fast hardware implementation; when hardware is available, DES is an excellent choice. However, a number of design decisions were made in DES reflecting the hardware orientation which result in slow software performance -- making the current extensive use of DES in software both unplanned-for and rather anomalous.

Having offered a rationale for an encryption function designed for software implementation, we now turn to the design principles, followed by the actual design.

Basic Principles

The basic design principles in DES seem sound. The fact that DES has not been publicly broken speaks in their favor. However, upon examining specific design decisions in DES, we find that several should be revised -- either in light of the software orientation of the new encryption function, or because of the decreased cost of hardware since the early '70's. Examining the basic design decisions one by one, and in no particular order, we can decide what reasonably should be changed.

The selection of a 56 bit key size is too small, a problem which can be easily remedied. This subject has already been debated extensively, and while 56 bits seems to offer just sufficient protection for many commercial applications, the negligible cost of increasing the key size virtually dictates that it be done.

The extensive use of permutations is expensive in software, and should be eliminated -- provided that a satisfactory alternative can be found. While permutations are cheap in hardware and provide an effective way to spread information (also called "diffusion" [21]) they are not the best choice for software. In the faster implementations of DES, the permutations are implemented by table look-ups on several bits at once. That is, the 48-to-32 bit permutation P is implemented by looking up several bits at once in a table -- where each individual table entry is 32 bits wide and the table has been pre-computed to contain the permutation of the bits looked up. Using a table-lookup in a software encryption function seems a good idea and can effectively provide the desired "diffusion" -- however there seems no reason to limit such a table to being a permutation. Having once paid the cost of looking up an entry in a table, it seems preferable that the entry should contain as much information as possible rather than being arbitrarily restricted to a small range of possibilities.

Each individual S-box in DES provides only 64 entries of 4 bits each, or 32 bytes per S-box. Memory sizes have greatly increased since the mid 1970's when DES was designed, and larger S-boxes seem appropriate. More subtly, DES uses 8 S-boxes and looks up 8 different values in them simultaneously. While this is appropriate for hardware (where the 8 lookups can occur in parallel) it seems an unreasonable restriction for software. In software, each table lookup must follow the preceding lookups anyway -- for that is the nature of sequential program execution. It seems more valuable cryptographically to make each lookup depend upon the preceding lookup. This means that the cascade of unpredictable changes that are so central to DES-type encryption functions can achieve greater depth with fewer lookups. Looked at another way, DES has a maximum circuit depth of 16 S-boxes, even though it has a total of 128 S-box lookups. If those same 128 S-box operations were done sequentially, with the output of each lookup operation altering the input to the next lookup, then the maximum circuit depth would be 128 S-boxes -- eight times as many and almost certainly providing greater cryptographic strength. This change would have very little impact on the running time of a software implementation on a typical sequential processor. We conclude that a larger S-box size and sequential (rather than parallel) S-box usage should be adopted.

The initial and final permutations in DES are widely viewed as cryptographically pointless -- or at least, not very important. They are therefore discarded.

The key schedule in DES has received mild criticism for not being sufficiently complicated[9]. In practice, all of the faster DES software implementations pre-compute the key schedule. This pre-computation seems a good idea when large volumes of data are being encrypted -- the pre-computation allows a more leisurely and careful arrangement of the encryption tables and means the actual encryption function can more rapidly scramble the data with less effort. A more complex key pre-computation therefore seems desirable.

Finally, the design criteria used for the DES S-boxes were kept secret. Even though there is no particular reason to believe that they conceal a trap door, it would seem better if the criteria for S-box selection were made explicit, and some sort of assurances provided that the S-boxes were actually chosen randomly in accordance with the published criteria. This would both quiet the concerns about trap doors, and also allow a fuller and more explicit consideration of the S-box selection criteria.

With this overview of design principles we can now proceed to the design.

Khufu, Khafre and Snefru

There are actually two encryption functions named Khufu and Khafre, and a one-way hash function named Snefru. All three names were taken from the Pharoahs of ancient Egypt following a suggestion by Dan Greene. To quote the Encyclopedia Britannica "The ideal pyramid was eventually built by Snefru's successor, Khufu, and the first --- the Great Pyramid at Giza --- was the finest and must successful." Khafre was Khufu's son.

The basic hardware model around which they are optimized is a 32-bit register oriented microprocessor. The basic operations are 32-bit load, store, shift, rotate, "xor" and "and".

The two encryption functions are optimized for somewhat different tasks, but use similar design principles. Khufu is designed for fast bulk encryption of large amounts of data. To achieve the fastest possible speed, the tables used in encryption are pre-computed. This pre-computation is moderately expensive, and makes Khufu unsuited for the encryption of small amounts of data. The other encryption function -- Khafre -- does not require any pre-computation. This means Khafre can efficiently encrypt small amounts of data. On the other hand, Khafre is somewhat slower than Khufu for the encryption of large volumes of data because it takes more time to encrypt each block.

The one-way hash function -- Snefru -- is designed to rapidly reduce large blocks of data to a small residue (perhaps 128 or 256 bits). Snefru requires no pre-computation and therefore can be efficiently applied to small arguments. Snefru provides authentication and does not provide secrecy. Snefru is discussed in a separate paper[24]. The C source for Snefru is available by anonymous ftp from arisia.xerox.com (13.1.100.206) in directory /pub/hash

We first discuss the design of Khufu.

Khufu

Khufu is a block cipher operating on 64-bit blocks. Although increasing block size was a very tempting design alternative, the 64-bit block size of DES has not been greatly criti-cized. More important, many systems built around DES assume that the block size is 64 bits. The pain of using a different encryption function is better minimized if the new encryption function can be easily "plugged in" in place of the old -- which can be done if the block size is the same and the key size is larger. The new encryption function essen-tially looks exactly like the old encryption function -- but with some new keys added to the key space. Increasing the block size might have forced changes in more than just a single subroutine -- it might (for example) have forced changes in data formats in a communications systems.

Khufu, like DES, is a multi-round encryption function in which two 32-bit halves (called L and R for Left and Right) are used alternately in the computations. Each half is used as input to a function F, whose output is XORed with the other half -- the two halves are exchanged and the computation repeated until the result appears to be random (no statistically detectable patterns). Khufu uses a different F-function than DES -- and uses multiple different F-functions during the course of encryption. One round of DES uses an F-function defined by 8 table lookups and associated permutations. By contrast, one round of Khufu uses a single table lookup in a larger S-box. In addition, in the first step of encryption (prior to the main loop) the plaintext is XORed with 64 bits of key material, and again in the final step of encryption (following the main loop) the 64-bit block is XORed with another 64 bits of key material to produce the ciphertext.

We will need to refer to the 4 bytes in a 32-bit word, and will adopt the "big-endian" convention. Byte 0 is the leftmost (most significant) byte while byte 3 is the rightmost (least significant) byte. The 8 bytes in a 64-bit block will be numbered 0 through 7, again with byte 0 being the leftmost (most significant) byte while byte 7 is the rightmost (least significant) byte.

The algorithm proceeds as follows: the 64-bit plaintext is first divided into two 32-bit words designated L and R. L is bytes 0 through 3, and R is bytes 4 through 7 of the 64-bit plaintext. L and R are then XORed with two 32-bit words of auxiliary key material. Then the main loop is started, in which byte 3 (the least significant byte) of L is used as the input to a 256-entry S-box. Each S-box entry is 32-bits wide. The selected 32-bit entry is XORed with R. L is then rotated to bring a new byte into position, after which L and R are swapped. The S-box itself is changed to a new S-box after every 8 rounds (we shall sometimes call 8 rounds an "octet"). This means that the number of S-boxes required depends on the number of rounds of encryption being used: one new S-box for every octet. Finally, after the main loop has been completed, we again XOR L and R with two new 32-bit auxiliary key values to produce the ciphertext.

For efficiency reasons, we restrict the number of rounds to be a multiple of 8, i.e., an integral number of octets. If the main encryption loop is always executed a multiple of 8 times, then it can be unrolled 8 times -- which is substantially more efficient than the definitionally correct but inefficient versions given in this paper. For this reason, the variable "enough" given below must be an exact multiple of 8. Various integer calculations will not work correctly for values of "enough" that are not multiples of 8. Encryption of a single 64-bit plaintext by Khufu can be viewed algorithmically as follows:

L, R: int32;

enough: integer; -- the security parameter, default of 16 seems appropriate.
                -- values of 8, 16, 24, 32, 40, 48, 56, and 64 are possible.
SBoxes: ARRAY [1 .. enough/8] OF ARRAY [0 .. 255] OF int32; -- key material
AuxiliaryKeys: ARRAY[1 .. 4] OF int32; -- additional key material
rotateSchedule: ARRAY [1 .. 8] = [16,16,8,8,16,16,24,24];
octet: integer; -- really (round+7)/8, it keeps track of which
                -- 8-round "octet" we are currently in

L = L XOR AuxiliaryKeys[1];
R = R XOR AuxiliaryKeys[2];

octet = 1;

FOR round = 1 TO enough DO -- Note that "enough" must be a multiple of 8
Begin
  R = R XOR SBoxes[octet] [L AND #FF];
  L = RotateRight[L, rotateSchedule[(round-1) mod 8 + 1]];
  SWAP[L,R];
  if (round mod 8 = 0) then octet = octet+1;

End;

```
L = L  XOR AuxiliaryKeys[3];
R = R  XOR AuxiliaryKeys[4];
```

Notationally, it will be convenient to index the different variables at different rounds. This indexing is explicitly given by re-writing the above algorithm and replacing L and R with arrays. In addition, we add the array "i" to denote the indices used to index into the S-box.

```
L, R: ARRAY [-1 .. enough+1] OF int32;
enough: integer;  -- the security parameter, default of 16 seems appropriate.
              -- values of 8, 16, 24, 32, 40, 48, 56, and 64 are possible.
i: ARRAY[0 .. enough] OF int8;  -- 8-bit bytes
SBoxes: ARRAY [1 .. enough/8] OF ARRAY [0 .. 255] OF int32;  -- key material
AuxiliaryKeys: ARRAY[1 .. 4] OF int32;  -- additional key material
rotateSchedule: ARRAY [1 .. 8] = [16,16,8,8,16,16,24,24];
octet: integer;  -- really (round+7)/8, it keeps track of which 8-round
              -- "octet" we are currently in

L[0] = L[-1] XOR AuxiliaryKeys[1];
R[0] = R[-1] XOR AuxiliaryKeys[2];

octet = 1;

FOR round = 1 TO enough DO  -- Note that "enough" must be a multiple of 8
Begin
    i[round] = L[round-1] AND #FF
    L[round] = R[round-1] XOR SBoxes[octet] [ i[round] ];
    R[round] = RotateRight[L[round-1], rotateSchedule[ (round-1) mod 8 + 1] ];
    if (round mod 8 = 0) then octet = octet+1;
End;
```

L[enough+1] = L[enough] XOR AuxiliaryKeys[3];

R[enough+1] = R[enough] XOR AuxiliaryKeys[4];

The plaintext is (by definition) [L[-1], R[-1]], while the ciphertext is [L[enough+1], R[enough+1]]. By definition, round 1 computes L[1] and R[1] from L[0] and R[0], using index 1 -- or i[1]. Similarly, round n computes L[n] and R[n] from L[n-1] and R[n-1] using i[n]. We shall sometimes say that "round" 0 computes L[0] and R[0] from L[-1] and R[-1], and that "round" enough+1 computes L[enough+1] and R[enough+1] from L[enough] and R[enough].

The primary purpose of the rotation schedule is to bring new bytes into position so that all 8 bytes of input are used in the first 8 rounds (or first octet). This means that a change in any single input bit is guaranteed to force the use of a different S-box entry within 8 rounds, and so initiate the cascade of unpredictable changes needed to scramble the input. A secondary purpose of the rotation schedule is to maximize the number of rotates by 16 because they tend to be faster on many microprocessors. For example, the 68000 has a SWAP instruction which is equivalent to rotating a 32-bit register by 16 bits. Also, rotation by 16 tends to be very fast on processors with 16 bit registers -- simply by altering one's viewpoint about which register contains the lower 16 bits and which register contains the upper 16 bits it is possible to perform this operation with no instructions at all. The final purpose of the rotation schedule is to restore the data to its original rotational position after each octet of 8 rounds. Thus, the sum of the rotations is equal to 0 modulo 32.

A different S-box is used after each octet of encryption. This has two beneficial effects: first, it means that the same S-box entry will never be used twice with the same rotational alignment. That is, if a single S-box were used for all octets, then it might be that i[1] (the index used to select an S-box entry on the first round) and i[9] might be the same -- and therefore the same S-box entry would be used in rounds 1 and 9. These identical S-box entries would cancel each other out because a value XORed with itself produces 0. (If i[1] = i[9], then SBox[i[1]] XOR ...stuff... XOR SBox[i[9]] would equal ...stuff...) Both i[1] and i[9] would have had no effect on the encryption process. This would weaken the encryption function. If, however, the S-box is changed after every octet then even if i[1] = i[9], cancellation is very unlikely to occur (because SBoxes[1][i[1]] is almost certainly different from SBoxes[2][i[9]], even though i[1]=i[9]). A second beneficial effect is to insure that the encryption process is entirely different during the second octet than in the first octet. If the same S-box were used, then the second octet would compute the same function as the first octet -- which can be a serious weakness.

The parameter "enough" is used because encryption must continue for enough rounds to obscure and conceal the data. The exact number of rounds that is sufficient will no doubt be a matter of considerable debate -- it is left as a parameter precisely so that those who wish greater security can use more rounds, while those who are satisfied with fewer rounds can encrypt and decrypt data more rapidly. It seems very unlikely that fewer than 8 rounds (one octet) will ever be used, nor more than 64 rounds (8 octets). The author expects that almost all applications will use 16, 24, or 32 rounds. Values of "enough" that are not multiples of 8 are banned.

It is interesting to note that DES uses 16 rounds, and that it requires 5 rounds before each bit of input and key influences every bit of the block being encrypted[17]. That is, a change in a single bit of the input or of the key will not influence all 64 bits in the block being encrypted for 5 rounds. We might refer to this number as the "mixing interval," and say that DES has a mixing interval of 5 rounds. In Khufu, it requires 9 rounds before every bit of input and key influences every bit of the block being encrypted. It requires 8 rounds before every bit influences the selection of an S-box entry, and a 9th round for that change to influence the other 32-bit half of the 64-bit block being encrypted. The mixing interval in Khufu would therefore be 9 rounds. An interesting number is the total number of rounds divided by the mixing interval, which we will call the "safety factor." In DES, the safety factor is $16/5 = 3.2$. In Khufu with 16 rounds, the safety factor is $16/9 = 1.8$. It would seem that Khufu with 16 rounds suffers in this comparison, although we need to remember that the S-boxes in Khufu are secret, whereas the S-boxes in DES are public. Secret S-boxes are presumably more effective than publicly known S-boxes in concealing the data. If we increase the number of rounds in Khufu to 32, then the safety factor becomes $32/9 = 3.6$, which seems more likely to be satisfactory. While this metric seems useful, it should be viewed with caution: a large safety factor is no guarantee of security, nor is there any guarantee that 3.2 (the safety factor for DES) should be imbued with special significance. Given, however, that the task of selecting the number of rounds is difficult, it seems plausible to seek guidance by examining related systems.

Pre-Computing the S-Boxes

While 128 bits of key material is used at the start and finish of the encryption process (e.g., 64 bits at the start and 64 bits at the finish from the 128-bit array "auxiliaryKeys"), most of the key material is mixed in implicitly during the encryption process by selection of entries from the S-boxes. All the S-boxes (along with the 128 bits of auxiliary key material) are pre-computed from a (presumably short) user supplied key. The S-boxes *are* most of the key. This raises the question of how the S-boxes are computed and what properties they have. While the specific method of computing the S-boxes is complex, the essential idea is simple: generate the S-boxes in a pseudo-random fashion from a user supplied key so that they satisfy one property: all four of the one-byte columns in each S-box must be permutations. Intuitively, we require that selection of a different S-box entry change all four bytes produced by the S-box. More formally, (where "#" means "not equal to" and SBoxes[o][i][k] refers to the kth byte in the ith 32-bit entry of the SBox used during octet "o"): for all o, i, j, k; i # j implies SBoxes[o][i][k] # SBoxes[o][j][k].

We can divide the pre-computation of a pseudo-random S-box satisfying the desired properties into two parts: first, we generate a stream of good pseudo-random bytes; second, we use the stream of pseudo-random bytes to generate four pseudo-random permutations that map 8 bits to 8 bits. These four pseudo-random permutations are the generated S-box. We repeat this process and compute additional S-boxes until we have enough for the number of rounds of encryption that we anticipate.

We could generate a stream of pseudo-random bytes using an encryption function -- but we have no S-box to use in such an encryption function! To circumvent this circularity problem, we can assume the existence of a single "initial" S-box. Although we must get this initial S-box from somewhere, for the moment we assume it exists and satisfies the properties described earlier. We will discuss where it comes from later.

We (rather arbitrarily) adopt a 64-byte "state" value for our pseudo-random byte-stream generator. That is, the user-provided key is used to initialize a 64-byte block (which effectively limits the key size to 512 bits -- this does not seem to be a significant limit). This 64-byte block is then encrypted using Khufu (using the standard S-box for all octets, and setting the auxiliary keys to 0) in cipher block chaining mode. (Although use of a single S-box for all rounds will result in occasional cancelations as described earlier, this is acceptable for this particular application.) This provides 64 pseudo-random bytes. When these 64 bytes have been used, the 64-byte block is again encrypted, providing an additional 64 pseudo-random bytes. This process is repeated as long as more pseudo-random bytes are needed.

Now that we have a stream of pseudo-random bytes, we must convert them into the needed permutations. We adopt the algorithm given in Knuth Vol II. In this algorithm, we start with some pre-existing (not neccessarily random) permutation. For our purposes, we can start with the initial S-box. We then interchange each element in the initial permutation with some other randomly chosen element, thus producing a random permutation. In a pseudo programming language we have:

```
FOR octet = 1 TO enough/8 DO
    SBox = initialSBox;
    FOR column = 0 TO 3 DO
      BEGIN
        FOR i = 0 TO 255 DO
        BEGIN
            randomRow = RandomInRange[i,255];  -- returns a random number
                                               -- between i and 255, inclusive
            SwapBytes[ SBox[i,column], SBox[randomRow,column] ];
```

```
        END;
      END;
    SBoxes[octet] = SBox;
END;
```

The routine "RandomInRange" uses the stream of random bytes to actually generate a number in the requested range.

Khafre

The design of Khafre is similar to the design of Khufu except that Khafre does not pre-compute its S-box. Instead, Khafre uses a set of standard S-boxes (discussed in the next section -- note that the standard S-boxes are different from the one initial S-box). The use of standard S-boxes means that Khafre can quickly encrypt a single 64-bit block without the lengthy pre-computation used in Khufu; however it also means that some new mechanism of mixing in key material must be adopted because the standard S-boxes can not serve as the key. The mechanism of key-mixing is simple -- key material is XORed with the 64-bit data block before the first round and thereafter following every 8 rounds. A consequence of this method is that the key must be a multiple of 64 bits -- it is expected that 64-bit and 128-bit key sizes will typically be used in commercial applications. Arbitrarily large key sizes can be used, though this will slow down encryption.

We can summarize Khafre as follows:

```
L, R: int32;
standardSBoxes: ARRAY [1 .. enough/8] OF ARRAY [0 .. 255] OF int32;
key:  ARRAY [0 .. keySize-1] OF ARRAY [0 .. 1] of int32;
keyIndex: [0 .. keySize-1];
rotateSchedule: ARRAY [1 .. 8] = [16,16,8,8,16,16,24,24];
```

```
L = L XOR key[0][0];
R = R XOR key[0][1];
keyIndex = 1 MOD keySize;
octet = 1;
FOR round = 1 TO enough DO
BEGIN
    L = L XOR standardSBoxes[octet] [R AND #FF];
    R = RotateRight[R, rotateSchedule[round mod 8 + 1] ];
    SWAP[L,R];
    IF round MOD 8 = 0 THEN
        BEGIN
            L = L XOR rotateRight[ key[keyIndex][0], octet];
            R = R XOR rotateRight[ key[keyIndex][1], octet];
            keyIndex = keyIndex + 1;
            IF keyIndex = keySize THEN keyIndex = 0;
            octet = octet+1;
        END;
END;
```

keySize is the number of 64-bit blocks of key material used for encryption.
rotateRight [a, b] rotates the 32-bit word "a" right by "b" bits.

We again require that the number of rounds be a multiple of 8 for efficiency reasons.

In order to decrypt correctly, we have to compute the correct value of "keyIndex" to use when decryption begins. For example, if we used a 128-bit key (keySize = 2) for 32 rounds to encrypt a 64-bit plaintext, then the final entry used in the key array would be key[1]. When we began to decrypt, we would have to begin with key[1] rather than key[0]. In general, we will have to start decryption from key[(enough/8 + 1) MOD keySize]. This computation is extremely easy in the common case where keySize is 1, for any integer taken modulo 1 is 0. The other common case, in which keySize is 2, is also very easy to compute. Computing an integer modulo 2 requires only that we examine the bottom bit of the integer. While the modulo operation is more complex in some other cases, these cases are likely to be rare. If a particular case should prove to be frequent, simple special case code could be used to insure that computing the MOD function would not take excessive computer time.

Khafre will probably require more rounds than Khufu to achieve a similar level of security because it uses a fixed S-box. In addition, each Khafre round is somewhat more complex than each Khufu round. As a consequence of these two factors, Khafre will take longer than Khufu to encrypt each 64-bit block. In compensation for this slower encryption speed, Khafre does not require pre-computation of the S-box and so will encrypt small amounts of data more quickly than Khufu.

In Khafre used with a 64-bit key, the mixing interval is again 9 rounds. Here, because the S-boxes are public as in DES, it seems that the safety factor of $16/9 = 1.8$ is more directly comparable with the safety factor of $16/5 = 3.2$ for DES. Increasing the number of rounds from 16 to 24 or 32, yielding safety factors of $24/9 = 2.7$ or $32/9 = 3.6$, would seem more in keeping with the DES values. Further increases would be justified either because a safety factor larger than that of DES would be viewed as prudent, or because the "quality" of the mixing done by 9 rounds of Khafre might be viewed as less effective than 5 rounds of DES. Use of a key with more than 64 bits increases the mixing interval, and so would presumably require increases in the total number of rounds to yield commensurate increases in real security. Further study of these issues is warranted.

Making the Initial and Standard S-Boxes

We need an initial S-box to generate a pseudo-random stream of bytes. We also need a set of standard S-boxes to use in Khafre during the encryption process. In both applications, we need assurances about how the S-boxes were generated. This was a major question in DES -- whether any structure (intentional or accidental) might be present in the S-boxes that would weaken the encryption function. Because the method of selecting the DES S-boxes was kept secret, the published articles on the structure of DES are necessarily incomplete. Published discussions of the structure in the DES S-boxes makes it clear that very strong selection criteria were used, and much of the structure actually found can reaonably be attributed to design principles intended to strengthen DES. The purpose behind some of the structure detected is unclear; though it does not appear to weaken DES it would be useful to know if the structure serves some purpose or whether it occured as an unintended consequence of the particular method chosen to actually generate the S-boxes.

To avoid these questions, the standard S-boxes will be generated from the initial S-box according to the standard (and public) algorithm for generating a set of S-boxes from a key. The key selected for the standard S-boxes will be the null (all 0) key. In this way, not only the standard S-boxes but also the algorithm for generating them are made public and can be examined to determine if there are any weaknesses.

The initial S-box must be generated from some stream of random numbers. In order to insure that the initial S-box does not have hidden or secret structure, we adopt the following rules:

1.) The program that generates the initial S-box from a stream of random numbers will be public.

2.) The stream of random numbers used as input to the program should be above reproach -- it should be selected in such a fashion that it could not reasonably have been tampered with in a fashion that might allow insertion of a trap-door or other weakness.

The first criteria can be met by making the code for generation of the S-boxes available along with the code for Khufu and Khafre. The second criteria is met by using the random numbers published in 1955 by the RAND corporation in "A Million Random Digits with 100,000 Normal Deviates" (available on magnetic tape for a nominal fee).

Methods of Cryptanalysis

Questions about the security of a new cryptographic algorithm are inevitable. Often, these questions are of the form "Have you considered the following attack..." It is therefore useful to describe the attacks that were considered during the design process. This serves two purposes. First, it reassures those who find their attack has already been considered (and presumably found non-threatening). Second, it tells those who are considering a new attack that the matter might not be settled and is worth pursuing further. A second question typically asked is "How many rounds are enough?" This will vary with three factors: the value of the data being encrypted, the encryption speed (delay) that is acceptable, and the estimated cost of cryptanalysis. This last cost is inferred by considering how many rounds are sufficient to thwart various certificational attacks.

Attacks can be broadly divided into a number of categories -- starting with chosen plaintext, known plaintext and ciphertext only. We shall primarily consider attacks of the chosen plaintext variety -- a system secure against chosen plaintext attacks is presumably also secure against the two weaker attacks. Some consideration will be given to known plaintext and ciphertext only attacks. Protection against casual browsers is valuable and can be provided more cheaply (i.e., with fewer rounds in the encryption process and hence less delay). An attack by a casual browser is better modeled by a ciphertext only attack. At the same time, the cryptographic resources the casual browser is likely to bring to bear are markedly inferior. Finally, the cost of encryption (in user inconvenience or delay) might be significant and the value of the data might not justify much inconvenience -- the choice might be between rapid encryption that offers protection against casual attack or no encryption at all.

Without further ado, and in no particular order, we discuss the major attacks considered during the design phase.

We first consider attacks against Khufu with a reduced number of rounds. We shall here consider attacks against an 8 round Khufu and will start with a chosen plaintext attack. We assume that the objective is to determine the entries in the S-box and the values of the auxiliary keys. While it might theoretically be possible to take advantage of the fact that the S-box was generated in a pseudo-random fashion from a smaller key (effectively limited to 64 bytes) this has so far not proven to be the case. The pseudo-random method of generating the S-box from the key is sufficiently complex that the 64-byte to 1024-byte expansion involved in this process appears quite strong. This is probably due to the relaxed computational time requirements on the pre-computation, i.e., the pre-computation is probably over-kill, but in most applications an additional fixed delay of some tens of milliseconds probably won't be noticed, so it wasn't further optimized.

An 8 round encryption can be readily broken under a chosen plaintext attack by noting that each round of the encryption process is affected by only a single byte of the initial plaintext. Therefore, given 8 rounds and 8 bytes of plaintext, some byte of plaintext is used last; e.g., in the 8th round. By encrypting two plaintext blocks that differ only in this last byte, we obtain two ciphertext blocks in which the encryption process differs only in the 8th round, and therefore in which the two left halves have the same difference as two S-box entries. That is, if the two ciphertext left halves are designated $L[8]$ and $L'[8]$ and if the indices of the S-box entries used in the 8th rounds are designated $i[8]$ and $i'[8]$, then $L[8]$ XOR $L'[8]$ equals $SBox[i[8]]$ XOR $SBox[i'[8]]$. $L[8]$ and $L'[8]$ are known, as are $i[8]$ and $i'[8]$, so this provides an equation about two S-box entries. After we recover roughly 256 equations we will almost be able to solve for the 256 entries in the S-box. At this point, the recovery of the S-box will not quite be complete -- we can arbitrarily set the value of a single S-box entry and determine values for the rest of the entries that will satisfy the equations we have. Further equations will not help us, for if we have one solution to the equations, we can generate another solution by complementing the ith bit in every proposed S-box entry. The new set of values will also satisfy the equations, for every equation XOR's two S-box entries, and hence complementing the ith bit in both entries will leave the XOR of the two bits unchanged. We need another method for resolving this last ambiguity. This is conceptually easy (in the worst case, we could simply examine all 2^{32} possibilities) but an efficient algorithm is difficult to explain in a short space -- we therefore leave this as an exercise for the reader. Once the S-box entries are known, it is also relatively simple to determine the auxiliary keys.

If we consider a known plaintext attack against an 8 round encryption, we find the problem is more difficult. Certainly, we could request a large number of plaintext-ciphertext pairs and hope that at least some of the pairs differed only in the final few bytes (e.g., the bytes that are used only on the 7th and 8th rounds of encryption) but this would require many millions of such pairs. This, of course, presumes that the plaintext is selected randomly -- which implies that cipher block chaining (or some other pseudo-randomization method) is used to insure that patterns in the plaintext are eliminated prior to encryption. Direct encryption (without some "whitening" or pre-randomization) of sufficient text would probably result in 8-byte blocks that differed only in a single byte -- which might allow use of the method described above.

Finally, a ciphertext only attack against an 8-round Khufu appears to be a difficult problem. More sophisticated attacks can be mounted[22] that use various "hill-climbing" strategies. While we have not directly mounted such an attack, we would speculate that it would succeed for 8 rounds, though this is not certain.

Fundamentally, statistical or "hill-climbing" attacks must rely on statistically detectable differences between various alternatives. If the statistics are flat, then such techniques will fail. An important question with Khufu is the number of rounds required to achieve a statistically flat distribution. Preliminary results indicate that 16 rounds produces flat statistics.

The use of auxiliary keys were largely adopted for three reasons: first, it seemed intuitively reasonable that randomization of the input by XORing an unknown quanitity would assist in the encryption process. Second, four additional register-to-register XOR operations are cheap to implement. Finally, the auxiliary keys foil a specific chosen plaintext attack. This attack depends on the observation that, although the S-box has 256 entries, the encryption process does not use all entries for each plaintext-ciphertext pair. Even worse, although a typical 8-round encryption will use 8 different S-box entries it doesn't have to: some entries could be repeated. In the worst case, a single entry would be repeated 8 times -- which would effectively mean that only 32 bits of key material was used. If the auxiliary keys were not present then we could simply guess at the value of one of the S-box entries, and then confirm our guess if we could find a plaintext-ciphertext pair that used only that entry for all 8 rounds. Because each of the 8 rounds uses a single byte from the plaintext, we could actually construct the plaintext needed to confirm our guess (if the auxiliary keys were not present). For example, if we guess that the 0th S-box entry has some specific value, then we would select the first byte of our specially-built plaintext (or i[1], the byte of plaintext used as an index into the S-box in the first round) to be 0. Then, knowing what happens in the first round, we can select the second byte of the plaintext (or i[2]) so that the 0th entry is again selected on the second round -- which would tell us what happens in the third round. By repeating this process for 8 rounds, we can construct a plaintext which, when enciphered, will tell us whether or not the 0th S-box entry does or does not have a specific value. After trying 2^{32} values we will surely find the correct one. If we then repeat this whole process for the 1st entry, and then the 2nd entry, etc. we could determine the values of all the entries in the S-box.

The auxiliary keys prevent this attack because they effectively inject 64 bits of key material into the encryption process prior to selecting S-box entries. Thus, correctly guessing a 32-bit S-box entry is insufficient because we would also have to guess the 64-bit value XORed with the plaintext prior to encryption. If we guessed a single such bit incorrectly, then the incorrectly guessed bit would (within the first 8 rounds) cause selection of an uncontrolled S-box entry which would then initiate the uncontrolled avalanche of changes that we rely upon to provide cryptographic strength.

Although this attack is actually rather inefficient compared with our first chosen ciphertext attack, it does point out that there is no guarantee that multiple different S-box entries have actually been used during encryption. Instead, we must assure ourselves that the risk of this occuring is sufficiently low by explicitly computing the probability of its occurence.

Another attack in this general class is the cancelation attack. In this attack, we alter the first byte of the 8 bytes in the plaintext, and then attempt to cancel the effects of this alteration by altering the other 32-bit half in a compensating fashion. That is, by altering the first byte of plaintext used in the first round, we cause a change in the second round that we can understand. Because we can also change the other 32-bit half, this understandable change in the second round can be cancelled. (Notice that the auxiliary keys have very little impact on this attack. We shall assume that the auxilliary keys are 0 for this analysis.). Now, if the first byte were 3, and we changed it to a 5, then this would produce a predictable change in the value XORed with the other 32-bit half, R, in the first round. This first round is computed as:

i[1] = L[0] AND #FF;
L[1] = R[0] XOR SBox[i[1]];

For the first plaintext we encrypted, this would become:

L[1] = R[0] XOR SBox[3];

while for the second plaintext encrypted, this would become:

L'[1] = R'[0] XOR SBox[5];

Therefore, if we select R'[0] = R[0] XOR SBox[3] XOR SBox[5], then the second equation becomes:

L'[1] = R[0] XOR SBox[3] XOR SBox[5] XOR SBox[5]

or

L'[1] = R[0] XOR SBox[3]

But this means that L'[1] = R[0] XOR SBox[3] = L[1]

In other words, L[1] and L'[1] are identical -- by knowing SBox[3] XOR SBox[5] we were able to cancel out the change that should have taken place in L[1]. This, of course, means that the avalanche of changes upon which encryption so critically depends has been thwarted at the very start. Notice that after the first round of encryption, the two blocks differ only in the first byte -- that is, the byte used in the first round. After 8 rounds of encryption, the resulting ciphertexts will also differ in only this one byte.

In practice, this attack seems to require that you first guess the correct value of SBox[i] XOR SBox[j] for two different values of i and j. This is a 32-bit value, and so on average it seems necessary to try 2^{32} different values before encountering the correct one. After 8 rounds of encryption, however, the fact that we have determined the correct 32-bit "cancelation value" will be obvious because the final 64 bits of ciphertext generated by the two different plaintexts will differ in only a single byte.

It might not at first be obvious, but we can in fact modify this attack so that only $2 * 2^{16}$ plaintext-ciphertext pairs are required in order to find the correct cancelation value. Although as described above, it would seem that we need 2^{32} pairs of plaintext-ciphertext pairs to test each possible 32-bit cancelation value, this is not the case. We can generate two lists of plaintext-ciphertext pairs, and then by selecting one plaintext-ciphertext pair from one list and the other plaintext-ciphertext pair from the other list, we can generate 2^{32} possible combinations of entries from the two lists. If we select the plaintexts used to generate the lists carefully, then every 32-bit cancelation value can be represented by one entry from the first list, and one entry from the second list.

When we consider this attack on a 16 round Khufu it is much weaker. If we can determine the correct 32-bit cancelation value it will cause collapse of the encryption process up until the changed byte is again used. If the first byte has been changed, then it will again be used on the 9th round -- this means that in a 16-round Khufu a cancelation attack will effectively strip off 8 rounds. The remaining 8 rounds must then provide sufficient cryptographic strength to resist attack. Empirical statistical tests indicate that 8 rounds in which changes take place in the first one or two rounds will result in apparently random output -- though of course, this result demonstrates only that the output was random with respect to the specific statistical tests used, not that all possible statistical tests would reveal no pattern.

An attack proposed by Dan Greene is based on the observation that each 32-bit half is being

XORed with values selected (possibly with a rotation) from the S-box. Once the key has been chosen this S-box is fixed -- so at most 256 different values can be used and each value can be rotated (in the first 8 rounds of Khufu) in only four different ways. That is, we are at best applying a fixed and rather limited set of operations to each half. If we focus on the right half, R, (and if we neglect the effect of the auxiliary keys) then we find that:

R8 = R0 XOR ROTATE[SBox[i1],0] XOR ROTATE[SBox[i3],16] XOR
      ROTATE[SBox[i5],24] XOR ROTATE[SBox[i7],8]]

R8 designates the right half following 8 rounds of Khufu, i.e., the right half of the cipher-text. R0 designates the right half before encryption begins, i.e., the right half of the plain-text. Although the indices used to select the S-box entries are computed during encryption, we are going to ignore their actual values. Instead, we will assume that i1, i3, i5 and i7 are selected randomly. This should not weaken the encryption function, so any cryptanalytic success we have using this assumption indicates weakness in the original system as well.

If we define

Y = Y[i1, i3, i5, i7] = ROTATE[SBox[i1],0] XOR ROTATE[SBox[i3],16] XOR
ROTATE[SBox[i5],24] XOR ROTATE[SBox[i7],8]]

we can re-express the earlier equation as:

R8 XOR R0 = Y[i1, i3, i5, i7]

The left side of this equation is readily computed from a plaintext-ciphertext pair, and with enough such pairs we can compute the probability distribution of (R8 XOR R0). The right side should determine the same distribution (if we assume the actual indices are more or less random -- which should be a good approximation if the plaintext is random!). The 4 8-bit indices clearly could generate at most 2^{32} possible values for Y, but it seems more plausible that some values for Y will be produced more than once while other values for Y will not be produced at all. That is to say, the distribution of Y's will not be uniform. If we can compute this distribution from enough plaintext-ciphertext pairs, and if it is non-uniform, could we then cryptanalyze an 8 round Khufu? Statistical evidence gathered on a 16-round Khufu suggests that this attack will fail for 16 rounds, but its success for 8 rounds is still unclear. Even given the distribution of Y's it is not clear (at the time of writing) how to determine the actual S-box entries.

Summary

An 8-round Khufu can be broken by several attacks, though it is somewhat resistant to ciphertext only attack. A 16-round Khufu has so far resisted the modest level of attack that has been mounted. Preliminary statistical analysis suggests that a 16-round Khufu produces random output. We are hopeful that a 16-round Khufu will be useful for general commercial encryption, but this conclusion is tentative. Increasing the number of rounds to 32 or more should be effective in increasing the complexity of cryptanalysis. Further study concerning the number of rounds required to prevent cryptanalysis is warranted.

The analysis of Khafre has been less detailed. It seems probable that Khafre will require more rounds of encryption to provide equivalent security than Khufu, because the S-boxes used with Khafre are public. Khufu, by contrast, generates different S-boxes for each key and keeps the S-boxes secret -- and so uses more key material per round than Khafre.

Any reader seriously considering use of these encryption functions is advised that (1) waiting for one to two years following their publication should allow sufficient time for their examination by the public cryptographic community and (2) current information about their status should be obtained by contacting the author.

Acknowledgements

The author would like to particularly thank Dan Greene for his many comments and the many hours of discussion about cryptography in general and the various design proposals for Khufu in particular. Thanks are also due to Luis Rodriguez, who implemented the C version of Khufu and gathered most of the statistics. Thanks are also due the many researchers at PARC who provided insight, technical comments, and encouragement. I would also like to thank Dan Swinehart, John White, Mark Weiser, Frank Squires, John Seely Brown, Ron Rider, and the rest of PARC management for their persistent support of this work.

Bibliography

1.) "Secrecy, Authentication, and Public Key Systems", Stanford Ph.D. thesis, 1979, by Ralph C. Merkle.

2.) "A Certified Digital Signature", Crypto '89.

3.) Moti Yung, private communication.

4.) "A High Speed Manipulation Detection Code", by Robert R. Jueneman, Advances in Cryptology - CRYPTO '86, Springer Verlag, Lecture Notes on Computer Science, Vol. 263, page 327 to 346.

5.) "Another Birthday Attack" by Don Coppersmith, Advances in Cryptology - CRYPTO '85, Springer Verlag, Lecture Notes on Computer Science, Vol. 218, pages 14 to 17.

6.) "A digital signature based on a conventional encryption function", by Ralph C. Merkle, Advances in Cryptology CRYPTO 87, Springer Verlag, Lecture Notes on Computer Science, Vol. 293, page 369-378.

7.) "Cryptography and Data Security", by Dorothy E. R. Denning, Addison-Wesley 1982, page 170.

8.) "On the security of multiple encryption", by Ralph C. Merkle, CACM Vol. 24 No. 7, July 1981 pages 465 to 467.

9.) "Results of an initial attempt to cryptanalyze the NBS Data Encryption Standard", by Martin Hellman et. al., Information Systems lab. report SEL 76-042, Stanford University 1976.

10.) "Communication Theory of Secrecy Systems", by C. E. Shannon, Bell Sys. Tech. Jour. 28 (Oct. 1949) 656-715

11.) "Message Authentication" by R. R. Jueneman, S. M. Matyas, C. H. Meyer, IEEE Communications Magazine, Vol. 23, No. 9, September 1985 pages 29-40.

12.) "Generating strong one-way functions with cryptographic algorithm", by S. M. Matyas, C. H. Meyer, and J. Oseas, IBM Technical Disclosure Bulletin, Vol. 27, No. 10A, March 1985 pages 5658-5659

13.) "Analysis of Jueneman's MDC Scheme", by Don Coppersmith, preliminary version June 9, 1988. Analysis of the system presented in [4].

14.) "The Data Encryption Standard: Past and Future" by M.E. Smid and D.K. Branstad, Proc. of the IEEE, Vol 76 No. 5 pp 550-559, May 1988

15.) "Defending Secrets, Sharing Data: New Locks and Keys for Electronic Information", U.S. Congress, Office of Technology Assessment, OTA-CIT-310, U.S. Government Printing Office, October 1987

16.) "Exhaustive cryptanalysis of the NBS data encryption standard", by Whitfield Diffie and Martin Hellman, Computer, June 1977, pages 74-78

17.) "Cryptography: a new dimension in data security", by Carl H. Meyer and Stephen M. Matyas , Wiley 1982.

18.) "One Way Hash Functions and DES", by Ralph C. Merkle, Crypto '89.

19.) "Data Encryption Standard (DES)", National Bureau of Standards (U.S.), Federal Information Processing Standards Publication 46, National Technical Information Service, Springfield, VA, Apr. 1977

21.) "Cryptography and Computer Privacy", by H. Feistel, Sci. Amer. Vol. 228, No. 5 pp 15-23, May 1973

22.) "Maximum Likelihood Estimation Applied to Cryptanalysis", by Dov Andelman, Stanford Ph.D. Thesis, 1979

23.) IBM has recently proposed a specific one-way hash function which has so far resisted attack.

24.) "A Fast Software One-Way Hash Function," submitted to the Journal of Cryptology. The C source for this method is available by anonymous FTP from arisia.xerox.com (13.1.100.206) in directory /pub/hash.

CORSAIR:
A Smart Card for Public Key Cryptosystems

Dominique de Waleffe & Jean-Jacques Quisquater

Philips Research Laboratory
Avenue Albert Einstein, 4
B–1348 Louvain-la-Neuve, Belgium
E-mail: {ddw, jjq}@prlb.philips.be

Abstract. *Algorithms best suited for flexible smart card applications are based on public key cryptosystems — RSA, zero-knowledge protocols ... Their practical implementation (execution in ≈ 1 second) entails a computing power beyond the reach of classical smart cards, since large integers (512 bits) have to be manipulated in complex ways (exponentiation). CORSAIR achieves up to 40 (8 bit) MIPS with a clock speed of 6 Mhz. This allows to compute X^E mod M, with 512 bit operands, in less than 1.5 second (0.4 sec for a signature). The new smart card is in the final design stage; the first test chips should be available by the end of 1990.*

Keywords: smart card, public key algorithms, RSA, digital signature, zero-knowledge protocols.

1 Introduction

A large number of security problems can be solved by correct use of cryptographic methods. However, all methods found to date are more or less computationally intensive.

- DES works by applying a complex multiround algorithm on medium size numbers.

- Diffie-Hellman key exchange protocol is based on modular exponentiation of large integers.

- RSA is based on the same exponentiation and needs large exponents.

- Zero-knowledge protocols like those of Fiat-Shamir [9] or Guillou-Quisquater [10] use large number exponentiation but the exponents are not as large as in RSA.

- Many identity-based systems also rely on modular exponentiation of large numbers.

Public key techniques are the most promising for the future as they provide more flexible solutions and impose less burden both on users and security management. Most practical techniques rely on large integer arithmetic.

Another important aspect is the increased use of smart cards [11] in the solutions: smart cards can hold secrets, do some secure computations albeit slowly and implement protocols. However the kind of computations feasible by current cards is quite limited due to their relatively slow CPU. Improving the performance of those devices is very challenging as the smart card context severely limits the solution space.

In this paper we present the architecture of a coprocessor which can be integrated in smart cards and roughly provides the equivalent of 40 (8 bit) MIPS for large number arithmetic. A smart card suitably interfaced with the cell can compute X^E mod M, with 512 bit operands, in less than 1.5 second (6Mhz). Such a device is being developed, the system layout is completed (the heart of the device takes less than 3 mm^2) and the first circuits, for testing purposes, are expected in October '90.

Section 2 describes the main features of the algorithms, section 3 presents a first model of the architecture. This model is enhanced in section 4 to improve performance and memory usage. The performance is assessed in section 5.

2 Algorithms

Assume in the following that identifiers beginning with an uppercase represent large integers, while those starting with a lowercase letter represent small integer operands.

As is quite well-known, the so-called *English method* for multiplication must be chosen to implement modular multiplication with little memory because it does not need large intermediate values. The algorithm that multiplies X by $Y = \sum_{i=0}^{n-1} y_i \cdot b^i$ modulo M, in base b, is the following (in C language):

```
Acc = 0;
for(i = n − 1; i ≥ 0; i − −){
    Tmp = X · yᵢ;
    Acc = Acc · b + Tmp;
    Acc = reduce(Acc, M);
}
```

The sequence of operations for a small example is illustrated in figure 1. The operand Y is 278, and is treated from left to right, the opposite of what is usual when most people do multiplications.

Formula	Accumulator	Reduced
$2 \cdot 7563 + 0 \cdot 10$	15126	6169
$7 \cdot 7563 + 6169 \cdot 10$	114631	7147
$8 \cdot 7563 + 7147 \cdot 10$	131974	6576

Figure 1: English method for $7563 \cdot 278$ mod 8957.

An important property of modular arithmetic is that one can always subtract an arbitrary multiple of the modulus at any time during a complex computation, and still be able to obtain the correct result at the end. This allows one to reduce the size of manipulated numbers without doing modulo reductions before the very last step.

Novel algorithms [1] exploit that property and the reduction step is a simple subtraction of an adequate multiple of the modulus. As is explained in [1], one can do a multiplication step with a 24 bit y then follow by a reduction step where the modulus is multiplied by a 32 bit number before the subtraction. Further, the algorithm guarantees that intermediate values are always positive.

When the modulus is stored in 2's complement form, both multiplication and reduction steps are based on the operation

$$B \leftarrow y \cdot X + A$$

where all operands are positive numbers. This formula is the basic operation performed by the special cell.

3 First model

The width of data words used in storage and handling of information in current smart cards is one major architectural constraint. Most cards are based on 8 bit CPU's and memories and there is no likely radical change in the foreseeable future, primarily due to the chip size limit of 25 mm^2 of the ISO standard.

Adding a cell based on a different word size would further imply a major redesign of many systems components and may not bring the best performance due to the discrepancy in size of items.

A consequence of these facts is a coprocessor which manipulates 8 bit quantities, both internally (size, complexity, delays issues) and externally (interfacing issues).

The needed arithmetic operations can be performed quite fast with random logic; thus the limiting factor of the coprocessor's performance appears to be its ability to read input operands and write back results, which all are large integers. One goal of the architecture was thus to optimize the use of the available bus bandwidth.

Once it was shown that arithmetic operations could be performed in less than one memory access cycle, a direct connection between the cell and the memory system was introduced. This interface also comprises a number of auto-(inc)decrement pointers which give the cell some independence. These features allow the cell to access memory 6 million times per second.

Let us leave these interfacing considerations and examine the internal architecture. Using 8 bit data naturally leads to an 8 by 8 multiplier; if one also remembers that $(b-1)^2+2(b-1) < b^2$, one knows that adding two 8 bit numbers to the multiplication result is still a 16 bit number. The architecture in figure 2 exploits this property.

Note that, y considered as an 8 bit constant, the operation performed, $B \leftarrow y \cdot X + A$, necessitates 3 memory accesses for each multiplication (two "read", one "write").

This cell contains 3 pointers, one for each large integer operand. These pointers have auto-decrementers, hence they are updated automatically after each access. There are a cycle counter, command and status registers. The cycle counter, y and the pointers are setup by the CPU which then writes the start bit of the command register, allowing the cell to start.

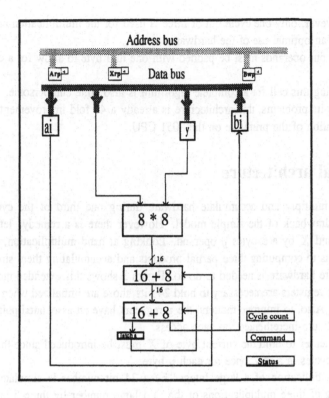

Figure 2: Simple cell

The sequencer for this cell can be summarized by the following algorithm[1]:

```
for(; cyclecount − −; ){
    / ∗ bus cycle 0 ∗ /
    ai = ∗Arp − −;
    / ∗ bus cycle 1 ∗ /
    parbegin
        tmp = ∗Xrp − − · yi + latcha + ai;
        latcha = highbyte(tmp); bi = lowbyte(tmp);
    parend
    / ∗ bus cycle 2 ∗ /
    ∗Bwp − − = bi;
}
```

Analysis of the sequencer shows that one memory access is made during each available bus

---

[1] A C-like syntax is adopted with *parbegin* and *parend* used to show the operations performed in parallel during one bus cycle. A temporary variable is introduced for simplicity. Pointers represent large integers, hence they start by an uppercase letter.

cycle. However, only one cycle out of three is used for the multiplication and accumulation. This is not an optimal use of the hardware.

Also, input operands must be padded with one null byte to allow for a correct last result byte.

Exploiting this cell for a complete algorithm is also quite cumbersome.

Despite its problems, this architecture is already a 40 fold improvement over a software implementation of the primitive on the 8051 CPU.

4 Final architecture

Using the multiply and accumulate hardware during one third of the cycles is the most important drawback of the simple model. However there is a remedy: let us multiply the large operand X by a 3 bytes y operand. Looking at hand multiplication, one can see that this amounts to computing three partial products and accumulating them simultaneously. Of course, more hardware is needed to do so. Figure 3 shows this extended model.

Three y registers are necessary to hold 24 bits, those are initialized when the cell starts its operations. Also, to improve matters, the y registers have an associated pointer (Yrp) which is used and auto-incremented[2] at each access.

A register xi to hold the current byte of X must be introduced since the same byte will be used 3 cycles in a row, once for each y byte.

The multiplication of a large integer by a 24 bit number is simulated by the proper interleaving of three multiplications of the said large number by three 8 bit numbers. This interleaving requires internal memory and datapaths which allow to recycle the temporary results into the final result. A pipeline structure for input and output also allows the interleave the memory accesses with the multiplications.

The sequencer is also quite easily described by a small algorithm, the reset cycles during which the y operand registers are loaded have been omitted (see also figure 4):

---

[2] The incrementer allows to easily implement the English method of multiplication, without reloading the Yrp register at each step.

```
for(; cyclecount − −; ){
    parbegin / * bus cycle 0 * /
        ai' = *Arp − −;
        tmp = zi · y[0] + latchd + ai;
        latchb = latcha;
        latcha = highbyte(tmp); bi = lowbyte(tmp);
    parend
    parbegin / * bus cycle 1 * /
        zi' = *Xrp − −;
        tmp = zi · y[1] + latchd + latcha;
        latchd = latchb;
        latcha = highbyte(tmp); latchb = lowbyte(tmp);
    parend
    parbegin / * bus cycle 2 * /
        *Bwp − − = bi;
        tmp = zi · y[2] + latchd + latcha;
        latchd = latchb;
        latcha = highbyte(tmp); latchb = lowbyte(tmp);
        zi = zi'; ai = ai';
    parend
}
```

Examining the sequencer (see figure 4 for a graphical view of the sequencer) and going through an example shows that all registers are necessary, and thus make up an optimal implementation of the algorithm.

Further, one also sees that during every available bus cycle, a multiplication step is performed as well as a memory access (read or write), the scheme is thus optimal in its use of the available hardware.

Unfortunately, the system as designed now prevents the CPU from doing anything while the cell is computing, turning it the other way around, the cell can not be used while the CPU works. If, somehow, both units could be active at the same time, the full capability of the novel algorithms could be used.

In these new algorithms there are no tests except for the number of loops to performs. Therefore, while one step, say multiplication, is being run by the cell, the next operation, reduction step, can be prepared by the CPU. This preparation consists in computing operand pointers, number of cycles, ...

A dedicated bus was thus introduced and is reserved to the cell. This allows the CPU to access ROM and EEPROM while the cell access the RAM at full speed.

This is not sufficient though, because the cell must receive new parameters at each step. By providing double control registers in the cell and making them accessible as internal CPU registers, the CPU can prepare the parameters, load them into the cell. Then as soon as the cell completes the current operation, the CPU can start it again. With this trick, the cell can be kept busy almost all the time during an exponentiation step.

As said in section 2, the algorithm also needs a multiplication of a large integer by a 32 bit number. The model has then been extended at the expense of optimality to provide such

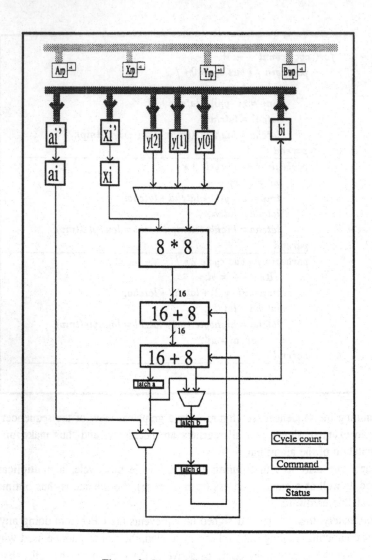

Figure 3: Intermediate architecture

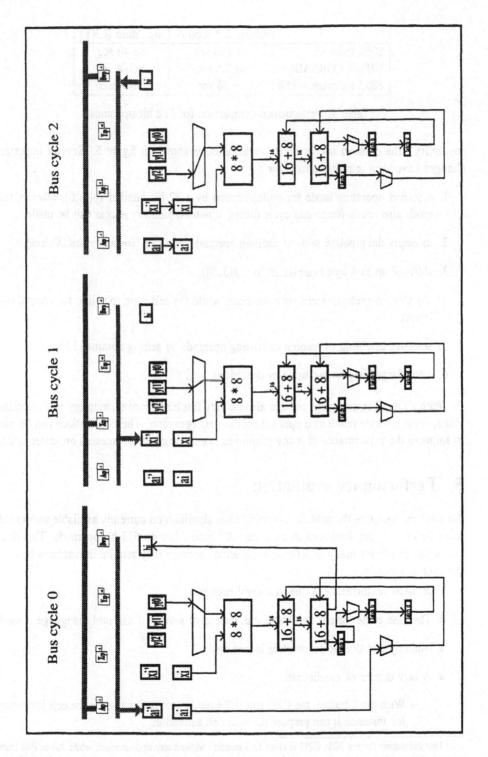

Figure 4: Activity during bus cycles

	trivial X^E mod N	signature (CRT)
8051 software	≈ 160 sec	≈ 40 sec
8051 + CORSAIR	≈ 1.5 sec	≈ 0.4 sec
6805 software + 8*8	≈ 36 sec	≈ 9 sec

Table 1: Performance comparison for 512 bit operands

capability. The detailed and complete architecture is shown in figure 5. Several important changes have been introduced to allow :

1. a second operating mode for multiplication by a 32 bit number ($y[3..0]$, *latchc*), this mode also needs fourth bus cycle during which no memory access can be made,

2. to empty the pipeline without padding operands (*read_A_lim* and *read_X_lim*),

3. shifts of up to 4 bytes (*write_B_lim*, $b[3..0]$),

4. the CPU to preload operation parameters while the cell runs (pipeline for control registers),

5. selective disabling of reading or writing operands by setting command bits,

6. allow large integers exclusive-or operations.

With all those features, the cell can also do very fast block moves, memory initializations, shifts, reuse a 4 byte result as y operand for the next operation. These operations can be used to improve the performance of many primitives manipulating large integers on smart cards.

5 Performance evaluation

An implementation of the modular exponentiation algorithm on currently available smart cards takes between 1 and 4 minutes to compute [3] X^E mod M, with 512 bit operands. This delay is not acceptable for many smart card applications because they require interactions between the user and system.

CORSAIR performance is due to several reasons:

• The base cycle time is one bus cycle, instead of several if assembly language is used.

• Multiply and double accumulate in one cycle.

• A high degree of parallelism:

    – With the 2 busses, the CPU can still execute instructions while the cell is running, for instance it can prepare the next cell activation;

---

[3] Our estimation for the 8051 CPU is close to 3 minutes without any optimization, while Amos Fiat (rump session of Crypto '90 and private communication) reported 9 seconds for a signature (CRT) on a 6805 enhanced by a 8 bit multiplier. Extrapolating gives a time of 36 seconds for the general case on the 6805.

511

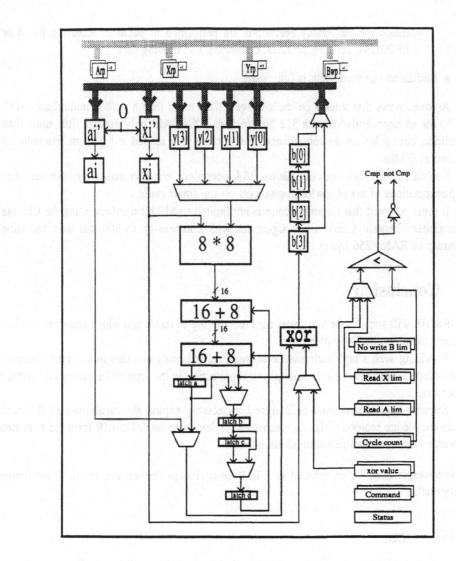

Figure 5: Final architecture

– Inside the cell, many operations are performed in parallel: accessing RAM or EEPROM, updating pointers, computing and moving data.

• Dedicated bus bandwidth is fully used.

As one knows that it takes on the average a little more than 8 million multiplications (8 by 8) for an exponentiation with 512 bit operands, CORSAIR only needs a little more than 8 million bus cycles for the computation, that is close to 1 second at 8 Mhz or less than 1.5 second at 6 Mhz.

Such a performance not only allows RSA operations but also makes possible very fast implementations of zero-knowledge protocols on the smart cards.

It must be noted that the architecture is not limited to 512 bit numbers, using the Chinese Remainder Theorem should allow signatures with numbers up to 800 bits with the same quantity of RAM (256 bytes).

6 Conclusion

CORSAIR will soon be the first smart card (complying to standards) which allows public key system to be practically implemented.

Providing such a high performance to smart cards is only one step in the right direction. The complete card must also include physical protection in the form of frequency and voltage detectors, ...

Security applications must be designed to securely exploit the capabilities of the card. Zero-knowledge protocols, signature schemes implemented on CORSAIR form the next step towards more manageable secure environments.

Acknowledgments: We are indebted to J.-P. Bournas (Philips Components, Paris) for his fruitful collaboration.

References

[1] J.-J. Quisquater, *"Fast modular exponentiation without division"*, Rump session of EUROCRYPT '90.

[2] J.-J. Quisquater, L. Guillou, *"Des procédés d'authentification basés sur une publication de problèmes complexes et personnalisés dont les solutions maintenues secrètes constituent autant d'accréditations"*, SECURICOM 89, Paris, April 1989.

[3] D. Denning, *"Cryptography and Data Security"*, Addison-Wesley Publishing Company, 1985.

[4] R. Rivest, A. Shamir, L. Adleman, *"A method for obtaining digital signatures and public-key cryptosystems"*, C. ACM, Vol. 21, No. 2, pp. 120–126, 1978.

[5] M. Gardner, *"A new kind of cipher that would take millions of years to break"*, Scientific American, Vol. 237, No. 2, pp. 120–124, Aug. 1977.

[6] R. Bright, *"Smart cards. Principles, practice, applications"*, Ellis Horwood Limited, 1988.

[7] W. Diffie, M. Hellman, *"New directions in cryptography"*, IEEE Trans. Informat. Theory, Vol. IT-22, pp. 644–654, Nov. 1976.

[8] J.-J. Quisquater, D. de Waleffe and J.-P. Bournas, *"CORSAIR: A chip card with fast RSA capability"*, Proceedings of Smart Card 2000, Amsterdam, 1989, to appear.

[9] A. Fiat, A. Shamir, *"How to prove yourself: practical solutions to identification and signature problems"*, Proc. of CRYPTO '86, Lecture notes in Computer Science, Springer Verlag, Vol. 263, pp. 186–194, 1987.

[10] L. C. Guillou, J.-J. Quisquater, *"A practical zero-knowledge protocol fitted to security microprocessor minimizing both transmission and memory"*, Proc. EUROCRYPT '88, Lecture notes in Computer Science, Springer Verlag, Vol. 330, pp. 123–128.

[11] L. C. Guillou, M. Ugon, *"Smart Card: a highly reliable and portable security device"*, Proc. of CRYPTO '86, Lecture notes in Computer Science, Springer Verlag, Vol. 263, pp. 464–489, 1987.

Design and Analysis I

Fast Checkers for Cryptography

Kireeti Kompella *   Leonard Adleman *

Department of Computer Science
University of Southern California
Los Angeles, CA 90089-0782

1 Introduction

Fast Checkers ...

Program correctness is a serious concern, and has consequently received considerable attention. This attention has taken three approaches:

- **mathematical:** *prove* programs correct;

- **empirical:** *test* programs for bugs; and

- **engineering:** *design* programs well.

While considerable progress has been made, the question of whether a given computation was performed correctly still has no practical solution. However, a new approach, proposed by Manuel Blum, promises to be both practical and of theoretical significance, and is intrinsically closer to a computer scientist's heart, since the approach is

- **algorithmic:** *check* every computation

using a *program checker.* Program checkers are designed for specific computational problems; a checker is then an algorithm such that, given a program that is supposed to solve that

---

*Research supported under NSF Grant # CCR 8519296

problem, and an input value, if the program computes correctly at that input, the checker says "CORRECT" (with a small probability of error); alternately, if the program has a bug, it says "BUGGY" (again, with a small chance of error).

Program checkers have the advantages that 1) they check entire computations (software + hardware + operating system); 2) they provide certificates on individual computations; and 3) the effort need not be duplicated if a different program for the same problem is to be checked. On the other hand, the price for increased confidence is increased computation, making *fast* checkers especially attractive.

... for Cryptography

If the average user is concerned about program correctness, how much more so the cryptographer, who, by the nature of his profession, deals with information of critical importance, making the correct manipulation of this information vital? How often is he willing to pay the price of slower speed for the sake of increased confidence? Program checkers make this choice available.

This paper describes a fast checker for modular exponentiation, the computational problem underlying RSA, one that, for modulus n, requires $O(\log \log n)$ queries and modular multiplications for a given confidence level. This paper also presents a hypothesis that implies the existence of a "constant-query" checker, requiring only a constant number of queries and modular multiplications, independent of the input. Finally, it is shown without hypothesis that in many practical cases, constant-query checkers can be obtained. Independently, Ronitt Rubinfeld [R] has devised a checker for a restricted version of modular exponentiation[1] that requires $O((\log \log n)^3)$ queries and $O((\log \log n)^4)$ modular multiplications for modulus n.

In passing, it is noted that this checker can be used in a number of cryptographic contexts, e.g., the Diffie-Hellman key exchange and discrete logarithm based systems. Furthermore, an entirely analogous checker can be used to check elliptic curve discrete logarithm systems, where exponentiation corresponds to multiplying points on the curve.

1.1 Definition of Program Checkers

For completeness, Blum's original definition of a program checker is given:

Definition 1 (Blum) *Let π be a computational problem. For x an input to π, let $\pi(x)$ denote the output of π. Call C_π a program checker for problem π, if for all programs P that halt on all inputs, for all instances I of π, and for all positive integers k (presented in unary), C_π^P is a probabilistic oracle Turing machine (with oracle P) such that:*

---

[1] This version requires that the number being exponentiated be relatively prime to the modulus.

1. If $P(x) = \pi(x)$ for all instances x of π, then with probability $\geq 1 - 1/2^k$, $C_\pi^P(I;k) = CORRECT$ (i.e., $P(I)$ is correct);

2. If $P(I) \neq \pi(I)$ then with probability $\geq 1 - 1/2^k$, $C_\pi^P(I;k) = BUGGY$ (i.e., P has a "bug").

Clearly, every computable problem π has a trivial checker: run a correct program for π, and check whether the given program produced the same answer. Thus, to obtain useful checkers, it will be required that the time for checking, apart from queries to the program, be $o(T_\pi)$, where T_π is the time complexity of solving π, i.e., that the checker run much faster than any program for π; such a checker will be called *fast*. If T_π is not known (as is often the case), one can aim for checkers that run in $o(U_\pi)$, where U_π is the best known upper bound for π; such checkers will be called *"fast"*. A *constant-query* checker is a fast (or "fast") checker that, for each value of the confidence parameter k, requires only a constant number of calls to the program being checked, and the arguments of each such call have size at most that of the original input. In such a case, one can transform any "reasonable" program for π to a "self-checking" program that has a running time of the same order of complexity.

2 Checking Modular Exponentiation

2.1 Problem Statement

Both RSA encryption/decryption and the Diffie-Hellman key exchange protocol have the same underlying computational problem, namely, modular exponentiation (ME), which can be described as follows:

> **Input:** a, b, m: positive integers, with $a < m$.
> **Output:** $c \equiv a^b \bmod m$.

The main result:

Theorem 1 (Fast Checkers for Modular Exponentiation Exist.) *There exists a program checker C_{ME} for modular exponentiation such that for all programs P which halt everywhere, and all inputs $a, b, m \in Z_{>0}$ with $a < m$,*

1. C_{ME}^P *makes* $O(\log \log b)$ *queries of the program P;*

2. C_{ME}^P *requires* $O(\log \log b + \log \log m)$ *multiplications modulo m.*

2.2 Remarks

The checker C_{ME} is based on the *tester-checker* paradigm, introduced in [AK]. That is, it follows a two-stage protocol, where, in the first stage, the checker *tests* that the program satisfies some statistical property (e.g., correctness on a certain fraction of the inputs); and in the second, it *checks* the program on the given input, making use of the property just verified.

To see whether C_{ME} is a *fast* checker, one has to compare the time to check against the time to compute. The fastest known algorithm for modular exponentiation takes $O(\log b)$ modular multiplications for exponent b. Thus, until an algorithm that takes $O(\log \log b)$ multiplications is invented, the given checker can be deemed fast. Independently, Ronitt Rubinfeld [R] discovered a checker that requires $O(\log \log b \cdot \log \log^3 m)$ modular multiplications and $O(\log \log b \log \log^2 m)$ calls to the program.

The checker C_{ME} can easily be modified to check exponentiation on any group, and in many semi-groups, again with $O(\log \log n)$ queries and group multiplications, where n is the exponent. Thus, for example, one can obtain fast checkers for exponentiation in polynomial rings and on elliptic curve groups.

2.3 Informal Description

(To simplify this description, the modulus m is assumed to be prime. This restriction is not required for the actual checker.)

At the heart of the checker for modular exponentiation lies the familiar algebraic identity:

$$a^e \cdot a^f \equiv a^{e+f} \bmod m; \tag{1}$$

Let P be a program that purports to perform modular exponentiation, and let (a, b, m) be the given input. Suppose that, for base a and modulus m, P exponentiates correctly at sufficiently many exponents f, i.e.,

$$P(a, f, m) \equiv a^f \bmod m \text{ for at least } 5/6 \text{ of } f \in \{0, \ldots, B\} \tag{2}$$

(where B is appropriately chosen), but, at the given input,

$$P(a, b, m) \not\equiv a^b \bmod m. \tag{3}$$

Then identity (1) suggests the following check: pick f randomly from $\{0, \ldots, B\}$, and check whether $P(a, b, m) \cdot P(a, f, m) \equiv P(a, b+f, m) \bmod m$. If f is such that $P(a, f, m) \equiv a^f \bmod m$ and $P(a, b+f, m) \equiv a^{b+f} \bmod m$, then (3) implies that the check will fail. Moreover, (2) implies that picking such an f is reasonably likely (provided that $b + f \leq B$). Thus, the tester-checker paradigm suggests itself: first, obtain confidence that the program P satisfies (2), then use identity (1) as outlined to obtain confidence that $P(a, b, m) \equiv a^b \bmod m$.

However, the "tester" phase of verifying that (2) holds needs to be performed carefully. Direct computation is clearly too slow, taking $O(\log b)$ multiplications, as opposed to the desired $O(\log \log b)$ multiplications. Thus, a more subtle approach is required: establish (2) for a much smaller interval, then inductively extend to larger intervals, using P itself to perform the checks.

For the inductive step, the identity used is the following:

$$a^{h \cdot 2^{2^j} + l} \equiv (a^h)^{2^{2^j}} \cdot a^l \bmod m$$

Thus, checking on exponents 2^{j+1} bits long (namely, $h \cdot 2^{2^j} + l$, with h and l of size 2^j) is reduced to checking on exponents of half this size (namely, h and l). However, one more check is needed: that $x^{2^{2^j}} \bmod m$ is computed correctly for arbitrary x. Again, the tester-checker paradigm is brought into play: first test that $P(y, 2^{2^j}, m) \equiv y^{2^{2^j}} \bmod m$, for most $y \in \{1, \ldots, m-1\}$, then use the identity

$$(xy)^e \equiv x^e \cdot y^e \bmod m$$

to check that $x^{2^{2^j}} \bmod m$ is computed correctly. Once again, the testing is done inductively: if P is tested for 2^{2^j}, then it can be tested for $2^{2^{j+1}}$ using:

$$y^{2^{2^{j+1}}} \equiv (y^{2^{2^j}})^{2^{2^j}} \bmod m.$$

Now consider the case when m is not prime. Then cancellation is no longer valid in general, and this introduces two problems: first, even if a "nice" f is picked, the check suggested by (1) may not work; and second, the check for $P(x, 2^{2^j}, m)$ also may not work. The former problem is circumvented by working modulo the largest factor of m relatively prime to a (without explicitly computing it), so that cancellation is reinstated; and the latter is solved by using a "generalized" cancellation law modulo m:

$$z(y^e) \equiv (xy)^e \ \& \ z(y+1)^e \equiv (x(y+1))^e \text{ implies } z \equiv x^e.$$

2.4 The Checker C_{ME}

The checker is presented below in detail. Note that the modulus m is no longer restricted to be prime.

The following notation will be used: for any positive integers m and a, write m as a product $\prod p_i^{e_i}$ of distinct primes, and denote by $m[a]$ the product $\prod_{p_i \mid a} p_i^{e_i}$, and let $\overline{m[a]} = m/m[a]$. Note that $(m[a], \overline{m[a]}) = (a, \overline{m[a]}) = 1$. Let $exp(m) = max_i\{e_i\}$; observe that $exp(m) \leq \log m$.

For $j \in \mathbb{Z}_{\geq 0}$, let $T_1(P, j, m)$ be the property that $\frac{\#\{y | 0 < y < m \& P(y, 2^{2^j}, m) \equiv y^{2^{2^j}} \bmod m\}}{\#\{y | 0 < y < m\}} \geq \frac{7}{8}$, and $T_2(P, a, j, m)$ that $\frac{\#\{f | 0 \leq f < 2^{2^j} \& P(a, f, m) \equiv a^f \bmod \overline{m[a]}\}}{\#\{f | 0 \leq f < 2^{2^j}\}} \geq \frac{5}{6}$. The checker first attempts to verify that $T_1(P, j, m)$ and $T_2(P, a, j, m)$ hold for $0 \leq j \leq \log \log b$. It then checks the program on the given input.

$C_{ME}^P(a, b, m; k)$:

Input: P: a program (supposedly for modular exponentiation) that halts on all inputs;
  a, b, m: positive integers such that $0 < a < m$;
  k: confidence parameter (given in unary).
Output: 'CORRECT' if $P(A, B, M) \equiv A^B \bmod M$ for all $A, B, M \in \mathbb{Z}_{>0}$ with $A < M$;
  'BUGGY' (with probability $\geq 1 - 1/2^k$) if $P(a, b, m) \not\equiv a^b \bmod m$.

```
begin
    Set c = exp(m), if known; else set c = ⌈log m⌉
    (* For small exponents b ≤ c, check by direct computation. *)
    if b ≤ exp(m), compute a^b mod m directly;
        if P(a, b, m) ≢ a^b mod m, output 'BUGGY'
        otherwise, output 'CORRECT';
        halt.

    set n = ⌈log log b⌉.
(* Tester stage *)
    test1(n, m, k)
    test2(a, n, m, k)

(* Checker stage: establish correctness at given input *)
    do k times
        check2(a, b, n, m) (* Check that P(a, b, m) ≡ a^b mod m̄[a] *)
        (* Then, that P(a, b, m) ≡ a^b mod m[a] *)
        directly compute a^c mod m
        if P(a, b − c, m) · a^c ≢ P(a, b, m) mod m then output 'BUGGY'
        else output 'CORRECT'
end
```

```
test1(n, m, k):
(* Test whether T₁(P, j, m) holds for 0 ≤ j ≤ n. *)
    begin
        (* The base case j = 0 is just squaring: test directly *)
            do 6k times
                pick x randomly from {1, ..., m − 1}
```

if $P(x, 2, m) \not\equiv x^2 \bmod m$ then output 'BUGGY' and halt

for $j \in \{1, \ldots, n\}$ do
    do $11k$ times:
        pick x randomly from $\{1, \ldots, m-1\}$
        check1$(x, j-1, m)$; let $y = P(x, 2^{2^{j-1}}, m)$
        check1$(y, j-1, m)$; let $z = P(y, 2^{2^{j-1}}, m)$
        if $P(x, 2^{2^j}, m) \not\equiv z \bmod m$ then output 'BUGGY' and halt
end

check1(x, j, m):
(* check that $P(x, 2^{2^j}, m) \equiv x^{2^{2^j}} \bmod m$, given that $T_1(P, j, m)$ holds. *)
begin
    pick y randomly from $\{1, \ldots, m-1\}$
    if $P(x, 2^{2^j}, m) \cdot P(y, 2^{2^j}, m) \not\equiv P(x \cdot y \bmod m, 2^{2^j}, m) \bmod m$ then
        output 'BUGGY' and halt.
    if $P(x, 2^{2^j}, m) \cdot P(y+1, 2^{2^j}, m) \not\equiv P(x \cdot (y+1) \bmod m, 2^{2^j}, m) \bmod m$ then
        output 'BUGGY' and halt.
end

test2(a, n, m, k):
(* Test whether $T_2(P, a, j, m)$ holds for $0 \le j \le n$. *)
begin
    (* The base case $j = 0$ is checked directly. *)
    if $P(a, 0, m) \not\equiv 1 \bmod m$ or $P(a, 1, m) \not\equiv a \bmod m$ then
        output 'BUGGY,' and halt.

    for $j \in \{1, \ldots, n\}$
        do $8k$ times
            pick e randomly from $\{0, \ldots, 2^{2^j} - 1\}$
            write $e = h \cdot 2^{2^{j-1}} + l$, with $0 \le h, l < 2^{2^{j-1}}$
            check2$(a, h, j-1, m)$; let $x = P(a, h, m)$
            check1$(x, j-1, m)$;   let $y = P(x, 2^{2^{j-1}}, m)$
            check2$(a, l, j-1, m)$; let $z = P(a, l, m)$
            if $y \cdot z \not\equiv P(a, e, m) \bmod m$ then output 'BUGGY' and halt
end

check2(a, e, j, m):
(* check that $P(a, e, m) \equiv a^e \bmod \overline{m[a]}$, given that $e < 2^{2^j}$ and $T_2(P, a, j, m)$ holds. *)
begin
    pick f randomly from $\{0, \ldots, 2^{2^j} - 1\}$

if $f > e$ then
      if $P(a, e, m) \cdot P(a, f - e, m) \not\equiv P(a, f, m) \bmod m$ then
          output 'BUGGY' and halt.
else
      if $P(a, f, m) \cdot P(a, e - f, m) \not\equiv P(a, e, m) \bmod m$ then
          output 'BUGGY' and halt.
end

2.5 Formal Proof of Theorem 1

In this section, Theorem 1 is proved. The proof proceeds via several lemmas that assert that the tests and checks given perform as desired:

Lemma 1 (check1 works) *For all $j \in Z_{\geq 0}$, for all $x, m \in Z_{>0}$ with $x < m$,*

1. *If $P(y, 2^{2^j}, m) \equiv y^{2^{2^j}} \bmod m$ for all $0 < y < m$, then* check1(x, j, m) *does nothing.*

2. *If $T_1(P, j, m)$ holds, but $P(x, j, m) \not\equiv x^{2^{2^j}} \bmod m$, then with probability $\geq 1/2$* check1(x, j, m) *outputs 'BUGGY' and halts.*

Proof: 1) Straightforward.

2) Assume the antecedent. For $0 < y < m$, let $S_y = \{y, xy \bmod m, y+1, x(y+1) \bmod m\}$; call y *bad* if S_y has a z such that $P(z, 2^{2^j}, m) \not\equiv z^{2^{2^j}} \bmod m$. Now, each z with $0 < z < m$ can appear in at most 4 S_y's; and since $\#\{z | 0 < z < m \ \& \ P(z, 2^{2^j}, m) \not\equiv z^{2^{2^j}} \bmod m\} < \frac{m-1}{8}$, there are less than $\frac{m-1}{2}$ bad y's. But if y is not bad, then check1 will output 'BUGGY' and halt, for otherwise, one must have

$$P(x, 2^{2^j}, m) \cdot y^{2^{2^j}} \equiv (xy)^{2^{2^j}} \equiv x^{2^{2^j}} \cdot y^{2^{2^j}} \bmod \overline{m[y]}$$

(since $\overline{m[y]}|m$), so that $P(x, 2^{2^j}, m) \equiv x^{2^{2^j}} \bmod \overline{m[y]}$ (since $(y, \overline{m[y]}) = 1$, one can cancel); and similarly, $P(x, 2^{2^j}, m) \equiv x^{2^{2^j}} \bmod m[y]$ (since $m[y]|m$, and $(y + 1, m[y]) = 1$), whence $P(x, 2^{2^j}, m) \equiv x^{2^{2^j}} \bmod m$ by the Chinese Remainder Theorem, a contradiction. Thus, with probability at least $1/2$, check1(x, j, m) will output 'BUGGY' and halt. $\square$

Lemma 2 (test1 works) *For all $n \in Z_{\geq 0}$, for all $m, k \in Z_{>0}$,*

1. *If $P(y, 2^{2^j}, m) \equiv y^{2^{2^j}} \bmod m$ for $0 < y < m$, then* test1(n, m, k) *does nothing.*

2. *If $T_2(P, a, j, m)$ fails to hold for some $0 \leq j \leq n$, then with probability at least $1 - 2^{-k}$,* test1(n, m, k) *will output 'BUGGY' and halt.*

Proof: 1) Straightforward.

2) Let j_0 be the smallest j such that $T_2(P, a, j, m)$ fails to hold. If $j_0 = 0$, then P squares incorrectly at least $1/8$ of the time, and in 6 passes through the first loop, an instance where $P(x, 2, m) \not\equiv x^2 \bmod m$ will be found with probability at least $1/2$. Therefore, at the end of the loop, with probability $\geq 1 - 2^{-k}$, test1 will output 'BUGGY' and halt.

Now suppose $j_0 > 0$. For random x, $\mathrm{Prob}[P(x, 2^{2^{j_0}}, m) \not\equiv x^{2^{2^{j_0}}} \bmod m] \geq 1/8$. For such an x, if $P(x, 2^{2^{j_0 - 1}}, m) \equiv x^{2^{2^{j_0 - 1}}} \bmod m$, and $P(x^{2^{2^{j_0 - 1}}}, 2^{2^{j_0 - 1}}, m) \equiv (x^{2^{2^{j_0 - 1}}})^{2^{2^{j_0 - 1}}} \equiv x^{2^{2^{j_0}}} \bmod m$, then test1 will output 'BUGGY' and halt. If either of these values is computed incorrectly, then with probability at least $1/2$, check1 will output 'BUGGY' and halt. So, every pass through the second loop will detect a bug with probability at least $1/16$. Thus, at the end of the loop, with probability $\geq 1 - 2^{-k}$, test1 will output 'BUGGY' and halt. $\square$

Lemma 3 (check2 works) *For all $e, j \in \mathbb{Z}_{\geq 0}$ with $e < 2^{2^j}$, for all $a, m \in \mathbb{Z}_{> 0}$ with $a < m$,*

1. *If $P(a, f, m) \equiv a^f \bmod m$ for all $0 \leq f < 2^{2^j}$, then check2(a, e, j, m) does nothing.*

2. *If $T_1(P, j, m)$ and $T_2(P, a, j, m)$ hold, but $P(a, e, m) \not\equiv a^e \bmod \overline{m[a]}$ then with probability $\geq 1/2$ check2(a, e, j, m) outputs 'BUGGY' and halts.*

Proof: 1) Straightforward.

2) Assume the antecedent. Arguing as in lemma 1, one can show that the probability of picking f such that, modulo $\overline{m[a]}$,

$$P(a, f, m) \equiv a^f, P(a, e - f, m) \equiv a^{e-f} \text{ (if } e \geq f), \text{ and } P(a, f - e, m) \equiv a^{f-e} \text{ (if } f \geq e)$$

is at least $1/2$. But for such an f (say $f \geq e$), $P(a, e, m) \cdot P(a, f - e, m) \not\equiv P(a, f, m) \bmod \overline{m[a]}$, since $P(a, e, m) \not\equiv a^e \bmod \overline{m[a]}$ and $(\overline{m[a]}, a) = 1$); thus, *a fortiriori*, the congruence cannot hold mod m. Therefore, with probability at least $1/2$, check2 will output 'BUGGY' and halt. $\square$

Lemma 4 (test2 works) *For all $n \in \mathbb{Z}_{\geq 0}$, for all $a, m, k \in \mathbb{Z}_{> 0}$,*

1. *If $P(a, f, m) \equiv a^f \bmod m$ for $0 \leq f < 2^{2^n}$, then test1(n, m, k) does nothing.*

2. *If $T_1(P, j, m)$ holds for all $0 \leq j \leq n$, and $T_2(P, a, j, m)$ fails to hold for some $0 \leq j \leq n$, then with probability at least $1 - 2^{-k}$, test2(a, n, m, k) will output 'BUGGY' and halt.*

Proof: 1) Straightforward.

2) Let j_0 be the smallest j such that $T_2(P, a, j, m)$ fails to hold. WLOG, assume $j_0 > 0$. Then, for random $e < 2^{2^{j_0}}$, $\mathrm{Prob}[P(a, e, m) \not\equiv a^e \bmod \overline{m[a]}] \geq 1/6$. If $x := P(a, h, m) \equiv$

$a^h \bmod \overline{m[a]}$, $P(x, 2^{2^{j_0-1}}, m) \equiv x^{2^{2^{j_0-1}}} \bmod m$ (and thus mod $\overline{m[a]}$), and $P(a, l, m) \equiv a^l \bmod \overline{m[a]}$, then **test2** will output 'BUGGY' and halt. If any of the congruences fails, then the corresponding check will catch the bug with probability at least $1/2$. Therefore, for random e, Prob[test2 finds a bug]$\geq 1/12$. Thus, after $11k$ choices of e, Prob[test2 says 'BUGGY'] $\geq 1 - 2^{-k}$. □

Proof of Theorem 1:
To show that C_{ME} is in fact a checker for modular exponentiation, observe first that for any correct program P, C_{ME}^P answers 'CORRECT' on all valid inputs. On the other hand, if P and $< a, b, m >$ are such that $P(a, b, m) \not\equiv a^b \bmod m$, then one of the following must hold (let $n = \lceil \log \log b \rceil$, and assume WLOG that $b \geq c = exp(m)$):

1. $T_1(P, j, m)$ fails to hold for some $0 \leq j \leq n$;

2. $T_1(P, j, m)$ holds for all $0 \leq j \leq n$, but $T_2(P, a, j, m)$ fails to hold for some $0 \leq j \leq n$;

3. $T_1(P, j, m)$ and $T_2(P, a, j, m)$ hold for all $0 \leq j \leq n$, but $P(a, b, m) \not\equiv a^b \bmod \overline{m[a]}$;

4. $T_1(P, j, m)$ and $T_2(P, a, j, m)$ hold for all $0 \leq j \leq n$, but $P(a, b, m) \not\equiv a^b \bmod m[a]$.

Case 1: Lemma 2 applies;
Case 2: Lemma 4 applies;
Case 3: Lemma 3 applies;
Case 4: For $b \geq c$, $a^b \equiv 0 \bmod m[a]$. Thus, $P(a, b - c, m) \cdot a^c \equiv 0 \bmod m[a]$. Hence, if $P(a, b, m) \not\equiv a^b \bmod m[a]$, then $P(a, b, m) \not\equiv P(a, b - c, m) \cdot a^c \bmod m[a]$, so the congruence fails mod m. Thus, in any case, $C_{ME}^P(a, b, m; k)$ will output 'BUGGY' with probability at least $1 - 2^{-k}$.

Verifying the running time is a straightforward task. □

Remark: when $exp(m)$ is bounded, C_{ME} requires only $O(\log \log b)$ queries and modular multiplications: checking for small exponents is done explicitly, and not by direct computation. This is the case when using the Diffie-Hellman key exchange protocol ($exp(m) = 1$ since the modulus is prime), and for the RSA cryptosystem (the modulus is usually square- or cube-free.)

2.6   Constant-Query Checkers for Modular Exponentiation

While C_{ME} is a "fast" (with respect to the current best upper bounds) checker, one can ask whether there exists a constant-query checker for modular exponentiation, i.e., a checker that requires a constant number of queries and modular multiplications. In this section, it is shown that, under a hypothesis, such a checker does indeed exist for what one might call the RSA problem: on input positive integers x, y, z with $x < z$ and $(x, z) = 1$, compute $x^y \bmod z$.

The hypothesis is now presented. Some definitions are required:

Definition 2 *For all $n \in Z_{>0}$, for all $f : Z \rightarrow Z$, for all $\gamma \in R$ with $0 \leq \gamma \leq 1$,*

1. *f is γ-homomorphic for n iff*

$$\frac{\#\{x \in Z | 0 \leq x < n \ \& \ f(x) \not\equiv 0 \bmod n\}}{\#\{x \in Z | 0 \leq x < n\}} \geq \gamma$$

and

$$\frac{\#\{x, y \in Z \mid 0 \leq x, y < n \ \& \ f(x+y) \equiv f(x) \cdot f(y) \bmod n\}}{\#\{x, y \in Z | 0 \leq x, y < n\}} \geq \gamma$$

and

$$\frac{\#\{x \in Z \mid 0 \leq x < n \ \& \ f(x+1) \equiv f(x) \cdot f(1) \bmod n\}}{\#\{x \in Z | 0 \leq x < n\}} \geq \gamma$$

2. *f is γ-exponential for n iff*

$$\frac{\#\{x \in Z | 0 \leq x < n \ \& \ f(x) \equiv f(1)^x \bmod n\}}{\#\{x \in Z | 0 \leq x < n\}} \geq \gamma$$

Hypothesis 1 *There exists $\gamma \in R$ with $0 \leq \gamma < 1$ such that for all $n \in Z_{>0}$ and for all $f : Z \rightarrow Z$, if f is γ-homomorphic for n, then f is $\frac{9}{10}$-exponential for n.*

In support of the hypothesis, note the following lemma (proof omitted):

Lemma 5 *For all $n \in Z_{>0}$, for all $f : Z/\phi(n)Z \rightarrow Z/nZ$, f is 1-homomorphic for n iff f is 1-exponential for n.*

Further, Don Coppersmith has shown that a similar hypothesis holds when the order of the multiplicative group $\phi(n)$ is known. Using this, Blum, Luby and Rubinfeld have demonstrated constant-query checkers for modular exponentiation when n is prime, or of known factorization ([BLR]).

Theorem 2 *Hypothesis 1 implies that there exists an RSA checker C_{RSA} such that for all programs P that halt on all inputs, and all instances $x, y, z \in Z_{>0}$ with $x, y < z$ and $(x, z) = 1$ and all $k \in Z_{>0}$,*

1. *$C^P(x, y, z; k)$ requires at most $O(k)$ queries to P;*

2. *$C^P(x, y, z; k)$ requires at most $O(k)$ multiplications mod z.*

First the checker is presented:

Given a program P that halts on all inputs (and supposedly computes RSA), and given $x, y, z \in Z_{>0}$ with $x, y < z$ and $(x, z) = 1$; $C^P_{RSA}(x, y, z; k)$ runs as follows:

$C_{RSA}^P(x, y, z; k)$:

Let $t_1 = \lceil -k \log_\gamma 2 \rceil$, and $t_2 = \lceil -k/\log_{4/5} 2 \rceil$, where γ is as in Hypothesis 1.

begin

    (Ensure that $f(1) \equiv x \bmod z$.)

    if $f(1) \not\equiv x \bmod z$, output 'BUGGY' and halt.

    (Establish γ-homomorphism for $f(s) = P(x, s, z)$.)

    repeat t_1 times:

        choose random $i \in Z$ with $0 \le i < z$.

        if $P(x, i, z) \equiv 0 \bmod z$, output 'BUGGY' and halt.

        choose random $i, j \in Z$ with $0 \le i, j < z$.

        if $P(x, i, z) \cdot P(x, j, z) \not\equiv P(x, i + j, z) \bmod z$, output 'BUGGY' and halt.

        choose random $i \in Z$ with $0 \le i < z$.

        if $P(x, i, z) \cdot P(x, 1, z) \not\equiv P(x, i + 1, z) \bmod z$, output 'BUGGY' and halt.

    (Establish correctness on given input.)

    repeat t_2 times:

        choose random $r \in Z$ with $0 \le r < z$.

        if $P(x, y, z) \cdot P(x, r, z) \not\equiv P(x, y + r, z) \bmod z$, output 'BUGGY' and halt.

    Output 'CORRECT'.

end

Proof of Theorem 2:

Clearly, if $P(x, y, z) \equiv x^y \bmod z$ for all $x, y, z \in Z_{>0}$, C_{RSA} outputs 'CORRECT'. It remains to verify that if $P(x, y, z) \not\equiv x^y \bmod z$, then $C_{RSA}^P(x, y, z; k)$ outputs 'BUGGY' with probability $\ge 1 - 1/2^k$.

Well, if f (as defined in Step 2) is not γ-homomorphic for z, then with probability $\ge 1 - 1/2^k$ (by the choice of t_1), C_{RSA} will find a bug. So, assume f is in fact γ-homomorphic. By Hypothesis 1, f is $\frac{9}{10}$-exponential. But then, for all $w \in Z$ with $0 \le w < z$,

$$\frac{\#\{r \in Z \mid 0 \le r < z \,\&\, f(r) \equiv f(1)^r \bmod z \,\&\, f(w + r) \equiv f(1)^{w+r} \bmod z\}}{\#\{r \in Z \mid 0 \le r < z\}} \ge \frac{4}{5}.$$

Thus, by the choice of t_2, the probability that C_{RSA} picks an r such that $f(r) \equiv f(1)^r \bmod z$, and $f(y + r) \equiv f(1)^{y+r} \bmod z$) is $\ge 1 - 1/2^k$. If such an r is picked, then $f(r) \cdot f(y) \not\equiv f(y + r) \bmod z$, since $f(1) \equiv x \bmod z$ by Step 1, and $(x, z) = 1$. $\qquad\square$

2.7 "Offline" Checking

In many situations, one has the situation where the modulus is fixed. Such is the case when two parties use the RSA cryptosystem to converse. In this case, checking can be done much more efficiently, without hypothesis, by performing the tester phase offline, i.e., the program to be checked is tested to see that it works reasonably well for a given modulus. Then, whenever the program is run, the output is checked using a checker that only guarantees correctness when used with tested programs.

A checker for tested programs is now presented. First, some definitions are needed:

Definition 3 *For all* $m \in Z_{>0}$, *for all programs* P, P *is* m-*tested iff*

$$\frac{\#\{x,y \in Z \mid 0 \leq x,y < m^2 \ \& \ (x,m) = 1 \ \& \ P(x,y) \equiv x^y \bmod m\}}{\#\{x,y \in Z \mid 0 \leq x,y < m^2 \ \& \ (x,m) = 1\}} \geq 99/100$$

Definition 4 (after Blum) *For all* $m \in Z_{>0}$, *call* TC_{RSA} *an RSA tester-checker for modulus* m, *iff for all* m-*tested programs* P *that halt on all inputs, for all* $x,y \in Z$ *with* $0 \leq x,y < m$ *and* $(x,m) = 1$, *and for all positive integers* k *(presented in unary),* TC_{RSA}^{P} *is a probabilistic oracle Turing machine (with oracle P) such that:*

1. *If* $P(w,v) \equiv w^v \bmod m$ *for all* $w,v \in Z$ *with* $0 \leq w,v < m$ *and* $(w,m) = 1$, *then with probability* $\geq 1 - 1/2^k$, $TC_{RSA}^{P}(x,y;k) = CORRECT$.

2. *If* $P(x,y) \not\equiv x^y \bmod m$ *then with probability* $\geq 1 - 1/2^k$, $TC_{RSA}^{P}(x,y;k) = BUGGY$.

For all $m \in Z_{>0}$ an RSA tester-checker for modulus m is now presented. Let R be a program (purported to have the property that for all $w,v \in Z$ with $0 \leq w,v < m^2$ and $(w,m) = 1$, on input w,v it outputs $w^v \bmod m$) to be checked.

First, the algorithm RSA-Tester below is run to eliminate with high probability programs which are not m-tested.

Algorithm RSA-Tester:

Input: R: a program (supposedly for RSA) that halts on all inputs;
  m: a positive integer;
  k: confidence parameter (given in unary).
  begin
  Set $t = \lceil (k+1) \log_{100/99} 2 \rceil$.
  repeat t times:
  Choose random $x,y \in Z$ with $0 \leq x,y < n^2$.
  If $R(x,y) \not\equiv x^y \bmod m$, output 'FAIL' and halt.
  Output 'PASS.'
  end

The checker phase follows only for 'm-tested' programs, for input $x, y \in \mathbb{Z}$, with $0 \leq x, y < m$ and $(x, m) = 1$. Let $\text{fail}(u, v, w, x, y, z)$ be the predicate

$$R(w \cdot z, v) \cdot R(u, y \cdot v) \not\equiv R(u \cdot x, y \cdot v) \cdot R(w, v) \bmod n$$

Algorithm RSA Tester-Checker

Input:	R: a m-tested program;
	x, y, m: positive integers as above;
	k: confidence parameter (given in unary).
Output:	'CORRECT' if $P(X, Y, m) \equiv X^Y \bmod m$ for all $X, Y \in \mathbb{Z}_{>0}$ with $X < m$ and $(X, m$
	'BUGGY' (with probability $\geq 1 - 1/2^k$) if $P(x, y, m) \not\equiv x^y \bmod m$.

begin
    Set $z = R(x, y)$.
    repeat $t = \lceil (k+1) \log_{25/24} 2 \rceil$ times:
        choose random $u, v, w \in \mathbb{Z}$, with $0 \leq u, v, w < m$.
        if $\text{fail}(u, v, w, x, y, z)$ or $\text{fail}(u+1, v, w, x, y, z)$
            or $\text{fail}(u, v+1, w, x, y, z)$ or $\text{fail}(u+1, v+1, w, x, y, z)$
            or $\text{fail}(u, v, w+1, x, y, z)$ or $\text{fail}(u+1, v, w+1, x, y, z)$
            or $\text{fail}(u, v+1, w, x, y, z)$ or $\text{fail}(u+1, v+1, w+1, x, y, z)$
            Output 'BUGGY' and halt.

    Output 'CORRECT.'
end

2.8 Open Problems

An important open problem is whether there exists a constant-query checker for modular exponentiation. Such a checker could prove useful in cryptography. One direction in which to pursue this question would be to prove that Hypothesis 1 holds.

A question of greater general interest is to characterize problems with constant-query checkers. Software practitioners could use this characterization for guidance in writing "checkable" programs.

References

[AK]   Leonard Adleman and Kireeti Kompella, Self-Checking RSA Programs, abstract submitted to *Advances in Cryptology* (CRYPTO 89).

[B]   Manuel Blum, Designing Programs to Check Their Work, Technical Report, ISRI, UC Berkeley, Nov. 1988.

[BLR]   Manuel Blum, Michael Luby, and Ronitt Rubinfeld, Self-Testing/Correcting with Applications to Numerical Problems, *Proc. of the 22nd Annual ACM Symposium on Theory of Computing*, 1990, pp. 73-83.

[DH]   Walt Diffie and Martin Hellman, New Directions in Cryptography, *IEEE Transcations on Information Theory*, vol. IT-22, 1976, pp. 644-654.

[RSA]   Ron Rivest, Adi Shamir, and Leonard Adleman, A Method for Obtaining Digital Signatures and Public-Key Cryptosystems, *Communications of the ACM*, vol. 21, no. 2, February 1978, pp. 120-126.

[R]   Ronitt Rubinfeld, private communication.

Complexity Theoretic Issues Concerning Block Ciphers Related to D.E.S.

*Richard Cleve**
Department of Computer Science
University of Calgary
Calgary, Canada T2N 1N4

Abstract

The D.E.S. cipher is naturally viewed as a composition of sixteen invertible transformations on 64-bit strings (where the transformations depend of the value of a 56-bit key). Each of the transformations has a special form and satisfies the particular property that each of its output bits is determined by a "small" number of its input bits. We investigate the computational power of block ciphers on n-bit strings that can be expressed as polynomial-length (with respect to n) compositions of invertible transformations that have a form similar to those of D.E.S. In particular, we require that the basic transformations have the property that each of their output bits depends on the value of a small number of their input bits (where "small" is somewhere in the range between $O(1)$ and $O(\log n)$). We present some sufficient conditions for ciphers of this type to be "pseudorandom function generators" and, thus, to yield private key cryptosystems that are secure against adaptive chosen plaintext attacks.

1 Introduction

The Data Encryption Standard (D.E.S.) was developed at IBM in the seventies to be used as a private key cryptosystem (i.e. a system that enables two parties, who share

---

*Research partially conducted while the author was at the University of Toronto, partially supported by an NSERC postgraduate scholarship, and at the International Computer Science Institute in Berkeley, CA.

a common "private key," to secretly communicate information over a channel that is possibly being monitored). Presently, D.E.S. is one of the most widely used commercial cryptosystems. In spite of this, and a significant amount of attention by the open research community, very little is actually known about the "security" of D.E.S. Although no method is publicly known that "breaks" D.E.S. more efficiently than a brute-force exhaustive key search, there is no formal justification for considering D.E.S. to be secure.

D.E.S. is a function that for each m-bit "key" (where $m = 56$) and n-bit "plaintext" (where $n = 64$) produces an n-bit "ciphertext." For each fixed value of the key, the resulting mapping on n-bit strings is invertible and the inverse map is easily obtained by changing the order of the key bits.

Luby and Rackoff [7] explain that the security of D.E.S. is related to whether or not D.E.S. passes the "black box" test, which is informally described as follows.

> Construct two black boxes that compute functions from n bits to n bits as follows. One of the functions is selected uniformly at random from all the $2^{n \cdot 2^n}$ possible functions from n bits to n bits. The other function is the D.E.S. function with the key set to a uniformly random m-bit string. We say that D.E.S. "passes" the black box test if, no algorithm that examines the two black boxes by repeatedly feeding inputs to them and examining the outputs can obtain, with a "feasible" amount of computation, a "significant" idea about which box is which.

If D.E.S. passes the black box test then D.E.S. is secure against an "adaptive chosen plaintext attack" (explained in [7]), which is one of the strongest kinds of cryptographic attacks known.

With n fixed at 64, the black box test as stated above is very informal, since the terms "feasible" and "significant" are imprecise, and would appear difficult to quantify precisely when the values of n and m are fixed. Nevertheless, in a vague sense, D.E.S. appears to pass the black box test, given our present knowledge and computing power.[1]

There is a rich theory of cryptography that concerns the asymptotic behavior of asymptotically large cryptosystems. In this theory, the black box test would apply to functions mapping n-bit strings to n-bit strings, for arbitrarily large values of n, and "feasible" means polynomially bounded with respect to n, and a "significant"

---

[1]Some researchers claim that, since the key is only 56 bits long, it is feasible to break D.E.S. by an exhaustive key search. Such an attack is clearly not feasible if D.E.S. is modified to "triple encryption" mode (explained by Coppersmith [5]).

quantity is one that is bounded below by a quantity that is larger than the inverse of a polynomially bounded quantity (i.e. $(\frac{1}{n})^{O(1)}$). A cipher (or "permutation generator") is any function that maps an $m(n)$-bit string (called the key) and an n-bit string (called the plaintext) to an n-bit string (called the ciphertext). It is reasonable to require that a cipher be feasibly computable (i.e. computable in time polynomial with respect to n). A cipher that passes the black box test is called a "pseudorandom permutation generator" and, when used as a private key cryptosystem, is secure against adaptive chosen plaintext attacks [7].

It is not clear how to naturally scale up D.E.S. for arbitrarily large block sizes; however, certain of its structural features do scale up naturally. The D.E.S. function is a composition of functions of the following forms. Let $F : \{0,1\}^n \rightarrow \{0,1\}^n$. Define the mapping $T_F : \{0,1\}^{2n} \rightarrow \{0,1\}^{2n}$ as $T_F(x,y) = (x, y \oplus F(x))$ and define the mapping $S : \{0,1\}^{2n} \rightarrow \{0,1\}^{2n}$ as $S(x,y) = (y,x)$. Let $\circ$ denote the composition operator. The D.E.S. cipher, for each value of its key, is of the form

$$T_{F_1} \circ S \circ T_{F_2} \circ S \circ \cdots \circ S \circ T_{F_{16}} \, ,$$

where n is set to 64, and where $F_1, ..., F_{16}$ also depend on the value of the key. Moreover, the functions F_i ($i \in \{1, ..., 16\}$) all satisfy the following restrictive property: each output bit of F_i depends on at most six of its input bits. These structural features scale up naturally with larger values of n to compositions of the form

$$T_{F_1} \circ S \circ T_{F_2} \circ S \circ \cdots \circ S \circ T_{F_{r(n)}} \, ,$$

where some bound may be placed on $r(n)$, the length of the composition, and a bound may be placed on the number of input bits that each output bit of F_i depends on.

We investigate the class of permutations that can be expressed as

$$T_{F_1} \circ S \circ T_{F_2} \circ S \circ \cdots \circ S \circ T_{F_{r(n)}} \, ,$$

where $r(n)$ is polynomial in n, and, for each $i \in \{1, ..., r(n)\}$, each output bit of F_i depends on a number of input bits that is bounded somewhere from $O(1)$ to $O(\log n)$. (For technical reasons, we consider it a realistic reflection of the design of D.E.S. to disallow F_i's whose output bits depend on more than $O(\log n)$ input bits. This is because, in the finer structure of the D.E.S. cipher, there are functions, called "S-boxes," that are expressed in tabular form. In asymptotic versions of D.E.S., in order for these tables to be of polynomial size, the number of inputs to the S-boxes must be logarithmically bounded. We do not elaborate further on this aspect of D.E.S. in this report.)

Our first observation is that, by a construction of Coppersmith and Grossman [4], and Even and Goldreich [6], the above class of permutations is robust in that the class obtained is the same when the bound on the number of input bits that the output bits depend on is $O(1)$ or $O(\log n)$. Also, applying a result of Luby and Rackoff [7], if using our basic permutations, we could feasibly simulate permutations of the form T_F, where F is an arbitrary polynomial-time computable function (that also depends on a key) then there would be a pseudorandom permutation generator in the above class (assuming a one-way function exists). Our main result shows how to simulate, in terms of our basic permutations, permutations of the form T_F where $F \in NC^1$, and we then extend this to permutations of the form T_F where F is computed in nonuniform logarithmic space. As a consequence, if there exists a pseudorandom function generator in nonuniform logarithmic space then there exists a "secure" cipher that is in our class, and therefore one that has a form similar to D.E.S.

2   Overview of Related Work

Coppersmith and Grossman [4] investigate certain special permutations on sets of strings that are different from—but related to—those permutations described above. They show that, by composing sufficiently many of their special permutations, any permutation of even parity can be constructed. Even and Goldreich [6] make the connection between the work of Coppersmith and Grossman, and D.E.S. more explicit. The resulting theorem is that any of the $\frac{1}{2}2^{2n}!$ permutations of even parity on $\{0,1\}^{2n}$ can be expressed as

$$T_{F_1} \circ S \circ T_{F_2} \circ S \circ \cdots \circ S \circ T_{F_{r(n)}} \,,$$

where $F_1, ..., F_{r(n)}$ have the property that each of their output bits depends on at most a constant number (in this case two is sufficient) of their input bits, and $r(n)$ is *exponentially* (in n) bounded. This implies that, allowing exponentially long compositions of the basic permutations, and allowing the functions $F_1, ..., F_{r(n)}$ to also depend on a key (which in this case would also have to be exponentially long), ciphers that pass the black box test can be constructed. This result is of some support to the security of D.E.S. in that if all compositions of the above form were in a sufficiently restricted class then this would expose an insecurity of D.E.S. For example, if we consider compositions of the above form where the functions $F_1, ..., F_{r(n)}$ have the property that each of their output bits depends on at most *one* input bit then the resulting permutations are all affine linear [4,6], and such transformations are easily defeated by the black box test. On the other hand, exponentially long compositions of permutations seem too long to realistically reflect the design of D.E.S. We consider it more realistic to investigate the permutations that can be generated by compositions of the above form where $r(n)$ is polynomial in n.

Luby and Rackoff [7] show that much shorter compositions of permutations yield ciphers that are in some sense pseudorandom, provided that one allows the basic permutations to be powerful enough. What they show is that permutations of the form

$$T_{F_1} \circ S \circ T_{F_2} \circ S \circ T_{F_3}$$

are pseudorandom, provided that F_1, F_2, F_3 are independently generated pseudorandom functions. Using other results and assuming that a one-way function exists, there exist functions F_1, F_2, F_3 (that also depend on keys) that are of polynomial time complexity and are pseudorandom. This is an interesting result because, prior to this work, there were no known constructions of pseudorandom permutation generators in terms of pseudorandom function generators. This result does not, however, explain a mechanism that works in D.E.S. In D.E.S., the functions $F_1, ..., F_{16}$ are definitely *not* pseudorandom. Any function that, like $F_1, ..., F_{16}$, has the property that each of its output bits does not depend on all of its input bits can be very easily distinguished from a random function. In fact, in the case of D.E.S., the individual functions F_i can each be broken in a much stronger sense: they can be *completely determined* in a simple manner by evaluating them at only 64 different inputs. Also, Biham and Shamir [8] show that if one varies D.E.S. by reducing the number of rounds then it quickly becomes insecure as the number of rounds decreases from 16. Thus, it appears necessary to use all 16 rounds in D.E.S.

The design principle in D.E.S. seems to be to employ simpler functions than those considered in [7] (more along the lines of those considered in [4,6]) and allow the length of the composition to be more than constant (yet shorter than the exponential lengths considered [4,6]).

3 Results

The main results are Theorem 5 and Theorem 6.

3.1 Function Generators

Definition 1: A *function generator* G is a function of the from $G = \bigcup_{n=1}^{\infty} G^n$, where, for each n, $G^n : \{0,1\}^{m(n)} \times \{0,1\}^n \to \{0,1\}^n$. We call the first input to G^n (the

$m(n)$-bit string) the *key*. Each value of the key determines a function from $\{0,1\}^n$ to $\{0,1\}^n$. When convenient, we will sometimes interchange the notation G and G^n when no ambiguity results.

We are interested in classes of function generators that have certain properties, such as having polynomial (in n) time complexity.

Definition 2: P is the class of function generators computed in polynomial time. More formally, a function generator G^n is in P (for polynomial-time) if, for each n, each output bit of G^n is computed by a Boolean circuit of size polynomial in n.

We are also interested in other classes of function generators. Each of the three classes defined below have the following properties. Each of the function generators G^n are expressible as $G^n(y, x) = F^n(H^n(y), x)$, where $H^n : \{0,1\}^{m(n)} \to \{0,1\}^{p(n)}$ and $F^n : \{0,1\}^{p(n)} \times \{0,1\}^n \to \{0,1\}^n$, and H is polynomial-time computable, and F satisfies a condition that depends on which of the three specific classes that G is in. H is called the *key preprocessing* phase of the computation. For convenience, we may regard F^n as a function from $\{0,1\}^{p(n)+n}$ to $\{0,1\}^n$.

Definition 3: $FAN\text{-}IN[k(n)]$ denotes the class of all function generators that, after polynomial-time preprocessing of key bits, are computed by a function with *fan-in* bounded above by $k(n)$, where the *fan-in* of a function is, informally, the maximum number of input bits that any output bit depends on. More formally, a function generator G^n has *fan-in* $k(n)$ if it is expressible as $G(y, x) = F(H(y), x)$, where $H : \{0,1\}^{m(n)} \to \{0,1\}^{p(n)}$ is polynomial-time computable, and $F : \{0,1\}^{p(n)+n} \to \{0,1\}^n$ has the following property. Each output bit of $F(z_1, ..., z_{p(n)+n})$ is determined by the values of at most $k(n)$ of the values $z_1, ..., z_{p(n)+n}$. That is, for all $i \in \{1, ..., n\}$, there exists $j_1, ..., j_{k(n)} \in \{1, ..., n\}$ and $f : \{0,1\}^{k(n)} \to \{0,1\}$ such that, for all $z_1, ..., z_{p(n)+n} \in \{0,1\}$, $[F(z_1, ..., z_{p(n)+n})]_i = f(z_{j_1}, ..., z_{j_{k(n)}})$.

Definition 4: NC^1 is the class of function generators that, after polynomial-time preprocessing of key bits, are computed by logarithmic-depth Boolean circuits. More formally, a function generator G^n is in NC^1 if it is expressible as $G(y, x) = F(H(y), x)$, where $H : \{0,1\}^{m(n)} \to \{0,1\}^{p(n)}$ is polynomial-time computable, and $F : \{0,1\}^{p(n)+n} \to \{0,1\}^n$ has the following property. Each output bit of $F(z_1, ..., z_{p(n)+n})$ is computed by a Boolean circuit of depth $O(\log n)$.

Definition 5: $SPACE[w(n)]$ is the class of all function generators that, after polynomial-time preprocessing of key bits, are computed by $w(n)$-space computations (which are defined formally below). Informally, when $w(n)$-space computations are analogous to non-uniform Turing machine computations that use $w(n)$-space and run in polynomial-time. Formally, a function generator G^n is in $SPACE[w(n)]$ if it is expressible as $G(y, x) = F(H(y), x)$, where $H : \{0,1\}^{m(n)} \rightarrow \{0,1\}^{p(n)}$ is polynomial-time computable, and $F : \{0,1\}^{p(n)+n} \rightarrow \{0,1\}^n$ has the following property. The computation of F on the inputs $(z_1, ..., z_{p(n)+n}) = (H(y), x)$ is defined in terms of a sequence

$$\Pi_1, ..., \Pi_{t(n)} : \{0,1\} \times \{0,1\}^{w(n)} \rightarrow \{0,1\}^{w(n)}$$

of *transition functions*, and a sequence

$$\alpha_1, ..., \alpha_{t(n)} : \{0,1\}^{w(n)} \rightarrow \{1, ..., p(n) + n\}$$

of *address functions*, where $t(n) \in n^{O(1)}$. The resulting computation is then a sequence $s_0, ..., s_{t(n)} \in \{0,1\}^{w(n)}$ of *configurations*, where the initial configuration s_0 is $0...0$, and, for $i \in \{1, ..., t(n)\}$,

$$s_i = \Pi_i(z_{\alpha_i(s_{i-1})}, s_{i-1}) \ .$$

This latter part means that, from each configuration, the following configuration is determined by the current configuration and the value of one input (which may depend on the current configuration). The *output* of the computation is 1 if the final configuration $s_{t(n)}$ is, say, $0...0$, and 0 otherwise.

We consider some relationships between the above classes of function generators. Clearly, $FAN\text{-}IN[O(1)] \subset FAN\text{-}IN[O(\log n)]$ and this containment is *proper*. Also, the following theorem is elementary to prove.

Theorem 1: $FAN\text{-}IN[O(\log n)] \subset NC^1$ and the containment is proper.

From Barrington's work [1], we can obtain the following.

Theorem 2 (Barrington [1]): $SPACE[4] = SPACE[O(1)] = NC^1$.

Finally, it is clear that $NC^1 \subset SPACE[O(\log n)] \subset P$ and it is not known whether any of these containments are proper (though they are widely believed to be so).

3.2 Permutation Generators

Definition 6: A *permutation generator* is a function of the form $A = \bigcup_{n=1}^{\infty} A^n$, where $A^n : \{0,1\}^{m(n)} \times \{0,1\}^{2n} \rightarrow \{0,1\}^{2n}$, and, for each $z \in \{0,1\}^{m(n)}$ (called a *key*), $A^n(z) : \{0,1\}^{2n} \rightarrow \{0,1\}^{2n}$ is a permutation (i.e. an invertible mapping). We call the first input G^n (the $m(n)$-bit string) the *key*, and the second input (the $2n$-bit string) the *plaintext*. Also, we call the $2n$-bit output string the *ciphertext*. (For technical reasons, that will soon become apparent, the sizes of the plaintext and ciphertext are $2n$ rather than n.) For convenience, we will sometimes interchange the notation A and A^n when no ambiguity results. The *composition* of two permutation generators A and B is $A \circ B : \{0,1\}^{m(n)} \times \{0,1\}^{2n} \to \{0,1\}^{2n}$, where the permutations are taken relative to the same key (i.e. $(A \circ B)(z) = A(z) \circ B(z)$, for each $z \in \{0,1\}^{m(n)}$).

We are interested in permutation generators that have a structure similar to that of D.E.S. To this end, we define the following.

Definition 7: For any function generator $G : \{0,1\}^{m(n)} \times \{0,1\}^n \to \{0,1\}^n$, define the associated permutation generator $T_G : \{0,1\}^{m(n)} \times \{0,1\}^{2n} \to \{0,1\}^{2n}$ as

$$T_G(z)(x,y) = (x, y \oplus G(z,x))$$

for all $z \in \{0,1\}^{m(n)}$ and $x,y \in \{0,1\}^n$ (where the $\oplus$ is taken bitwise). Note that T_G is clearly a permutation generator since $T_G \circ T_G$ is the identity permutation for each value of the key. Also, define the permutation $S : \{0,1\}^{2n} \to \{0,1\}^{2n}$ as

$$S(x,y) = (y,x)$$

for all $x, y \in \{0,1\}^n$.

Definition 8: For any class of function generators B (e.g. *FAN-IN*$[k(n)]$, NC^1, *SPACE*$[w(n)]$, or P), define *DES*$[B]$ as the class of permutation generators of the form

$$T_{G_1} \circ S \circ T_{G_2} \circ S \circ \cdots \circ S \circ T_{G_{r(n)}} ,$$

where $r(n)$ is polynomial in n and $G_1, G_2, ..., G_{r(n)}$ are all in B.

It should be noted that the D.E.S. cipher is expressible in the form of the above definition with $n = 64$, $m(n) = 56$, $r(n) = 16$, and $B = $ *FAN-IN*$[12]$ (6 key bits and 6 plaintext bits contribute to the fan-in).

We also note that the form of the permutations in Definition 8 need not strictly alternate between T_G permutations and S permutations, since T_ϕ and $S \circ T_\phi \circ S$ are both the identity permutation if ϕ is the zero function generator (i.e. always zero).

We consider any class that contains a realistic asymptotic extension of D.E.S. to be in *DES*$[$*FAN-IN*$[k(n)]]$, where $k(n)$ is somewhere between $O(1)$ and $O(\log n)$.

Luby and Rackoff [7] show the following (we do not formally define pseudorandom permutation generators or one-way functions; the reader is referred to [7] for more details about this).

Theorem 3 (Luby and Rackoff [7]): *If there exists a one-way function then there exists a pseudorandom permutation generator in DES[P].*

As noted, we consider $DES[P]$ to be too powerful to reflect the design principles of D.E.S. In this report, we are primarily interested in $DES[FAN\text{-}IN[O(1)]]$ and $DES[FAN\text{-}IN[O(\log n)]]$. If we could show that one of these classes is equivalent to $DES[P]$ then, by the result of Luby and Rackoff, it would follow that there exists a pseudorandom permutation generator in $DES[FAN\text{-}IN[O(1)]]$ or $DES[FAN\text{-}IN[O(\log n)]]$ (provided a one-way function exists).

If one could, for any $G \in P$, construct a permutation of the form T_G in terms of polynomially many permutations of the form S and T_H, where $H \in FAN\text{-}IN[O(\log n)]$, then we would have $DES[FAN\text{-}IN[O(\log n)]] = DES[P]$ and a pseudorandom permutation generator would exist in $DES[FAN\text{-}IN[O(\log n)]]$.

Coppersmith and Grossman [4], and Even and Goldreich [6] considered a class similar to $DES[FAN\text{-}IN[2]]$, but without the polynomial bound on the length of compositions of the permutations. Nevertheless, by analyzing their constructions, we find that permutations of the form T_F where $F \in FAN\text{-}IN[O(\log n)]$ can be expressed as polynomial-length compositions of permutations of the form S, and T_G, where $G \in FAN\text{-}IN[2]$. Thus, we have the following theorem (which is also a consequence of Theorem 5 below).

Theorem 4 (Coppersmith and Grossman [4]; Even and Goldreich [6]): $DES[FAN\text{-}IN[2]] = DES[FAN\text{-}IN[O(\log n)]]$.

Thus, we obtain the same complexity class if the fan-in is anywhere in the between $O(1)$ and $O(\log n)$. Note that this is in spite of the fact that $FAN\text{-}IN[2]$ is a proper subset of $FAN\text{-}IN[O(\log n)]$.

We do not know whether $DES[FAN\text{-}IN[2]] = DES[P]$, but we can show that, for some interesting complexity classes B that are much more powerful than $FAN\text{-}IN[O(\log n)]$ $DES[FAN\text{-}IN[2]] = DES[B]$. Our first result along these lines is the following (bear in mind that $FAN\text{-}IN[O(\log n)]$ is a proper subset of NC^1).

Theorem 5: $DES[FAN\text{-}IN[2]] = DES[NC^1]$.

Proof: It is sufficient to show that, for every function generator G that is in NC^1, the permutation generator T_G is in $DES[FAN\text{-}IN[2]]$. Some parts of our constructions are related to those used by Ben-Or and Cleve in [2].

For $i, j, k \in \{1, ..., n\}$, define $\Phi_{i,j}^k : \{0,1\}^{2n} \to \{0,1\}^{2n}$ as, for all $x, y \in \{0,1\}^n$, $\Phi_{i,j}^k(x, y) = (x, z)$, where

$$z_r = \begin{cases} y_k \oplus (y_i \wedge y_j) & \text{if } r = k \\ y_r & \text{if } r \neq k . \end{cases}$$

We first show that, for any $i, j, k \in \{1, ..., n\}$ for which with i and j are both distinct from k, $\Phi_{i,j}^k \in DES[FAN\text{-}IN[2]]$. To do this, define $\Delta_{i,j}^k : \{0,1\}^n \to \{0,1\}^n$ ($i, j, k \in \{1, ..., n\}$) as

$$[\Delta_{i,j}^k(x)]_r = \begin{cases} (x_i \wedge x_j) & \text{if } r = k \\ 0 & \text{if } r \neq k \end{cases}$$

for all $x \in \{0,1\}^n$. Note that $\Delta_{i,j}^k \in FAN\text{-}IN[2]$. Also, it is straightforward to verify that, for all $i, j, k \in \{1, ..., n\}$ with $i, j \neq k$,

$$\Phi_{i,j}^k = S \circ T_{\Delta_{i,j}^1} \circ S \circ T_{\Delta_{1,1}^k} \circ S \circ T_{\Delta_{i,j}^1} \circ S \circ T_{\Delta_{1,1}^k} .$$

Therefore, $\Phi_{i,j}^k \in DES[FAN\text{-}IN[2]]$, as claimed.

Now, for $g : \{0,1\}^{m(n)} \times \{0,1\}^n \to \{0,1\}$ and $i \in \{1, ..., n\}$, define the permutation generator $\Gamma_{g,i} : \{0,1\}^{m(n)} \times \{0,1\}^{2n} \to \{0,1\}^{2n}$ as $\Gamma_{g,i} = T_A$, where $A : \{0,1\}^{m(n)} \times \{0,1\}^n \to \{0,1\}^n$ is defined as

$$[A(y, x)]_r = \begin{cases} g(y, x) & \text{if } r = i \\ 0 & \text{if } r \neq i , \end{cases}$$

for all $y \in \{0,1\}^{m(n)}$ and $x \in \{0,1\}^n$.

Now, let $G \in NC^1$ be given and let $F : \{0,1\}^{p(n)} \times \{0,1\}^n \to \{0,1\}^n$ and $H : \{0,1\}^{m(n)} \to \{0,1\}^{p(n)}$ be as in Definition 4. In particular, the depth complexity of F over the basis $\{\wedge, \oplus, 1\}$ is $O(\log n)$. Let $(z_1, ..., z_{p(n)+n}) = (H(y), x)$.

We shall show that, for each $i \in \{1, ..., n\}$, $\Gamma_{[G]_i, i} \in DES[FAN\text{-}IN[2]]$. First, note that, for each $i \in \{1, ..., n\}$ and $j \in \{1, ..., p(n) + n\}$,

$$\Gamma_{1,i} \in DES[FAN\text{-}IN[0]] \subset DES[FAN\text{-}IN[2]]$$

and

$$\Gamma_{z_j, i} \in DES[FAN\text{-}IN[1]] \subset DES[FAN\text{-}IN[2]] .$$

Therefore, if the depth complexity of $[F]_i$ is 0 then $\Gamma_{[G]_i, i} \in DES[FAN\text{-}IN[2]]$. Also, for any two functions f_1 and f_2, it is straightforward to verify that the identities

$$\Gamma_{(f_1 \oplus f_2), i} = \Gamma_{f_1, i} \circ \Gamma_{f_2, i}$$

and

$$\Gamma_{(f_1 \wedge f_2),k} = \Phi_{i,j}^k \circ \Gamma_{f_1,i} \circ \Phi_{i,j}^k \circ \Gamma_{f_2,j} \circ \Phi_{i,j}^k \circ \Gamma_{f_1,i} \circ \Phi_{i,j}^k \circ \Gamma_{f_2,j} ,$$

for all $i, j, k \in \{1, ..., n\}$ with $i, j \neq k$, hold. Therefore, if the depth complexity of $[F]_i$ is d then, by recursively applying the above identities, $\Gamma_{[G]_i,i}$ is expressible as a composition of length $O(4^d)$ of elements of $DES[FAN\text{-}IN[2]]$. Therefore, since, for each $i \in \{1, ..., n\}$, the depth complexity of $[F]_i$ is $O(\log n)$, the composition is of polynomial length, so $\Gamma_{[G]_i,i} \in DES[FAN\text{-}IN[2]]$, as claimed.

Finally, since $\Gamma_{[G]_1,1}, \Gamma_{[G]_2,2}, ..., \Gamma_{[G]_n,n} \in DES[FAN\text{-}IN[2]]$, it follows that

$$T_G = \Gamma_{[G]_1,1} \circ \Gamma_{[G]_2,2} \circ \cdots \circ \Gamma_{[G]_n,n} \in DES[FAN\text{-}IN[2]] .$$

$\square$

In is conceivable that NC^1 is equivalent to $SPACE[O(\log n)]$ —or even P—but, given our current knowledge, such equivalences are considered unlikely. Thus, the following theorem extends Theorem 5.

Theorem 6: $DES[FAN\text{-}IN[2]] = DES[SPACE[\frac{1}{2}\log(\frac{n}{3})]]$.

Prior to proving Theorem 6, we prove the following lemma.

Lemma 7: If a function generator G^n is in $SPACE[w(n)]$ then it is expressible as $G(y,x) = F(H(y),x)$, where $H : \{0,1\}^{m(n)} \to \{0,1\}^{p(n)}$ is polynomial-time computable, and $F : \{0,1\}^{p(n)+n} \to \{0,1\}^n$ has the following property. For each $i \in \{1, ..., n\}$, there exists a sequence of $2^{w(n)} \times 2^{w(n)}$ matrices over $\{0, 1, z_1, ..., z_{p(n)+n}, \neg z_1, ..., \neg z_{p(n)+n}\}$, namely

$$M_1, M_2, ..., M_{t(n)}$$

(where $t(n) \in n^{O(1)}$), such that

$$[F(z_1, ..., z_{p(n)+n})]_i = [M_1 \cdot M_2 \cdot ... \cdot M_{t(n)}]_{1,1} ,$$

where the iterated matrix product on the right is defined relative to modulo 2 arithmetic.

Proof: The idea of the proof is to associate each configuration $s \in \{0,1\}^{w(n)}$ with a unique vector of length $2^{w(n)}$ that consists of a 1 in one position and 0s in all other positions. Then the transition functions for any computation are easily expressible in terms of the desired matrices.

More formally, for the function generator G, let $H : \{0,1\}^{m(n)} \to \{0,1\}^{p(n)}$, and $F : \{0,1\}^{p(n)+n} \to \{0,1\}^n$ be as in Definition 5. Fix $i \in \{1,...,n\}$ and let

$$\Pi_1, ..., \Pi_{t(n)} : \{0,1\} \times \{0,1\}^{w(n)} \to \{0,1\}^{w(n)} ,$$

and

$$\alpha_1, ..., \alpha_{t(n)} : \{0,1\}^{w(n)} \to \{1, ..., p(n) + n\}$$

be as in Definition 5 for the i-th output bit of F.

For $s \in \{0,1\}^{w(n)}$, associate the vector $\mu(s) \in \{0,1\}^{2^{w(n)}}$ as follows. For $r \in \{1, ..., 2^{w(n)}\}$,

$$[\mu(s)]_r = \begin{cases} 1 & \text{if } r = 1 + [s]_1 + 2[s]_2 + \cdots + 2^{w(n)-1}[s]_{w(n)} \\ 0 & \text{otherwise} . \end{cases}$$

Clearly, μ is a one-to-one mapping.

Now, for each $j \in \{1,...,t(n)\}$, we define M_j so as to simulate the effect that Π_j and α_j have on each $s \in \{0,1\}^{w(n)}$. For each $k \in \{1,...,2^{w(n)}\}$, the k-th row of M_j has the following form. If $\Pi_j(0, \mu^{-1}(k)) = \Pi_j(1, \mu^{-1}(k))$ then the row has a 1 in position $\mu\left(\Pi_j(0, \mu^{-1}(k))\right)$, and 0s in all other positions. Otherwise (if $\Pi_j(0, \mu^{-1}(k)) \neq \Pi_j(1, \mu^{-1}(k))$), the row has $z_{\alpha_j(\mu^{-1}(k))}$ in position $\mu\left(\Pi_j(1, \mu^{-1}(k))\right)$, and $\neg z_{\alpha_j(\mu^{-1}(k))}$, in position $\mu\left(\Pi_j(0, \mu^{-1}(k))\right)$, and 0s in all other positions. It is then straightforward to verify that, for all $s \in \{0,1\}^{w(n)}$,

$$\mu\left(\Pi_j(z_{\alpha_j(s)}, s)\right) = \mu(S) \cdot M_j .$$

Therefore, the final configuration of the computation is

$$s_{t(n)} = \mu^{-1}\left(\mu(0...0) \cdot M_1 \cdot M_2 \cdot ... \cdot M_{t(n)}\right),$$

and $s_{t(n)} = 0...0$ if and only if

$$1 = [[1\ 0\ ...\ 0] \cdot M_1 \cdot M_2 \cdot ... \cdot M_{t(n)}]_1 = [M_1 \cdot M_2 \cdot ... \cdot M_{t(n)}]_{1,1} ,$$

as required. $\square$

Proof of Theorem 6: It is sufficient to show that, for every function generator G that is in $SPACE[\frac{1}{2}\log(\frac{n}{3})]$, the permutation generator T_G is in $DES[FAN\text{-}IN[2]]$. The construction used here can be viewed as an extension of the construction of Theorem 5.

Let $G \in SPACE[\frac{1}{2}\log(\frac{n}{3})]$ be given, and let $H : \{0,1\}^{m(n)} \to \{0,1\}^{p(n)}$, and $F : \{0,1\}^{p(n)+n} \to \{0,1\}^n$ be as in Lemma 7. Let $(z_1, ..., z_{p(n)+n}) = (H(y), x)$.

For any $\sqrt{\frac{n}{3}} \times \sqrt{\frac{n}{3}}$ matrix M whose entries are polynomials over $(z_1, ..., z_{p(n)+n})$, define the permutation generators $\Lambda_M^1, \Lambda_M^2, \Lambda_M^3 : \{0,1\}^{m(n)} \times \{0,1\}^{2n} \to \{0,1\}^{2n}$ as follows. For $e \in \{1,2,3\}$, let $\Lambda_M^e = T_D$, where $D : \{0,1\}^{m(n)} \times \{0,1\}^n \to \{0,1\}^n$ is defined as

$$[D(y,x)]_r = \begin{cases} M_{\beta((r \bmod \frac{n}{3})+1)} & \text{if } 1 + (e-1)(\frac{n}{3}) \leq r \leq e(\frac{n}{3}) \\ 0 & \text{otherwise}, \end{cases}$$

for all $y \in \{0,1\}^{m(n)}$ and $x \in \{0,1\}^n$. Here,

$$\beta : \{1, ..., \tfrac{n}{3}\} \to \{1, ..., \sqrt{\tfrac{n}{3}}\} \times \{1, ..., \sqrt{\tfrac{n}{3}}\}$$

is the natural bijection defined as

$$\beta(r) = (((r-1) \bmod \sqrt{\tfrac{n}{3}}) + 1, ((r-1)\operatorname{div}\sqrt{\tfrac{n}{3}}) + 1) .$$

As in the proof of Theorem 5, it is sufficient to show that, for any $i \in \{1, ..., n\}$, $\Gamma_{[G]_{i,i}} \in DES[FAN\text{-}IN[2]]$. Let $i \in \{1, ..., n\}$ be given, and let $M_1, M_2, ..., M_{t(n)}$ be the corresponding $\sqrt{\frac{n}{3}} \times \sqrt{\frac{n}{3}}$ matrices over $\{0, 1, z_1, ..., z_{p(n)+n}, \neg z_1, ..., \neg z_{p(n)+n}\}$ that exist from the application of Lemma 7.

We shall show that, for each $e \in \{1,2,3\}$, $\Lambda_{M_1 \cdot M_2 \cdots M_{t(n)}}^e \in DES[FAN\text{-}IN[2]]$. First note that, for each $j \in \{1, ..., t(n)\}$, since the entries of M_j are in $\{0, 1, z_1, ..., z_{p(n)+n}, \neg z_1, ..., \neg z_{p(n)+n}\}$, it follows that $\Lambda_{M_j}^e \in DES[FAN\text{-}IN[1]] \subset DES[FAN\text{-}IN[2]]$ ($e \in \{1,2,3\}$).

At this point, we define the permutations $\Theta_1, \Theta_2, \Theta_3 : \{0,1\}^{2n} \to \{0,1\}^{2n}$. First, we introduce the following permutations in $DES[FAN\text{-}IN[2]]$. Let $\Phi_{i,j}^k : \{0,1\}^{2n} \to \{0,1\}^{2n}$ (for $i,j,k \in \{1, ..., n\}$) be as in the proof of Theorem 5. Also, define $\Upsilon_1, \Upsilon_2, \Upsilon_3 : \{0,1\}^{2n} \to \{0,1\}^{2n}$ as, for all $x \in \{0,1\}^n$, and $u, v, w \in \{0,1\}^{\frac{n}{3}}$,

$$\Upsilon_1(x, u, v, w) = (x, u, v, w)$$

$$\Upsilon_2(x, u, v, w) = (x, w, u, v)$$

$$\Upsilon_3(x, u, v, w) = (x, v, w, u) .$$

It is easily shown that $\Upsilon_1, \Upsilon_2, \Upsilon_3 \in DES[FAN\text{-}IN[2]]$. Finally, for $e \in \{1,2,3\}$, define $\Theta_e : \{0,1\}^{2n} \to \{0,1\}^{2n}$ as the composition

$$\text{for } a = 1 \text{ to } \sqrt{\tfrac{n}{3}} \left(\text{for } b = 1 \text{ to } \sqrt{\tfrac{n}{3}} \left(\Upsilon_e \circ \Phi_{\beta(a,1),\beta(1,b)+\frac{n}{3}}^{\beta(a,b)+2\frac{n}{3}} \circ \cdots \circ \Phi_{\beta(a,\sqrt{\frac{n}{3}}),\beta(\sqrt{\frac{n}{3}},b)+\frac{n}{3}}^{\beta(a,b)+2\frac{n}{3}} \circ \Upsilon_e^{-1} \right.\right.$$

Since $\Theta_1, \Theta_2, \Theta_3$ are polynomial-length compositions of elements of $DES[FAN\text{-}IN[2]]$, $\Theta_1, \Theta_2, \Theta_3 \in DES[FAN\text{-}IN[2]]$.

Now, the key part of our construction is the identity, for $e \in \{1, 2, 3\}$,

$$\Lambda_{M \cdot M'}^{(e+2)\bmod 3} = \Theta_e \circ \Lambda_{M'}^{(e+1)\bmod 3} \circ \Theta_e \circ \Lambda_M^e \circ \Theta_e \circ \Lambda_{M'}^{(e+1)\bmod 3} \circ \Theta_e \circ \Lambda_M^e .$$

By applying this identity recursively, and using the fact that, for each $j \in \{1, ..., t(n)\}$, $\Lambda_{M_j}^e \in DES[FAN\text{-}IN[2]]$ ($e \in \{1, 2, 3\}$), it follows that $\Lambda_{M_1 \cdot M_2 \cdot ... \cdot M_{t(n)}}^e \in DES[FAN\text{-}IN[2]]$ ($e \in \{1, 2, 3\}$).

Since

$$[F(z_1, ..., z_{p(n)+n})]_i = [M_1 \cdot M_2 \cdot ... \cdot M_{t(n)}]_{1,1} ,$$

it follows that

$$T_{[G]_i, i} = \Phi_{1+(e-1)(\frac{n}{3}), 1+(e-1)(\frac{n}{3})}^i \circ \Lambda_{M_1 \cdot M_2 \cdot ... \cdot M_{t(n)}}^e \circ \Phi_{1+(e-1)(\frac{n}{3}), 1+(e-1)(\frac{n}{3})}^i ,$$

whenever $i \notin \{1 + (e-1)(\frac{n}{3}), ..., e(\frac{n}{3})\}$ and, therefore, $T_{[G]_i, i} \in DES[FAN\text{-}IN[2]]$.

Finally, since $\Gamma_{[G]_1, 1}, \Gamma_{[G]_2, 2}, ..., \Gamma_{[G]_n, n} \in DES[FAN\text{-}IN[2]]$, it follows that

$$T_G = \Gamma_{[G]_1, 1} \circ \Gamma_{[G]_2, 2} \circ \cdots \circ \Gamma_{[G]_n, n} \in DES[FAN\text{-}IN[2]] .$$

$\square$

It would be interesting to extend this work to showing that $DES[FAN\text{-}IN[2]] = DES[B]$ for more powerful complexity classes B. In particular, the following problem is of interest.

Open Problem: *Determine whether or not $DES[FAN\text{-}IN[2]] = DES[P]$.*

4 Further Work

We can extend our results to function generators G in $SPACE[c \cdot \log n]$, for arbitrary $c > 0$, and for function generators in a nonuniform version of *nondeterministic* logarithmic space. We cannot show that for such function generators G, $T_G \in DES[FAN\text{-}IN[2]]$, but we can show that, given a pseudorandom function generator in one of these classes, we can nevertheless construct a pseudorandom permutation generator in $DES[FAN\text{-}IN[2]]$. Some of these results are explained in [3] and will appear in the final paper.

5 Acknowledgement

Thanks to Charles Rackoff for suggesting this direction of research.

References

[1] D. A. Barrington, "Bounded-Width Polynomial-Size Branching Programs Recognize Exactly Those Languages in NC^1," *J. Computer System Sci.* Vol. 38, pp. 150–164, 1989.

[2] M. Ben-Or, and R. Cleve, "Computing Algebraic Formulas Using a Constant Number of Registers," *Proc. 20th Ann. ACM Symp. on Theory of Computing*, pp. 254–257, 1988.

[3] R. Cleve, *Methodologies for Designing Block Ciphers and Cryptographic Protocols (Part I)*, Ph.D. Thesis, University of Toronto, 1989.

[4] D. Coppersmith, and E. Grossman, "Generators for Certain Alternating Groups with Applications to Cryptography," *SIAM J. Appl. Math.*, pp. 624-627, 1975.

[5] D. Coppersmith, "Cryptography," *IBM J. Res. Develop.*, Vol. 31, No. 2, pp. 244–248, 1987.

[6] S. Even, and O. Goldreich, "DES-Like Functions Can Generate the Alternating Group," *IEEE Trans. on Information Theory*, pp. 863–865, 1983.

[7] Luby, M., and C. Rackoff, "How to Construct Pseudorandom Permutations From Pseudorandom Functions," *SIAM J. Comput.*, Vol. 17, No. 2, pp. 373–386, 1988.

[8] E. Biham, and A. Shamir, "Differential Cryptanalysis of DES-like Cryptosystems," these proceedings, 1990.

THE REDOC II CRYPTOSYSTEM

Thomas W. Cusick
Department of Mathematics
State University of New York at Buffalo
Buffalo, New York 14214
York 14701

Michael C. Wood
Cryptech, Inc.
508 Lafayette Street
Jamestown, New

ABSTRACT. *A new cryptosystem called REDOC II is introduced. Analysis of a miniature (one—round) version of this system is given.*

INTRODUCTION.

This report discusses the REDOC II cryptosystem developed by Michael C. Wood and the one round attack performed on the cryptosystem by Dr. Thomas Cusick.

REDOC II is a high—speed Shannon confusion diffusion arithmetic cryptosystem capable of enciphering 800 kilobits per second on a 20 MHz clock. The current implementation involves a 10—round procedure performed on a 10—byte (80 bit) data block.

The REDOC II cryptosystem possesses exceptional cryptographic strength. The most direct attack developed to date against a single round requires approximately 2^{30} operations for the original REDOC II implementation. This attack is discussed in full detail below.

Recently, design modifications have been made to the REDOC II cryptosystem. While these changes do not affect the encryption speed, the work factor for a single round attack appears to be greatly increased. Presently, an upper bound for the work factor for a single round modified REDOC II stands at 2^{44} operations.

As with the DES, the work factor for REDOC II appears to multiply with each successive round. Achieving such an unusually high work factor after one round gives strong evidence for extraordinary cryptographic strength to be possessed by the complete 10 round system.

With the promise of great strength and efficiency, REDOC II cryptosystems warrant further investigation.

BRIEF DESCRIPTION OF REDOC II.

Figure 1 summarizes the REDOC II system. As shown there, REDOC II is a block cipher which operates on ten–byte plaintext blocks. In Figure 1, R is the round number. Carrying out ten rounds (as shown in Figure 1) on a given plaintext block produces the ciphertext. The permutation, substitution, and enclave tables are all chosen prior to implementing the cryptosystem. The key table and mask table are generated after the cryptosystem is implemented.

The original REDOC II contains 128 permutation table entries [see Sample Table 1]. Each entry specifies a position change for each of the 10 bytes to be enciphered. For example, if perm 0 were performed on data block : **90 27 11 41 114 117 56 33 72 122** : the result would be : **90 117 72 122 56 27 11 33 41 114** :. Thus, with REDOC II, permutations are performed on the byte, rather than the bit, level.

Sixteen substitution table entries were included in the original REDOC II [see Sample Table 2]. Each entry specifies a new value for every possible value in the alphabet space.

The enclave function is a procedure unique to the REDOC family of cryptosystems. The original REDOC II contained 32 enclave table entries, each with four subsections (a, b, c, & d) [see Sample Table 3]. Each subsection specifies how the enclave function will be performed on a half block (five bytes). Subsections 'a' and 'b' alter the right half block while 'c' and 'd' direct the procedure for the left block.

Figure 2 illustrates how the enclave procedure transforms an entire 10 byte data block. First, the block is divided in half (left block and right block). The right block is then transformed by subsection 'a' of the enclave entry chosen. The right block is then transformed again by subsection 'b'. The resulting right block is then exclusive or–ed with the original left block to produce a new left block. This left block is then transformed by subsection 'c' , which in turn is altered again by subsection 'd' . The resulting left block is then exclusive or–ed with the right block to produce a new right block. The two blocks are then combined yielding the new 10 byte data block.

Figure 3 illustrates how each subsection functions to alter a half block. Each subsection consists of five rows and three columns. For encryption, the tables are read row by row from top to bottom. The first value in each row specifies the position of the byte to be changed. The second and third values specify the postions of the bytes used to transform the byte specified by the first value. Transformation is accomplished by replacing the first byte specified by the sum of the three bytes (mod 128). The original REDOC II cryptosystem only encrypted the first 7 bits of each byte. Thus the alphabet space for each byte ranges from 0 to 127. Therefore, all addition is performed by modulo 128.

After the permutation, substitution, and enclave tables are chosen, a key must be selected. The original key length for REDOC II was 10 bytes. However, since only the first seven bits were used, the effective key size was 70 bits. However, REDOC II can support a key size ranging from 70 to 17,920 bits. Current implementations use a 140 bit key.

INITIALIZATION

The REDOC II cryptosystem must be initialized every time a new key is selected. The initialization process consists of the creation of the key table and the Mask table.

In the original REDOC II, 128 ten byte keys are generated from the installed ten byte key [see Sample Table 4]. These keys are created from a series of one way functions performed on the installed and previously generated keys. Since the attack on a one round system does not rely on the key generation methodology, a detailed description is omitted from this paper.

The Mask table consists of 4 ten byte blocks [see Sample Table 5]. The Masks are generated by exclusive or–ing a large number of values from the key table. The first Mask is created from the first thirty–two keys in the key table. The second Mask is created from the next thirty–two, and so on.

The Masks are used to choose which entry in the function and key tables will be chosen. The first Mask is used to choose the permutation entry. The second Mask chooses the keys from the key table. Mask three selects an enclave entry, and Mask four selects a substitution entry.

Each of the ten bytes for every Mask corresponds to the round of encryption. The first byte of each Mask is used during round one. The second byte is used during round two. For each round, the corresponding byte is used.

After the key table and Mask table are created, encryption and decryption can begin.

REDOC II ENCRYPTION

Figure 1 contains an overview of the REDOC II encryption process. For each round, entries from the function and key tables are determined by the values of at least one byte in the internal ciphertext and one byte from the Mask table . For each round:

1. An entry from the permutation table is selected.
2. The internal ciphertext is permuted according to the selected entry.
3. A key is selected from the key table.
4. Each byte in the internal ciphertext is exclusive or–ed with the corresponding byte in the key except the byte used in selecting the key.
5. Another key is selected from the key table.
6. Each byte in the internal ciphertext is exclusive or–ed with the corresponding byte in the key except the byte used in selecting the key.
7. An enclave entry is selected.
8. The internal ciphertext is transformed by the selected enclave procedure.
9. An entry from the substitution table is selected.
10. Every byte in the internal ciphertext is substituted except the byte used in choosing the entry
11. Another entry from the substitution table is selected.
12. Every byte in the internal ciphertext is substituted except the byte used in choosing the entry.

NOMENCLATURE

A : Block 'A'

A_w = Byte 'w' of Block 'A' $\{0 \leq w \leq 10\}$

P_w : Permutation entry 'w'

$P_w(A) = B$: Perform Permutation 'w' on 'A' to produce 'B' $\{0 \leq w \leq 127\}$

K_w : Denotes KEY 'w' $\{0 \leq w \leq 127\}$

$K_{w,y}$: Denotes byte 'y' of Key 'w' e.g. fourth byte of Key 32 = $K_{32,4}$

$K_{w,y}$ xor A_y where $\{y=z$ and $0 \leq y \leq 10\} = B$: XOR every byte in block 'A' with corresponding byte in Key 'w' except for byte 'z' to produce block 'B'.

E_w : Denotes Enclave entry 'w'

$E_w(A) = B$: Perform Enclave as directed by table 'w' on Block A producing output B

S_w : Denotes Substitution table 'w'

$S_w(A_y)$ where $\{y=z$ and $0 \leq y \leq 10\} = B$: Substitute the corresponding value in table 'w' for the corresponding byte value of every byte in the block except byte 'z'.

SUM $(A) = w$: Sum all the values of block 'A' (mod 128) to obtain value 'w'.

MATHEMATICAL DESCRIPTION OF ROUNDS

Input block 'A' for round 'r'

1. SUM (A) xor $Mask_{1,r} = w$
2. $P_w(A) = B$
3. B_r xor $Mask_{2,r} = W$
4. $K_{w,y}$ xor B_y where $\{y=r$ and $0 \leq y \leq 10\} = C$
5. $X = (r \bmod 10) + 1$
6. C_x xor $Mask_{2,x} = W$
7. $K_{w,y}$ xor C_y where $\{y=r$ and $0 \leq y \leq 10\} = D$
8. D_r xor $Mask_{3,r} = W$
9. $E_w(D) = E$
10. E_r xor $Mask_{4,r} = W$

11. $S_w(E_y)$ where $\{y=z$ and $0 \leq y \leq 10\} = F$

12. $(r \bmod 10) + 1 = x$

13. F_x xor $Mask_{4,x} = W$

14. $S_w(F_y)$ where $\{y=x$ and $0 \leq y \leq 10\} = G$

Output Block 'G';

[Output Block 'G' becomes the Input Block 'A' of the next round.]

ATTACK ON ONE–ROUND VERSION OF REDOC II

For convenience of reference, we divide up the one–round REDOC algorithm into "stages", which we label as follows:

Stage 1 – Variable permutation

Stage 2 – First variable key add

Stage 3 – Second variable key add

Stage 4 – Enclave

Stage 5 – First variable substitution

Stage 6 – Second variable substitution

We let $B = (B_1, B_2, ..., B_{10})$ denote a typical plaintext block of ten 7–bit bytes B_i and we let $C = (C_1, C_2, ..., C_{10})$ denote a typical ciphertext block of ten 7–bit bytes C_i.

We begin our attack by assuming that we have enough plaintext blocks and corresponding ciphertext so that we can choose 256 plaintext blocks B_i $(1 \leq i \leq 256)$ with

(i)   values of B_1 and B_2 identical in all 256 blocks

(ii)   values of $B_1 + ... + B_{10}$ mod 128 give each of the 128 possibilities exactly twice.

The purpose of (i) is to guarantee that the two keys used in stages 2 and 3 of the REDOC encryption are the same for all 256 blocks B_i (by definition of the

REDOC algorithm). The purpose of (ii) is to guarantee that at least one of the variable permutations which keep B_1 and B_2 fixed is used twice in the set of 256 encryptions of blocks B_i. We assume for definiteness that there are exactly 2 permutations which fix B_1 and B_2, namely permutations #8 and #29. It will be clear from what follows that our attack does not depend on this specific feature of the particular permutation table which we happen to be using. Our use here of a particular property of permutations #8 and #29 merely makes it easier to describe the attack.

We let C_i $(1 \leq i \leq 256)$ denote the ciphertext blocks corresponding to the plaintext blocks B_i. We let

$$W_j = (W_{j,1}, W_{j,2}, ..., W_{j,10}) \quad (j = 1 \text{ or } 2)$$

denote the two keys which are used at stages 2 and 3, respectively, of the encryptions of the blocks B_i. *If* we have chosen a block B_i such that permutation #8 or #29 is used in stage 1 of the encryption, then the result at each of the first 3 stages is as follows:

$$
\begin{array}{lll}
\text{Stage 1:} & B_1, B_2, B_{3,p}, B_{4,p}, ..., B_{10,p} & (p = 8 \text{ or } 29) \\
(1) \quad \text{Stage 2:} & B_1, B_2 \oplus W_{1,2}, B_{3,p} \oplus W_{1,3}, ..., B_{10,p} \oplus W_{1,10} \\
\text{Stage 3:} & B_1 \oplus W_{2,1}, B_2 \oplus W_{1,2}, B_{3,p} \oplus W_{1,3} \oplus W_{2,3}, ..., B_{10,p} \oplus \\
& W_{1,10} \oplus W_{2,10}
\end{array}
$$

(Here $\oplus$ is component-wise addition mod 2, i.e. xor.) Here the value of p indicates which of the permutations #8 or #29 is actually used at stage 1.

The object of our attack is to locate, among the 256 blocks B_i which we shall denote by

$$B_i = (B_1^{(i)}, B_2^{(i)}, ..., B_{10}^{(i)}) \quad (1 \leq i \leq 256),$$

two blocks which encipher using the same key values $W_{1,2}$ and $W_{2,1}$ and the same variable permutation (which will be #8 or #29). The attack proceeds by applying a process which we shall call "reversal" to each of the 256 blocks of ciphertext C_i . Reversal consists in taking a ciphertext block C_i after stage 6 of REDOC, then inverting the two variable substitutions of stages 5 and 6 in all $16^2 = 2^8 = 256$ possible ways, and finally applying to each of these blocks the inverse of each of the 32 possible enclaves of stage 4. Thus applying reversal to a block C_i gives $2^{13} = 8{,}192$ blocks which are candidates for the actual block which results at Stage 3 in (1) above when the corresponding plaintext block B_i is enciphered.

Only the unique candidate which corresponds to the actual choice of the enclave and the two variable substitutions at Stages 4, 5 and 6 of the encryption is the correct one.

It is clear from the form of the block B_i after Stage 3 of the encryption process (see (1) above) that each candidate block arising from reversal of block C_i uniquely determines values for $W_{2,1}$ and $W_{1,2}$ (of course these values may be incorrect if the candidate is not the right one). Thus we can associate with each candidate block arising from reversal of C_i a triple $(W_{1,2}(i,j,n), W_{2,1}(i,j,n), n)$, where n $(1 \leq n \leq 32)$ is the number of the enclave whose inverse is used to obtain the candidate and j $(1 \leq j \leq 256)$ is an index which identifies the pair of substitutions whose inverses are used to obtain the candidate. The grouping of the triples according to the enclave used is important for the analysis which follows. Using the above notation for the triples, we can schematically show the reversal process on the blocks of ciphertext as follows:

$$(W_{1,2}(1,j,n), W_{2,1}(1,j,n), n) \qquad\qquad (W_{1,2}(256,j,n), W_{2,1}(256,j,n), n)$$

(2) $\qquad\qquad\qquad \uparrow \qquad\qquad \cdots \qquad\qquad \uparrow$

$$C_1 \qquad\qquad\qquad\qquad\qquad\qquad C_{256}$$

Given two identical triples in the list of $256 \times 2^{13} = 2^{21}$ triples generated by the reversal (2), we set the corresponding 20 bytes in the two blocks associated with the two triples equal to the respective 20 bytes which arise at stage 3 (see (1) above) in the encryption of the corresponding two plaintext blocks B_i . To do this we must guess the needed two values of p in (1), which is possible in 4 different ways. Thus we obtain 4 systems of 20 linear equations in the 20 unknowns $W_{1,j}$ and $W_{2,j}$ ($1 \le j \le 10$). Suppose that the two identical triples in (2) correspond to ciphertexts C_i and C_j, and suppose that the reversal process which leads to the two identical triples gives the blocks

$$(d_{i,1}, d_{i,2}, ..., d_{i,10})$$

and

$$(d_{j,1}, d_{j,2}, ..., d_{j,10}),$$

respectively. Now each of the 4 systems of 20 linear equations has the form

$$B_1^{(i)} \oplus W_{2,1} = d_{i,1}$$

$$B_2^{(i)} \oplus W_{1,2} = d_{i,2}$$
$$B_{3,p}^{(i)} \oplus W_{1,3} \oplus W_{2,3} = d_{i,3}$$

$$\cdots\cdots\cdots\cdots\cdots$$

(3) $\qquad\qquad B_{10,p}^{(i)} \oplus W_{1,10} \oplus W_{2,10} = d_{i,10}$

$$B_1^{(j)} \oplus W_{2,1} = d_{j,1}$$

$$B_2^{(j)} \oplus W_{1,2} = d_{j,2}$$

$$B_{3,p}^{(j)} \oplus W_{1,3} \oplus W_{2,3} = d_{j,3}$$

$$\cdots\cdots\cdots\cdots\cdots$$

$$B_{10,p}^{(j)} \oplus W_{1,10} \oplus W_{2,10} = d_{j,10}$$

We shall analyze a typical system of equations (3) later, but first we show that we can reduce the number of candidate permutation pairs to 2 instead of 4 for each pair of identical triples in (2) and also reduce the number of identical triples that need to be considered, by a closer analysis. In particular, suppose we have two identical triples $(W_{1,2}, W_{2,1}, n)$ corresponding to ciphertext blocks C_i and C_j. If the encipherments of the corresponding plaintext blocks B_i and B_j actually both use permutation #8 or both use permutation #29 at stage 1, then we have

$$(4) \qquad B_1^{(i)} + ... + B_{10}^{(i)} \equiv B_1^{(j)} + ... + B_{10}^{(j)} \bmod 128$$

If, on the other hand, when B_i and B_j are enciphered permutation #8 is used at stage 1 for one of the encipherments and permutation #29 is used for the other, then we have

$$(5) \qquad 8 \oplus 29 = (B_1^{(i)} + ... + B_{10}^{(i)} \bmod 128) \oplus (B_1^{(j)} + ... + B_{10}^{(j)} \bmod 128) = 21 \ .$$

Thus a pair of identical triples in (2) can only lead to a genuine system of equations (3) if either (4) or (5) is true; this will allow us to eliminate some pairs of identical triples from further consideration. If (4) is true for a given pair of identical triples, then we need only consider the cases where $p = 8$ for both of the corresponding encipherments or where $p = 29$ for both of the encipherments. Similarly, if (5) is true for the given pair of triples, we need only consider the two cases where $p = 8$ for one of the encipherments and $p = 29$ for the other. Thus each pair of identical triples in (2) leads to at most two systems of equations (3).

Now we need a count of the number of pairs of identical triples in (2). For each fixed n, there are $256 \times 2^8 = 2^{16}$ triples in (2) but there are only 2^{14} distinct triples for any given n, so there will be many duplicated triples. However, the maximum possible number of pairs of distinct plaintext blocks B_i and B_j which satisfy one of the necessary conditions (4) or (5) is 768. This follows since, for each B_i $(1 \leq i \leq 256)$, if we have

$$(6) \qquad B_1^{(i)} + ... + B_{10}^{(i)} \equiv m \bmod 128 \quad (0 \leq m \leq 127)$$

then there is a unique B_j such that (6) holds with $i = j$ and the same m; and there is a unique pair B_h, B_k such that (5) holds with j equal to h or k. (Here we are using our initial assumption (ii) about the 256 plaintext blocks B_i.) Now any of the 6 possible pairs chosen from the set $\{B_h, B_i, B_j, B_k\}$ will satisfy either (4) or (5) and this gives ≤ 768 distinct pairs as i varies, $1 \leq i \leq 256$.

Let us consider one of the 768 pairs – say B_i and B_j – of the plaintext blocks for which (4) or (5) is satisfied. In the corresponding system of equations (3), we must have $B_1^{(i)} = B_1^{(j)}$ and $B_2^{(i)} = B_2^{(j)}$ by our assumption (i), so the system is inconsistent unless we also have $d_{i,1} = d_{j,1}$ and $d_{i,2} = d_{j,2}$. If the pairs $d_{j,1}$, $d_{j,2}$ were randomly distributed in our 768 pairs, the probability of matching the pair $d_{i,1}$, $d_{i,2}$ would be $768/128^2$, i.e. we would not expect to find any matches.

However, by our assumptions (i) and (ii) we know that exactly 4 of the encryptions of our 256 blocks B use either permutation #8 or permutation #29. Suppose the set $\{B_h, B_i, B_j, B_k\}$ of the previous paragraph corresponds to these blocks B. Then by the discussion in the previous paragraph this set gives 6 pairs of distinct blocks B which must give consistent systems of equations of form (3). Thus it is very likely that exactly 6 of the 768 pairs give consistent systems of equations of form (3), and these systems will involve just 4 of the 256 blocks B. Thus we have determined the values of

$$(7) \qquad W_{1,2}, W_{2,1}, W_{1,3} \oplus W_{2,3}, W_{1,4} \oplus W_{2,4}, ..., W_{1,10} \oplus W_{2,10}.$$

By the definition of REDOC decryption, the number of the variable substitution at stage 6 is determined by the ciphertext and the mask byte $Mask_{4,1}$; the number of the variable substitution at stage 5 is determined by the ciphertext and $Mask_{4,1}$; and the number of the enclave at stage 4 is simply $Mask_{3,1}$. Since we know the enclave number and the variable substitution numbers corresponding to the systems (3) which determine the numbers in (7), we can also determine

$$(8) \qquad Mask_{3,1} \text{ and } Mask_{4,1}.$$

Since the number of the variable permutation at stage 1 is given by

$$(B_1 + \ldots + B_{10} \bmod 128) \oplus \text{Mask}_{1,1},$$

we can also determine $\text{Mask}_{1,1}$ from the known fact that the encryptions of the blocks B_h, B_i, B_j, B_k above use either permutation #8 or permutation #29.

An upper bound for the number of operations needed to reach this point is $2^{29} \approx 5 \times 10^8$. We arrive at this number as follows: We estimate that 150 is an upper bound for the number of operations needed to carry out an inverse enclave and two inverse substitutions. Thus at most $150 \times 2^{21} < 3.2 \times 10^8$ operations are needed to produce the list of 2^{21} triples needed for the reversals in (2). By our work above, we must examine at most 768 ciphertext pairs C_i, C_j in order to find identical triples in the list of 2^{21} triples. For each such ciphertext pair, we must look for matches in 32 pairs of sets of 2^8 triples; these 32 pairs arise because we need only try to match triples with the same enclave number in (2), and there are 2^{13} triples associated with each C_i in (2). We can estimate that checking one such pair of sets takes $\leq 2^{12}$ operations. Thus checking all 32 pairs of sets for the ≤ 768 ciphertext pairs can be done in $\leq 768 \times 2^{17} \approx 10^8$ operations. Finally, testing for consistency of the systems (3) will require few operations. This gives our bound of 2^{29} operations.

We note that 2^{29} operations could be done in about 30 seconds on an inexpensive 20 megahertz personal computer. The attack to this point could be done in parallel with many processors (see (2) for a natural use of 256 processors) and so could be greatly speeded up by a large investment in hardware.

Stage 1 — Variable permutation number is $(B_1 + \ldots + B_{10} \bmod 128) \oplus \text{Mask}_{1,1}$

Stage 2 — Key number is $B_1 \oplus \text{Mask}_{2,1}$

Stage 3 — Key number is $B_2 \oplus \text{Mask}_{2,1}$

Stage 4 — Enclave number is $\text{Mask}_{3,1}$

Stage 5 — Variable substitution number is $(\text{Byte 1} \oplus \text{Mask}_{4,1}) \bmod 32$

Stage 6 — Variable substitution number is $(\text{Byte 2} \oplus \text{Mask}_{4,1}) \bmod 32$

Table 1. Use of mask values in one—round REDOC

Table 1 shows that, since we know the mask values in (8), we can apply the reversal process to any ciphertext block $(C_1, ..., C_{10})$ and obtain the numerical values of the ten bytes in the stage 3 block of the encipherment of the corresponding plaintext block $(B_1, ..., B_{10})$. Since we also know $Mask_{1,1}$, the block at stage 3 will have the form (see (1) above)

(9) $B_{p(1)} \oplus W_{j,1}, B_{p(2)} \oplus W_{i,2}, B_{p(3)} \oplus W_{i,3} \oplus W_{j,3}, ..., B_{p(10)} \oplus W_{i,10} \oplus W_{j,10}$

where $(p(1), ..., p(10))$ is a certain permutation of $(1, ..., 10)$, and i and j are the numbers of the keys used at stages 2 and 3, respectively. Here and in all that follows we slightly change our earlier notation and let

$$W_j = (W_{j,1}, W_{j,2}, ..., W_{j,10}) \quad (0 \le j \le 127)$$

denote the j–th key in the REDOC key table. Thus when we convert (7) to our new notation, we see that our work above has determined the values of

(10) $\qquad W_{j,1}, W_{i,2}, W_{i,3} \oplus W_{j,3}, ..., W_{i,10} \oplus W_{j,10}$

with $i = I$ and $j = J$, where I and J are certain key numbers which we do not know (of course we do know that

(11) $\qquad I = B_1 \oplus Mask_{2,1}$ and $J = B_2 \oplus Mask_{2,1}$,

where B_1 and B_2 are the special values from the assumption (i) made at the beginning of our attack).

It is evident from (9) that if we know the key numbers i and j being used, and if we know the values for the ten bytes in (10) above, then we can immediately recover the plaintext block $(B_1, ..., B_{10})$ from knowledge of the values of the 10 bytes in (9), as follows: We xor the known values in (10) with the 10 bytes in (9) and thus recover the values of $B_{p(1)}, ..., B_{p(10)}$. Then we compute the number

$$(B_{p(1)} + ... + B_{p(10)} \bmod 128) \oplus Mask_{1,1}$$

of the permutation $(p(1), ..., p(10))$ (since we know the value of $Mask_{1,1}$); now by consulting the REDOC permutation table we invert this permutation and recover $B_1, ..., B_{10}$.

It is now clear that any ciphertext block whose corresponding plaintext happens to begin with the same bytes B_1 and B_2 that appear in (11) can be immediately decrypted by the above procedure. Furthermore, if we can produce a table of values of the 10 bytes in (10) for a large number of pairs (i, j) of key numbers, then we can very quickly decrypt a large number of blocks of ciphertext. We simply apply the reversal process to the ciphertext blocks and so obtain the values of the bytes in (9). Then we xor the bytes in (9) with values of the bytes in (10) for various pairs (i, j). Each xor gives a candidate for the bytes $B_{p(1)}, ...,$ $B_{p(10)}$ and also determines the permutation number in stage 1, so we can immediately tell if we have sensible plaintext. If we do not get sensible plaintext, we continue trying entries from the sum table until the plaintext emerges or until we run out of pairs (i,j) to try; the larger our table is, the less likely it is that the latter possibility occurs. Even if the latter possibility does occur, we are defeated only for the single block under consideration.

Since most of the bytes in (10) are sums of key bytes rather than actual key bytes, let us call a table of values of the 10 bytes in (10) for a large number of pairs (i, j) of key numbers, a *sum table*. Using plaintext blocks **B** and corresponding ciphertext blocks **C**, we can rapidly produce a large sum table, as follows: We apply the reversal process to all of the ciphertext blocks in our list of known plaintext and ciphertext. Each plaintext block

$$B^{(1)} = (B_1^{(1)}, B_2^{(1)}, ..., B_{10}^{(1)})$$

will give values of the 10 bytes in (10) for key numbers

$$(12) \qquad i = B_1^{(1)} \oplus Mask_{2,1} \text{ and } j = B_2^{(1)} \oplus Mask_{2,1}.$$

It is easy to make a large sum table even from modest amounts of known plaintext and ciphertext because, for example, if we know the values for $W_{i,3} \oplus W_{j,3}$ and $W_{i,3} \oplus W_{k,3}$, then we immediately have the value of $W_{j,3} \oplus W_{k,3}$ by xor.

We do not know the value of $Mask_{2,1}$, but we do not need this in order to produce our sum table, or to use the sum table in decrypting REDOC ciphertext. We simply arrange the entries in the sum table according to the blocks $B_1^{(1)}$ and $B_2^{(1)}$ instead of the actual key numbers (12).

The creation of a large sum table in the last part of the attack certainly takes less time than the first part of the attack in which the mask values in (8) were found. A generous upper bound on the extra time involved is to say that the total time is doubled. It is clear that once the sum table has been created, decryption of given ciphertext can be done very rapidly (i.e., the vast majority of the effort in the attack is setting up the sum table).

It is interesting to note that in attacking the one–round REDOC we do **not** need to reconstruct the key table, and indeed we do not need to find any of the keys in the key table; we only need a large sum table as described above. It follows that complicating the process by which the key table is generated will not strengthen one–round REDOC.

Sample Table 1
Permutation Table

Original	=	1	2	3	4	5	6	7	8	9	10
Perm 0	=	1	6	7	9	10	2	5	8	3	4
Perm 1	=	10	4	8	3	1	7	2	9	5	6
Perm 2	=	1	6	4	9	8	5	10	2	3	7
Perm 3	=	9	8	3	4	5	10	6	1	7	2
. . .											
Perm 86	=	9	7	2	6	5	8	3	10	1	4
Perm 87	=	5	3	8	1	9	7	10	2	4	6
. . .											
Perm 126	=	9	8	3	7	1	10	5	6	2	4
Perm 127	=	7	8	5	10	9	3	4	2	1	6

Sample Table 2
Substitution Table

Original Value	Sub 0	Sub 1	Sub 4	Sub 10	Sub 14	Sub 15
0	90	47	25	66	73	0
1	46	89	51	13	36	52
2	66	87	103	31	107	44
3	21	20	116	7	43	83
. . .	. . .	. . .	. . .	. . .	. . .	. . .
126	24	14	105	114	77	6
127	122	62	11	63	49	79

Sample Table 3
Enclave Table

	a	b	c	d
Entry 0:	5 2 3	3 5 2	5 4 2	5 4 2
	4 3 1	1 3 5	4 3 1	2 5 1
	2 5 4	2 4 1	1 5 3	1 3 5
	1 4 5	5 1 4	3 2 5	3 2 4
	3 1 2	4 2 3	2 1 4	4 1 3
Entry 1:	3 1 2	3 2 5	4 2 1	4 2 3
	4 3 1	5 1 4	3 4 5	5 3 1
	2 5 4	2 4 3	5 1 4	2 1 5
	5 2 3	4 3 1	1 3 2	3 5 4
	1 4 5	1 5 2	2 5 3	1 4 2
...	...	...	...	...
Entry 31:	2 4 1	2 4 3	1 5 3	4 1 5
	3 5 4	4 1 2	2 4 1	3 5 2
	5 1 3	3 5 4	4 3 2	1 4 3
	1 2 5	5 2 1	5 2 4	2 3 4
	4 3 2	1 3 5	3 1 5	5 2 1

Sample Table 4
Key Table

KEY	0	=	0	34	5	63	9	73	74	107	109	33
KEY	1	=	10	62	48	85	32	101	8	0	63	56
KEY	2	=	26	59	75	97	33	80	8	6	73	26
...												
KEY	107	=	36	123	45	10	55	59	109	45	98	24
...												
KEY	118	=	95	25	48	47	1	20	117	55	19	67
...												
KEY	126	=	62	110	70	27	124	31	119	97	9	2
KEY	127	=	11	54	25	87	107	73	4	118	62	34

Sample Table 5
Mask Table

Mask 1	=	48	2	121	18	60	105	33	50	11	60
Mask 2	=	26	78	24	72	69	13	77	43	9	99
Mask 3	=	64	113	72	61	37	13	49	71	24	60
Mask 4	=	104	62	69	87	18	31	102	101	32	125

561

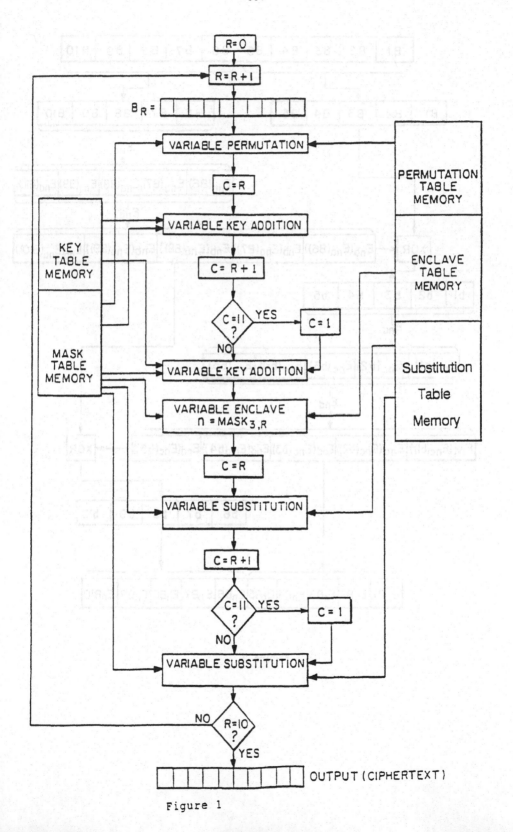

Figure 1

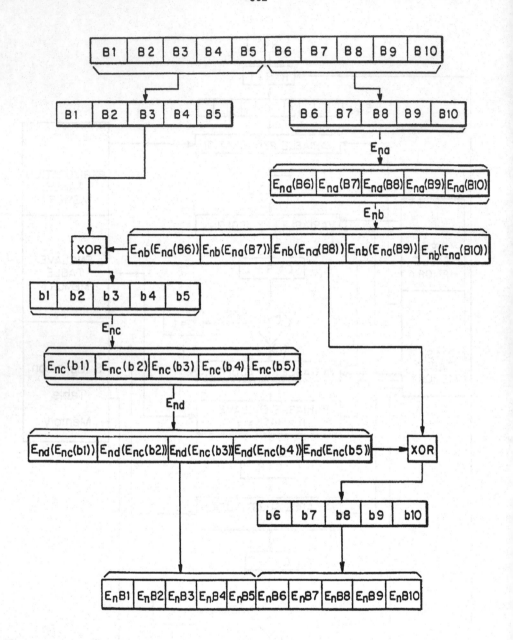

Figure 2

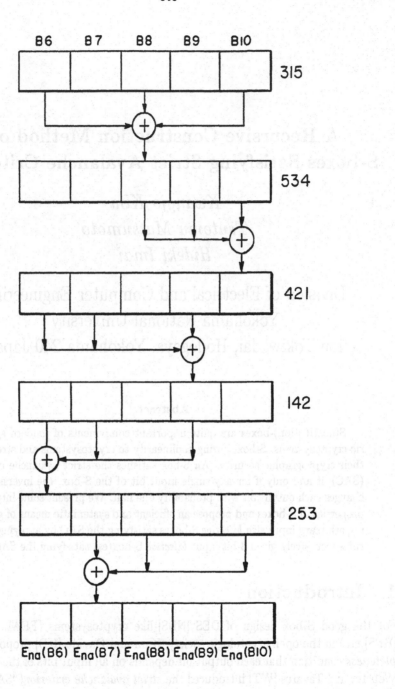

Figure 3

A Recursive Construction Method of S-boxes Satisfying Strict Avalanche Criterion

Kwangjo Kim

Tsutomu Matsumoto

Hideki Imai

Division of Electrical and Computer Engineering

Yokohama National University

156 Tokiwadai, Hodogaya, Yokohama 240 Japan

Abstract

S(ubstitution)-boxes are quite important components of modern symmetric cryptosystems. S-boxes bring nonlinearity to cryptosystems and strengthen their cryptographic security. An S-box satisfies the strict avalanche criterion (SAC), if and only if for any single input bit of the S-box, the inversion of it changes each output bit with probability one half. We present some interesting properties of S-boxes and propose an efficient and systematic means of generating arbitrary input size *bijective* S-boxes satisfying the SAC by applying simple rules recursively given 3-bit input *bijective* S-box(es) satisfying the SAC.

1   Introduction

For the good S-box design of DES [NBS]-like cryptosystems (FEAL [MSS],LOKI [BPS],etc) in the open cryptologic society, Kam and Davida [KD] proposed the *completeness* condition that each output bit depends on all input bits of the substitution. Webster and Tavares [WT] introduced the *strict avalanche criterion*("SAC") in order to combine the notions of the *completeness* and the *avalanche effect* [Fe]. Moreover, Forré [Fo] discussed the Walsh spectral properties of S-boxes satisfying the SAC and extended the concept of SAC to the subfunctions obtained from the original function by keeping one or more input bits constant, in order to prevent partial approximation cryptanalysis. Lloyd [Ll] re-stated the Forré's extended SAC and suggested the counting functions satisfying a higher order SAC.

Some results [GR],[Ay] were published to design S-boxes by randomly selecting from all possible reversible transformations. Recently, Pieprzyk [Pi] has proposed one construction method of S-box satisfying maximum nonlinearity[1] by exponentiation over $GF(2^n)$.

However in the open literature there are sparse publications concerning the systematic design methods for the generation of S-boxes satisfying the SAC. The main purpose of this paper is to suggest the properties of S-boxes satisfying the SAC and to propose the recursive construction methods of S-boxes satisfying the SAC.

2 Basic Definitions

We summarize here the formal definition of the related criteria. Let Z denote the set of integers and Z_2^n denote the n-dimensional vector space over the finite field $Z_2 = GF(2)$. Also let $\oplus$ denote the addition over Z_2^n, or, the bit-wise exclusive-or.

Definition 1 *For a positive integer n, define $c_1^{(n)}, c_2^{(n)}, \ldots c_n^{(n)} \in Z_2^n$ by*

$$
\begin{aligned}
c_1^{(n)} &= [0, 0, \ldots, 0, 0, 1] \\
c_2^{(n)} &= [0, 0, \ldots, 0, 1, 0] \\
&\vdots \\
c_n^{(n)} &= [1, 0, \ldots, 0, 0, 0].
\end{aligned}
$$

Definition 2 (Completeness) *A function $f : Z_2^n \rightarrow Z_2^m$ is complete if and only if*

$$
\sum_{x \in Z_2^n} f(x) \oplus f(x \oplus c_i^{(n)}) > (0, 0, \ldots, 0)
$$

for all i $(1 \leq i \leq n)$, where both the summation and the greater-than are component-wise over Z^m.

This means that each output bit depends on all of the input bits. Thus, if it were possible to find the simplest Boolean expression for each output bit in terms of the input bits, each of those expressions would have to contain all of the input bits if the function is *complete*.

Definition 3 (Avalanche effect) *A function $f : Z_2^n \rightarrow Z_2^m$ exhibits the avalanche effect if and only if*
$$
\sum_{x \in Z_2^n} wt(f(x) \oplus f(x \oplus c_i^{(n)})) = m2^{n-1}
$$
for all i $(1 \leq i \leq n)$. Here $wt(\ )$ denotes the Hamming weight function.

---

[1]Defined as the Hamming distance between the function in question and the set of all linear functions.

This means that an average of one half of the output bits change whenever a single input bit is complemented.

Definition 4 (SAC, Strong S-box) *We say that a function* $f : Z_2^n \to Z_2^m$ *satisfies the SAC, or* f *is a strong S-box, if for all* i *(*$1 \leq i \leq n$*) there hold the following equations :*

$$\sum_{\mathbf{x} \in Z_2^n} f(\mathbf{x}) \oplus f(\mathbf{x} \oplus \mathbf{c}_i^{(n)}) = (2^{n-1}, 2^{n-1}, \ldots, 2^{n-1}).$$

If a function satisfies the SAC, each of its output bits should change with a probability of one half whenever a single input bit is complemented. Clearly, a strong S-box is *complete* and exhibits the *avalanche effect*.

If some output bits depend on only a few input bits, then, by observing a significant number of input-output pairs such as chosen plaintext attack, a cryptanalyst might be able to detect these relations and use this information to aid the search for the key. And because any lower-dimensional space approximation of a mapping yields a wrong result in 25 % [Ba] of the cases, strong S-boxes play significant roles in cryptography.

Notation For a function $f : Z_2^n \to Z_2^m$, denote by f_j ($1 \leq j \leq m$) the function $Z_2^n \to Z_2$ such that $f(\mathbf{x}) = (f_m(\mathbf{x}), f_{m-1}(\mathbf{x}), \ldots, f_2(\mathbf{x}), f_1(\mathbf{x}))$. We identify an element $\mathbf{z} = (z_k, z_{k-1}, \ldots, z_2, z_1)$ of Z_2^k with an integer $\sum_{i=1}^k z_i 2^{i-1}$. To represent a function $f : Z_2^n \to Z_2^m$, we often use the integer tuple $< f >= [f(0), f(1), f(2), \ldots, f(2^n - 1)]$ and call it the integer representation of f. This representation can be obtained by combining $< f_m >, < f_{m-1} >, \ldots, < f_2 >, < f_1 >$ as $< f >= \sum_{j=1}^m < f_j > \cdot 2^{j-1}$.

3 Properties of Strong S-box

Let us discuss the cryptographic properties of strong S-boxes *or* functions satisfying the SAC.

3.1 Some Functions Never Satisfy the SAC

Definition 5 (Linearity, Affinity) *A function* f *from* Z_2^n *into* Z_2^m *is affine if there exist an* $n \times m$ *matrix* $\mathbf{A}_f$ *over* Z_2 *and an* m-*dimensional vector* $\mathbf{b}_f$ *over* Z_2 *such that*

$$f(\mathbf{x}) = \mathbf{x}\mathbf{A}_f + \mathbf{b}_f$$

where $\mathbf{x}$ *denotes the indeterminate* n-*dimensional vector. A function* f *is linear if it is affine with* $\mathbf{b}_f = \mathbf{0}$.

It is well known[HM] that any cryptosystem which implements linear or affine functions can be easily broken. This fact brings us the question : Are there linear or affine functions satisfying the SAC ? The answer is of course "no".

Theorem 1 *A strong S-box is neither linear nor affine.*

And also it is easy to see that

Theorem 2 *For $n = 1$, or 2, any bijective function f from Z_2^n into Z_2^n never satisfy the SAC.*

Thus in order to obtain *bijective* strong S-boxes, we must treat at least quadratic function of at least three variables.

3.2 Use of Single Output Strong S-box

When $m = 1$, and $n = 3$ or 4, the experiments tell us that we can easily generate many strong S-boxes $f : Z_2^n \to Z_2$ by random search on an engineering workstation (SONY NWS810) in a few microseconds. But for the case of $n \geq 5$ it becomes rather difficult to efficiently generate single output strong S-boxes in the same computational environment.

Example 1 For $n = 3$ and $m = 1$,

$$< p >= [1, 0, 1, 1, 1, 0, 0, 0],$$

$$< q >= [1, 1, 1, 0, 0, 0, 1, 0],$$

$$< r >= [1, 1, 0, 1, 0, 1, 0, 0]$$

are integer representations of strong S-boxes p, q and r respectively. By complementing the output bit of the single output strong S-box p, q and r, we have

$$< p' >= [0, 1, 0, 0, 0, 1, 1, 1],$$

$$< q' >= [0, 0, 0, 1, 1, 1, 0, 1],$$

$$< r' >= [0, 0, 1, 0, 1, 0, 1, 1].$$

It is easy to check that all of these functions are strong S-boxes.

By the definition of the SAC and by the above observation, we can readily show the following.

Theorem 3 *Let e (g, resp.) denote an affine function from Z_2^n (Z_2^m, resp.) into itself with a permutation matrix and an arbitrary binary vector. Then, a function $f : Z_2^n \to Z_2^m$ satisfies the SAC if and only if the composite function $g \circ f \circ e : Z_2^n \to Z_2^m$ satisfies the SAC.*

Given some single output strong S-boxes, we can generate multiple output strong S-boxes using the idea summarized in the above theorem. (However, note that a strong S-box of $m = n$ generated by this method is not guaranteed to be *bijective*.)

Example 2 The 3-input 3-output S-box f defined by $f(\mathbf{x}) = (r(\mathbf{x}), p(\mathbf{x}), q'(\mathbf{x}))$ is strong, *i.e.*, satisfies the SAC. Since

$$< r >= [1, 1, 0, 1, 0, 1, 0, 0],$$

$$< p >= [1, 0, 1, 1, 1, 0, 0, 0],$$

$$< q' >= [0, 0, 0, 1, 1, 1, 0, 1],$$

then, the integer representation of f is

$$< r > \cdot 4 + < p > \cdot 2 + < q' >= [6, 4, 2, 7, 3, 5, 0, 1].$$

Thus we can conclude this section by describing that there are no difficulties to efficiently generate many strong S-boxes up to the 4-bit input case.

4 Enlargement of Strong S-box

4.1 Construction

Next we discuss the expandable properties of strong S-boxes and present the recursive construction of strong S-boxes of arbitrary n and m.

Let us construct $(n+1)$-bit input S-boxes using n-bit input S-boxes.

Definition 6 *For a function $f : Z_2^n \to Z_2$, an integer $k \in \{1, 2, \ldots, n\}$ and a constant $b \in Z_2$, define a function $\mathbf{D}_b^k[f] : Z_2^{n+1} \to Z_2$ by $\mathbf{D}_b^k[f](0, \mathbf{x}) = f(\mathbf{x})$ and $\mathbf{D}_b^k[f](1, \mathbf{x}) = f(\mathbf{x} \oplus \mathbf{c}_k^{(n)}) \oplus b$ for all $\mathbf{x} \in Z_2^n$.*

Definition 7 *For a function $f : Z_2^n \to Z_2^n$ such that $f(\mathbf{x}) = (f_n(\mathbf{x}), f_{n-1}(\mathbf{x}), \ldots, f_1(\mathbf{x}))$, and a function $g : Z_2^n \to Z_2$ and an integer $k \in \{1, 2, \ldots, n\}$, define the function $\mathbf{E}^k[g, f] : Z_2^{n+1} \to Z_2^{n+1}$ by*

$$\mathbf{E}^k[g, f](\mathbf{y}) = (\mathbf{D}_1^k[g](\mathbf{y}), \mathbf{D}_0^k[f_n](\mathbf{y}), \mathbf{D}_0^k[f_{n-1}](\mathbf{y}), \ldots, \mathbf{D}_0^k[f_1](\mathbf{y}))$$

for all $\mathbf{y} \in Z_2^{n+1}$.

We can show that the constructed S-boxes have nice properties.

Theorem 4 *If a function $f : Z_2^n \to Z_2$ satisfies the SAC, then for any $k \in \{1, 2, \ldots, n\}$ and any $b \in Z_2$, $\mathbf{D}_b^k[f]$ also satisfies the SAC.*

Proof: Since f satisfies the SAC, it holds that

$$\sum_{\mathbf{x} \in Z_2^n} f(\mathbf{x}) \oplus f(\mathbf{x} \oplus \mathbf{c}_i^{(n)}) = 2^{n-1}$$

for any $i \in \{1, 2, \ldots, n\}$. Thus it also holds that

$$\sum_{\mathbf{x} \in Z_2^n} f(\mathbf{x}) \oplus f(\mathbf{x} \oplus \mathbf{c}_i^{(n)}) \oplus 1$$

$$= 2^n - \sum_{\mathbf{x} \in Z_2^n} f(\mathbf{x}) \oplus f(\mathbf{x} \oplus \mathbf{c}_i^{(n)})$$

$$= 2^n - 2^{n-1}$$

$$= 2^{n-1}$$

To prove the theorem, we denote $\mathbf{D}_b^k[f]$ by g and show that for any $i \in \{1, 2, \ldots, n+1\}$,

$$\sum_{\mathbf{y} \in Z_2^{n+1}} g(\mathbf{y}) \oplus g(\mathbf{y} \oplus \mathbf{c}_i^{(n+1)}) = 2^n$$

(Case 1) $i \in \{1, 2, \ldots, n\}$.

$$\sum_{\mathbf{y} \in Z_2^{n+1}} g(\mathbf{y}) \oplus g(\mathbf{y} \oplus \mathbf{c}_i^{(n+1)})$$

$$= \sum_{\mathbf{x} \in Z_2^n} g(0, \mathbf{x}) \oplus g(0, \mathbf{x} \oplus \mathbf{c}_i^{(n)}) + \sum_{\mathbf{x} \in Z_2^n} g(1, \mathbf{x}) \oplus g(1, \mathbf{x} \oplus \mathbf{c}_i^{(n)})$$

$$= \sum_{\mathbf{x} \in Z_2^n} f(\mathbf{x}) \oplus f(\mathbf{x} \oplus \mathbf{c}_i^{(n)}) + \sum_{\mathbf{x} \in Z_2^n} (f(\mathbf{x} \oplus \mathbf{c}_k^{(n)}) \oplus b) \oplus (f((\mathbf{x} \oplus \mathbf{c}_i^{(n)}) \oplus \mathbf{c}_k^{(n)}) \oplus b)$$

$$= \sum_{\mathbf{x} \in Z_2^n} f(\mathbf{x}) \oplus f(\mathbf{x} \oplus \mathbf{c}_i^{(n)}) + \sum_{\mathbf{x} \in Z_2^n} f(\mathbf{x} \oplus \mathbf{c}_k^{(n)}) \oplus f((\mathbf{x} \oplus \mathbf{c}_k^{(n)}) \oplus \mathbf{c}_i^{(n)})$$

$$= 2 \cdot \sum_{\mathbf{x} \in Z_2^n} f(\mathbf{x}) \oplus f(\mathbf{x} \oplus \mathbf{c}_i^{(n)})$$

$$= 2 \cdot 2^{n-1}$$

$$= 2^n$$

(Case 2) $i = n+1$

$$\sum_{\mathbf{y} \in Z_2^{n+1}} g(\mathbf{y}) \oplus g(\mathbf{y} \oplus \mathbf{c}_{n+1}^{(n+1)})$$

$$= \sum_{\mathbf{x} \in Z_2^n} g(0, \mathbf{x}) \oplus g(1, \mathbf{x}) + \sum_{\mathbf{x} \in Z_2^n} g(1, \mathbf{x}) \oplus g(0, \mathbf{x})$$

$$= 2 \cdot \sum_{\mathbf{x} \in Z_2^n} g(0, \mathbf{x}) \oplus g(1, \mathbf{x})$$

$$= 2 \cdot \sum_{\mathbf{x} \in Z_2^n} f(\mathbf{x}) \oplus f(\mathbf{x} \oplus \mathbf{c}_k^{(n)}) \oplus b$$

$$= 2 \cdot 2^{n-1}$$

$$= 2^n$$

Thus, we complete the proof. $\qquad \square$

Theorem 5 *For a bijection* $f \colon Z_2^n \to Z_2^n$, *a function* $g \colon Z_2^n \to Z_2$, *and an integer* $k \in \{1, 2, \ldots, n\}$, *the function* $\mathbf{E}^k[g, f] \colon Z_2^{n+1} \to Z_2^{n+1}$ *is bijective.*

Proof: By the definition of $\mathbf{E}^k[g, f]$ we have for any $\mathbf{x} \in Z_2^n$,

$$
\begin{aligned}
\mathbf{E}^k[g, f](0, \mathbf{x}) &= (g(\mathbf{x}), f(\mathbf{x})), \\
\mathbf{E}^k[g, f](1, \mathbf{x} \oplus \mathbf{c}_k^{(n)}) &= (g(\mathbf{x}) \oplus 1, f(\mathbf{x})).
\end{aligned}
$$

For any $\mathbf{u} \in Z_2^n$ and $\mathbf{v} \in Z_2^n$, let

$$
\begin{aligned}
A(\mathbf{u}, \mathbf{v}) &= \mathbf{E}^k[g, f](0, \mathbf{u}) \oplus \mathbf{E}^k[g, f](0, \mathbf{v}), \\
B(\mathbf{u}, \mathbf{v}) &= \mathbf{E}^k[g, f](1, \mathbf{u} \oplus \mathbf{c}_k^{(n)}) \oplus \mathbf{E}^k[g, f](1, \mathbf{v} \oplus \mathbf{c}_k^{(n)}), \\
C(\mathbf{u}, \mathbf{v}) &= \mathbf{E}^k[g, f](0, \mathbf{u}) \oplus \mathbf{E}^k[g, f](1, \mathbf{v} \oplus \mathbf{c}_k^{(n)}).
\end{aligned}
$$

We have

$$
\begin{aligned}
A(\mathbf{u}, \mathbf{v}) &= B(\mathbf{u}, \mathbf{v}) \\
&= (g(\mathbf{u}) \oplus g(\mathbf{v}), f(\mathbf{u}) \oplus f(\mathbf{v})) \\
C(\mathbf{u}, \mathbf{v}) &= (g(\mathbf{u}) \oplus g(\mathbf{v}) \oplus 1, f(\mathbf{u}) \oplus f(\mathbf{v}))
\end{aligned}
$$

Since f is *bijective*, $f(\mathbf{u}) \oplus f(\mathbf{v}) = 0$ if and only if $\mathbf{u} = \mathbf{v}$. Therefore, if $\mathbf{u} \neq \mathbf{v}$, we have $A(\mathbf{u}, \mathbf{v}) = B(\mathbf{u}, \mathbf{v}) \neq (0, 0)$ and $C(\mathbf{u}, \mathbf{v}) \neq (0, 0)$. And if $\mathbf{u} = \mathbf{v}$, we have $A(\mathbf{u}, \mathbf{v}) = B(\mathbf{u}, \mathbf{v}) = (0, 0)$ and $C(\mathbf{u}, \mathbf{v}) = (1, 0) \neq (0, 0)$. Thus, $A(\mathbf{u}, \mathbf{v})$ and $B(\mathbf{u}, \mathbf{v})$ equals to zero if and only if $\mathbf{u} = \mathbf{v}$, and $C(\mathbf{u}, \mathbf{v})$ never equals to zero for any $\mathbf{u}$ and $\mathbf{v}$. These facts show that for any $\mathbf{s} \in Z_2^{n+1}$ and $\mathbf{t} \in Z_2^{n+1}$, $\mathbf{E}^k[g, f](\mathbf{s}) = \mathbf{E}^k[g, f](\mathbf{t})$ if and only if $\mathbf{s} = \mathbf{t}$, in other words, that $\mathbf{E}^k[g, f]$ is *bijective*. $\quad \square$

Theorem 6 *If both a bijection* $f \colon Z_2^n \to Z_2^n$ *and a function* $g \colon Z_2^n \to Z_2$ *satisfy the SAC, then for any integer* $k \in \{1, 2, \ldots, n\}$, *the function* $\mathbf{E}^k[g, f] \colon Z_2^{n+1} \to Z_2^{n+1}$ *is a bijection satisfying the SAC.*

Proof: This theorem follows directly from **Theorems 4** and **5**. $\quad \square$

For the explanatory purpose, we illustrate this method like Fig.1 in the **Appendix**.

Remark: Define $f_i \colon Z_2^n \to Z_2$ $(i = 1, 2, \ldots, n)$ by $f(\mathbf{x}) = (f_n(\mathbf{x}), f_{n-1}(\mathbf{x}), \ldots, f_1(\mathbf{x}))$ from the *bijection* $f \colon Z_2^n \to Z_2^n$ satisfying the SAC. Noting that f_i satisfies the SAC, **Theorem 6** tells us that given a *bijection* $f \colon Z_2^n \to Z_2^n$ satisfies the SAC we can construct a *bijection* $\mathbf{E}^k[f_i, f] \colon Z_2^{n+1} \to Z_2^{n+1}$ satisfying the SAC using only f (See Fig.2 in the **Appendix**). $\quad \square$

By using these construction methods, we can generate strong S-boxes in an efficient and systematic way. We give some examples in the next section.

4.2 Examples

Here we give detailed examples to generate strong S-boxes.

Example 3 A function $f : Z_2^3 \rightarrow Z_2$ which satisfies the SAC is given as $< f > = [1, 1, 0, 0, 0, 1, 0, 1]$. Then,

$$< D_0^1[f] > = [1, 1, 0, 0, 0, 1, 0, 1, 1, 1, 0, 0, 1, 0, 1, 0],$$

and

$$< D_1^1[f] > = [1, 1, 0, 0, 0, 1, 0, 1, 0, 0, 1, 1, 0, 1, 0, 1].$$

By **Theorem 4**, these expanded functions also satisfy the SAC.

Example 4 When a strong S-box $g : Z_2^3 \rightarrow Z_2$ is $[1, 0, 0, 0, 1, 1, 0, 1]$ and a *bijective* strong S-box $f : Z_2^3 \rightarrow Z_2^3$ is $[3, 1, 4, 0, 2, 5, 6, 7]$,

$$< D_1^1[g] > = [1, 0, 0, 0, 1, 1, 0, 1, 1, 0, 1, 1, 0, 0, 0, 1],$$

and

$$< D_0^1[f] > = [3, 1, 4, 0, 2, 5, 6, 7, 1, 3, 0, 4, 5, 2, 7, 6].$$

By **Theorem 6**, we can get a strong *bijective* S-box :

$$< E^1[g, f] > = [11, 1, 4, 0, 10, 13, 6, 15, 9, 3, 8, 12, 5, 2, 7, 14].$$

Also by applying **Thereom 6** two times, we can get 6-bit input *bijective* strong S-boxes :

$$[4, 53, 16, 57, 43, 45, 2, 6, 12, 55, 63, 33, 8, 26, 30, 51,$$
$$37, 20, 41, 0, 61, 59, 22, 18, 39, 28, 49, 47, 10, 24, 35, 14,$$
$$21, 36, 25, 48, 13, 11, 38, 34, 23, 44, 1, 31, 58, 40, 19, 62,$$
$$52, 5, 32, 9, 27, 29, 50, 54, 60, 7, 15, 17, 56, 42, 46, 3],$$

and

$$[36, 21, 48, 57, 43, 45, 2, 38, 12, 23, 63, 1, 8, 58, 30, 19,$$
$$37, 20, 9, 0, 29, 27, 22, 50, 39, 60, 49, 15, 10, 56, 35, 46,$$
$$53, 4, 25, 16, 13, 11, 6, 34, 55, 44, 33, 31, 26, 40, 51, 62,$$
$$52, 5, 32, 41, 59, 61, 18, 54, 28, 7, 47, 17, 24, 42, 14, 3].$$

As stated earlier, the experiments on the random search show that we can easily find 3-bit input *bijective* strong S-boxes, but when the number of input is increased, it becomes more and more difficult to find even a 5-bit input *bijective* strong S-box.

By applying **Theorem 6** recursively, however, we can generate arbitrary input size *bijective* strong S-boxes given 3-bit input *bijective* strong S-boxes. This method is very useful in designing a *bijective* strong S-box with a larger input size.

5 Concluding Remarks

We have summarized the cryptographically significant criteria for S-boxes of symmetric cryptosystems and proved several interesting theorems of strong S-boxes. Moreover, we proposed two recursive construction methods from 3-bit input *bijective* strong S-box(es) to an arbitrary input size *bijective* strong S-box.

The generated strong S-boxes can be useful for a basic building block of symmetric cryptosystems or pseudorandom generators, etc.

Acknowledgment The first author is supported in part by Electronics and Telecommunications Research Institute.

References

[NBS] NBS, "Data Encryption Standard(DES)", FIPS PUB 46, US National Bureau of Standards, Washinston DC, Jan., 1977.

[MSS] S.Miyaguchi, A.Shiraishi and A.Shimizu, "Fast data encryption algorithm FEAL–8 (in Japanese)", Electr. Comm. Lab. Tech. J., NTT, Vol.37, No.4/5, pp.321–327, 1988.

[BPS] L. Brown, J.Pieprzyk and J. Seberry, "LOKI – a cryptographic primitive for authentication and secrecy", Proc. of AUSCRYPT90, 1990.

[KD] J.B. Kam and G.I. Davida, "Structured design of substitution–permutation encryption network", IEEE Trans. on Comput., Vol.C-28, No.10, pp.747–753, Oct., 1979.

[WT] A.F. Webster and S.E. Tavares, "On the design of S-boxes", Proc. of CRYPTO85, Springer-Verlag, 1985.

[Fe] H. Feistel, "Cryptography and computer privacy", Scientific American, Vol.228, No.5, pp 15–23, 1973.

[Fo] R.Forré, "The strict avalanche criterion : spectral properties of Boolean functions and an extended definition", Proc.of CRYPTO88, Springer-Verlag, 1988.

[Ll] S.Lloyd, "Counting functions satisfying a higher order strict avalanche criterion", Proc. of EUROCYRPT89, Springer-Verlag, 1989.

[GR] J.A.Gordon and H. Retkin, "Are big S-boxes best ? ", IEEE workshop on computer security, pp.257–262, 1981.

[Ay] F.Ayoub, "Probabilistic completeness of substitution–permutation encryption networks", IEE, Vol.129, E, 5, pp195–199, Sep., 1982.

[Pi]   J.P.Pieprzyk, "Non-linearity of exponent permutations", Proc. of EURO-CRYPTO89, Springer-Verlag, 1989.

[Ba]   S.Babbage, "On the relevance of the strict avalanche criterion", Electronics Letters, Vol.26, No.7, pp.461-462, 29th Mar., 1990.

[HM]   M. Hellman, R. Merkle ,R. Schroeppel, L. Washington, W. Diffie, S. Pohlig and P. Schweitzer, "Results of an initial attempt to analyze the NBS data encryption standard", Information Systems Laboratory Report, Stanford University, 1976.

Appendix

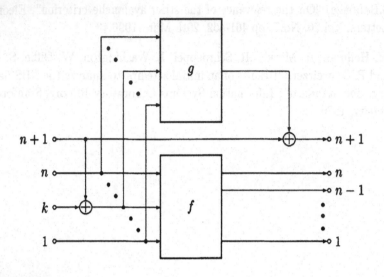

Figure 1: Construction method using f and g ($1 \leq k \leq n$).

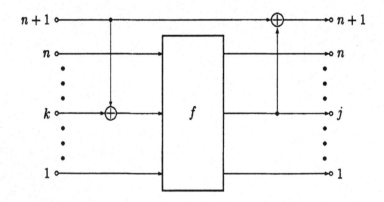

Figure 2: Construction method using only f ($1 \leq k, j \leq n$).

Session 12

Design and Analysis II

Chair: J. Buchmann, Universität des Saarlandes

A Comparison of Practical Public-Key Cryptosystems based on Integer Factorization and Discrete Logarithms

(extended abstract)

Paul C. van Oorschot †

Bell-Northern Research, Ottawa, Canada

Since its inception in the mid 1970's, public-key cryptography has flourished as a research activity, and significant theoretical advances have been made. In more recent years, many public-key concepts have gained acceptance in the commercial world. Without question, the best-known public-key cryptosystem is the RSA system of Rivest, Shamir and Adleman [28]. Although not as well-known, another public-key cryptosystem of practical interest is that due to ElGamal [11]. The latter system and its variations use a basic extension of Diffie-Hellman key exchange [9] for encryption, together with an accompanying signature scheme. Elliptic curve cryptosystems, introduced by Miller [24] and Koblitz [12], have also recently received much attention as cryptographic alternatives.

The security of the RSA and ElGamal cryptosystems is generally equated to the difficulty of integer factorization and that of the computation of discrete logarithms in finite fields, respectively. Based on the current literature, this survey considers a detailed analysis of a version of the multiple polynomial quadratic sieve integer factorization algorithm [26], and a variation of the Coppersmith algorithm for computing discrete logarithms in $GF(2^n)$ [6]. The analysis is used for a practical security comparison between the RSA cryptosystem and the ElGamal cryptosystem in fields of characteristic two. By "practical" we mean a comparison suitable for dealing with particular problem instances of practical interest, rather than dwelling exclusively on asymptotic complexities. The algorithms analyzed are the best general practical algorithms currently known for the respective problems, for problem sizes of cryptographic interest. Other aspects of the cryptosystems are considered in addition to relative security, including practical efficiency. The security of elliptic curve cryptosystems, which is generally equated to the difficulty of extracting elliptic curve logarithms (the elliptic curve analogue of the discrete logarithm problem), is also discussed and related to that of the previously mentioned cryptosystems. The recent reduction [23] of

†Partial support for this work was provided by the University of Waterloo, Waterloo, Ontario, and by Newbridge Microsystems, Kanata, Ontario.

the elliptic curve logarithm problem, for certain elliptic curves, to the discrete logarithm problem in extension fields of the underlying field, has made an understanding of the relative difficulty of the discrete logarithm problem and that of integer factorization of even greater importance.

This abstract serves to overview and provide references to recent research related to the cryptosystems in question and their underlying problems. The full version of this paper will appear in a book of survey articles edited by Gus Simmons [33].

It is well known that the computation of discrete logarithms in $GF(2^n)$ is easier than the factorization of n-bit integers N, using the best currently known algorithms for each problem. The resulting security difference between the RSA and ElGamal cryptosystem in $GF(2^n)$ can be addressed by using larger bitlengths n in the latter. The price is somewhat larger key sizes, and any implications that result from this. Asymptotic running times for the best practical algorithms for integer factorization and discrete logarithms in $GF(2^n)$ reveal that for similar levels of security, the relative bitlength by which the $GF(2^n)$ system must exceed the bitlength in RSA increases with the bitlength of the RSA system.

The analysis of the Coppersmith algorithm for computing discrete logarithms is largely based on that of Odlyzko [25]. Similarly, the practical analysis of the quadratic sieve factorization algorithm is based on the analysis of Pomerance et al. [27]. The analysis in the full paper suggests that for levels of security equivalent to integer factorization at 100 and 155 digits (332 and 512 bits), the discrete logarithm problem in $GF(2^n)$ currently requires bitlengths of approximately 400 and 700 bits respectively. Estimates of algorithmic parameters, the size of the resulting linear system, and operation counts are tabulated for problems of these sizes. We focus on the relative difficulty of these different problems, as opposed to absolute running times. For the latter, see Lenstra and Manasse [18,19,17] and Silverman [32,5] for factorization, and Coppersmith [6] for logarithms in $GF(2^n)$.

Integer factorization has been the subject of intense research in recent years. An early survey of progress is given by Davis et al. [8]. Since then, the quadratic sieve algorithm has been carefully examined with an eye to specialized hardware (e.g. [27]) and networks of distributed processors ([5,18]). More recently, dramatic theoretical progress has resulted in the elliptic curve method [20] and the number field sieve [17]. Each of the algorithms resulting from these latter two advances is most efficient when applied to specific classes of composite integers, although the number field sieve may eventually prove to be a competitive factoring technique for general integers of sizes of cryptographic interest. Elliptic curve factorization allows extraction of smaller factors (up to 30 or 40 digits) from relatively large numbers (up to 200 digits). The number field sieve applies to a small class of numbers including those of the form $N = r^e \pm s$ for small integers r and s, and runs in heuristic expected time $\exp((c+o(1))(\ln N)^{1/3}(\ln\ln N)^{2/3})$, where $c \approx 1.526$; it has been used to factorize the 155-digit ninth Fermat number, $2^{512}+1$. The generalized number field sieve applies to general integers, and has a running time constant of $c = 3^{2/3} \approx 2.08$; further research is underway to improve upon this constant. While asymptotically significantly faster than all previous general factoring algorithms, the generalized number field sieve is not currently practical for integers of cryptographic interest.

While the elliptic curve method and the number field sieve have been used to factor numbers of special form much larger than can be factored at present using the quadratic sieve, such numbers can be easily avoided in cryptographic applications. The quadratic sieve (in particular, the multiple polynomial version, suggested by Davis and independently by Montgomery) remains the most efficient general purpose factoring algorithm in 1990. Two important new ideas that apply to the quadratic sieve have been demonstrated by A.K. Lenstra and Manasse. The first is the use of electronic mail to coordinate the activities of large networks of "anonymous" workstations [18]; this has changed the rules somewhat regarding what should generally be considered as computationally feasible. The second is the "two large prime" version used for collecting sparse equations [19].

The discrete logarithm problem has also been the subject of much study in recent years. The computation of discrete logarithms in odd prime fields GF(p) is discussed by Coppersmith et al. [7] and by LaMacchia and Odlyzko [15]. The latter paper indicates that in practice the computation of discrete logarithms in GF(p), using the best currently known techniques, is slightly harder than factorization of integers N (where $N \approx p$) via the multiple polynomial quadratic sieve. We restrict attention primarily to fields of characteristic two - these traditionally being of practical interest, as arithmetic in such fields is particularly amenable to efficient hardware implementation. Early work by Blake et al. [3] rendered the field GF(2^{127}) totally inadequate for cryptographic security; a key size of 127 bits, which corresponds to 38 digits, is simply insufficient. Subsequent work by Coppersmith [6] and Odlyzko [25] led to further improvements in the index-calculus techniques for computing logarithms in larger fields GF(2^n). There has been a lack of further practical work in fields of characteristic two, although it appears there is renewed interest of late. Recent surveys discussing discrete logarithms include [16], [1], and [21].

Efficient techniques for the solution of large sparse linear systems over finite fields are important in both factoring and extracting discrete logarithms. Progress on this front has been made by Wiedemann [34], and LaMacchia and Odlyzko [14].

The Diffie-Hellman key exchange technique and the related ElGamal cryptosystem can be carried out using the group of points of an elliptic curve over a finite field, resulting in elliptic curve cryptosystems as noted above. The apparent absence of efficient attacks on elliptic curve systems (and efficient general algorithms for computing elliptic curve logarithms) has resulted in the belief that these systems with relatively short keylengths may afford greater security than alternative cryptosystems with larger keylengths. Shorter keylengths imply simpler implementations of arithmetic, and smaller bandwidth and memory requirements - important in smart card applications, among others.

Menezes, Okamoto and Vanstone [23] have recently shown that for certain classes of curves over fields $GF(q)$, the elliptic curve logarithm problem can be reduced to the discrete logarithm problem in an extension field $GF(q^k)$. In general k is exponentially large and the reduction takes exponential time, but for *supersingular* curves, k is small and the reduction is probabilistic polynomial time - yielding a subexponential-time elliptic curve logarithm algorithm. The cryptographic impact of this is that special care must now be taken in the particular choice of elliptic curve, either avoiding the supersingular curves or compensating for the new algorithm by using appropriately larger fields to preserve security. These larger fields in the latter case may still be smaller than those required for equivalent security in other types of cryptosystems, in which case even these elliptic curve systems remain attractive in practice. Ironically, the classes of curves susceptible to the new attack include many of those which have previously been recommended for use, including curves originally suggested by Miller [24], Koblitz [12], Bender and Castagnoli [2], and Menezes and Vanstone [22].

Significant advances have also been made in recent years, in theory and in practice, on techniques for efficient implementation of the cryptosystems in question. For RSA modular exponentiation, these include custom VLSI chips (see Brickell's survey [4]), efficient digital signal processor software implementations (e.g. Dussé and Kaliski [10]), and a Programmable Active Memory implementation by Shand et al. [31]. Custom VLSI chips for arithmetic operations in $GF(2^n)$ are now also available (see Rosati [29]). Schnorr has recently proposed a signature scheme for ElGamal-like cryptosystems resulting in shorter signatures that can be both constructed and verified more efficiently than in ElGamal's original proposal [30]. Implementation of elliptic curve cryptosystems over fields of characteristic two has recently been studied by Menezes and Vanstone [22] and Koblitz [13].

References

[1] E. Bach, "Intractable problems in number theory", *Advances in Cryptology - Crypto 88*, S. Goldwasser (ed.), *Lecture Notes in Computer Science* 403, Springer-Verlag (1990), 77-93.

[2] A. Bender and G. Castagnoli, "On the implementation of elliptic curve cryptosystems", *Advances in Cryptology - Crypto 89*, G. Brassard (ed.), *Lecture Notes in Computer Science* 435, Springer-Verlag (1990), 186-192.

[3] I.F. Blake, R. Fuji-Hara, R.C. Mullin, and S.A. Vanstone, "Computing logarithms in finite fields of characteristic two", *SIAM J. Alg. Disc. Meth.* 5 (2), June 1984, 276-285.

[4] E.F. Brickell, "A survey of hardware implementations of RSA (abstract)", *Advances in Cryptology - Crypto 89*, G. Brassard (ed.), *Lecture Notes in Computer Science* 435, Springer-Verlag (1990), 368-370.

[5] T.T. Caron and R.D. Silverman, "Parallel Implementation of the quadratic sieve", *J. Supercomput.* 1 (1988), 273-290.

[6] D. Coppersmith, "Fast evaluation of logarithms in fields of characteristic two", *IEEE Transactions on Information Theory* IT-30 (4), July 1984, 587-594.

[7] D. Coppersmith, A.M. Odlyzko, and R. Schroeppel, "Discrete logarithms in GF(p)", *Algorithmica* 1 (1), 1986, 1-15.

[8] J.A. Davis, D.B. Holdridge, and G.J. Simmons, "Status report on factoring", *Advances in Cryptology - Eurocrypt 84*, T. Beth, N. Cot, I. Ingemarsson (eds.), *Lecture Notes in Computer Science* 209, Springer-Verlag (1985), 183-215.

[9] W. Diffie and M. Hellman, "New directions in cryptography", *IEEE Transactions on Information Theory* IT-22 (6), Nov. 1976, 644-654.

[10] S.R. Dussé and B.S. Kaliski, Jr., "A cryptographic library for the Motorola DSP56000", *Advances in Cryptology - Eurocrypt 90*, I. Damgard (ed.), to appear.

[11] T. ElGamal, "A public key cryptosystem and a signature scheme based on discrete logarithms", *IEEE Transactions on Information Theory* IT-31 (4), July 1985, 469-472.

[12] N. Koblitz, "Elliptic curve cryptosystems", *Math. Comp.* 48 (1987), 203-209.

[13] N. Koblitz, "Constructing elliptic curve cryptosystems in characteristic 2", *Advances in Cryptology - Crypto 90*, S.A. Vanstone (ed.), to appear.

[14] B.A. LaMacchia and A.M. Odlyzko, "Solving large sparse linear systems over finite fields", *Advances in Cryptology - Crypto 90*, S.A. Vanstone (ed.), to appear.

[15] B.A. LaMacchia and A.M. Odlyzko, "Computation of discrete logarithms in prime fields", *Advances in Cryptology - Crypto 90*, S.A. Vanstone (ed.), to appear.

[16] A.K. Lenstra and H.W. Lenstra, Jr., "Algorithms in number theory", in *Handbook of theoretical computer science*, A. Meyer, M. Nivat, M. Paterson, D. Perrin (eds.), North Holland, Amsterdam, to appear.

[17] A.K. Lenstra, H.W. Lenstra, Jr., M.S. Manasse and J.M. Pollard, "The number field sieve", *Proc. 22nd ACM Symp. Theory of Computing* (1990), 564-572.

[18] A.K. Lenstra and M.S. Manasse, "Factoring by electronic mail", *Advances in Cryptology - Eurocrypt 89*, J.-J. Quisquater and J. Vandewalle (eds.), *Lecture Notes in Computer Science* 434, Springer-Verlag (1990), 355-371.

[19] A.K. Lenstra and M.S. Manasse, "Factoring with two large primes", *Advances in Cryptology - Eurocrypt 90*, I. Damgard (ed.), to appear.

[20] H.W. Lenstra, Jr., "Factoring with elliptic curves", *Ann. of Math.* 126 (1987), 649-673.

[21] K.S. McCurley, "The discrete logarithm problem", in *Cryptography and Computational Number Theory*, C. Pomerance (ed.), *Proc. Symp. Appl. Math.*, Amer. Math. Soc. (1990), to appear.

[22] A. Menezes and S. Vanstone, "The implementation of elliptic curve cryptosystems", *Advances in Cryptology - Auscrypt 90*, J. Seberry and J. Pieprzyk (eds.), *Lecture Notes in Computer Science* 453, Springer-Verlag (1990), 2-13.

[23] A. Menezes, S. Vanstone and T. Okamoto, "Reducing elliptic curve logarithms to logarithms in a finite field", presented at *Crypto 90*; to appear in *Proc. 23rd ACM Symp. Theory of Computing* (1991).

[24] V. Miller, "Uses of elliptic curves in cryptography", *Advances in Cryptology - Crypto 85*, H. Williams (ed.), *Lecture Notes in Computer Science* 218, Springer-Verlag (1986), 417-426.

[25] A.M. Odlyzko, "Discrete logarithms in finite fields and their cryptographic significance", *Advances in Cryptology - Eurocrypt 84*, T. Beth, N. Cot, I. Ingemarsson (eds.), *Lecture Notes in Computer Science* 209, Springer-Verlag (1985), 224-314.

[26] C. Pomerance, "Analysis and comparison of some integer factoring algorithms", in *Computational Methods in Number Theory*, H.W. Lenstra, Jr. and R. Tijdeman (eds.), Math. Centrum Tract 154, 1982, 89-139.

[27] C. Pomerance, J.W. Smith and R. Tuler, "A pipeline architecture for factoring large integers with the quadratic sieve algorithm", *SIAM J. Computing* 17 (2), Apr. 1988, 387-403.

[28] R. Rivest, A. Shamir and L. Adleman, "A method for obtaining digital signatures and public-key cryptosystems", *Communications of the ACM* 21 (1978), 120-126.

[29] T. Rosati, "A High Speed Data Encryption Processor for Public Key Cryptography", *Proceedings of the IEEE Custom Integrated Circuits Conference*, May 1989.

[30] C.P. Schnorr, "Efficient identification and signatures for smart cards", *Advances in Cryptology - Crypto 89*, G. Brassard (ed.), *Lecture Notes in Computer Science* 435, Springer-Verlag (1990), 239-251.

[31] M. Shand, P. Bertin and J. Vuillemin, "Hardware speedups in long integer multiplication", *Proceedings of the 2nd ACM Symposium on Parallel Algorithms and Architectures*, Crete, July 2-6, 1990, to appear.

[32] R.D. Silverman, "The multiple polynomial quadratic sieve", *Math. Comp.* 48 (1987), 329-339.

[33] G.J. Simmons (ed.), *Contemporary Cryptology: The Science of Information Integrity*, IEEE press, to appear.

[34] D.H. Wiedemann, "Solving sparse linear equations over finite fields", *IEEE Transactions on Information Theory* IT-32 (1), Jan. 1986, 54-62.

Nonlinear Parity Circuits and their Cryptographic Applications

Kenji Koyama and Routo Terada[1]

NTT Research Laboratories
Musashino-shi, Tokyo 180, Japan

ABSTRACT

This paper proposes a new family of nonlinear cryptographic functions called parity circuits. These parity circuits compute a one-to-one Boolean function, and they can be applied to symmetric block ciphers. In this paper, parity circuits are first defined. Next, these circuits are proven to satisfy some of the properties required in cryptography; involution, nonlinearity, the probability of bit complementation, avalanche effect, equivalent keys and computational efficiency. Finally, the speed of parity circuits implemented using the current hardware technology is estimated to show they can achieve 160 Mbps with a 64-bit block size, 8 rounds, and 3.2 K gates.

1. Introduction

Although the Data Encryption Standard (DES) [NBS77] is widely used and standardized today, there is an increasing interest on alternative cryptographic functions. A few DES-type symmetric block ciphers, for example FEAL [MSS88], or Khufu [Me89], or LOKI [BPS90], have been proposed. In order to achieve systematic design and exact evaluation of symmetric ciphers, cryptographic functions may have to be mathematically simple and cryptographically secure, as well as asymmetric (public key) cryptosystems like RSA.

This paper proposes a new family of nonlinear cryptographic functions called parity circuits. The proposed functions have a simple structure. These parity circuits compute a one-to-one function from $\{0,1\}^n$ to $\{0,1\}^n$, and they can be applied to symmetric block ciphers. This paper first defines parity circuits. Next, their cryptographic properties; involution, nonlinearity, randomness, the probability of bit complementation, avalanche effect, equivalent keys are clarified. Based on an analysis of these, design criteria are shown for parity circuit parameters that can keep cryptosystem secure and rapid. Finally, the speed of parity circuits implemented using the current hardware technology is estimated.

2. Parity Layers and Circuits

First, some basic concepts need to be defined that will be used in later sections.

---

[1]On a special leave of absence from the University of S. Paulo, Brazil, E-mail address: roterada@brusp.bitnet
This author was partially supported by grant FAPESP 89/2983-0

2.1 Parity Circuit Layer L(n)

Definition 1 A *parity circuit layer of length* n, or simply an $L(n)$ *circuit layer*, is a Boolean device with an n-bit input and an n-bit output, characterized by a *key* that is a sequence of n symbols from $\{0, 1, -, +\}$. □

It is convenient to think of each circuit layer as a sequence of n *cells*, each one with an input bit and an output bit, containing a key symbol. Cells with 0 and 1 are called *testers*, while cells with − are called *odd inverters* and with + are called *even inverters*.

Informally, the effects of an $L(n)$ parity circuit layer are:

(1) to verify whether or not the input bits corresponding to tester cell positions are equal to tester symbols at the same positions;

(2) if an even number of the testers are successful (*i.e.*, an *even parity event* occurs), the input bits at the even inverters are complemented; otherwise, the input bits at the odd inverters are complemented.

(3) in either case, the input bits at tester cells with 1 are complemented, but not changed at tester cells with 0; in other words, the input bits are "exclusive-or-ed" with the tester cells.

More formally, we have the following:

Definition 2 Function $B = f(K, A)$, as computed by an $L(n)$ circuit layer with key

$$K = k_1 k_2 \cdots k_n \in \{0, 1, -, +\}^n$$

is the relation from an n-bit input sequence

$$A = a_1 a_2 \cdots a_n \in \{0, 1\}^n$$

to an n-bit output sequence

$$B = b_1 b_2 \cdots b_n \in \{0, 1\}^n$$

defined below. An $L(n)$ circuit layer first computes first variable T modulo 2 such that:

$$T = \sum_{j=1}^{n} t_j \bmod 2 \quad \text{where} \quad t_j = \begin{cases} 1 & \text{if } (k_j = 0 \text{ and } a_j = 0) \text{ or } (k_j = 1 \text{ and } a_j = 1) \\ 0 & \text{otherwise.} \end{cases}$$

Note that $T = 0$ if there are no testers in K.

When $T = 0$ an *even parity event* is said to have occurred; otherwise, an *odd parity event* occurred.

Output $B = b_1 b_2 \cdots b_n$ of the circuit layer is then

$$b_j = \begin{cases} \overline{a}_j & \text{if } \begin{cases} k_j = - \text{ and } T = 1 \text{ (odd event)} \\ \text{or} \\ k_j = + \text{ and } T = 0 \text{ (even event)} \\ \text{or} \\ k_j = 1 \end{cases} \\ a_j & \text{otherwise.} \end{cases}$$

□

Some examples of $L(n)$ parity circuit layers for $n = 10$ are as follows:

Table 1. $L(n)$

Example 1. $T = 1$ (odd event)

Input	1	0	1	1	0	0	1	0	0	1
Key	−	0	1	−	+	+	1	1	−	+
Output	0	0	0	0	0	0	0	1	1	1

Example 2. $T = 0$ (even event)

Input	1	0	0	1	0	0	1	0	0	1
Key	−	0	1	−	+	+	1	1	−	+
Output	1	0	1	1	1	1	0	1	0	0

2.2 Parity Circuits C(n, d)

To obtain the so-called cascade effect, we compose the parity circuit layers as follows.

Definition 3 A *parity circuit of width n and depth d*, or simply a $C(n, d)$ *circuit*, is a matrix of d $L(n)$ circuit layers with keys denoted by $\mathbf{K} = K_1 \parallel K_2 \parallel \cdots \parallel K_d$ for which the n output bits of the $(i - 1)$-th circuit layer are the n input bits for the i-th circuit layer for $2 \leq i \leq d$. The *key* for the $C(n, d)$ circuit is a $d \times n$ matrix whose d lines contain the circuit layer keys. □

In other words, given n-bit input A and key $\mathbf{K}$, the $C(n, d)$ circuit computes function $F(\mathbf{K}, A)$ from $\{0, 1\}^n$ to $\{0, 1\}^n$ and defines it as:

$$F(\mathbf{K}, A) = f(K_d, f(K_{d-1}, \cdots, f(K_1, A) \cdots))$$

where each $f(K_i, .)$ is computed by the i-th circuit layer.
An example of $C(n, d)$ parity circuit is shown below.

Table 2. $C(n, d)$ when $n = 10$ and $d = 3$

Input	1	0	1	1	0	0	1	0	0	1
K_1	−	0	1	−	+	+	1	1	−	+
Output	0	0	0	0	0	0	0	1	1	1
K_2	+	1	0	1	1	+	0	−	+	−
Output	1	1	0	1	1	1	0	1	0	1
K_3	−	0	1	+	+	0	−	+	+	-
Output	1	1	1	0	0	1	0	0	1	1

3. Basic Properties of C(n, d) Circuits and Inversion

We must first define the inverse circuit layer in order to decrypt the output of an $L(n)$ circuit layer. The inverse layer operates exactly the same as the $L(n)$ layer, except that exclusive-or using the tester cells is performed before the even or odd parity event is computed.

Definition 4 Function $B = f^{-1}(K, A)$, as computed by an $L^{-1}(n)$ *inverse* circuit layer with key

$$K = k_1 k_2 \cdots k_n$$

is the relation from $\{0,1\}^n$ to $\{0,1\}^n$ defined below. Given input

$$A = a_1 a_2 \cdots a_n,$$

it first computes intermediate output:

$$A' = a'_1 a'_2 \cdots a'_n,$$

defined by:

$$a'_j = \begin{cases} \bar{a}_j & \text{if } k_j = 1 \\ \\ a_j & \text{otherwise.} \end{cases}$$

Then, variable T is computed for A' as in Definition 2, and output $B = b_1 b_2 \cdots b_n$ of the circuit layer is then:

$$b_j = \begin{cases} \bar{a}'_j & \text{if} \begin{cases} k_j = - & \text{and } T = 1 \\ \\ k_j = + & \text{and } T = 0 \end{cases} \\ \\ a'_j & \text{otherwise.} \end{cases}$$

□

The correctness of this definition is established by the following lemma.

Lemma 1 *Every $L(n)$ circuit layer that computes f has an inverse layer, $L^{-1}(n)$, to compute f^{-1} (as in Definition 4 above); i.e. , $f^{-1}(K, f(K, A)) = A$, for any n-bit input A and any key K.*

Proof. This lemma is an immediate consequence of Definitions 2 and 4. Notice that after the intermediate output A' is computed as in Definition 4, the entries in A' affecting parity value T (in $L^{-1}(n)$) are the same as for the input to the $L(n)$ layer, and so the $L^{-1}(n)$ layer will compute the same T value, and $L^{-1}(n)$ will again complement the input bits complemented by $L(n)$ (if any). □

Lemma 2 *Let $F(.)$ be the function from $\{0, 1\}^n$ to $\{0, 1\}^n$ computed by a $C(n, d)$ circuit with key $K_1 \parallel K_2 \parallel \cdots \parallel K_d$. Inverse function $F^{-1}(.)$ is computed by the "inverted" circuit, $C^{-1}(n, d)$, with key:*

$$K_d \parallel K_{d-1} \parallel \cdots \parallel K_1.$$

Proof. This lemma immediately follows from consecutive application of Lemma 1 until concatenation of the two circuits characterized by:

$$\underbrace{K_1 \parallel K_2 \parallel \cdots \parallel K_d} \underbrace{\parallel K_d \parallel K_{d-1} \parallel \cdots \parallel K_1.}$$

□

It can be concluded that:

Theorem 1 *Every $C(n, d)$ circuit computes a one-to-one function from $\{0,1\}^n$ to $\{0,1\}^n$.*

Proof. By Lemma 2, the $C(n, d)$ circuit computes function $F(.)$, which always admits an inverse $F^{-1}(.)$, so this lemma follows. □

Next, we show a basic property of $L(n)$ ciurcuit layer. If the $L(n)$ circuit layers re randomly generated, with uniform distribution of symbols $\{0, 1, -, +\}$, an average of $n/4$ symbols for each type will occur in the key, and thus, about $n/2$ cells will be testers. According to this hypothesis, it can be seen that around half of all the possible input values imply an even event (*i.e.*, variable T in Definition 2 will be 0), and the other half imply an odd one. More precisely, we can prove the following:

Theorem 2 *If the $L(n)$ circuit layers are uniformly generated, then*

$$Prob\{\text{even event}\} = \frac{1}{2} + \frac{1}{2^{n+1}}, \quad Prob\{\text{odd event}\} = \frac{1}{2} - \frac{1}{2^{n+1}}.$$

Proof. First, assume that each $L(n)$ circuit layer contains at least one tester cell. Let k_j be one of the tester cells. By uniform distribution of the keys, we have

$$Prob\{k_j = 0\} = 1/2, \quad Prob\{k_j = 1\} = 1/2,$$

so that

$$Prob\{t_j = 0\} = 1/2, \quad Prob\{t_j = 1\} = 1/2.$$

This conclusion independently holds for any tester cell in the key. Thus, by summing t_j modulo 2 over all the tester key positions, we have

$$Prob\{T = 0 \text{ (even event)}\}=1/2, \quad Prob\{T =1 \text{ (odd event)}\}=1/2.$$

That is, the probability of an even as well as odd event is $1/2$ for the layer, if it contains at least one tester cell.

There are 4^n keys, but 2^n of these keys have no tester. So, there are $(4^n - 2^n)$ keys implying an even event with a probability of $1/2$. Additionally, there are 2^n keys without a tester which always implies an even event. Therefore, we have the following probability of even event:

$$Prob\{\text{even event}\} = \frac{(4^n - 2^n)}{2 \times 4^n} + \frac{2^n}{4^n} = \frac{1}{2} + \frac{1}{2^{n+1}},$$

and the case for $T = 0$ is proved.

The case for $T = 1$ is complementary. There are $(4^n - 2^n)$ keys that imply an odd event with a probability of $1/2$. Therefore, we have the following probability of odd event:

$$Prob\{\text{odd event}\} = \frac{(4^n - 2^n)}{2 \times 4^n} = \frac{1}{2} - \frac{1}{2^{n+1}}. \quad □$$

4. Cryptographic Properties

We will now consider certain properties of the $C(n, d)$ circuits that are relevant to their use as cryptographic devices. It will be shown how n and d affect nonlinearity, the probability of bit complementation, avalanche effect, output randomness, and the existence of equivalent keys. Furthermore, the n and d values can be increased as necessary to properly secure a cryptosystem.

4.1 Nonlinearity

Strictly speaking, *exclusive or* operations are *nonlinear* in the sense that

$$f(K,\ I_1 + I_2) \neq f(K,\ I_1) + f(K,\ I_2).$$

Thus, almost all of the $L(n)$ circuit layers are *nonlinear* except for particular cases where a key contains only $-$ or only 0 symbols. These particular keys equalize the input and output, and the occurrence probability is given by $1 - (1 - (1/4)^n)^2 = 2^{1-2n} - 2^{-4n}$. Note that the parity circuit has *non-affine* transformation. Whenever a key contains at least one tester cell and one inverter cell, the function computed by its $L(n)$ circuit layer is a *non-homomorphism* in the sense that

$$f(K,\ I_1 \circ I_2) \neq f(K,\ I_1) \circ f(K,\ I_2).$$

If a key contains only $\{-, +\}$ symbols or only $\{0, 1\}$ symbols, then we have

$$f(K,\ I_1 \oplus I_2) = f(K,\ I_1) \oplus f(K,\ I_2).$$

This case is the so-called Vernam cipher, and the occurrence probability is given by $1 - (1 - (1/2)^n)^2 = 2^{1-n} - 2^{-2n}$. Properties such as strict nonlinearity, non-affineness and non-homomorphism are called nonlinearity in this paper. When randomly chosen $L(n)$ circuit layers are combined in circuits $C(n, d)$, nonlinear behavior is preserved with a high probability. This nonlinear characteristic is a desirable attribute in any cryptographic function [Ru86, MS89], since it increases the difficulty of breaking the cipher.

The *order* of Boolean canonical form of a nonlinear function, defined to be the maximum of the order of its product terms, is often applied as a measure of nonlinearity [Ru86]. For instance, the Boolean expressions for $L(n)$ when $n = 2$ and $k_1 \in \{0, 1\}$ are

$$b_2 = \bar{a}_1 \bar{a}_2\ k_1 + \bar{a}_1 a_2 \bar{k}_1 + a_1 \bar{a}_2 \bar{k}_1 + a_1 a_2 k_1 \quad \text{if } k_2 = +,$$

$$b_2 = \bar{a}_1 \bar{a}_2\ \bar{k}_1 + \bar{a}_1\ a_2\ k_1 + a_1 \bar{a}_2\ k_1 + a_1 a_2 \bar{k}_1 \quad \text{if } k_2 = -.$$

The order of the $C(n, d)$ circuit increases exponentially as n or d increases. It would be practically infeasible to cryptoanalyze $C(n, d)$ using its Boolean expression if $n \geq 64$ and $d \geq 8$.

4.2 Probability of Complementation

Now we are going to prove a complementation property regarding the influence of the parameters d and n on the behavior of a $C(n, d)$ circuit.

Lemma 3 *If a $C(n, d)$ circuit is uniformly generated, then we have the following formulas for the times that one input element a_j $(1 \leq j \leq n)$ will be complemented by the d circuit layers. Probability that one or more complementations occur is:*

$$1 - \left(\frac{147}{256} - \frac{3}{2^{2n+8}}\right)^d \approx 1 - (0.57)^d.$$

The average of complementation times is:

$$d\left(1 - \frac{147}{256} + \frac{3}{2^{2n+8}}\right) \approx 0.43d.$$

The variance of complementation times is:

$$d\left(1 - \frac{147}{256} + \frac{3}{2^{2n+8}}\right)\left(\frac{147}{256} - \frac{3}{2^{2n+8}}\right) \approx 0.25d.$$

Proof: First consider any uniformly generated $L(n)$ layer of a $C(n, d)$ circuit. For fixed position j, $1 \le j \le n$, we have

$$Prob\{k_j = 0\} = 1/4, \quad Prob\{k_j = 1\} = 1/4,$$
$$Prob\{k_j = -\} = 1/4, \quad Prob\{k_j = +\} = 1/4.$$

Let X be event "$k_j = +$ and $T = 0$" in the $L(n)$ layer, and a_j will be complemented by the *even inverter*. For this compound event, by Theorem 2, we have

$$Prob\{X\} = \frac{1}{4} \times \left(\frac{1}{2} + \frac{1}{2^{n+1}}\right) = \frac{1}{8} + \frac{1}{2^{n+3}},$$

and

$$Prob\{not\ X\} = 1 - \left(\frac{1}{8} + \frac{1}{2^{n+3}}\right) = \frac{7}{8} - \frac{1}{2^{n+3}}.$$

Similarly, let Y be event "$k_j = -$ and $T = 1$"; i.e., a_j will be complemented by the *odd inverter*. Again, by Theorem 2, we have

$$Prob\{Y\} = \frac{1}{8} - \frac{1}{2^{n+3}}, \quad Prob\{not\ Y\} = \frac{7}{8} + \frac{1}{2^{n+3}}.$$

Let Z be event "$k_j = 1$ "; i.e., a_j will be complemented by the tester.

$$Prob\{Z\} = 1/4, \quad Prob\{not\ Z\} = 3/4.$$

By combining these three bounds, we have

$$Prob\{not\ (X\ or\ Y\ or\ Z)\} = \left(\frac{7}{8} - \frac{1}{2^{n+3}}\right) \times \left(\frac{7}{8} + \frac{1}{2^{n+3}}\right) \times \frac{3}{4}$$
$$= \frac{147}{256} - \frac{3}{2^{2n+8}}$$

Now, considering that d circuit layers are uniformly and independently generated, we have

$$Prob\{a_j\text{ be complemented one or more times in }d\text{ circuit layers}\}$$

$$= 1 - \left(\frac{147}{256} - \frac{3}{2^{2n+8}}\right)^d \approx 1 - (0.57)^d.$$

This probability quickly converges to one as d increases. Let p be the probability that the input element is complemented in one layer:

$$p = 1 - \frac{147}{256} + \frac{3}{2^{2n+8}}$$

Considering now d layers, we have:

$$Prob\{i \text{ complementations in } d \text{ layers}\} = \binom{d}{i} p^i (1-p)^{(d-i)}.$$

Using well known results of binomial distribution, the average of complementation times in d layers is dp, and their variance is $dp(1-p)$.

□

The probability of any input bit being complemented an odd or an even number of times by a circuit is established as follows.

Theorem 3 *If a $C(n, d)$ circuit is uniformly generated, the element a_j, for any $1 \le j \le n$ of the input sequence, is complemented an odd number of times with a probability asymptotic to 0.5; and an even number of times with the same probability.*

Proof. As in the Lemma 3 proof, we have:

$$Prob\{i \text{ complementations in } d \text{ layers}\} = \binom{d}{i} p^i (1-p)^{(d-i)}.$$

Let P_C be the probability that input element a_j is complemented in d layers of $C(n, d)$:

$$P_C = Prob\{b_j = \bar{a}_j\}.$$

This P_C is computable by summing the above expression over all the odd $i's$, $0 \le i \le d$:

$$P_C = Prob\{\text{odd number of complementations in } d \text{ layers}\}$$

$$= \sum_{i \text{ is odd, } i=0}^{d} \binom{d}{i} p^i (1-p)^{(d-i)}$$

Note that the probability of non-complementation is given by $1 - P_C$, which is the one summed over all the even $i's$ for $0 \le i \le d$. Both of these probabilities very quickly converge to $1/2$ as d increases. □

For example, if $n = 10$, we have

$$P_C = 0.425781253 \quad \text{if } d = 1$$

$$P_C = 0.499757258 \quad \text{if } d = 4$$

$$P_C = 0.499999862 \quad \text{if } d = 8$$

$$P_C = 0.500000000 \quad \text{if } d = 16$$

4.3 Avalanche Effect and Output Randomness

It is desirable that a cryptographic function exhibits the so-called *avalanche effect*; i.e., a small change in the plaintext or the key gives rise to a large change in the ciphertext [Fe73, Ko81]. This avalanche effect will be analized for our proposed function F.

4.3.1 Avalanche Effect between Plaintext and Ciphertext

First, the avalanche effect between the input (plaintext) and output (ciphertext) is analyzed. Given a $C(n, d)$ circuit and input pair (A_1, A_2) with Hamming distance of i $(1 \leq i \leq n)$, the *average Hamming distance of output pairs* $(F(K, A_1), F(K, A_2))$ is denoted by $H_I(n, d, i)$. This average $H_I(n, d, i)$ is defined over all inputs and keys as; $\binom{n}{i}$ input pairs and 4^n keys. When $d = 1$, average output distance $H_I(n, 1, i)$ for any n can be directly derived as follows.

Lemma 4 *If a $L(n)$ circuit layer is uniformly distributed, then $H_I(n, 1, i)$ is explicitly expressed by*

$$H_I(n, 1, 1) = \frac{n}{4} + \frac{3}{4},$$

$$H_I(n, 1, i) = \frac{n}{4} + \frac{i}{2} \quad \text{if } i \geq 2.$$

Proof. Let $\mathcal{K}$ be a set of keys corresponding to changes in an input pair. Let $\overline{\mathcal{K}}$ be $K - \mathcal{K}$. Note $\mathcal{K}$ and $\overline{\mathcal{K}}$ have cardinalities i and $n - i$, respectively. Consequently, we have two possible cases.

(1) $\mathcal{K}$ has an *odd* number of tester keys.

> In this case, the i-bit change in the input implies the conversion of a parity event between odd and even. Thus, only the following output bits are complemented by the change in the input.

(i) Output bits at the inverter keys in $\overline{\mathcal{K}}$ whose average number is $(n - i)/2$.

(ii) Output bits at the tester keys in $\mathcal{K}$ whose average number is: 1 if $i = 1$, $i/2$ if $i \geq 2$.

Thus, the average Hamming distance of the output pair in this case is:

$$\frac{n-1}{2} + 1 = \frac{n}{2} + \frac{1}{2} \quad \text{if } i = 1, \qquad \frac{n-i}{2} + \frac{i}{2} = \frac{n}{2} \quad \text{if } i \geq 2.$$

(2) $\mathcal{K}$ has an *even* number of tester keys.

> In this case, the i-bit change in the input *never* converts the parity event between odd and even. Thus, only the following output bits are complemented by the change in the input.

(i) Output bits at the inverter keys in $\mathcal{K}$ whose average number is: 1 if $i = 1$, $i/2$ if $i \geq 2$.

(ii) Output bits at the tester keys in $\mathcal{K}$ whose average number is: 0 if $i = 1$, $i/2$ if $i \geq 2$.

Thus, the average Hamming distance of the output pair in this case is:

$$1 + 0 = 1 \quad \text{if } i = 1, \qquad \frac{i}{2} + \frac{i}{2} = i \quad \text{if } i \geq 2.$$

For the above cases, we have

$$Prob\{\mathcal{K} \text{ has } odd \text{ number of tester keys}\} = 1/2,$$

$$Prob\{\mathcal{K} \text{ has } even \text{ number of tester keys}\} = 1/2.$$

In summation, the average Hamming distance of the output pair is:

$$H_I(n, 1, i) = \frac{1}{2}(\frac{n}{2} + \frac{1}{2}) + \frac{1}{2} \times 1 = \frac{n}{4} + \frac{3}{4} \quad \text{if } i = 1,$$

$$H_I(n, 1, i) = \frac{1}{2} \times \frac{n}{2} + \frac{1}{2} \times i = \frac{n}{4} + \frac{i}{2} \quad \text{if } i \geq 2.$$

Thus, the lemma has been proved. □

Examples of $H_I(n, 1, i)$ are shown in Table 3.

Table 3. Average output distances $H_I(n, 1, i)$

	n=1	n=2	n=3	n=4	n=5	n=6
$i = 1$	1.00	1.25	1.50	1.75	2.00	2.25
$i = 2$	—	1.50	1.75	2.00	2.25	2.50
$i = 3$	—	—	2.25	2.50	2.75	3.00
$i = 4$	—	—	—	3.00	3.25	3.50
$i = 5$	—	—	—	—	3.75	4.00
$i = 6$	—	—	—	—	—	4.50

If only the average distances of the intermediate values are used without analysis of the exact distribution of the distances, then $H_I(n, d, i)$ when $d \geq 2$ can be approximately estimated as follows:

Lemma 5 *If a $C(n, d)$ circuit is uniformly distributed, then $H_I(n, d, i)$ is approximately expressed by*

$$\frac{n}{2} + (\frac{1}{2})^d(i - \frac{n}{2}) \leq H_I(n, d, i) \leq \frac{n+1}{2} + (\frac{1}{2})^d(i - \frac{n+1}{2}).$$

Proof. Since we only consider the average distances of the intermediate values, then $H_I(n, d, i)$ when $d \geq 2$ can be approximately estimated by using $H_I(n, 1, i)$ as

$$H_I(n, d, i) = \overbrace{H_I(n, 1, H_I(n, 1, H_I(..., H_I(n, 1, i))))}^{d \text{ times}}.$$

From Lemma 4, $H_I(n, 1, i)$ is generally expressed by

$$\frac{n}{4} + \frac{i}{2} \leq H_I(n, 1, i) \leq \frac{n}{4} + \frac{1}{4} + \frac{i}{2} \quad \text{for all } i.$$

Thus, we have

$$H_I(n, d, i) \geq \frac{n}{4}(1 + \frac{1}{2} + (\frac{1}{2})^2 + \cdots + (\frac{1}{2})^{d-1}) + i(\frac{1}{2})^d,$$

$$H_I(n, d, i) \leq \frac{n+1}{4}(1 + \frac{1}{2} + (\frac{1}{2})^2 + \cdots + (\frac{1}{2})^{d-1}) + i(\frac{1}{2})^d.$$

By rewriting a finite geometric sum for $H_I(n, d, i)$, we have

$$\frac{n}{2} + (\frac{1}{2})^d(i - \frac{n}{2}) \leq H_I(n, d, i) \leq \frac{n+1}{2} + (\frac{1}{2})^d(i - \frac{n+1}{2}). \quad □$$

Note that $H_I(n, d, i)$ converges to a value between $n/2$ and $(n+1)/2$ as $d \to \infty$ regardless of the i value. Using the formula in Lemma 5, we can observe the dependency of n, d and i for the avalanche effect.

To obtain the exact $H_I(n, d, i)$ when $d \geq 2$, an analysis is needed that includes intermediate distance distribution. Thus, we introduce a transition probability based on the Markov chain theory. Given input pair (A_1, A_2) with Hamming distance of i ($1 \leq i \leq n$), then *the probability that the Hamming distance of output pairs* $(f(K, A_1), f(K, A_2))$ *is* j ($0 \leq j \leq n$) is denoted by $P_n(i, j)$. This transition probability, $P_n(i, j)$, is defined over all the inputs and keys as; $\binom{n}{i}$ input pairs and 4^n keys, and it satisfies

$$0 \leq P_n(i, j) \leq 1, \quad \sum_{j=0}^{n} P_n(i, j) = 1.$$

Since our proposed function f is a one-to-one mapping, note that

$$P_n(i, 0) = 0 \quad \text{if } i > 0.$$

We have obtained some of the $P_n(i, j)$ values through computer simulation. Some examples of $[P_n(i, j)]$ matrices such that $2 \leq n \leq 6$ are as follows.

$$[P_2(i, j)] = \begin{pmatrix} 3/4 & 1/4 \\ 1/2 & 1/2 \end{pmatrix}, \quad [P_3(i, j)] = \begin{pmatrix} 5/8 & 2/8 & 1/8 \\ 1/4 & 3/4 & 0 \\ 3/8 & 0 & 5/8 \end{pmatrix},$$

$$[P_4(i, j)] = \begin{pmatrix} 9/16 & 3/16 & 3/16 & 1/16 \\ 1/8 & 6/8 & 1/8 & 0 \\ 3/16 & 3/16 & 9/16 & 1/16 \\ 1/4 & 0 & 1/4 & 2/4 \end{pmatrix}, \quad [P_5(i, j)] = \begin{pmatrix} 17/32 & 4/32 & 6/32 & 4/32 & 1/32 \\ 1/16 & 11/16 & 3/16 & 1/16 & 0 \\ 3/32 & 6/32 & 20/32 & 2/32 & 1/32 \\ 1/8 & 1/8 & 1/8 & 5/8 & 0 \\ 5/32 & 0 & 10/32 & 0 & 17/32 \end{pmatrix},$$

$$[P_6(i, j)] = \begin{pmatrix} 33/64 & 5/64 & 10/64 & 10/64 & 5/64 & 1/64 \\ 1/32 & 20/32 & 6/32 & 4/32 & 1/32 & 0 \\ 3/64 & 9/64 & 42/64 & 6/64 & 3/64 & 1/64 \\ 1/16 & 2/16 & 2/16 & 10/16 & 1/16 & 0 \\ 5/64 & 5/64 & 10/64 & 10/64 & 33/64 & 1/64 \\ 3/32 & 0 & 10/32 & 0 & 3/32 & 16/32 \end{pmatrix}.$$

Using the $[P_n(i, j)]$ matrices, an exact $H_I(n, d, i)$ is generally expressed by

$$H_I(n, d, i) = \sum_{j=1}^{n} j G_{n,d}(i, j), \quad \text{where} \quad [G_{n,d}(i, j)] = [P_n(i, j)]^d.$$

If $d = 1$ and $i \geq 1$, then $H_I(n, 1, i)$ can be simply expressed as

$$H_I(n, 1, i) = \sum_{j=1}^{n} j G_{n,1}(i, j) = \sum_{j=1}^{n} j P_n(i, j),$$

and its explicit formula using n and i can be obtained in Lemma 4.

Since a Markov chain with a transition probability of $[P_n(i, j)]$ is ergodic (i.e. irreducible and non-periodic), it has a stable limit distribution, $[G_{n,\infty}(i, j)]$, defined by

$$[G_{n,\infty}(i, j)] = [P_n(i, j)]^{\infty}.$$

Since $[G_{n,\infty}(i, j)]$ is rewritten as $[P_n(i, j)]^m$ to satisfy

$$[P_n(i, j)]^{m+1} = [P_n(i, j)]^m,$$

the elements of $G_{n,\infty}(i, j)$ are directly derived from $P_n(i, j)$ by solving a system of linear equations

$$[G_{n,\infty}(i, j)] \times [I - [P_n(i, j)]] = 0,$$

$$\sum_{j=1}^{n} G_{n,\infty}(i, j) = 1,$$

where I and 0 denote a unit matrix and a zero matrix, respectively.

Table 4 shows average output distances for $H_I(n, d, i)$ when $i = 1$. The values for $H_I(n, d, 1)$ when $n \leq 6$ and $d = 2, 3, 16$, and ∞ are calculated by the transition probability matrices. The analytical results coincide with the ones obtained by exhaustive computer simulation. The values for $H_I(n, d, 1)$ when $n \geq 8$ in Table 4 are the results of 1 million random samplings.

Table 4. Average output distance $H_I(n, d, 1)$

	n=1	n=2	n=3	n=4	n=6	n=8	n=16	n=32	n=64
$d = 1$	1	1.2500	1.5000	1.7500	2.2500	2.7500	4.7500	8.7500	16.750
$d = 2$	1	1.3125	1.6563	2.0156	2.7539	3.5469	6.3750	11.750	22.508
$d = 3$	1	1.3281	1.7031	2.1055	2.9502	3.9625	7.4625	14.463	28.463
$d = 16$	1	1.3331	1.7141	2.1331	3.0474	4.0021	8.0000	16.000	32.000
$d = \infty$	1	1.3333	1.7143	2.1333	3.0476	4.0023	8.0000	16.000	32.000

In Table 4, we can observe that the $H_I(n, d, i)$ estimate in Lemma 5 seems to be a "good" approximation, and that the average output distance $H_I(n, d, i)$ converges to $n/2$ as both n and d increase.

4.3.2 Avalanche Effect between Key and Ciphertext

Given two sequences, $K = (k_1, k_2, ..., k_m)$ and $K' = (k'_1, k'_2, ..., k'_m)$, of m symbols from $\{0, 1, -, +\}$, key symbol distance s is defined as

$$s = \sum_{\ell=1}^{m} c_\ell \quad \text{where } c_\ell = \begin{cases} 0 & \text{if } k_\ell = k'_\ell \\ 1 & \text{otherwise.} \end{cases}$$

Given a $C(n, d)$ circuit and a key pair (K, K') whose key symbol distance is i, the average Hamming distance of output pairs $(F(K, A), F(K', A))$ is denoted by $H_K(n, d, i)$.

When $d = 1$, average output distance $H_K(n, d, i)$ for any n can be directly derived as follows.

Lemma 6 If an input (plaintext) to an $L(n)$ circuit layer is uniformly distributed and fixed, and the keys of the key pair (K, K') are also uniformly distributed, then $H_K(n, 1, i)$ is explicitly expressed by

$$H_K(n, 1, 1) = \frac{n}{4} + \frac{5}{12},$$

$$H_K(n, 1, i) = \frac{n}{4} + \frac{i}{3} \quad \text{if } i \geq 2.$$

Proof. (Proof is similar to the analysis of Lemma 4 proof, and will be given in the full paper.)

If we only consider key changes in the first layer of $C(n, d)$ circuit, then $H_K(n, d, i)$ when $d \geq 2$ can be approximately estimated as follows.

Lemma 7 *If an input (plaintext) to a $C(n, d)$ circuit is uniformly distributed and fixed, and the keys of the key pair $(\mathbf{K}, \mathbf{K'})$ are also uniformly distributed where $K_1 \neq K_1'$, $K_\ell = K_\ell'$ $(2 \leq \ell \leq d)$, then $H_K(n, d, i)$ is approximately expressed by*

$$\frac{n}{2} + \left(\frac{1}{2}\right)^{d-1}\left(\frac{i}{3} - \frac{n}{4}\right) \leq H_K(n, d, i) \leq \frac{n}{2} + \left(\frac{1}{2}\right)^{d-1}\left(\frac{1}{12} + \frac{i}{3} - \frac{n}{4}\right).$$

Proof. By combining the results of Lemmas 4 and 6, $H_K(n, d, i)$ can be estimated similarly to Lemma 5. □

In this subsection, we discussed the avalanche effect between an *internal key* and the output of one $L(n)$ layer. From a practical viewpoint, it is necessary to clarify the avalanche effect between an *external key* and an output. The avalanche effect depends on a *key generation scheme* or *key schedule calculation scheme*, which will be described in Section 5.1. The results obtained in Section 4.3 are useful to design an optimal scheme.

4.3.3 Completeness and Avalanche Effect

The notion of avalanche effect has a close relationship with *completeness* defined as:

Definition 5 (Completeness)
A function is complete if and only if each output bit depends on all of the input bits. □

Kam and Davida [KD79] showed a method of designing substitution-permutation encryption scheme to meet the *completeness* condition. As for function F based on a $C(n, d)$ circuit, the completeness condition is expressed as follows:

Lemma 8 *Let $\mathbf{K} = K_1 K_2 \cdots K_d$ and $K_\ell = k_{\ell 1} k_{\ell 2} \cdots k_{\ell n}$ $(1 \leq \ell \leq d)$. Function $F(\mathbf{K}, .)$ based on a $C(n, d)$ circuit is complete if and only if*

$$\left(k_{\ell i} = \{\text{inverter}\}, \ k_{\ell j} = \{\text{tester}\} \ 1 \leq i, j \leq n, \ i \neq j, \ \exists \ell \right) \ \forall i, \forall j.$$

Proof. (Sketch) If $k_{\ell i} = \{\text{inverter}\}$, and $k_{\ell j} = \{\text{tester}\}$ in the same layer, then i-th output bit depends on j-th input bit. If this relation satisfies in any one layer of d layers for all i and for all j $(1 \leq i, j \leq n)$, then function F is complete, vice versa. □

From Lemma 8 , we get a necessary and sufficient condition of completeness as follows:

Lemma 9 *There exists a complete function F based on a $C(n, d)$ circuit if and only if $d \geq n$.*

Proof. If $d < n$, it is impossible to construct a parity circuit satisfying complete condition described in Lemma 8. If $d \geq n$, we have an instance of complete function such that

$$k_{\ell\ell} = \{\text{inverter}\}, \ k_{\ell j} = \{\text{tester}\}, \ \ell \neq j, \ 1 \leq \ell, j \leq n. \quad \square$$

Webster and Tavares [WT86] introduced the *strict avalanche criterion* in order to combine the notions of the completeness and the so-called *avalanche effect* [Fe73]. Forre [Fo88] and Lloyd [Ll89] discussed this strict avalanche criterion for some cryptographic functions. Definitions of these criteria are summarized as follows.

Definition 6 (Avalanche Effect)

A function exhibits the *avalanche effect* if and only if an average of half of output bits change whenever a single input bit is complemented. □

Definition 7 (Strict Avalanche Criterion)

A function satisfies the *strict avalanche criterion* if and only if each output bit changes with probability $1/2$ whenever a single input bit is complemented. □

In Sections 4.3.1 and 4.3.2., we showed that *avalance effect* is satisfied for function F based on $C(n, d)$ circuit for large n and d. Furthermore, the relationship between completeness and the strict avalanche effect is obtained for $C(n, d)$ circuit as follows.

Lemma 10 *If function F based on $C(n, d)$ circuit is complete, then it satisfies the strict avalanche criterion.*

Proof. It is clear from the definitions and Lemma 8. □

4.4 Equivalent Keys

Let π_n be the group of all permutations on $\{0, 1\}^n$, the set of n-bit messages. For a given key K, function $F(K, .)$ defines an element of π_n. Note that the group π_n has cardinality $(2^n)!$. The key space generates a subset of π_n. Since a K key defining $F(K, .)$ is a sequence of nd symbols from $\{ 0, 1, -, + \}$, the number of distinct K keys is 4nd. That is, the cardinality of the key space is 4nd. If $d > n/2$, then $4^{nd} > 2^n!$, so equivalent keys must exist.

4.4.1 Equivalent Keys for One Input-Output Pair

When an input-output pair (I, O) is given, we need to know how many distinct equivalent keys exist. Distinct equivalent keys for pair (I_i, O_j) are defined as K_1 and K_2 such that:

$$O_j = F(K_1, I_i) = F(K_2, I_i), \quad K_1 \neq K_2.$$

Table 5 shows all the distinct equivalent keys when $n = 2$, $d = 1$.

Table 5. Distinct equivalent keys when $n = 2$, $d = 1$

$O\backslash I$	(0,0)	(0,1)	(1,0)	(1,1)
(0,0)	(0,0), $(-,-)$ (0,+), (+,0)	(0,1), $(-,+)$ (0,$-$), (+,1)	(1,0), (+,$-$) ($-$,0), (1,+)	(1,1), (+,+) ($-$,1), (1,$-$)
(0,1)	(0,1), $(-,+)$ ($-$,1), (0,$-$)	(0,0), $(-,-)$ ($-$,0), (0,+)	(1,1), (+,+) (+,1), (1,$-$)	(1,0), (+,$-$) (+,0), (1,+)
(1,0)	(1,0), (+,$-$) ($-$,0), (1,$-$)	(1,1), (+,+) ($-$,1), (1,+)	(0,0), $(-,-)$ (0,$-$), (+,0)	(0,1), $(-,+)$ (0,+), (+,1)
(1,1)	(1,1), (+,+) (+,1), (1,+)	(1,0), (+,$-$) (+,0), (1,$-$)	(0,1), $(-,+)$ ($-$,1), (0,+)	(0,0), $(-,-)$ ($-$,0), (0,$-$)

Let $N_{ij}(n, d)$ be the number of distinct K keys such that $O_j = F(K, I_i)$ for fixed input I_i $(1 \le i \le 2^n)$ and fixed output O_j $(1 \le j \le 2^n)$. From Table 5, we can observe that $N_{ij}(2, 1) = 4$ for all i and j. As for $N_{ij}(n, d)$, we get the following theorem.

Theorem 4 *For all (n, d) pairs, number $N_{ij}(n, d)$ is the same for all i and j. Number $N_{ij}(n, d)$ can be abbreviated as $N(n, d)$, and expressed by*

$$N(n, d) = 2^{(2d-1)n}.$$

Proof. Note that the cardinality of the key space is 4nd. Assume that an input is fixed as I_i. When $F(\mathbf{K}, I_i)$ is computed with 4nd distinct keys, output values $\{0, 1\}^n$ are classified into 2^n distinct classes. Since the K keys are uniformly distributed, the output values are also uniformly distributed by the complementation property shown in Theorem 3. Thus, $N_{ij}(n, d)$ is the same for a fixed i and for all j ($1 \leq j \leq n$). Furthermore, it is expressed by

$$N_{ij}(n, d) = \frac{4^{nd}}{2^n} = 2^{(2d-1)n} \quad \text{for all } j.$$

It is clear that this holds for all i. Thus, the theorem has been proved. $\quad\square$

Through computer simulation, we have confirmed that Theorem 4 holds. Table 6 shows $N(n, d)$ values such that $1 \leq n \leq 4$, $1 \leq d \leq 3$.

Table 6. Number of distinct equivalent keys
for one input-output pair

	n=1	n=2	n=3	n=4
$d = 1$	2	4	8	16
$d = 2$	8	64	512	4096
$d = 3$	32	1024	32768	1048576

Furthemore, the following can be observed:

(1) Ratio R of number $N(n, d)$ to the cardinality of the key space is:

$$R = N(n, d)/4^{nd} = 2^{(2d-1)n}/4^{nd} = 1/2^n.$$

Ratio R converges to 0 as $n \to \infty$.

(2) If a key size is fixed as $c = nd$, then $N(n, d)$ value is maxmized as $2^{2c-1} = 2^{2nd-1}$ when $n = 1$ and $d = c$, and minmized as $2^c = 2^{nd}$ when $n = c$ and $d = 1$.

4.4.2 Completely Equivalent Keys

Key pair $(\mathbf{K_1}, \mathbf{K_2})$ is called *completely equivalent* if

$$F(\mathbf{K_1}, I) = F(\mathbf{K_2}, I), \quad \mathbf{K_1} \neq \mathbf{K_2} \quad \text{for all } I.$$

Lemma 11 *Let* $\mathbf{K}^{\pm} = k_1^{\pm} k_2^{\pm} \ldots k_{nd}^{\pm}$ *be a sequence of symbols from* $\{-, +\}$, *and* $\mathbf{K}^{\oslash} = k_1^{\oslash} k_2^{\oslash} \ldots k_{nd}^{\oslash}$ *be a sequence of symbols from* $\{0, 1\}$. *If*

either $(k_i^{\pm} = -, \ k_i^{\oslash} = 0)$ or $(k_i^{\pm} = +, \ k_i^{\oslash} = 1)$ for all i such that $1 \leq i \leq nd$,

then, pair $(\mathbf{K}^{\pm}, \mathbf{K}^{\oslash})$ *is completely equivalent.*

Proof. If $\mathbf{K}^{\pm}$ is used, then only even events occur for all I, which implies that the input entry corresponding to $+$ is complemented and the one corresponding to $-$ is not. If $\mathbf{K}^{\oslash}$ is used, then the input entry corresponding to 1 is complemented and the one corresponding to 0 is not. Thus we have

$$F(\mathbf{K}^{\pm}, I) = F(\mathbf{K}^{\oslash}, I), \quad \mathbf{K}^{\pm} \neq \mathbf{K}^{\oslash} \quad \text{for all } I. \quad\square$$

The number of keys for both $K^{\pm}$ and $K^{\oslash}$ is 2nd. The number of pairs of completely equivalent keys is also 2nd. Thus, the number of completely equivalent keys is $2 \cdot 2^{nd}$ ($= 2^{nd+1}$). Note that the ratio of the number of completely equivalent keys to the cardinality of the key space is $2^{nd+1}/2^{2nd} = 2^{1-nd}$.

4.5 Complementation Property

Let $\overline{X}$ denote the complement of X. When X is a sequence of bits, $\overline{X}$ represents the bitwise inverse of X. In Particular, the complement of symbols $-$ and $+$ are defined as $+$ and $-$. Our proposed function f has the following complementation property:

Property 1: $f(K, I) = f(\overline{K}, \overline{I})$ for all K keys and I inputs.

It can be proved that Property 1 holds: For the tester positions of the keys, it is clear that $(K) \oplus (I) = (\overline{K}) \oplus (\overline{I})$. Since the complementation of both key K and input I does not change the parity event, the output bits at the inverter keys do not change. Notice that the above complementation property does not always hold for function F when $d \geq 2$.

We can now make the following remarks. DES cipher algorithm E has the following complementation property.

Property 2:   If $O = E(K, I)$, then $\overline{O} = E(\overline{K}, \overline{I})$ for all K keys and I inputs,

Using this property and the weak keys, it is easy to find collisions for hash functions based on DES and the Meyer-Matyas chaining scheme [MOI90]. If a hash function is designed based on $C(n, d)$ circuit and a certain chaining scheme, it is desirable that $d \geq 2$.

5. Applications

5.1 Key Generation

Each circuit layer key $\in \{0, 1, -, +\}$ is coded as 2-bit information so that "00" $\leftrightarrow$ "0", "01" $\leftrightarrow$ "1", "10" $\leftrightarrow$ "$-$", "11" $\leftrightarrow$ "$+$". Since each j iteration ($1 \leq j \leq d$) of the $L(n)$ parity layer uses a different $2n$-bit key, the $C(n, d)$ parity circuits use $2nd$-bit *internal keys*. The internal key size is determined to be as large as needed to secure the cryptosystem.

Internal keys, $K = (K_1, K_2, \cdots K_d)$, are generated from *external key* K_E (supplied by the user). Thus, a key generation scheme (or, so-called key schedule calculation scheme) is needed to map from the external key to the internal one. In DES, a 768 ($= 48 \times 16$)-bit internal key is generated from a 56-bit external key by using the algorithm described in [NBS77]. However, it is said that the 56-bit key length is *not* sufficiently secure against exhaustive search attacks [Ma88] or chosen plaintext attacks [Si90]. External key size, of say 64-bits or 128-bits, is determined from the viewpoints of security, compatibility and standardization. Our circuit easily generates internal key K from external key K_E by applying the $C(n, d)$ circuit itself as in [Me89]. Thus, the $L(n)$ circuit layer is recursively used for both data randomization and key generation. There are a lot of variants for key generation schemes. One possibility uses the CBC mode with external key K_E and initial fixed key K_I, which is randomly chosen and shared between the sender and the receiver.

5.2 Design Principles and Criteria

The $C(n, d)$ parity circuit can be used in any *mode of operation* currently defined by ISO.

Thus, the circuit of n-bit width is directly applicable to block ciphers whose block size is n bits. Furthermore, $C(n, d)$ parity circuit can be also applied to the *F-function* of Feistel type ciphers whose block size is $2n$ bits. In any application schemes of $C(n, d)$, the block size can be flexible, say 64-bits, which is compatible with DES or FEAL.

If a block cipher is used as the hashing function in a certain chaining mode, the size of the hashed value (or *digest*) must be chosen securely. It is recommended [MOI90] that the size of the hashed value must be 128-bits to counter "meet-in-the-middle attacks". Thus, block size must be 128-bits. The $C(n, d)$ parity circuit, when $n = 128$, can achieve much faster speed while preserving security.

Recently, Quisquarter and Delescaille have found 21 equivalence key pairs for DES (64-bit input and 56-bit key),for fixed input-output pairs [QD89]. These key pairs are also called keys with collision. Their collision search algorithm is based on Pollard's ρ method. Even if we apply their collision search algorithm, it appears difficult to search for collisions in our $F(., .)$, with, say, 128-bit inputs and 128-bit external keys that generate 4nd symbols of internal keys.

5.3 Hardware Implementation

The $C(n, d)$ circuits can be implemented with high performance in hardware as well as in software.

We estimated the encryption/decryption speed of our proposed $C(n, d)$ parity circuits according to the current hardware technology. Assume that $C(n, d)$ circuits are implemented by 1.5 μm CMOS gate-arrays. The encryption speed will nearly equal the decryption speed. The amount of the encryption time is mainly taken up by comparisons and calculations for bits corresponding to the *tester cells*. These operations are carried out for each $L(n)$ layer by EXOR gates. The time for one EXOR calculation can be estimated as 4 nano seconds. Assume that data randomization and key generation are simultaneously carried out using an $L(n)$ module of $L(n)$ with feedback registers. Since one EXOR requires 3 gates and one register requires 5.5 gates, the total hardware amount can be estimated as $50n$ gates. In the $C(n, d)$ circuit, the encryption time is $d\,(4\lceil \log_2 n \rceil + 25)$ nano seconds. Thus, the encryption speed S is expressed by

$$S = \frac{n}{d\,(4\lceil \log_2 n \rceil + 25)} \times 10^9 \text{ bps.}$$

Some reasonable implementation examples are shown in Table 7. Note that FEAL-8 LSI achieves 96 Mega bps with 4 Kilo gates for the core parts.

Also note that the n and d parameters for the $C(n, d)$ parity circuit can be flexibly designed while still preserving "good" cryptographic properties. Furthermore, encryption speed S increases as width n increases while still ensuring randomness. Circuit modules with a fixed n and d have a regular structure so the structure can be expanded by multiple modular connections at a minimal cost. This advanced feature is not found in any other existing block ciphers.

Table 7. Hardware Performance

Width n (bits)	Depth d (rounds)	Speed S (M bps)	Size (K gates)
64	8	160	3.2
64	16	80	3.2
128	8	300	6.4
128	16	150	6.4

6. Conclusions

A new family of cryptographic functions called parity circuits has been presented. Furthermore, we have clarified cryptographic properties such as involution, nonlinearity, the probability of bit complementation, avalanche effect, equivalent keys. Some recommended parameter values to preserve security have been shown. In addition, we estimated the speed of the parity circuits when implemented using the current hardware technology.

Acknowledgement

The authors would like to thank Hikaru Morita at NTT for valuable discussions.

References

[BPS90] Brown, L., J. Pieprzyk and J. Seberry: "LOKI - A cryptographic primitive for authentication and secrecy applications", Abstract of Auscrypt 90, U. of New South Wales, Sydney, Australia, January (1990).

[Fe73] Feistel, H.: "Cryptography and computer privacy", Scientic American, Vol.228, No.5, pp.15-23, (1973).

[Fo88] Forre, R.: "The strict avalanche criterion: spectral properties of Boolean functions and an extended definition", Proc. of CRYPTO'88, (1988).

[KD79] Kam, J. B. and G. I. Davida: "Structured design of substitution-permutation encryption network", IEEE Trans. on Computers, Vol.28, No.10, pp.747-753, Oct., (1979).

[Ko81] Konheim, A. G.: "Cryptography: A Primer", John Wiley & Sons, New York, (1981).

[Ll89] Lloyd, S.: "Counting functions satisfying a higher order strict avalanche criterion", Proc. of Eurocrypt'89, (1989).

[Ma89] Massey J.: "An introduction to contemporary cryptology", Proc. IEEE, Vol.76, no.5, pp.533-549, May (1988).

[MS89] Meier, M. and O. Staffelbach: "Nonlinearity criteria for cryptographic functions", Proc. of Eurocrypt'89 (1989).

[MOI90] Miyaguchi, S. , K. Ohta and M. Iwata:"128-bit hash function (N-Hash)", Proc. of Securicom'90 (1990).

[NBS77] National Bureau of Standards: " Data Encryption Standard", FIPS Publication 46, U. S. Dept. of Commerce, January (1977).

[Me89] Merkle, R. C.: "A software encryption function", private communication, (1989).

[MSS88] Miyaguchi, S., A. Shiraishi, and A. Shimizu: "Fast data encipherment algorithm FEAL-8", Review of the Electrical Communication Laboratories, vol. 36-4, (1988).

[QD89] Quisquarter, J. J. and J. P. Delescaille: "How easy is collision search? New results and applications to DES", Proc. of CRYPTO'89 (1989).

[Ru86] Rueppel R. A.: "Analysis and design of stream ciphers", Springer-Verlag, Berlin, (1986).

[Si90] Simmons, G. J.:"Predictions for the 1990's ", IACR Newsletter, vol. 7, No.1, January (1990).

[WT86] Webster, A. F. and S. E. Tavares.:"On the design of S-box ", Proc. of CRYPTO'85, Springer, (1986).

Cryptographic Significance of the Carry for Ciphers Based on Integer Addition

Othmar Staffelbach [1]   Willi Meier [2]

[1] GRETAG, Althardstrasse 70
CH-8105 Regensdorf, Switzerland

[2] HTL Brugg-Windisch
CH-5200 Windisch, Switzerland

Abstract

Integer addition has been proposed for use in cryptographic transformations since this operation is nonlinear when considered over GF(2). In these applications nonlinearity or confusion is achieved via the carry. If the carry happens to be biased, there result correlations to linear functions which can be cryptanalytically exploited.

The aim of the present paper is to investigate the probability distribution of the carry for integer addition with an arbitrary number n of inputs. It is shown that asymptotically the carry is balanced for even n and biased for odd n. As a result, for $n = 3$ the carry is strongly biased, whereas for increasing n it is shown that the bias tends to 0.

1 Introduction

Several cryptographic transformations are known which use integer addition as a primitive. In [5,6] the summation principle has been formulated in order to generate cryptographically strong binary sequences out of given (cryptographically weak) sequences. In another direction we mention that knapsack type ciphers are also based on integer addition.

In these ciphers nonlinearity or confusion is achieved via the carry. In fact if the carry happens to be zero, integer addition is linear when considered over $GF(2)$, or there result correlations to linear functions if the carry is biased. Therefore the strength of these ciphers heavily relies on the randomness of the carry. In particular it is required that the least significant bit (l.s.b.) of the carry is balanced or nearly balanced. However it may happen that this postulate is satisfied in the average, but is violated locally. In fact for the summation combiner with $n = 2$ inputs it has been shown in [4] that the carry is balanced in the average, but is strongly biased in runs of consecutive equal output digits. Furthermore in [4] it is indicated how the resulting correlations may be cryptanalytically exploited. As a consequence the (l.s.b. of the) carry should also be balanced (or nearly balanced) when probabilities are conditioned on side information, e.g. on known output digits.

The aim of the present paper is to investigate the probability distribution of the carry for a summation combiner with an arbitrary number n of inputs. It is shown that for any probability distribution of the initial carry σ_0, the probability distribution of the j-th carry σ_j converges to a unique asymptotic distribution. It turns out that asymptotically for $n = 3$ the (l.s.b. of the) carry is strongly biased. This contrasts to the case $n = 2$ where the carry is balanced. More generally it is proved that the carry is balanced for even n and biased for odd n. We develop a method which allows to compute the bias numerically as a normalized correlation $\delta(n)$, where $-1 \leq \delta(n) \leq 1$. In these terms the bias $\delta(n)$ is shown to converge to 0 as n tends to ∞.

If the probability distribution of the carry is conditioned on the output, a corresponding bias is introduced. This bias is denoted by $\delta'(n)$, and it is proved that $\delta'(n) = \delta(n-1)$. As a special case we have $\delta'(2) = \delta(1) = 1$, which further illuminates the observation that for $n = 2$ the carry is strongly biased in runs of consecutive equal output digits.

In order to derive the above results, the probability distribution of the carry σ_j is described as a n-vector $\mathbf{q}_j$ over the reals. Then the evolution of the probability distribution of the carry is given by an equation of the form $\mathbf{q}_{j+1} = A\mathbf{q}_j$, where A is a $n \times n$ transition matrix. An explicit description of the matrix A is given in terms of binomial coefficients (cf. (17)). In order to study the asymptotic behaviour of $\mathbf{q}_j$, one has to find the eigenvalues and eigenvectors of A.

For the existence of a unique asymptotic probability distribution it is sufficient to show that $\lambda = 1$ is an eigenvalue (with multiplicity 1), and that all other eigenvalues have absolute value strictly smaller than 1. In fact we show that the eigenvalues are given by $\lambda_i = 2^{-i}$, for $0 \leq i \leq n - 1$ (Theorem 3.1). The fact that the eigenvalues can be computed for general n is remarkable and is based on particular properties of the transition matrix A. As a result the unique asymptotic probability distribution is described by the eigenvector $\mathbf{x}$ to the eigenvalue 1, normalized by $\sum_s x_s = 1$. Moreover the bias $\delta(n)$ of the carry is expressed as a property of this eigenvector (Theorem 4.1).

2 Integer Addition with Two or Three Inputs

2.1 Integer Addition with Two Inputs

To recall the summation principle consider two binary sequences $\mathcal{A} = (a_0, a_1, a_2, \ldots)$ and $\mathcal{B} = (b_0, b_1, b_2, \ldots)$. For every m the first m digits are viewed as the binary representation of an integer, i.e. $a = a_{m-1}2^{m-1} + \cdots + a_1 2 + a_0$ and $b = b_{m-1}2^{m-1} + \cdots + b_1 2 + b_0$. Then the integer sum $z = a + b$ defines the first m digits of the resulting sequence $\mathcal{Z} = (z_0, z_1, z_2, \ldots)$. If $\mathcal{A}$ and $\mathcal{B}$ are semi-infinite then $\mathcal{Z}$ is also defined as a semi-infinite sequence. The digit z_j is recursively computed by

$$z_j = f_0(a_j, b_j, \sigma_{j-1}) = a_j + b_j + \sigma_{j-1} \tag{1}$$

$$\sigma_j = f_1(a_j, b_j, \sigma_{j-1}) = a_j b_j + a_j \sigma_{j-1} + b_j \sigma_{j-1} \tag{2}$$

where in (1) σ_{j-1} denotes the carry bit, and $\sigma_{-1} = 0$.

Suppose that the input to the adder, i.e. the integers a and b, are uniformly distributed. In statistical terms this means that the corresponding input sequences $\mathcal{A}$ and $\mathcal{B}$ are considered as *independent and uniformly distributed* sequences of random variables. Then, as is shown in [4], the probability distribution of the carry bit σ_j converges exponentially to the uniform distribution. Moreover, if the initial carry σ_{-1} is assumed to be uniformly distributed this is also the case for all successive carries σ_j distributed as well. With regard to *correlation immunity*, knowledge of the output z_j does not give any information about the inputs a_j, b_j or the sum $a_j + b_j$. However it is shown in [4] that this is no longer true when z_j is observed in a run of consecutive equal output digits, as in this case the carry bit is expected to be biased.

To recall some results proved in [4], let $q_j(0)$ and $q_j(1)$ denote the probability that the carry bit σ_j is in state 0, or state 1, respectively. According to [4], the probability distributions $\mathbf{q}_j = (q_j(0), q_j(1))$ and $\mathbf{q}_{j-1} = (q_{j-1}(0), q_{j-1}(1))$ are related by

$$\begin{pmatrix} q_j(0) \\ q_j(1) \end{pmatrix} = \begin{pmatrix} \frac{3}{4} & \frac{1}{4} \\ \frac{1}{4} & \frac{3}{4} \end{pmatrix} \begin{pmatrix} q_{j-1}(0) \\ q_{j-1}(1) \end{pmatrix} \tag{3}$$

However if z_j is known to be 0, the relation between the conditional probabilities $\mathbf{q}_j$ and $\mathbf{q}_{j-1}$ is given by

$$\begin{pmatrix} q_j(0) \\ q_j(1) \end{pmatrix} = \begin{pmatrix} \frac{1}{2} & 0 \\ \frac{1}{2} & 1 \end{pmatrix} \begin{pmatrix} q_{j-1}(0) \\ q_{j-1}(1) \end{pmatrix} \tag{4}$$

Now assume that a run of s consecutive output digits 0 has been observed, e.g. $z_{j+1} = z_{j+2} = \cdots = z_{j+s} = 0$. Then the (conditional) probabilities $\mathbf{q}_{j+s}$ and $\mathbf{q}_j$ are related by $\mathbf{q}_{j+s} = A^s \mathbf{q}_j$ where the transition matrix A^s is obtained as

$$A^s = \begin{pmatrix} \frac{1}{2} & 0 \\ \frac{1}{2} & 1 \end{pmatrix}^s = \begin{pmatrix} \frac{1}{2^s} & 0 \\ 1 - \frac{1}{2^s} & 1 \end{pmatrix} \tag{5}$$

Thus, for any value of $\mathbf{q}_j$, the probability distribution $\mathbf{q}_{j+s}$ satisfies the inequalities

$$q_{j+s}(0) \leq \frac{1}{2^s} \quad \text{and} \quad q_{j+s}(1) \geq 1 - \frac{1}{2^s} \tag{6}$$

Therefore the carry prefers to be 1 in a run of consecutive 0's, similarly it prefers to be 0 in a run of consecutive 1's. Hence, there result strong correlations between a single output digit z_j and the sum $a_j + b_j$.

2.2 Integer Addition with Three Inputs

Consider the addition of 3 integers $a = a_{m-1}2^{m-1} + \cdots + a_1 2 + a_0$, $b = b_{m-1}2^{m-1} + \cdots + b_1 2 + b_0$ and $c = c_{m-1}2^{m-1} + \cdots + c_1 2 + c_0$. Denote by $\mathcal{A} = (a_0, a_1, a_2, \ldots)$, $\mathcal{B} = (b_0, b_1, b_2, \ldots)$ and $\mathcal{C} = (c_0, c_1, c_2, \ldots)$ the corresponding binary input sequences. Then the integer sum $z = a + b + c$ defines the first m digits of the output sequence $\mathcal{Z} = (z_0, z_1, z_2, \ldots)$. Denote by $I_j = a_j + b_j + c_j$ the integer sum of the inputs a_j, b_j and c_j. For independent and uniformly distributed input sequences, I_j can take the values 0,1,2 or 3 with the following probabilities

I_j	0	1	2	3
p	0.125	0.375	0.375	0.125

(7)

The value of the carry σ_j can be 0, 1 or 2, and is given as a function of σ_{j-1} and I_j as shown in Table 1, where the entries for σ_j in the frames indicate that the corresponding output z_j is 0.

	I_j			
σ_{j-1}	0	1	2	3
0	$\boxed{0}$	0	$\boxed{1}$	1
1	0	$\boxed{1}$	1	$\boxed{2}$
2	$\boxed{1}$	1	$\boxed{2}$	2

Table 1: σ_j as function of σ_{j-1} and I_j

For $j = 0, 1, 2, \ldots$ denote by $q_j(0)$, $q_j(1)$ and $q_j(2)$ the probability that the carry σ_j is in state 0, 1 or 2. From Table 1 and (7) we conclude that the probability vectors $\mathbf{q}_j = (q_j(0), q_j(1), q_j(2))$ and $\mathbf{q}_{j-1} = (q_{j-1}(0), q_{j-1}(1), q_{j-1}(2))$ are related by

$$\begin{pmatrix} q_j(0) \\ q_j(1) \\ q_j(2) \end{pmatrix} = \begin{pmatrix} \frac{1}{2} & \frac{1}{8} & 0 \\ \frac{1}{2} & \frac{3}{4} & \frac{1}{2} \\ 0 & \frac{1}{8} & \frac{1}{2} \end{pmatrix} \begin{pmatrix} q_{j-1}(0) \\ q_{j-1}(1) \\ q_{j-1}(2) \end{pmatrix}$$

(8)

Therefore $\mathbf{q}_j = A^j \mathbf{q}_0$, where A denotes the transition matrix in (8). This equation describes the propagation of the probability distribution of the carry from a given initial distribution. In this context it is of interest to know how $\mathbf{q}_j$ behaves asymptotically and whether $\lim_{j \to \infty} \mathbf{q}_j$ does exist. To settle this question we observe that the transition matrix A is *diagonalizable*, i.e. it can be written in the form $A = S^{-1}DS$, where D is a diagonal matrix, namely

$$A = \begin{pmatrix} \frac{1}{2} & \frac{1}{8} & 0 \\ \frac{1}{2} & \frac{3}{4} & \frac{1}{2} \\ 0 & \frac{1}{8} & \frac{1}{2} \end{pmatrix} = \begin{pmatrix} \frac{1}{6} & 1 & -\frac{1}{2} \\ \frac{2}{3} & 0 & 1 \\ \frac{1}{6} & -1 & -\frac{1}{2} \end{pmatrix} \begin{pmatrix} 1 & 0 & 0 \\ 0 & \frac{1}{2} & 0 \\ 0 & 0 & \frac{1}{4} \end{pmatrix} \begin{pmatrix} 1 & 1 & 1 \\ \frac{1}{2} & 0 & -\frac{1}{2} \\ -\frac{2}{3} & \frac{1}{3} & -\frac{2}{3} \end{pmatrix} \qquad (9)$$

Then we have $\mathbf{q}_j = A^j \mathbf{q}_0 = S^{-1} D^j S \mathbf{q}_0$. As the diagonal entries of D are 1, 1/2, 1/4, we arrive at

$$\lim_{j \to \infty} \mathbf{q}_j = \lim_{j \to \infty} A^j \mathbf{q}_0 = S^{-1} \lim_{j \to \infty} D^j S \mathbf{q}_0 = \left(\frac{1}{6}, \frac{2}{3}, \frac{1}{6}\right) \qquad (10)$$

Observe that the diagonal entries of D are the eigenvalues of A, and that the limit in (10) is the (normalized) eigenvector to the eigenvalue 1.

Formula (10) implies that (asymptotically) the carry is 0, 1 or 2 with probability 1/6, 2/3 or 1/6, respectively. Therefore the least significant bit of the carry is strongly biased. As a consequence, in the average the output z_j is correlated to $a_j + b_j + c_j + 1$ with probability 2/3. This result contrasts to the addition with 2 inputs, where the carry is balanced in the average.

Our analysis shows that the summation combiner with 3 inputs still has unpleasant properties with respect to correlation. Therefore we arc lead to investigate whether the situation improves as n increases.

3 Integer Addition with n Inputs

3.1 The Transition Matrix

Consider n integers $x_1, x_2, \ldots, x_n$, and denote by $\mathcal{X}_k = (x_{k0}, x_{k1}, x_{k2}, \ldots)$, $1 \le k \le n$, the corresponding binary sequences, i.e. $x_k = x_{k,m-1} 2^{m-1} + \cdots + x_{k1} 2 + x_{k0}$. Then the integer sum $z = x_1 + \cdots + x_n$ defines the first m digits of the output sequence $\mathcal{Z} = (z_0, z_1, z_2, \ldots)$. Denote by $I_j = x_{1j} + \cdots + x_{nj}$ the integer sum of the j-th input digits. Again the $\mathcal{X}_k$'s are assumed to be independent and uniformly distributed sequences of random variables. Then I_j can take the values i, $0 \le i \le n$, with probability

$$P(I_j = i) = \binom{n}{i} \frac{1}{2^n} \qquad (11)$$

The values of the output z_j and the carry σ_j are given as a function of the input I_j and the previous carry σ_{j-1}:

$$z_j = f_0(I_j, \sigma_{j-1}) \qquad (12)$$
$$\sigma_j = f_1(I_j, \sigma_{j-1}) \qquad (13)$$

The carry σ_j can take the values 0, 1, ..., n-1, and is computed according to Table 2, where the entry for σ_j in the frames indicate that the corresponding output z_j is 0.

σ_{j-1}	0	1	2	3	4	5	$\cdots$	$n-1$	n
0	$\boxed{0}$	0	$\boxed{1}$	1	$\boxed{2}$	2	·		
1	0	$\boxed{1}$	1	$\boxed{2}$	2	·			
2	$\boxed{1}$	1	$\boxed{2}$	2	·				
3	1	$\boxed{2}$	2	·					
4	$\boxed{2}$	2	·						
5	2	·							
·	·						·		$n-2$
$n-2$							·	$n-2$	$\boxed{n-1}$
$n-1$							$n-2$	$\boxed{n-1}$	$n-1$

Table 2: σ_j as function of σ_{j-1} and I_j

For $j = 0, 1, 2, \ldots$, and $0 \le s \le n-1$ denote by $q_j(s)$ the probability that the carry σ_j is in state s, and let $\mathbf{q}_j = (q_j(0), \ldots, q_j(n-1))$. The vectors $\mathbf{q}_j$ and $\mathbf{q}_{j-1}$ are related by the formula

$$q_j(s) = \sum_{\substack{i,t \\ f_1(i,t) = s}} P(I_j = i)\, q_{j-1}(t) \tag{14}$$

Thus we have the linear relation $\mathbf{q}_j = A\mathbf{q}_{j-1}$ where the $n \times n$ transition matrix A, according to Table 2 and formula (11), is computed as follows.

$$A = \frac{1}{2^n} \begin{pmatrix} \binom{n}{1}+\binom{n}{0} & \binom{n}{0} & 0 & 0 & \cdots & 0 \\ \binom{n}{3}+\binom{n}{2} & \binom{n}{2}+\binom{n}{1} & \binom{n}{1}+\binom{n}{0} & \binom{n}{0} & \cdots & 0 \\ \binom{n}{5}+\binom{n}{4} & \binom{n}{4}+\binom{n}{3} & \binom{n}{3}+\binom{n}{2} & \binom{n}{2}+\binom{n}{1} & \cdots & 0 \\ & & \vdots & & & \\ 0 & & \cdots & 0 & \binom{n}{0} & \binom{n}{0}+\binom{n}{1} \end{pmatrix} \tag{15}$$

The entry a_{st} of the matrix A is expressed as

$$a_{st} = \frac{1}{2^n}\left(\binom{n}{2s-t} + \binom{n}{2s-t-1}\right) = \frac{1}{2^n}\binom{n+1}{2s-t} \tag{16}$$

whereby (16) also holds for $2s - t < 0$ or $2s - t > n + 1$, in which case the binomial coefficients are defined to be 0. Therefore the matrix A can be written in the form

$$
A = \frac{1}{2^n}
\begin{pmatrix}
\binom{n+1}{1} & \binom{n+1}{0} & 0 & 0 & 0 & \cdots & 0 \\
\binom{n+1}{3} & \binom{n+1}{2} & \binom{n+1}{1} & \binom{n+1}{0} & 0 & \cdots & 0 \\
\binom{n+1}{5} & \binom{n+1}{4} & \binom{n+1}{3} & \binom{n+1}{2} & \binom{n+1}{1} & \cdots & 0 \\
& & & \vdots & & & \\
0 & & \cdots & & 0 & \binom{n+1}{0} & \binom{n+1}{1}
\end{pmatrix}
\tag{17}
$$

3.2 Eigenvectors and Eigenvalues of the Transition Matrix

In Section 2.2 the evolution of the probability distribution of the carry is obtained by considering the diagonalization of the transition matrix. In order to find a representation of the matrix A in diagonal form, $A = S^{-1}DS$, one has to find the eigenvalues and the eigenvectors of A. Recall that the eigenvalues of A coincide with the diagonal entries of D, and the columns of the matrix S^{-1} are the corresponding eigenvectors.

Observe that the diagonalization of (9) for $n = 3$ is based on the fact that the eigenvalues of the transition matrix are all distinct. Moreover a unique asymptotic probability distribution (see (10)) of the carry exists as a consequence of the fact that, apart from the eigenvalue 1, all other other eigenvalues have absolute value strictly smaller than 1. Our aim is to generalize both of these facts to the transition matrix in (17) for arbitrary n.

First observe that A is a stochastic matrix, i.e. its satisfies $\sum_{s=1}^{n} a_{st} = 1$. Thus for any vector $\mathbf{x} = (x_1, \ldots, x_n)$ the sum $\sum_s x_s$ is preserved by A, i.e. if $\mathbf{x}' = A\mathbf{x}$ then $\sum_s x'_s = \sum_s x_s$. Suppose that $\mathbf{x}$ is an eigenvector of A to the eigenvalue λ, i.e. $\mathbf{x}' = A\mathbf{x} = \lambda\mathbf{x}$. Then $\sum_s x'_s = \lambda\sum_s x_s = \sum_s x_s$ implies either $\lambda = 1$ or $\sum_s x_s = 0$. Hence all eigenvectors to eigenvalues $\lambda \neq 1$ satisfy $\sum_s x_s = 0$.

The matrix A has an additional symmetry—it is compatible with the the transformation M defined by $M(x_1, \ldots, x_n) = (x_n, \ldots, x_1)$. This means that $MA\mathbf{x} = AM\mathbf{x}$ holds for all $\mathbf{x}$. If $\mathbf{x}$ is an eigenvector, $M\mathbf{x}$ is also an eigenvector to the same eigenvalue λ. For eigenvectors $\mathbf{x}$ with multiplicity 1 this implies that

$$
M\mathbf{x} = \mathbf{x} \quad \text{or} \quad M\mathbf{x} = -\mathbf{x}, \tag{18}
$$

i.e. the eigenvector is either symmetric or antisymmetric.

Theorem 3.1 *The matrix $A = A(n)$ as given by (17) has n different eigenvalues*

$$
\lambda_k = 2^{-k}, \quad 0 \leq k \leq n - 1 \tag{19}
$$

and the corresponding eigenvectors $\mathbf{x}_k$ satisfy

$$Mx_k = (-1)^k x_k \tag{20}$$

Moreover the components of the eigenvector $\mathbf{x} = \mathbf{x}_0$ to the eigenvalue $\lambda_0 = 1$ satisfy $x_s > 0$ for all s.

Proof. For $n = 1$ the claim of the theorem is trivial, and for $n > 1$ we proceed by induction on n. Denote by A the matrix in dimension n, and by A' the matrix in dimension $n - 1$. According to (16) A and A' are computed as

$$a_{st} = \frac{1}{2^n} \binom{n+1}{2s-t} \quad \text{and} \quad a'_{st} = \frac{1}{2^{n-1}} \binom{n}{2s-t} \tag{21}$$

In the following computations it makes sense to consider a_{st}, as defined in (21), also for values $s < 1$ or $s > n$, and similarly a'_{st} for $s < 1$ or $s > n - 1$. To establish a relationship between A and A' consider, for $1 \leq t \leq n - 1$,

$$
\begin{aligned}
a_{st} - a_{s,t+1} &= \frac{1}{2^n} \left(\binom{n+1}{2s-t} - \binom{n+1}{2s-t-1} \right) \\
&= \frac{1}{2^n} \left(\binom{n}{2s-t} + \binom{n}{2s-t-1} - \binom{n}{2s-t-1} - \binom{n}{2s-t-2} \right) \\
&= \frac{1}{2^n} \left(\binom{n}{2s-t} - \binom{n}{2s-t-2} \right) \\
&= \frac{1}{2} a'_{st} - \frac{1}{2} a'_{s-1,t} \tag{22}
\end{aligned}
$$

Since for $1 \leq t \leq n - 1$, $s = 0$ or $s = n$, we have $a'_{st} = 0$, formula (22) for $s = 1$ or $s = n$ writes as

$$a_{1t} - a_{1,t+1} = \frac{1}{2} a'_{1t} \tag{23}$$

$$a_{nt} - a_{n,t+1} = -\frac{1}{2} a'_{n-1,t} \tag{24}$$

Now suppose that $\mathbf{y} = (y_1, \ldots, y_{n-1})$ is an eigenvector of A' to the eigenvalue λ. Consider the vector $\mathbf{x} = (x_1, \ldots, x_n)$ defined by

$$
\begin{aligned}
x_1 &= y_1 \\
x_s &= y_s - y_{s-1}, \quad 2 \leq s \leq n - 1 \\
x_n &= -y_{n-1}
\end{aligned} \tag{25}
$$

We claim that $\mathbf{x}$ is an eigenvector of A. The image $\mathbf{x}' = A\mathbf{x}$ is computed as

$$x'_s = \sum_{t=1}^{n} a_{st} x_t = a_{s1} y_1 + \sum_{t=2}^{n-1} a_{st}(y_t - y_{t-1}) - a_{sn} y_{n-1} = \sum_{t=1}^{n-1} (a_{st} - a_{s,t+1}) y_t \tag{26}$$

According to (22) one obtains for $2 \leq s \leq n - 1$,

$$
\begin{aligned}
x'_s &= \frac{1}{2} \sum_{t=1}^{n-1} (a'_{st} - a'_{s-1,t})\, y_t = \frac{1}{2} \sum_{t=1}^{n-1} a'_{st}\, y_t - \frac{1}{2} \sum_{t=1}^{n-1} a'_{s-1,t}\, y_t \\
&= \frac{1}{2} \lambda y_s - \frac{1}{2} \lambda y_{s-1} = \frac{\lambda}{2} x_s
\end{aligned}
\tag{27}
$$

Similarly, according to (23) and (24), for $s = 1$ or $s = n$ we get

$$
x'_1 = \frac{1}{2} \sum_{t=1}^{n-1} a'_{1t}\, y_t = \frac{\lambda}{2} y_1 = \frac{\lambda}{2} x_1
\tag{28}
$$

$$
x'_n = -\frac{1}{2} \sum_{t=1}^{n-1} a'_{n-1,t}\, y_t = -\frac{\lambda}{2} y_{n-1} = \frac{\lambda}{2} x_n
\tag{29}
$$

Thus by (25) we have a (linear) mapping $Q : \mathbf{R}^{n-1} \to \mathbf{R}^n$ which maps an eigenvector (to the eigenvalue λ) in dimension $n - 1$ to an eigenvector (to the eigenvalue $\lambda/2$) in dimension n. Moreover if $\mathbf{y}$ is symmetric, $\mathbf{x} = Q\mathbf{y}$ is antisymmetric; if $\mathbf{y}$ is antisymmetric, $\mathbf{x} = Q\mathbf{y}$ is symmetric. By induction hypothesis, A' has $n - 1$ eigenvectors $\mathbf{y}_k$, $0 \leq k \leq n - 2$, to the eigenvalues $\lambda_k = 2^{-k}$ with $M\mathbf{y}_k = (-1)^k \mathbf{y}_k$. Therefore $\mathbf{x}_k = Q\mathbf{y}_{k-1}$, $1 \leq k \leq n - 1$, are $n - 1$ eigenvectors of A to eigenvalues $\lambda_k = 2^{-k}$ with $M\mathbf{x}_k = (-1)^k \mathbf{x}_k$.

It remains to consider the eigenvalue $\lambda_0 = 1$. Let $I = (\delta_{st})$ denote the identity matrix. Since A is a stochastic matrix, we have $\sum_s (a_{st} - \delta_{st}) = 0$. Hence $A - I$ is a singular matrix and $\lambda = 1$ is an eigenvalue of A. This completes the proof of (19). Moreover, as the eigenvalues are all distinct, the corresponding eigenvectors are determined up to a scalar factor. It follows that the matrix A is diagonalizable, i.e. it can be written in the form

$$
A = S^{-1} D S = S^{-1}
\begin{pmatrix}
\lambda_0 & & 0 \\
& \ddots & \\
0 & & \lambda_{n-1}
\end{pmatrix}
S
\tag{30}
$$

with $\lambda_k = 2^{-k}$ and where the k-the column in S^{-1} is an eigenvector to the eigenvalue λ_k. It remains to show that the eigenvector $\mathbf{x} = \mathbf{x}_0$ to the eigenvalue $\lambda_0 = 1$ is symmetric, and that its components x_s are strictly positive.

Let $\mathbf{y} \in \mathbf{R}^n$ be any vector, and denote by α the first component of $S\mathbf{y}$. Then by (30)

$$
\lim_{m \to \infty} A^m \mathbf{y} = \alpha \mathbf{x}
\tag{31}
$$

Since $\sum_s y_s$ is preserved by A, we have $\sum_s y_s = \alpha \sum_s x_s$. By choosing $\sum_s y_s \neq 0$, we conclude that $\sum_s x_s \neq 0$. Thus we may normalize the eigenvector $\mathbf{x} = \mathbf{x}_0$ such that $\sum_s x_s = 1$. In this case we have $\alpha = \sum_s y_s$, and hence for any $\mathbf{y}$ with $\sum_s y_s = 1$,

$$
\lim_{m \to \infty} A^m \mathbf{y} = \mathbf{x}
\tag{32}
$$

In order to show that all components x_s of $\mathbf{x}$ are strictly positive, consider the set

$$G = \{\mathbf{y} \in \mathbf{R}^n \,|\, \sum_{s=1}^{n} y_s = 1, \; y_s > 0\} \tag{33}$$

and its closure in the topological space $\mathbf{R}^n$,

$$\overline{G} = \{\mathbf{y} \in \mathbf{R}^n \,|\, \sum_{s=1}^{n} y_s = 1, \; y_s \geq 0\} \tag{34}$$

Note that $\overline{G}$ is the set of all probability distributions for n–ary random variables. It is easy to see that the matrix A maps $\overline{G}$ into $\overline{G}$. Thus for any $\mathbf{y} \in \overline{G}$ and for all m, we have $A^m\mathbf{y} \in \overline{G}$ and hence $\mathbf{x} = \lim_{m\to\infty} A^m\mathbf{y} \in \overline{G}$. In order to show that actually $\mathbf{x}$ is in G we observe that $A^m(\overline{G}) \subset G$ for m sufficiently large (e.g. $m \geq n$). This claim follows from the fact that the entries of A in the diagonal and next to the diagonal are strictly positive. Hence for any $\mathbf{y} \in \overline{G}$ with $y_s > 0$, also the components y'_{s-1}, y'_s, y'_{s+1} of the image $\mathbf{y}' = A\mathbf{y}$ are strictly positive. Iterating this argument, we conclude that $A^m\mathbf{y} \in G$ for $m \geq n-1$. In particular for $\mathbf{y} = \mathbf{x}$ we have $\mathbf{x} = A^m\mathbf{x} \in G$, i.e. $x_s > 0$ for all s.

Moreover by (18) either $M\mathbf{x} = \mathbf{x}$ or $M\mathbf{x} = -\mathbf{x}$. As $\mathbf{x} \in G$, we must have $M\mathbf{x} = \mathbf{x}$, which means that the eigenvector to the eigenvalue 1 is symmetric. This completes the proof of the theorem. $\square$

4 Probability Distribution of the Carry

4.1 Asymptotic Probability Distribution

According to (32), for any probability distribution $\mathbf{q}_0$ of the initial carry σ_0, the probability distribution of the j–th carry σ_j converges (exponentially) to a unique asymtotic probability distribution

$$\mathbf{x} = \lim_{j\to\infty} A^j \mathbf{q}_0 \tag{35}$$

where $\mathbf{x} = (x_1, \ldots, x_n)$ is the eigenvector of A to the eigenvalue 1, normalized by $\sum_s x_s = 1$. Since $z_j = x_{1j} + \cdots + x_{nj}$ for even carry σ_j and $z_j \neq x_{1j} + \cdots + x_{nj}$ for odd carry, z_j is correlated to the sum $x_{1j} + \cdots + x_{nj}$ of inputs with probability $p_0 = P(z_j = x_{1j} + \cdots + x_{nj}) = x_1 + x_3 + x_5 + \cdots$, or $p_1 = P(z_j \neq x_{1j} + \cdots + x_{nj}) = x_2 + x_4 + x_6 + \cdots$. The normalized correlation (see [3]) caused by the "bias" of the carry is expressed as the difference

$$\delta(n) = p_0 - p_1 = -\sum_{s=1}^{n} (-1)^s x_s \tag{36}$$

The correlation $\delta(n)$ decreases for larger n as is shown in the following theorem.

Theorem 4.1 *For an even number n of inputs there is no bias of the carry, i.e.*

$$\delta(n) = 0, \tag{37}$$

and for an odd number of inputs we have

$$|\delta(n)| < 2^{-(n-1)/2} \tag{38}$$

and in particular $\lim_{n\to\infty} \delta(n) = 0$.

Proof. According to Theorem 3.1 the eigenvector $\mathbf{x}$ of A to the eigenvalue 1 is symmetric. For even n this implies

$$\sum_{s=1}^{n}(-1)^s x_s = 0$$

and hence $\delta(n) = 0$. For odd n the equality $A\mathbf{x} = \mathbf{x}$ can be applied to estimate $\delta(n)$, e.g. as follows

$$\sum_{s=1}^{n}(-1)^s x_s = \sum_{s=1}^{n}(-1)^s \sum_{t=1}^{n} a_{st} x_t = \sum_{t=1}^{n}\left(\sum_{s=1}^{n}(-1)^s a_{st}\right)x_t \tag{39}$$

For the evaluation of $\sum_s(-1)^s a_{st}$ in (39), according to (17) the two sums

$$S_0 = S_0(n+1) = \binom{n+1}{0} - \binom{n+1}{2} + \binom{n+1}{4} - \cdots \pm \binom{n+1}{n+1} \tag{40}$$

$$S_1 = S_1(n+1) = \binom{n+1}{1} - \binom{n+1}{3} + \binom{n+1}{5} - \cdots \pm \binom{n+1}{n} \tag{41}$$

are to be computed. Then $\sum_s(-1)^s a_{st}$ is equal to $\pm 2^{-n}S_0$ for even s, and to $\pm 2^{-n}S_1$ for odd s, such that

$$\sum_{s=1}^{n}(-1)^s x_s = 2^{-n}(S_1 x_1 + S_0 x_2 - S_1 x_3 - S_0 x_4 + \cdots \pm S_1 x_n) \tag{42}$$

The values $S_0(n+1)$ and $S_1(n+1)$ are given in the following lemma.

Lemma 4.2 *For even m, $m = 2k$, we have*

$$S_0(2k) = \begin{cases} 2^k & k \equiv 0 \pmod 4 \\ 0 & k \equiv 1 \pmod 4 \\ -2^k & k \equiv 2 \pmod 4 \\ 0 & k \equiv 3 \pmod 4 \end{cases} \qquad S_1(2k) = \begin{cases} 0 & k \equiv 0 \pmod 4 \\ 2^k & k \equiv 1 \pmod 4 \\ 0 & k \equiv 2 \pmod 4 \\ -2^k & k \equiv 3 \pmod 4 \end{cases}$$

This lemma immediately follows from the equation

$$S_0 + S_1 i = (1+i)^m = \left(\sqrt{2}e^{i\pi/4}\right)^m = 2^k\left(e^{i\pi/2}\right)^k = 2^k i^k. \tag{43}$$

Therefore by Lemma 4.2 and (42) we get

$$\sum_{s=1}^{n}(-1)^s x_s = \begin{cases} 2^{-n}S_1(x_1 - x_3 + x_5 - \cdots \pm x_n) & n \equiv 1 \pmod 4 \\ 2^{-n}S_0(x_2 - x_4 + x_6 - \cdots \pm x_{n-1}) & n \equiv 3 \pmod 4 \end{cases} \tag{44}$$

Since $|x_1 - x_3 + x_5 - \cdots \pm x_n|$ and $|x_2 - x_4 + x_6 - \cdots \pm x_{n-1}|$ are strictly less than 1, this implies $|\delta(n)| < 2^{-n}2^{(n+1)/2} = 2^{-(n-1)/2}$, hence the theorem. $\square$

4.2 Probability Distribution of the Carry Conditioned on the Output

Now suppose that the output z_j is known to be 0. Then the input I_j and the carry σ_{j-1} are restricted to the values as indicated by the frames in Table 2. Thus I_j is restricted to either even or odd values depending on whether σ_{j-1} is even or odd. This means that the conditional probability $P(I_j = i)$ is either 0 or the double of the value as given in (11). Therefore the conditional probabilities q_j and q_{j-1} are related by the formula $q_j = Cq_{j-1}$ where the transition matrix C, according to Table 2 is given as

$$
C = \frac{1}{2^{n-1}}
\begin{pmatrix}
\binom{n}{0} & 0 & 0 & 0 & 0 & \cdots & 0 \\
\binom{n}{2} & \binom{n}{1} & \binom{n}{0} & 0 & 0 & \cdots & 0 \\
\binom{n}{4} & \binom{n}{3} & \binom{n}{2} & \binom{n}{1} & \binom{n}{0} & \cdots & 0 \\
& & & \vdots & & & \\
0 & & \cdots & & 0 & \binom{n}{0} & \binom{n}{1}
\end{pmatrix}
\tag{45}
$$

The matrix (45) is of the form

$$
C =
\begin{pmatrix}
2^{-(n-1)} & 0 & \cdots & 0 \\
* & & & \\
\vdots & & A & \\
* & & &
\end{pmatrix}
\tag{46}
$$

where A is the transition matrix for the unconditioned probability distribution of the carry for $n - 1$ inputs as given in (17). By (46) it follows that $\lambda_{n-1} = 2^{-(n-1)}$ is an eigenvalue of C, and for any eigenvector y of A the vector $(0, y)$ is an eigenvector of C to the same eigenvalue. Thus Theorem 3.1 implies

Corollary 4.3 *The matrix $C = C(n)$ as given by (45) has n different eigenvalues $\lambda_k = 2^{-k}$, $0 \leq k \leq n - 1$. For $0 \leq k \leq n - 2$ the corresponding eigenvectors x_k are of the form $x_k = (0, y_k)$, where y_k is an eigenvector to λ_k of the matrix $A(n - 1)$ as given in (17).*

If a run of t consecutive output digits $z_{j+1} = z_{j+2} = \ldots = z_{j+t} = 0$ has been observed, the (conditional) probabilities q_{j+t} and q_j are related by $q_{j+t} = C^t q_j$. Similar as in the proof of Theorem 3.1 we conclude that for any probability distribution q_j, in a run of consecutice output digits 0, the probability distribution of the carry tends to the asymptotic value

$$
x' = \lim_{t \to \infty} C^t q_j = (0, x)
\tag{47}
$$

where **x** is the (unconditioned) asymptotic probability distribution of the carry for $n-1$ inputs. In such a run, for $m = j + t$, the output digit z_m is asymptotically correlated to $x_{1m} + \cdots + x_{nm}$ with correlation coefficient

$$\delta'(n) = -\sum_{s=1}^{n}(-1)^s x'_s = \sum_{s=1}^{n-1}(-1)^s x_s = -\delta(n-1) \qquad (48)$$

A similar result holds for runs of consecutive output digits 1. In fact if z_j is assumed to be 1, the transition matrix of the conditional probabilities is of the form

$$C = \begin{pmatrix} \boxed{\quad A \quad} & \begin{matrix} * \\ \vdots \\ * \end{matrix} \\ 0 \;\cdots\; 0 & 2^{-(n-1)} \end{pmatrix} \qquad (49)$$

where $A = A(n-1)$ is the transition matrix for the probability distribution of the carry for $n-1$ inputs. Then Theorem 3.1 is applied as in Corrolary 4.3 to determine eigenvectors and eigenvalues. In particular $\mathbf{x}' = (\mathbf{x}, 0)$ is an eigenvector of C to the eigenvalue 1. Thus in a run of consecutice output digits 1, the probability distribution of the carry tends to the asymptotic value $\mathbf{x}' = (\mathbf{x}, 0)$. Therefore the asymptotic correlation of z_m to $x_{1m} + \cdots + x_{nm}$ in a run of consecutive output digits 1 is obtained as

$$\delta'(n) = -\sum_{s=1}^{n}(-1)^s x'_s = -\sum_{s=1}^{n-1}(-1)^s x_s = \delta(n-1) \qquad (50)$$

4.3 Numerical Values of $\delta(n)$ for Small n

For small numbers of inputs n the eigenvectors **x** of $A = A(n)$ to the eigenvalue 1 are obtained as shown in Table 3. The eigenvectors are normalized by $x_1 = 1$.

n	Eigenvectors to the eigenvalue 1	$\sum_{s=1}^{n} x_s$
1	(1)	1
2	(1, 1)	2
3	(1, 4, 1)	6
4	(1, 11, 11, 1)	24
5	(1, 26, 66, 26, 1)	120
6	(1, 57, 302, 302, 57, 1)	720
7	(1, 120, 1191, 2416, 1191, 120, 1)	5,040
8	(1, 247, 4293, 15619, 15619, 4293, 247, 1)	40,320
9	(1, 502, 14608, 88234, 156190, 88234, 14608, 502, 1)	362,880
10	(1, 1013, 47840, 455192, 1310354, 1310354, 455192, 47840, 1013, 1)	3,628,800

Table 3: Eigenvectors to the eigenvalue 1

To obtain the corresponding asymptotic probability distribution of the carry the eigenvectors have to be divided by $\sum_s x_s$, i.e. by the entry in the last column. For odd n the resulting values of $\delta(n)$ are given in Table 4—by Theorem 4.1 for even n the values $\delta(n)$ are 0.

n	1	3	5	7	9	11
$\delta(n)$	1.0000	-0.3333	0.1333	-0.0540	0.0219	-0.0088

Table 4: Values of $\delta(n)$ for odd n

As already pointed out in Theorem 4.1 the bias of the carry diminishes as n gets larger. This means that the resulting correlation probability approaches 0.5. For example from Table 4 one can deduce that the deviation of $\delta(n)$ from 0.5 decreases from 0.1667 for 3 inputs to 0.0044 for 11 inputs.

A closer look at the last column in Table 3 shows that the eigenvectors to the eigenvalue 1 satisfy the equation

$$\sum_{s=1}^{n} x_s = n! \tag{51}$$

In subsequent work, W.-A. Jackson and K. Martin [1], and independently S. Lloyd and C. Mitchell [2], were able to prove that equation (51) holds for arbitrary n. Furthermore in [2] closed formulas for the eigenvectors and the values of $\delta(n)$, as well as some nice combinatorial interpretations have also been derived.

References

[1] W.-A. Jackson, K. Martin, *Private communication*, 1990.

[2] S. Lloyd, C. Mitchell, *Calculating Some Eigenvectors*, Preprint 1990.

[3] W. Meier, O. Staffelbach, *Nonlinearity Criteria for Cryptographic Functions*, Proceedings of Eurocrypt'89, Springer-Verlag, to appear.

[4] W. Meier, O. Staffelbach, *Correlation Properties of Combiners with Memory in Stream Ciphers*, Journal of Cryptology, to appear.

[5] R.A. Rueppel, *Correlation Immunity and the Summation Generator*, Advances in Cryptology—Crypto'85, Proceedings, pp. 260–272, Springer-Verlag, 1986.

[6] R.A. Rueppel, *Analysis and Design of Stream Ciphers*, Springer-Verlag, 1986.

Rump Session
Impromptu Talks
Chair: W. Diffie, Bell Northern

Computation of Discrete Logarithms in Prime Fields

(Extended Abstract[†])

B. A. LaMacchia[*]
A. M. Odlyzko

AT&T Bell Laboratories
Murray Hill, New Jersey 07974

1. Introduction

If p is a prime and g and x integers, then computation of y such that

$$y \equiv g^x \bmod p, \ \ 0 \leq y \leq p - 1 \tag{1.1}$$

is referred to as *discrete exponentiation*. Using the successive squaring method, it is very fast (polynomial in the number of bits of $|p| + |g| + |x|$). On the other hand, the inverse problem, namely, given p, g, and y, to compute some x such that Equation 1.1 holds, which is referred to as the *discrete logarithm* problem, appears to be quite hard in general. Many of the most widely used public key cryptosystems are based on the assumption that discrete logarithms are indeed hard to compute, at least for carefully chosen primes.

The current state of knowledge about discrete logarithms is surveyed in [3, 4]. If certain precautions concerning the choice of p are observed, then the best published algorithms [1] for computing discrete logarithms modulo a prime p have running time

$$\exp((1 + o(1))(\log p)^{\frac{1}{2}}(\log \log p)^{\frac{1}{2}}) \ \ \text{as } p \to \infty. \tag{1.2}$$

The estimate given by Equation 1.2 is of roughly the same form as that of most of the fast practical algorithms for factoring composite integers of about the same size as p. An important feature of the estimate above is that it applies to a precomputation phase that has to be carried out once for each prime p. Once that phase is completed, individual discrete logarithms modulo that prime are much easier to compute.

[†]Full text of this paper to appear in *Designs, Codes, and Cryptography* **1** (1991).
[*]Present address: MIT, Cambridge, MA 02139

The complexity of computing discrete logs in prime fields is of substantial practical interest, since it provides an estimate of the size of the prime that has to be used. Sun Microcomputers, Inc., has implemented a secure identification feature as part of their Network File System (NFS). The Sun scheme uses discrete exponentiation modulo a prime of 192 bits. Our work shows that it is quite easy to compute discrete logs modulo that prime, which makes it possible to break the NFS security in a very clean way. In a few days on a moderately fast machine it is possible to prepare a database of less than a megabyte that will then enable the cryptanalyst to obtain any particular user's secret key in a matter of at most a few minutes.

2. Discrete Logarithms in Prime Fields

All of the fast algorithms known for computing discrete logarithms are forms of the index-calculus algorithm [4]. In the index-calculus algorithm, an initial processing stage computes the discrete logarithms of a set Q of elements in the field. These logarithms are found by obtaining a number of equations in the logarithms of elements of Q, and solving the resulting system modulo the prime factors of $p-1$. Once this table of logarithms has been computed, any other logarithm may be found relatively quickly utilizing the information in the table.

Our experiments were performed using the method of Gaussian integers [1]. The Gaussian integer scheme maps the field $GF(p)$ to a subset of $\mathbf{Z}^2$. Let r be a small negative integer which is also a quadratic residue modulo p, let S be an integer such that $S^2 \equiv r \bmod p$, and let s represent the imaginary number $\sqrt{r}$. Choose two integers $T, V \lesssim \sqrt{p}$ such that $T^2 \equiv rV^2 \bmod p$. Let the factor base Q consist of small complex primes $x + ys$ in $Z[s]$, small real primes q (some of which will factor into two complex primes), and the integer V. Now, let $p' = T + Vs$, and choose $g = e + fs$ to be a complex prime which generates $(Z[s]/p')^*$. This g is the new base for logarithms.

In order to generate logarithm equations, we search for pairs of integers (c_1, c_2) such that their residue $c_1V - c_2T$ is smooth with respect to the real primes q in the factor base Q. Notice that we may write

$$c_1 V - c_2 T \;=\; V(c_1 + c_2 s) - c_2(T + Vs) \equiv V(c_1 + c_2 s) \bmod p'.$$

If $c_1 V - c_2 T$ is smooth with respect to the real primes in Q, and $(c_1 + c_2 s)$ is smooth with respect to the complex primes in Q, we may write a related equation in logarithms to base g. When we map complex numbers $a + bs$ to $a + bS$ and the base $g = e + fs$ to $e + fS$, the logarithms are preserved.

3. Sieving and Linear Algebra

We used a sieve to find pairs of integers (c_1, c_2) whose residues $c_1 V - c_2 T$ were smooth over the small real primes in Q. For each pair (c_1, c_2) with a smooth residue, the corresponding equation $c_1 V - c_2 T \equiv V(c_1 + c_2 s) \bmod p'$ was factored (if possible) over the extended (complex) factor base. The sieve considered approximately 2.7×10^{10} (c_1, c_2) pairs, of which 288,017 yielded equations.

The various algorithms that are available for solving large sparse linear systems over finite fields are surveyed in [2]. Here we will only mention briefly how they performed on our problem. The system of 288,017 equations in 96,321 unknowns was reduced by the structured Gaussian elimination method to a smaller system of 7,262 equations in 6,006 unknowns. The resulting smaller system was then solved modulo 2 using a conjugate gradient program, and modulo $\frac{p-1}{2}$ using the Lanczos algorithm. These results suggest that linear algebra is likely to be a significant but not an insurmountable problem in computing discrete logarithms modulo large primes.

4. Conclusions

Our experiments with the 192-bit Sun prime as well as with a 224-bit prime demonstrate that the discrete log algorithms of [1] are indeed practical. Using the same amount of computing power that is used to factor a generally hard 115 decimal digit integer by the multiple polynomial quadratic sieve method, one can compute discrete logarithms modulo a prime of at least 100 decimal digits.

References

[1] D. Coppersmith, A. Odlyzko, and R. Schroeppel, Discrete logarithms in $GF(p)$, *Algorithmica* **1** (1986), 1-15.

[2] B. A. LaMacchia and A. M. Odlyzko, Solving large sparse linear systems over finite fields, *Advances in Cryptology: Proceedings of Crypto '90*, A. Menezes, S. Vanstone, eds., to be published.

[3] K. S. McCurley, The discrete logarithm problem, in *Cryptography and Computational Number Theory*, C. Pomerance, ed., *Proc. Symp. Appl. Math.*, Amer. Math. Soc., 1990, to appear.

[4] A. M. Odlyzko, Discrete logarithms in finite fields and their cryptographic significance, *Advances in Cryptology: Proceedings of Eurocrypt '84*, T. Beth, N. Cot, I. Ingemarsson, eds., *Lecture Notes in Computer Science* **209**, Springer-Verlag, NY (1985), 224-314.

Systolic Modular Multiplication

Shimon Even*

Bellcore
445 South St.
Morristown, NJ 07960-1910

Abstract. *A simple systolic array for achieving the effect of modular reduction, in linear time, is described. This circuit, in conjunction with Atrubin's multiplier, performs modular multiplication in linear time.*

1. Introduction

With the increasing interest in using number theoretic cryptographic systems, the quest for fast and inexpensive circuits for performing modular multiplication of long integers continues. It is possible to perform integer multiplication, as well as dividing by a fixed modulus, in logarithmic time. However, the corresponding circuits tend to be complex.

A systolic array, for performing multiplication of long integers, was proposed by Atrubin [A] over 25 years ago. The two positive integers to be multiplied are represented in binary. They are fed serially to the first cell of the array, least significant bit first. The product is supplied serially by the first cell, least significant bit first, without delay. Thus, the time required to get the product is linear. The structure of the cell of Atrubin's array is very simple, and it uses no long-distance communications; i.e. each cell (a finite automaton) communicates only with its neighbors. Thus, very high clock rates are possible.**

I propose a systolic array, with similar characteristics, which performs, in effect, modular reduction. This array is based on a modular reduction system proposed by Montgomery [M].

The design of a chip for performing number-theoretic cryptographic operations, based on these two systolic arrays, is simple, and allows very high clock rates. I believe that these two advantages make such a chip competitive with currently known designs;

---

* On leave from Computer Science Dept., Technion, Haifa, Israel 32000. Csnet: even@cs.technion.ac.il

** Note that if the two multiplicands are of length n, the product is of length $2 \cdot n$, and no pipelining is possible.

see, for example, the relevant abstracts from EuroCrypt 90 [DK, OSA].

2. Montgomery's modular system

Let N be an odd integer, the *modulus*. We wish to be able to perform modular multiplications quickly. Montgomery suggested a system which avoids "regular" division, and replaces it by an operation which requires less time. We describe the system in the binary case*.

Assume all integer representations are in binary; i.e. the radix is 2. Let n be the number of bits in the representation of N; i.e. $2^{n-1} < N < 2^n$. Let $R = 2^n$. For every $x \in Z_N$ let $\overline{x} \equiv x \cdot R \pmod{N}$. $\overline{x}$ is called the *image* of x. Throughout, a representation of an image has at most n bits; it may exceed N, but is nonnegative.

The idea is to do all the modular operations with images. Thus, given $\overline{x}$ and $\overline{y}$, images of x and y, respectively, we want to compute $\overline{z}$, where $z \equiv x \cdot y \pmod{N}$. However, by multiplying $\overline{x}$ and $\overline{y}$, we get

$$T = \overline{x} \cdot \overline{y}$$
$$\equiv x \cdot y \cdot R^2 \pmod{N}$$
$$\equiv \overline{z} \cdot R \pmod{N},$$

and we need to divide T by R in order to get $\overline{z}$. This division is meaningful, in the ring of integers modulo N, since R and N are relatively prime. Note that there are at most $2n$ bits in the representation of T, and we want the representation of $\overline{z}$ to be nonnegative and have at most n bits. Observe that division by R, modulo N, is also useful for returning from an image to its source.

For a given binary representation K of an integer, let K_0 be its least significant bit.

The computation of $T \cdot R^{-1} \bmod N$ is performed by the following procedure:

begin
    $M \leftarrow T$;
    for $i = 1$ *to* n *do*
    begin
        $M \leftarrow M + N \cdot M_0$;
        Shift-right M, one bit
    end
    if $M \geq 2^n$ *then* $M \leftarrow M - N$
end

---

* The system is slightly modified, following a suggestion of Ami Litman, in order to simplify its description.

Observe that since N is odd, the addition of $N \cdot M_0$ to M, causes the new M_0 to be 0, and this 0 is then shifted away, affecting a division by 2. Denote by $M_0^{(i)}$ the least significant bit of M, just before the i-th application of the loop. It follows that the value of M, upon the termination of the inner loop, satisfies

$$M = \tfrac{1}{2}(\cdots\tfrac{1}{2}(\tfrac{1}{2}(T + M_0^{(1)} \cdot N) + M_0^{(2)} \cdot N) \cdots + M_0^{(n)} \cdot N).$$

Thus,

$$T = 2(\cdots(2(2 \cdot M - M_0^{(n)} \cdot N) - M_0^{(n-1)} \cdot N) \cdots) - M_0^{(1)} \cdot N.$$
$$= 2^n \cdot M - N \cdot (M_0^{(n)} \cdot 2^{n-1} + M_0^{(n-1)} \cdot 2^{n-2} + \cdots + M_0^{(1)}). \qquad (1.1)$$

and

$$T \equiv R \cdot M \pmod{N},$$

or,

$$M \equiv T \cdot R^{-1} \pmod{N}.$$

Further, let us show that equation (1.1) indicates the number of bits in the representation of M. Denote

$$\mu \triangleq M_0^{(n)} \cdot 2^{n-1} + M_0^{(n-1)} \cdot 2^{n-2} + \cdots + M_0^{(1)}.$$

Now, equation (1.1) can be rewritten as

$$M \cdot 2^n = T + N \cdot \mu.$$

Since $\mu < 2^n$ and $T < 2^{2n}$,

$$M \cdot 2^n < 2^{2n} + N \cdot 2^n,$$

or

$$M - N < 2^n.$$

If $M < 2^n$, then no correction of its representation is necessary. Otherwise, a subtraction of N leaves it positive, and its representation uses at most n bits. This completes the proof of validity of the procedure.

3. A Systolic Array for $T \cdot R^{-1} \pmod{N}$

The systolic array for computing $T \cdot R^{-1} \pmod{N}$ consists of n identical cells, $C_1, C_2, \cdots, C_n$. The design of the cell is depicted in the diagram. The inputs to C_1 are supplied from the outside, and for every $1 \le i < n$, the outputs of C_i are the corresponding inputs to C_{i+1}. The T-output line of the last cell, C_n, is the output of the whole array.

The D boxes are *delay flip-flops*; i.e. their output at time $t+1$ is equal to their input at time t. There is a global clock whose pulses reach each of the flip-flops, but its lines and ports are not shown in the diagram.

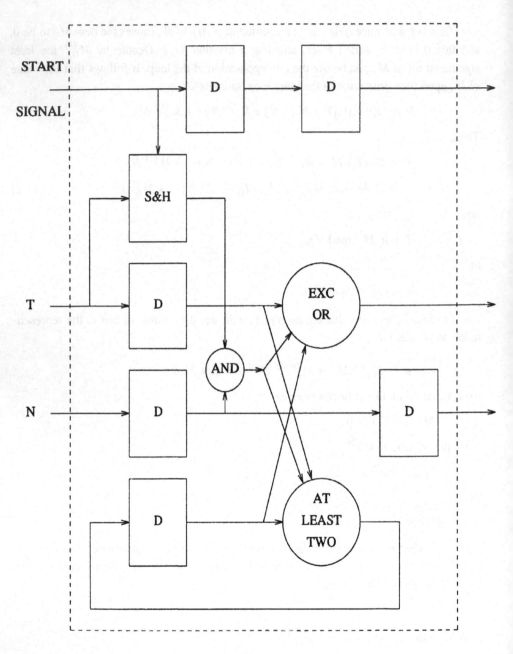

Typical cell of systolic array

for computing T/R mod N.

The *start signal*, as seen by C_1, is the sequence $1 \cdot 0^{2n-1}$, i.e. a 'one' pulse followed by $2n-1$ 'zero' pulses. Clearly, C_i gets the 'one' at time $2 \cdot i - 1$.

The *sample and hold* flip-flop, S&H, samples the input entering from the l.h.s., when it gets the 'one' from the top, and holds it. All flip-flops are set to produce a 'zero' output, at time $t=1$, by a *reset* signal which reaches them; the reset lines and ports are not shown in the diagram.

The EXC-OR (exclusive or) circuit and the AT-LEAST-TWO circuit, in conjunction with the lower-left delay flip-flop, constitute the serial adder function of the cell; the current bit of the sum $(M + N \cdot M_0)$ is the output of the EXC-OR, the carry bit is the output of the AT-LEAST-TWO -- it is delayed by lower-left delay flip-flop. The adder adds the two numbers which appear serially and simultaneously, least significant bit first, on the T and N lines. If the first bit on T, sampled at time $2 \cdot i - 1$, is 'one', then starting from time $2 \cdot i$, the AND gate is enabled. In this case, the number appearing on the N line goes through the enabled AND gate and is added serially to the number appearing on the T line. If the first bit on T is 'zero' then the AND gate remains disabled and the number on the T line goes through the adder unchanged, since the disabled AND gate blocks the number on the N line from entering the adder. In either case, the first output bit on the T line appears at time $2 \cdot i$ and is always 'zero'. However, it is ignored by C_{i+1}, which samples its input T line at time $2 \cdot i + 1$, thus affecting a shift-right operation on the output of C_i. The bits of N are delayed twice, and thus the least significant bit of N appears at the output together with the least significant bit of the number on the T line, after its "right-shift".

Thus, the cell performs the operations of one instance of the inner loop of the algorithm, and a systolic array of n cells performs all its iterations. The remaining operation, of subtracting N, if necessary, is not shown. It requires storing all $n+1$ bits of M, and going through a one-cell subtractor, if necessary. The total time to do a modular multiplication consists, therefore, of the following addends: Feeding the two multiplicands to Atrubin's array, the first output bit comes out immediately (or one tick later, depending on the particular design). The last bit of output, from the systolic array proposed here, comes out $3 \cdot n$ ticks later. Subtracting N, if necessary, can then start without further delay, and the final result can already be fed back to Atrubin's multiplier, for the next step of the modular exponentiation. Thus, the number of clock ticks per one modular multiplication is, effectively, $3 \cdot n$.

Remark

Ami Litman has shown me a method for removal of the need to store the $n+1$ bits before starting the subtraction. Using his method, effectively, one modular multiplication takes $2n+4$ ticks, instead of $3n$.

4. Acknowledgments

I would like to thank Yacov Yacobi for getting me interested in the subject, Ami Litman for useful discussions, Arjen K. Lenstra and Richard F. Graveman for commenting on an earlier version.

5. References

[A]   Atrubin, A. J., "A One-Dimensional Real-Time Iterative Multiplier", *IEEE Tran. on Electronic Computers*, Vol. 14, 1965, pp. 394-399.

[DK]   Dusse, S. R., and B. S. Kaliski Jr., "A Cryptographic Library for the Motorola DSP 56000", *EuroCrypt 90 - Abstracts*, May 21-24, 1990, Scanticon, Arhus, Denmark, pp. 213-217.

[OSA] Orup, H., Svendsen, E., and E. Andreasen, "VICTOR, An Efficient RSA Hardware Implementation", *EuroCrypt 90 - Abstracts*, May 21-24, 1990, Scanticon, Arhus, Denmark, pp. 219-227.

[M]   Montgomery, P. L., "Modular Multiplication Without Trial Division", *Math. of Computation*, Vol. 44, 1985, pp. 519-521.

Finding Four Million Large Random Primes

Ronald L. Rivest[*]

Laboratory for Computer Science

Massachusetts Institute of Technology

Cambridge, MA 02139

A number n is a (base two) *pseudoprime* if it is composite and satisfies the identity

$$2^{n-1} \equiv 1 \pmod{n} . \tag{1}$$

Every prime satisifies (1), but very few composite numbers are pseudoprimes. If pseudoprimes are *very* rare, then one could even find large "industrial strength" primes (say for cryptographic use) by simply choosing large random values for n until an n is found that satisfies (1). How rare are pseudoprimes? We performed an experiment that attempts to provide an answer. We also provide some references to the literature for theoretical analyses.

Using a network of 33 SUN Sparcstations, approximately 718 million random 256-bit values were tested by a "small divisor test", followed (if the small divisor test was passed) by a test of equation (1), followed (if the equation (1) was satisified) by 8 iterations of the Miller-Rabin probabilistic primality test. A number passes the small divisor test if it has no divisors smaller than 10^4. Of the numbers tested, 43,741,404 of them passed the small-divisor test. Of those, 4,058,000 satisfied equation (1). Of those, *all* passed 8 iterations of the Miller-Rabin probabilistic primality test. That is, *no pseudoprimes were found.* In other words, every number that passed the small-divisor test and satisfied equation (1) was found to be (probably) prime. Empirically, therefore, pseudoprimes are very rare, at least among numbers with no small divisors.

The available theory also suggests that pseudoprimes are rare. On the basis of extensive experience and analysis, Pomerance [5, 8] conjectures that the number of pseudoprimes less than n is at most

$$n/L(n)^{1+o(1)} \tag{2}$$

where

$$L(n) = \exp\left(\frac{\log n \log \log \log n}{\log \log n}\right) .$$

---

[*]Supported by NSF grant CCR-8914428, and RSA Data Security.   email address: rivest@theory.lcs.mit.edu

If this conjecture is correct, and we make the (unjustified) additional assumption that the $o(1)$ in conjecture (2) can be ignored, then the number of pseudoprimes less than 2^{256} is conjectured to be at most

$$4 \times 10^{52}$$

whereas the number of 256-bit primes is approximately

$$6.5 \times 10^{74} .$$

Thus, if Pomerance's conjecture is correct (and if the $o(1)$ term can safely be ignored), the chance that a randomly chosen 256-bit number that satisfies equation (1) is in fact composite is less than 1 in 10^{22}. For "practical purposes" pseudoprimality may be a sufficient guarantee of primality. (Of course, it is easy to improve the test to provide higher reliability.) Our experiments are consistent with these theoretical conjectures. For further information on finding large primes and on the density of pseudoprimes, see [1, 2, 3, 4, 5, 6, 7, 8].

Acknowledgments

I'd like to thank Carl Pomerance for bringing some of his work to my attention, and William Ang for helping with the running of the programs.

References

[1] Pierre Beauchemin, Gilles Brassard, Claude Crépeau, Claude Goutier, and Carl Pomerance. The generation of random numbers that are probably prime. *Journal of Cryptology*, 1:53–64, 1988.

[2] Pomerance C., J. L. Selfridge, and S. Wagstaff, Jr. The pseudoprimes to $25 \cdot 10^9$. *Mathematics of Computation*, 35(151):1003–1026, July 1980.

[3] Paul Erdös and Carl Pomerance. On the number of false witnesses for a composite number. *Mathematics of Computation*, 46(173):259–279, January 1986.

[4] Su Hee Kim and Carl Pomerance. The probability that a random probable prime is composite. *Mathematics of Computation*, 53(188):721–741, October 1989.

[5] Carl Pomerance. On the distribution of pseudoprimes. *Mathematics of Computation*, 37(156):587–593, 1981.

[6] Carl Pomerance. A new lower bound for the pseudoprime counting function. *Illinois Journal of Mathematics*, 26(1):4–9, Spring 1982.

[7] Carl Pomerance. On the number of false witnesses for a composite number. *Mathematics of Computation*, 46(173):259–279, January 1986.

[8] Carl Pomerance. Two methods in elementary analytic number theory. In R. A. Mollin, editor, *Number Theory and Applications*, pages 135–161. Kluwer Academic Publishers, 1989.

The FEAL Cipher Family

Shoji MIYAGUCHI

Communications and Information Processing Laboratories, NTT
1-2356, Take, Yokosuka-shi, Kanagawa, 238-03 Japan

1 FEAL cipher family

FEAL-8 has been expanded to FEAL-N (N round FEAL with 64-bit key), where FEAL-N with N=4/8 is identical to FEAL-4/-8 which have been previously published respectively. N is a user defined parameter (N$\geq$4, N:even, N=2^x, $x \geq 2$ is recommended). FEAL-N has also been expanded to FEAL-NX (X: expansion, N round FEAL with 128-bit key) that accepts 128-bit keys. When the right half of the 128-bit key is all zeros, FEAL-NX works as FEAL-N. Upward compatibility is an important concept of the FEAL cipher family [1].

2 Round number N

The author believes that most cipher applications can avoid chosen plaintext attacks by the countermeasures described in Annex-1. Increased N in FEAL-N or FEAL-NX can avoid chosen plaintext attacks. Where the countermeasures are applicable, small values of N (eg. N=8) should be used. If none of the countermeasures can be applied or their effectiveness is unclear, the value of N in FEAL-N or FEAL-NX should be increased.

3 64-bit key and 128-bit key

The author thinks that exhaustive searches for FEAL-N 64-bit keys may be possible if LSI technology advances sufficiently, as shown in Annex-2. He feels that FEAL-N may weaken against exhaustive search within one to two decades. Therefore, FEAL-NX which accepts 128-bit keys has been designed.

Annex-3 discusses a comparison of chosen plaintext attack and exhaustive attack.

4 Implementation

The processing speed of the FEAL-8 LSI chip is 96 Mbps (CMOS, 1.5μm, f=12MHz, 88'). FEAL-N program speeds are shown in Table 1 using a 16-bit μp (i80286). The number of dynamic steps per stage of FEAL-N data randomization is about only **25 steps** for both 16-bit microprocessors (i80286) and 32-bit general purpose computers (IBM370) if assembly programs are used (†). Programming techniques are outlined in Annex-4. FEAL-N and FEAL-NX are still efficient even when N=32 or N=64. (†: An 80286 assembly program of DES needs about several hundred dynamic steps per stage.)

Table 1. Enciphering speed of FEAL-N program

Round number N	4	8	1 6	3 2	6 4
Speed (kilo-bps)	1,000	670	440	220	120

CPU: i80286, f=10MHz, assembler program(430+2N bytes, N:Max value)

References [1]: S. Miyaguchi et al, 'Expansion of FEAL cipher', Vol 2, No.6, NTT REVIEW, November 1990

Annex-1   Chosen plaintext attack
1   Flow of chosen plaintext attack

There may be two typical cases of attack possible. Here, the cipher user is called the victim.

Case-1: The victim enciphers the chosen plaintexts

The attacker sends the chosen plaintexts to the victim through a communication line or in storage media. The victim enciphers the chosen plaintexts in the ECB mode (a basic mode without feedback, see ISO8372) and returns the generated ciphertexts to the attacker. This case includes the situation where the attacker provides the victim with a program to generate the chosen plaintexts.

Case-2: The attacker enciphers the chosen plaintexts

The victim provides the attacker with an enciphement tool (encipherment equipment, a smart card including cipher module etc.) that has the victim's secret key. The attacker inputs the chosen plaintexts into the tool and obtains the ciphertexts generated in the

ECB mode. This case includes the situation where the attacker uses the tool without permission of the victim.

2   Countermeasures

One of the following may be effective to prevent the attack.

(1)   Elimination of cooperation and improper use

A cipher user should not encipher data from outside (possible chosen plaintexts) in the ECB mode using his secret key, and then return the ciphertexts so generated. He also should not provide an encipherment tool that outputs data enciphered in the ECB mode using the user's secret key, i.e. eliminate user cooperation with the attacker, improper uses of the cipher as in Case-1 or Case-2 above.

(2)   Inhibition of the ECB

ECB mode should be inhibited, and CBC or CFB modes (feedback modes, see ISO8372) should be used(†). Initial values of each mode are changed with each use of the cipher. The cipher user determines the initial value, IV, with his rule that is secret to others (possible attackers). The value of IV may be revealed after the first block of plaintexts is given. If the initial value IV must be sent to the receiver, it can be appended to the head of the ciphertext.

† : International standards, ISO8732, ISO9160 and ISO10126, recommend the use of CBC or CFB modes in cipher communications.

(3)   Key changes :   The key, the target of chosen plaintext

attack should be changed after each key use (††).

†† : International standard, ISO8732, recommends that the key be changed for each communication session.

(4)   Miscellaneous: Individual countermeasures can be developed for each cipher application. For instance, if the volume of chosen plaintexts is 1 Mega-byte, maximum data is limited to a lesser volume (eg. 100 kilo-byte) within one key lifetime.

Annex-2   Exhaustive search for 64-bit keys

1   Progress of LSI C-MOS technology

A rough approximation is that LSI processing speed is inversely proportional to the channel width while LSI integrated transistor density is inversely proportional to the square of the channel width. The past decade has shown that LSI channel width has decreased to one third of the original width; consequently, processing speeds have roughly tripled and the transister density has increased by a factor of 10. It is predicted that similar LSI technology advances will continue in the future.

2 FEAL-attack LSI chip

Assume that a special FEAL-attack LSI chip can be fabricated, i.e., enciphering speed of the chip is 3 times the current speed, 300 Mbps $\approx 3 \times 96$ Mbps ($3 \times$ speed of current FEAL-8 chip). The chip has ten FEAL-N processing elements, while chip price is 20 US dollars.

3 Exhaustive search equipment

The equipment includes 100,000 FEAL-attack chips. The eqipment inputs one plaintext (P) and its ciphertext (C) which was enciphered by a secret key, and enciphers P repeatedly and in parallel using key K_i for i from i=1 to 2^{64}, producing ciphertext C_i and comparing C_i to C. Here, the key K_i is generated in the equipment. If the equipment finds $C_i = C$, it outputs the value of K_i. The enciphering speed (V) of the equipment is $V = 300 \times 10^6$ (bps)$\times 10^5$(chips)$\times 10$ (FEAL-8 processing elements/chip) = 300 Tera-bps. Assume that the equipment price is ten times the total chip cost. For reference, *the equipment cannot be re-designed to input and/or output texts at a speed of 300 Tera-bps* because it is technically impossible.

4 Equipment performance

Let p be the probability to discover the secret key. Then the price of the equipment and the time to discover the key are given as: (a) the price = 20 US (dollars/chip)$\times$ 100,000 (chips) $\times$ 10 (times) = 20 million US dollars, (b) the time = $((2^{64} \times 64$(bits))$/(300 \times 10^6$ (bps)$\times 10^5$(chips)$\times 10$ (FEAL-8 processing elements/chip)$\times 8.64 \times 10^4$ (sec/day)) $\times$ p ≈ 45 days $\times$ p).

That is: Equipment price (million dollars) $\times$ Time to discover the key (days) $\approx 20 \times 45 \times$ p (million dollars$\times$days)

5 Conclusion

FEAL-N (64-bit key) may weaken against exhaustive search within one to two decades.

Reference: Exhaustive search for DES 56-bit keys
(a) the price: 20 million US dollars (the same as above)
(b) the time = $((2^{56} \times 64$ (bits))$/(3 \times 20(\dagger) \times 10^6(bps)\times 10^5$ (chips) $\times 10$ (DES elements/chip)$\times 8.64 \times 10^4$ (sec/day)) ≈ 1 days).
   $\dagger$ 20 Mbps (approximate speed of DES chip)

Annex-3   Comparison of Chosen plaintext attack and Exhaustive search

The author believes that a chosen plaintext attack (CPA) on 2^{64} blocks is extremely ineffective, and cannot be equated with exhaustive search on 2^{64} keys, *even if the countermearsures to CPA described in Anndex-1 are ignored.* The reasons are:

(a) A cipher user (victim) or attacker has to use encipherment equipment that input/outputs texts at a speed of 300 Tera-bps which cannot be realized, if the speed of CPA is comparable with that for exhaustive search (see Clause 3 of Annex-2).
(b) The sheer volume of data to be transferred, $2^{64} \times 8$ bytes (1.47×10^{20} bytes), prevents CPA within any reasonable period or price.

To the author, it seems to be questionable to compare the number of chosen plaintext attacks with *that of exhaustive search* when the number is very big such as 2^{64}. This comparison may lead to the misunderstanding that both attacks might be equally strong.

Annex-4   Programming techniques for FEAL
Programming examples of S functions of FEAL are shown below.

1   Program example using 1-bit left rotation instruction
If a 1-bit (or 2-bit) left rotation is used, S_0/S_1 functions can be coded easily. $S_1(X_1, X_2) = \text{Rot2}((X_1 + X_2 + 1) \bmod 256)$ is given below in typical 16-bit μp assembly language.

```
add    R1, R2    ; R1 ← (R1) + (R2) mod 256,
                   where X₁/X₂ is in R1/R2.
inc    R1        ; R1 ← (R1) + 1
rot    R1        ; R1 ← 1-bit left rotation on (R1)
rot    R1        ; R1 ← 1-bit left rotation on (R1)
```

2   Table search technique: This is suitable for processors
that have a base register to point the table. The idea is shown for
$S_1(X_1, X_2) = \text{Rot2}((X_1 + X_2 + 1) \bmod 256)$
Step-1: $X \leftarrow X_1 + X_2$ (add X_1 and X_2, then sum is stored into X)
Step-2: $Y \leftarrow$ 2-bit left rotation on (X+1) from table pointed X

3   Note: Program coding of paired stages in FEAL data randomization is very useful to decrease dynamic program steps.

Annex-5   FEAL Specifications

This Annex uses the following conventions and notations.

(1) A,Ar,... : blocks

(2) $(A, B, ...)$: concatenation of blocks in this order

(3) A B: exclusive-or operation of A and B

(4) ϕ : zero block, 32-bits long

(5) =: Transfer from left side to right side

(6) Bit position: 1,2,3,... from the first left side bit (MSB) in a block towards the right.

1 FEAL options

(1) Round number (N): Determines the round number (N) for FEAL data randomization, where $N \geq 4$ and even. 2^x, $x \geq 2$ is recommended.

(2) Key parity: Indicates: (a) Use of key parity bits in a key-block, or (b) Non-use of key parity bits in a key-block

2 Enciphering algorithm

Plaintext P is separated into L_0 and R_0 of equal lengths (32 bits), i.e., $P = (L_0, R_0)$.

First, $(L_0, R_0) = (L_0, R_0) \oplus (K_N, K_{N+1}, K_{N+2}, K_{N+3})$

Next, $(L_0, R_0) = (L_0, R_0) \oplus (\phi, L_0)$

Next, and calculate the equations below for r from 1 to N iteratively,

$$R_r = L_{r-1} \oplus f(R_{r-1}, K_{r-1})$$
$$L_r = R_{r-1}$$

where extended keys K_is are defined in Clause 4, and function f is defined in Clause 5. Output of r-th round is (L_r, R_r).

Interchange the final output of the iterative calculation, (L_N, R_N), into (R_N, L_N). Next calculate:

$$(R_N, L_N) = (R_N, L_N) \oplus (\phi, R_N)$$

Lastly, $\quad (R_N, L_N) = (R_N, L_N) \oplus (K_{N+4}, K_{N+5}, K_{N+6}, K_{N+7})$

Ciphertext is given as (R_N, L_N).

3 Deciphering algorithm

Ciphertext (R_N, L_N) is separated into R_N and L_N of equal lengths.

First, $\quad (R_N, L_N) = (R_N, L_N) \oplus (K_{N+4}, K_{N+5}, K_{N+6}, K_{N+7})$

Next, $\quad (R_N, L_N) = (R_N, L_N) \oplus (\phi, R_N)$

Next, calculate the equations below for r from N to 1 iteratively,

$$L_{r-1} = R_r \oplus f(L_r, K_{r-1})$$
$$R_{r-1} = L_r$$

Interchange the final output of the iterative calculation, (R_0, L_0), into (L_0, R_0). Next calculate:

$$(L_0, R_0) = (L_0, R_0) \oplus (\phi, L_0)$$

Lastly, $\quad (L_0, R_0) = (L_0, R_0) \oplus (K_N, K_{N+1}, K_{N+2}, K_{N+3})$

Plaintext is given as (L_0, R_0). Data randomization for the enciphering / deciphering algorithms is shown in Figure 1.

4 Key schedule

First, the key schedule of FEAL-NX is described, where the functions used are defined in clause 5. The key schedule yields the extended key K_i (i=0,1,2,...,N+7) from the 128-bit key.

4.1 Definition of left key K_L and right key K_R

Inputted 128-bit key is equally divided into a 64-bit left key, K_L, and a 64-bit right key, K_R, i.e., (K_L, K_R) is the inputted 128-bit key.

4.2 Parity bit processing

(1) Non-use of key parity bits: There is no special processing here.

(2) Use of key parity bits: Bit positions, 8, 16, 24, 32, 40, 48, 56, 64, of both K_L and K_R are set to zeros, i.e., all parity bits in the key block are set to zero.

Note: How to use parity bits is outside the scope of the FEAL-NX.

4.3 Iterative calculation

(1) Processing of the right key K_R

K_R is divided into left half K_{R1} and right half K_{R2}, $(K_R = (K_{R1}, K_{R2}))$ and the temporary variable, Q_r, is defined as: $\quad Q_r = K_{R1} \oplus K_{R2} \quad$ for r=1,4,7,..., (r=3i+1; i=0,1,...)

$\quad\quad Q_r = K_{R1} \quad$ for r=2,5,8,..., (r=3i+2; i=0,1,...)

$\quad\quad Q_r = K_{R2} \quad$ for r=3,6,9,..., (r=3i+3; i=0,1,...)

Where $1 \leq r \leq (N/2)+4$. ($N \geq 4$, N:even)

Note: For FEAL-N, $K_R = (\phi, \phi)$ (64 zeros) and $Q_r = \phi$ (32 zeros).

(2) Processing of the left key K_L

Let A_0 be the left half of K_L and let B_0 be the right half, i.e., $K_L = (A_0, B_0)$ and $D_0 = \phi$. Then calculate K_i(i = 0 to N+7) for r = 1 to $(N/2) + 4$, ($N \geq 4$, N:even)

$$D_r = A_{r-1}, \quad A_r = B_{r-1}$$
$$B_r = f_K(\alpha, \beta) = f_K(A_{r-1}, (B_{r-1} \oplus D_{r-1} \oplus Q_r))$$
$$K_{2(r-1)} = (B_{r0}, B_{r1}), \quad K_{2(r-1)+1} = (B_{r2}, B_{r3})$$

where A_r, B_r, D_r and Q_r are auxiliary variables. $B_r = (B_{r0}, B_{r1}, B_{r2}, B_{r3})$. $B_{r0}, \ldots, B_{r3}$ are each 8 bits long. Function f_K is the same as in FEAL-N. The key schedule of FEAL-NX is shown in Figure 2.

4.4 Key schedule of FEAL-N

The FEAL-N key schedule is equivalent to the FEAL-NX key schedule when K_L is the 64-bit key of FEAL-N and K_R is all zeros, where the temporary variable $Q_r = \phi$.

Let A_0 be the left half of the 64-bit key and let B_0 be the right, i.e., the 64-bit key$= (A_0, B_0)$ and $D_0 = \phi$. Then calculate $K_i'($ i $= 0$ to N+7) for r $= 1$ to $(N/2) + 4$, $(N \geq 4$, N:even)

$$D_r = A_{r-1}, \quad A_r = B_{r-1}$$
$$B_r = f_K(\alpha, \beta) = f_K(A_{r-1}, (B_{r-1} \oplus D_{r-1}))$$
$$K_{2(r-1)} = (B_{r0}, B_{r1}), \quad K_{2(r-1)+1} = (B_{r2}, B_{r3})$$

5 Functions

5.1 Function f (see also Figure 3)

$f(\alpha, \beta)$ is shortened to f. α and β are divided as follows, where α_i, and β_i are 8-bits long. Functions S_0 and S_1 are defined in clause 5.3.

$$\alpha = (\alpha_0, \alpha_1, \alpha_2, \alpha_3), \quad \beta = (\beta_0, \beta_1).$$

$f = (f_0, f_1, f_2, f_3)$ are calculated in the sequence (1) to (8).

(1) $f_1 = \alpha_1 \oplus \beta_0$,   (2) $f_2 = \alpha_2 \oplus \beta_1$

(3) $f_1 = f_1 \oplus \alpha_0$,   (4) $f_2 = f_2 \oplus \alpha_3$

(5) $f_1 = S_1(f_1, f_2)$,   (6) $f_2 = S_0(f_2, f_1)$

(7) $f_0 = S_0(\alpha_0, f_1)$,   (8) $f_3 = S_1(\alpha_3, f_2)$

Example in hex: Inputs: $\alpha = $ 00FF FF00, $\beta = $ FFFF,

Output: $f = $ 1004 1044

5.2 Function f_K (see also Figure 4)

Inputs of function f_K, α and β, are divided into four 8-bit blocks as:

$$\alpha = (\alpha_0, \alpha_1, \alpha_2, \alpha_3), \quad \beta = (\beta_0, \beta_1, \beta_2, \beta_3).$$

$f_K(\alpha, \beta)$ is shortened to f. $f_K = (f_{K0}, f_{K1}, f_{K2}, f_{K3})$ are calculated in the sequence (1) to (6).

(1) $f_{K1} = \alpha_1 \oplus \alpha_0$,   (2) $f_{K2} = \alpha_2 \oplus \alpha_3$

(3) $f_{K1} = S_1(f_{K1}, (f_{K2} \oplus \beta_0))$,   (4) $f_{K2} = S_0(f_{K2}, (f_{K1} \oplus \beta_1))$

(5) $f_{K0} = S_0(\alpha_0, (f_{K1} \oplus \beta_2))$,   (6) $f_{K3} = S_1(\alpha_3, (f_{K2} \oplus \beta_3))$

Example in hex: Inputs: $\alpha = $ 0000 0000, $\beta = $ 0000 0000,

$$f_K = 1004\ 1044$$

5.3 Function S

S_0 and S_1 are defined as follows:

$$S_0(X_1, X_2) = \text{Rot2}((X_1 + X_2) \bmod 256)$$
$$S_1(X_1, X_2) = \text{Rot2}((X_1 + X_2 + 1) \bmod 256)$$

where $X_1 and X_2$ are 8-bit blocks and $Rot2(T)$ is the result of a 2-bit left rotation operation on 8-bit block, T.

Example: Suppose $X_1 = 00010011$, $X_2 = 11110010$ then

$$T = (X_1 + X_2 + 1) \bmod 256 = 00000110$$
$$S_1(X_1, X_2) = Rot2(T) = 00011000$$

6 Example of working data in hex

(1) Working data for FEAL-8

Parameters: Round number N=8 and non-use of key parity bits.

(a) Key: K = 0123 4567 89AB CDEF

(b) Extended key:

K_0 = DF3B, K_1 = CA36, K_2 = F17C, K_3 = 1AEC

K_4 = 45A5, K_5 = B9C7, K_6 = 26EB, K_7 = AD25

K_8 = 8B2A, K_9 = ECB7, K_{10} = AC50, K_{11} = 9D4C

K_{12} = 22CD, K_{13} = 479B, K_{14} = A8D5, K_{15} = 0CB5

(c) Plaintext: P = 0000 0000 0000 0000

(d) Ciphertext: C = CEEF 2C86 F249 0752

(2) Working data for FEAL-4X/-8X/-16X/-32X/-64X

Parameters: N=4,8,16,32,64 and non-use of key parity bits.

(a) Key: K =0123 4567 89AB CDEF 0123 4567 89AB CDEF

(b) Plaintext: P = 0000 0000 0000 0000

(c) Ciphertext:

C_4 = DF7B EDD3 D59C 7C4B , C_8 = 92BE B65D 0E93 82FB

C_{16} = 01A9 4383 EB19 BA07 , C_{32} = 9C9B 5497 3DF6 85F8

C_{64} = E2B0 F1C2 98EB 5030

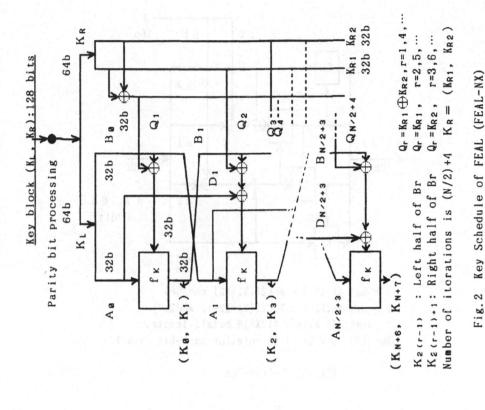

Key block (K$_L$,K$_R$):128 bits

Parity bit processing

Fig.2 Key Schedule of FEAL (FEAL-NX)

K$_{2(r-1)}$: Left half of B$_r$
K$_{2(r-1)+1}$: Right half of B$_r$
Number of iterations is (N/2)+4

Q$_r$=K$_{R1}$⊕K$_{R2}$,r=1,4,···
Q$_r$=K$_{R1}$, r=2,5,···
Q$_r$=K$_{R2}$, r=3,6,···
K$_R$ = (K$_{R1}$, K$_{R2}$)

Plaintext (Ciphertext) block

( ) : Deciphering   (K$_{N+4}$ to K$_{N+7}$)
                    ((K$_N$ to K$_{N+3}$))
Ciphertext (Plaintext) block

Fig.1 Data Randomization

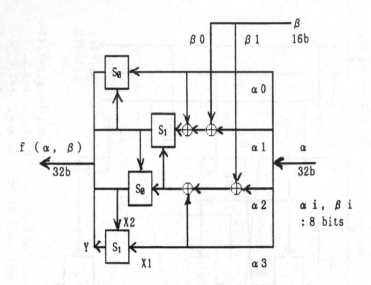

$$Y = S_0(X1,X2) = Rot2((X1+X2) \bmod 256)$$
$$Y = S_1(X1,X2) = Rot2((X1+X2+1) \bmod 256)$$

Y: output(8 bits), X1/X2(8 bits): inputs,

Rot2(Y): a 2-bit left rotation on 8-bit data Y

Fig. 3   f -function

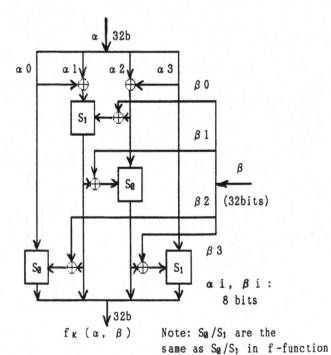

Fig. 4   f_K-function

Discrete-Log With Compressible Exponents

Yacov Yacobi

Bellcore

445 South St., Morristown, NJ 07960

Abstract

Many key distribution systems are based on the assumption that the Discrete-Log (DL) problem is hard. The implementations could be more efficient if a significantly smaller exponent could be used, without lowering the complexity of the DL problem. When the exponent is known to reside in interval of size w, the DL problem can be computed in time $O(\sqrt{w})$, using Pollard's "Lambda method for catching Kangaroos".

Suppose we want a level of security of 300 years on a 1 MIP machine, with 1K bit operations per instruction. Then $w = 2^{127}$ currently seems sufficient (with 512 bit modulus). It is not clear, however, whether methods other than "Kangaroo" exist, with lower complexity.

Let s and m denote the number of squarings and multiplications, respectively, required to exponentiate. It is well known that s roughly equals the size in bits of the exponent (L), and m is roughly $1.5 \cdot L/lg_2(L)$, for the most efficient methods, in the practical range.

We show that by using an exponent which is known to be compressible by a factor η, using the Ziv-Lempel method, we reduce m exponentially in η, on the average (integer multiplications may be more than twice as expensive as squarings, hence this is not negligible).

This can be used to speed up cryptographic key distribution systems of the Diffie-Hellman family. However, it is not clear how safe compressible exponents are.

1   Introduction

Many key distribution systems are based on the assumption that the Discrete-Log (DL) problem is hard. The implementations could be more efficient if a significantly smaller exponent could be used, without lowering the complexity of the DL problem. When the exponent is known to reside in interval of size w, the DL problem can be computed in time $O(\sqrt{w})$, using Pollard's "Lambda method for catching Kangaroos" [P]. This is a randomized algorithm, with controllable error probability $\epsilon > 0$, which can be made arbitrarily small, at the cost of increasing the runtime. The increase is linear in $\sqrt{log(1/\epsilon)}$.

Suppose we want a level of security of 300 years on a 1 MIP machine, with 1K bit operations per instruction. Then $w = 2^{127}$ currently seems sufficient (with a 512 bit modulus). It is not clear, however, whether methods other than "Kangaroo" exist, with lower complexity.

Problem 1: What is the complexity of DL with 512 bit prime modulus, and 127 bit exponent?

Let s and m denote the number of squarings and multiplications, respectively, required to exponentiate. It is well known that s roughly equals the size in bits of the exponent (L), and m is roughly $1.5 \cdot L/lg_2(L)$, for the most efficient methods, in the practical range.

We show that by using an exponent which is known to be compressible by a factor η, using the Ziv-Lempel method, we reduce m exponentially in η, on the average.

Problem 2: What is the complexity of DL with 512 bit prime modulus, and 127 bit exponent, when the exponent is known to be ZL-compressible by a ratio of η?

The new exponentiation method was described in [Y], and is repeated briefly in section 2. Section 3 shows that the actual gain in m is exponential in η. The above problems 1 and 2 where not explicitly stated in [Y].

2   The new method

The intuition behind the method is that if some patterns in the binary representation of the exponent reappear, then we don't have to recompute their contribution, if we already stored it. The method is similar to the m-ary method [L], with two differences. First, in the m-ary method we may do some precomputations, which are not used later, while in the new method we precompute exactly those subexponents that we are about to use. Second, we do not bound our precomputations to a fixed predetermined length. Rather our algorithm is adaptive to the particular exponent at hand. A similar intuition led to the Ziv-Lempel [ZL] compression algorithm.

We parse n right to left (i.e., from low order to high order bits) the way Ziv-Lempel [ZL] do in their compression method, i.e., we create a binary "compression" tree, where the path e_i from the root to node i is a segment of the exponent, and node i contains the partial result x^{e_i}. The structure of the tree makes it easy to add a new leaf, given its parent. We describe first a subroutine that creates the binary tree, and then the main program, which uses the tree to compute x^n.

The exponent is called here *seq*, and is treated sometimes as an integer, and sometimes as a sequence of bits. Each segment e_i of the exponent is an odd number of length $L_i \geq 1$, and is preceded (to the right) by $Z_i \geq 0$ zeroes.

subroutine **build-tree**

begin

- **Init:** Store $e_0 = 1$; $Z_0 \leftarrow L_{-1} \leftarrow 0$ in node 0, and set $L_0 \leftarrow 0$. Put parse 0 right of *seq*; $i \leftarrow 1$;

- **While** there are more symbols in *seq* **do**

- **begin**

  - $L_i \leftarrow 0$; $Z_i \leftarrow 0$.
  - Scan *seq* from the $i - 1_{th}$ parse to the left.
  - While the new symbol (ns) $= 0$ $Z_i \leftarrow Z_i + 1$.
  - (ns=1) $L_i \leftarrow L_i + 1$; start following the path of the tree defined by *seq*, incrementing L_i, until a leaf is reached.
  - Scan one more symbol (ns), add a new arc from the last visited leaf, label it ns, add a new leaf and a new parse, and label them i. e_i is the integer represented by the segment which starts at parse $i - 1$ and ends at parse i, not including leading zeroes to the right.
  - Compute x^{e_i}, and store it together with $L_{i-1} = |e_{i-1}|$, e_{i-1}, and Z_i in leaf i.
  - $i \leftarrow i + 1$;

- **end;**

end.

Let $k = max(i)$. The exponent looks as follows. $n = e_k 0^{z_k} e_{k-1} 0^{z_{k-1}} ... e_1 0^{z_1}$

Algorithm 1:
begin

- Call **build-tree** subroutine.

- $x^n \leftarrow ((...((x^{e_k})^{2^{z_k}+L_{k-1}} \cdot x^{e_{k-1}})^{2^{z_{k-1}}+L_{k-2}} \cdot x^{e_{k-2}}...)^{2^{z_2}+L_1} \cdot x^{e_1})^{2^{z_1}}$

end.

Remarks :

- e_{i-1} is stored in "node e_i" as a back pointer, later used by algorithm 1 to determine the right sequencing of the partial results.

- The method is general, and applies to any multiplicative group.

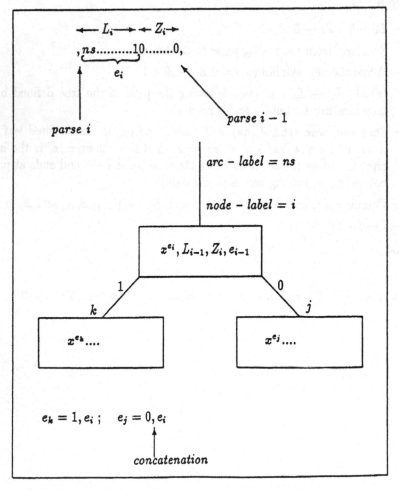

The general structure of the tree

The following theorem and its proof appear in [Y]. As before, let $L = log(n)$ the length of the exponent.

Theorem: The average time complexity of Algorithm 1 is
$$l(n) = L - (log(L) - loglog(L))/2 + 1.5 \cdot (L/log(L) + o(L/log(L))).$$

3 Compressible exponents

Roughly speaking, if a sequence is ZL-compressible then its compression tree is not balanced, and on the average, node-names are shorter than the corresponding exponent segments, i.e. the tree has relatively few nodes. Let k be the number of nodes of a noncompressible sequence, and k' the number of nodes of another sequence of the same length, which is compressible by a factor $\eta < 1$. Let N denote the expected length of a node-name (similarly N' for the compressible case). Then roughly $k = 2^N$, and since $N' = \eta \cdot N$, we get $k' = 2^{N'} = k^\eta$. The number of multiplications in the compressible case is $m' = c \cdot k'$, $1 < c < 2$ compared with $m = 1.5 \cdot k$, i.e. the saving is asymptotically exponential in η.

If the tree is skewed to the right (fewer ones), then $c < 1.5$, while if the tree is skewed to the left, $c > 1.5$.

Some implementors use exponents of low Hamming weight; thus gaining in the linear factor ($c < 1.5$), this may be combined with the new algorithm to gain twice: use low weight exponents ($c < 1.5$), which are also ZL-compressible ($\eta < 1$).

4 References

[L] A.K. Lenstra, and H.W. Lenstra, Jr.: "Algorithms in Number Theory," Technical Report 87-008, Univ. of Chicago, Dept. of CS, May 1987

[P] J.M. Pollard, "Monte Carlo Methods for Index Computation (mod p)," Math. Comp. 32 (1978), 918-924

[Y] Y. Yacobi,"Exponentiating faster with addition chains," Proceedings of Eurocrypt'90.

[ZL] J. Ziv, and A. Lempel: "Compression of individual sequences via variable rate coding," IEEE Trans. Inf. Th. Vol. IT-24, No. 5, Sep. 1978

Author Index

Lecture Notes in Computer Science

For information about Vols. 1–466
please contact your bookseller or Springer-Verlag

Vol. 509: A. Endres, H. Weber (Eds.), Software Development Environments and CASE Technology. Proceedings, 1991. VIII, 286 pages. 1991.

Vol. 510: J. Leach Albert, B. Monien, M. Rodríguez (Eds.), Automata, Languages and Programming. Proceedings, 1991. XII, 763 pages. 1991.

Vol. 511: A. C. F. Colchester, D.J. Hawkes (Eds.), Information Processing in Medical Imaging. Proceedings, 1991. XI, 512 pages. 1991.

Vol. 512: P. America (Ed.), ECOOP '91. European Conference on Object-Oriented Programming. Proceedings, 1991. X, 396 pages. 1991.

Vol. 513: N. M. Mattos, An Approach to Knowledge Base Management. IX, 247 pages. 1991. (Subseries LNAI).

Vol. 514: G. Cohen, P. Charpin (Eds.), EUROCODE '90. Proceedings, 1990. XI, 392 pages. 1991.

Vol. 515: J. P. Martins, M. Reinfrank (Eds.), Truth Maintenance Systems. Proceedings, 1990. VII, 177 pages. 1991. (Subseries LNAI).

Vol. 516: S. Kaplan, M. Okada (Eds.), Conditional and Typed Rewriting Systems. Proceedings, 1990. IX, 461 pages. 1991.

Vol. 517: K. Nökel, Temporally Distributed Symptoms in Technical Diagnosis. IX, 164 pages. 1991. (Subseries LNAI).

Vol. 518: J. G. Williams, Instantiation Theory. VIII, 133 pages. 1991. (Subseries LNAI).

Vol. 519: F. Dehne, J.-R. Sack, N. Santoro (Eds.), Algorithms and Data Structures. Proceedings, 1991. X, 496 pages. 1991.

Vol. 520: A. Tarlecki (Ed.), Mathematical Foundations of Computer Science 1991. Proceedings, 1991. XI, 435 pages. 1991.

Vol. 521: B. Bouchon-Meunier, R. R. Yager, L. A. Zadek (Eds.), Uncertainty in Knowledge-Bases. Proceedings, 1990. X, 609 pages. 1991.

Vol. 522: J. Hertzberg (Ed.), European Workshop on Planning. Proceedings, 1991. VII, 121 pages. 1991. (Subseries LNAI).

Vol. 523: J. Hughes (Ed.), Functional Programming Languages and Computer Architecture. Proceedings, 1991. VIII, 666 pages. 1991.

Vol. 524: G. Rozenberg (Ed.), Advances in Petri Nets 1991. VIII, 572 pages. 1991.

Vol. 525: O. Günther, H.-J. Schek (Eds.), Advances in Spatial Databases. Proceedings, 1991. XI, 471 pages. 1991.

Vol. 526: T. Ito, A. R. Meyer (Eds.), Theoretical Aspects of Computer Software. Proceedings, 1991. X, 772 pages. 1991.

Vol. 527: J.C.M. Baeten, J. F. Groote (Eds.), CONCUR '91. Proceedings, 1991. VIII, 541 pages. 1991.

Vol. 528: J. Maluszynski, M. Wirsing (Eds.), Programming Language Implementation and Logic Programming. Proceedings, 1991. XI, 433 pages. 1991.

Vol. 529: L. Budach (Ed.), Fundamentals of Computation Theory. Proceedings, 1991. XII, 426 pages. 1991.

Vol. 530: D. H. Pitt, P.-L. Curien, S. Abramsky, A. M. Pitts, A. Poigné, D. E. Rydeheard (Eds.), Category Theory and Computer Science. Proceedings, 1991. VII, 301 pages. 1991.

Vol. 531: E. M. Clarke, R. P. Kurshan (Eds.), Computer-Aided Verification. Proceedings, 1990. XIII, 372 pages. 1991.

Vol. 532: H. Ehrig, H.-J. Kreowski, G. Rozenberg (Eds.), Graph Grammars and Their Application to Computer Science. Proceedings, 1990. X, 703 pages. 1991.

Vol. 533: E. Börger, H. Kleine Büning, M. M. Richter, W. Schönfeld (Eds.), Computer Science Logic. Proceedings, 1990. VIII, 399 pages. 1991.

Vol. 534: H. Ehrig, K. P. Jantke, F. Orejas, H. Reichel (Eds.), Recent Trends in Data Type Specification. Proceedings, 1990. VIII, 379 pages. 1991.

Vol. 535: P. Jorrand, J. Kelemen (Eds.), Fundamentals of Artificial Intelligence Research. Proceedings, 1991. VIII, 255 pages. 1991. (Subseries LNAI).

Vol. 536: J. E. Tomayko, Software Engineering Education. Proceedings, 1991. VIII, 296 pages. 1991.

Vol. 537: A. J. Menezes, S. A. Vanstone (Eds.), Advances in Cryptology – CRYPTO '90. Proceedings. XIII, 644 pages. 1991.